Mastering PostgreSQL Administration

Internals, Operations, Monitoring, and Oracle Migration Strategies

Y V Ravi Kumar
Arun Kumar Samayam
Phani Kadambari

Apress®

Mastering PostgreSQL Administration: Internals, Operations, Monitoring, and Oracle Migration Strategies

Y V Ravi Kumar
Irving, TX, USA

Arun Kumar Samayam
Dallas, TX, USA

Phani Kadambari
Lewisville, TX, USA

ISBN-13 (pbk): 979-8-8688-1506-5
https://doi.org/10.1007/979-8-8688-1507-2

ISBN-13 (electronic): 979-8-8688-1507-2

Copyright © 2025 by Y V Ravi Kumar, Arun Kumar Samayam, and Phani Kadambari

This work is subject to copyright. All rights are reserved by the Publisher, whether the whole or part of the material is concerned, specifically the rights of translation, reprinting, reuse of illustrations, recitation, broadcasting, reproduction on microfilms or in any other physical way, and transmission or information storage and retrieval, electronic adaptation, computer software, or by similar or dissimilar methodology now known or hereafter developed.

Trademarked names, logos, and images may appear in this book. Rather than use a trademark symbol with every occurrence of a trademarked name, logo, or image we use the names, logos, and images only in an editorial fashion and to the benefit of the trademark owner, with no intention of infringement of the trademark.

The use in this publication of trade names, trademarks, service marks, and similar terms, even if they are not identified as such, is not to be taken as an expression of opinion as to whether or not they are subject to proprietary rights.

While the advice and information in this book are believed to be true and accurate at the date of publication, neither the authors nor the editors nor the publisher can accept any legal responsibility for any errors or omissions that may be made. The publisher makes no warranty, express or implied, with respect to the material contained herein.

Managing Director, Apress Media LLC: Welmoed Spahr
Acquisitions Editor: Shaul Elson
Development Editor: Laura Berendson
Coordinating Editor: Gryffin Winkler

Cover designed by eStudioCalamar

Cover Photo by Mylon Ollila on Unsplash

Distributed to the book trade worldwide by Springer Science+Business Media New York, 1 New York Plaza, New York, NY 10004. Phone 1-800-SPRINGER, fax (201) 348-4505, e-mail orders-ny@springer-sbm.com, or visit www.springeronline.com. Apress Media, LLC is a Delaware LLC and the sole member (owner) is Springer Science + Business Media Finance Inc (SSBM Finance Inc). SSBM Finance Inc is a **Delaware** corporation.

For information on translations, please e-mail booktranslations@springernature.com; for reprint, paperback, or audio rights, please e-mail bookpermissions@springernature.com.

Apress titles may be purchased in bulk for academic, corporate, or promotional use. eBook versions and licenses are also available for most titles. For more information, reference our Print and eBook Bulk Sales web page at http://www.apress.com/bulk-sales.

Any source code or other supplementary material referenced by the author in this book is available to readers on GitHub (https://github.com/Apress). For more detailed information, please visit https://www.apress.com/gp/services/source-code.

If disposing of this product, please recycle the paper

Table of Contents

About the Authors xi

About the Technical Reviewers xiii

Acknowledgments xv

Chapter 1: PostgreSQL System Architecture 1

    Introduction 1

    PostgreSQL Components 2

    PostgreSQL Server Process Tree 14

    PostgreSQL Architecture Flow 16

    Summary 18

Chapter 2: PostgreSQL Installation and Initialization 19

    Introduction 19

    PostgreSQL Available Versions and Supported OS Platforms 20

    System Requirements for PostgreSQL Installation on Linux 20

    Environment Details 21

    Downloading PostgreSQL Software 22

    Installing PostgreSQL Using the Binary Packages (RPMs) 22

        Exploring a few files under the data directory 40

    Shutdown Modes in PostgreSQL Database Cluster 47

    Uninstallation of PostgreSQL Server (Installed Using RPMs) 50

    Installing PostgreSQL Server Using Source Code 55

    Uninstallation of PostgreSQL Server (Installed Using Source Code) 73

    Summary 74

TABLE OF CONTENTS

Chapter 3: PostgreSQL Physical Structures **75**

Introduction 75

PostgreSQL Database Cluster 76

PostgreSQL Directory Structure 77

Databases in PostgreSQL 88

Tablespaces in PostgreSQL 99

Default Tablespaces 100

Creating a New Tablespace 102

Changing Default Tablespace 103

Page Structure and Layout in PostgreSQL Database Cluster 110

Query Processing in PostgreSQL 112

    Connection Request Stage 112

    Query Execution Stage 113

    Parser Stage 113

    Execution Plan Generation Stage 113

    Execution Stage 114

Inspecting Physical Data with the *pg_filedump* Utility 114

Other Administrative Operations 121

    Altering a Tablespace 121

    Dropping a Tablespace 122

    Temporary Tablespaces 124

    Index Objects on Separate Tablespace 128

    Advantages of Tablespaces 131

    Cloning a Database 131

    Dropping a Database in a Cluster 134

    Dropping Default Databases 135

Summary 136

Chapter 4: PostgreSQL Management of Database Server 137

Introduction 137
Creating Database Using OS Command 138
Schemas in PostgreSQL 140
Creating a Schema 142
Accessing Schema Objects in PostgreSQL 148
Database Local Connectivity by User 154
User Attributes 157
User Renaming 162
Schema Ownership 162
Database Remote Connectivity by User 165
The pg_hba.conf File 173
Authentication Method – Trust and Reject 189
Predefined Roles in PostgreSQL 192
Extensions in PostgreSQL 197
Dropping Users in PostgreSQL 205
Dropping a Schema in PostgreSQL 206
Dropping Database Using OS Command 209
Summary 211

Chapter 5: PostgreSQL Backup and Recovery 213

Introduction 213
Why Backup a Database? 215
Importance of a Backup Strategy 216
Backup Types in PostgreSQL 217
SQL Dump 218
File System-Level Backup 219
Continuous Archiving and Point-in-Time Recovery (PITR) 220
Using External Tools 221

TABLE OF CONTENTS

Barman 221
Installing Barman 223
Configuring Barman 224
pgBackRest 233
Installation and Configuration of pgBackRest Tool 233
Real-World Practical Backup and Recovery Scenarios 244
Scenario 1: Backup and Restore a Single Table 244
Scenario 2: Backup and Restore a Table Structure Without the Data 249
Scenario 3: Backup and Restore the Table Data Without the Structure 253
Scenario 4: Backup and Restore Multiple Tables at a Time 257
Scenario 5: Backup and Restore a Table in Custom Format 263
Scenario 5a: Backup and Restore a Table Using *pg_dump* in *tar* Format 265
Scenario 5b: Backup and Restore a Table Using *pg_dump* in *dir* Format 266
Scenario 6: Backup Multiple Tables and Restore One Table in Custom Format 268
Scenario 7: Backup and Restore a Schema Within a Database 270
Scenario 8: Backup Multiple Schemas and Restore a Single Schema Within a Database .. 274
Scenario 9: Backup and Restore an Entire Database 279
Scenario 10: Restore a Backup to a New Database 284
Scenario 11: Improve Backup Performance with Parallel Jobs 287
Scenario 12: Restore a Single Table from a Full Database Backup 287
Scenario 13: Logical Backup of a Complete Server and Restore Specific Databases 289
Scenario 14: Backup of Global Database Objects 292
Scenario 15: Physical Backup of the Complete Server 292
Scenario 15a: Verification of Physical Backups (pg_verifybackup) Before Restore 294
Scenario 16: Restore Procedures 298
Scenario 16a: Restore to a New Instance 298
Scenario 16b: Restore to an Existing Instance 302
Scenario 17: Perform a Point-in-Time Recovery (PITR) 305
Scenario 18: Backup and Restore Using Barman 316
Scenario 19: Backup and Restore Using pgBackRest 333
Summary 358

Chapter 6: PostgreSQL Routine Maintenance 359

Introduction 359

Analyze 360

Vacuum in PostgreSQL 365

    Key Purposes of vacuum 365

    Types of vacuum 366

    VACUUM FULL in PostgreSQL 383

    Key Points About VACUUM FULL 383

    PostgreSQL vacuum Commands – Summary Table 388

    Vacuum and Analyze Threshold Settings in postgresql.conf 388

    vacuumdb Commands for Various Scenarios 390

Reindexing in PostgreSQL 392

    TIP: REINDEX TABLE <table_name> 396

    Reindexing in PostgreSQL – Key Options 398

PostgreSQL Catalog Views for Size Monitoring 398

Finding the Largest Tables in the Database 399

Finding and Removing Unused Tables and Indexes 400

Clear Write-Ahead Logging (WAL) Logs to Free Up Space in Database Server 400

Best Practices to Prevent Disk Space Issues in PostgreSQL Cluster 401

Log File Maintenance in PostgreSQL 402

Summary 403

Chapter 7: PostgreSQL Monitoring Using PgAdmin and Grafana 405

Introduction 405

Monitoring System Resources and OS-Level Metrics 405

Understanding Real-Time System Behavior 413

PostgreSQL System Views: Real-Time Insights, No Extra Setup 423

Administering Databases Using pgAdmin 428

    Installation and Configuration of pgAdmin 428

    Installing pgAdmin 4 on Windows 431

    Connectivity Between pgAdmin and pg_server 434

    Registering PostgreSQL Server in pgAdmin 435

Integrating PostgreSQL with Monitoring Solutions (Grafana) 458
Installation and Configuration of Grafana 458
    Downloading Grafana on Windows 458
    Installing Grafana on Windows 459
    Connecting to Grafana 464
    Adding a PostgreSQL Data Source in Grafana 465
    Building a Dashboard in Grafana 470
    Creating a Bar Chart in the Dashboard 471
    Adding a New Bar Chart Panel to the Existing Dashboard 473
    Adding a New XY Chart Panel to the Existing Dashboard 476
    Adding Multiple Series to the XY Chart 478
    Mapping Series of Multi-country Visualization 479
Summary 484

Chapter 8: Data Migration from Oracle to PostgreSQL Using Ora2Pg 485

Introduction 485
Why Migrate to PostgreSQL 485
Migration Tools 486
Migration Best Practices 487
Oracle to PostgreSQL Migration Using Ora2Pg 488
Migration Approach 489
Migration Prerequisites 490
Pre-migration Phase: Prepare Environment for Migration 491
Install Perl Modules Required for DBD::Oracle and Ora2Pg 494
Install Ora2Pg 504
Migration Phase: Migrate Oracle Schemas to PostgreSQL Database 509
Migrating HR Schema Using Direct Load Method 513
Migrating CO Schema Using COPY (Bulk Load) Method 531
Migrating SH Schema Using INSERT Method 543
Migration Issues 553
Summary 573

Chapter 9: Data Replication from Oracle to PostgreSQL Using Oracle GoldenGate 575

Introduction 575

GoldenGate Replication Configuration Prerequisites 578

    Configure Source Database (Oracle) Ready for Replication 578

    Configure Target Database (PostgreSQL) Ready for Replication 583

Configure Oracle GoldenGate Hub 586

    What Is Oracle GoldenGate Hub? 586

    Install Oracle Client 587

    Install GoldenGate Software 594

    Install Oracle GoldenGate for Oracle Database 595

    Install Oracle GoldenGate for PostgreSQL 601

Create the Deployments 607

    Create Deployment for Source Oracle Database 607

    Create Deployment for Target PostgreSQL Database 619

    Configure GoldenGate on Target Deployment 646

Replication Configuration – Create Dist Path in Source Deployment 658

Summary 672

Chapter 10: New Features of PostgreSQL 17 673

Introduction 673

Downloading PostgreSQL 17 Software Binaries 674

Installing PostgreSQL Using Binary Packages (RPMs) 674

New Features: Incremental Backups in PostgreSQL 17 697

New Features: Logical Replication from Standby Servers in PostgreSQL 17 716

New Features: Combining I/Os in PostgreSQL 17 717

New Features: Query Planner Improvements in PostgreSQL 17 718

New Features: Introducing Split and Merge Partitions in PostgreSQL 17 719

Summary 719

Index 721

About the Authors

Y. V. Ravi Kumar is a recipient of the prestigious EB1-A "Einstein Visa" for Extraordinary Ability in the United States. He brings over 27 years of multinational leadership experience across the United States, Seychelles, and India in the banking, financial services, and insurance (BFSI) sectors. A seasoned technologist, Ravi is an Oracle Certified Master, Oracle ACE Director Alum, Snowflake Data Superhero, and Snowflake Squad Member. He holds a wide range of certifications, including Oracle Certified Professional (OCP) in versions 8i through 19c and Oracle Certified Expert (OCE) in GoldenGate, RAC, Performance Tuning, Oracle Cloud Infrastructure (OCI), Terraform, and Oracle Engineered Systems (Exadata, ZDLRA, and ODA). He is also certified in Oracle Security, Maximum Availability Architecture (MAA), Snowflake Pro, PostgreSQL, MySQL, and MySQL HeatWave and is a multi-cloud architect certified in OCI, AWS, and GCP. In addition, he is TOGAF certified and a Senior Member of the IEEE.

Ravi Kumar has co-authored six books, including *Oracle Database Upgrade and Migration Methods*; *Oracle High Availability, Disaster Recovery, and Cloud Services*; and *Mastering MySQL Administration*, and has served as a technical reviewer on six more titles: *Oracle 19c AutoUpgrade Best Practices, Oracle Autonomous Database in Enterprise Architecture, End-to-End Observability with Grafana, Maximum Availability Architecture (MAA) with Oracle GoldenGate MicroServices in HUB Architecture, The Cloud Computing Journey: Design and Deploy Resilient and Secure Multi-cloud Systems with Practical Guidance,* and *Azure FinOps Essentials*.

Ravi Kumar has published over 100 technical articles across platforms such as Oracle Technology Network, ORAWORLD Magazine, UKOUG, and Redgate. A frequent speaker at international conferences, he has presented at Oracle OpenWorld four times and delivered sessions at numerous user groups including IOUG, NYOUG, AUSOUG, and Quest. His work includes designing data centers and implementing mission-critical databases for central banks, and his contributions have been recognized by Oracle in their OCM list and Spotlight on Success stories.

ABOUT THE AUTHORS

Arun Kumar Samayam is an experienced technology architect and a seasoned database professional with a profound passion for innovation. He is a Principal Cloud Solutions Architect in the Cloud and Engineering platform team at a global airline company. He is part of the Cloud Center of Excellence (CCoE) team, where he drives the organization's cloud transformation journey through cloud governance practices.

Before this role, Arun worked as a Product Technical Leader for the Enterprise Database Services team, where he had the opportunity to develop and hone his technical proficiency through engineering, managing, and supporting multiple database platforms like Oracle, MySQL, PostgreSQL, SQL server, and MongoDB. In addition, Arun is a multi-cloud certified professional, and his industry knowledge and experience have made him a speaker at prestigious events like Oracle OpenWorld, where he shared his insights and expertise on database products.

Sri Ram Phani Kiran Kadambari is a seasoned IT professional with over 16 years of experience in database management, cloud solutions, and diverse technology domains. Passionate about databases, he specializes in Oracle (including Engineered Systems), PostgreSQL, MySQL with HeatWave, and Snowflake, along with extensive expertise in cloud platforms such as Oracle Cloud Infrastructure (OCI), AWS, and Azure. Phani's technical skills have been instrumental in helping organizations successfully migrate their databases and mission-critical applications to the cloud.

Phani's journey began as a database trainer, and his passion for knowledge-sharing has driven him to mentor and train countless professionals, guiding them to build successful careers in database engineering. He holds multiple certifications in Oracle, MySQL, PostgreSQL, Snowflake, and Oracle Cloud Infrastructure.

A respected contributor to the database community, Phani shared his insights as a speaker at KSAOUG Connect – 2024, where he presented on MySQL High Availability and Disaster Recovery. He has also served as a technical reviewer for the book *Mastering MySQL Administration* (Apress, 2024), further showcasing his commitment to advancing the field. Phani's blend of technical expertise, industry experience, and dedication to mentoring makes him a valuable contributor to the IT and database community.

About the Technical Reviewers

Velu Natarajan is a seasoned expert with over 20 years of experience architecting scalable, high-performance data and database solutions across a wide range of platforms. His passion lies in the relentless pursuit of modernizing data platforms – ensuring they are not only efficient and high-performing but also scalable and durable to meet the evolving needs of the industry. As an industry trailblazer, Velu has been an early advocate for Cloud FinOps frameworks, leveraging them to drive business success and achieve significant cost savings.

As a leader in the Database Cloud Center of Excellence (CCoE), Velu plays a crucial role in advancing his organization's cloud transformation journey. His deep expertise in database practices enables him to lead initiatives that ensure seamless migrations, business continuity, and operational efficiency.

Velu's pioneering work with Cloud FinOps has been instrumental in delivering measurable business outcomes. His application of the FinOps framework to control costs in cloud-based data platforms earned him the Discover President Award in 2024. Through effective collaboration with cross-functional teams, he has optimized performance, managed costs, and established best practices – developing self-service tools and processes, identifying potential issues, and creating comprehensive cost management plans.

A respected contributor to the data and financial operations community, Velu has shared his insights at prestigious events such as Snowflake Summit 2024, where he spoke on optimizing performance and cost on Snowflake, maximizing business value, reducing budget risk, and enhancing the user experience. He served as a technical reviewer for *Azure FinOps Essentials* and is currently co-authoring *FinOps for Snowflake* – further demonstrating his commitment to advancing financial operations and data platform excellence.

ABOUT THE TECHNICAL REVIEWERS

Velu holds certifications as an AWS Certified Database Specialty, FinOps Certified Practitioner, and Snowflake Architect and is widely recognized for his expertise in data products and his dedication to excellence. Outside of work, he enjoys playing soccer and watching epic movies.

Raghavendra S (Raghav) is a Database Cloud Architect who specializes in designing and implementing cloud-based database solutions for organizations. With a deep understanding of both database management systems and cloud computing technologies, he helps businesses leverage the power of the cloud to optimize their database operations.

His expertise lies in developing architecture strategies that align with business goals, ensuring scalability, high availability, and performance of database systems in the cloud. He has hands-on experience with leading cloud platforms, including Oracle Cloud Infrastructure (OCI), Amazon Web Services (AWS), and Google Cloud Platform (GCP).

Raghav works closely with stakeholders to assess their database requirements, plan migration strategies, and design secure and cost-effective cloud-based database solutions. He possesses a strong understanding of database technologies such as Oracle Database, MySQL, and PostgreSQL, enabling him to provide expert guidance on data modeling, schema design, and query optimization.

He also has a solid understanding of big data technologies, including Hadoop, HDFS, Hive, HBase, Kafka, and Data Lake/Lakehouse architectures.

Acknowledgments

I am grateful to God who gave me all the strength, courage, perseverance, and patience in this sincere and honest attempt of knowledge sharing. This seventh book of mine as a co-author would not have been possible without the following people: Shri Yenugula Venkata Pathi and Smt. Yenugula Krishna Kumari, my parents who instilled in me good thoughts and values, and Shri B. Suresh Kamath (founder of LaserSoft and Patterns Cognitive), my mentor, my guru, my strength, and my guide, who has inspired me for the last 27 years.

B. Suresh Kamath is an immensely talented and technically sound individual. He taught me how to be well read with no compromises. He led by example in being content yet hungry for knowledge. He motivated me to go that extra mile in attempting and experimenting with newer technologies/environments and in being regularly out of my comfort zone.

Anitha Ravi Kumar, my wife, was immensely tolerant with me. "Behind every successful man, there is a good woman," as they say. I believe she is the embodiment of this well-known belief. Special thanks to my daughter, Sai Hansika, and my son, Sai Theeraz, for giving me time to write a seventh book in the last seven years.

I would like to thank Velu Natarajan and Raghavendra S (Raghav) for accepting to be technical reviewers for this book. Special thanks to Shaul Elson, Gryffin Winkler, Nirmal Selvaraj, Celestin Suresh John, and Laura Berendson at Apress for giving me the opportunity to write my sixth book for Apress. Thank you to the readers for picking up this book. We have attempted to be as simple and straightforward as possible when sharing this knowledge, and we truly believe that it will help you to steadily deep dive into various interesting concepts and procedures.

I would also like to thank the complete Infolob Global team – Vijay Cherukuri, Tim Fox, Josh Turnbull, Nivas Nadimpalli, Satyendra Pasalapudi – and LaserSoft colleagues.

—**Venkata Ravi Kumar Yenugula**

I am forever grateful for the love and support of those who have shaped my life journey and made this book possible.

ACKNOWLEDGMENTS

To my parents, Ram Kumar and Lakshmi Sarada, for nurturing me with unwavering love, kindness, and the freedom to pursue my passions. Your encouragement and support have fueled my determination to pursue my dreams.

To my beloved wife, Ramya, and our daughter, Iraa, whose boundless love and unwavering support have been the bedrock of strength in my life. Your belief in me has propelled me forward, urging me to strive for excellence in all endeavors.

To my mentor, Venkata Ravi Kumar Yenugula, for recognizing my potential, guiding me through challenges, and opening doors to new opportunities. Your wisdom, dedication, and noble pursuit of knowledge have been a constant source of inspiration.

To my co-authors, Venkata Ravi Kumar Yenugula and Phani Kadambari, and technical reviewers, Velu Natarajan and Raghavendra S – your dedication, collaboration, and unwavering support throughout the writing process have enriched this book and made it truly special.

To my esteemed American Airlines leaders, Rasika Vaidya and Echo Jiang, for their unwavering support and encouragement on this journey.

To my Apress publishing team – Shaul Elson, Gryffin Winkler, and Nirmal Selvaraj – thank you for entrusting me with the opportunity. I am confident this book will be a practical guide for many aspiring database technologists.

Thank you all for being an integral part of this incredible journey.

—**Arun Kumar Samayam**

Writing the very first book in my career has been an incredible journey, and I am deeply grateful to the many people who supported me along the way.

I want to use this opportunity to express my gratitude to God and bow down to my parents, Shri Kadambari Rama Badri Raju and Smt. Satyavathi, for this life, their teachings, and invaluable lessons at every phase of my life. Special mention to my sister, Smt. Poornima Garimella, whose sacrifice, support, and encouragement inspired me to strive for my achievements.

Special thanks to my beloved wife, Praneetha Kadambari, undoubtedly the pillar in my life for providing unconditional love and support in whatever I do and the decisions I take. I thank our daughters Aadhya and Nihidaa for their mature understanding and giving me space and time to complete this book.

ACKNOWLEDGMENTS

My respectful obeisance and my heartfelt gratitude to my gurus:

- Shri Namburi Bhima Shankar Acharya, a revered individual, whose blessings have brought me here today.

- M.V. Madhusudan, Founder and M.D. of Wilshire Software Technologies, who offered me my first opportunity as a Database Administrator and played a pivotal role in shaping my career.

- Venkata Ramakrishna Gandi, more of a brother than a mentor. His guidance has inspired me to continuously learn and maintain a calm, composed mindset in every situation.

- Venkata Ravi Kumar Yenugula, an inspiration to many aspirants whose mentorship has played a significant role in shaping my professional growth.

I am grateful to my co-authors, Arun Kumar Samayam and Y V Ravi Kumar, and the technical reviewers, Velu Natarajan and Raghavendra S, for considering me for this project and for their time and efforts in contributing to and producing great content.

I extend my thanks to all my friends, well-wishers, and my colleagues at work for their continuous encouragement and support to develop individually and professionally.

To my Apress publishing team – Shaul Elson, Gryffin Winkler, Nirmal Selvaraj, and Laura Berendson – thank you for your trust and the opportunity given to write my first book.

—**Sri Ram Phani Kiran Kadambari**

CHAPTER 1

PostgreSQL System Architecture

Introduction

In this chapter, we learn about the origin of PostgreSQL, its architecture, and its components and understand the various components of PostgreSQL during a client connection request.

We cover the following topics:

- Origin of PostgreSQL
- PostgreSQL key architectural components
- PostgreSQL server process tree
- PostgreSQL architecture flow

PostgreSQL is one of the most popular open source object-relational database management systems (ORDBMS). It is based on POSTGRES, Version 4.2, initially developed at the University of California at Berkeley's Computer Science department. PostgreSQL is based on the Berkeley code and follows the SQL standard, offering various features we will cover in this book.

The PostgreSQL architecture is designed to handle transactions efficiently and maintain data integrity, supporting concurrent sessions. In this chapter, we will learn about the various components of the PostgreSQL internal architecture and their functions.

PostgreSQL follows a typical client/server architecture. The client and server are usually on different hosts and communicate over a TCP/IP network connection. Several core components work together to handle queries, manage data storage, and ensure efficient execution of the query operations.

CHAPTER 1   POSTGRESQL SYSTEM ARCHITECTURE

PostgreSQL Components

The key components in a PostgreSQL architecture are

1. Server process
2. Utility process
3. System memory
4. Physical files

Each of these core components further relies on several minor components. Let's learn about each core component in detail and its function.

1. **Server process**

    A server process consists of the following components:

    Postmaster process: This is the central process that starts and controls all other PostgreSQL processes. It listens for incoming client connections and spawns background processes to handle each connection.

    postgres background process: Each incoming client connection is served by a dedicated backend process responsible for query parsing, planning, execution, and client interaction.

    The server process is represented in the figure below.

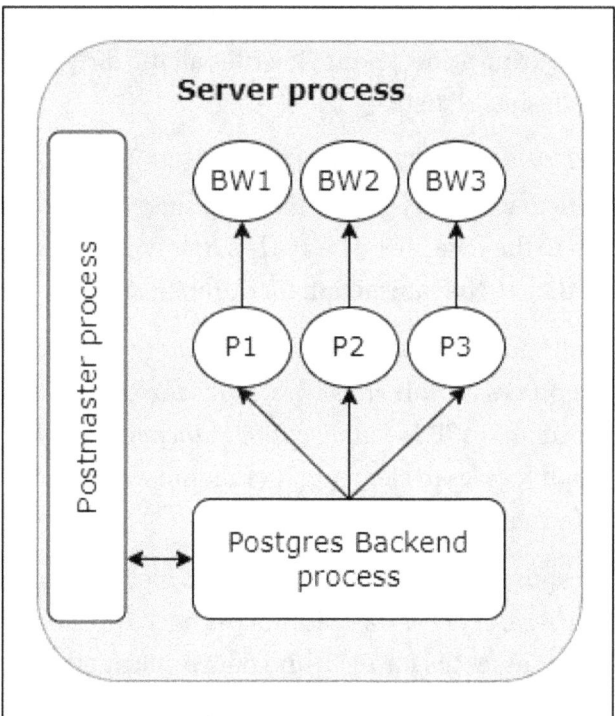

Figure 1-1. *PostgreSQL server process*

In Figure 1-1, P1/P2/P3 are the backend processes, and BW1/BW2/BW3 are the corresponding background worker processes.

2. **Utility process**

   The utility process is a collection of auxiliary processes. These secondary or supplementary processes perform all the tasks initiated by the server process. Let's learn about the different auxiliary processes.

   Background writer: The background writer handles periodic writes of dirty buffers from shared memory to the disk. *Dirty buffers* are modified data that has yet to be written to the disk and can get lost if a server restart happens. So flushing the data from the shared buffers is essential, and the background writer handles this periodically, freeing up space from the shared buffer.

Checkpoint: This process ensures that checkpoints occur periodically. During a checkpoint, it writes all the dirty pages to the disk and flushes all data.

WAL Writer: *Write-Ahead Logging* is a transaction logging method in PostgreSQL that records changes to data files in a log before writing them to the data files. The *WAL Writer* writes changes made to the data to the transaction for durability.

Autovacuum: Vacuum is data that is no longer needed. The autovacuum process automatically reclaims the storage by removing dead tuples. The *Autovacuum launcher* spawns autovacuum processes to clean up the vacuum and ensure optimal performance.

Archiver: Responsible for archiving the WAL files to support *point-in-time recovery (PITR)*. This process backs up all the WAL records that are essential for PITR and data replication.

Statistics collector: Collects statistics about database usage and query performance and provides insights for the query planner to optimize query execution.

Log writer: Responsible for writing debug logs and error logs to the log file that are important for troubleshooting and monitoring.

Logical replication launcher: Responsible for periodically checking the *pg_subscription* catalog table to see if any subscriptions have been added or enabled and ensuring the logical replication workers are started for every enabled subscription making use of the background worker infrastructure.

Figure 1-2 shows the collection of all the auxiliary processes.

CHAPTER 1 POSTGRESQL SYSTEM ARCHITECTURE

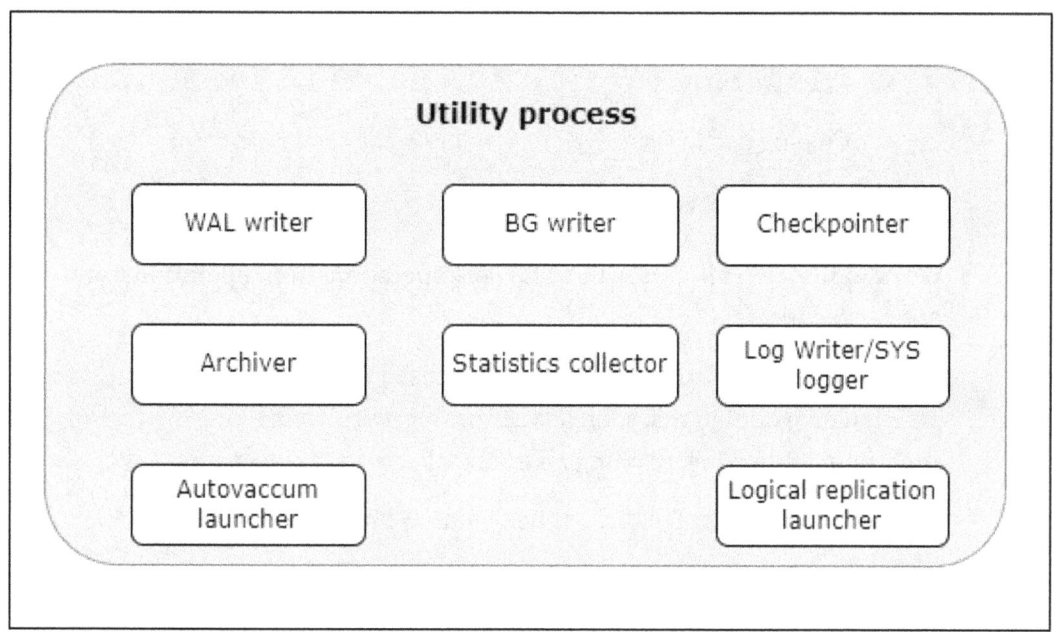

Figure 1-2. *PostgreSQL Utility process*

3. **System memory**

    PostgreSQL memory architecture is divided into two categories:

    - Local memory
    - Shared memory

    Local memory

    Local memory is private to each background process used for query processing. It is further divided into several sub-areas, whose sizes are either fixed or variable.

    The sub-areas include

    - Work memory
    - Maintenance work memory
        - Autovacuum work memory

- Temporary buffers
  - Effective cache size
  - Catalog cache
  - Operating system cache

Work memory: This area is used for sort operations, join operations, and query execution.

Maintenance work memory: This area is used for all maintenance operations, such as vacuuming, vacuuming full, analyzing, reindexing, creating an index, altering a table, etc.

Effective cache size: This area is used to make index usage more effective.

Shared memory

A shared memory is usually allocated by a PostgreSQL server when it starts up. This area is subdivided into several fixed-size sub-areas and accessible by all background processes.

- Shared buffers
- WAL buffers
- Temp buffers
- Other buffers

Shared buffers: PostgreSQL uses this area to load pages within tables and indexes from the disks and operate on them. For example, to view the current allocation, you may issue the command below:

postgres=# **show shared_buffers;**

shared_buffers

128MB

(1 row)

WAL buffers: This area stores transaction log entries before they are written to the disk to ensure that server failures have lost no data. For example, to view the current allocation, you may issue the command below:

postgres=# **SHOW wal_buffers;**

wal_buffers

4MB

(1 row)

Temp buffers: This area stores temporary tables required during an operation and when more temporary result sets are needed during multiple join operations. It is also used whenever *Work memory* can no longer support the query operation. For example, to view the current allocation, you may issue the command below:

postgres=# **SHOW temp_buffers;**

temp_buffers

8MB

(1 row)

Other buffers: Besides these buffers, PostgreSQL allocates other areas for transaction processing, such as savepoints and two-phase commit, background processes, like checkpoints and autovacuum, and different access control mechanisms, like shared and exclusive locks, etc.

The figure below represents the various components involved in the memory architecture.

CHAPTER 1 POSTGRESQL SYSTEM ARCHITECTURE

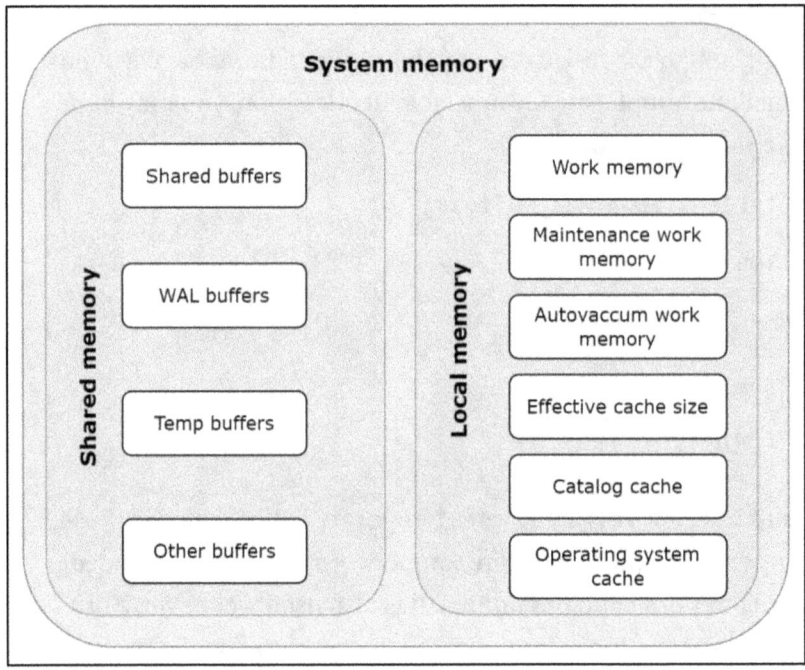

Figure 1-3. *PostgreSQL system memory*

4. **Physical files**

   The physical files are the actual files stored in the *base* directory. It contains several different subdirectories and many files. In general, all the physical files are grouped into the below categories:

   - Data files
   - WAL log files
   - Log files
   - Archived log files

   Data files

   The data files usually include the configuration files and data files used by the database cluster and are stored in the cluster's data directory, such as *PGDATA*. This directory further contains several

CHAPTER 1 POSTGRESQL SYSTEM ARCHITECTURE

subdirectories, control files, and other configuration files required to run the database cluster. To view the default location, issue the command below:

```
postgres=# SHOW data_directory;
     data_directory
------------------------
/var/lib/pgsql/16/data
(1 row)
```

```
[postgres@pg_server ~]$ ls -lrth /var/lib/pgsql/16/data
total 220K
drwx------. 2 postgres postgres    6 Jun  1  2024 tablespace1
-rwx------. 1 postgres postgres  29K Jun  1  2024 postgresql.conf_bkp
drwx------. 2 postgres postgres   18 Jun  1  2024 pg_xact
-rwx------. 1 postgres postgres    3 Jun  1  2024 PG_VERSION
drwx------. 2 postgres postgres    6 Jun  1  2024 pg_twophase
drwx------. 2 postgres postgres    6 Jun  1  2024 pg_snapshots
drwx------. 2 postgres postgres    6 Jun  1  2024 pg_serial
drwx------. 2 postgres postgres    6 Jun  1  2024 pg_notify
drwx------. 4 postgres postgres   36 Jun  1  2024 pg_multixact
-rwx------. 1 postgres postgres 2.6K Jun  1  2024 pg_ident.conf
-rwx------. 1 postgres postgres 5.4K Jun  1  2024 pg_hba.conf_bkp
drwx------. 2 postgres postgres    6 Jun  1  2024 pg_dynshmem
drwx------. 2 postgres postgres    6 Jun  1  2024 pg_commit_ts
-rw-------. 1 postgres postgres   38 Jun  6  2024 tablespace_map.old
-rw-------. 1 postgres postgres  227 Jun  6  2024 backup_label.old
-rwx------. 1 postgres postgres  30K Jun  6  2024 postgresql.conf_bkp2
-rw-------. 1 postgres postgres  187 Jun  6  2024 logfile
drwx------. 2 postgres postgres   18 Jun  6  2024 pg_subtrans
drwx------. 2 postgres postgres  188 Jun 17  2024 log
-rwx------. 1 postgres postgres 6.3K Nov 26 18:53 pg_hba.conf_new
drwx------. 2 postgres postgres    6 Nov 28 00:20 pg_stat
-rwx------. 1 postgres postgres 6.1K Dec 24 21:10 pg_hba.conf_bkp122424
drwx------. 2 postgres postgres   60 Mar  7 23:44 pg_tblspc
-rwx------. 1 postgres postgres  30K Mar 17 14:35 postgresql.conf_bkp03172025
-rw-------. 1 postgres postgres  348 Mar 20 09:44 postgresql.auto.conf
-rwx------. 1 postgres postgres  30K Apr 27 16:53 postgresql.conf
-rwx------. 1 postgres postgres 6.5K Apr 27 17:45 pg_hba.conf
drwx------. 8 postgres postgres   76 May 12 11:55 base
drwx------. 2 postgres postgres    6 May 12 12:07 pg_replslot
drwx------. 2 postgres postgres  28K May 12 12:07 archive
drwx------. 3 postgres postgres 4.0K May 12 12:12 pg_wal
drwx------. 2 postgres postgres   35 May 13 17:17 pg_stat_tmp
-rw-------. 1 postgres postgres   30 May 13 17:17 current_logfiles
-rw-------. 1 postgres postgres   58 May 13 17:17 postmaster.opts
drwx------. 4 postgres postgres   68 May 13 17:17 pg_logical
-rw-------. 1 postgres postgres   91 May 13 17:17 postmaster.pid
drwx------. 2 postgres postgres 4.0K May 13 17:23 global
[postgres@pg_server ~]$
```

Figure 1-4. *PostgreSQL data directory layout*

WAL log files

The *Write-Ahead Logging (WAL)* files are usually referred to as transaction logs as they ensure data durability and help avoid data loss in case of server failures for point-in-time recovery and data replication. The default location for WAL log files is /var/lib/pgsql/16/data/pg_wal.

[postgres@pg_server ~]$ ls -lrth /var/lib/pgsql/16/data/pg_wal
```
total 705M
rw-------. 1 postgres postgres 16M Apr 28 17:50 000000010000000400000006E -rw-------. 1 postgres postgres 16M Apr 28 17:50 000000010000000400000006F -rw-------. 1 postgres postgres 16M Apr 28 17:50 0000000100000004000000070 -rw-------. 1 postgres postgres 16M Apr 28 17:50 0000000100000004000000071 -rw-------. 1 postgres postgres 16M Apr 28 17:50 0000000100000004000000068 -rw-------. 1 postgres postgres 16M Apr 28 17:50 0000000100000004000000069 -rw-------. 1 postgres postgres 16M Apr 28 17:50 000000010000000400000006A -rw-------. 1 postgres postgres 16M Apr 28 17:50 000000010000000400000006B -rw-------. 1 postgres postgres 16M Apr 28 17:51 000000010000000400000006C -rw-------. 1 postgres postgres 16M Apr 28 17:51 000000010000000400000006D -rw-------. 1 postgres postgres 16M Apr 28 17:51 000000010000000400000007D -rw-------. 1 postgres postgres 16M Apr 28 17:51 0000000100000004000000073 -rw-------. 1 postgres postgres 16M Apr 28 17:51 0000000100000004000000074 -rw-------. 1 postgres postgres 16M Apr 28 17:51 0000000100000004000000075 -rw-------. 1 postgres postgres 16M Apr 28 17:51 0000000100000004000000076 -rw-------. 1 postgres postgres 16M Apr 28 17:51 0000000100000004000000077 -rw-------. 1 postgres postgres 16M Apr 28 17:51 0000000100000004000000078 -rw-------. 1 postgres postgres 16M Apr 28 17:51 0000000100000004000000079 -rw-------. 1 postgres postgres 16M Apr 28 17:51 000000010000000400000007A -rw-------. 1 postgres postgres 16M Apr 28 17:51 000000010000000400000007B -rw-------. 1 postgres postgres 16M Apr 28 17:51 000000010000000400000007C -rw-------. 1 postgres postgres 341 May 12 12:07 0000000100000004000000066.00000028.backup
```

CHAPTER 1 POSTGRESQL SYSTEM ARCHITECTURE

```
drwx------. 2 postgres postgres 59 May 12 12:12 archive_status
rw-------. 1 postgres postgres 16M May 13 17:17
000000010000000400000067
```

<<< OUTPUT TRUNCATED >>>

Log files

The log files are where we can view all the diagnostic information required for troubleshooting, monitoring, and analytical purposes. Every action performed within the database is written to the log file to track all the changes within the database. To view log file location:

```
postgres=# SHOW log_directory;
log_directory
---------------
log
(1 row)
```

```
[postgres@pg_server log]$ ls -lrth /var/lib/pgsql/16/data/log
total 96K
-rwx------. 1 postgres postgres 3.5K May  1 17:34 postgresql-Thu.log
-rwx------. 1 postgres postgres 6.9K May  2 22:17 postgresql-Fri.log
-rwx------. 1 postgres postgres    0 May  3 12:10 postgresql-Sat.log
-rw-------. 1 postgres postgres  19K May  4 12:49 postgresql-Sun.log
-rwx------. 1 postgres postgres 5.0K May  7 21:37 postgresql-Wed.log
-rw-------. 1 postgres postgres  42K May 12 12:12 postgresql-Mon.log
-rwx------. 1 postgres postgres 8.7K May 13 17:23 postgresql-Tue.log
[postgres@pg_server log]$
```

```
postgres=# SHOW log_filename;
   log_filename
-------------------
postgresql-%a.log
(1 row)

postgres=# SHOW logging_collector;
logging_collector
-------------------
on
(1 row)
```

Archived log files

The archived log files are nothing but WAL log files that have been moved to an archive location after they have been written to the disk. We must archive the WAL log files as they help maintain data integrity, backup and recovery, and support replication. To view the default location:

```
postgres=# SHOW archive_command;
            archive_command
------------------------------------------
cp %p /var/lib/pgsql/16/data/archive/%f
(1 row)
```

[postgres@pg_server ~]$ ls -lrth /var/lib/pgsql/16/data/archive/
```
total 1.7G
-rw-------. 1 postgres postgres 16M Apr 28 17:50
000000010000000400000000
-rw-------. 1 postgres postgres 16M Apr 28 17:50
000000010000000400000001
-rw-------. 1 postgres postgres 16M Apr 28 17:50
000000010000000400000002
-rw-------. 1 postgres postgres 16M Apr 28 17:50
000000010000000400000003
-rw-------. 1 postgres postgres 16M Apr 28 17:50
000000010000000400000004
```

CHAPTER 1   POSTGRESQL SYSTEM ARCHITECTURE

```
-rw-------. 1 postgres postgres 16M Apr 28 17:50
000000010000000400000005
-rw-------. 1 postgres postgres 16M Apr 28 17:50
000000010000000400000006
-rw-------. 1 postgres postgres 16M Apr 28 17:50
000000010000000400000007
```

<<< OUTPUT TRUNCATED >>>

The figure below shows the physical files stored in the *base* directory.

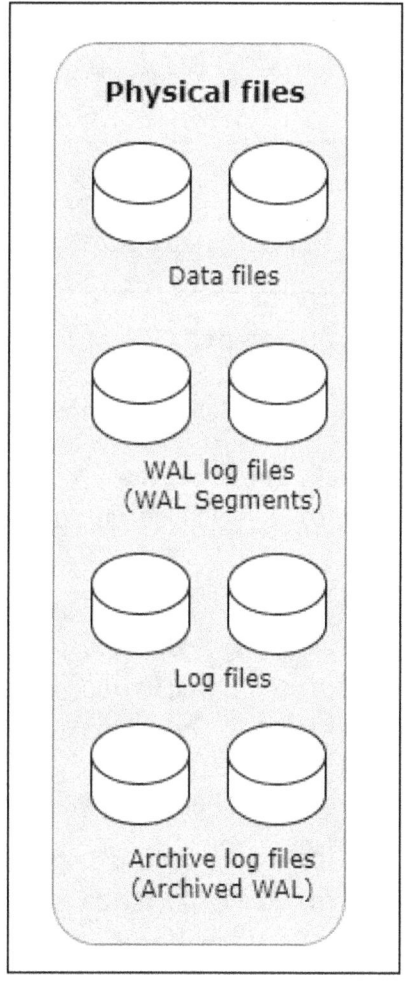

Figure 1-5. *PostgreSQL physical files*

CHAPTER 1 POSTGRESQL SYSTEM ARCHITECTURE

PostgreSQL Server Process Tree

Now that we have seen each architectural component, let's understand the steps involved in the architectural flow when a connection is initiated and look at the PostgreSQL process tree.

A typical PostgreSQL server process tree looks like below:

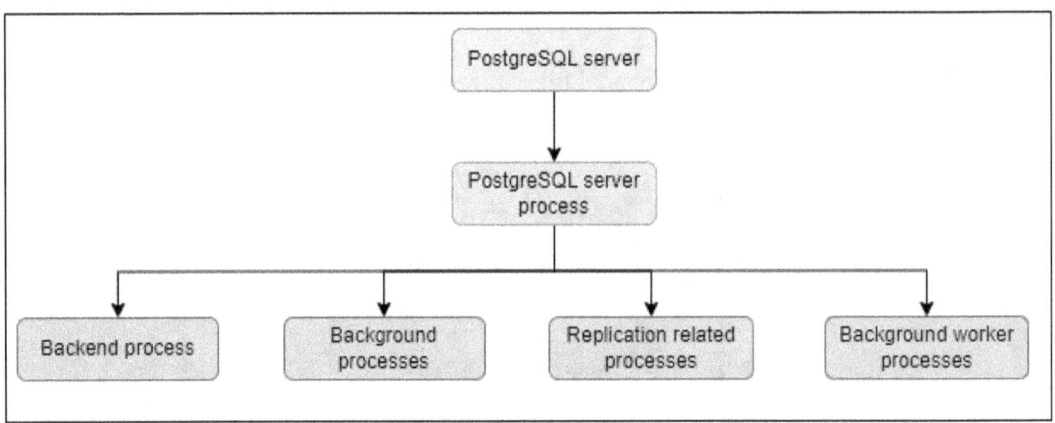

Figure 1-6. PostgreSQL server process tree

Here is a sample output of the PostgreSQL server process tree:

```
[postgres@pg_server ~]$ ps -ef|grep postgres
postgres    1335     1  0 21:07 ?        00:00:00 /usr/pgsql-16/bin/postgres -D /var/lib/pgsql/16/data/
postgres    1489  1335  0 21:07 ?        00:00:00 postgres: logger
postgres    1537  1335  0 21:07 ?        00:00:00 postgres: checkpointer
postgres    1538  1335  0 21:07 ?        00:00:00 postgres: background writer
postgres    3300  1335  0 21:07 ?        00:00:00 postgres: walwriter
postgres    3301  1335  0 21:07 ?        00:00:00 postgres: autovacuum launcher
postgres    3302  1335  0 21:07 ?        00:00:00 postgres: archiver
postgres    3303  1335  0 21:07 ?        00:00:00 postgres: logical replication launcher
root        4409  4289  0 21:10 pts/0    00:00:00 su - postgres
postgres    4410  4409  0 21:10 pts/0    00:00:00 -bash
postgres    5832  4410  0 21:37 pts/0    00:00:00 ps -ef
```

```
postgres    5833  4410  0 21:37 pts/0  00:00:00 grep --color=auto postgres
[postgres@pg_server ~]$

[postgres@pg_server ~]$ systemctl status postgresql-16
● postgresql-16.service - PostgreSQL 16 database server
   Loaded: loaded (/usr/lib/systemd/system/postgresql-16.service; enabled;
           vendor preset: disabled)
   Active: active (running) since Wed 2025-05-07 21:07:44 CDT; 33min ago
     Docs: https://www.postgresql.org/docs/16/static/
  Process: 1299 ExecStartPre=/usr/pgsql-16/bin/postgresql-16-check-db-dir
           ${PGDATA} (code=exited, status=0/SUCCESS)
 Main PID: 1335 (postgres)
    Tasks: 8 (limit: 35703)
   Memory: 39.3M
   CGroup: /system.slice/postgresql-16.service
           ├─1335 /usr/pgsql-16/bin/postgres -D /var/lib/pgsql/16/data/
           ├─1489 postgres: logger
           ├─1537 postgres: checkpointer
           ├─1538 postgres: background writer
           ├─3300 postgres: walwriter
           ├─3301 postgres: autovacuum launcher
           ├─3302 postgres: archiver
           └─3303 postgres: logical replication launcher
[postgres@pg_server ~]$
```

PostgreSQL server: This is a collection of all the processes within one database cluster.

PostgreSQL server process: This is the parent of all processes and is called *postmaster*. This is started at server startup and is allocated a shared memory area in the memory, starts various background processes, starts replication-associated processes and background worker processes where necessary, and then waits for connection requests from clients.

Backend process: This process is called *postgres* and handles all queries issued by one connected client. Each client has its backend process and its corresponding background processes.

Background process: This is a group of all individual processes that perform a specific action.

Replication-related processes: These processes perform all processing related to streaming replication.

Background worker processes: These processes perform any user processing, including user-supplied code.

PostgreSQL Architecture Flow

In this section, let's combine all the different architectural components we have learned so far to understand how a typical architectural flow happens when a client request is initiated.

Please follow the flow by looking at the numbers in Figure 1-7 to understand the flow better.

1. A client initiates a connection request to the database. A client can be any application or interface communicating with the PostgreSQL server to send queries and receive results. This can be command-line tools (like SQL), graphical user interfaces (GUIs), or other applications using PostgreSQL client interface libraries. Clients connect to the PostgreSQL server using a network protocol, typically TCP/IP. In some cases, Unix domain sockets are also used for local connections. Every connection is authenticated and authorized on PostgreSQL default port 5432. The *postmaster* server process continuously listens for every new incoming connection.

2. The *postmaster* connection then hands off the processing to the *postgres* backend process. Each connection from a client is handled by a separate backend process, which executes queries, manages transactions, and retrieves data.

3. Each backend process spawns separate background worker processes as needed, depending on the type of client request received. It communicates with the client over a single TCP/IP connection and terminates when the connection is disconnected or terminated.

CHAPTER 1 POSTGRESQL SYSTEM ARCHITECTURE

4. Each process the server initiates requires a memory component to perform its processing. So a memory area is allocated depending on the needed processing type.

5. The server process also spawns subsequent auxiliary processes to perform various background actions needed for database management, each serving a specific purpose.

6. After all the processing is complete, wherever the committed data needs persistence, the corresponding auxiliary and memory processes store the data in physical files.

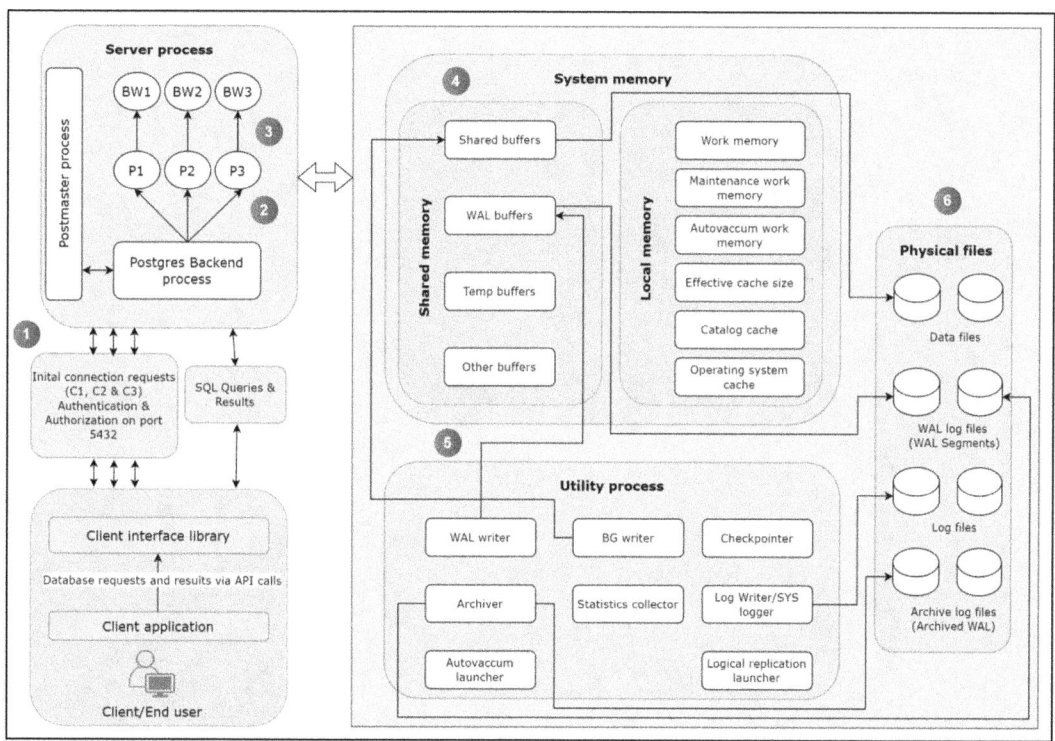

Figure 1-7. *PostgreSQL architecture flow*

Summary

In summary, we learned about the different core components of PostgreSQL architecture, its subcomponents, and its functionality. We also learned about the PostgreSQL process-based architecture flow and saw how a client request is handled. This architecture ensures efficient handling of client requests, data integrity, and robust performance across concurrent sessions.

CHAPTER 2

PostgreSQL Installation and Initialization

Introduction

Database software installation is one of the key and essential steps in setting up and working with a database system. This chapter provides a deep intuitive understanding of PostgreSQL installation and uninstallation and initializing the database server. PostgreSQL is compatible with multiple operating system platforms, and the software can be installed using binary packages (RPMs) or using source code.

In this chapter, the following topics are covered:

- System requirements for PostgreSQL installation on Linux
- Environment details and how to download PostgreSQL
- Learn how to install PostgreSQL using RPMs and source code
- Learn about additional packages required for version PostgreSQL 16.3/16.2
- How to initialize a database cluster
- How to uninstall PostgreSQL
- Connecting to PostgreSQL using the psql utility
- Learn various commands and options to use at CLI

CHAPTER 2　POSTGRESQL INSTALLATION AND INITIALIZATION

PostgreSQL Available Versions and Supported OS Platforms

PostgreSQL is available in multiple versions: 17 (current, released in 09/2024), 16, 15, 14, 13, and 12.

PostgreSQL can be downloaded from www.postgresql.org/downloads.

PostgreSQL is supported widely on various operating systems including cloud-based platforms. Some of the supported platforms are listed in Table 2-1.

Table 2-1. *PostgreSQL supported platforms*

Operating system family	Distribution
Linux	Debian, Red Hat/Rocky/AlmaLinux, SUSE, Ubuntu, Other Linux
macOS	macOS 11 (Big Sur), macOS 12 (Monterey), macOS 13 (Ventura)
Windows	Windows 10 and 11, Windows Server 2016, 2019, and 2022
BSD	OpenBSD, FreeBSD, NetBSD
Solaris	Solaris
Cloud Platform	Amazon Relational Database Service (RDS) for PostgreSQL, Amazon Aurora PostgreSQL, Google Cloud (Cloud SQL), Microsoft Azure (Azure Database for PostgreSQL), Oracle Cloud Infrastructure (OCI) Database for PostgreSQL, IBM Cloud

System Requirements for PostgreSQL Installation on Linux

- The minimum hardware configuration required for PostgreSQL installation is as mentioned in Table 2-2.

Table 2-2. *Hardware configuration for PostgreSQL installation*

CPU	1 GHz or faster processor
RAM	2 GB of RAM
Disk Space	512 MB of HDD

CHAPTER 2 POSTGRESQL INSTALLATION AND INITIALIZATION

- Root or sudo user access is required.

Note Based on various factors such as database size, workloads, application requirements, concurrent sessions, and performance expectations, the system configuration required to install PostgreSQL and to maintain the database differs. It is highly recommended to perform the infrastructure designing and capacity planning before proceeding with PostgreSQL installation and database configuration as it will impact or benefit PostgreSQL performance significantly.

Environment Details

Note OS installation is not shown as part of the practical scenarios described in this chapter and subsequent chapters.

PostgreSQL 16 will be installed on a system with details mentioned in Table 2-3.

Table 2-3. System details

Machine hostname	Machine type	IP address
pg_server	Database server	192.168.2.24

System configuration can be checked using below os commands:

```
[root@pg_server ~]# hostname; hostname -i
pg_server
192.168.2.24
[root@pg_server ~]# cat /etc/os-release
NAME="Oracle Linux Server"
VERSION="8.7"
VARIANT="Server"
PLATFORM_ID="platform:el8"
```

```
[root@pg_server ~]# lscpu
Architecture:          x86_64
CPU op-mode(s):        32-bit, 64-bit
Byte Order:            Little Endian
CPU(s):                8
On-line CPU(s) list:   0-7
Thread(s) per core:    2
Core(s) per socket:    4
Socket(s):             1
```

Downloading PostgreSQL Software

PostgreSQL offers several ways to download and install binaries. We will discuss the two most used approaches for installing PostgreSQL:

- Installing PostgreSQL using the binary packages (RPMs)
- Installing PostgreSQL using source code

Installing PostgreSQL Using the Binary Packages (RPMs)

In this method, we will see how the binary packages are used to install PostgreSQL. PostgreSQL provides RPM packages, which are the precompiled binaries, for different versions compatible with most of the commonly used operating systems. The suitable RPM packages specific to the operating system are selected, which can be used to install PostgreSQL.

In this section, we will go over the step-by-step process of installing PostgreSQL version 16.3 using the RPMs.

Step 1: Browse the PostgreSQL website, which is the source for multiple releases of PostgreSQL (www.postgresql.org/downloads).

Step 2: On the downloads page, select the operating system as **Linux**.

CHAPTER 2 POSTGRESQL INSTALLATION AND INITIALIZATION

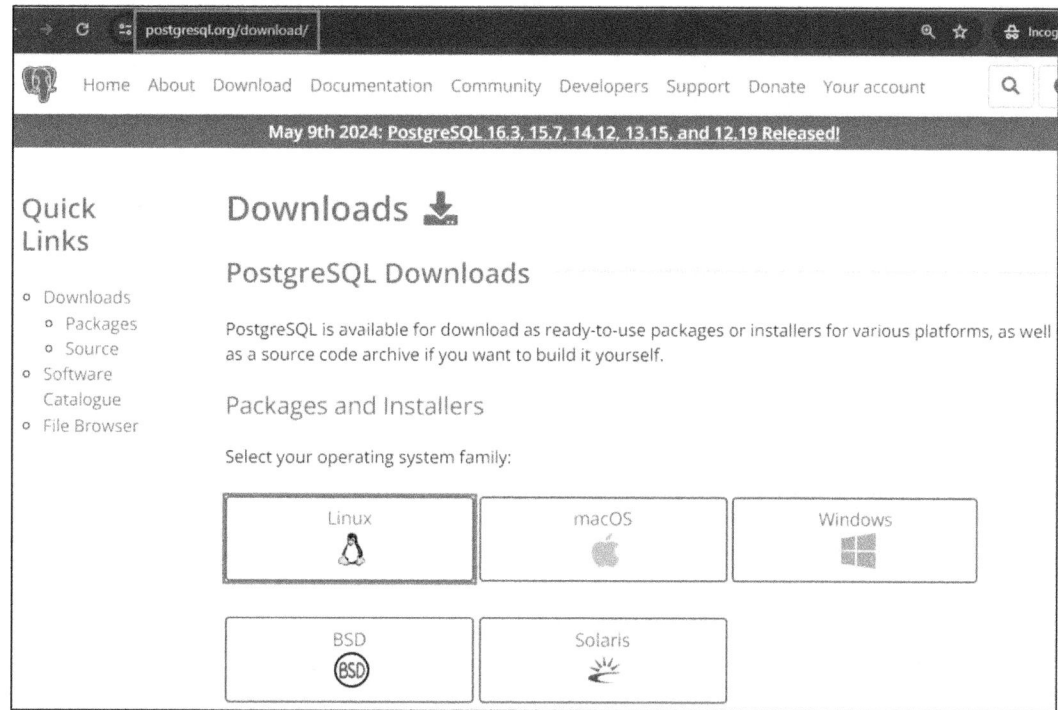

Figure 2-1. *Operating system family selection*

Once the Linux option is selected, a list will expand to choose the required Linux distribution.

Step 3: Select appropriate Linux distribution (in this case, choose **Red Hat/Rocky/AlmaLinux**).

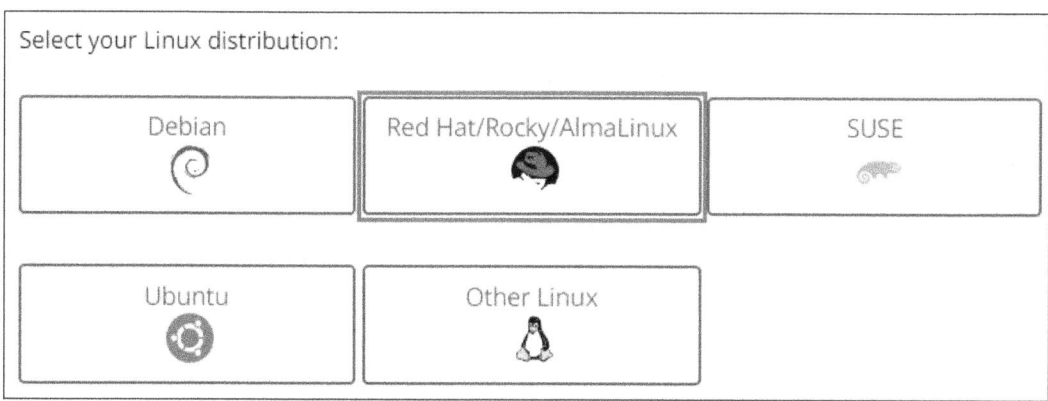

Figure 2-2. *Linux distribution selection*

Selection of the "Red Hat/Rocky/AlmaLinux" option will redirect to PostgreSQL Yum Repository.

Step 4: In the PostgreSQL Yum Repository section, select

Version – **16**

Platform – **Red Hat Enterprise, Rocky, AlmaLinux or Oracle version 8**

Architecture – **x86_64**

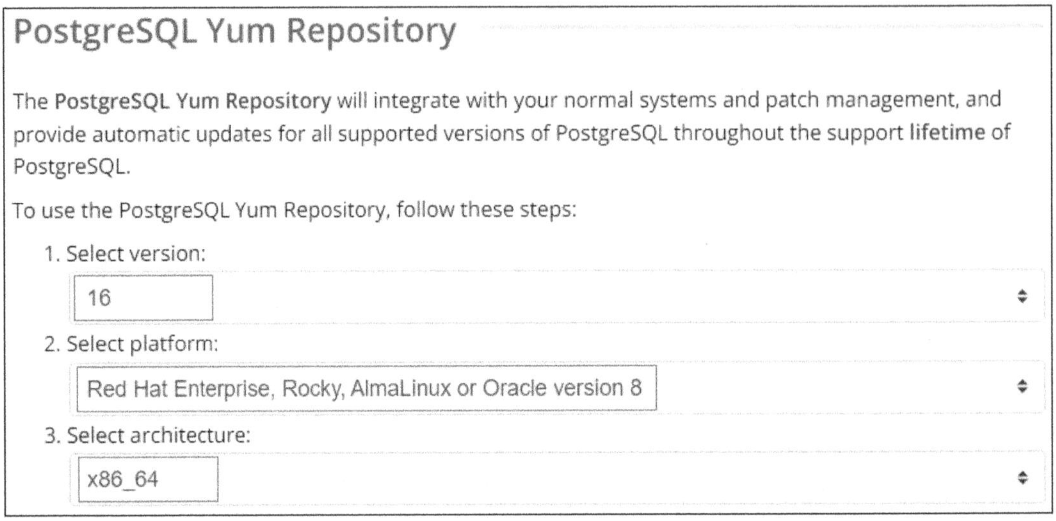

Figure 2-3. PostgreSQL version, OS platform, and architecture selection

Once version, platform, and architecture are selected, a setup script will be displayed, which can be copied and used in subsequent tasks.

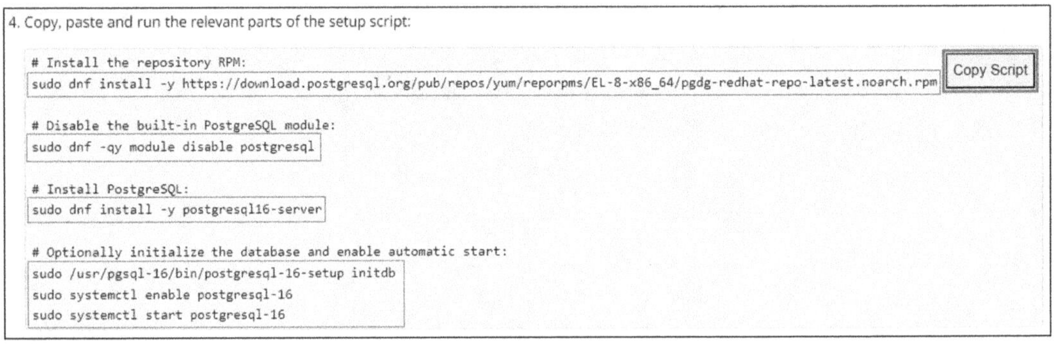

Figure 2-4. Installation and initialization setup script

The setup script has four sections, and each plays its part in installing PostgreSQL.

> **Note** To install RPMs, either YUM (Yellowdog Updater, Modified) or DNF (Dandified Yum) can be used. YUM is used in our case.

The first section has the command to download and install the RPM repository.

 # Install the repository RPM:

```
sudo yum install -y https://download.postgresql.org/pub/repos/yum/reporpms/EL-8-x86_64/pgdg-redhat-repo-latest.noarch.rpm
```

The second section has a command to disable the built-in PostgreSQL module.

 # Disable the built-in PostgreSQL module:

```
sudo yum -qy module disable postgresql
```

The third section has the command that will actually install the PostgreSQL server binaries.

 # Install PostgreSQL:

```
sudo yum install -y postgresql16-server
```

The fourth section has three separate commands.

 # Optionally initialize the database and enable automatic start:

```
sudo /usr/pgsql-16/bin/postgresql-16-setup initdb
sudo systemctl enable postgresql-16
sudo systemctl start postgresql-16
```

```
sudo /usr/pgsql-16/bin/postgresql-16-setup initdb
```

- This command will initialize the storage area and create the data directories.

    ```
    sudo systemctl enable postgresql-16
    ```

- This command is to enable the auto start of the PostgreSQL server every time when the system restarts.

    ```
    sudo systemctl start postgresql-16
    ```

- This command is to start the PostgreSQL.

CHAPTER 2   POSTGRESQL INSTALLATION AND INITIALIZATION

Step 5: In the system, create an OS superuser with the name "postgres".

As root user, create the OS superuser postgres and validate. *postgres* user will own the binaries and data directory.

[root@pg_server ~]# useradd postgres

[root@pg_server ~]# grep -i postgres /etc/passwd
postgres:x:1001:1001::/home/postgres:/bin/bash

Change the password of newly created user postgres.

[root@pg_server ~]# passwd postgres
Changing password for user postgres.
New password:
BAD PASSWORD: The password is shorter than 8 characters
Retype new password:
passwd: all authentication tokens updated successfully.

Note   *postgres* user will be created during the PostgreSQL server installation but with no password. The password can be reset or the user can be created in advance to installation.

Step 6: Add the superuser "postgres" in the /etc/sudoers configuration file.

Adding a user to sudoers list allows the user to execute a few commands that need to be run as root user.

[root@pg_server ~]# vi /etc/sudoers

--Add the following entry
postgres   ALL=(ALL)   ALL

[root@pg_server ~]# grep -i postgres /etc/sudoers
postgres   ALL=(ALL)   ALL

Step 7: Install the PostgreSQL repository packages required for the system.

As root user or as postgres user (using sudo), install the repository rpm using yum (a package management command).

26

CHAPTER 2   POSTGRESQL INSTALLATION AND INITIALIZATION

Run the command copied from the first section of setup script earlier (**Step 4**).

yum install -y https://download.postgresql.org/pub/repos/yum/reporpms/
EL-8-x86_64/pgdg-redhat-repo-latest.noarch.rpm

This rpm will not install PostgreSQL; instead, it generates a repository with all the available PostgreSQL versions as *pgdg-redhat-all.repo* in the */etc/yum.repos.d* directory.

One of the advantages of installing using RPM method is the RPM package managers will handle the dependencies automatically.

[root@pg_server ~]# yum install -y https://download.postgresql.org/pub/repos/yum/reporpms/EL-8-x86_64/pgdg-redhat-repo-latest.noarch.rpm
```
Last metadata expiration check: 2:26:32 ago on Tue 21 May 2024 08:20:29 PM CDT.
pgdg-redhat-repo-latest.noarch.rpm            25 kB/s |  15 kB     00:00
Dependencies resolved.
================================================================================
 Package              Architecture   Version           Repository        Size
================================================================================
Installing:
 pgdg-redhat-repo     noarch         42.0-43PGDG       @commandline      15 k

Transaction Summary
================================================================================
Install  1 Package

Total size: 15 k
Installed size: 15 k
Downloading Packages:
Running transaction check
Transaction check succeeded.
Running transaction test
Transaction test succeeded.
Running transaction
  Preparing        :                                                      1/1
  Installing       : pgdg-redhat-repo-42.0-43PGDG.noarch                  1/1
  Verifying        : pgdg-redhat-repo-42.0-43PGDG.noarch                  1/1
```

```
Installed:
  pgdg-redhat-repo-42.0-43PGDG.noarch
```

Complete!

```
[root@pg_server ~]# ls -lrt /etc/yum.repos.d/pgdg-redhat-all.repo
total 32
-rw-r--r--. 1 root root 13280 Apr 10 02:00 pgdg-redhat-all.repo
```

The *pgdg-redhat-all.repo* repository file will have the list of all available PostgreSQL versions and the instructions to download the RPMs.

```
[root@pg_server ~]# cat /etc/yum.repos.d/pgdg-redhat-all.repo
#######################################################
# PGDG Red Hat Enterprise Linux / Rocky repositories   #
#######################################################

# PGDG Red Hat Enterprise Linux / Rocky stable common repository for all PostgreSQL versions

[pgdg-common]
name=PostgreSQL common RPMs for RHEL / Rocky / AlmaLinux $releasever - $basearch
baseurl=https://download.postgresql.org/pub/repos/yum/common/redhat/rhel-$releasever-$basearch
enabled=1
gpgcheck=1
gpgkey=file:///etc/pki/rpm-gpg/PGDG-RPM-GPG-KEY-RHEL
repo_gpgcheck = 1
.
```

<<< output truncated >>>

```
.
# PGDG Red Hat Enterprise Linux / Rocky stable repositories:

[pgdg16]
name=PostgreSQL 16 for RHEL / Rocky / AlmaLinux $releasever - $basearch
baseurl=https://download.postgresql.org/pub/repos/yum/16/redhat/rhel-$releasever-$basearch
```

```
enabled=1
gpgcheck=1
gpgkey=file:///etc/pki/rpm-gpg/PGDG-RPM-GPG-KEY-RHEL
repo_gpgcheck = 1
.
<<< output truncated >>>
.
[pgdg12-updates-testing-debuginfo]
name=PostgreSQL 12 for RHEL / Rocky / AlmaLinux $releasever - $basearch -
Debuginfo
baseurl=https://dnf-debuginfo.postgresql.org/testing/debug/12/redhat/
rhel-$releasever-$basearch
enabled=0
gpgcheck=1
gpgkey=file:///etc/pki/rpm-gpg/PGDG-RPM-GPG-KEY-RHEL
repo_gpgcheck = 1
```

So when the actual PostgreSQL server version installation is performed, the repository file */etc/yum.repos.d/pgdg-redhat-all.repo* is referred for version specific recommendations for the current OS platform.

Step 8: Install Extra Packages for Enterprise Linux (EPEL) repository.

For PostgreSQL 16, it is recommended to install EPEL repository configuration. EPEL repository provides additional packages that are not included in the default repositories.

Install epel-release using yum as below:

```
[root@pg_server ~]# yum install epel-release
Last metadata expiration check: 2:32:59 ago on Tue 21 May 2024
08:20:29 PM CDT.
Dependencies resolved.
================================================================
Package                   Architecture Version      Repository         Size
================================================================
Installing:
oracle-epel-release-el8   x86_64       1.0-5.el8    ol8_baseos_latest  15 k
```

```
Transaction Summary
========================================================================
Install  1 Package

Total download size: 15 k
Installed size: 18 k
```
Is this ok [y/N]: y
```
Downloading Packages:
oracle-epel-release-el8-1.0-5.el8.x86_64.rpm 78 kB/s |  15 kB     00:00
------------------------------------------------------------------------
Total                                        75 kB/s |  15 kB     00:00
Running transaction check
Transaction check succeeded.
Running transaction test
Transaction test succeeded.
Running transaction
  Preparing        :                                                 1/1
  Installing       : oracle-epel-release-el8-1.0-5.el8.x86_64        1/1
  Verifying        : oracle-epel-release-el8-1.0-5.el8.x86_64        1/1

Installed:
  oracle-epel-release-el8-1.0-5.el8.x86_64
```
Complete!

> **Step 9**: Disable built-in PostgreSQL module.

Red Hat Linux 8, CentOS 8, and Oracle Linux 8 ship with the default PostgreSQL module, which may conflict with the new installation. Hence, disable built-in PostgreSQL module to prevent conflicts.

[root@pg_server ~]# yum -qy module disable postgresql
```
Importing GPG key 0x08B40D20:
 Userid     : "PostgreSQL RPM Repository <pgsql-pkg-yum@lists.
              postgresql.org>"
 Fingerprint: D4BF 08AE 67A0 B4C7 A1DB CCD2 40BC A2B4 08B4 0D20
 From       : /etc/pki/rpm-gpg/PGDG-RPM-GPG-KEY-RHEL
[root@pg_server ~]#
```

CHAPTER 2   POSTGRESQL INSTALLATION AND INITIALIZATION

Step 10: Install PostgreSQL 16 server.

Install PostgreSQL 16 server binaries using yum. When yum is run, the pgdg-redhat-all.repo file will be referred for download and install recommendations for PostgreSQL 16 and the required dependencies for OEL 8.

```
[root@pg_server ~]# yum install -y postgresql16-server
Last metadata expiration check: 3:02:21 ago on Tue 21 May 2024
08:20:29 PM CDT.
Dependencies resolved.
================================================================
 Package              Architecture  Version             Repository  Size
================================================================
Installing:
 postgresql16-server  x86_64        16.3-1PGDG.rhel8    pgdg16      6.7 M
Installing dependencies:
 postgresql16         x86_64        16.3-1PGDG.rhel8    pgdg16      1.9 M
 postgresql16-libs    x86_64        16.3-1PGDG.rhel8    pgdg16      329 k

Transaction Summary
================================================================
Install  3 Packages

Total download size: 8.9 M
Installed size: 39 M
Downloading Packages:
(1/3):postgresql16-libs-16.3-1PGDG.rhel8.x86_64.rpm    184 kB/s | 329
                                                       kB 00:01
(2/3):postgresql16-16.3-1PGDG.rhel8.x86_64.rpm         883 kB/s |
                                                       1.9 MB 00:02
(3/3):postgresql16-server-16.3-1PGDG.rhel8.x86_64.rpm  2.6 MB/s |
                                                       6.7 MB 00:02
----------------------------------------------------------------
Total                                                  3.4 MB/s | 8.9
                                                       MB   00:02
PostgreSQL 16 for RHEL/Rocky/AlmaLinux 8 - x86_64      2.4 MB/s | 2.4
                                                       kB   00:00
```

CHAPTER 2 POSTGRESQL INSTALLATION AND INITIALIZATION

```
Importing GPG key 0x08B40D20:
 Userid     : "PostgreSQL RPM Repository <pgsql-pkg-yum@lists.
             postgresql.org>"
 Fingerprint: D4BF 08AE 67A0 B4C7 A1DB CCD2 40BC A2B4 08B4 0D20
 From       : /etc/pki/rpm-gpg/PGDG-RPM-GPG-KEY-RHEL
Key imported successfully
Running transaction check
Transaction check succeeded.
Running transaction test
Transaction test succeeded.
Running transaction
  Preparing        :                                                    1/1
  Installing       : postgresql16-libs-16.3-1PGDG.rhel8.x86_64          1/3
  Running scriptlet: postgresql16-libs-16.3-1PGDG.rhel8.x86_64          1/3
  Installing       : postgresql16-16.3-1PGDG.rhel8.x86_64               2/3
  Running scriptlet: postgresql16-16.3-1PGDG.rhel8.x86_64               2/3
  Running scriptlet: postgresql16-server-16.3-1PGDG.rhel8.x86_64        3/3
  Installing       : postgresql16-server-16.3-1PGDG.rhel8.x86_64        3/3
  Running scriptlet: postgresql16-server-16.3-1PGDG.rhel8.x86_64        3/3
  Verifying        : postgresql16-16.3-1PGDG.rhel8.x86_64               1/3
  Verifying        : postgresql16-libs-16.3-1PGDG.rhel8.x86_64          2/3
  Verifying        : postgresql16-server-16.3-1PGDG.rhel8.x86_64        3/3
Installed:
  postgresql16-16.3-1PGDG.rhel8.x86_64
  postgresql16-libs-16.3-1PGDG.rhel8.x86_64
  postgresql16-server-16.3-1PGDG.rhel8.x86_64
```

Complete!

PostgreSQL 16 server binaries are installed in default location '**/usr/pgsql-16/bin**'. All the executables are located here.

[root@pg_server ~]# ls -lrt /usr/pgsql-16/bin
```
total 13132
-rwxr-xr-x. 1 root root      9617 May  8 04:30 postgresql-16-setup
-rwxr-xr-x. 1 root root    757560 May  8 04:30 psql
```

CHAPTER 2   POSTGRESQL INSTALLATION AND INITIALIZATION

```
-rwxr-xr-x. 1 root root 9118408 May  8 04:30 postgres
.
<<< output truncated >>>
.
-rwxr-xr-x. 1 root root   63736 May  8 04:30 pg_controldata
-rwxr-xr-x. 1 root root   46984 May  8 04:30 pg_config
-rwxr-xr-x. 1 root root  157392 May  8 04:30 initd
-rwxr-xr-x. 1 root root   77328 May  8 04:30 dropdb
-rwxr-xr-x. 1 root root   86312 May  8 04:30 createuser
-rwxr-xr-x. 1 root root   85912 May  8 04:30 createdb
```

Also, we can see that the RPMs below have been installed as part of the installation.

```
[root@pg_server ~]# rpm -qa |grep -i postgres
postgresql16-libs-16.3-1PGDG.rhel8.x86_64
postgresql16-server-16.3-1PGDG.rhel8.x86_64
postgresql16-16.3-1PGDG.rhel8.x86_64
```

postgresql16-libs-16.3-1PGDG.rhel8.x86_64	Contains shared libraries
postgresql16-server-16.3-1PGDG.rhel8.x86_64	Contains PostgreSQL server binaries
postgresql16-16.3-1PGDG.rhel8.x86_64	Contains core utilities and client programs Switch to postgres user to verify the version of PostgreSQL server binaries installed on the system

Use the below command to check the PostgreSQL version:

```
[root@pg_server ~]# su - postgres
[postgres@pg_server ~]$ /usr/pgsql-16/bin/postgres --version
postgres (PostgreSQL) 16.3
```

From the output, it is confirmed that PostgreSQL version 16.3 is installed.

Before initializing the storage area and database cluster, an additional RPM named postgresql16-contrib needs to be installed. The contrib package provides additional extension modules like new data types, utilities, tools, functions, etc., for PostgreSQL to enhance its functionality.

CHAPTER 2   POSTGRESQL INSTALLATION AND INITIALIZATION

Step 11: Install the contrib package.

As root user, install the postgresql16-contrib package using yum.

[root@pg_server ~]# yum install -y postgresql16-contrib
Last metadata expiration check: 3:08:45 ago on Tue 21 May 2024 08:20:29 PM CDT.
Dependencies resolved.
==
 Package   Architecture Version   Repository   Size
==
Installing:
 postgresql16-contrib   x86_64   16.3-1PGDG.rhel8 pgdg16   761 k

Transaction Summary
==
Install 1 Package

Total download size: 761 k
Installed size: 2.7 M
Downloading Packages:
postgresql16-contrib-16.3-1PGDG.rhel8.x86_64.rpm 1.5 MB/s | 761 kB   00:00

Total   1.5 MB/s | 761 kB   00:00
Running transaction check
Transaction check succeeded.
Running transaction test
Transaction test succeeded.
Running transaction
  Preparing   :   1/1
  Installing   : postgresql16-contrib-16.3-1PGDG.rhel8.x86_64   1/1
  Running scriptlet: postgresql16-contrib-16.3-1PGDG.rhel8.x86_64   1/1
  Verifying   : postgresql16-contrib-16.3-1PGDG.rhel8.x86_64   1/1

Installed:
  postgresql16-contrib-16.3-1PGDG.rhel8.x86_64

Complete!

CHAPTER 2 POSTGRESQL INSTALLATION AND INITIALIZATION

Now, check the additional packages installed with contrib using the "rpm -qa" command.

```
[root@pg_server ~]# rpm -qa |grep postgres
postgresql16-libs-16.3-1PGDG.rhel8.x86_64
postgresql16-16.3-1PGDG.rhel8.x86_64
postgresql16-server-16.3-1PGDG.rhel8.x86_64
postgresql16-contrib-16.3-1PGDG.rhel8.x86_64
```

postgresql16-contrib-16.3-1PGDG.rhel8.x86_64 contains extension modules.

With this step, installation of PostgreSQL 16 server with extension modules is complete.

The RPMs (postgresql16-server and postgresql16-contrib) just install the PostgreSQL binaries and extension modules but don't configure or start the PostgreSQL server.

Let us proceed with initializing the storage area and database.

Step 12: Initialize the database cluster.

Before we proceed with using the postgres server, we must initialize a database storage area on the disk; this is called a database cluster. A database cluster is a collection of databases that are managed by a single instance of the database server. For this, the program "initdb", which is installed with PostgreSQL, is used.

Now, initialize the database cluster with data directory.

As root user, run the command /usr/pgsql-16/bin/postgresql-16-setup initdb:

```
[root@pg_server ~]# /usr/pgsql-16/bin/postgresql-16-setup initdb
Initializing database ... OK
```

When the database cluster is initiated, PostgreSQL by default creates three databases in the cluster.

The database named *postgres* is the default database meant for use by users, utilities, and third-party applications.

The other two databases, *template0* and *template1*, are meant as source or template databases to be used for creating new databases using the CREATE DATABASE command.

Also, as part of database cluster creation, the default data directory created by postgres is */var/lib/pgsql/16/data*. The subdirectory, 16 in this case, is created based on the postgres server version installed.

We can see that various configuration files have been created in the default data directory, */var/lib/pgsql/16/data*.

```
[root@pg_server ~]# ls -lrth /var/lib/pgsql/16/data
total 56K
drwx------. 2 postgres postgres    6 May 21 23:39 pg_twophase
drwx------. 2 postgres postgres    6 May 21 23:39 pg_tblspc
drwx------. 2 postgres postgres    6 May 21 23:39 pg_snapshots
drwx------. 2 postgres postgres    6 May 21 23:39 pg_serial
-rw-------. 1 postgres postgres    3 May 21 23:39 PG_VERSION
.
<<< output truncated >>>
.
-rw-------. 1 postgres postgres  29K May 21 23:39 postgresql.conf
-rw-------. 1 postgres postgres 5.4K May 21 23:39 pg_hba.conf
drwx------. 2 postgres postgres 4.0K May 21 23:39 global
drwx------. 4 postgres postgres  68 May 21 23:39 pg_logical
drwx------. 2 postgres postgres  25 May 21 23:39 pg_stat
drwx------. 2 postgres postgres   6 May 21 23:39 log
```

Step 13: Starting and stopping PostgreSQL server.

PostgreSQL installation doesn't start PostgreSQL server automatically. Initially the PostgreSQL service needs to be enabled. Enabling the service automates the startup during system restarts.

In order to manage a database's life cycle, the "*systemctl*" command is used to perform operations like enable, disable, start, stop, reload, and restart PostgreSQL server.

systemctl is a command-line utility mostly used in Linux distributions and not specific to PostgreSQL.

As root user, use the systemctl enable command to enable PostgreSQL service initially.

```
[root@pg_server ~]# systemctl status postgresql-16
• postgresql-16.service - PostgreSQL 16 database server
   Loaded: loaded (/usr/lib/systemd/system/postgresql-16.service; disabled;
   vendor preset: disabled)
   Active: inactive (dead)
     Docs: https://www.postgresql.org/docs/16/static/
```

[root@pg_server ~]#

[root@pg_server ~]# systemctl enable postgresql-16
Created symlink /etc/systemd/system/multi-user.target.wants/postgresql-16.service ? /usr/lib/systemd/system/postgresql-16.service.

PostgreSQL service can be started using systemctl start, and the status can be checked using systemctl status commands.

[root@pg_server ~]# systemctl start postgresql-16

[root@pg_server ~]# systemctl status postgresql-16
- postgresql-16.service - PostgreSQL 16 database server
  Loaded: loaded (/usr/lib/systemd/system/postgresql-16.service; enabled; vendor preset: disabled)
  Active: active (running) since Tue 2024-05-21 23:51:51 CDT; 40s ago
    Docs: https://www.postgresql.org/docs/16/static/
  Process: 10815 ExecStartPre=/usr/pgsql-16/bin/postgresql-16-check-db-dir ${PGDATA} (code=exited, status=0/SUCCESS)
 Main PID: 10821 (postgres)
    Tasks: 7 (limit: 35703)
   Memory: 17.7M
   CGroup: /system.slice/postgresql-16.service
           ├─10821 /usr/pgsql-16/bin/postgres -D /var/lib/pgsql/16/data/
           ├─10822 postgres: logger
           ├─10823 postgres: checkpointer
           ├─10824 postgres: background writer
           ├─10826 postgres: walwriter
           ├─10827 postgres: autovacuum launcher
           └─10828 postgres: logical replication launcher

May 21 23:51:51 pg_server systemd[1]: Starting PostgreSQL 16 database server...
May 21 23:51:51 pg_server postgres[10821]: 2024-05-21 23:51:51.282 CDT [10821] LOG: redirecting log output to logging collector process
May 21 23:51:51 pg_server postgres[10821]: 2024-05-21 23:51:51.282 CDT [10821] HINT: Future log output will appear in directory "log".
May 21 23:51:51 pg_server systemd[1]: Started PostgreSQL 16 database server.

CHAPTER 2   POSTGRESQL INSTALLATION AND INITIALIZATION

Once the PostgreSQL server is started, we can see that all the default auxiliary processes are started and running, which was explained in Figure 1-2.

```
[root@pg_server ~]# ps -ef |grep -i postgres
postgres    10821       1  0 23:51 ?        00:00:00 /usr/pgsql-16/bin/
postgres -D /var/lib/pgsql/16/data/
postgres    10822   10821  0 23:51 ?        00:00:00 postgres: logger
postgres    10823   10821  0 23:51 ?        00:00:00 postgres: checkpointer
postgres    10824   10821  0 23:51 ?        00:00:00 postgres: background writer
postgres    10826   10821  0 23:51 ?        00:00:00 postgres: walwriter
postgres    10827   10821  0 23:51 ?        00:00:00 postgres: autovacuum
                                                              launcher
postgres    10828   10821  0 23:51 ?        00:00:00 postgres: logical
                                                              replication
                                                              launcher
```

There are few more ***systemctl*** command options available for other admin operations like

- To stop PostgreSQL to completely bring down the service

    # systemctl stop postgresql-16

- To restart PostgreSQL after any configuration changes

    # systemctl restart postgresql-16

- To reload PostgreSQL after any configuration changes but do not require full restart

    # systemctl reload postgresql-16

- To disable PostgreSQL in order to prevent it from starting automatically during system restarts

    # systemctl disable postgresql-16

Step 14: Verifying database and data directory as postgres user.

As postgres user, we can use the command-line client, "psql", a primary interface to interact with the database engine.

```
[root@pg_server ~]# su - postgres
[postgres@pg_server ~]$
[postgres@pg_server ~]$ psql
psql (16.3)
Type "help" for help.

postgres=#
```

From the above output, we can see psql command execution as postgres user connects to the PostgreSQL console. The default behavior of psql is to show the client utility current version during server connectivity. Connecting to PostgreSQL prompt allows us to interact with the database management system.

PostgreSQL provides a wide range of commands to execute at CLI to perform administrative tasks like creating and managing databases, performing database activities, etc. Let us explore a few out of many commands available to use at postgres user prompt.

The *help* command displays options to use and get familiarized with PostgreSQL environment.

```
postgres=# help
You are using psql, the command-line interface to PostgreSQL.
Type:  \copyright for distribution terms
       \h for help with SQL commands
       \? for help with psql commands
       \g or terminate with semicolon to execute query
       \q to quit
```

To see the list of databases that are available on server, use the \l command.

<<< output truncated >>>

```
postgres=# \l
List of databases
   Name    |  Owner   |   Ctype    |   Access privileges
-----------+----------+------------+----------------------
 postgres  | postgres | en_US.UTF-8 |
 template0 | postgres | en_US.UTF-8 | =c/postgres         +
           |          |             | postgres=CTc/postgres
 template1 | postgres | en_US.UTF-8 | =c/postgres         +
           |          |             | postgres=CTc/postgres
(3 rows)
```

As discussed in previous steps, when PostgreSQL cluster is initialized, these databases are automatically created in the system.

When the PostgreSQL server is initialized using *initdb*, the default data directory is created.

Below commands help us see the default location *initdb* used for data directory.

postgres=# show data_directory;
```
    data_directory
------------------------
 /var/lib/pgsql/16/data
(1 row)
```

postgres=# select setting from pg_settings where name='data_directory';
```
        setting
------------------------
 /var/lib/pgsql/16/data
(1 row)
```

To check the version of the installed PostgreSQL:

postgres=# select version();
```
version
--------------------------------------------------------------------
PostgreSQL 16.3 on x86_64-pc-linux-gnu, compiled by gcc (GCC) 8.5.0
20210514 (Red Hat 8.5.0-20), 64-bit
(1 row)
```

Exploring a few files under the data directory

All the PostgreSQL configuration files along with log directory are stored under the data directory location */var/lib/pgsql/16/data*.

postgresql.conf is one of the main configuration files that has all the parameters commented out by default. The parameters can be uncommented, and values can be set as per the requirement.

CHAPTER 2   POSTGRESQL INSTALLATION AND INITIALIZATION

We will explore various parameters from postgresql.conf throughout this book.

One of the parameters is port; opening the port allows the clients to connect to PostgreSQL instance/database remotely.

```
[postgres@pg_server ~]$ cd /var/lib/pgsql/16/data/

[postgres@pg_server data]$ grep -i port postgresql.conf
#port = 5432                    # (change requires restart)
```

As postgres user, uncomment the port in /var/lib/pgsql/16/data//postgresql.conf.

```
[postgres@pg_server data]$ vi postgresql.conf

[postgres@pg_server data]$ grep -i port postgresql.conf
port = 5432                     # (change requires restart)
```

postmaster.opts is another key file created automatically in the PostgreSQL configuration. This file records the command-line options used to start PostgreSQL server and helps during troubleshooting.

```
[postgres@pg_server data]$ cat postmaster.opts
/usr/pgsql-16/bin/postgres "-D" "/var/lib/pgsql/16/data/"
```

pg_controldata is another utility of PostgreSQL that provides the information of the PostgreSQL control file, which contains critical metadata like checkpoint information, database block size, WAL block size, etc.

```
[root@pg_server bin]# /usr/pgsql-16/bin/pg_controldata -D /var/lib/pgsql/16/data
pg_control version number:            1300
Catalog version number:               202307071
Database system identifier:           7371678965862218025
Database cluster state:               in production
pg_control last modified:             Tue 21 May 2024 11:56:55 PM CDT
Latest checkpoint location:           0/156F438
Latest checkpoint's REDO location:    0/156F400
Latest checkpoint's REDO WAL file:    000000010000000000000001
Latest checkpoint's TimeLineID:       1
Latest checkpoint's PrevTimeLineID:   1
Latest checkpoint's full_page_writes: on
```

CHAPTER 2 POSTGRESQL INSTALLATION AND INITIALIZATION

```
Latest checkpoint's NextXID:            0:738
Latest checkpoint's NextOID:            24576
Latest checkpoint's NextMultiXactId:    1
Latest checkpoint's NextMultiOffset:    0
Latest checkpoint's oldestXID:          722
Latest checkpoint's oldestXID's DB:     1
Latest checkpoint's oldestActiveXID:    738
Latest checkpoint's oldestMultiXid:     1
Latest checkpoint's oldestMulti's DB:   1
Latest checkpoint's oldestCommitTsXid:0
Latest checkpoint's newestCommitTsXid:0
Time of latest checkpoint:              Tue 21 May 2024 11:56:51 PM CDT
Fake LSN counter for unlogged rels:     0/3E8
Minimum recovery ending location:       0/0
Min recovery ending loc's timeline:     0
Backup start location:                  0/0
Backup end location:                    0/0
End-of-backup record required:          no
wal_level setting:                      replica
wal_log_hints setting:                  off
max_connections setting:                100
max_worker_processes setting:           8
max_wal_senders setting:                10
max_prepared_xacts setting:             0
max_locks_per_xact setting:             64
track_commit_timestamp setting:         off
Maximum data alignment:                 8
Database block size:                    8192
Blocks per segment of large relation:   131072
WAL block size:                         8192
Bytes per WAL segment:                  16777216
Maximum length of identifiers:          64
Maximum columns in an index:            32
Maximum size of a TOAST chunk:          1996
Size of a large-object chunk:           2048
```

```
Date/time type storage:           64-bit integers
Float8 argument passing:          by value
Data page checksum version:       0
Mock authentication nonce:        51a6acb120409951b6350b1439955692278f
2432e1a8289b53ddd99b53935e4f
[root@pg_server bin]#
```

Step 15: Update the *.bash_profile* of the postgres user with environment variables.

Adding variables related to path of binaries and data directory in *.bash_profile* will automatically set the PostgreSQL environment every time when logged in as postgres user.

As postgres user, add the below two lines to the *.bash_profile* file under home (/home/postgres) directory.

```
[postgres@pg_server ~]$ vi .bash_profile
export PATH=$PATH:/usr/pgsql-16/bin
export PGDATA=/var/lib/pgsql/16/data/
```

Log out and log in back as postgres user.

```
[postgres@pg_server ~]$ exit
logout
[root@pg_server data]#
[root@pg_server data]# su - postgres
[postgres@pg_server ~]$
[postgres@pg_server ~]$ echo $PATH
/home/postgres/.local/bin:/home/postgres/bin:/usr/share/Modules/bin:/usr/local/bin:/usr/bin:/usr/local/sbin:/usr/sbin:/usr/pgsql-16/bin
[postgres@pg_server ~]$ echo $PGDATA
/var/lib/pgsql/16/data/
```

Step 16: Alternative option for stopping and starting the PostgreSQL server.

In addition to using "systemctl" commands as root user, a PostgreSQL utility called *pg_ctl* can be used as an alternative to perform administrative operations like start, stop, status, restart, reload, etc. using postgres user.

Syntax:

```
[postgres@pg_server ~]$ which pg_ctl
/usr/pgsql-16/bin/pg_ctl

[postgres@pg_server ~]$ pg_ctl --help
pg_ctl is a utility to initialize, start, stop, or control a
PostgreSQL server.

Usage:
  pg_ctl init[db]   [-D DATADIR] [-s] [-o OPTIONS]
  pg_ctl start      [-D DATADIR] [-l FILENAME] [-W] [-t SECS] [-s]
                    [-o OPTIONS] [-p PATH] [-c]
  pg_ctl stop       [-D DATADIR] [-m SHUTDOWN-MODE] [-W] [-t SECS] [-s]
  pg_ctl restart    [-D DATADIR] [-m SHUTDOWN-MODE] [-W] [-t SECS] [-s]
                    [-o OPTIONS] [-c]
  pg_ctl reload     [-D DATADIR] [-s]
  pg_ctl status     [-D DATADIR]
  pg_ctl promote    [-D DATADIR] [-W] [-t SECS] [-s]
  pg_ctl logrotate  [-D DATADIR] [-s]
  pg_ctl kill       SIGNALNAME PID
```

- To check the status of the PostgreSQL server

  ```
  [postgres@pg_server ~]$ pg_ctl status
  pg_ctl: server is running (PID: 10821)
  /usr/pgsql-16/bin/postgres "-D" "/var/lib/pgsql/16/data/"
  ```

  or

  ```
  [postgres@pg_server ~]$ pg_ctl -D /var/lib/pgsql/16/data status
  pg_ctl: server is running (PID: 10821)
  /usr/pgsql-16/bin/postgres
  ```

- To stop the PostgreSQL server

  ```
  [postgres@pg_server ~]$ pg_ctl stop
  waiting for server to shut down.... done
  server stopped
  ```

CHAPTER 2   POSTGRESQL INSTALLATION AND INITIALIZATION

or

[postgres@pg_server ~]$ pg_ctl -D /var/lib/pgsql/16/data stop
waiting for server to shut down.... done
server stopped

- To verify the status after stop

[postgres@pg_server ~]$ pg_ctl status
pg_ctl: no server running

or

[postgres@pg_server ~]$ pg_ctl -D /var/lib/pgsql/16/data status
pg_ctl: no server running

- To start the PostgreSQL server

[postgres@pg_server ~]$ pg_ctl start
waiting for server to start....2024-05-22 00:10:29.005 CDT [12667] LOG: redirecting log output to logging collector process
2024-05-22 00:10:29.005 CDT [12667] HINT: Future log output will appear in directory "log".
 done
server started

or

[postgres@pg_server ~]$ pg_ctl -D /var/lib/pgsql/16/data start
waiting for server to start....2024-05-22 00:15:27.605 CDT [12797] LOG: redirecting log output to logging collector process
2024-05-22 00:15:27.605 CDT [12797] HINT: Future log output will appear in directory "log".
 done
server started

- To verify the status after start

[postgres@pg_server ~]$ pg_ctl status
pg_ctl: server is running (PID: 12667)
/usr/pgsql-16/bin/postgres "-D" "/var/lib/pgsql/16/data/"

45

or

[postgres@pg_server ~]$ pg_ctl -D /var/lib/pgsql/16/data status
```
pg_ctl: server is running (PID: 12797)
/usr/pgsql-16/bin/postgres "-D" "/var/lib/pgsql/16/data"
```

- To restart the PostgreSQL server

  We can use the restart command directly to stop/start the PostgreSQL server.

  [postgres@pg_server ~]$ pg_ctl -D /var/lib/pgsql/16/data restart
  ```
  waiting for server to shut down.... done
  server stopped
  waiting for server to start....2024-05-22 00:17:07.065 CDT [12843] LOG:  redirecting log output to logging collector process
  2024-05-22 00:17:07.065 CDT [12843] HINT: Future log output will appear in directory "log".
   done
  server started
  ```

- To verify the status after restart

  [postgres@pg_server ~]$ pg_ctl -D /var/lib/pgsql/16/data status
  ```
  pg_ctl: server is running (PID: 12843)
  /usr/pgsql-16/bin/postgres "-D" "/var/lib/pgsql/16/data"
  ```

  or

  [postgres@pg_server ~]$ pg_ctl -D /var/lib/pgsql/16/data status
  ```
  pg_ctl: server is running (PID: 12843)
  /usr/pgsql-16/bin/postgres "-D" "/var/lib/pgsql/16/data"
  ```

We often run into scenarios where we want to modify the configuration of the already-running or active PostgreSQL server, and some of the parameter changes will require reloading the server whereas some require restart of the server. To reload the configuration, we can use the command below:

[postgres@pg_server ~]$ pg_ctl -D /var/lib/pgsql/16/data reload
```
server signaled
```

CHAPTER 2   POSTGRESQL INSTALLATION AND INITIALIZATION

Step 17: Auto start of the PostgreSQL server.

To ensure the PostgreSQL server is automatically started on system boot, the pg_ctl startup command can be added to the rc.local script file.

As root user, add the below line to the /etc/rc.d/rc.local file:

su - postgres -c '/usr/pgsql-16/bin/pg_ctl -D /var/lib/pgsql/16/data start'

[root@pg_server ~]# ls -lrt /etc/rc.d/rc.local
-rwxr-xr-x. 1 root root 549 May 23 10:53 /etc/rc.d/rc.local

[root@pg_server ~]# vi /etc/rc.d/rc.local

[root@pg_server ~]# grep -i postgres /etc/rc.d/rc.local
su - postgres -c '/usr/pgsql-16/bin/pg_ctl -D /var/lib/pgsql/16/data start'

Shutdown Modes in PostgreSQL Database Cluster

Usually, the PostgreSQL database cluster is stopped using normal options, which we have seen in previous sections. But there are shutdown modes available that can be used based on need.

Smart: When the PostgreSQL server is stopped using smart option, the server does not allow any new connections but allows the existing or connected sessions to complete the transactions. Once the transactions are complete and all the sessions are disconnected, the server proceeds for shutdown. This is considered to be a graceful shutdown, and the system doesn't need no recovery during the next startup.

[postgres@pg_server ~]$ pg_ctl stop -D /var/lib/pgsql/16/data -m smart
waiting for server to shut down... done
server stopped

The server stop waited for the existing session to be disconnected.

Log output:
[1194] LOG: received smart shutdown request
[16854] FATAL: the database system is shutting down
[1194] LOG: background worker "logical replication launcher" (PID 3744) exited with exit code 1
[1639] LOG: shutting down
[1639] LOG: checkpoint starting: shutdown immediate

47

[1639] LOG: checkpoint complete: wrote 0 buffers (0.0%); 0 WAL file(s) added, 1 removed, 0 recycled; write=0.001 s, sync=0.001 s, total=0.103 s; sync files=0, longest=0.000 s, average=0.000 s; distance=3845 kB, estimate=8399 kB; lsn=3/73000028, redo lsn=3/73000028
[1194] LOG: database system is shut down

When a user is trying to connect during the stop operation, below error is received.

psql: error: connection to server at "192.168.2.24", port 5432 failed:
FATAL: the database system is shutting down

Fast: When the PostgreSQL server is stopped using fast option, the server does not allow any new connections and terminates the existing connected sessions and immediately proceeds with server shutdown. This is considered to be a consistent shutdown as the ongoing transactions are aborted, and the system doesn't need any recovery during the next startup. This is the default stop mode.

[postgres@pg_server ~]$ pg_ctl stop -D /var/lib/pgsql/16/data -m fast
waiting for server to shut down.... done
server stopped

The server is stopped immediate, did not wait for the connected session to disconnect.

Log output:

[16877] LOG: received fast shutdown request
[16877] LOG: **aborting any active transactions**
[17015] FATAL: terminating connection due to administrator command
[16877] LOG: background worker "logical replication launcher" (PID 16885) exited with exit code 1
[16879] LOG: shutting down
[16879] LOG: checkpoint starting: shutdown immediate
LOG: checkpoint complete: wrote 0 buffers (0.0%); 0 WAL file(s) added, 1 removed, 0 recycled; write=0.001 s, sync=0.001 s, total=0.018 s; sync files=0, longest=0.000 s, average=0.000 s; distance=16383 kB, estimate=16383 kB; lsn=3/74000028, redo lsn=3/74000028
[16877] LOG: database system is shut down

Immediate: When the PostgreSQL server is stopped using immediate option, the server gets abruptly terminated. This is considered to be an inconsistent shutdown as the buffers are not written to disk and the system needs recovery during the next startup.

[postgres@pg_server ~]$ pg_ctl stop -D /var/lib/pgsql/16/data -m immediate
waiting for server to shut down.... done
server stopped

The server is stopped abruptly.

<u>Log output:</u>

[18183] LOG: checkpoint starting: time
[18183] LOG: checkpoint complete: wrote 3 buffers (0.0%); 0 WAL file(s) added, 0 removed, 0 recycled; write=0.001 s, sync=0.003 s, total=0.025 s; sync files=2, longest=0.002 s, average=0.002 s; distance=0 kB, estimate=0 kB; lsn=3/74000110, redo lsn=3/740000D8
[18181] LOG: received immediate shutdown request
[18181] LOG: database system is shut down

Subsequent startup performs system recovery

[19034] LOG: starting PostgreSQL 16.3 on x86_64-pc-linux-gnu, compiled by
               gcc (GCC) 8.5.0 20210514 (Red Hat 8.5.0-20), 64-bit
[19034] LOG: listening on IPv4 address "0.0.0.0", port 5432
[19034] LOG: listening on IPv6 address "::", port 5432
[19034] LOG: listening on Unix socket "/run/postgresql/.s.PGSQL.5432"
[19034] LOG: listening on Unix socket "/tmp/.s.PGSQL.5432"
[19038] LOG: database system was interrupted; last known up at 2024-10-17 18:55:06 CDT
[19038] LOG: database system was not properly shut down; automatic recovery in progress
[19038] LOG: redo starts at 3/740000D8
[19038] LOG: invalid record length at 3/740001C0: expected at least 24, got 0
[19038] LOG: redo done at 3/74000188 system usage: CPU: user: 0.00 s, system: 0.00 s, elapsed: 0.00 s

```
[19036] LOG:    checkpoint starting: end-of-recovery immediate wait
[19036] LOG:    checkpoint complete: wrote 3 buffers (0.0%); 0 WAL
                file(s) added
[19034] LOG:    database system is ready to accept connections
```

With this step, we conclude some of the administrative tasks of the PostgreSQL server.

One of the key points to remember is that whenever the PostgreSQL server is installed using YUM installation, the binaries and data will be hosted in the default location. Installation does not provide an option to select a different path either for the binaries or for the data directory. Even with this limitation, this is standard method followed in the enterprise organizations during PostgreSQL installation.

Uninstallation of PostgreSQL Server (Installed Using RPMs)

In this section, we will see how PostgreSQL server is uninstalled by removing the binaries from the system.

Step 1: Stop the PostgreSQL server.

```
[root@pg_server ~]# systemctl stop postgresql-16
[root@pg_server ~]#
[root@pg_server ~]# systemctl status postgresql-16
● postgresql-16.service - PostgreSQL 16 database server
    Loaded: loaded (/usr/lib/systemd/system/postgresql-16.service; enabled;
    vendor preset: disabled)
    Active: inactive (dead) since Wed 2024-05-22 00:10:16 CDT; 16min ago
      Docs: https://www.postgresql.org/docs/16/static/
   Process: 10821 ExecStart=/usr/pgsql-16/bin/postgres -D ${PGDATA}
   (code=exited, status=0/SUCCESS)
   Process: 10815 ExecStartPre=/usr/pgsql-16/bin/postgresql-16-check-db-dir
   ${PGDATA} (code=exited, status=0/SUCCESS)
  Main PID: 10821 (code=exited, status=0/SUCCESS)
```

CHAPTER 2   POSTGRESQL INSTALLATION AND INITIALIZATION

```
May 21 23:51:51 pg_server systemd[1]: Starting PostgreSQL 16 database
server...
May 21 23:51:51 pg_server postgres[10821]: 2024-05-21 23:51:51.282 CDT
[10821] LOG:  redirecting log output to logging collector process
May 21 23:51:51 pg_server postgres[10821]: 2024-05-21 23:51:51.282 CDT
[10821] HINT:  Future log output will appear in directory "log".
May 21 23:51:51 pg_server systemd[1]: Started PostgreSQL 16
database server.
May 22 00:10:16 pg_server systemd[1]: postgresql-16.service: Killing
process 10822 (postgres) with signal SIGKILL.
May 22 00:10:16 pg_server systemd[1]: postgresql-16.service: Succeeded.
[root@pg_server ~]#
```

Step 2: Remove the PostgreSQL software using the YUM remove command.

```
[root@pg_server ~]# yum remove postgresql16-server
Dependencies resolved.
================================================================================
 Package                  Architecture  Version              Repository   Size
================================================================================
Removing:
 postgresql16-server      x86_64        16.3-1PGDG.rhel8     @pgdg16      28 M
Removing dependent packages:
 postgresql16-contrib     x86_64        16.3-1PGDG.rhel8     @pgdg16      2.7 M
Removing unused dependencies:
 postgresql16             x86_64        16.3-1PGDG.rhel8     @pgdg16      10 M

Transaction Summary
================================================================================
Remove  3 Packages

Freed space: 41 M
Is this ok [y/N]: y
Running transaction check
Transaction check succeeded.
Running transaction test
```

CHAPTER 2 POSTGRESQL INSTALLATION AND INITIALIZATION

```
Transaction test succeeded.
Running transaction
  Preparing         :                                                1/1
  Running scriptlet: postgresql16-contrib-16.3-1PGDG.rhel8.x86_64     1/1
  Erasing           : postgresql16-contrib-16.3-1PGDG.rhel8.x86_64    1/3
  Running scriptlet: postgresql16-server-16.3-1PGDG.rhel8.x86_64      2/3
  Erasing           : postgresql16-server-16.3-1PGDG.rhel8.x86_64     2/3
  Running scriptlet: postgresql16-server-16.3-1PGDG.rhel8.x86_64      2/3
  Erasing           : postgresql16-16.3-1PGDG.rhel8.x86_64            3/3
  Running scriptlet: postgresql16-16.3-1PGDG.rhel8.x86_64             3/3
  Verifying         : postgresql16-16.3-1PGDG.rhel8.x86_64            1/3
  Verifying         : postgresql16-contrib-16.3-1PGDG.rhel8.x86_64    2/3
  Verifying         : postgresql16-server-16.3-1PGDG.rhel8.x86_64     3/3

Removed:
  postgresql16-16.3-1PGDG.rhel8.x86_64
  postgresql16-contrib-16.3-1PGDG.rhel8.x86_64
  postgresql16-server-16.3-1PGDG.rhel8.x86_64
```

Complete!

Step 3: Remove residue RPMs.

Below are the additional RPM packages that are still present after removing postgres from the server.

[root@pg_server ~]# rpm -qa |grep -i postgres
postgresql16-libs-16.3-1PGDG.rhel8.x86_64
pcp-pmda-postgresql-5.3.7-7.el8.x86_64

Remove the residue packages using the "rpm -e" command.

[root@pg_server ~]# rpm -e postgresql16-libs-16.3-1PGDG.rhel8.x86_64 pcp-pmda-postgresql-5.3.7-7.el8.x86_64
[root@pg_server ~]#
[root@pg_server ~]# rpm -qa |grep -i postgres
[root@pg_server ~]#

Step 4: Remove binary and data directories.

As root user, remove the directories.

```
[root@pg_server ~]# ls -ld /usr/pgsql-16/
drwxr-xr-x. 6 root root 52 May 21 23:29 /usr/pgsql-16/

[root@pg_server ~]# ls -ld /var/lib/pgsql/16
drwx------. 3 postgres postgres 36 May 22 00:27 /var/lib/pgsql/16

[root@pg_server ~]# rm -rf /usr/pgsql-16/ /var/lib/pgsql/16

[root@pg_server ~]# ls -ld /var/lib/pgsql/16 /var/lib/pgsql/16
ls: cannot access '/var/lib/pgsql/16': No such file or directory
ls: cannot access '/var/lib/pgsql/16': No such file or directory
```

This completes cleanup of PostgreSQL from server.

Please note that if we want to install the previous versions of the RPMs, we will have to first search for specific version RPMs in the repository and download it.

- Below is the repository URL:

    https://download.postgresql.org/pub/repos/yum/

- To select specific version:

    https://download.postgresql.org/pub/repos/yum/16/

- To select the distribution:

    https://download.postgresql.org/pub/repos/yum/16/redhat/

- To select specific family:

    https://download.postgresql.org/pub/repos/yum/16/redhat/rhel-8.7-x86_64/

Once we select the family, it will take us to the complete list of available repositories where we can search for specific version and download the required RPMs and install them. Once we download the specific required RPM packages, we can then install the repository package using YUM commands as root. Like in the below example, we downloaded the 16.3 RPMs and we can install them using the rpm command.

List of 16.3 RPMs.

postgresql16-libs-16.3-3PGDG.rhel8.x86_64.rpm
postgresql16-16.3-3PGDG.rhel8.x86_64.rpm
postgresql16-server-16.3-3PGDG.rhel8.x86_64.rpm
postgresql16-contrib-16.3-3PGDG.rhel8.x86_64.rpm

Installing 16.3 using rpm command.

rpm -ivh postgresql16-libs-16.3-3PGDG.rhel8.x86_64.rpm
rpm -ivh postgresql16-16.3-3PGDG.rhel8.x86_64.rpm
rpm -ivh postgresql16-server-16.3-3PGDG.rhel8.x86_64.rpm
rpm -ivh postgresql16-contrib-16.3-3PGDG.rhel8.x86_64.rpm

Once we know the exact path, specific version files can be directly downloaded to the server using the *wget* command as shown below:

Downloading 16.3 RPMs directly to the server.

wget https://download.postgresql.org/pub/repos/yum/16/redhat/rhel-8.7-x86_64/postgresql16-libs-16.3-3PGDG.rhel8.x86_64.rpm --no-check-certificate
wget https://download.postgresql.org/pub/repos/yum/16/redhat/rhel-8.7-x86_64/postgresql16-16.3-3PGDG.rhel8.x86_64.rpm --no-check-certificate
wget https://download.postgresql.org/pub/repos/yum/16/redhat/rhel-8.7-x86_64/postgresql16-server-16.3-3PGDG.rhel8.x86_64.rpm --no-check-certificate
wget https://download.postgresql.org/pub/repos/yum/16/redhat/rhel-8.7-x86_64/ postgresql16-contrib-16.3-3PGDG.rhel8.x86_64.rpm --no-check-certificate

Once we have the required RPMs, we can install them using rpm command.

rpm -ivh postgresql16-libs-16.3-3PGDG.rhel8.x86_64.rpm
rpm -ivh postgresql16-16.3-3PGDG.rhel8.x86_64.rpm
rpm -ivh postgresql16-server-16.3-3PGDG.rhel8.x86_64.rpm
rpm -ivh postgresql16-contrib-16.3-3PGDG.rhel8.x86_64.rpm

Initialize the database cluster and start the PostgreSQL instance.

/usr/pgsql-16/bin/postgresql-16-setup initdb

systemctl enable postgresql-16
systemctl start postgresql-16
systemctl status postgresql-16

Installing PostgreSQL Server Using Source Code

PostgreSQL can also be installed using the source code as an alternate method to binary (RPM) installation.

In this section, we will see how PostgreSQL can be installed using the source code. The main advantage of installing PostgreSQL with source code over binary (RPM) method is that we can install the PostgreSQL in desired location along with an option to select user-defined path for the data directory.

Let us see the process involved in installing PostgreSQL version 16.2 using source code.

Step 1: Create the required OS directories.

We need to create three directories for the purpose mentioned below.

Directory for staging PostgreSQL software - */usr/local/software*
Installation directory for the PostgreSQL binaries - */var/postgres/postgres16.2*
Location of the data directory - */var/pgdata/postgres16/data*

```
[root@pg_server ~]# mkdir -p /usr/local/software
[root@pg_server ~]# mkdir -p /var/postgres/postgres16.2
[root@pg_server ~]# ls -lrt /usr/local/software
[root@pg_server ~]# ls -lrt /var/postgres/postgres16.2
```

Step 2: Download the required source code for specific PostgreSQL version 16.2.

We can download the source code for all the available versions from the URL below:

https://ftp.postgresql.org/pub/source/

In the home page of the above URL, we can navigate across different versions that we want to download. In this case, we will check 16.2 by navigating to the URL below:

https://ftp.postgresql.org/pub/source/v16.2/

CHAPTER 2 POSTGRESQL INSTALLATION AND INITIALIZATION

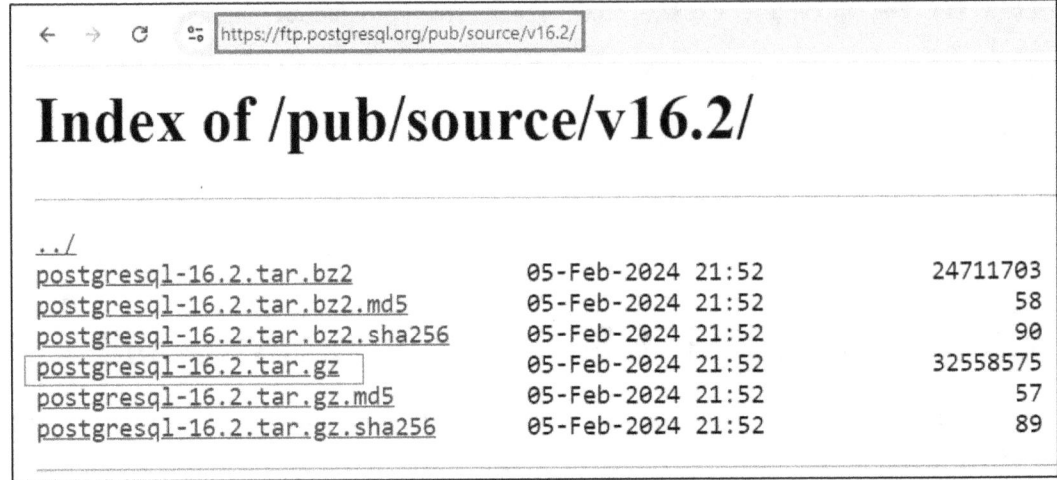

Figure 2-5. *Source code downloadable location and file*

We can download the file, postgresql-16.2.tar.gz, and copy it to the server or the wget command can be used on the server to download the file (postgresql-16.2.tar.gz) directly.

In this example, let us download the tar file using the wget command on the server.

As root user, run the wget command being in software stage directory created earlier.

[root@pg_server ~]# cd /usr/local/software

[root@pg_server software]# wget https://ftp.postgresql.org/pub/source/ v16.2/postgresql-16.2.tar.bz2 --no-check-certificate
--2024-05-22 22:15:25-- https://ftp.postgresql.org/pub/source/v16.2/ postgresql-16.2.tar.bz2
Resolving ftp.postgresql.org (ftp.postgresql.org)... 147.75.85.69, 217.196.149.55, 72.32.157.246, ...
Connecting to ftp.postgresql.org (ftp.postgresql.org)|147.75.85.69|:443... connected.
HTTP request sent, awaiting response... 200 OK
Length: 24711703 (24M) [application/octet-stream]
Saving to: 'postgresql-16.2.tar.bz2'

postgresql-16.2.tar.bz2   100%[========>]   23.57M   6.46MB/s   in 4.0s

CHAPTER 2 POSTGRESQL INSTALLATION AND INITIALIZATION

```
2024-05-22 22:15:31 (5.88 MB/s) - 'postgresql-16.2.tar.bz2' saved
[24711703/24711703]
```

[root@pg_server software]# ls -lrt
```
total 24136
-rw-r--r--. 1 root root 24711703 Feb  5 15:52 postgresql-16.2.tar.bz2
```

Step 3: Extract the downloaded source code file.

```
[root@pg_server software]# tar -xvf postgresql-16.2.tar.bz2
postgresql-16.2/
.
```
<<< output truncated >>>
```
.
postgresql-16.2/INSTALL
```

[root@pg_server software]# ls -lrt
```
total 24140
drwxrwxrwx. 6 1107 1107       4096 Feb  5 15:52 postgresql-16.2
-rw-r--r--. 1 root root   24711703 Feb  5 15:52 postgresql-16.2.tar.bz2
```

Go to the unzipped location and check files.

[root@pg_server software]# cd postgresql-16.2
[root@pg_server postgresql-16.2]# ls -lrt
```
total 872
-rw-r--r--.  1 1107 1107    1213 Feb  5 15:41 README
-rw-r--r--.  1 1107 1107    6266 Feb  5 15:41 meson_options.txt
-rw-r--r--.  1 1107 1107    1875 Feb  5 15:41 Makefile
-rw-r--r--.  1 1107 1107     277 Feb  5 15:41 HISTORY
-rw-r--r--.  1 1107 1107    4288 Feb  5 15:41 GNUmakefile.in
-rw-r--r--.  1 1107 1107    1192 Feb  5 15:41 COPYRIGHT
-rw-r--r--.  1 1107 1107   87279 Feb  5 15:41 configure.ac
-rwxr-xr-x.  1 1107 1107  584547 Feb  5 15:41 configure
-rw-r--r--.  1 1107 1107     365 Feb  5 15:41 aclocal.m4
-rw-r--r--.  1 1107 1107  102111 Feb  5 15:50 meson.build
drwxrwxrwx. 61 1107 1107    4096 Feb  5 15:51 contrib
drwxrwxrwx.  2 1107 1107    4096 Feb  5 15:51 config
```

57

CHAPTER 2   POSTGRESQL INSTALLATION AND INITIALIZATION

```
drwxrwxrwx.  3 1107 1107     87 Feb  5 15:51 doc
-rw-r--r--.  1 1107 1107  64601 Feb  5 15:52 INSTALL
drwxrwxrwx. 16 1107 1107   4096 Feb  5 15:52 src
```

[root@pg_server postgresql-16.2]# pwd
/usr/local/software/postgresql-16.2

We will use three commands to install the PostgreSQL server as described in Table 2-4.

Table 2-4. PostgreSQL install commands

Configure	This command will check if all the required libraries are available or not
Make	Make command will export all the required library paths and ensures that the system is ready for installation
Make Install	'Make Install' (running INSTALL): Installs PostgreSQL

Step 4: Run the configure command.

The *configure* command will check if all the required libraries are available or not, and it will configure the downloaded PostgreSQL source code on the server. We can check the options that we can provide with the configure command using the --help option.

Below is the trimmed output of the *"configure --help"* command.

[root@pg_server postgresql-16.2]# ./configure --help
```
`configure' configures PostgreSQL 15.4 to adapt to many kinds of systems.

Usage: ./configure [OPTION]... [VAR=VALUE]...

To assign environment variables (e.g., CC, CFLAGS...), specify them as
VAR=VALUE.   See below for descriptions of some of the useful variables.

Defaults for the options are specified in brackets.

Configuration:
  -h, --help              display this help and exit
      --help=short        display options specific to this package
      --help=recursive    display the short help of all the included
                          packages
```

```
-V, --version           display version information and exit
-q, --quiet, --silent   do not print `checking ...' messages
    --cache-file=FILE   cache test results in FILE [disabled]
-C, --config-cache      alias for `--cache-file=config.cache'
-n, --no-create         do not create output files
    --srcdir=DIR        find the sources in DIR [configure dir or `..']

Installation directories:
  --prefix=PREFIX       install architecture-independent files in PREFIX
                        [/usr/local/pgsql]
  --exec-prefix=EPREFIX install architecture-dependent files in EPREFIX
                        [PREFIX]

By default, `make install' will install all the files in
`/usr/local/pgsql/bin', `/usr/local/pgsql/lib' etc.  You can specify
an installation prefix other than `/usr/local/pgsql' using `--prefix',
for instance `--prefix=$HOME'.

For better control, use the options below.

Fine tuning of the installation directories:
  --bindir=DIR          user executables [EPREFIX/bin]
  --sbindir=DIR         system admin executables [EPREFIX/sbin]
```

The configure step will allow the option to specify non-default installation path for the build process.

If we want to go with the default installation path of "/usr/local/pgsql", we can just run the "./configure" command without any options as root user.

Now we want to install the postgres in a specific location, i.e., non-default location, /var/postgres/postgres16.2; hence, we need to pass the location with the "prefix" option.

./configure --prefix=/var/postgres/postgres16.2/

The above command will check for the libraries, and it will fail for these two libraries if they are not already installed.

1. readline-devel
2. zlib-devel

CHAPTER 2   POSTGRESQL INSTALLATION AND INITIALIZATION

As root user, install these two libraries using the yum command.

[root@pg_server postgresql-16.2]# yum install readline-devel
Last metadata expiration check: 0:24:40 ago on Wed 22 May 2024 10:53:26 PM CDT.
Dependencies resolved.
==
 Package   Architecture Version   Repository   Size
==
Installing:
 readline-devel   x86_64   7.0-10.el8   ol8_baseos_latest 204 k
Installing dependencies:
 ncurses-c++-libs x86_64   6.1-9.20180224.el8   ol8_baseos_latest   58 k
 ncurses-devel   x86_64   6.1-9.20180224.el8   ol8_baseos_latest 528 k

Transaction Summary
==
Install 3 Packages

Total download size: 789 k
Installed size: 1.4 M
Is this ok [y/N]: y
Downloading Packages:
(1/3):ncurses-c++-libs-6.1-9.20180224.el8.x86_64.rpm   176 kB/s | 58 kB 00:00
(2/3): readline-devel-7.0-10.el8.x86_64.rpm   599 kB/s | 204 kB 00:00
(3/3): ncurses-devel-6.1-9.20180224.el8.x86_64.rpm   1.5 MB/s | 528 kB 00:00

Total   2.0 MB/s | 789 kB 00:00
Running transaction check
Transaction check succeeded.
Running transaction test
Transaction test succeeded.
Running transaction
  Preparing   :   1/1
  Installing   : ncurses-c++-libs-6.1-9.20180224.el8.x86_64   1/3
  Installing   : ncurses-devel-6.1-9.20180224.el8.x86_64   2/3
  Installing   : readline-devel-7.0-10.el8.x86_64   3/3

```
  Running scriptlet: readline-devel-7.0-10.el8.x86_64                    3/3
  Verifying        : ncurses-c++-libs-6.1-9.20180224.el8.x86_64          1/3
  Verifying        : ncurses-devel-6.1-9.20180224.el8.x86_64             2/3
  Verifying        : readline-devel-7.0-10.el8.x86_64                    3/3

Installed:
  ncurses-c++-libs-6.1-9.20180224.el8.x86_64
  ncurses-devel-6.1-9.20180224.el8.x86_64
  readline-devel-7.0-10.el8.x86_64

Complete!
```

[root@pg_server postgresql-16.2]# yum install zlib-devel
```
Last metadata expiration check: 0:26:37 ago on Wed 22 May 2024 10:53:26 PM CDT.
Package zlib-devel-1.2.11-20.el8.x86_64 is already installed.
Dependencies resolved.
================================================================================
 Package          Architecture      Version              Repository       Size
================================================================================
Upgrading:
 zlib             x86_64            1.2.11-25.el8        ol8_baseos_latest 102 k
 zlib-devel       x86_64            1.2.11-25.el8        ol8_baseos_latest  57 k

Transaction Summary
================================================================================
Upgrade  2 Packages

Total download size: 160 k
Is this ok [y/N]: y
Downloading Packages:
(1/2): zlib-1.2.11-25.el8.x86_64.rpm           329 kB/s | 102 kB     00:00
(2/2): zlib-devel-1.2.11-25.el8.x86_64.rpm     181 kB/s |  57 kB     00:00
--------------------------------------------------------------------------------
Total                                          483 kB/s | 160 kB     00:00
Running transaction check
Transaction check succeeded.
Running transaction test
```

CHAPTER 2 POSTGRESQL INSTALLATION AND INITIALIZATION

```
Transaction test succeeded.
Running transaction
  Preparing        :                                                1/1
  Upgrading        : zlib-1.2.11-25.el8.x86_64                      1/4
  Upgrading        : zlib-devel-1.2.11-25.el8.x86_64                2/4
  Cleanup          : zlib-devel-1.2.11-20.el8.x86_64                3/4
  Cleanup          : zlib-1.2.11-20.el8.x86_64                      4/4
  Running scriptlet: zlib-1.2.11-20.el8.x86_64                      4/4
  Verifying        : zlib-1.2.11-25.el8.x86_64                      1/4
  Verifying        : zlib-1.2.11-20.el8.x86_64                      2/4
  Verifying        : zlib-devel-1.2.11-25.el8.x86_64                3/4
  Verifying        : zlib-devel-1.2.11-20.el8.x86_64                4/4
Upgraded:
  zlib-1.2.11-25.el8.x86_64
  zlib-devel-1.2.11-25.el8.x86_64
```

Complete!

As root user, we can now run the configure command with prefix option for non-default binary location.

[root@pg_server postgresql-16.2]# ./configure --prefix=/var/postgres/postgres16.2
```
checking build system type... x86_64-pc-linux-gnu
checking host system type... x86_64-pc-linux-gnu
.
```

<<< output truncated >>>
```
.
config.status: linking src/include/port/linux.h to src/include/pg_config_os.h
config.status: linking src/makefiles/Makefile.linux to src/Makefile.port
[root@pg_server postgresql-16.2]#
```

Once the configure command is complete, it will log its status into a file with name *"configure.log"* in the same directory. We can open the file, and we should see the exit status "0".

CHAPTER 2   POSTGRESQL INSTALLATION AND INITIALIZATION

[root@pg_server postgresql-16.2]# ls -ltr config.log
-rw-r--r--. 1 root root 440972 May 22 22:58 config.log

We can do a tail on this log file.

[root@pg_server postgresql-16.2]# tail -10 config.log
#define HAVE_GCC__ATOMIC_INT64_CAS 1
#define HAVE__GET_CPUID 1
#define USE_SSE42_CRC32C_WITH_RUNTIME_CHECK 1
#define USE_UNNAMED_POSIX_SEMAPHORES 1
#define USE_SYSV_SHARED_MEMORY 1
#define MEMSET_LOOP_LIMIT 1024
#define PG_VERSION_STR "PostgreSQL 16.2 on x86_64-pc-linux-gnu, compiled by gcc

configure: exit 0
[root@pg_server postgresql-16.2]#

Since we see exit 0, it means that configuring step is completed successfully and so we can proceed with the next step in installation.

Step 5: Building PostgreSQL from the source code with the "make" command.

When we run the "make" command, it will export all the required library paths and ensure that the system is ready for installation and then starts the PostgreSQL build using the series of predefined tasks in the file, *Makefile*, which is in the same unzipped location.

As root user, execute the make command. The execution will take some time for completion.

[root@pg_server postgresql-16.2]# pwd
/usr/local/software/postgresql-16.2

[root@pg_server postgresql-16.2]# ls -ltr Makefile*
-rw-r--r--. 1 1107 1107 1875 Aug 7 15:08 Makefile

[root@pg_server postgresql-16.2]# make
make -C ./src/backend generated-headers
make[1]: Entering directory '/usr/local/software/postgresql-16.2/src/backend'
make -C catalog distprep generated-header-symlinks
.

63

<<< output truncated >>>

-

```
make -C config all
make[1]: Entering directory '/usr/local/software/postgresql-16.2/config'
make[1]: Nothing to be done for 'all'.
make[1]: Leaving directory '/usr/local/software/postgresql-16.2/config'
[root@pg_server postgresql-16.2]#
```

Step 6: Install PostgreSQL using the "make install" command.

The make command in the previous step basically compiles the source code to executable code, which is now ready to be run to install the PostgreSQL using the "make install" command. The "make install" command basically executes the compiled source code and will copy the built program along with all its libraries and documentations to the correct location.

```
[root@pg_server postgresql-16.2]# make install
make -C ./src/backend generated-headers
make[1]: Entering directory '/usr/local/software/postgresql-16.2/src/backend'
make -C catalog distprep generated-header-symlinks
```

-

<<< output truncated >>>

-

```
make -C config install
make[1]: Entering directory '/usr/local/software/postgresql-16.2/config'
/usr/bin/mkdir -p '/var/postgres/postgres16.2/lib/pgxs/config'
/usr/bin/install -c -m 755 ./install-sh '/var/postgres/postgres16.2/lib/pgxs/config/install-sh'
/usr/bin/install -c -m 755 ./missing '/var/postgres/postgres16.2/lib/pgxs/config/missing'
make[1]: Leaving directory '/usr/local/software/postgresql-16.2/config'
[root@pg_server postgresql-16.2]#
```

This step will install PostgreSQL in the location defined using prefix option when the configure command was run; in this case, it will install the PostgreSQL in */var/postgres/postgres16.2*.

CHAPTER 2   POSTGRESQL INSTALLATION AND INITIALIZATION

```
[root@pg_server postgresql-16.2]# cd /var/postgres/postgres16.2/
[root@pg_server postgresql-16.2]# ls -lrt
total 24156
-rw-r--r--. 1 root root 24711703 Feb  5 15:52 postgresql-16.2.tar.bz2
drwxrwxrwx. 6 1107 1107     4096 May 22 23:43 postgresql-16.2
drwxr-xr-x. 6 root root     4096 May 23 00:14 include
drwxr-xr-x. 2 root root     4096 May 23 00:14 bin
drwxr-xr-x. 6 root root     4096 May 23 00:14 share
drwxr-xr-x. 4 root root     4096 May 23 00:14 lib
[root@pg_server postgresql-16.2]# cd bin
[root@pg_server bin]# ls -lrt
total 14948
-rwxr-xr-x. 1 root root 9687904 May 23 00:14 postgres
-rwxr-xr-x. 1 root root 1026632 May 23 00:14 ecpg
-rwxr-xr-x. 1 root root  182328 May 23 00:14 initdb
-rwxr-xr-x. 1 root root  124720 May 23 00:14 pg_amcheck
-rwxr-xr-x. 1 root root   58080 May 23 00:14 pg_archivecleanup
-rwxr-xr-x. 1 root root  185728 May 23 00:14 pg_basebackup
-rwxr-xr-x. 1 root root  132960 May 23 00:14 pg_receivewal
-rwxr-xr-x. 1 root root  128632 May 23 00:14 pg_recvlogical
-rwxr-xr-x. 1 root root   93808 May 23 00:14 pg_checksums
-rwxr-xr-x. 1 root root   56528 May 23 00:14 pg_config
-rwxr-xr-x. 1 root root   71168 May 23 00:14 pg_controldata
-rwxr-xr-x. 1 root root   86512 May 23 00:14 pg_ctl
-rwxr-xr-x. 1 root root  445040 May 23 00:14 pg_dump
.
```

<<< output truncated >>>

```
.
-rwxr-xr-x. 1 root root  224960 May 23 00:14 pgbench
-rwxr-xr-x. 1 root root  745248 May 23 00:14 psql
-rwxr-xr-x. 1 root root  101832 May 23 00:14 createdb
-rwxr-xr-x. 1 root root   92688 May 23 00:14 dropdb
-rwxr-xr-x. 1 root root   98144 May 23 00:14 createuser
-rwxr-xr-x. 1 root root   92632 May 23 00:14 dropuser
-rwxr-xr-x. 1 root root   93456 May 23 00:14 clusterdb
```

CHAPTER 2   POSTGRESQL INSTALLATION AND INITIALIZATION

```
-rwxr-xr-x. 1 root root   111408 May 23 00:14 vacuumdb
-rwxr-xr-x. 1 root root   102584 May 23 00:14 reindexdb
-rwxr-xr-x. 1 root root    88184 May 23 00:14 pg_isready
```

Step 7: Build and install contrib module using the make command.

We can install the additional packages like contrib using the same *make* and *make install* commands but from contrib directory.

As root user, run the make and make install commands.

[root@pg_server ~]# cd /usr/local/software/postgresql-16.2/contrib

[root@pg_server contrib]# make
```
make -C ../src/backend generated-headers
make[1]: Entering directory '/usr/local/software/postgresql-16.2/src/backend'
make -C catalog distprep generated-header-symlinks Make install
```
.

<<< output truncated >>>
.
```
make[1]: Leaving directory '/usr/local/software/postgresql-16.2/contrib/vacuumlo'
[root@pg_server contrib]#
```
[root@pg_server contrib]# make install
```
make -C ../src/backend generated-headers
make[1]: Entering directory '/usr/local/software/postgresql-16.2/src/backend'
make -C catalog distprep generated-header-symlinks
```
.

<<< output truncated >>>
.
```
/usr/bin/mkdir -p '/var/postgres/postgres16.2/bin'
/usr/bin/install -c   vacuumlo '/var/postgres/postgres16.2/bin'
make[1]: Leaving directory '/usr/local/software/postgresql-16.2/contrib/vacuumlo'
```

The information about build and installation of PostgreSQL instance can be checked using a utility, pg_config.

```
[root@pg_server ~]# /var/postgres/postgres16.2/bin/pg_config
BINDIR = /var/postgres/postgres16.2/bin
DOCDIR = /var/postgres/postgres16.2/share/doc
HTMLDIR = /var/postgres/postgres16.2/share/doc
INCLUDEDIR = /var/postgres/postgres16.2/include
PKGINCLUDEDIR = /var/postgres/postgres16.2/include
INCLUDEDIR-SERVER = /var/postgres/postgres16.2/include/server
LIBDIR = /var/postgres/postgres16.2/lib
PKGLIBDIR = /var/postgres/postgres16.2/lib
LOCALEDIR = /var/postgres/postgres16.2/share/locale
MANDIR = /var/postgres/postgres16.2/share/man
SHAREDIR = /var/postgres/postgres16.2/share
SYSCONFDIR = /var/postgres/postgres16.2/etc
PGXS = /var/postgres/postgres16.2/lib/pgxs/src/makefiles/pgxs.mk
CONFIGURE =  '--without-icu'
CC = gcc
CPPFLAGS = -D_GNU_SOURCE
CFLAGS = -Wall -Wmissing-prototypes -Wpointer-arith -Wdeclaration-after-
statement -Werror=vla -Wendif-labels -Wmissing-format-attribute -Wimplicit-
fallthrough=3 -Wcast-function-type -Wshadow=compatible-local -Wformat-
security -fno-strict-aliasing -fwrapv -fexcess-precision=standard -Wno-
format-truncation -Wno-stringop-truncation -O2
CFLAGS_SL = -fPIC
LDFLAGS = -Wl,--as-needed -Wl,-rpath,'/var/postgres/postgres16.2/
lib',--enable-new-dtags
LDFLAGS_EX =
LDFLAGS_SL =
LIBS = -lpgcommon -lpgport -lz -lreadline -lpthread -lrt -ldl -lm
VERSION = PostgreSQL 16.2
[root@pg_server ~]#
```

With this step, we have successfully installed PostgreSQL 16.2 using the source code. As root user, create a directory for data and change its ownership.

CHAPTER 2 POSTGRESQL INSTALLATION AND INITIALIZATION

[root@pg_server ~]# mkdir -p /var/pgdata/postgres16/data

[root@pg_server ~]# chown -R postgres:postgres /var/pgdata/postgres16/data

[root@pg_server ~]# chown -R postgres:postgres /var/postgres/postgres16.2

Step 8: Initialize the storage area/data directory in specific location.

As mentioned earlier, if we use source code for installing PostgreSQL, we can use custom location for the data directory. Let's see if we can initialize the storage in a specific user-defined location.

We will use the directory */var/pgdata/postgres16/data* created earlier.

As postgres user, run the below command to initialize data directory:

[root@pg_server ~]# su - postgres

[postgres@pg_server ~]$ /var/postgres/postgres16.2/bin/initdb -D /var/pgdata/postgres16/data

```
The files belonging to this database system will be owned by user
"postgres".
This user must also own the server process.

The database cluster will be initialized with locale "en_US.UTF-8".
The default database encoding has accordingly been set to "UTF8".
The default text search configuration will be set to "english".

Data page checksums are disabled.

fixing permissions on existing directory /var/pgdata/postgres16/data ... ok
creating subdirectories ... ok
selecting dynamic shared memory implementation ... posix
selecting default max_connections ... 100
selecting default shared_buffers ... 128MB
selecting default time zone ... America/Chicago
creating configuration files ... ok
running bootstrap script ... ok
performing post-bootstrap initialization ... ok
syncing data to disk ... ok
```

CHAPTER 2 POSTGRESQL INSTALLATION AND INITIALIZATION

initdb: warning: enabling "trust" authentication for local connections
initdb: hint: You can change this by editing pg_hba.conf or using the
option -A, or --auth-local and --auth-host, the next time you run initdb.

Success. You can now start the database server using:

    /var/postgres/postgres16.2/bin/pg_ctl -D /var/pgdata/postgres16/data -l logfile start

List the files/directories in data directory location.

```
[postgres@pg_server ~]$ cd /var/pgdata/postgres16/data
[postgres@pg_server data]$ ls -lrt
total 56
drwx------. 2 postgres postgres    6 May 23 00:35 pg_twophase
drwx------. 2 postgres postgres    6 May 23 00:35 pg_snapshots
drwx------. 2 postgres postgres    6 May 23 00:35 pg_serial
drwx------. 2 postgres postgres    6 May 23 00:35 pg_notify
drwx------. 4 postgres postgres   36 May 23 00:35 pg_multixact
drwx------. 2 postgres postgres    6 May 23 00:35 pg_dynshmem
drwx------. 2 postgres postgres    6 May 23 00:35 pg_commit_ts
-rw-------. 1 postgres postgres    3 May 23 00:35 PG_VERSION
drwx------. 2 postgres postgres    6 May 23 00:35 pg_tblspc
.
<<< output truncated >>>
.
drwx------. 5 postgres postgres   33 May 23 00:35 base
drwx------. 4 postgres postgres   68 May 23 00:35 pg_logical
drwx------. 2 postgres postgres   25 May 23 00:35 pg_stat
```

We can start the PostgreSQL and verify the data directory locations.

As postgres user, start the PostgreSQL server.

Check the status of PostgreSQL server

```
[postgres@pg_server data]$ /var/postgres/postgres16.2/bin/pg_ctl -D /var/pgdata/postgres16/data status
pg_ctl: no server running
```

Start the PostgreSQL server

```
[postgres@pg_server data]$ /var/postgres/postgres16.2/bin/pg_ctl -D /var/pgdata/postgres16/data start -l /tmp/server.log
waiting for server to start.... done
server started
```

Check the status again

```
[postgres@pg_server data]$ /var/postgres/postgres16.2/bin/pg_ctl -D /var/pgdata/postgres16/data status
pg_ctl: server is running (PID: 25555)
/var/postgres/postgres16.2/bin/postgres "-D" "/var/pgdata/postgres16/data"
```

Step 9: Add the startup command in the rc.local script.

To ensure the PostgreSQL server is automatically started on system boot, the pg_ctl startup command can be added to the rc.local script file.

As root user, add the below line to the /etc/rc.d/rc.local file:

su - postgres -c '/var/postgres/postgres16.2/bin/pg_ctl -D /var/pgdata/postgres16/data start'

```
[root@pg_server ~]# vi /etc/rc.d/rc.local
```

```
[root@pg_server ~]# grep -i postgres /etc/rc.d/rc.local
su - postgres -c '/var/postgres/postgres16.2/bin/pg_ctl -D /var/pgdata/postgres16/data start'
```

Step 10: Update the *.bash_profile* of the postgres user with environment variables

Adding variables related to path of binaries and data directory in *.bash_profile* will automatically set the PostgreSQL environment every time when logged in as postgres user.

As postgres user, add the below two lines to the *.bash_profile* file under home (/home/postgres) directory:

```
[postgres@pg_server ~]$ vi .bash_profile
export PATH=$PATH: /var/postgres/postgres16.2/bin
export PGDATA=/var/pgdata/postgres16/data
```

CHAPTER 2   POSTGRESQL INSTALLATION AND INITIALIZATION

Log out and log in back as postgres user.

[postgres@pg_server ~]$ exit
logout
[root@pg_server data]#
[root@pg_server data]# su - postgres
[postgres@pg_server ~]$
[postgres@pg_server ~]$ echo $PATH
/home/postgres/.local/bin:/home/postgres/bin:/usr/share/Modules/bin:/usr/local/bin:/usr/bin:/usr/local/sbin:/usr/sbin:**/var/postgres/postgres16.2/bin**
[postgres@pg_server ~]$ echo $PGDATA
/var/pgdata/postgres16/data

[postgres@pg_server ~]$ pg_ctl status
pg_ctl: server is running (PID: 1976)
/var/postgres/postgres16.2/bin/postgres "-D" "/var/pgdata/postgres16/data"

Step 11: Checking a few commands in PostgreSQL instance.

Connect to the PostgreSQL instance using the psql utility and list the current databases.

<<< output truncated >>>

[postgres@pg_server ~]$ psql
psql (16.2)
Type "help" for help.

postgres=# \l

```
                                           List of databases
   Name    |  Owner   | Encoding | Ctype        |   Access privileges
-----------+----------+----------+--------------+-----------------------
 postgres  | postgres | UTF8     | en_US.UTF-8  |
 template0 | postgres | UTF8     | en_US.UTF-8  | =c/postgres          +
           |          |          |              | postgres=CTc/postgres
 template1 | postgres | UTF8     | en_US.UTF-8  | =c/postgres          +
           |          |          |              | postgres=CTc/postgres
(3 rows)

postgres=#
```

CHAPTER 2   POSTGRESQL INSTALLATION AND INITIALIZATION

Step 12: Perform few administrative operations.

Stop the PostgreSQL server using the "pg_ctl stop" command.

[postgres@pg_server ~]$ pg_ctl status
```
pg_ctl: server is running (PID: 1976)
/var/postgres/postgres16.2/bin/postgres "-D" "/var/pgdata/postgres16/data"
```

[postgres@pg_server ~]$ pg_ctl stop
```
waiting for server to shut down.... done
server stopped
```

[postgres@pg_server ~]$ pg_ctl status
```
pg_ctl: no server running
```

Start the PostgreSQL instance using the pg_ctl command.

[postgres@pg_server ~]$ pg_ctl status
```
pg_ctl: no server running
```

[postgres@pg_server ~]$ pg_ctl start
```
waiting for server to start....2024-05-23 09:27:41.306 CDT [5091]
LOG:  starting PostgreSQL 16.2 on x86_64-pc-linux-gnu, compiled by gcc
(GCC) 8.5.0 20210514 (Red Hat 8.5.0-15.0.1), 64-bit
2024-05-23 09:27:41.308 CDT [5091] LOG:  listening on IPv6 address "::1",
port 5432
2024-05-23 09:27:41.308 CDT [5091] LOG:  listening on IPv4 address
"127.0.0.1", port 5432
2024-05-23 09:27:41.315 CDT [5091] LOG:  listening on Unix socket "/
tmp/.s.PGSQL.5432"
2024-05-23 09:27:41.321 CDT [5094] LOG:  database system was shut down at
2024-05-23 09:27:09 CDT
2024-05-23 09:27:41.325 CDT [5091] LOG:  database system is ready to accept
connections
 done
server started
```

[postgres@pg_server ~]$ pg_ctl status
```
pg_ctl: server is running (PID: 5091)
/var/postgres/postgres16.2/bin/postgres
```

CHAPTER 2 POSTGRESQL INSTALLATION AND INITIALIZATION

Uninstallation of PostgreSQL Server (Installed Using Source Code)

We can uninstall PostgreSQL as mentioned in our earlier section.

Stop the PostgreSQL server.

[postgres@pg_server ~]$ pg_ctl status
pg_ctl: server is running (PID: 5091)
/var/postgres/postgres16.2/bin/postgres

[postgres@pg_server ~]$ pg_ctl stop
waiting for server to shut down....2024-05-23 09:28:17.481 CDT [5091] LOG: received fast shutdown request
2024-05-23 09:28:17.534 CDT [5091] LOG: aborting any active transactions
2024-05-23 09:28:17.535 CDT [5091] LOG: background worker "logical replication launcher" (PID 5097) exited with exit code 1
2024-05-23 09:28:17.535 CDT [5092] LOG: shutting down
2024-05-23 09:28:17.538 CDT [5092] LOG: checkpoint starting: shutdown immediate
2024-05-23 09:28:17.551 CDT [5092] LOG: checkpoint complete: wrote 3 buffers (0.0%); 0 WAL file(s) added, 0 removed, 0 recycled; write=0.001 s, sync=0.005 s, total=0.016 s; sync files=2, longest=0.003 s, average=0.003 s; distance=0 kB, estimate=0 kB; lsn=0/150F408, redo lsn=0/150F408
2024-05-23 09:28:17.554 CDT [5091] LOG: database system is shut down
 done
server stopped

[postgres@pg_server ~]$ pg_ctl status
pg_ctl: no server running

Remove the PostgreSQL software from the installed location and data directories.
Uninstall any RPMs related to postgres.

[root@pg_server ~]# rm -rf /usr/local/software/

[root@pg_server ~]# rm -rf /var/pgdata

[root@pg_server ~]# rpm -qa |grep -i postgres

```
[root@pg_server ~]# rpm -qa |grep -i pgdg
pgdg-redhat-repo-42.0-43PGDG.noarch

[root@pg_server ~]# rpm -e pgdg-redhat-repo-42.0-43PGDG.noarch

[root@pg_server ~]# rpm -qa |grep -i pgdg
```

With this step, we have successfully completed uninstallation of PostgreSQL.

Summary

In this chapter, we explored the installation of PostgreSQL on an Oracle Enterprise Linux (OEL) system. In the first section, we walked through the process of installing PostgreSQL using RPM packages, and in the later section, we saw how to install PostgreSQL using the source code method. In addition to installation, we have gained knowledge about downloading previous versions of PostgreSQL as required and the process of uninstalling the PostgreSQL software.

CHAPTER 3

PostgreSQL Physical Structures

Introduction

PostgreSQL physical storage is structured into many important components that exist on the file system. The structures are important to the database's functionality. In this chapter, let us take a detailed look at the physical storage topology and key physical components of PostgreSQL as well as database cluster and tablespace relationships.

The following topics are covered in this chapter:

- PostgreSQL database cluster
- PostgreSQL directory structure
- Changes to the directory structure when a database and tables are created
- Subdirectories, configuration files, and their purpose
- Concept of databases and their management
- Concept of tablespaces
- Default tablespaces
- Administering tablespaces
- Temporary tablespaces
- Advantages of using tablespaces
- Query processing in PostgreSQL

CHAPTER 3   POSTGRESQL PHYSICAL STRUCTURES

In the previous chapter, after installing the PostgreSQL server, we initialized the database cluster using the *initdb* utility. In PostgreSQL, a database cluster is nothing but a collection of databases and is managed by a single PostgreSQL server instance. The database server program called postgres must be started before a database can be accessed.

PostgreSQL Database Cluster

In PostgreSQL cluster, the databases, tablespaces, and users/groups/roles are independent objects and are defined at the cluster level. A cluster will host multiple databases, and each database will support creation and management of one or more schemas. Each schema will store objects like tables, views, functions, etc.

Each database is independent or isolated from each other but can still access the cluster-level objects. Also, the data inserted in the database will be stored in the default tablespace pg_global unless an exclusive tablespace is mapped.

The PostgreSQL cluster can have multiple tablespaces, and a tablespace, on the other hand, will store data from multiple databases, i.e., a single tablespace is not confined to any specific database.

An individual user or a group of users or roles can be granted access to one or more databases using the access control through configuration files and access permissions using roles.

More information about the schemas, users, roles, objects, and access control will be explained in subsequent chapters.

Below is the high-level object hierarchy in PostgreSQL database cluster.

CHAPTER 3 POSTGRESQL PHYSICAL STRUCTURES

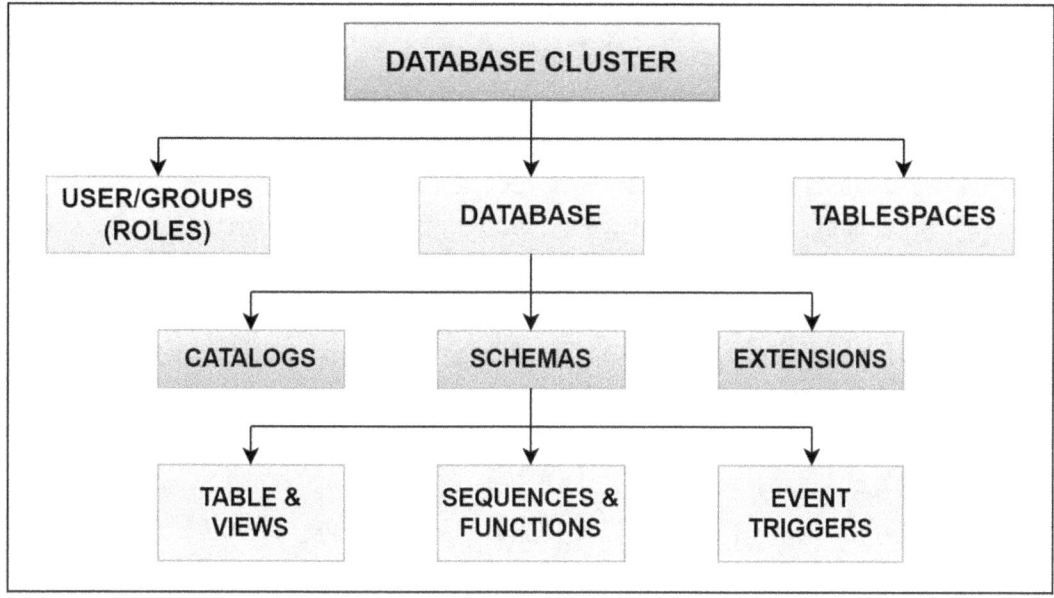

Figure 3-1. PostgreSQL cluster hierarchy

PostgreSQL Directory Structure

When a PostgreSQL server is initialized, it creates a single directory structure containing many subdirectories and files. This single directory is called the *data directory or data area* where PostgreSQL stores all the data. The path of the cluster data directory is usually set to the environment variable *PGDATA*.

For example, in a PostgreSQL 16 server, the data directory will look like the following:

```
[postgres@pg_server bin]$ echo $PGDATA
/var/lib/pgsql/16/data

[postgres@pg_server bin]$ cd $PGDATA

[postgres@pg_server data]$ ls -ltr
total 68
-rw-------. 1 postgres postgres    3 Oct 13 16:39 PG_VERSION
drwx------. 2 postgres postgres    6 Oct 13 16:39 pg_twophase
drwx------. 2 postgres postgres    6 Oct 13 16:39 pg_tblspc
drwx------. 2 postgres postgres    6 Oct 13 16:39 pg_stat_tmp
drwx------. 2 postgres postgres    6 Oct 13 16:39 pg_snapshots
```

```
drwx------. 2 postgres postgres      6 Oct 13 16:39 pg_serial
drwx------. 2 postgres postgres      6 Oct 13 16:39 pg_replslot
drwx------. 2 postgres postgres      6 Oct 13 16:39 pg_notify
drwx------. 4 postgres postgres     36 Oct 13 16:39 pg_multixact
drwx------. 2 postgres postgres      6 Oct 13 16:39 pg_dynshmem
drwx------. 2 postgres postgres      6 Oct 13 16:39 pg_commit_ts
-rw-------. 1 postgres postgres  29691 Oct 13 16:39 postgresql.conf
-rw-------. 1 postgres postgres     88 Oct 13 16:39 postgresql.auto.conf
-rw-------. 1 postgres postgres   2640 Oct 13 16:39 pg_ident.conf
-rw-------. 1 postgres postgres   5499 Oct 13 16:39 pg_hba.conf
drwx------. 3 postgres postgres     60 Oct 13 16:39 pg_wal
drwx------. 2 postgres postgres     18 Oct 13 16:39 pg_xact
drwx------. 2 postgres postgres     18 Oct 13 16:39 pg_subtrans
drwx------. 5 postgres postgres     33 Oct 13 16:39 base
drwx------. 2 postgres postgres     32 Oct 13 16:40 log
-rw-------. 1 postgres postgres     30 Oct 13 16:40 current_logfiles
-rw-------. 1 postgres postgres     58 Oct 13 16:40 postmaster.opts
drwx------. 2 postgres postgres      6 Oct 13 16:40 pg_stat
-rw-------. 1 postgres postgres     99 Oct 13 16:40 postmaster.pid
drwx------. 4 postgres postgres     68 Oct 13 16:45 pg_logical
drwx------. 2 postgres postgres   4096 Oct 13 16:51 global
[postgres@pg_server data]$
```

Here is a pictorial representation of the above folder structure for a better understanding.

CHAPTER 3 POSTGRESQL PHYSICAL STRUCTURES

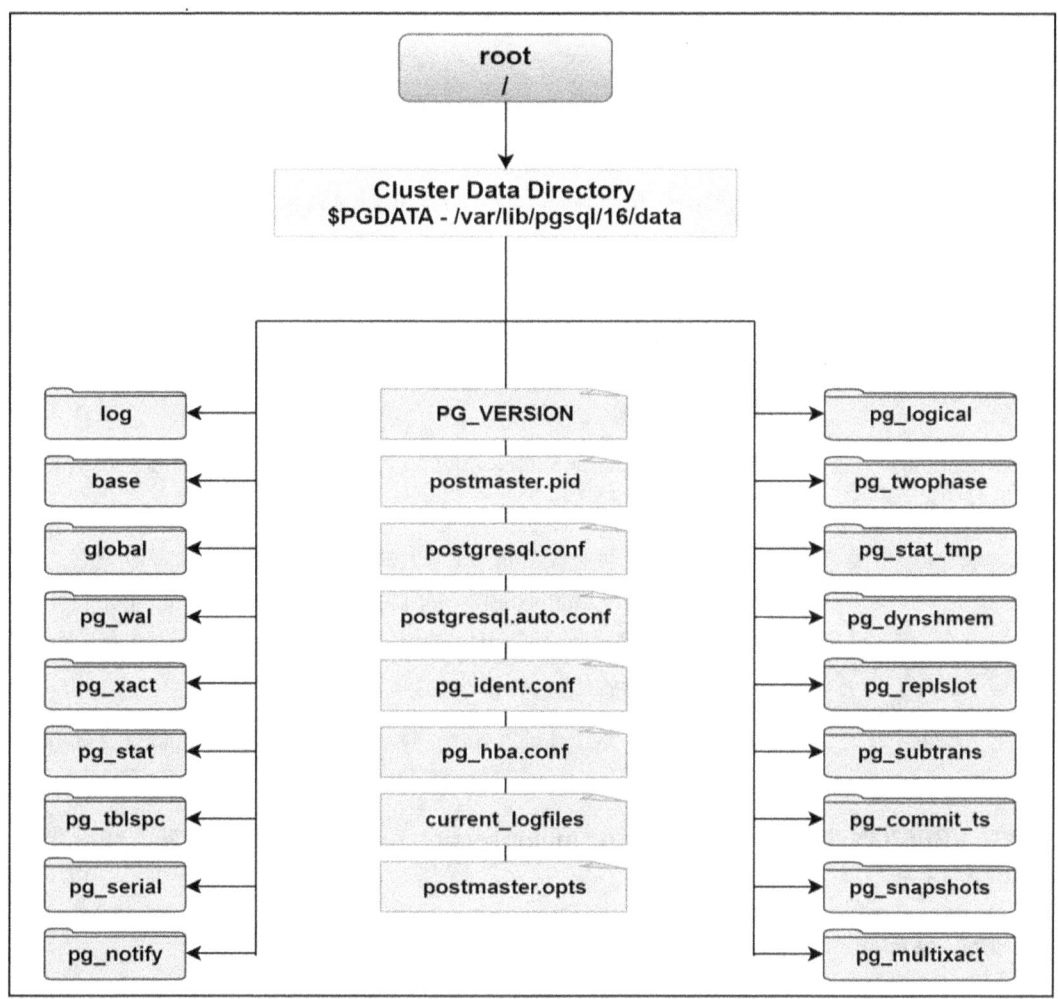

Figure 3-2. *PostgreSQL cluster data directory layout*

Let us learn more about the purpose of each file and subdirectory within the cluster data directory *PGDATA* as listed in Table 3-1 and 3-2.

Table 3-1. PostgreSQL file contents in the cluster data directory PGDATA

File name	Description
PG_VERSION	This file contains the major version number of PostgreSQL
pg_hba.conf	This file controls PostgreSQL's client authentication
pg_ident.conf	This file controls PostgreSQL's user name mapping
postgresql.conf	This file is used to set server configuration parameters
postgresql.auto.conf	This file is used for storing configuration parameters that are set in ALTER SYSTEM
postmaster.opts	This file records the number of command-line options the server was last started with
postmaster.pid	This is a lock file recording the current postmaster process ID (PID), cluster directory path, postmaster start timestamp, port number, first valid listen_address, Unix-domain socket directory path (if in use), and shared memory segment ID
current_logfiles	File recording the log files currently written to by the logging collector

PG_VERSION: This file contains the major version number of PostgreSQL running on the system.

```
[root@pg_server ~]# cd /var/lib/pgsql/16/data
[root@pg_server data]# ls -lrt PG_VERSION
-rwx------. 1 postgres postgres 3 Jun  1 04:43 PG_VERSION
[root@pg_server data]# cat PG_VERSION
16
```

pg_hba.conf: This is one of the key configuration files in PostgreSQL database cluster.

- This configuration file is created under the cluster data directory when the database cluster is initiated.
- **hba** stands for host-based authentication, and this host-based access control file mainly enables client authentication between the client application and the PostgreSQL server.

CHAPTER 3 POSTGRESQL PHYSICAL STRUCTURES

- This file controls the operations like which hosts are allowed to connect, how clients are authenticated, which PostgreSQL user names they can use, which database they can access, etc.

- This file contains a set of authentication records, and each record maintains connection type, database name, user name, client IP, and authentication method.

- The file is read at the server startup and when the server receives a SIGHUP signal. Subsequent changes to the file require server reload either using command pg_ctl or function pg_reload_conf.

- PostgreSQL rejects any connection if the entry with respect to address is not found in this file.

```
[root@pg_server data]# ls -lrt pg_hba.conf
-rw-------. 1 postgres postgres  5499 Oct 13 16:39 pg_hba.conf
[root@pg_server data]# cat pg_hba.conf
# PostgreSQL Client Authentication Configuration File
# ====================================================
.
<<< output truncated >>>
.
# TYPE   DATABASE        USER            ADDRESS                 METHOD

host     all             all             192.168.2.1/32          trust

# "local" is for Unix domain socket connections only
local    all             all                                     peer
# IPv4 local connections:
host     all             all             127.0.0.1/32            scram-sha-256
# IPv6 local connections:
host     all             all             ::1/128                 scram-sha-256
# Allow replication connections from localhost, by a user with the
# replication privilege.
local    replication     all                                     peer
host     replication     all             127.0.0.1/32            scram-sha-256
host     replication     all             ::1/128                 scram-sha-256
```

- The first field is the connection **TYPE**, and it allows the below values:
  - local: A Unix-domain socket, allows connection from only local db server
  - host: A TCP/IP socket (encrypted or not)
  - hostssl: A TCP/IP socket that is SSL-encrypted
  - hostnoss: A TCP/IP socket that is not SSL-encrypted
  - hostgssenc: A TCP/IP socket that is GSSAPI-encrypted
  - hostnogssenc: A TCP/IP socket that is not GSSAPI-encrypted
- **DATABASE** field can have values like all, specific db name or comma-separated db list, and replication.
- **USER** field can have values like all, a specific username, a group name prefixed with "+", or a comma-separated user list.
- **ADDRESS** field can be a host name, specific IP address and a CIDR mask, IP address and netmask in separate columns to specify the set of hosts.
- Method field can accept values as below:
  - **trust**: This allows authentication without providing a password provided the user is available on the PostgreSQL side.
  - **reject**: The connection will be rejected.
  - **password** or **md5**: Connections are allowed when password is used and md5 uses hashing algorithm and it was default before scram-sha-256 is introduced.
  - **scram-sha-256**: An advanced and highly secure password authentication. This authentication method provides more security than md5 method and uses a far more secure hash than the previous version.

CHAPTER 3 POSTGRESQL PHYSICAL STRUCTURES

- **ident**: This authentication method is used primarily for local connections where PostgreSQL checks the OS username of the client and compares with the PostgreSQL user.

- **peer**: Used for local connections and allows the already OS level authenticated user to connect without password.

pg_ident.conf: This file controls PostgreSQL user name mapping. It maps external user names to their corresponding PostgreSQL user names.

- No map names are defined in the default configuration.

- Records are mapped using fields MAPNAME, SYSTEM-USERNAME, and PG-USERNAME.

- MAPNAME is the map name that was used in pg_hba.conf.

- SYSTEM-USERNAME is the detected user name of the client.

- PG-USERNAME is the requested PostgreSQL user name.

- If any map record exist in this file, then SYSTEM-USERNAME may connect as PG-USERNAME.

- If all system user names and PostgreSQL user names are the same, no map records are required in this file.

- The file is read at the server startup and when the postmaster receives a SIGHUP signal. Subsequent online changes to the file require server reload using command pg_ctl reload.

```
[root@pg_server data]# ls -lrt pg_ident.conf
-rwx------. 1 postgres postgres 2640 Jun  1 04:43 pg_ident.conf
[root@pg_server data]# cat pg_ident.conf
# PostgreSQL User Name Maps
# ==========================

# MAPNAME    SYSTEM-USERNAME    PG-USERNAME
```

postgresql.conf: This file is another important and main configuration file for PostgreSQL located inside the data directory and is created as part of cluster initialization.

83

- This file contains parameters that are used by PostgreSQL cluster.
- The configuration parameters in this file control and affect the behavior of the PostgreSQL server such as
  - **authentication and security**: Parameters related to password encryption, ssl, ssl key file, etc.
  - **networking**: Parameters like port, listen_address, max_connections, etc.
  - **logging**: Parameters that define destination or directory location for the log files, log file names, etc.
  - **resource management**: Parameters used for memory allocation for individual components that supports operations like sorts, vacuum, indexes, and table alterations
  - **performance tuning**: Few parameters like max_wal_size, wal_buffers, etc., which improve the performance of the system
- All the configuration parameters are case insensitive.
- This file is manually edited based on the system's needs.
- For some parameters, if the value is changed, the PostgreSQL server needs to be reloaded or restarted for the new settings to take effect.

```
postgres=# show config_file;
          config_file
-----------------------------------------
 /var/lib/pgsql/16/data/postgresql.conf
(1 row)

[root@pg_server data]# ls -lrt postgresql.conf
-rwx------. 1 postgres postgres 29767 Jun  6 18:17 postgresql.conf

[root@pg_server data]# cat postgresql.conf
# -----------------------------
# PostgreSQL configuration file
# -----------------------------
#
```

```
# This file consists of lines of the form:
listen_addresses = '*'                  # what IP address(es) to listen on;
                                        # comma-separated list of
                                          addresses;
                                        # defaults to 'localhost'; use
                                          '*' for all
                                        # (change requires restart)
port = 5432                             # (change requires restart)
max_connections = 100                   # (change requires restart)
.
<<< output truncated >>>
.
shared_buffers = 128MB                  # min 128kB
dynamic_shared_memory_type = posix      # the default is usually the
                                          first option
max_wal_size = 1GB
min_wal_size = 80MB
log_filename = 'postgresql-%a.log'      # log file name pattern,
```

postgresql.auto.conf: This configuration file is also created during PostgreSQL cluster initialization.

- This file is located in the data directory alongside postgresql.conf.

- This is an automatically managed configuration file where the parameters are stored when set using the "**ALTER SYSTEM**" command.

- Unlike postgresql.conf, this file is a dynamic configuration file and is updated directly by PostgreSQL when configuration changes are made using the "**ALTER SYSTEM**" command.

- Postgresql.auto.conf configuration file is given priority over postgresql.conf. If any parameter is defined in both the files, then the parameter value from postgresql.auto.conf takes precedence, i.e., parameter value in postgresql.conf is overridden by parameter value in postgresql.auto.conf.

CHAPTER 3 POSTGRESQL PHYSICAL STRUCTURES

```
[root@pg_server data]# ls -lrt postgresql.auto.conf
-rw-------. 1 postgres postgres 197 Oct 17 22:22 postgresql.auto.conf

[root@pg_server data]# cat postgresql.auto.conf
# Do not edit this file manually!
# It will be overwritten by the ALTER SYSTEM command.
archive_mode = 'on'
archive_command = 'cp %p /var/lib/pgsql/16/data/archive/%f'
```

Apart from the configuration files, the current parameter values can also be checked from the cluster as below:

<<< output truncated >>>

```
postgres=# select * from pg_file_settings;
 sourcefile                  | name              | setting
-----------------------------+-------------------+------------------------
 $PGDATA/postgresql.conf     | max_connections   | 100
 $PGDATA/postgresql.conf     | shared_buffers    | 128MB
 $PGDATA/postgresql.conf     | max_wal_size      | 1GB
 $PGDATA/postgresql.conf     | min_wal_size      | 80MB
 $PGDATA/postgresql.conf     | restore_command   | cp $PGDATA/archive/%f %p
 $PGDATA/postgresql.conf     | log_destination   | stderr
 $PGDATA/postgresql.conf     | logging_collector | on
 $PGDATA/postgresql.conf     | log_directory     | log
 $PGDATA/postgresql.conf     | log_filename      | postgresql-%a.log
 $PGDATA/postgresql.conf     | log_rotation_age  | 1d
 $PGDATA/postgresql.conf     | log_rotation_size | 0
 $PGDATA/postgresql.conf     | log_line_prefix   | %m [%p]
 $PGDATA/postgresql.conf     | log_timezone      | America/Chicago
 $PGDATA/postgresql.conf     | datestyle         | iso, mdy
 $PGDATA/postgresql.conf     | timezone          | America/Chicago
 $PGDATA/postgresql.conf     | lc_messages       | en_US.UTF-8
 $PGDATA/postgresql.conf     | lc_monetary       | en_US.UTF-8
 $PGDATA/postgresql.conf     | lc_numeric        | en_US.UTF-8
 $PGDATA/postgresql.conf     | lc_time           | en_US.UTF-8
```

CHAPTER 3   POSTGRESQL PHYSICAL STRUCTURES

```
$PGDATA/postgresql.auto.conf | archive_mode      | on
$PGDATA/postgresql.auto.conf | archive_command   | cp %p $PGDATA/archive/%f
```

postmaster.opts: This file contains the command-line option used for the PostgreSQL server (postmaster) startup.

- It will capture the options like data path, port, config-file location, etc., if used during the server startup.
- Helpful during troubleshooting server startup-related issues.

[root@pg_server data]# ls -lrt postmaster.opts
-rw-------. 1 postgres postgres 58 Oct 19 16:39 postmaster.opts

[root@pg_server data]# cat postmaster.opts
/usr/pgsql-16/bin/postgres "-D" "/var/lib/pgsql/16/data/"

postmaster.pid: This is a lock file recording the current postmaster process ID (PID), cluster data directory path, postmaster start timestamp, port number, first valid listen_ address, Unix-domain socket directory path (if in use), and shared memory segment ID.

[root@pg_server data]# ls -lrt postmaster.pid
-rw-------. 1 postgres postgres 91 Oct 19 16:39 postmaster.pid

[root@pg_server data]# cat postmaster.pid
1187
/var/lib/pgsql/16/data
1729373949
5432
/run/postgresql
*
  36898398   0
Ready

[postgres@pg_server ~]$ pg_ctl status
pg_ctl: server is running (PID: **1187**)
/usr/pgsql-16/bin/postgres "-D" "/var/lib/pgsql/16/data/"

Table 3-2. *PostgreSQL subdirectories in the cluster data directory PGDATA*

Subdirectory name	Description
pg_twophase	Contains state files for prepared transactions
pg_tblspc	Contains symbolic links to tablespaces
pg_stat_tmp	Contains temporary files for the statistics subsystem
pg_snapshots	Contains exported snapshots created by *pg_export_snapshot()* function
pg_serial	Contains information about committed serializable transactions
pg_replslot	Contains replication slot data
pg_notify	Contains LISTEN/NOTIFY status data
pg_multixact	Contains multitransaction status data
pg_dynshmem	Contains files used by the dynamic shared memory subsystem
pg_commit_ts	Contains transaction commit timestamp data
pg_wal	Contains WAL segment files
pg_xact	Contains transaction commit state data
pg_subtrans	Contains subtransaction status data
Log	Contains log files
pg_stat	Contains permanent files for the statistics subsystem
pg_logical	Contains status data for logical decoding
Global	Contains cluster-wide tables, such as *pg_database* and *pg_control*
Base	Contains per-database subdirectories

You may refer to the official documentation page by visiting https://www.postgresql.org/docs/16/storage-file-layout.html for detailed information.

Databases in PostgreSQL

PostgreSQL by default creates three databases in the cluster when PostgreSQL cluster is initialized.

CHAPTER 3　POSTGRESQL PHYSICAL STRUCTURES

The database named *postgres* is the default database meant for use by users, utilities, and third-party applications.

The other two databases, *template0* and *template1*, are meant as source or template databases to be used for creating new databases using the CREATE DATABASE command.

PostgreSQL allows the creation of objects under *template1* database, and if any new user databases are created using *template1*, then all the objects from *template1* database will be copied into newly created user databases.

On the other hand, PostgreSQL recommends not to modify or change or add anything to *template0* database once the database cluster is initialized. But *template0* database can still be used as a copy to create new databases, and this newly created user database is called "pristine" database since it will have un-altered system objects inherited from *template0* database and as obvious no under-defined objects exist.

```
postgres=# \l
List of databases
   Name    |  Owner   |   Ctype    |   Access privileges
-----------+----------+------------+-----------------------
 postgres  | postgres | en_US.UTF-8 |
 template0 | postgres | en_US.UTF-8 | =c/postgres          +
           |          |             | postgres=CTc/postgres
 template1 | postgres | en_US.UTF-8 | =c/postgres          +
           |          |             | postgres=CTc/postgres
(3 rows)
```

Or

```
postgres=# select oid,datname from pg_database;
  oid | datname
------+-----------
    1 | template1
    4 | template0
    5 | postgres
(3 rows)
```

CHAPTER 3   POSTGRESQL PHYSICAL STRUCTURES

The PostgreSQL default databases and every user database we create are a subdirectory under the base directory of cluster data directory *PGDATA*, and each of the tables, indexes, free space maps (FSMs), and visibility maps (VMs) are stored as a single file under the subdirectory of the corresponding database.

```
[postgres@pg_server ~]$ echo $PGDATA
/var/lib/pgsql/16/data/

[postgres@pg_server ~]$ ls -lrt $PGDATA/base
total 60
drwx------. 2 postgres postgres 8192 Jun  1 04:43 1
drwx------. 2 postgres postgres 8192 Jun  1 04:43 4
drwx------. 2 postgres postgres 8192 Jun  1 04:43 5

[postgres@pg_server ~]$ oid2name
All databases:
    Oid  Database Name  Tablespace
    ---------------------------------
      5        postgres  pg_default
      4       template0  pg_default
      1       template1  pg_default
```

In the above output, we can see under $PGDATA/base the subdirectories got created with name same as database OID (object identifier).

CHAPTER 3 POSTGRESQL PHYSICAL STRUCTURES

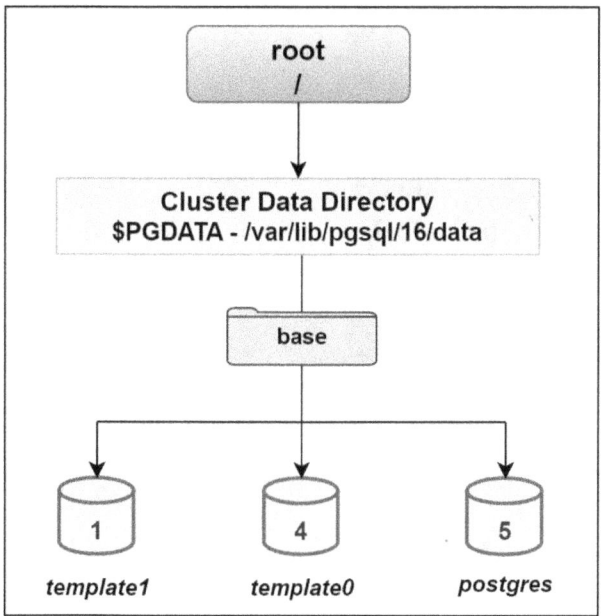

Figure 3-3. *PostgreSQL cluster database layout*

Let us understand more about the physical layout by creating a few databases and other objects in the cluster.

postgres=# select oid,datname from pg_database;
```
  oid  |  datname
-------+-----------
     5 | postgres
     1 | template1
     4 | template0
 98428 | pgdb1
 98429 | pgdb2
(5 rows)
```

[postgres@pg_server ~]$ ls -lrt $PGDATA/base
```
total 60
drwx------. 2 postgres postgres 8192 Jun  1 04:43 1
drwx------. 2 postgres postgres 8192 Jun  1 04:43 4
drwx------. 2 postgres postgres 8192 Jun  1 04:43 5
drwx------. 2 postgres postgres 8192 Oct 18 14:23 98428
drwx------. 2 postgres postgres 8192 Oct 18 14:23 98429
```

91

CHAPTER 3   POSTGRESQL PHYSICAL STRUCTURES

```
[postgres@pg_server ~]$ oid2name
All databases:
    Oid  Database Name  Tablespace
    ----------------------------------
  98428          pgdb1  pg_default
  98429          pgdb2  pg_default
      5       postgres  pg_default
      4      template0  pg_default
      1      template1  pg_default
```

From the above output, we can see each newly created user database is created as a separate subdirectory in the *base* directory. In this example, **pgdb1** is created in **98428** and *pgdb2* in *98429*.

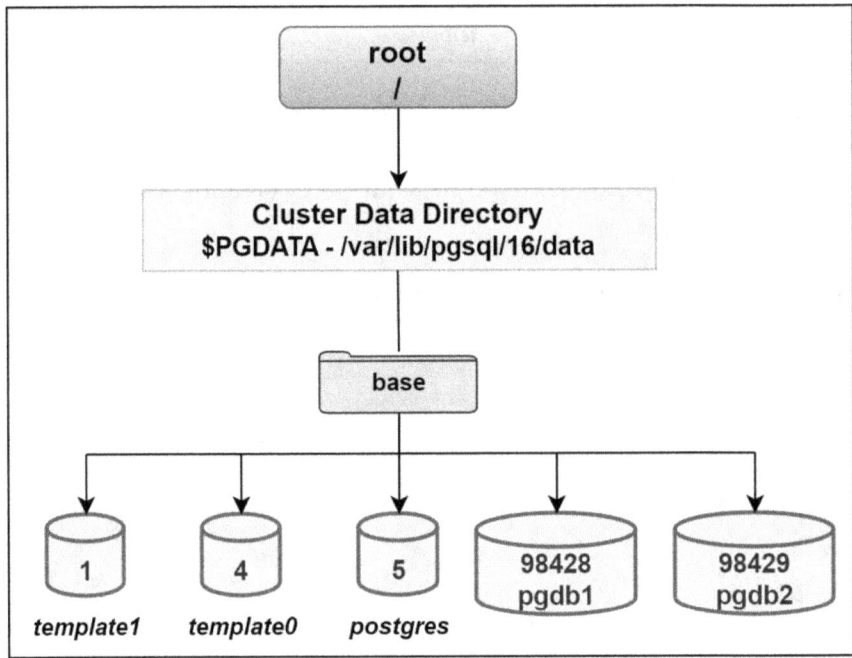

Figure 3-4. *PostgreSQL cluster database layout*

Now, let us create a few tables under these databases and see which physical path the tables take.

CHAPTER 3 POSTGRESQL PHYSICAL STRUCTURES

In database pgdb1:

```
postgres=# \c pgdb1
```
You are now connected to database "pgdb1" as user "postgres".

```
pgdb1=# create table db1t1 (x int, y int);
CREATE TABLE
pgdb1=# insert into db1t1 values (1,2), (3,4);
INSERT 0 2
pgdb1=# select * from db1t1;
 x | y
---+---
 1 | 2
 3 | 4
(2 rows)

pgdb1=# create table db1t2 (a int, b int);
CREATE TABLE
pgdb1=# insert into db1t2 values (5,6), (7,8);
INSERT 0 2
pgdb1=# select * from db1t2;
 a | b
---+---
 5 | 6
 7 | 8
(2 rows)
```

In database pgdb2:

```
pgdb1=# \c pgdb2
```
You are now connected to database "pgdb2" as user "postgres".

```
pgdb2=# create table db2t1 (x int, y int);
CREATE TABLE
pgdb2=# insert into db2t1 values (9,10), (11,12);
INSERT 0 2
pgdb2=# select * from db2t1;
```

93

CHAPTER 3 POSTGRESQL PHYSICAL STRUCTURES

```
  x  |  y
----+----
  9 | 10
 11 | 12
(2 rows)

pgdb2=#
pgdb2=# create table db2t2 (a int, b int);
CREATE TABLE
pgdb2=# insert into db2t2 values (13,14), (15,16);
INSERT 0 2
pgdb2=# select * from db2t2;
  a  |  b
----+----
 13 | 14
 15 | 16
(2 rows)
```

Since the tables are created in respective databases, their physical structure should fall under the corresponding database directories. So tables **db1t1** and **db1t2** should get created under **$PGDATA/base/98428** (physical path of **pgdb1** database), and tables **db2t1** and **db2t2** should get created under **$PGDATA/base/98429** (physical path of **pgdb2** database).

You might ask, how do I confirm that this is the case? To confirm this, we can use the **pg_relation_filepath()** system function to obtain the file path of a relation relative to the data directory. To verify, let us check the relative data directory path of the tables created in **pgdb1** and **pgdb2** databases.

```
postgres=# \c pgdb1
You are now connected to database "pgdb1" as user "postgres".
pgdb1=# select pg_relation_filepath('db1t1');
 pg_relation_filepath
----------------------
 base/98428/98430
(1 row)
```

CHAPTER 3 POSTGRESQL PHYSICAL STRUCTURES

```
pgdb1=# select pg_relation_filepath('db1t2');
 pg_relation_filepath
----------------------
 base/98428/98433
(1 row)

pgdb1=# \c pgdb2
You are now connected to database "pgdb2" as user "postgres".

pgdb2=# select pg_relation_filepath('db2t1');
 pg_relation_filepath
----------------------
 base/98429/98436
(1 row)

pgdb2=# select pg_relation_filepath('db2t2');
 pg_relation_filepath
----------------------
 base/98429/98439
(1 row)
```

From the above output, we can confirm that the relative file path in the data directory for **pgdb1** database table **db1t1** is **base/98428/98430**, and for table **db1t2**, it is **base/98428/98433**. Similarly, for pgdb2 database table db2t1, it is **base/98429/98436**, and for table db2t2, it is **base/98429/98439.**

95

CHAPTER 3 POSTGRESQL PHYSICAL STRUCTURES

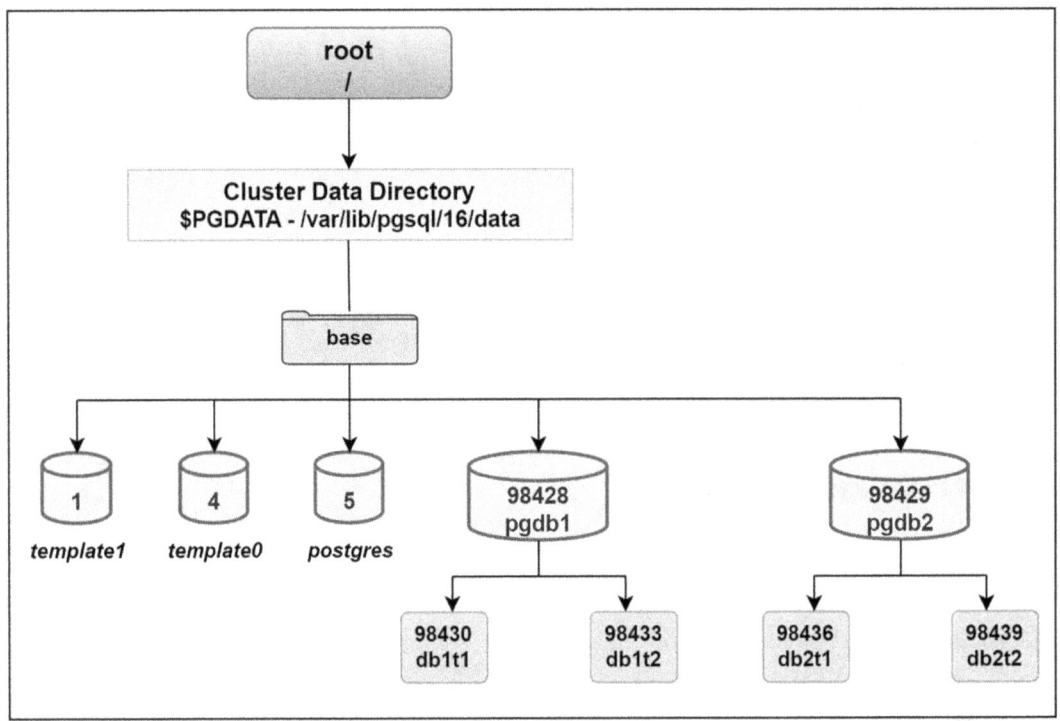

Figure 3-5. *PostgreSQL cluster database object layout*

Now, let us create a few other objects like indexes, views, and materialized views in databases *pgdb1* and *pgdb2* and check the physical layout.

In database pgdb1:

pgdb1=# create index db1t1_i1 on db1t1(x);
CREATE INDEX

pgdb1=# select pg_relation_filepath('db1t1_i1');
 pg_relation_filepath
----
 base/98428/98442
(1 row)

pgdb1=# create index db1t2_i2 on db1t2(b);
CREATE INDEX

CHAPTER 3 POSTGRESQL PHYSICAL STRUCTURES

```
pgdb1=# select pg_relation_filepath('db1t2_i2');
 pg_relation_filepath
----------------------
 base/98428/98443
(1 row)

pgdb1=# create view db1t1_v1 as select * from db1t1;
CREATE VIEW

pgdb1=# select pg_relation_filepath('db1t1_v1');
 pg_relation_filepath
----------------------

(1 row)


pgdb1=# create materialized view db1t1_mv1 as select * from db1t1;
SELECT 2

pgdb1=# select pg_relation_filepath('db1t1_mv1');
 pg_relation_filepath
----------------------
 base/98428/98448
(1 row)
```

Check the tablespace details of each object in database:

```
pgdb1=# SELECT spcname,relname,
pgdb1-# CASE WHEN relpersistence = 't' THEN 'temp '
pgdb1-# WHEN relpersistence = 'u' THEN 'unlogged '
pgdb1-# ELSE '' END ||
pgdb1-# CASE
pgdb1-# WHEN relkind = 'r' THEN 'table'
pgdb1-# WHEN relkind = 'p' THEN 'partitioned table'
pgdb1-# WHEN relkind = 'f' THEN 'foreign table'
pgdb1-# WHEN relkind = 't' THEN 'TOAST table'
pgdb1-# WHEN relkind = 'v' THEN 'view'
pgdb1-# WHEN relkind = 'm' THEN 'materialized view'
pgdb1-# WHEN relkind = 'S' THEN 'sequence'
pgdb1-# WHEN relkind = 'c' THEN 'type'
```

```
pgdb1-# ELSE 'index' END as objtype
pgdb1-# FROM pg_class c join pg_tablespace ts
pgdb1-# ON (CASE WHEN c.reltablespace = 0 THEN
pgdb1(# (SELECT dattablespace FROM pg_database WHERE datname = current_database())
pgdb1(# ELSE c.reltablespace END) = ts.oid
pgdb1-# WHERE relname NOT LIKE 'pg_toast%'
pgdb1-# AND relnamespace NOT IN
pgdb1-# (SELECT oid FROM pg_namespace
pgdb1(# WHERE nspname IN ('pg_catalog', 'information_schema'));
  spcname   |  relname  |      objtype
------------+-----------+-------------------
 pg_default | db1t1     | table
 pg_default | db1t2     | table
 pg_default | db1t1_i1  | index
 pg_default | db1t2_i2  | index
 pg_default | db1t1_v1  | view
 pg_default | db1t1_mv1 | materialized view
(6 rows)
```

In database pgdb2:

```
pgdb1=# \c pgdb2
You are now connected to database "pgdb2" as user "postgres".

pgdb2=# create index db2t1_i1 on db2t1(x);
CREATE INDEX

pgdb2=# select pg_relation_filepath('db2t1_i1');
 pg_relation_filepath
----------------------
 base/98429/98452
(1 row)

pgdb2=# create materialized view db2t2_mv1 as select * from db2t2;
SELECT 2
```

CHAPTER 3   POSTGRESQL PHYSICAL STRUCTURES

pgdb2=# select pg_relation_filepath('db2t2_mv1');
 pg_relation_filepath
 ----
 base/98429/98453
(1 row)

From the above output, we can see clearly that every object except view has a relative file path. Since a view is a logical object and doesn't hold any data of its own, there is no physical file created for the view.

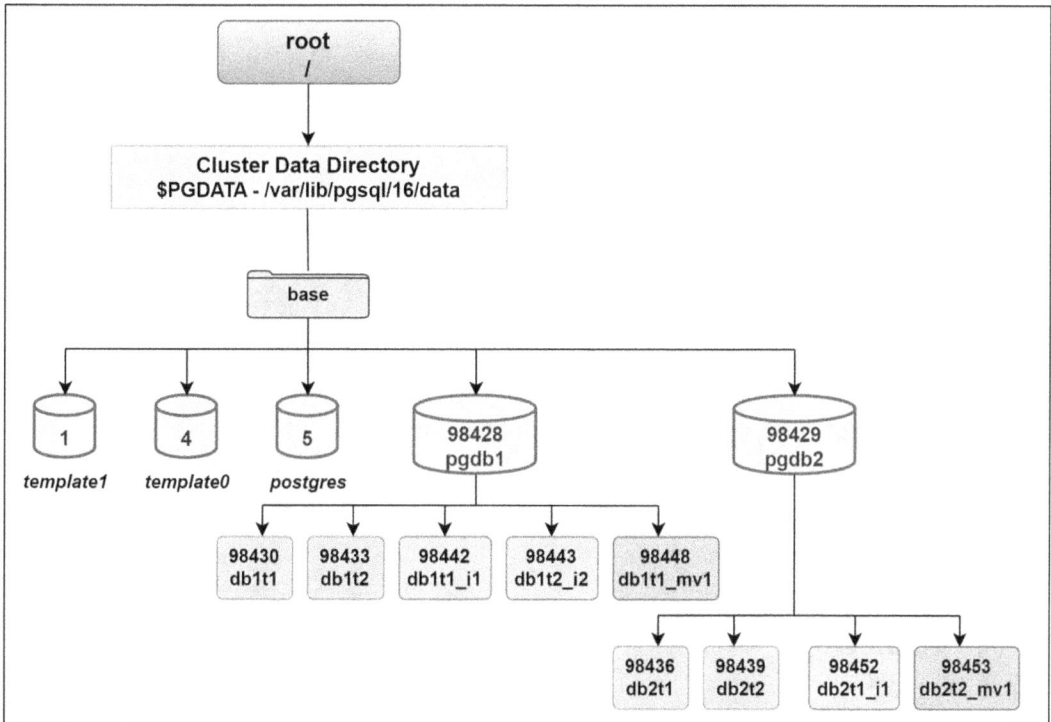

Figure 3-6. PostgreSQL cluster database object layout

Tablespaces in PostgreSQL

A tablespace in PostgreSQL is another area outside the base cluster data directory *PGDATA*. Each tablespace created has a symbolic link to a physical database directory under the *PGDATA/pg_tblspc* directory, named after the tablespace's object identifier (OID). In simpler terms, a tablespace in PostgreSQL is nothing but a directory that

99

contains the datafiles on a physical filesystem. These datafiles contain the data from the database objects like tables, indexes, materialized views, etc. The name of the tablespace must be distinct from the name of any other existing tablespaces in the database cluster.

Default Tablespaces

PostgreSQL has *two* default tablespaces:

- **pg_default**: Tablespace used to store user data
- **pg_global**: Tablespace used to store global data

A tablespace can be created using the syntax below:

```
create tablespace <tablespace_name> location '<path>';
```

At the beginning of this chapter, we created two databases named *pgdb1* and *pgdb2*.

[postgres@pg_server data]$ psql
```
psql (16.3)
Type "help" for help.
```

postgres=# select oid,datname from pg_database;
```
  oid  |  datname
-------+-----------
     5 | postgres
     1 | template1
     4 | template0
 98428 | pgdb1
 98429 | pgdb2
(5 rows)
```

Let us look for the default tablespaces in database cluster.

[postgres@pg_server ~]$ psql
```
psql (16.3)
Type "help" for help.
```

```
postgres=# \db
                List of tablespaces
    Name    |  Owner   |           Location
------------+----------+------------------------------
 pg_default | postgres |
 pg_global  | postgres |
(2 rows)
```

Or

```
postgres=# select * from pg_tablespace;
  oid  |  spcname   | spcowner | spcacl | spcoptions
-------+------------+----------+--------+------------
  1663 | pg_default |       10 |        |
  1664 | pg_global  |       10 |        |

postgres=# SELECT spcname AS "Name",
postgres-# pg_catalog.pg_get_userbyid(spcowner) AS "Owner",
postgres-# pg_catalog.pg_tablespace_location(oid) AS "Location",
postgres-# pg_catalog.array_to_string(spcacl, E'\n') AS "Access privileges",
postgres-# spcoptions AS "Options",
postgres-# pg_catalog.pg_size_pretty (pg_catalog.pg_tablespace_size(oid)) AS "Size",
postgres-# pg_catalog.shobj_description(oid,'pg_tablespace') AS "Description"
postgres-# FROM pg_catalog.pg_tablespace
postgres-# ORDER BY 1;
    Name    |  Owner   | Location | Access privileges | Options |  Size  | Description
------------+----------+----------+-------------------+---------+--------+-------------
 pg_default | postgres |          |                   |         | 75 MB  |
 pg_global  | postgres |          |                   |         |        |
(2 rows)
```

CHAPTER 3   POSTGRESQL PHYSICAL STRUCTURES

As we can see, the database cluster has two default tablespaces: *pg_default* and *pg_global*.

Creating a New Tablespace

Since tablespace has a symbolic link to a physical directory outside of the base cluster data directory, let us first create a directory that we can use for a new tablespace.

As **root** user:

```
[root@pg_server ~]# mkdir -p /u01/pgsql16/pgdata/tablespace1
[root@pg_server ~]# chown -R postgres:postgres /u01/pgsql16/pgdata/tablespace1
[root@pg_server ~]# chmod -R 700 /u01/pgsql16/pgdata/tablespace1
[root@pg_server ~]# ls -ld /u01/pgsql16/pgdata/tablespace1
drwx------. 2 postgres postgres 6 Oct 18 17:45 /u01/pgsql16/pgdata/tablespace1
```

Now, let us create a new tablespace by logging into the default *postgres* database.

```
[postgres@pg_server ~]$ psql
psql (16.3)
Type "help" for help.
```

postgres=# create tablespace tspace1 location '/u01/pgsql16/pgdata/tablespace1';
CREATE TABLESPACE

postgres=# \db
```
                List of tablespaces
    Name    |  Owner   |           Location
------------+----------+-------------------------------
 pg_default | postgres |
 pg_global  | postgres |
 tspace1    | postgres | /u01/pgsql16/pgdata/tablespace1
(3 rows)
```

Or

CHAPTER 3   POSTGRESQL PHYSICAL STRUCTURES

```
postgres=# select * from pg_tablespace;
  oid  |  spcname   | spcowner | spcacl | spcoptions
-------+------------+----------+--------+------------
  1663 | pg_default |       10 |        |
  1664 | pg_global  |       10 |        |
 98457 | tspace1    |       10 |        |
(3 rows)

postgres=# \q
[postgres@pg_server ~]$ cd $PGDATA/pg_tblspc/

[postgres@pg_server pg_tblspc]$ ls -lrt
total 0
lrwxrwxrwx. 1 postgres postgres 31 Oct 18 17:49 98457 -> /u01/pgsql16/pgdata/tablespace1

[postgres@pg_server ~]$ ls -lrt /u01/pgsql16/pgdata/tablespace1
total 0
drwx------. 2 postgres postgres 6 Oct 18 17:49 PG_16_202307071
```

From the above output, we need to notice two things. One, for the newly created tablespace *tspace1*, the physical subdirectory with tablespace OID name is created under *$PGDATA/pg_tblspc*. And this subdirectory is a symbolic link to the actual physical directory we have created for this non-default tablespace *tspace1*.

The other one is once we issue the *create tablespace* command by mentioning the physical file location */u01/pgsql16/pgdata/tablespace1*, a subdirectory named *PG_16_202307071* is created, which will store the object data from the corresponding databases, i.e., databases that are assigned default tablespace as *tspace1*.

Changing Default Tablespace

Let us create a new database named *pgdb3* and change the default tablespace for the database.

```
postgres=# create database pgdb3;
CREATE DATABASE
```

103

CHAPTER 3 POSTGRESQL PHYSICAL STRUCTURES

```
postgres=# select oid,datname from pg_database;
  oid  |  datname
-------+-----------
     5 | postgres
     1 | template1
     4 | template0
 98428 | pgdb1
 98429 | pgdb2
 98458 | pgdb3
(6 rows)
```

Check the default tablespaces for databases:

```
postgres=# select d.oid,d.datname,d.dattablespace tsoid,t.oid
tsoid,t.spcname tsname from pg_database d join pg_tablespace t on
d.dattablespace=t.oid;
  oid  |  datname  | tsoid | tsoid |   tsname
-------+-----------+-------+-------+------------
     5 | postgres  |  1663 |  1663 | pg_default
     1 | template1 |  1663 |  1663 | pg_default
     4 | template0 |  1663 |  1663 | pg_default
 98428 | pgdb1     |  1663 |  1663 | pg_default
 98429 | pgdb2     |  1663 |  1663 | pg_default
 98458 | pgdb3     |  1663 |  1663 | pg_default
(6 rows)
```

or

```
[postgres@pg_server ~]$ oid2name
All databases:
    Oid  Database Name  Tablespace
----------------------------------
  98428          pgdb1  pg_default
  98429          pgdb2  pg_default
  98458          pgdb3  pg_default
```

```
    5      postgres   pg_default
    4      template0  pg_default
    1      template1  pg_default
```

Now change the default tablespace for database pgdb3:

postgres=# alter database pgdb3 set tablespace tspace1;
ALTER DATABASE

Check again the default tablespaces for databases:

postgres=# select d.oid,d.datname,d.dattablespace tsoid,t.oid tsoid,t.spcname tsname from pg_database d join pg_tablespace t on d.dattablespace=t.oid;

```
  oid  |  datname  | tsoid | tsoid |   tsname
-------+-----------+-------+-------+------------
     5 | postgres  |  1663 |  1663 | pg_default
     1 | template1 |  1663 |  1663 | pg_default
     4 | template0 |  1663 |  1663 | pg_default
 98428 | pgdb1     |  1663 |  1663 | pg_default
 98429 | pgdb2     |  1663 |  1663 | pg_default
 98458 | pgdb3     | 98457 | 98457 | tspace1
(6 rows)
```

Or

[postgres@pg_server ~]$ oid2name
```
All databases:
   Oid   Database Name   Tablespace
----------------------------------
 98428          pgdb1    pg_default
 98429          pgdb2    pg_default
 98458          pgdb3    tspace1
     5       postgres    pg_default
     4      template0    pg_default
     1      template1    pg_default
```

CHAPTER 3   POSTGRESQL PHYSICAL STRUCTURES

By issuing an *"ALTER DATABASE <DB_NAME> SET TABLESPACE <TABLESPACE_ NAME>;"* command, we can change the default tablespace of a database.

Now, if we check the mapping between the database and the tablespace at the physical layer, a directory with name as database OID, in this case **98458 (pgdb3)**, will be created under the tablespace **tspace1** physical location (**/u01/pgsql16/pgdata/ tablespace1/PG_16_202307071**).

[postgres@pg_server ~]$ ls -lrt /u01/pgsql16/pgdata/tablespace1/ PG_16_202307071
```
total 12
drwx------. 2 postgres postgres 8192 Oct 18 18:01 98458
```

Also, in general, it is a best practice to assign a default tablespace in a separate physical directory for various benefits, which we will learn shortly after. For example, at the time of a database creation, we issue the below command:

postgres=# create database pgdb4 tablespace = 'tspace1';
CREATE DATABASE

postgres=# select oid,datname from pg_database;
```
  oid  | datname
-------+-----------
     5 | postgres
     1 | template1
     4 | template0
 98428 | pgdb1
 98429 | pgdb2
 98458 | pgdb3
 98459 | pgdb4
(7 rows)
```

postgres=# select d.oid,d.datname,d.dattablespace tsoid,t.spcname tsname from pg_database d join pg_tablespace t on d.dattablespace=t.oid;
```
  oid  | datname   | tsoid | tsname
-------+-----------+-------+------------
     5 | postgres  |  1663 | pg_default
     1 | template1 |  1663 | pg_default
     4 | template0 |  1663 | pg_default
```

```
98428 | pgdb1     |   1663 | pg_default
98429 | pgdb2     |   1663 | pg_default
98458 | pgdb3     |  98457 | tspace1
98459 | pgdb4     |  98457 | tspace1
(7 rows)
```

The physical file structure looks like the following:

[postgres@pg_server ~]$ oid2name
```
All databases:
   Oid  Database Name  Tablespace
---------------------------------
  98428          pgdb1  pg_default
  98429          pgdb2  pg_default
  98458          pgdb3     tspace1
  98459          pgdb4     tspace1
      5       postgres  pg_default
      4      template0  pg_default
      1      template1  pg_default
```

[postgres@pg_server ~]$ cd /u01/pgsql16/pgdata/tablespace1/PG_16_202307071

[postgres@pg_server PG_16_202307071]$ ls -lrt
```
total 24
drwx------. 2 postgres postgres 8192 Oct 18 18:01 98458
drwx------. 2 postgres postgres 8192 Oct 18 18:26 98459
```

Now, let us create few objects in databases *pgdb3* and *pgdb4* that have default tablespace as *tspace1* and observe the layout.

In database pgdb3:

postgres=# \c pgdb3
```
You are now connected to database "pgdb3" as user "postgres".
```

pgdb3=# create table db3t1 (a int, b int);
```
CREATE TABLE
```
pgdb3=# insert into db3t1 values (17,18), (19,20);
```
INSERT 0 2
```

CHAPTER 3 POSTGRESQL PHYSICAL STRUCTURES

```
pgdb3=# select * from db3t1;
 a  | b
----+----
 17 | 18
 19 | 20
(2 rows)

pgdb3=# select pg_relation_filepath('db3t1');
            pg_relation_filepath
---------------------------------------------
 pg_tblspc/98457/PG_16_202307071/98458/98460
(1 row)

pgdb3=# create index db3t1_i1 on db3t1(a);
CREATE INDEX

pgdb3=# select pg_relation_filepath('db3t1_i1');
            pg_relation_filepath
---------------------------------------------
 pg_tblspc/98457/PG_16_202307071/98458/98463
(1 row)
```

In database pgdb4:

```
pgdb3=# \c pgdb4
You are now connected to database "pgdb4" as user "postgres".

pgdb4=# create table db4t1 (x int, y int);
CREATE TABLE
pgdb4=# insert into db4t1 values (21,22), (23,24);
INSERT 0 2
pgdb4=# select * from db4t1;
 x  | y
----+----
 21 | 22
 23 | 24
(2 rows)
```

CHAPTER 3 POSTGRESQL PHYSICAL STRUCTURES

pgdb4=# select pg_relation_filepath('db4t1');
```
          pg_relation_filepath
-------------------------------------------
 pg_tblspc/98457/PG_16_202307071/98459/98464
(1 row)
```

pgdb4=# create materialized view db4t1_mv1 as select * from db4t1;
SELECT 2

pgdb4=# select pg_relation_filepath('db4t1_mv1');
```
          pg_relation_filepath
-------------------------------------------
 pg_tblspc/98457/PG_16_202307071/98459/98467
(1 row)
```

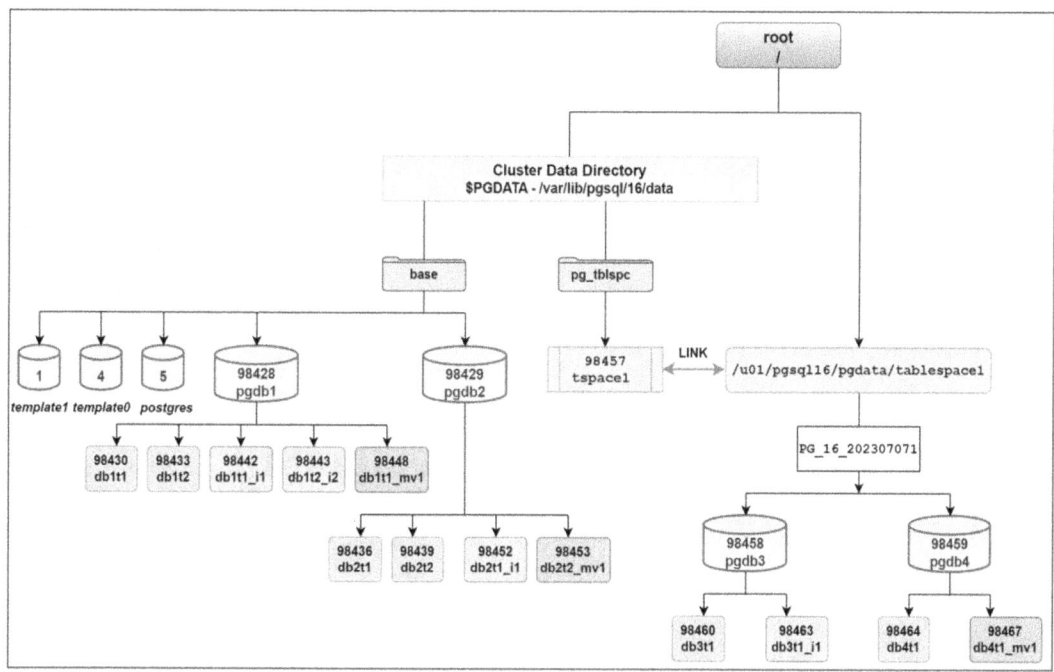

Figure 3-7. PostgreSQL cluster and database objects layout

From the above figure, we can see the complete physical layout of the cluster data directory with databases and the corresponding objects we have created.

CHAPTER 3   POSTGRESQL PHYSICAL STRUCTURES

The below table format figure shows the storage location of the objects we have created in each database. Objects of databases pgdb1 and pgdb2 are under subdirectories of base directory in $PGDATA due to the default tablespace, which is pg_default. For the other two databases, pgdb3 and pgdb4, since the default tablespace is set to tspace1, the object files are stored in $PGDATA/pg_tblspc having symbolic link pointers to the actual relative path /u01/pgsql16/pgdata/tablespace1.

Database Name	Table Name	Index Name	View Name	Mview Name	Default Tablespace	Storage Location
pgdb1	db1t1	db1t1_i1	db1t1_v1	db1t1_mv1	pg_default	base/98428/98430 (table db1t1)
	db2t2	db1t2_i2				base/98428/98433 (table db1t2)
						base/98428/98442 (index db1t1_i1)
						base/98428/98443 (index db1t2_i2)
						base/98428/98448 (mview db1t1_mv1)
pgdb2	db2t1	db2t1_i1			pg_default	base/98429/98436 (table db2t1)
	db2t2			db2t2_mv1		base/98429/98439 (table db2t2)
						base/98429/98452 (index db2t1_i1)
						base/98429/98453 (mview db2t2_mv1)
pgdb3	db3t1	db3t1_i1			tspace1	pg_tblspc/98457/PG_16_202307071/98458/98460 (table db3t1)
						/u01/pgsql16/pgdata/tablespace1/PG_16_202307071/98458/98460
						pg_tblspc/98457/PG_16_202307071/98458/98463 (index db3t1_i1)
						/u01/pgsql16/pgdata/tablespace1/PG_16_202307071/98458/98463
pgdb4	db4t1			db4t1_mv1	tspace1	pg_tblspc/98457/PG_16_202307071/98459/98464 (table db4t1)
						/u01/pgsql16/pgdata/tablespace1/PG_16_202307071/98459/98464
						pg_tblspc/98457/PG_16_202307071/98459/98467 (mview db4t1_mv1)
						/u01/pgsql16/pgdata/tablespace1/PG_16_202307071/98459/98467

Figure 3-8. PostgreSQL database objects storage directory

In addition to these directory structures, another important aspect of the physical structure we need to learn is about page structure in PostgreSQL.

Page Structure and Layout in PostgreSQL Database Cluster

In PostgreSQL, the data is stored on the disk in the form of a **data page**, which is considered to be the basic or fundamental unit of storage on disk.

The data pages are fixed-size pages with a default size of 8KB. The tables, indexes, and other data structures are organized into these fixed-size pages.

Each data page has different areas like page header data, item identifiers, free space, items, and special space as described in Table 3-3.

The initial 24 bytes are occupied by page header data. The page header data maintains metadata of the page in the form of multiple fields where it stores details related to WAL entries, unallocated space (i.e., free space) within the page, page size and layout version number, etc. Page header data is followed by item identifiers that are the pointers to the actual item (an individual data value) stored in a page. Free space within the page is a placeholder used to accommodate the items through inserts or updates. The items (rows/tuples) in the page are stored in the space allocated backward from the end of unallocated space. The other area within the page is special section used only by index pages; regular table pages do not use this area.

Table 3-3. Data page layout

Item	Description
PageHeaderData	24 bytes long. Contains general information about the page, including free space pointers
ItemIdData	Array of item identifiers pointing to the actual items
Free Space	The unallocated space. New item identifiers are allocated from the start of this area, new items from the end
Items	The actual items
Special Space	Index access method specific data. Different methods store different data

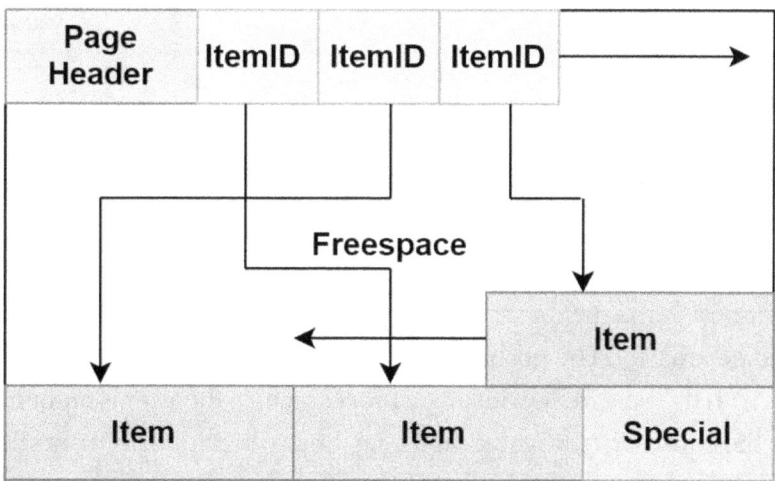

Figure 3-9. PostgreSQL data page layout

Query Processing in PostgreSQL

Since we have seen the physical storage layout of the PostgreSQL cluster, let us see the high-level sequence of operations happening in the backend during the query processing. Any query or transaction executed by the user undergoes various internal tasks like parsing, generation of execution plan, plan execution, row fetch, and results back to the user.

Below is the graphical representation of how a user accesses the table's data that is stored in the tablespace's datafile.

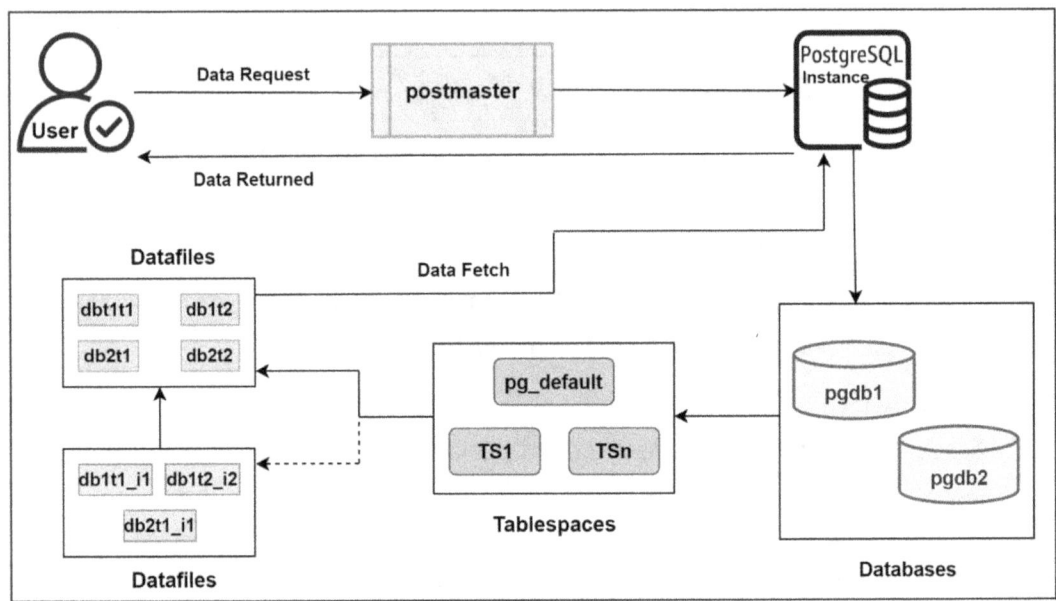

Figure 3-10. Path of a query

Connection Request Stage

In a client/server architecture, let us assume a remote application user sends a connection request to the database; the request will be acknowledged by a supervisor process called postmaster. The postmaster spawns a new dedicated background process that interacts with the PostgreSQL instance process. Once the user is authenticated by validating the entries in configuration file pg_hba.conf and certain permissions in the database, a connection will be established between the client user and the PostgreSQL server.

In order to get a successful connection, the user has to use correct username/password, port, and database details. The connections will not be established if the authentication fails.

Query Execution Stage

Once connection is established, the user session is allowed to run queries against the database.

Assume the connected user has executed a SELECT statement to fetch rows from one of the tables.

This query by the client will be handled by the dedicated background process on the PostgreSQL server.

Once the query is transmitted to the server, the user session awaits the results.

Parser Stage

The query received at the server end as a plain text will undergo syntax validation by parser. If the syntax is incorrect, then an error will be returned, else it proceeds with building a parse tree.

In the next stage, the transformation process evaluates the parse tree shared by parser, i.e., it performs a semantic check to identify the tables or views or other objects used in the query and the conditions, operators, etc., used in the query. A query tree is built based on the output of transformation process evaluation.

Execution Plan Generation Stage

Using the query tree details, the planner or optimizer will generate an execution plan for the query. The optimizer's responsibility is to generate an optimal execution plan. So for every query, the optimizer will generate multiple execution plans and evaluate each plan to understand the time it takes for the execution, which depends on various factors like number of tables involved, size of tables, conditions used, etc. Also, the optimizer needs to scan the metadata to understand the physical storage location of the objects involved.

For a simple query, generation of optimal execution plan is easier. But when a complex query involving multiple tables, join conditions, aggregate functions, comparison operators, etc., is used, then deriving an optimal plan involves excessing internal testing as the optimizer has to generate various possible combinations to fetch the rows.

Execution Stage

The plan tree will have an actual execution path to use to fetch the rows and return to the user.

The execution plan will have information like whether to use indexes or go for full table scan, or for complex queries, the types of join operations to be performed, etc.

The executor will use the plan tree and fetch or extract the necessary rows and return to the user.

Finally, the rows satisfying the query will be displayed to the user.

Inspecting Physical Data with the *pg_filedump* Utility

The Page Header contains metadata about the page, including the following components:

1. Number of tuples

2. Offset of free space

3. Log Sequence Number (LSN), Checksum, flags, etc.

Tuple Insertion Process in PostgreSQL
When you insert a row in PostgreSQL, the following will happen automatically:

- PostgreSQL checks for available space on the page, i.e., when inserting a new row, PostgreSQL looks for a page with enough free space (using FSM – free space map).

- A line pointer is added to the page header.

- The tuple is inserted at the bottom of the page, and the tuple's location is identified/represented by **ctid** (combination of Block Number + Line Pointer Offset).

Tuple Identifier (ctid)

Every row in PostgreSQL has a ***ctid*** field.

ctid = (block_number, offset_number)

- block_number: Which 8KB block (page) the tuple is in
- offset_number: Index of the line pointer in the page header

Let's see an example below by installing the *pg_filedump* utility.

Install pg_filedump for the corresponding PostgreSQL version.

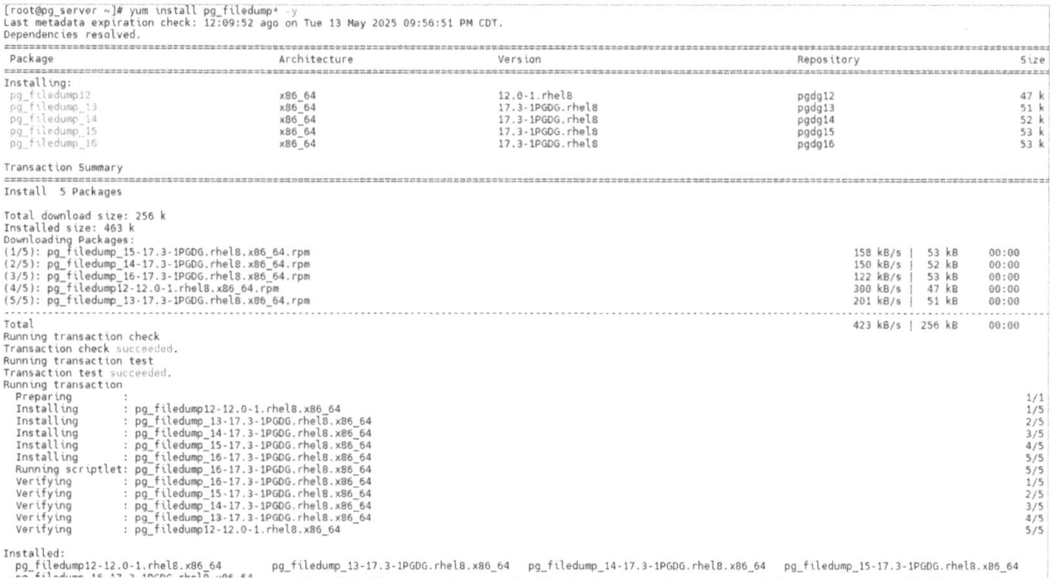

```
[root@pg_server ~]# yum install pg_filedump* -y
Last metadata expiration check: 12:09:52 ago on Tue 13 May 2025 09:56:51 PM CDT.
Dependencies resolved.
================================================================================
 Package              Architecture      Version                 Repository      Size
================================================================================
Installing:
 pg_filedump12        x86_64            12.0-1.rhel8            pgdg12          47 k
 pg_filedump_13       x86_64            17.3-1PGDG.rhel8        pgdg13          51 k
 pg_filedump_14       x86_64            17.3-1PGDG.rhel8        pgdg14          52 k
 pg_filedump_15       x86_64            17.3-1PGDG.rhel8        pgdg15          53 k
 pg_filedump_16       x86_64            17.3-1PGDG.rhel8        pgdg16          53 k

Transaction Summary
================================================================================
Install  5 Packages

Total download size: 256 k
Installed size: 463 k
Downloading Packages:
(1/5): pg_filedump_15-17.3-1PGDG.rhel8.x86_64.rpm       158 kB/s |  53 kB     00:00
(2/5): pg_filedump_14-17.3-1PGDG.rhel8.x86_64.rpm       150 kB/s |  52 kB     00:00
(3/5): pg_filedump_16-17.3-1PGDG.rhel8.x86_64.rpm       122 kB/s |  53 kB     00:00
(4/5): pg_filedump12-12.0-1.rhel8.x86_64.rpm            300 kB/s |  47 kB     00:00
(5/5): pg_filedump_13-17.3-1PGDG.rhel8.x86_64.rpm       201 kB/s |  51 kB     00:00
--------------------------------------------------------------------------------
Total                                                   423 kB/s | 256 kB     00:00
Running transaction check
Transaction check succeeded.
Running transaction test
Transaction test succeeded.
Running transaction
  Preparing        :                                                        1/1
  Installing       : pg_filedump12-12.0-1.rhel8.x86_64                      1/5
  Installing       : pg_filedump_13-17.3-1PGDG.rhel8.x86_64                 2/5
  Installing       : pg_filedump_14-17.3-1PGDG.rhel8.x86_64                 3/5
  Installing       : pg_filedump_15-17.3-1PGDG.rhel8.x86_64                 4/5
  Installing       : pg_filedump_16-17.3-1PGDG.rhel8.x86_64                 5/5
  Running scriptlet: pg_filedump_16-17.3-1PGDG.rhel8.x86_64                 5/5
  Verifying        : pg_filedump_16-17.3-1PGDG.rhel8.x86_64                 1/5
  Verifying        : pg_filedump_15-17.3-1PGDG.rhel8.x86_64                 2/5
  Verifying        : pg_filedump_14-17.3-1PGDG.rhel8.x86_64                 3/5
  Verifying        : pg_filedump_13-17.3-1PGDG.rhel8.x86_64                 4/5
  Verifying        : pg_filedump12-12.0-1.rhel8.x86_64                      5/5

Installed:
  pg_filedump12-12.0-1.rhel8.x86_64    pg_filedump_13-17.3-1PGDG.rhel8.x86_64    pg_filedump_14-17.3-1PGDG.rhel8.x86_64    pg_filedump_15-17.3-1PGDG.rhel8.x86_64
```

Figure 3-11. *Installation of pg_filedump*

Check the following after installation of the pg_filedump utility.

```
[root@pg_server ~]# rpm -qa |grep pg_filedump
pg_filedump12-12.0-1.rhel8.x86_64
pg_filedump_15-17.3-1PGDG.rhel8.x86_64
pg_filedump_14-17.3-1PGDG.rhel8.x86_64
pg_filedump_16-17.3-1PGDG.rhel8.x86_64
pg_filedump_13-17.3-1PGDG.rhel8.x86_64

[root@pg_server ~]# ls -lrth /usr/pgsql-16/bin/pg_filedump
-rwxr-xr-x. 1 root root 87K Apr 16 14:08 /usr/pgsql-16/bin/pg_filedump
```

Connect to the pgdb1 database and create db1t1 and db1t2 tables and insert rows.

```
[root@pg_server ~]# su - postgres
[postgres@pg_server ~]$ psql
psql (16.3)
Type "help" for help.
postgres=#
```

postgres=# \c pgdb1
```
You are now connected to database "pgdb1" as user "postgres".
pgdb1=#
```

pgdb1=# create table db1t1 (x int, y int);
```
CREATE TABLE
```

pgdb1=# insert into db1t1 values (1,2), (3,4);
```
INSERT 0 2
```

pgdb1=# select * from db1t1;
```
 x | y
---+---
 1 | 2
 3 | 4

(2 rows)
```

pgdb1=# create table db1t2 (a int, b int);
```
CREATE TABLE
```

pgdb1=# insert into db1t2 values (5,6), (7,8);
```
INSERT 0 2
```

pgdb1=# select * from db1t2;
```
 a | b
---+---
 5 | 6
 7 | 8

(2 rows)
```

CHAPTER 3 POSTGRESQL PHYSICAL STRUCTURES

Find the file path for both the tables (db1t1 and db1t2).

pgdb1=# select pg_relation_filepath('db1t1');

```
        pg_relation_filepath
----------------------------------------
base/98428/172200 (1 row)
```

pgdb1=# select pg_relation_filepath('db1t2');

```
        pg_relation_filepath
----------------------------------------
base/98428/172203 (1 row)
```

pgdb1=#

Check the Page (Before Checkpoint) for the tables (db1t1 and db1t2)

[postgres@pg_server ~]$ /usr/pgsql-16/bin/pg_filedump -f /var/lib/pgsql/16/data/base/98428/172200

- PostgreSQL File/Block Formatted Dump Utility
- File: /var/lib/pgsql/16/data/base/98428/172200
- Options used: -f

Notice: Block size determined from reading block 0 is zero, using default 8192 instead. Hint: Use -S to specify the size manually.

Block 0 **

----- Block Offset: 0x00000000 Offsets: Lower 0 (0x0000) Block: Size 0 Version 0 Upper 0 (0x0000) LSN: logid 0 recoff 0x00000000 Special 0 (0x0000) Items: 0 Free Space: 0 Checksum: 0x0000 Prune XID: 0x00000000 Flags: 0x0000 () Length (including item array): 24

Error: Invalid header information.

0000: 00000000 00000000 00000000 00000000 .... 0010: 00000000 00000000 ....

CHAPTER 3 POSTGRESQL PHYSICAL STRUCTURES

```
----- Empty block - no items listed
----- Error: Invalid special section encountered. Error: Special section
points off page. Unable to dump contents.

*** End of File Encountered. Last Block Read: 0 ***
[postgres@pg_server ~]$
```

> **Note** This is because the changes haven't been flushed to disk yet. Please execute the command "CHECKPOINT".

Log in to the pgdb1 database and force checkpoint and retry again the same command for both the tables (db1t1 and db1t2).

postgres-# \c pgdb1
```
You are now connected to database "pgdb1" as user "postgres".
pgdb1-#
```

pgdb1=# CHECKPOINT;
```
CHECKPOINT
pgdb1=#
pgdb1=# exit
```

[postgres@pg_server ~]$ /usr/pgsql-16/bin/pg_filedump -f /var/lib/pgsql/16/data/base/98428/172200

- PostgreSQL File/Block Formatted Dump Utility
- File: /var/lib/pgsql/16/data/base/98428/172200
- Options used: -f

```
Block 0 ********************************************************
----- Block Offset: 0x00000000 Offsets: Lower 32 (0x0020) Block: Size 8192
Version 4 Upper 8128 (0x1fc0) LSN: logid 4 recoff 0x670302b0 Special 8192
(0x2000) Items: 2 Free Space: 8096 Checksum: 0x0000 Prune XID: 0x00000000
Flags: 0x0000 () Length (including item array): 32
```

```
0000: 04000000 b0020367 00000000 2000c01f  .......g.... ...  0010: 00200420
00000000 e09f4000 c09f4000                 . . ......@...@.
```

----- Item 1 -- Length: 32 Offset: 8160 (0x1fe0) Flags: NORMAL 1fe0:
45080000 00000000 00000000 00000000 E............... 1ff0: 01000200
00091800 01000000 02000000 ....

Item 2 -- Length: 32 Offset: 8128 (0x1fc0) Flags: NORMAL 1fc0: 45080000
00000000 00000000 00000000 E............... 1fd0: 02000200 00091800
03000000 04000000 ....

*** End of File Encountered. Last Block Read: 0 ***

[postgres@pg_server ~]$ /usr/pgsql-16/bin/pg_filedump -f /var/lib/pgsql/16/data/base/98428/172203

- PostgreSQL File/Block Formatted Dump Utility
- File: /var/lib/pgsql/16/data/base/98428/172203
- Options used: -f

Block 0 **
----- Block Offset: 0x00000000 Offsets: Lower 32 (0x0020) Block: Size 8192
Version 4 Upper 8128 (0x1fc0) LSN: logid 4 recoff 0x67031578 Special 8192
(0x2000) Items: 2 Free Space: 8096 Checksum: 0x0000 Prune XID: 0x00000000
Flags: 0x0000 () Length (including item array): 32

```
0000: 04000000 78150367 00000000 2000c01f  ....x..g.... ...  0010: 00200420
00000000 e09f4000 c09f4000                 . . ......@...@.
```

----- Item 1 -- Length: 32 Offset: 8160 (0x1fe0) Flags: NORMAL 1fe0:
47080000 00000000 00000000 00000000 G............... 1ff0: 01000200
00091800 05000000 06000000 ....

Item 2 -- Length: 32 Offset: 8128 (0x1fc0) Flags: NORMAL 1fc0: 47080000
00000000 00000000 00000000 G............... 1fd0: 02000200 00091800
07000000 08000000 ....

*** End of File Encountered. Last Block Read: 0 ***

Checking the *ctid* for both the tables (db1t1 and db1t2)

```
postgres=# \c pgdb1
You are now connected to database "pgdb1" as user "postgres".
pgdb1=# pgdb1=# \dt+
List of relations | Name  | Type  | Owner    | Persistence | Access  | Size       |
Description
Schema                                                     method
-----------------+-------+-------+----------+-------------+---------+------------+-
public            | db1t1 | table | postgres | permanent   | heap    | 8192 bytes |
public            | db1t2 | table | postgres | permanent   | heap    | 8192 bytes |
(2 rows)
pgdb1=#

pgdb1=# select ctid from db1t1 where x=1;
ctid
----
(0,1)
(1 row)

pgdb1=#
pgdb1=# select ctid from db1t2 where a=5;
ctid
----
(0,1)

(1 row)
pgdb1=# exit
[postgres@pg_server ~]$
```

In PostgreSQL, data inserted into a table isn't immediately flushed to disk. Instead, it is first stored in memory buffers for performance optimization. The actual write to disk is deferred and controlled by background processes and configuration settings. Parameters like checkpoint_timeout determine how often full checkpoints are triggered, ensuring data is flushed at regular intervals. The bgwriter_delay controls how frequently

CHAPTER 3   POSTGRESQL PHYSICAL STRUCTURES

the background writer process flushes dirty buffers to disk in small batches. Additionally, max_wal_size influences when checkpoints are forced based on the growth of the Write-Ahead Log (WAL). Together, these settings help balance system performance with data durability and recovery needs.

Understanding how PostgreSQL manages its internal page structure is vital for fine-tuning performance, diagnosing complex issues, and conducting thorough database analysis. This section explained how data is stored in 8KB pages on disk, the organization of tuples within those pages, and how to examine physical storage using tools like pg_filedump. With this foundational knowledge, you'll gain deeper visibility into PostgreSQL's inner mechanics, empowering you to make more informed optimization and troubleshooting decisions.

Other Administrative Operations
Altering a Tablespace

We can change the definition of tablespace using the *ALTER TABLESPACE* command. In order to change the definition of the tablespace, one must be an owner of the tablespace. Please see examples below where we can rename the existing tablespace name from *db1_tbs1* to *tbs1_pgdb1*.

```
postgres=# select * from pg_tablespace;
  oid  |  spcname   | spcowner | spcacl | spcoptions
-------+------------+----------+--------+------------
 98457 | tspace1    |       10 |        |

postgres=# alter tablespace tspace1 rename to tspace_new;
ALTER TABLESPACE

postgres=# select * from pg_tablespace;
  oid  |  spcname   | spcowner | spcacl | spcoptions
-------+------------+----------+--------+------------
 98457 | tspace_new |       10 |        |
```

```
postgres=# \db
                     List of tablespaces
    Name    |  Owner   |           Location
------------+----------+-------------------------------
 tspace_new | postgres | /u01/pgsql16/pgdata/tablespace1
```

```
[postgres@pg_server ~]$ oid2name
All databases:
    Oid  Database Name  Tablespace
----------------------------------
  98428          pgdb1  pg_default
  98429          pgdb2  pg_default
  98458          pgdb3  tspace_new
  98459          pgdb4  tspace_new
      5       postgres  pg_default
      4      template0  pg_default
      1      template1  pg_default
```

Dropping a Tablespace

To remove a tablespace, use the *DROP TABLESPACE* command. You must be the owner or the superuser, and it must be empty of all database objects before it can be dropped. For example, let us drop the tablespace tspace_new.

```
postgres=# select * from pg_tablespace;
  oid  |  spcname   | spcowner | spcacl | spcoptions
-------+------------+----------+--------+------------
  1663 | pg_default |       10 |        |
  1664 | pg_global  |       10 |        |
 98457 | tspace_new |       10 |        |
```

```
postgres=# drop tablespace tspace_new;
ERROR:  tablespace "tspace_new" is not empty
```

```
postgres=# drop tablespace if exists tspace_new;
ERROR:  tablespace "tspace_new" is not empty
pgdb1=#
```

If you notice, the drop tablespace command returned an error since there are some mapped database objects. So we had to first drop the database objects before we could drop the tablespace.

postgres=# \c pgdb3
You are now connected to database "pgdb3" as user "postgres".
pgdb3=# drop table db3t1;
DROP TABLE

pgdb3=# \c pgdb4
You are now connected to database "pgdb4" as user "postgres".

pgdb4=# drop table db4t1 cascade;
NOTICE: drop cascades to materialized view db4t1_mv1
DROP TABLE

postgres=# drop tablespace tspace_new;
ERROR: tablespace "tspace_new" is not empty

postgres=# select d.oid,d.datname,d.dattablespace tsoid,t.spcname tsname from pg_database d join pg_tablespace t on d.dattablespace=t.oid;
```
  oid  |  datname  | tsoid |   tsname
-------+-----------+-------+------------
 98458 | pgdb3     | 98457 | tspace_new
 98459 | pgdb4     | 98457 | tspace_new
```

postgres=# alter database pgdb3 set tablespace pg_default;
ALTER DATABASE

postgres=# alter database pgdb4 set tablespace pg_default;
ALTER DATABASE

postgres=# select d.oid,d.datname,d.dattablespace tsoid,t.spcname tsname from pg_database d join pg_tablespace t on d.dattablespace=t.oid;
```
  oid  |  datname  | tsoid |   tsname
-------+-----------+-------+------------
 98458 | pgdb3     |  1663 | pg_default
 98459 | pgdb4     |  1663 | pg_default
```

postgres=# drop tablespace tspace_new;
DROP TABLESPACE

CHAPTER 3 POSTGRESQL PHYSICAL STRUCTURES

```
postgres=# select * from pg_tablespace;
  oid  |  spcname   | spcowner | spcacl | spcoptions
-------+------------+----------+--------+------------
  1663 | pg_default |       10 |        |
  1664 | pg_global  |       10 |        |
```

From the above output, if we observe, after the objects are dropped from the databases, still we are not able to drop the tablespace. This is because there are still databases mapped to the tablespaces. Hence, the database's default tablespace has to be changed before attempting tablespace drop. In this case, we have changed the default tablespace of databases pgdb3 and pgdb4 to pg_default from tspace_new, which allowed the dropping of tablespace.

Other option is to drop the databases themselves followed by tablespace drop.

Temporary Tablespaces

If the allocated work memory is not enough, PostgreSQL uses temporary files for the sorting operation in the query. By default, it creates temporary files in the "pgsql_tmp" directory under $PGDATA/base.

However, we can create a tablespace and use it for temp file operations.

Let us see how a regular tablespace can be assigned for temporary options.

Once temp_tablespaces parameter value is set to a tablespace value, then the tablespace is available for temporary operations like sorting, temporary tables, etc.

```
[postgres@pg_server ~]$ mkdir -p /u01/pgsql16/pgdata/temp_files
[postgres@pg_server ~]$ cd /u01/pgsql16/pgdata/temp_files
[postgres@pg_server temp_files]$ psql
(16.3)
Type "help" for help.

postgres=# \c db1
You are now connected to database "db1" as user "postgres".

db1=# show temp_tablespaces;
 temp_tablespaces
------------------
```

```
(1 row)
db1=# create tablespace temp_ts location '/u01/pgsql16/pgdata/temp_files';
CREATE TABLESPACE

postgres-# \db+
                              List of tablespaces
    Name    |  Owner   |            Location              | Options |  Size   |
------------+----------+----------------------------------+---------+---------+
 pg_default | postgres |                                  |         | 37 MB   |
 pg_global  | postgres |                                  |         | 621 kB  |
 temp_ts    | postgres | /u01/pgsql16/pgdata/temp_files   |         | 0 bytes |

db1=# alter system set temp_tablespaces = 'temp_ts';
ALTER SYSTEM

db1=# select pg_reload_conf();
 pg_reload_conf
----------------
 t
(1 row)

db1=# show temp_tablespaces ;
 temp_tablespaces
------------------
 temp_ts
(1 row)
```

From the above output, we can see a function named ***pg_reload_config()*** is used. This function is used to reload the auto configuration file when any dynamic parameter is modified, while still connected to PostgreSQL, provided the connected user is granted privilege on this function or by a superuser.

Now if any temporary table is created in the database, they are created under the temporary tablespace directory created in the previous section.

```
db1=# create temporary table tempt1 (x int, y int, z int);
CREATE TABLE

db1=# select pg_relation_filepath ('tempt1');
           pg_relation_filepath
--------------------------------------------------
```

CHAPTER 3   POSTGRESQL PHYSICAL STRUCTURES

 pg_tblspc/90272/PG_16_202307071/90234/t4_90273
(1 row)

db1=# create temporary table tempt2 (a int, b int, c int);
CREATE TABLE

db1=# select pg_relation_filepath ('tempt2');
             pg_relation_filepath
----
 pg_tblspc/90272/PG_16_202307071/90234/t4_90276
(1 row)

[postgres@pg_server data]$ ls -l pg_tblspc/90272
lrwxrwxrwx. 1 postgres postgres 30 Oct 17 22:22 **pg_tblspc/90272 -> /u01/pgsql16/pgdata/temp_files**

[postgres@pg_server data]$ ls -lrt pg_tblspc/90272/PG_16_202307071/90234/t4_90273
-rw-------. 1 postgres postgres 0 Oct 17 22:23 pg_tblspc/90272/PG_16_202307071/90234/t4_90273

[postgres@pg_server data]$ ls -lrt pg_tblspc/90272/PG_16_202307071/90234/t4_90276
-rw-------. 1 postgres postgres 0 Oct 17 22:23 pg_tblspc/90272/PG_16_202307071/90234/t4_90276

[postgres@pg_server data]$ ls -lrt /u01/pgsql16/pgdata/temp_files/PG_16_202307071/90234
total 0
-rw-------. 1 postgres postgres 0 Oct 17 22:23 t4_90273
-rw-------. 1 postgres postgres 0 Oct 17 22:23 t4_90276

From the above output, we can see that the temporary tables are created under the subdirectories of the **$PGDATA/pg_tblspc/90272** directory, which is a soft link to /u01/pgsql16/pgdata/temp_files.

So the temporary tables are actually created under the directory structure created for temporary operations, i.e., **/u01/pgsql16/pgdata/temp_files**.

db1=# \dt
            List of relations

```
 Schema   |  Name  | Type  | Owner
-----------+--------+-------+----------
 pg_temp_4 | tempt1 | table | postgres
 pg_temp_4 | tempt2 | table | postgres
(2 rows)

db1=# exit
```
[postgres@pg_server ~]$ psql
```
psql (16.3)
Type "help" for help.
```

postgres=# \c db1
```
You are now connected to database "db2" as user "postgres".
```

db1=# \dt
Did not find any relations.

[postgres@pg_server data]$ ls -l pg_tblspc/90272
```
lrwxrwxrwx. 1 postgres postgres 30 Oct 17 22:22 pg_tblspc/90272 -> /u01/
pgsql16/pgdata/temp_files
```

[postgres@pg_server data]$ ls -lrt pg_tblspc/90272/PG_16_202307071/90234/t4_90273
```
ls: cannot access 'pg_tblspc/90272/PG_16_202307071/90234/t4_90273': No such
file or directory
```

[postgres@pg_server data]$ ls -lrt pg_tblspc/90272/PG_16_202307071/90234/t4_90276
```
ls: cannot access 'pg_tblspc/90272/PG_16_202307071/90234/t4_90276': No such
file or directory
```

[postgres@pg_server data]$ ls -lrt /u01/pgsql16/pgdata/temp_files/
```
PG_16_202307071/90234
total 0
[postgres@pg_server data]$
```

From the above output, we can see that the temporary tables don't exist in the database when checked after reconnecting, reason being a temporary table is visible only to the session that creates it. In other words, it is invisible to other sessions. Also, the temporary tables get dropped automatically when the session ends.

Index Objects on Separate Tablespace

It is advised to place index objects on a different tablespace other than tablespaces where corresponding tables are stored. This will help reduce the I/O contention on disk and improve storage management.

Let us see an example of how indexes' default tablespace can be changed.

```
[root@pg_server ~]# mkdir -p /u01/pgsql16/pgdata/ind_ts
[root@pg_server ~]# chown -R postgres:postgres /u01/pgsql16/pgdata/ind_ts
[root@pg_server ~]# chmod -R 700 /u01/pgsql16/pgdata/ind_ts
[root@pg_server ~]#
[root@pg_server ~]# ls -ld /u01/pgsql16/pgdata/ind_ts
drwx------. 2 postgres postgres 6 Oct 21 13:22 /u01/pgsql16/pgdata/ind_ts

[postgres@pg_server ~]$ psql

postgres=# create tablespace ind_ts location '/u01/pgsql16/pgdata/ind_ts';
CREATE TABLESPACE

postgres=# SELECT spcname AS "Name",pg_catalog.pg_get_userbyid(spcowner) AS
"Owner",pg_catalog.pg_tablespace_location(oid) AS "Location",pg_catalog.pg_
size_pretty(pg_catalog.pg_tablespace_size(oid)) AS "Size" FROM pg_catalog.
pg_tablespace ORDER BY 1;

    Name    |  Owner   |          Location           |   Size
------------+----------+-----------------------------+----------
 ind_ts     | postgres | /u01/pgsql16/pgdata/ind_ts  | 0 bytes
 pg_default | postgres |                             | 75 MB
 pg_global  | postgres |                             | 621 kB
(3 rows)

postgres=# \c pgdb1
You are now connected to database "pgdb1" as user "postgres".

pgdb1=# SELECT spcname,relname,
pgdb1-# CASE WHEN relpersistence = 't' THEN 'temp '
pgdb1-# WHEN relpersistence = 'u' THEN 'unlogged '
pgdb1-# ELSE '' END ||
pgdb1-# CASE
```

CHAPTER 3 POSTGRESQL PHYSICAL STRUCTURES

```
pgdb1-# WHEN relkind = 'r' THEN 'table'
pgdb1-# WHEN relkind = 'p' THEN 'partitioned table'
pgdb1-# WHEN relkind = 'f' THEN 'foreign table'
pgdb1-# WHEN relkind = 't' THEN 'TOAST table'
pgdb1-# WHEN relkind = 'v' THEN 'view'
pgdb1-# WHEN relkind = 'm' THEN 'materialized view'
pgdb1-# WHEN relkind = 'S' THEN 'sequence'
pgdb1-# WHEN relkind = 'c' THEN 'type'
pgdb1-# ELSE 'index' END as objtype
pgdb1-# FROM pg_class c join pg_tablespace ts
pgdb1-# ON (CASE WHEN c.reltablespace = 0 THEN
pgdb1(# (SELECT dattablespace FROM pg_database WHERE datname =
current_database())
pgdb1(# ELSE c.reltablespace END) = ts.oid
pgdb1-# WHERE relname NOT LIKE 'pg_toast%'
pgdb1-# AND relnamespace NOT IN
pgdb1-# (SELECT oid FROM pg_namespace
pgdb1(# WHERE nspname IN ('pg_catalog', 'information_schema'));
   spcname   |  relname  |      objtype
------------+-----------+--------------------
 pg_default | db1t1     | table
 pg_default | db1t2     | table
 pg_default | db1t1_i1  | index
 pg_default | db1t2_i2  | index
(4 rows)

pgdb1=# alter index db1t1_i1 set tablespace ind_ts;
ALTER INDEX
pgdb1=#
pgdb1=# alter index db1t2_i2 set tablespace ind_ts;
ALTER INDEX
pgdb1=#
pgdb1=# SELECT spcname,relname,
CASE WHEN relpersistence = 't' THEN 'temp '
WHEN relpersistence = 'u' THEN 'unlogged '
```

```
ELSE '' END ||
CASE
WHEN relkind = 'r' THEN 'table'
ELSE 'index' END as objtype
FROM pg_class c join pg_tablespace ts
ON (CASE WHEN c.reltablespace = 0 THEN
(SELECT dattablespace FROM pg_database WHERE datname = current_database())
ELSE c.reltablespace END) = ts.oid
WHERE relname NOT LIKE 'pg_toast%'
AND relnamespace NOT IN
(SELECT oid FROM pg_namespace
WHERE nspname IN ('pg_catalog', 'information_schema'));
   spcname   |  relname  | objtype
-------------+-----------+---------
 pg_default  | db1t1     | table
 pg_default  | db1t2     | table
 ind_ts      | db1t1_i1  | index
 ind_ts      | db1t2_i2  | index
(4 rows)

pgdb1=# SELECT spcname AS "Name",pg_catalog.pg_get_userbyid(spcowner) AS
"Owner",pg_catalog.pg_tablespace_location(oid) AS "Location",pg_catalog.pg_
size_pretty(pg_catalog.pg_tablespace_size(oid)) AS "Size" FROM pg_catalog.
pg_tablespace ORDER BY 1;
    Name    |  Owner   |            Location             |   Size
------------+----------+---------------------------------+---------
 ind_ts     | postgres | /u01/pgsql16/pgdata/ind_ts      | 32 kB
 pg_default | postgres |                                 | 75 MB
 pg_global  | postgres |                                 | 621 kB
(3 rows)
```

Or during the index creation, we can specify the tablespace where the index is to be stored.

Advantages of Tablespaces

So why do we need to use tablespaces if it's just an extension of our data into a different physical directory? What benefit does it offer?

Imagine your disks are standard hard drives that have lesser IOPS (I/O operations per second) and your application is performing a lot of reads and writes to your database. How do we improve performance?

Imagine you have a lot of database objects written in one single file? What about the I/O throughput?

It is in these cases the concept of tablespaces helps us. Tablespaces in PostgreSQL can offer several advantages to enhance database management and performance. Here are a few key benefits:

Storage management
Tablespaces provide us the flexibility to control where the data is stored on the disk. It helps with distributing I/O load across multiple disks.

Performance
It even provides us flexibility to write/read data from a faster disk (SSDs, Flash, etc.) with higher IOPS.

Data management
It helps organizing the data logically, grouping specific application or schema data into dedicated tablespaces, making it easier to manage and even provide flexibility with backup and restore processes without having to impact the complete database

Improved maintenance
It helps with maintenance tasks like vacuuming and indexing on a per-tablespace level leading to more efficient use of database resources and less downtime for the database.

Cloning a Database

In a PostgreSQL cluster, a new database can be created using an existing database as a template; this will copy all the objects of a template database into a cloned database.

Chapter 3 PostgreSQL Physical Structures

Check the size of the existing database:

postgres=# select pg_database_size('pgdb1');
```
 pg_database_size
------------------
          8008163
(1 row)
```

Check the objects in the existing database:

postgres=# \c pgdb1
You are now connected to database "pgdb1" as user "postgres".

pgdb1=# \dt
```
        List of relations
 Schema | Name  | Type  | Owner
--------+-------+-------+----------
 public | db1t1 | table | postgres
 public | db1t2 | table | postgres
(2 rows)
```

pgdb1=# \dmv
```
                List of relations
 Schema |   Name    |       Type        | Owner
--------+-----------+-------------------+----------
 public | db1t1_mv1 | materialized view | postgres
 public | db1t1_v1  | view              | postgres
```

pgdb1=# \di
```
             List of relations
 Schema |  Name    | Type  | Owner    | Table
--------+----------+-------+----------+-------
 public | db1t1_i1 | index | postgres | db1t1
 public | db1t2_i2 | index | postgres | db1t2
(2 rows)
```

CHAPTER 3 POSTGRESQL PHYSICAL STRUCTURES

Now, make a copy of database pgdb1 on the same PostgreSQL cluster using template method.

postgres=# create database pgdb1_clone template pgdb1;
```
CREATE DATABASE
postgres=#
```
postgres=# select datname from pg_database;
```
   datname
-------------
 postgres
 template1
 template0
 pgdb1
 pgdb2
 pgdb3
 pgdb4
 pgdb1_clone
```

postgres=# select pg_database_size('pgdb1_clone');
```
 pg_database_size
------------------
          7848463
(1 row)
```

Validate the objects in new database pgdb1_clone.

postgres=# \c pgdb1_clone
```
You are now connected to database "pgdb1_clone" as user "postgres".
```

pgdb1_clone=# \dt
```
        List of relations
 Schema | Name  | Type  |  Owner
--------+-------+-------+----------
 public | db1t1 | table | postgres
 public | db1t2 | table | postgres
(2 rows)
```

Chapter 3 PostgreSQL Physical Structures

```
pgdb1_clone=# \dmv
            List of relations
 Schema |   Name    |       Type        |  Owner
--------+-----------+-------------------+----------
 public | db1t1_mv1 | materialized view | postgres
 public | db1t1_v1  | view              | postgres
(2 rows)

pgdb1_clone=# \di
              List of relations
 Schema |   Name   | Type  |  Owner   | Table
--------+----------+-------+----------+-------
 public | db1t1_i1 | index | postgres | db1t1
 public | db1t2_i2 | index | postgres | db1t2
(2 rows)

pgdb1_clone=#
```

The limitation of cloning a database using template is the template database must not be opened for write operations while performing cloning. PostgreSQL cannot copy a database while it is being modified or with active connections to database. An error will be thrown when an attempt is made to copy an active database.

```
postgres=# create database pgdb1_clone template pgdb1;
ERROR:  source database "pgdb1" is being accessed by other users
DETAIL:  There is 1 other session using the database.
```

Dropping a Database in a Cluster

A database can be dropped from a PostgreSQL cluster as below:

```
postgres=# select datname from pg_database;
   datname
-------------
 postgres
 template1
 template0
 pgdb1
```

```
  pgdb2
  pgdb3
  pgdb4
  pgdb1_clone
```

postgres=# drop database pgdb1_clone;
```
DROP DATABASE
```

postgres=# select datname from pg_database;
```
   datname
 -----------
  postgres
  template1
  template0
  pgdb1
  pgdb2
  pgdb3
  pgdb4
```

postgres=# \c pgdb1_clone
```
connection to server on socket "/run/postgresql/.s.PGSQL.5432" failed:
FATAL:  database "pgdb1_clone" does not exist
Previous connection kept
postgres=#
```

Dropping Default Databases

PostgreSQL will not allow the dropping of default databases.

postgres=# drop database template0;
```
ERROR:  cannot drop a template database
postgres=#
```
postgres=# drop database template1;
```
ERROR:  cannot drop a template database
postgres=#
```

Summary

Overall, in this chapter, we have learned about the PostgreSQL cluster storage structure, the importance of configuration files in data directory, database and tablespace management, as well as the process involved during an execution of a query along with the storage unit called data page.

CHAPTER 4

PostgreSQL Management of Database Server

Introduction

This chapter mainly discusses the management of schemas and users in PostgreSQL and explains the key differences between a schema and a user and how to create and manage them using authentication and privilege management with support of roles and privileges. Also, this chapter illustrates different ways on how a user can connect to the PostgreSQL database both from within a database server and from a remote host. After reading this chapter, you will understand the authentication methods defined in PostgreSQL and options to use when connecting to PostgreSQL databases.

In this chapter, the following topics are explained:

- Schema and user in PostgreSQL
- How to create and manage a schema and a user
- Authentication methods available and their usage
- Accessing schema objects using users
  - **Scenario 1**: The user accesses all databases/schemas/tables from both client machines.
  - **Scenario 2**: The user accesses only one database and its corresponding schema and table from both client machines.
  - **Scenario 3**: The user accesses only one database and its corresponding schema and table from only a single client machine.

CHAPTER 4   POSTGRESQL MANAGEMENT OF DATABASE SERVER

- Local and remote database connectivity
- Predefined roles and extensions in PostgreSQL

In the previous chapter, we created a database by connecting to postgres prompt; we can also create a new database at operating system command prompt as postgres user.

Creating Database Using OS Command

In PostgreSQL, for creating a database from command prompt, we can use the following syntax:

Syntax:
CREATEDB [OPTION]... [DBNAME] [DESCRIPTION]

The following is the list of complete options available for the *createdb* command:

```
[postgres@pg_server ~]$ createdb --help
createdb creates a PostgreSQL database.

Usage:
  createdb [OPTION]... [DBNAME] [DESCRIPTION]

Options:
  -D, --tablespace=TABLESPACE  default tablespace for the database
.
<<<<< OUTPUT TRUNCATED >>>>>
.
  -O, --owner=OWNER            database user to own the new database
  -T, --template=TEMPLATE      template database to copy
  -V, --version                output version information, then exit
  -?, --help                   show this help, then exit

Connection options:
  -h, --host=HOSTNAME          database server host or socket directory
  -p, --port=PORT              database server port
  -U, --username=USERNAME      user name to connect as
  -w, --no-password            never prompt for password
  -W, --password               force password prompt
  --maintenance-db=DBNAME      alternate maintenance database

By default, a database with the same name as the current user is created.
```

Report bugs to <pgsql-bugs@lists.postgresql.org>.
PostgreSQL home page: <https://www.postgresql.org/>
[postgres@pg_server ~]$
```

Using this command, let us create a database *pgdbhrm*.

**[postgres@pg_server ~]$ createdb pgdbhrm**

**[postgres@pg_server ~]$ psql**
```
psql (16.3)

postgres=# \l
```
               List of databases
   Name    |  Owner   | Encoding |   Access privileges
-----------+----------+----------+-----------------------------------
 pgdb1     | postgres | UTF8     |
 pgdb2     | postgres | UTF8     |
 pgdb3     | postgres | UTF8     |
 pgdb4     | postgres | UTF8     |
 pgdbhrm   | postgres | UTF8     |
 postgres  | postgres | UTF8     |
 template0 | postgres | UTF8     | =c/postgres + postgres=CTc/postgres
 template1 | postgres | UTF8     | =c/postgres + postgres=CTc/postgres
(8 rows)
```

postgres=# \c pgdbhrm
```
You are now connected to database " pgdbhrm" as user "postgres".
```

As we can see from the output, the owner of all the default databases and the user-defined databases is the superuser, postgres.

We can change the owner for a database from the default user *postgres* to any other user. For this, let us create a new user with the name *pguseradm* and make the new user the owner of the *pgdbhrm* database.

Syntax:
CREATE USER <USERNAME>;
du – This command lists the users or roles available in the database.

[postgres@pg_server ~]$ psql
```
psql (16.3)
```

```
postgres=# \du
                              List of roles
 Role name |                         Attributes
-----------+------------------------------------------------------------
 postgres  | Superuser, Create role, Create DB, Replication, Bypass RLS

postgres=# CREATE USER pguseradm;
CREATE ROLE

postgres=# \du
                              List of roles
 Role name |                         Attributes
-----------+------------------------------------------------------------
 pguseradm |
 postgres  | Superuser, Create role, Create DB, Replication, Bypass RLS

postgres=# ALTER DATABASE pgdbhrm OWNER TO PGUSERADM;
ALTER DATABASE

postgres=# \l pgdbhrm
                List of databases
   Name    |   Owner   | Encoding | Access privileges
-----------+-----------+----------+-------------------
 pgdbhrm   | pguseradm | UTF8     |
(1 row)
```

So we were able to create a new database and new user and change the owner of the database.

In the next sections, we will learn about schemas and users in PostgreSQL.

Schemas in PostgreSQL

In PostgreSQL, a schema is a namespace that contains objects like tables, indexes, views, functions, etc. A database can contain one or more schemas, but each schema belongs to only one database. Just like in other RDBMS, multiple schemas can have database objects with same name, and to access the specific objects from a specific schema, we just have to use the fully qualified name, i.e., a prefix of schema name to the object name, *<schemaname>.<objectname>*. The main advantage of creating schemas is that it allows the users to organize the objects into logical groups, which will be easy to manage.

Every database in PostgreSQL comes with a default schema called *public*.

Syntax:

conninfo – Provides the output of connection information.

dn – Lists the schemas available in a database.

dt – Lists the tables available in a schema.

current_database() – This function lists the database name the current session is connected to.

[postgres@pg_server ~]$ psql
psql (16.3)

postgres=# \c pgdbhrm
You are now connected to database "pgdbhrm" as user "postgres".

pgdbhrm=# \conninfo
You are connected to database "pgdbhrm" as user "postgres" via socket in "/run/postgresql" at port "5432".

pgdbhrm=# select current_database();
```
 current_database
------------------
 pgdbhrm
(1 row)
```

pgdbhrm=# \dn
```
      List of schemas
  Name  |       Owner
--------+-------------------
 public | pg_database_owner
(1 row)
```

CHAPTER 4   POSTGRESQL MANAGEMENT OF DATABASE SERVER

pgdbhrm=# select current_schema();
```
 current_schema
----------------
 public
(1 row)
```

pgdbhrm=# \dt public.*
Did not find any relation named "public.*".

Creating a Schema

To create a new schema in a PostgreSQL database, the following is the syntax.

Syntax:
CREATE SCHEMA <SCHEMANAME>;

Let us create a schema *hrmschema* in database *pgdbhrm*.

pgdbhrm=# select current_database();
```
 current_database
------------------
 pgdbhrm
(1 row)
```

pgdbhrm=# \dn
```
     List of schemas
  Name  |      Owner
--------+------------------
 public | pg_database_owner
(1 row)
```

pgdbhrm=# CREATE SCHEMA HRMSCHEMA;
CREATE SCHEMA

Now, if we list the current schemas in this database using the meta command, "\dn", it will list the newly created schema as well.

pgdbhrm=# \dn
```
     List of schemas
```

```
   Name    |       Owner
-----------+--------------------
 hrmschema | postgres
 public    | pg_database_owner
(2 rows)
```

When multiple schemas exist in the database, any database object created without prefixing the schema name in the create command, PostgreSQL will place the object in the default schema, *public*.

Create a table with name *ptab1* in database *pgdbhrm* using the *"create table"* command.

List the current tables in a public schema in pgdbhrm database.

pgdbhrm=# \dt public.*
```
Did not find any relation named "public.*".
```

pgdbhrm=# CREATE TABLE PTAB1 (NUMBER INT);
```
CREATE TABLE
```

pgdbhrm=# \dt public.*
```
         List of relations
 Schema | Name  | Type  | Owner
--------+-------+-------+----------
 public | ptab1 | table | postgres
(1 row)
```

pgdbhrm=# \dt
```
         List of relations
 Schema | Name  | Type  | Owner
--------+-------+-------+----------
 public | ptab1 | table | postgres
(1 row)
```

From the above output, we can see that the newly created table is placed in a public schema. So to create an object in a non-public schema, the schema name should be prefixed to the object name.

Syntax:
CREATE <OBJECT_TYPE> <SCHEMANAME>.<OBJECT_NAME>;

CHAPTER 4 POSTGRESQL MANAGEMENT OF DATABASE SERVER

For example, if we want to create a table with name *hrmstaff* in schema *hrmschema* in *pgdbhrm* database, we can create it as shown below:

```
pgdbhrm=# select current_database();
 current_database
------------------
 pgdbhrm
(1 row)

pgdbhrm=# CREATE TABLE HRMSCHEMA.HRMSTAFF (NAME VARCHAR, ID INT);
CREATE TABLE

pgdbhrm=# \dt hrmschema.hrmstaff
           List of relations
  Schema   |   Name   | Type  |  Owner
-----------+----------+-------+----------
 hrmschema | hrmstaff | table | postgres
(1 row)
```

If we want to list all the tables in a specific schema, we can use the meta command, "*\dt <schemaname>.**".

```
pgdbhrm=# \dt hrmschema.*
           List of relations
  Schema   |   Name   | Type  |  Owner
-----------+----------+-------+----------
 hrmschema | hrmstaff | table | postgres
(1 row)
```

We can also give the database name as prefix, like <database name>.<schema name>.<object name>, but database name allowed as the one that the current session is connected to. Cross database references are not allowed.

```
pgdbhrm=# CREATE TABLE PGDBHRM.HRMSCHEMA.HRMJOB (POSITION VARCHAR,
EXP INT);
CREATE TABLE

pgdbhrm=# \dt hrmschema.*
```

```
          List of relations
  Schema    |   Name    | Type  |  Owner
------------+-----------+-------+----------
 hrmschema  | hrmjob    | table | postgres
 hrmschema  | hrmstaff  | table | postgres
(2 rows)
```

pgdbhrm=# \c postgres
You are now connected to database "postgres" as user "postgres".

Being connected to *postgres* database, if we try to create a table in *pgdbhrm* database, it reports an error.

postgres=# CREATE TABLE PGDBHRM.HRMSCHEMA.HRMHOL (HOLIDAY VARCHAR, HOL_DATE DATE);
ERROR: cross-database references are not implemented: "pgdbhrm.hrmschema.hrmhol"
LINE 1: CREATE TABLE PGDBHRM.HRMSCHEMA.HRMHOL (HOLIDAY VARCHAR, HOL_...
                     ^

Another option to create an object in a schema without prefixing the schema name to the object name is by using schema *search path* option.

A schema search path is a parameter that accepts one or more schema names as a value. Setting a search path tells the system to determine the list of schemas to look in sequence for objects. Also, it considers the first schema in the list to create a new table if the CREATE TABLE command is used with no schema name prefix.

pgdbhrm=# SELECT CURRENT_DATABASE();
```
 current_database
------------------
 pgdbhrm
(1 row)
```

pgdbhrm=# SELECT CURRENT_SCHEMA();
```
 current_schema
----------------
 public
(1 row)
```

CHAPTER 4 POSTGRESQL MANAGEMENT OF DATABASE SERVER

```
pgdbhrm=# SHOW SEARCH_PATH;
  search_path
-----------------
 "$user", public
(1 row)

pgdbhrm=# SET SEARCH_PATH TO HRMSCHEMA;
SET

pgdbhrm=# SHOW SEARCH_PATH;
 search_path
-------------
 hrmschema
(1 row)

pgdbhrm=# SELECT CURRENT_SCHEMA();
 current_schema
----------------
 hrmschema
(1 row)

pgdbhrm=# CREATE TABLE HRMHOL (HOLIDAY VARCHAR, HOL_DATE DATE);
CREATE TABLE

pgdbhrm=# \dt
           List of relations
  Schema   |  Name    | Type  | Owner
-----------+----------+-------+----------
 hrmschema | hrmhol   | table | postgres
 hrmschema | hrmjob   | table | postgres
 hrmschema | hrmstaff | table | postgres
(3 rows)
```

From the above output, we can see that the newly created table is placed in *hrmschema* instead of default *public* schema even though schema prefix is not used; the reason is the setting of *search path* to *hrmschema*.

Let us see the function of search path parameter for other operations.

CHAPTER 4   POSTGRESQL MANAGEMENT OF DATABASE SERVER

```
pgdbhrm=# SHOW SEARCH_PATH;
 search_path
-------------
 hrmschema
(1 row)

pgdbhrm=# SET SEARCH_PATH TO HRMSCHEMA, PUBLIC;
SET

pgdbhrm=# SHOW SEARCH_PATH;
    search_path
-------------------
 hrmschema, public
(1 row)

pgdbhrm=# SELECT CURRENT_SCHEMA();
 current_schema
----------------
 hrmschema
(1 row)

pgdbhrm=# \dt public.*
         List of relations
 Schema | Name  | Type  | Owner
--------+-------+-------+----------
 public | ptab1 | table | postgres
(1 row)

pgdbhrm=# insert into ptab1 values (1),(2),(3);
INSERT 0 3

pgdbhrm=# select * from ptab1;
 number
--------
      1
      2
      3
(3 rows)
```

From the above output, the following is observed:

- The search_path accepts multiple schema names.

- The first schema name in the list will always act as the current schema.

- System searches along the schema list in the search path to identify the table mentioned in insert and select statements. Since there is no table named *ptab1* in *hrmschema*, the system continued to search for *ptab1* in *public* schema since it is the second schema in the list.

- The matching table in *public* schema is considered for insert and select operations.

- The unqualified table names, i.e., the table names without schema name prefix, can be carefully used when the search path is set.

Accessing Schema Objects in PostgreSQL

The important thing to remember about schemas in postgres is that even though schemas own the database objects, we cannot really connect to the postgres databases using schemas. So how can we access schema objects? That's where a *user* comes into the picture. To access the schema objects in postgres, we must initially connect to the database as a *user* and then access the schema data. PostgreSQL has a default user (superuser) named *postgres* that can connect to any database and access any schema object; this can be observed in the previous scenarios explained earlier in this chapter.

For any user to access database objects in a schema, there are different levels of privileges that we must provide. Below are high level privilege types available to grant:

- Server level or database level

- Schema level privileges

- Object level privileges

Server Level or Database Level

This is the first level of privilege a user is required, which can be assigned or granted using authentication mechanisms and certain permissions and access controls defined at the server and database level as roles.

Schema Level Privileges

Just granting access to connect to a database will not allow a user to access data unless the next level of privileges at schema level is granted. The schema level privileges allow or restrict a user to perform certain types of operations.

Object Level Privileges

This is a fine-grained access control that manages user privileges at the database objects level, which is essential in a multi-user environment.

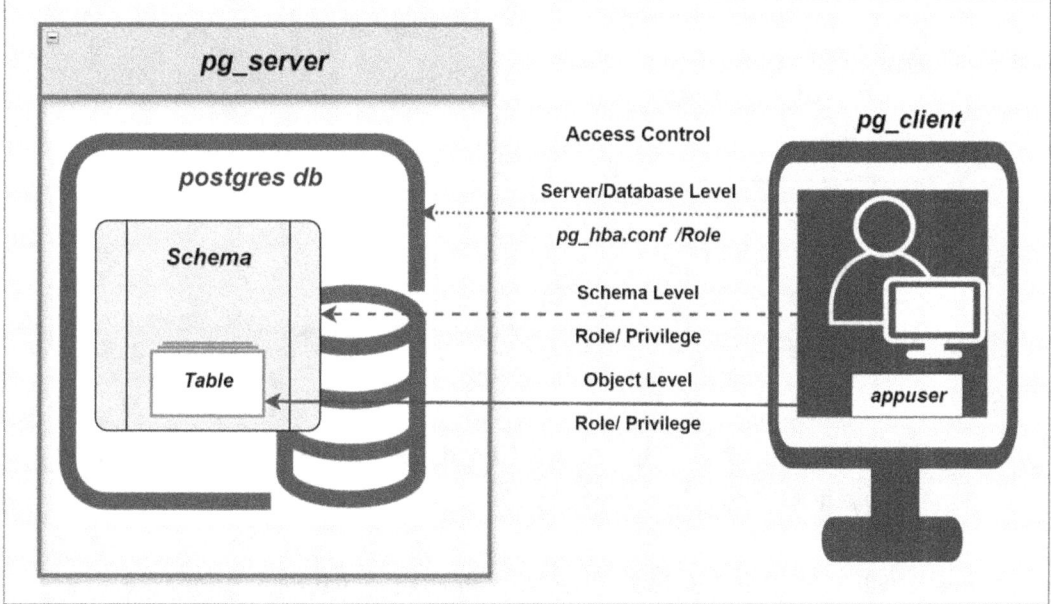

Figure 4-1. *PostgreSQL authentication and privilege process*

For example, in *pgdbhrm* database, we have a schema named *hrmschema*. Let us perform the below operations to understand the working of privileges.

- Create a table named *teaminfo* in *hrmschema* schema of *pgdbhrm* database.
- Insert rows into the *teaminfo* table.
- Create a user named *grpaccount*
- Grant necessary privileges on the *hrmschema.teaminfo* table to user *grpaccount*.
- Try to access the *teaminfo* table as user *grpaccount*.

CHAPTER 4 POSTGRESQL MANAGEMENT OF DATABASE SERVER

[postgres@pg_server ~]$ psql
psql (16.3)

postgres=# \c pgdbhrm
You are now connected to database "pgdbhrm" as user "postgres".

pgdbhrm=# CREATE TABLE HRMSCHEMA.TEAMINFO (EMPNAME VARCHAR, EMPID INT, DEPTNAME VARCHAR);
CREATE TABLE

pgdbhrm=# \dt hrmschema.*
```
          List of relations
  Schema   |   Name   | Type  |  Owner
-----------+----------+-------+----------
 hrmschema | hrmhol   | table | postgres
 hrmschema | hrmjob   | table | postgres
 hrmschema | hrmstaff | table | postgres
 hrmschema | teaminfo | table | postgres
(4 rows)
```

pgdbhrm=# INSERT INTO HRMSCHEMA.TEAMINFO VALUES ('Peter J',1000,'Sales'),
         ('Robin M',1001,'Accounts');
INSERT 0 2
pgdbhrm=# INSERT INTO HRMSCHEMA.TEAMINFO VALUES ('David S',1002,'Sales'),
         ('Stefeny R',1003,'Marketing');
INSERT 0 2
pgdbhrm=# INSERT INTO HRMSCHEMA.TEAMINFO VALUES ('Marshal G',1004,'Sales'),
         ('Ross T',1006,'Accounts');
INSERT 0 2
pgdbhrm=# INSERT INTO HRMSCHEMA.TEAMINFO VALUES ('Leanord D',1200,'Sales'),
         ('Mark W',1030,'Sales');
INSERT 0 2
pgdbhrm=# INSERT INTO HRMSCHEMA.TEAMINFO VALUES ('Mark S',1022,'Marketing'),
         ('Carl M',1094,'Sales');
INSERT 0 2
pgdbhrm=# INSERT INTO HRMSCHEMA.TEAMINFO VALUES ('Katy P',1098,'Accounts');
INSERT 0 1

```
pgdbhrm=# SELECT * FROM HRMSCHEMA.TEAMINFO;
  empname   | empid | deptname
------------+-------+-----------
 Peter J    |  1000 | Sales
 Robin M    |  1001 | Accounts
 David S    |  1002 | Sales
 Stefeny R  |  1003 | Marketing
 Marshal G  |  1004 | Sales
 Ross T     |  1006 | Accounts
 Leanord D  |  1200 | Sales
 Mark W     |  1030 | Sales
 Mark S     |  1022 | Marketing
 Carl M     |  1094 | Sales
 Katy P     |  1098 | Accounts
(11 rows)
```

To create a user, we can use the below mentioned syntax:

Syntax:

CREATE USER <USERNAME> WITH PASSWORD '<PASSWORD>'

\du – This command is to check the users available in the database.

Let us create a user named *grpaccount*.

```
pgdbhrm=# \du
                             List of roles
 Role name  |                         Attributes
------------+-----------------------------------------------------------
 pguseradm  |
 postgres   | Superuser, Create role, Create DB, Replication, Bypass RLS

pgdbhrm=# CREATE USER grpaccount WITH PASSWORD 'account';
CREATE ROLE

pgdbhrm=# \du
                             List of roles
 Role name  |                         Attributes
------------+-----------------------------------------------------------
 grpaccount |
 pguseradm  |
 postgres   | Superuser, Create role, Create DB, Replication, Bypass RLS
```

Now, if the user *grpaccount* wants to access the *hrmschema* objects, the user should have two privileges:

> **USAGE privilege**: This is a schema level privilege that is to be granted to a user who wants to access the database objects that are created in a schema.

> **DML privileges**: Apart from the USAGE privilege, the user should also have the necessary object level privileges, like insert/update/delete (DML privileges) on a specific object or all objects of a schema.

In our case, let us grant both these privileges to the *grpaccount* user as shown below:

[postgres@pg_server ~]$ psql
psql (16.3)

postgres=# \c pgdbhrm
You are now connected to database "pgdbhrm" as user "postgres".

pgdbhrm=# GRANT USAGE ON SCHEMA hrmschema TO grpaccount;
GRANT

pgdbhrm=# GRANT SELECT,INSERT,UPDATE,DELETE ON hrmschema.teaminfo TO grpaccount;
GRANT

pgdbhrm=# SELECT * FROM INFORMATION_SCHEMA.ROLE_TABLE_GRANTS WHERE GRANTEE='grpaccount';

```
 grantor  | grantee    | table_   | table_    | table_name | privilege_type
                       | catalog  | schema
----------+------------+----------+-----------+------------+---------------
 postgres | grpaccount | pgdbhrm  | hrmschema | teaminfo   | INSERT
 postgres | grpaccount | pgdbhrm  | hrmschema | teaminfo   | SELECT
 postgres | grpaccount | pgdbhrm  | hrmschema | teaminfo   | UPDATE
 postgres | grpaccount | pgdbhrm  | hrmschema | teaminfo   | DELETE
(4 rows)
```

We can also provide all the privileges on all tables in the schema using the command below:

```
pgdbhrm=# GRANT ALL ON ALL TABLES IN SCHEMA hrmschema TO grpaccount;
GRANT

pgdbhrm=# SELECT * FROM INFORMATION_SCHEMA.ROLE_TABLE_GRANTS WHERE GRANTEE='grpaccount';
```

grantor	grantee	table_catalog	table_schema	table_name	privilege_type
postgres	grpaccount	pgdbhrm	hrmschema	hrmstaff	INSERT
postgres	grpaccount	pgdbhrm	hrmschema	hrmstaff	SELECT
postgres	grpaccount	pgdbhrm	hrmschema	hrmstaff	UPDATE
postgres	grpaccount	pgdbhrm	hrmschema	hrmstaff	DELETE
postgres	grpaccount	pgdbhrm	hrmschema	hrmstaff	TRUNCATE
postgres	grpaccount	pgdbhrm	hrmschema	hrmstaff	REFERENCES
postgres	grpaccount	pgdbhrm	hrmschema	hrmstaff	TRIGGER
postgres	grpaccount	pgdbhrm	hrmschema	teaminfo	INSERT
postgres	grpaccount	pgdbhrm	hrmschema	teaminfo	SELECT
postgres	grpaccount	pgdbhrm	hrmschema	teaminfo	UPDATE
postgres	grpaccount	pgdbhrm	hrmschema	teaminfo	DELETE
postgres	grpaccount	pgdbhrm	hrmschema	teaminfo	TRUNCATE
postgres	grpaccount	pgdbhrm	hrmschema	teaminfo	REFERENCES
postgres	grpaccount	pgdbhrm	hrmschema	teaminfo	TRIGGER
postgres	grpaccount	pgdbhrm	hrmschema	hrmjob	INSERT
postgres	grpaccount	pgdbhrm	hrmschema	hrmjob	SELECT
postgres	grpaccount	pgdbhrm	hrmschema	hrmjob	UPDATE
postgres	grpaccount	pgdbhrm	hrmschema	hrmjob	DELETE
postgres	grpaccount	pgdbhrm	hrmschema	hrmjob	TRUNCATE
postgres	grpaccount	pgdbhrm	hrmschema	hrmjob	REFERENCES
postgres	grpaccount	pgdbhrm	hrmschema	hrmjob	TRIGGER
postgres	grpaccount	pgdbhrm	hrmschema	hrmhol	INSERT
postgres	grpaccount	pgdbhrm	hrmschema	hrmhol	SELECT
postgres	grpaccount	pgdbhrm	hrmschema	hrmhol	UPDATE
postgres	grpaccount	pgdbhrm	hrmschema	hrmhol	DELETE

CHAPTER 4 POSTGRESQL MANAGEMENT OF DATABASE SERVER

```
 postgres | grpaccount | pgdbhrm | hrmschema | hrmhol    | TRUNCATE
 postgres | grpaccount | pgdbhrm | hrmschema | hrmhol    | REFERENCES
 postgres | grpaccount | pgdbhrm | hrmschema | hrmhol    | TRIGGER
(28 rows)
```

Now, if you connect to *pgdbhrm* database as user *grpaccount* and run a select or insert/delete operation on table *hrmschema.teaminfo*, it will run without any issues. Let us test the table access.

Database Local Connectivity by User

Being on the PostgreSQL system, if a user wants to connect to a PostgreSQL database locally, the user requires an authentication. Also, the same psql utility needs to be used with additional options to connect to the database.

Below is the psql utility with additional options available to use for database connectivity.

Syntax:
psql [OPTION]... [DBNAME [USERNAME]]

[postgres@pg_server ~]$ psql --help
```
psql is the PostgreSQL interactive terminal.

Usage:
  psql [OPTION]... [DBNAME [USERNAME]]

General options:
  -d, --dbname=DBNAME      database name to connect to (default:
  "postgres")

Connection options:
  -h, --host=HOSTNAME      database server host or socket directory
  (default: "local socket")
  -p, --port=PORT          database server port (default: "5432")
  -U, --username=USERNAME  database user name (default: "postgres")
  -w, --no-password        never prompt for password
  -W, --password           force password prompt (should happen
                           automatically)
```

CHAPTER 4 POSTGRESQL MANAGEMENT OF DATABASE SERVER

As discussed in the previous chapters, the authentication for database connectivity happens through a very important configuration file, i.e., *pg_hba.conf*. In our case, *grpaccount* is a normal user, and we need to enable password-based authentication to allow the database connectivity.

Edit the pg_hba.conf file to include the below line:

```
[postgres@pg_server ~]$ vi /var/lib/pgsql/16/data/pg_hba.conf
# TYPE   DATABASE    USER         ADDRESS      METHOD
# "local" is for Unix domain socket connections only
local    pgdbhrm     grpaccount                md5              <<<<< Add this line
```

TYPE:local – Local value defines local authentication

DATABASE:pgdbhrm – Allows connectivity to specific database *pgdbhrm*

USER:grpaccount – Allows connectivity only for specific user *grpaccount*

METHOD:md5 – Enables password-based authentication for local connections

Once the pg_hba.conf file is updated, restart the PostgreSQL service, either using "pg_ctl reload" or "systemctl stop/start".

```
[root@pg_server ~]# systemctl stop postgresql-16

[root@pg_server ~]# systemctl start postgresql-16

[root@pg_server ~]# systemctl status postgresql-16
```
- postgresql-16.service - PostgreSQL 16 database server
  Loaded: loaded (/usr/lib/systemd/system/postgresql-16.service; enabled; vendor preset: disabled)
  Active: active (running) since Tue 2024-11-26 22:16:08 CST; 4s ago

Now, try to connect to *pgdbhrm* database as user *grpaccount* locally, i.e., being on PostgreSQL server.

```
[postgres@pg_server ~]$ psql -U grpaccount -d pgdbhrm
Password for user grpaccount:
psql (16.3)

pgdbhrm=> SELECT CURRENT_DATABASE();
 current_database
------------------
```

CHAPTER 4 POSTGRESQL MANAGEMENT OF DATABASE SERVER

```
 pgdbhrm
(1 row)
```

pgdbhrm=> SELECT CURRENT_SCHEMA();
```
 current_schema
----------------
 public
(1 row)
```

pgdbhrm=> SELECT CURRENT_USER;
```
 current_user
--------------
 grpaccount
(1 row)
```

pgdbhrm=> SELECT * FROM hrmschema.teaminfo;
```
  empname   | empid | deptname
------------+-------+-----------
 Peter J    |  1000 | Sales
 Robin M    |  1001 | Accounts
 David S    |  1002 | Sales
 Stefeny R  |  1003 | Marketing
 Marshal G  |  1004 | Sales
 Ross T     |  1006 | Accounts
 Leanord D  |  1200 | Sales
 Mark W     |  1030 | Sales
 Mark S     |  1022 | Marketing
 Carl M     |  1094 | Sales
 Katy P     |  1098 | Accounts
(11 rows)
```

pgdbhrm=> INSERT INTO HRMSCHEMA.TEAMINFO VALUES ('DARREN L',2002,'Sales');
```
INSERT 0 1
```

pgdbhrm=> SELECT * FROM hrmschema.teaminfo;
```
  empname   | empid | deptname
------------+-------+-----------
 Peter J    |  1000 | Sales
```

```
Robin M      |  1001 | Accounts
David S      |  1002 | Sales
Stefeny R    |  1003 | Marketing
Marshal G    |  1004 | Sales
Ross T       |  1006 | Accounts
Leanord D    |  1200 | Sales
Mark W       |  1030 | Sales
Mark S       |  1022 | Marketing
Carl M       |  1094 | Sales
Katy P       |  1098 | Accounts
DARREN L     |  2002 | Sales
(12 rows)
```

Please note that in postgres, all the transactions are auto committed; we don't have to exclusively issue the commit command.

Since the *grpaccount* user is granted the necessary server level, schema level, and object level privileges, it can connect to a database, access objects of a schema, and perform DML operations on the objects.

User Attributes

User attributes in PostgreSQL define the capabilities and permissions of a user in database system. Setting the attributes to any user defines the actions of the user with the database.

We can set various attributes for the users in the postgres database. For example, we can set the expiry for the password of the users.

```
[postgres@pg_server ~]$ psql
psql (16.3)

postgres=# \c pgdbhrm

pgdbhrm=# \du grpaccount
                List of roles
 Role name  |          Attributes
------------+-----------------------------------
 grpaccount |
```

```
pgdbhrm=# select rolname,rolvaliduntil from pg_roles where
rolname='grpaccount';
  rolname   |     rolvaliduntil
------------+------------------------
 grpaccount |
(1 row)
```

pgdbhrm=# ALTER USER grpaccount VALID UNTIL '12-31-2024';
```
ALTER ROLE
```

pgdbhrm=# \du grpaccount
```
                       List of roles
 Role name  |                  Attributes
------------+---------------------------------------------
 grpaccount | Password valid until 2024-12-31 00:00:00-06
```

pgdbhrm=# select rolname,rolvaliduntil from pg_roles where rolname='grpaccount';
```
  rolname   |     rolvaliduntil
------------+------------------------
 grpaccount | 2024-12-31 00:00:00-06
(1 row)
```

Now, let us set a few more attributes to the user, *grpaccount*.

pgdbhrm=# \du grpaccount
```
                       List of roles
 Role name  |                  Attributes
------------+---------------------------------------------
 grpaccount | Password valid until 2024-12-31 00:00:00-06
```

pgdbhrm=# select rolname,rolcreaterole,rolcreatedb,rolreplication from pg_roles where rolname='grpaccount';
```
  rolname   | rolcreaterole | rolcreatedb | rolreplication
------------+---------------+-------------+----------------
 grpaccount | f             | f           | f
(1 row)
```

pgdbhrm=# ALTER USER grpaccount WITH CREATEDB CREATEROLE REPLICATION;
ALTER ROLE

pgdbhrm=# \du grpaccount
```
                   List of roles
 Role name  |              Attributes
------------+-------------------------------------------
 grpaccount | Create role, Create DB, Replication       +
            | Password valid until 2024-12-31 00:00:00-06
```

pgdbhrm=# select rolname,rolcreaterole,rolcreatedb,rolreplication from pg_roles where rolname='grpaccount';
```
  rolname   | rolcreaterole | rolcreatedb | rolreplication
------------+---------------+-------------+----------------
 grpaccount | t             | t           | t
(1 row)
```

Let us add another attribute to limit the max connections for the user, *grpaccount*.

pgdbhrm=# \du grpaccount
```
                   List of roles
 Role name  |              Attributes
------------+-------------------------------------------
 grpaccount | Create role, Create DB, Replication       +
            | Password valid until 2024-12-31 00:00:00-06
```

pgdbhrm=# select rolname,rolcanlogin,rolconnlimit from pg_roles where rolname='grpaccount';
```
  rolname   | rolcanlogin | rolconnlimit
------------+-------------+--------------
 grpaccount | t           |           -1
(1 row)
```

pgdbhrm=# ALTER USER grpaccount CONNECTION LIMIT 1;
ALTER ROLE

```
pgdbhrm=# \du grpaccount
                       List of roles
 Role name  |                Attributes
------------+--------------------------------------------
 grpaccount | Create role, Create DB, Replication        +
            | 1 connection                               +
            | Password valid until 2024-12-31 00:00:00-06
```

pgdbhrm=# select rolname,rolcanlogin,rolconnlimit from pg_roles where rolname='grpaccount';

```
  rolname   | rolcanlogin | rolconnlimit
------------+-------------+--------------
 grpaccount | t           |            1
(1 row)
```

From the output, we can see the connection limit was -1, which indicates the user *grpaccount* can connect to the database through unlimited sessions. Setting attribute connection limit as 1 restricts the user to create only one session to the database. If the user tries to create more than one session, it reports an error during the connection request.

Let's test the connections.

Session 1

[postgres@pg_server ~]$ psql -U grpaccount -d pgdbhrm
Password for user grpaccount:
psql (16.3)

pgdbhrm=>

Session 2

[postgres@pg_server ~]$ psql -U grpaccount -d pgdbhrm
Password for user grpaccount:
psql: error: connection to server on socket "/run/postgresql/.s.PGSQL.5432" failed: FATAL: **too many connections for role "grpaccount"**

From the output, we can clearly see a rejection of the connection request since there is already an active connection by the user.

Below is the list of available attribute options in version 16.3.

postgres=# \h alter user
```
Command:     ALTER USER
Description: change a database role
Syntax:
ALTER USER role_specification [ WITH ] option [ ... ]

where option can be:

      SUPERUSER     | NOSUPERUSER
    | CREATEDB      | NOCREATEDB
    | CREATEROLE    | NOCREATEROLE
    | INHERIT       | NOINHERIT
    | LOGIN         | NOLOGIN
    | REPLICATION   | NOREPLICATION
    | BYPASSRLS     | NOBYPASSRLS
    | CONNECTION LIMIT connlimit
    | [ ENCRYPTED ] PASSWORD 'password' | PASSWORD NULL
    | VALID UNTIL 'timestamp'

ALTER USER name RENAME TO new_name

ALTER USER { role_specification | ALL } [ IN DATABASE database_name ] SET
configuration_parameter { TO | = } { value | DEFAULT }
ALTER USER { role_specification | ALL } [ IN DATABASE database_name ]
RESET ALL

where role_specification can be:

    role_name
  | CURRENT_ROLE
  | CURRENT_USER
  | SESSION_USER

URL: https://www.postgresql.org/docs/16/sql-alteruser.html
```

User Renaming

In postgres, we do have an option to change the name of an existing user. In the example below, we have a user with name *grpaccount* and will change the name of this user to *grpaccnew*.

```
postgres=# \du grpaccount
                  List of roles
 Role name |                  Attributes
-----------+---------------------------------------------
 grpaccount | Create role, Create DB, Replication       +
            | 1 connection                              +
            | Password valid until 2024-12-31 00:00:00-06
```

For changing the username, we will use the below mentioned syntax:

Syntax:
ALTER USER oldname RENAME TO newname

```
postgres=# ALTER USER grpaccount RENAME TO grpaccnew;
ALTER ROLE

postgres=# \du grpaccount
    List of roles
 Role name | Attributes
-----------+------------

postgres=# \du grpaccnew
                  List of roles
 Role name |                  Attributes
-----------+---------------------------------------------
 grpaccnew | Create role, Create DB, Replication        +
           | 1 connection                               +
           | Password valid until 2024-12-31 00:00:00-06
```

Schema Ownership

By default, when a schema is created in any PostgreSQL database, the *postgres* user will automatically be assigned and acted as the schema owner.

CHAPTER 4   POSTGRESQL MANAGEMENT OF DATABASE SERVER

But if we need to manage the schemas individually and want them to be owned by a non-default postgres user, PostgreSQL provides an option to change the owner of a schema.

Syntax:

ALTER SCHEMA schemaname OWNER TO username

In the example below, the owner of *hrmschema* schema is *postgres* user. We will change the owner of this schema to *grpaccnew*.

```
[postgres@pg_server ~]$ psql
psql (16.3)

postgres=# \c pgdbhrm
You are now connected to database "pgdbhrm" as user "postgres".

pgdbhrm=# \dn hrmschema
    List of schemas
   Name    |  Owner
-----------+----------
 hrmschema | postgres
(1 row)

pgdbhrm=# ALTER SCHEMA hrmschema OWNER TO grpaccnew;
ALTER SCHEMA

pgdbhrm=# \dn hrmschema
    List of schemas
   Name    |   Owner
-----------+-----------
 hrmschema | grpaccnew
(1 row)
```

As the owner of the schema, the *grpaccnew* user will have the privilege to create objects in the schema *hrmschema*.

```
[postgres@pg_server ~]$ psql -U grpaccnew -d pgdbhrm
Password for user grpaccnew:
psql (16.3)
```

```
pgdbhrm=> SELECT CURRENT_DATABASE();
 current_database
------------------
 pgdbhrm
(1 row)

pgdbhrm=> SELECT CURRENT_USER;
 current_user
--------------
 grpaccnew
(1 row)

pgdbhrm=> CREATE TABLE HRMSCHEMA.TAB1 (A INT, B VARCHAR, C DATE);
CREATE TABLE

pgdbhrm=> INSERT INTO HRMSCHEMA.TAB1 VALUES (1,'THIS IS TEST','26-NOV-2024');
INSERT 0 1

pgdbhrm=> SELECT * FROM HRMSCHEMA.TAB1;
 a |      b       |     c
---+--------------+------------
 1 | THIS IS TEST | 2024-11-26
(1 row)

pgdbhrm=> CREATE TABLE HRMSCHEMA.TAB2 (A INT, B TEXT, C DATE);
CREATE TABLE

pgdbhrm=> INSERT INTO HRMSCHEMA.TAB2 SELECT i,i::text,now() FROM GENERATE_SERIES(1,1000) i;
INSERT 0 1000
```

So far in the earlier scenarios, we have seen a user connecting to the database from the same database server, *pg_server*, using local authentication. In the next sections, we will see how we can make a user connect to a postgres database from remote machines.

Database Remote Connectivity by User

What happens when a user connects to the PostgreSQL database from a remote server. How does PostgreSQL server authentication happen for all the incoming client connections? We will check the authentication procedures and the user remote connectivity from a client server in the following sections.

In this explanation, we will use the database server *pg_server* and two client servers, *pg_client1* and *pg_client2*, as described in Table 4-1. We will try to connect to the databases running on the *pg_server* server from remote machines, *pg_client1* and *pg_client2*.

Table 4-1. *Server and client machine details*

Server name	Machine type	PostgreSQL version	IP address
pg_server	Database server	16.3	192.168.2.24
pg_client1	Client server	16.3 (no initdb)	192.168.2.30
Pg_client2	Client server	16.3 (no initdb)	192.168.2.40

On these two client machines, we have installed PostgreSQL binaries but have not initialized the data area or started PostgreSQL as we don't need them. We just need the binaries so that we can use the psql utility to connect to the databases on PostgreSQL server.

Let us prepare the database server environment so that we can test multiple scenarios for client authentication and database remote access.

On the pg_server database server, we will use databases *pgdb1*, *pgdb2*, *pgdb3*, and *pgdb4*, which were created in the previous chapter for these scenarios.

In pg_server:

```
[postgres@pg_server ~]$ echo $PG_HOME
/usr/pgsql-16

[postgres@pg_server ~]$ echo $PGDATA
/var/lib/pgsql/16/data

[postgres@pg_server ~]$ psql
psql (16.3)
```

CHAPTER 4   POSTGRESQL MANAGEMENT OF DATABASE SERVER

postgres=# \l
```
          List of databases
   Name    |  Owner   | Encoding | Access privileges
-----------+----------+----------+--------------------
 pgdb1     | postgres | UTF8     |
 pgdb2     | postgres | UTF8     |
 pgdb3     | postgres | UTF8     |
 pgdb4     | postgres | UTF8     |
```

Let us create a schema in each of these databases.

In database pgdb1:

postgres=# \c pgdb1
You are now connected to database "pgdb1" as user "postgres".

pgdb1=# CREATE SCHEMA pgdb1sch1;
CREATE SCHEMA

pgdb1=# \dn pgdb1sch1
```
    List of schemas
   Name    |  Owner
-----------+----------
 pgdb1sch1 | postgres
(1 row)
```

In database pgdb2:

pgdb1=# \c pgdb2
You are now connected to database "pgdb2" as user "postgres".

pgdb2=# CREATE SCHEMA pgdb2sch2;
CREATE SCHEMA

pgdb2=# \dn pgdb2sch2
```
    List of schemas
   Name    |  Owner
-----------+----------
 pgdb2sch2 | postgres
(1 row)
```

CHAPTER 4   POSTGRESQL MANAGEMENT OF DATABASE SERVER

In database pgdb3:

pgdb2=# \c pgdb3
You are now connected to database "pgdb3" as user "postgres".

pgdb3=# CREATE SCHEMA pgdb3sch3;
CREATE SCHEMA

pgdb3=# \dn pgdb3sch3
```
   List of schemas
    Name    |  Owner
------------+----------
 pgdb3sch3  | postgres
(1 row)
```

In database pgdb4:

pgdb3=# \c pgdb4
You are now connected to database "pgdb4" as user "postgres".

pgdb4=# CREATE SCHEMA pgdb4sch4;
CREATE SCHEMA

pgdb4=# \dn pgdb4sch4
```
   List of schemas
    Name    |  Owner
------------+----------
 pgdb4sch4  | postgres
(1 row)
```

pgdb4=#

After the creation of schemas in each of the databases, we have the layout below.

CHAPTER 4   POSTGRESQL MANAGEMENT OF DATABASE SERVER

Table 4-2. *Databases and schema details*

Database name	Schema name
pgdb1	pgdb1sch1
pgdb2	pgdb2sch2
pgdb3	pgdb3sch3
pgdb4	pgdb4sch4

Now, let us create one table in each of these schemas in each database and insert few rows.

In database pgdb1:

postgres=# \c pgdb1
You are now connected to database "pgdb1" as user "postgres".

pgdb1=# create table pgdb1sch1.db1s1t1 (name varchar, id int);
CREATE TABLE

pgdb1=# insert into pgdb1sch1.db1s1t1 values ('d1s1t1a',1), ('d1s1t1b',2);
INSERT 0 2

pgdb1=# select * from pgdb1sch1.db1s1t1;
```
  name   | id
---------+----
 d1s1t1a |  1
 d1s1t1b |  2
(2 rows)
```

In database pgdb2:

pgdb1=# \c pgdb2
You are now connected to database "pgdb2" as user "postgres".

pgdb2=# create table pgdb2sch2.db2s2t2 (name varchar, id int);
CREATE TABLE

pgdb2=# insert into pgdb2sch2.db2s2t2 values ('d2s2t2a',3), ('d2s2t2b',4);
INSERT 0 2

```
pgdb2=# select * from pgdb2sch2.db2s2t2;
  name   | id
---------+----
 d2s2t2a |  3
 d2s2t2b |  4
(2 rows)
```

In database pgdb3:

```
pgdb2=# \c pgdb3
You are now connected to database "pgdb3" as user "postgres".

pgdb3=# create table pgdb3sch3.db3s3t3 (name varchar, id int);
CREATE TABLE

pgdb3=# insert into pgdb3sch3.db3s3t3 values ('d3s3t3a',5), ('d3s3t3b',6);
INSERT 0 2

pgdb3=# select * from pgdb3sch3.db3s3t3;
  name   | id
---------+----
 d3s3t3a |  5
 d3s3t3b |  6
(2 rows)
```

In database pgdb4:

```
pgdb3=# \c pgdb4
You are now connected to database "pgdb4" as user "postgres".

pgdb4=# create table pgdb4sch4.db4s4t4 (name varchar, id int);
CREATE TABLE

pgdb4=# insert into pgdb4sch4.db4s4t4 values ('d4s4t4a',7), ('d4s4t4b',8);
INSERT 0 2
```

CHAPTER 4   POSTGRESQL MANAGEMENT OF DATABASE SERVER

pgdb4=# select * from pgdb4sch4.db4s4t4;
```
  name  | id
--------+----
 d4s4t4a |  7
 d4s4t4b |  8
(2 rows)
```

After the creation of tables in each of the database's schemas, we have the layout below.

Table 4-3. *Databases along with schema and table details*

Database name	Schema name	Table name
pgdb1	pgdb1sch1	db1s1t1
pgdb2	pgdb2sch2	db2s2t2
pgdb3	pgdb3sch3	db3s3t3
pgdb4	pgdb4sch4	db4s4t4

Let us now create three users in the PostgreSQL cluster and work with them for the remote database connectivity. Please note that the users are global entities and they do not belong to any individual databases.

In pg_server:

[postgres@pg_server ~]$ psql
psql (16.3)

postgres=# create user appuser1 with password 'pgappuser1';
CREATE ROLE
postgres=# create user appuser2 with password 'pgappuser2';
CREATE ROLE
postgres=# create user appuser3 with password 'pgappuser3';
CREATE ROLE

CHAPTER 4 POSTGRESQL MANAGEMENT OF DATABASE SERVER

postgres=# \du
```
                List of roles
 Role name |            Attributes
-----------+------------------------------------------------
 appuser1  |
 appuser2  |
 appuser3  |
```

So let us see a few scenarios where we can allow or restrict application users accessing databases from different client machines.

- **Scenario 1**: User *appuser1* accesses all databases/schemas/tables from both client machines.

- **Scenario 2**: User *appuser2* accesses only database *pgdb2* and its corresponding schema and table from both client machines.

- **Scenario 3**: User *appuser3* accesses only database *pgdb4* and its corresponding schema and table from only client machine *pg_client2*.

Figure 4-2 is the pictorial representation of the setup and testing the scenarios mentioned above.

CHAPTER 4 POSTGRESQL MANAGEMENT OF DATABASE SERVER

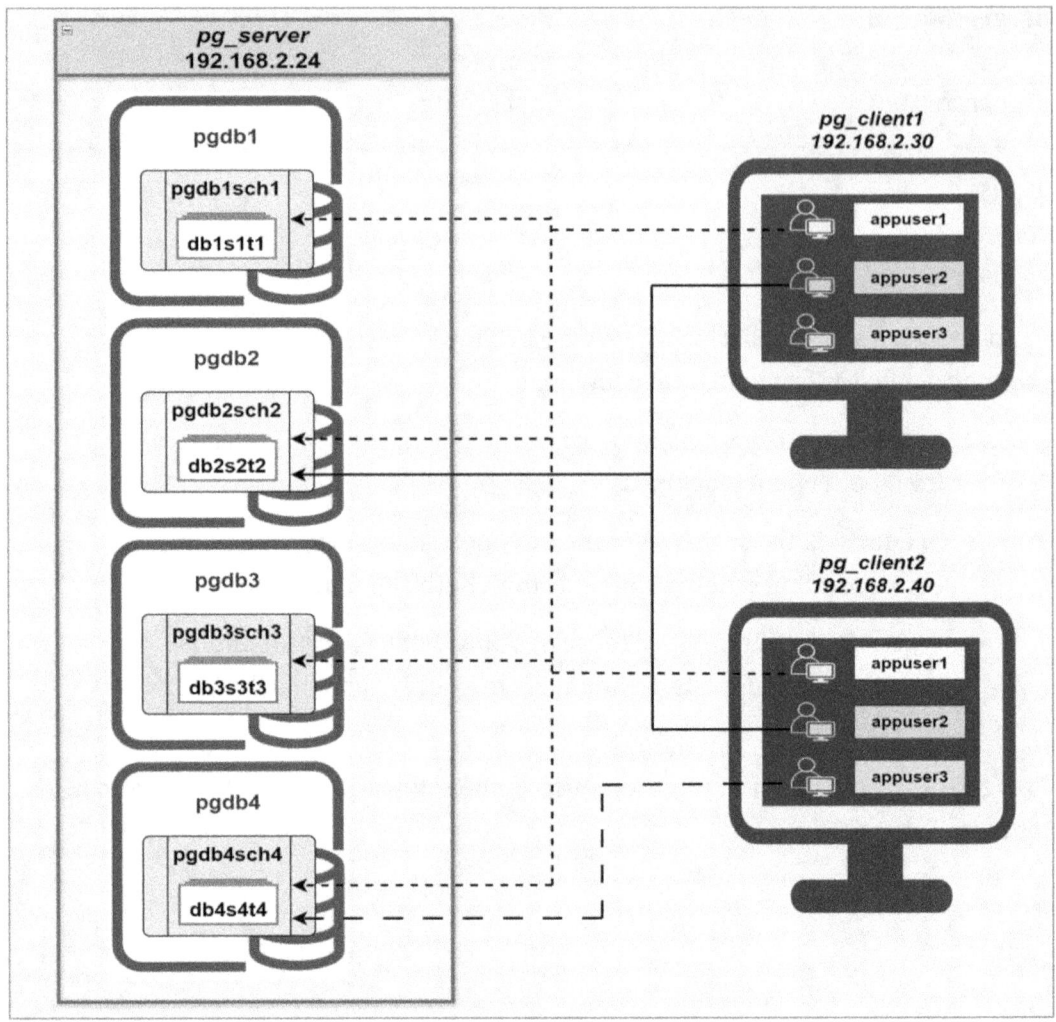

Figure 4-2. *Remote connectivity from client to server*

As mentioned earlier, we have installed PostgreSQL software on both the client machines so that we can use the ***psql*** utility to connect to the databases. Below is the syntax for connecting to a specific database.

Syntax:
psql -U USERNAME -d DBNAME -h HOSTNAME -p PORT
USERNAME – Username that we are trying to connect with
DBNAME – Database to which we are trying to connect
HOSTNAME – Server that is hosting the database
PORT – Port on the database server where it's accepting the connections

Scenario 1: User *appuser1* accesses all databases/schemas/tables from both client machines.

Log in to the first client server, *pg_client1*, and try to connect to database *pgdb1* as user *appuser1*.

In pg_client1:

```
[postgres@pg_client1 ~]$ which psql
/usr/bin/psql

[postgres@pg_client1 ~]$ psql -d pgdb1 -U appuser1 -p 5432 -h 192.168.2.24
psql: error: connection to server at "192.168.2.24", port 5432 failed:
FATAL:  no pg_hba.conf entry for host "192.168.2.30", user "appuser1",
database "pgdb1", no encryption

[postgres@pg_client1 ~]$
```

From the above output, it is observed that the connection request to the database *pgdb1* failed with error.

It is complaining about missing entry of client ip (192.168.2.30) in the configuration file *pg_hba.conf*. So what is this file?

The pg_hba.conf File

As explained in the previous chapter, the *pg_hba.conf* is a configuration file on the database server that controls the authentication of all the client connections. This gets created when the database cluster is initialized. **pg** in the *pg_hba.conf* file stands for postgres, and **hba** stands for host-based authentication. This file along with other configuration files will be present in the **data** directory of the database server. It is possible to place the pg_hba.conf file in a different location. If we want to place the file pg_hba.conf in a different location, we must specify the file location to the parameter, *hba_file*, in the main configuration file, *postgresql.conf*, which is also in the data directory.

The host-based authentication configuration file, pg_hba.conf, controls how the clients are authenticated and which servers are allowed to connect. When a user tries to connect the postgres database, postmaster process on the database server will check the pg_hba.conf file to see if it has all the details of the incoming user connection, which include the database username which it's trying to connect with, client server info from which the user is initiating the connection, and database name the user is trying to connect. Only when it finds all this information in the pg_hba.conf file, the postmaster process will allow the connections or else it will reject the user connection. Below is the general format of the details that we must keep in the pg_hba.conf file.

```
# TYPE    DATABASE          USER              ADDRESS                   METHOD
```

In our case, since we are trying to connect to the database from remote servers, we should add both the client server information in the pg_hba.conf file and reload PostgreSQL server.

In pg_server:

```
[postgres@pg_server ~]$ vi /var/lib/pgsql/16/data/pg_hba.conf
```

```
[postgres@pg_server ~]$ cat /var/lib/pgsql/16/data/pg_hba.conf
```

```
# TYPE   DATABASE   USER       ADDRESS          METHOD
# IPv4 local connections:
host     all        appuser1   192.168.2.30/32  scram-sha-256   << Add
```
this line
```
host     all        appuser1   192.168.2.40/32  scram-sha-256   << Add
```
this line

By adding these two lines in *pg_hba.conf*, we tell the system that if user *appuser1* tries to connect to any database from server 192.168.2.30, postmaster process on the database server allows the connection after the user *appuser1* enters the password since we have used password-based authentication method, scram-sha-256.

Whenever we modify the *pg_hba.conf* file, we must reload the configuration. This can be done either by running the "pg_ctl reload" command or by executing "select pg_reload_conf()" from psql. Both commands will not stop the postgres server; they will just reload the configuration. We will use pg_ctl reload for modified configuration.

```
[postgres@pg_server ~]$ pg_ctl reload
server signaled
```

Apart from pg_hba.conf, we need to validate a couple more parameters in the main configuration file, *postgresql.conf*, which are directly related to the database remote connectivity.

CHAPTER 4   POSTGRESQL MANAGEMENT OF DATABASE SERVER

- Validate that listen_addresses = '*' is set, which allows connections from any remote host.

- Validate that port = 5432 is set, the default standard port on which PostgreSQL server listens for connections.

In pg_server:

```
[root@pg_server ~]# egrep -i 'listen_addresses|port' /var/lib/pgsql/16/data/postgresql.conf
listen_addresses = '*'           # what IP address(es) to listen on;
port = 5432                      # (change requires restart)
```

Anytime when *postgresql.conf* file is updated, the server needs to be reloaded either by running the "pg_ctl reload" command or by executing "select pg_reload_conf()" from psql for the changes to take effect. In this case, the parameter values are already set, hence no reload required.

Now, let us retry the connection to database as user *appuser1* from client machine, *pg_client1*.

In pg_client1:

```
[postgres@pg_client1 ~]$ psql -d pgdb1 -U appuser1 -p 5432 -h 192.168.2.24
Password for user appuser1:
psql (16.3)

pgdb1=> \conninfo
You are connected to database "pgdb1" as user "appuser1" on host "192.168.2.24" at port "5432".

pgdb1=> select current_database(), current_user;
 current_database | current_user
------------------+--------------
 pgdb1            | appuser1
(1 row)
```

We can see from the output above, the *appuser1* authentication was successful and it prompted for a password as we have used password-based authentication method, scram-sha-256. In the connected session, let us try to run a select command on the table, *pgdb1sch1.db1s1t1* in the *pgdb1* database.

```
pgdb1=> select * from pgdb1sch1.db1s1t1;
ERROR:  permission denied for schema pgdb1sch1
LINE 1: select * from pgdb1sch1.db1s1t1;
                      ^
pgdb1=>
```

Though the user *appuser1* connected to database *pgdb1*, accessing the table reported permission denied error because we haven't provided any schema level and object level privileges on the table to user *appuser1*. Let us grant necessary privileges, now. As discussed earlier, we should provide two privileges; the first one is USAGE grant on schema *pgdb1sch1* and object level privileges on table, *db1s1t1*, or on all tables in the schema, *pgdb1sch1* to user *appuser1*.

In *pgdb1*, grant all privileges on all tables in schema *pgdb1sch1* to user *appuser1*.

In pg_server:

```
[postgres@pg_server ~]$ psql
psql (16.3)

postgres=# \c pgdb1
You are now connected to database "pgdb1" as user "postgres".

pgdb1=# grant usage on schema pgdb1sch1 to appuser1;
GRANT

pgdb1=# grant all on all tables in schema pgdb1sch1 to appuser1;
GRANT

pgdb1=# \dp pgdb1sch1.db1s1t1
                    Access privileges
  Schema    |  Name   | Type  |     Access privileges
------------+---------+-------+---------------------------
 pgdb1sch1  | db1s1t1 | table | postgres=arwdDxt/postgres+
            |         |       | appuser1=arwdDxt/postgres
(1 row)
```

From the above output of privilege details, we can see the table level privileges granted to users under "Access privileges". Below are details of each letter representing privileges.

CHAPTER 4 POSTGRESQL MANAGEMENT OF DATABASE SERVER

a: Allows the user to append/insert data into a table

r: Allows the user to read/select data from a table

w: Allows the user to write/update rows in a table

d: Allows the user to delete rows from a table

D: Allows the user to truncate a table

x: Allows the user to create foreign keys referencing the table

t: Allows the user to create triggers on a table

Since the necessary schema and object level privileges are granted to the user, let us retry the select command.

In pg_client1:

```
[postgres@pg_client1 ~]$ psql -d pgdb1 -U appuser1 -p 5432 -h 192.168.2.24
Password for user appuser1:
psql (16.3)
```

pgdb1=> \conninfo
```
You are connected to database "pgdb1" as user "appuser1" on host
"192.168.2.24" at port "5432".
```

pgdb1=> select * from pgdb1sch1.db1s1t1;
```
  name   | id
---------+----
 d1s1t1a |  1
 d1s1t1b |  2
(2 rows)
```

Hurray! It worked. Let us validate the same from another client machine, pg_client2.

In pg_client2:

```
[postgres@pg_client2 ~]$ which psql
/usr/bin/psql

[postgres@pg_client2 ~]$ psql -d pgdb1 -U appuser1 -p 5432 -h 192.168.2.24
Password for user appuser1:
psql (16.3)
```

CHAPTER 4   POSTGRESQL MANAGEMENT OF DATABASE SERVER

pgdb1=> \conninfo
You are connected to database "pgdb1" as user "appuser1" on host "192.168.2.24" at port "5432".

pgdb1=> select current_database(), current_user;
```
 current_database | current_user
------------------+--------------
 pgdb1            | appuser1
(1 row)
```

pgdb1=> select * from pgdb1sch1.db1s1t1;
```
  name   | id
---------+----
 d1s1t1a |  1
 d1s1t1b |  2
(2 rows)
```

Since password-based authentication is granted and with privileges already existing, the *appuser1* had connected to database *pgdb1* and accessed the table *pgdb1sch1.db1s1t1* from another client machine, *pg_client2*.

Now, let us validate whether *appuser1* can connect to other databases from both client machines.

In pg_client1:

Pgdb2 connectivity:

```
[postgres@pg_client1 ~]$ psql -d pgdb2 -U appuser1 -p 5432 -h 192.168.2.24
Password for user appuser1:
psql (16.3)
Type "help" for help.
```

pgdb2=> \conninfo
You are connected to database "pgdb2" as user "appuser1" on host "192.168.2.24" at port "5432".

pgdb2=> select current_database(), current_user;
```
 current_database | current_user
------------------+--------------
 pgdb2            | appuser1
(1 row)
```

Pgdb3 connectivity:

```
[postgres@pg_client1 ~]$ psql -d pgdb3 -U appuser1 -p 5432 -h 192.168.2.24
Password for user appuser1:
psql (16.3)

pgdb3=> \conninfo
You are connected to database "pgdb3" as user "appuser1" on host
"192.168.2.24" at port "5432".

pgdb3=> select current_database(), current_user;
 current_database | current_user
------------------+--------------
 pgdb3            | appuser1
(1 row)
```

Pgdb4 connectivity:

```
[postgres@pg_client1 ~]$ psql -d pgdb4 -U appuser1 -p 5432 -h 192.168.2.24
Password for user appuser1:
psql (16.3)

pgdb4=> \conninfo
You are connected to database "pgdb4" as user "appuser1" on host
"192.168.2.24" at port "5432".

pgdb4=> select current_database(), current_user;
 current_database | current_user
------------------+--------------
 pgdb4            | appuser1
(1 row)
```

From the above output, we can confirm that *appuser1* can connect to all the other databases, *pgdb2*, *pgdb3*, and *pgdb4*, in the cluster.

Now, what if a new table is created in schema *pgdb1sch1* in database *pgdb1*? Can user *appuser1* still be able to access it with existing privileges?

Let us verify this by creating a new table, *pgdb1sch1.db1s1t2*, in the *pgdb1* database.

CHAPTER 4 POSTGRESQL MANAGEMENT OF DATABASE SERVER

In pg_server:

```
[postgres@pg_server ~]$ psql
psql (16.3)

postgres=# \c pgdb1
You are now connected to database "pgdb1" as user "postgres".

pgdb1=# \dt pgdb1sch1.*
          List of relations
  Schema   |  Name   | Type  |  Owner
-----------+---------+-------+----------
 pgdb1sch1 | db1s1t1 | table | postgres
(1 row)

pgdb1=# create table pgdb1sch1.db1s1t2 (name varchar, id int);
CREATE TABLE

pgdb1=# insert into pgdb1sch1.db1s1t2 values ('db1s1t2a',100),
        ('db1s1t2b',101);
INSERT 0 2

pgdb1=# select * from pgdb1sch1.db1s1t2;
   name   | id
----------+-----
 db1s1t2a | 100
 db1s1t2b | 101
(2 rows)
```

Now, let us try to access the newly created table *pgdb1sch1.db1s1t2* using *appuser1*.

In pg_client1:

```
[postgres@pg_client1 ~]$ psql -d pgdb1 -U appuser1 -p 5432 -h 192.168.2.24
Password for user appuser1:
psql (16.3)

pgdb1=> \conninfo
You are connected to database "pgdb1" as user "appuser1" on host
"192.168.2.24" at port "5432".
```

CHAPTER 4 POSTGRESQL MANAGEMENT OF DATABASE SERVER

```
pgdb1=> select current_database(), current_user;
 current_database | current_user
------------------+--------------
 pgdb1            | appuser1
(1 row)

pgdb1=> \dt pgdb1sch1.*
          List of relations
  Schema   |  Name   | Type  |  Owner
-----------+---------+-------+----------
 pgdb1sch1 | db1s1t1 | table | postgres
 pgdb1sch1 | db1s1t2 | table | postgres
(2 rows)

pgdb1=> select * from pgdb1sch1.db1s1t2;
ERROR:  permission denied for table db1s1t2
pgdb1=>
pgdb1=>
pgdb1=> \dp pgdb1sch1.*
                  Access privileges
  Schema   |  Name   | Type  |     Access privileges
-----------+---------+-------+---------------------------
 pgdb1sch1 | db1s1t1 | table | postgres=arwdDxt/postgres+
           |         |       | appuser1=arwdDxt/postgres
 pgdb1sch1 | db1s1t2 | table |
(2 rows)
```

So the error from the above output confirms that even though the user *appuser1* is granted the necessary privileges at schema level on the schema *pgdb1sch1*, *appuser1* will not have object level privileges on the newly created objects.

Hence, PostgreSQL provided a way to address this issue. postgres provided the below method where we can grant all the privileges on a schema, which include grants on all future objects as well.

We can use the "ALTER DEFAULT PRIVILEGES" command for this.

CHAPTER 4 POSTGRESQL MANAGEMENT OF DATABASE SERVER

In pg_server:

```
pgdb1=# select current_database(), current_user;
 current_database | current_user
------------------+--------------
 pgdb1            | postgres
(1 row)

pgdb1=# alter default privileges in schema pgdb1sch1 grant
select,insert,update,delete on tables to appuser1;
ALTER DEFAULT PRIVILEGES
```

Let us create a new table and see whether *appuser1* can access it.

```
pgdb1=# create table pgdb1sch1.db1s1t3 (name varchar, id int);
CREATE TABLE

pgdb1=# insert into pgdb1sch1.db1s1t3 values ('db1s1t3a',10),
('db1s1t3b',20);
INSERT 0 2

pgdb1=# select * from pgdb1sch1.db1s1t3;
   name   | id
----------+----
 db1s1t3a | 10
 db1s1t3b | 20
(2 rows)
```

Test the table access by appuser1.

In pg_client1:

```
[postgres@pg_client1 ~]$ psql -d pgdb1 -U appuser1 -p 5432 -h 192.168.2.24
Password for user appuser1:
psql (16.3)

pgdb1=> \conninfo
You are connected to database "pgdb1" as user "appuser1" on host
"192.168.2.24" at port "5432".
```

CHAPTER 4   POSTGRESQL MANAGEMENT OF DATABASE SERVER

```
pgdb1=> select current_database(), current_user;
 current_database | current_user
------------------+--------------
 pgdb1            | appuser1
(1 row)

pgdb1=> \dt pgdb1sch1.*
          List of relations
  Schema   |  Name   | Type  |  Owner
-----------+---------+-------+----------
 pgdb1sch1 | db1s1t1 | table | postgres
 pgdb1sch1 | db1s1t2 | table | postgres
 pgdb1sch1 | db1s1t3 | table | postgres
(3 rows)

pgdb1=> select * from pgdb1sch1.db1s1t3;
   name   | id
----------+----
 db1s1t3a | 10
 db1s1t3b | 20
(2 rows)
```

Ok, that works, good.

But what happened to earlier table *pgdb1sch1.db1s1t2*? Does the "ALTER DEFAULT PRIVILEGE" grant take care of the table that was created before providing the default privilege? Let's see.

In pg_client1:

```
pgdb1=> select * from pgdb1sch1.db1s1t2;
ERROR:  permission denied for table db1s1t2
pgdb1=>

pgdb1=> \dp pgdb1sch1.*
                 Access privileges
  Schema   |  Name   | Type  |    Access privileges
-----------+---------+-------+---------------------------
 pgdb1sch1 | db1s1t1 | table | postgres=arwdDxt/postgres+
           |         |       | appuser1=arwdDxt/postgres
```

183

```
 pgdb1sch1 | db1s1t2 | table |
 pgdb1sch1 | db1s1t3 | table | postgres=arwdDxt/postgres+
           |         |       | appuser1=arwd/postgres
(3 rows)
```

From the output above, we can see that *appuser1* still cannot access the table since the user does not have any access privileges on table *pgdb1sch1.db1s1t2*. This means that the *ALTER DEFAULT PRIVILEGE* grant will take care of only the future objects that are created after providing this grant. For the existing objects, i.e., objects created after initial privileges granted and before the default privilege granted, we still need to provide exclusive privileges on those tables to the users.

Scenario 2: User *appuser2* accesses only database *pgdb2* and its corresponding schema and table from both client machines.

To make the *appuser2* connect to a specific database, i.e., *pgdb2*, let us perform the prerequisite tasks on a database server, i.e., add the necessary entries in pg_hba.conf and grant appropriate privileges.

Update the *pg_hba.conf* with the authentication entries and reload the postgres server.

In pg_server:

[postgres@pg_server ~]$ vi /var/lib/pgsql/16/data/pg_hba.conf

[postgres@pg_server ~]$ cat /var/lib/pgsql/16/data/pg_hba.conf

```
# TYPE   DATABASE   USER        ADDRESS            METHOD

# IPv4 local connections:
host     pgdb2      appuser2    192.168.2.30/32    scram-sha-256    << Add this line
host     pgdb2      appuser2    192.168.2.40/32    scram-sha-256    << Add this line

[postgres@pg_server ~]$
```
[postgres@pg_server ~]$ pg_ctl reload
```
server signaled
[postgres@pg_server ~]$
```

Grant the privileges on the schema *pgdb2sch2* in database *pgdb2* to *appuser2*.

[postgres@pg_server ~]$ psql
```
psql (16.3)
```

CHAPTER 4   POSTGRESQL MANAGEMENT OF DATABASE SERVER

postgres=# \c pgdb2
You are now connected to database "pgdb2" as user "postgres".

pgdb2=# grant usage on schema pgdb2sch2 to appuser2;
GRANT

pgdb2=# grant all on all tables in schema pgdb2sch2 to appuser2;
GRANT

Now, test the database connectivity and table access for user appuser2 from both the client machines.

In pg_client1:

[postgres@pg_client1 ~]$ psql -d pgdb2 -U appuser2 -p 5432 -h 192.168.2.24
Password for user appuser2:
psql (16.3)

pgdb2=> \conninfo
You are connected to database "pgdb2" as user "appuser2" on host "192.168.2.24" at port "5432".

pgdb2=> select current_database(), current_user;
```
 current_database | current_user
------------------+--------------
 pgdb2            | appuser2
(1 row)
```

pgdb2=> select * from pgdb2sch2.db2s2t2;
```
  name   | id
---------+----
 d2s2t2a |  3
 d2s2t2b |  4
(2 rows)
```

pgdb2=>

In pg_client2:

[postgres@pg_client2 ~]$ psql -d pgdb2 -U appuser2 -p 5432 -h 192.168.2.24
Password for user appuser2:
psql (16.3)

pgdb2=> \conninfo
You are connected to database "pgdb2" as user "appuser2" on host "192.168.2.24" at port "5432".

pgdb2=> select current_database(), current_user;
```
 current_database | current_user
------------------+--------------
 pgdb2            | appuser2
(1 row)
```

pgdb2=> select * from pgdb2sch2.db2s2t2;
```
  name   | id
---------+----
 d2s2t2a |  3
 d2s2t2b |  4
(2 rows)
```

From both the outputs above, we can see the user *appuser2* was successfully able to log in to database *pgdb2* and access schema table.

But the client authentication for *appuser2* was only allowed for database *pgdb2*, so any attempts to connect a different database would lead to connectivity errors. Let us test the same from *pg_client1* and *pg_client2* machines.

In pg_client1:

```
[postgres@pg_client1 ~]$ psql -d pgdb1 -U appuser2 -p 5432 -h 192.168.2.24
psql: error: connection to server at "192.168.2.24", port 5432 failed:
FATAL:  no pg_hba.conf entry for host "192.168.2.30", user "appuser2",
database "pgdb1", no encryption

[postgres@pg_client1 ~]$ psql -d pgdb3 -U appuser2 -p 5432 -h 192.168.2.24
psql: error: connection to server at "192.168.2.24", port 5432 failed:
FATAL:  no pg_hba.conf entry for host "192.168.2.30", user "appuser2",
database "pgdb3", no encryption

[postgres@pg_client1 ~]$ psql -d pgdb4 -U appuser2 -p 5432 -h 192.168.2.24
psql: error: connection to server at "192.168.2.24", port 5432 failed:
FATAL:  no pg_hba.conf entry for host "192.168.2.30", user "appuser2",
database "pgdb4", no encryption
```

CHAPTER 4   POSTGRESQL MANAGEMENT OF DATABASE SERVER

In pg_client2:

```
[postgres@pg_client2 ~]$ psql -d pgdb1 -U appuser2 -p 5432 -h 192.168.2.24
psql: error: connection to server at "192.168.2.24", port 5432 failed:
FATAL:  no pg_hba.conf entry for host "192.168.2.40", user "appuser2",
database "pgdb1", no encryption

[postgres@pg_client2 ~]$ psql -d pgdb3 -U appuser2 -p 5432 -h 192.168.2.24
psql: error: connection to server at "192.168.2.24", port 5432 failed:
FATAL:  no pg_hba.conf entry for host "192.168.2.40", user "appuser2",
database "pgdb3", no encryption

[postgres@pg_client2 ~]$ psql -d pgdb4 -U appuser2 -p 5432 -h 192.168.2.24
psql: error: connection to server at "192.168.2.24", port 5432 failed:
FATAL:  no pg_hba.conf entry for host "192.168.2.40", user "appuser2",
database "pgdb4", no encryption
[postgres@pg_client2 ~]$
```

Looking at the reported errors, we can confirm that the user can only log in to database *pgdb2* and from both the client machines, which is authenticated on the server.

Scenario 3: User *appuser3* accesses only database *pgdb4* and its corresponding schema and table from only client machine *pg_client2*.

To make *appuser3* connect to the database *pgdb4* and access the objects, let us perform the prerequisite tasks on a database server, i.e., add the necessary entries in pg_hba.conf and grant appropriate privileges.

Update the *pg_hba.conf* with the authentication entries and reload the postgres server.

In pg_server:

```
[postgres@pg_server ~]$ vi /var/lib/pgsql/16/data/pg_hba.conf

[postgres@pg_server ~]$ cat /var/lib/pgsql/16/data/pg_hba.conf
# TYPE   DATABASE    USER       ADDRESS           METHOD

# IPv4 local connections:
host     pgdb4       appuser3   192.168.2.40/32   scram-sha-256   << Add
this line
```

CHAPTER 4   POSTGRESQL MANAGEMENT OF DATABASE SERVER

```
[postgres@pg_server ~]$
[postgres@pg_server ~]$ pg_ctl reload
server signaled
[postgres@pg_server ~]$
```

Grant the privileges on the schema *pgdb4sch4 in database pgdb4* to *appuser3*.

In pg_server:

```
[postgres@pg_server ~]$ psql
psql (16.3)

postgres=# \c pgdb4
You are now connected to database "pgdb4" as user "postgres".

pgdb4=# grant usage on schema pgdb4sch4 to appuser3;
GRANT

pgdb4=# grant all on all tables in schema pgdb4sch4 to appuser3;
GRANT
```

Now, verify the connectivity and table access for user *appuser3* from client machine *pg_client2*.

In pg_client2:

```
[postgres@pg_client2 ~]$ psql -d pgdb4 -U appuser3 -p 5432 -h 192.168.2.24
Password for user appuser3:
psql (16.3)

pgdb4=> \conninfo
You are connected to database "pgdb4" as user "appuser3" on host
"192.168.2.24" at port "5432".

pgdb4=> select current_database(), current_user;
 current_database | current_user
------------------+--------------
 pgdb4            | appuser3
(1 row)

pgdb4=> select * from pgdb4sch4.db4s4t4;
```

```
  name   | id
---------+----
 d4s4t4a |  7
 d4s4t4b |  8
(2 rows)
```

Now, verify the connectivity and table access for user *appuser3* from client machine *pg_client1*.

In pg_client1:

```
[postgres@pg_client1 ~]$ psql -d pgdb4 -U appuser3 -p 5432 -h 192.168.2.24
psql: error: connection to server at "192.168.2.24", port 5432 failed:
FATAL:  no pg_hba.conf entry for host "192.168.2.30", user "appuser3",
database "pgdb4", no encryption
```

Even though the user *appuser3* has access granted for database *pgdb4*, they cannot connect to the database from *pg_client1* since the user is not authenticated to connect from the *pg_client1* server.

Authentication Method – Trust and Reject

In the previous scenarios, we have seen how a user is authenticated using password-based authentication method, "scram-sha-256".

When password-based authentication is used, the user must provide password while connecting to a database.

Let us now see a couple more authentication methods available.

Update the pg_hba.conf file to include a couple of lines with authentication methods as "trust" and "reject" and reload the service.

In pg_server:

```
[postgres@pg_server ~]$ vi /var/lib/pgsql/16/data/pg_hba.conf

[postgres@pg_server ~]$ cat /var/lib/pgsql/16/data/pg_hba.conf
# TYPE  DATABASE   USER       ADDRESS            METHOD
# IPv4 local connections:
host    pgdb4      appuser3   192.168.2.40/32    scram-sha-256
host    pgdb4      appuser3   192.168.2.30/32    trust           << Add this line
host    pgdb3      appuser3   192.168.2.40/32    reject          << Add this line
```

```
[postgres@pg_server ~]$
[postgres@pg_server ~]$ pg_ctl reload
server signaled
[postgres@pg_server ~]$
```

Please note the authentication types that we used, trust and reject.

When trust authentication is specified, PostgreSQL assumes that anyone who can connect to the server is authorized to connect to the database without any additional authentication.

So *appuser3* can connect to database *pgdb4* from client machine *pg_client1* without providing any password.

In pg_client1:

```
[postgres@pg_client1 ~]$ psql -d pgdb4 -U appuser3 -p 5432 -h 192.168.2.24
psql (16.3)

pgdb4=> \conninfo
You are connected to database "pgdb4" as user "appuser3" on host "192.168.2.24" at port "5432".

pgdb4=> select current_database(), current_user;
 current_database | current_user
------------------+--------------
 pgdb4            | appuser3
(1 row)
```

Let us perform the database connectivity from client machine pg_client2.

In pg_client2:

```
[postgres@pg_client2 ~]$ psql -d pgdb3 -U appuser3 -p 5432 -h 192.168.2.24
psql: error: connection to server at "192.168.2.24", port 5432 failed:
FATAL:  pg_hba.conf rejects connection for host "192.168.2.40", user
"appuser3", database "pgdb3", no encryption
```

From the above output, it is evident that the *appuser3* user connection request to the database server is rejected. This is because in the pg_hba.conf on the server, the authentication method value used is "*reject*". The *reject* method tells that if there is any connection request from specific users, hosts, or for a specific database, the client should be denied access to the database server and database.

To understand how the authentication policy is implemented in a PostgreSQL cluster, we can list the current list of authenticated users by using the below SQL.

Below is the sample output of the above command. Basically, this command will pull all the entries from the host-based configuration file, pg_hba.conf.

[postgres@pg_server ~]$ psql
psql (16.3)

postgres=# select * from pg_hba_file_rules;

file_name	line_ number	type	database	user_name	address	auth_method
pg_hba.conf	113	local	{pgdbhrm}	{grpaccnew}		md5
pg_hba.conf	117	host	{all}	{appuser1}	192.168.2.30	scram-sha-256
pg_hba.conf	118	host	{all}	{appuser1}	192.168.2.40	scram-sha-256
pg_hba.conf	119	host	{pgdb2}	{appuser2}	192.168.2.30	scram-sha-256
pg_hba.conf	120	host	{pgdb2}	{appuser2}	192.168.2.40	scram-sha-256
pg_hba.conf	121	host	{pgdb4}	{appuser3}	192.168.2.40	scram-sha-256
pg_hba.conf	122	host	{pgdb4}	{appuser3}	192.168.2.30	trust
pg_hba.conf	123	host	{pgdb3}	{appuser3}	192.168.2.40	reject

So this explains how the authentication process works in the PostgreSQL server. The client host details along with the username and the authentication method must be added to the host-based configuration file *pg_hba.conf* on the database server. If an entry is missing in this file, postmaster process will deny any request for the database connection. Depending upon the client info in the *pg_hba.conf* file, the user will be authenticated and will be granted access to a database. Once the user is connected to the database, the user account still needs additional privileges at schema level and at object level so that it will be able to access the data of a particular schema.

Apart from the password-based authentication methods, postgres also supports various other authentication methods. Kindly refer to Chapter 3, "PostgreSQL Directory Structure" section.

Predefined Roles in PostgreSQL

PostgreSQL provides a few predefined roles that we can assign to the users. Roles are global objects that work for all databases in a cluster. Below are a few of the predefined roles.

- **pg_read_all_data**: This role provides the read access to all the tables in a database. It is like providing SELECT access on all the tables and USAGE privilege on all the schemas within a database.

- **pg_write_all_data**: This role provides the write access to all the tables in a database. It is like providing INSERT, UPDATE, and DELETE privileges on all the tables and USAGE right on all the schemas within a database.

- **pg_read_all_stats**: Provides read access on all the pg_stat* views.

- **pg_read_all_settings**: This role provides read access on the configuration variables.

- **pg_monitor**: Provides read access and executes monitoring functions and views.

- **pg_read_server_files**: Provides read access for the files from any location that the database can access on the server.

- **pg_write_server_files**: Provides write access for the files from any location that the database can access on the server.

- **pg_database_owner**: This role cannot be assigned to other users; it is only assigned by default to the database owner.

Let us prepare the environment and verify the function of a couple of these roles. In database *pgdb4*, create a new schema and a table with rows inserted.

In pg_server:

```
[postgres@pg_server ~]$ psql
psql (16.3)
```

postgres=# \c pgdb4
```
You are now connected to database "pgdb4" as user "postgres".
```

```
pgdb4=# \dn
       List of schemas
   Name    |       Owner
-----------+--------------------
 pgdb4sch4 | postgres
 public    | pg_database_owner
(2 rows)

pgdb4=# create schema pgdb4sch5;
CREATE SCHEMA

pgdb4=# \dn
       List of schemas
   Name    |       Owner
-----------+--------------------
 pgdb4sch4 | postgres
 pgdb4sch5 | postgres
 public    | pg_database_owner
(3 rows)

pgdb4=# create table pgdb4sch5.db4s5t5 (name varchar, id int);
CREATE TABLE

pgdb4=# insert into pgdb4sch5.db4s5t5 values ('d4s5t5a',9), ('d4s5t5b',10);
INSERT 0 2

pgdb4=# select * from pgdb4sch5.db4s5t5;
   name   | id
----------+----
 d4s5t5a  |  9
 d4s5t5b  | 10
(2 rows)
```

```
pgdb4=# \dt pgdb4*.*
           List of relations
  Schema    |   Name   | Type  |  Owner
------------+----------+-------+----------
 pgdb4sch4  | db4s4t4  | table | postgres
 pgdb4sch5  | db4s5t5  | table | postgres
(2 rows)
```

Create a new user, *appuser4*, in the cluster and grant role *pg_read_all_data*.

In pg_server:

```
postgres=# create user appuser4 with password 'pgappuser4';
CREATE ROLE

postgres=# \c pgdb4
You are now connected to database "pgdb4" as user "postgres".

pgdb4=# grant pg_read_all_data to appuser4;
GRANT ROLE

pgdb4=# SELECT r2.rolname grantee,r1.rolname AS granted_role
        FROM pg_roles r1
        JOIN pg_auth_members m ON r1.oid = m.roleid
        JOIN pg_roles r2 ON m.member = r2.oid
        WHERE r2.rolname = 'appuser4';
 grantee  |   granted_role
----------+-------------------
 appuser4 | pg_read_all_data
(1 row)
```

Update the pg_hba.conf file to include the authentication details for user *appuser4*.

In pg_server:

```
[postgres@pg_server ~]$ vi /var/lib/pgsql/16/data/pg_hba.conf

[postgres@pg_server ~]$ cat /var/lib/pgsql/16/data/pg_hba.conf
# TYPE   DATABASE    USER        ADDRESS            METHOD
# IPv4 local connections:
host     pgdb4       appuser4    192.168.2.30/32    trust    << Add this line
```

```
[postgres@pg_server ~]$ pg_ctl reload
server signaled
[postgres@pg_server ~]$
```

Now, let us see what *appuser4* can do with the help of the role granted.

In pg_client1:

```
[postgres@pg_client1 ~]$ psql -d pgdb4 -U appuser4 -p 5432 -h 192.168.2.24
psql (16.3)

pgdb4=> \conninfo
You are connected to database "pgdb4" as user "appuser4" on host
"192.168.2.24" at port "5432".

pgdb4=> select current_database(), current_user;
 current_database | current_user
------------------+--------------
 pgdb4            | appuser4
(1 row)

pgdb4=> select * from pgdb4sch4.db4s4t4;
  name   | id
---------+----
 d4s4t4a |  7
 d4s4t4b |  8
(2 rows)

pgdb4=> select * from pgdb4sch5.db4s5t5;
  name   | id
---------+----
 d4s5t5a |  9
 d4s5t5b | 10
(2 rows)

pgdb4=> insert into pgdb4sch5.db4s5t5 values ('d4s5t5c',11);
ERROR:  permission denied for table db4s5t5
```

CHAPTER 4   POSTGRESQL MANAGEMENT OF DATABASE SERVER

From the above output, we can see that *appuser4* can access the tables (read data) from multiple schemas within database *pgdb4*. The granted role pg_read_all_data made this possible, which is an alternate to granting select privilege on individual objects of multiple schemas within a database.

Also, we can observe there is an error reported when the *appuser4* user tried to perform a DML (insert) operation on one of the tables which it had access to. This is because the *appuser4* is not granted any write privileges as the *pg_read_all_data* role allows only the select operation on the schema tables.

Let us grant role *pg_write_all_data* to the *appuser4* user.

In pg_server:

```
[postgres@pg_server ~]$ psql
psql (16.3)

postgres=# \c pgdb4
You are now connected to database "pgdb4" as user "postgres".

pgdb4=# grant pg_write_all_data to appuser4;
GRANT ROLE

pgdb4=# SELECT r2.rolname grantee,r1.rolname AS granted_role
        FROM pg_roles r1
        JOIN pg_auth_members m ON r1.oid = m.roleid
        JOIN pg_roles r2 ON m.member = r2.oid
        WHERE r2.rolname = 'appuser4';
 grantee  |   granted_role
----------+--------------------
 appuser4 | pg_read_all_data
 appuser4 | pg_write_all_data
(2 rows)
```

Now, retry the DML operation that reported an error earlier.

In pg_client1:

```
[postgres@pg_client1 ~]$ psql -d pgdb4 -U appuser4 -p 5432 -h 192.168.2.24
psql (16.3)
```

```
pgdb4=> select current_database(), current_user;
 current_database | current_user
------------------+--------------
 pgdb4            | appuser4
(1 row)

pgdb4=> insert into pgdb4sch5.db4s5t5 values ('d4s5t5c',11);
INSERT 0 1

pgdb4=> select * from pgdb4sch5.db4s5t5;
   name   | id
----------+----
 d4s5t5a  |  9
 d4s5t5b  | 10
 d4s5t5c  | 11
(3 rows)
```

From the above output, we can observe the user *appuser4* is now able to perform DML operations on the schema objects, only after the grant of the pg_write_all_data role, which is an alternate option to providing insert/update/delete object level privileges.

Extensions in PostgreSQL

Extensions in PostgreSQL are pre-built modules that add additional functionality to the database system and provide an enhancement to the PostgreSQL's core capabilities.

In pg_server:

To check the available extensions in PostgreSQL:

```
postgres=# select * from pg_available_extensions order by name;
       name         |default_|installed_|            comment
                    |version | version  |
--------------------+--------+----------+---------------------------------
 adminpack          |  2.1   |          | administrative functions for
                    |        |          |   PostgreSQL
 amcheck            |  1.3   |          | functions for verifying relation
                    |        |          |   integrity
```

```
file_fdw              | 1.0  |       | foreign-data wrapper for flat
                                       file access
insert_username       | 1.0  |       | functions for tracking who
                                       changed a table
lo                    | 1.1  |       | Large Object maintenance
pg_buffercache        | 1.4  |       | examine the shared buffer cache
pg_freespacemap       | 1.2  |       | examine the free space map (FSM)
pg_prewarm            | 1.2  |       | prewarm relation data
pg_stat_statements    | 1.10 |       | track planning and execution
                                       statistics of all SQL statements
                                       executed
```

<<< OUTPUT_TRUNCATED>>>

```
pgrowlocks            | 1.2  |       | show row-level locking information
pgstattuple           | 1.5  |       | show tuple-level statistics
plpgsql               | 1.0  | 1.0   | PL/pgSQL procedural language
sslinfo               | 1.2  |       | information about SSL certificates
```

To check the installed extensions in PostgreSQL:

```
postgres=# select * from pg_extension;
  oid  | extname | extowner | extversion
-------+---------+----------+-------------
 14482 | plpgsql |       10 | 1.0
(1 row)
```

Let us see the function of a couple of extensions.

pgstattuple: This module in PostgreSQL is an extension that helps to analyze the space utilization, identify fragmentation, etc., in tables or indexes with the help of statistics on the physical storage of a table or index.

Let's create a table with the name *db1s1tnew* and insert data into this table using generate_series in database *pgdb1*.

CHAPTER 4   POSTGRESQL MANAGEMENT OF DATABASE SERVER

We will also create an index on the newly created table as shown below:

In pg_server:

[postgres@pg_server ~]$ psql
psql (16.3)

postgres=# \c pgdb1
You are now connected to database "pgdb1" as user "postgres".

pgdb1=# select * from pg_extension;
```
  oid  | extname | extowner | extversion
-------+---------+----------+------------
 14482 | plpgsql |       10 | 1.0
(1 row)
```

pgdb1=# create table pgdb1sch1.db1s1tnew (id int);
CREATE TABLE

pgdb1=# \dt pgdb1sch1.db1s1tnew
```
           List of relations
  Schema   |   Name    | Type  |  Owner
-----------+-----------+-------+----------
 pgdb1sch1 | db1s1tnew | table | postgres
(1 row)
```

pgdb1=# insert into pgdb1sch1.db1s1tnew values (generate_series(1,1000000));
INSERT 0 1000000

pgdb1=# select count(*) from pgdb1sch1.db1s1tnew;
```
  count
---------
 1000000
(1 row)
```

pgdb1=# create index s1tnewidx on pgdb1sch1.db1s1tnew (id);
CREATE INDEX

CHAPTER 4   POSTGRESQL MANAGEMENT OF DATABASE SERVER

```
pgdb1=# \di pgdb1sch1.*
                List of relations
  Schema    |    Name    | Type  |  Owner   |   Table
------------+------------+-------+----------+-----------
 pgdb1sch1  | s1tnewidx  | index | postgres | db1s1tnew
(1 row)

pgdb1=# insert into pgdb1sch1.db1s1tnew values (generate_
series(1,1000000));
INSERT 0 1000000

pgdb1=# select count(*) from pgdb1sch1.db1s1tnew;
  count
---------
 2000000
(1 row)

pgdb1=# update pgdb1sch1.db1s1tnew set id=9999 where id < 500000;
UPDATE 999998
pgdb1=#
```

Now, run the below SQL, to understand the statistics of an index.

```
pgdb1=# select * from pgstatindex('pgdb1sch1.s1tnewidx');
ERROR:  function pgstatindex(unknown) does not exist
LINE 1: select * from pgstatindex('pgdb1sch1.s1tnewidx');
                      ^
HINT:  No function matches the given name and argument types. You might
need to add explicit type casts.
pgdb1=#
```

From the above output, we can see an error reported when trying to access *pgstatindex* as it does not exist in the database.

Let's create the extension *pgstattuple* as shown below:

```
pgdb1=# create extension pgstattuple;
CREATE EXTENSION

pgdb1=# \dx
                List of installed extensions
```

```
    Name     | Version |  Schema    |         Description
-------------+---------+------------+------------------------------
 pgstattuple | 1.5     | public     | show tuple-level statistics
 plpgsql     | 1.0     | pg_catalog | PL/pgSQL procedural language
(2 rows)

pgdb1=# select * from pg_extension;
   oid   |  extname    | extowner | extnamespace | extversion
---------+-------------+----------+--------------+------------
  14482  | plpgsql     |    10    |      11      | 1.0
 131266  | pgstattuple |    10    |     2200     | 1.5
(2 rows)

pgdb1=# \df public.*
                   List of functions
 Schema |           Name            | Result data type | Type
--------+---------------------------+------------------+------
 public | pgstatginindex            | record           | func
 public | pgstathashindex           | record           | func
 public | pgstatindex               | record           | func
 public | pgstatindex               | record           | func
 public | pgstattuple               | record           | func
 public | pgstattuple               | record           | func
 public | pgstattuple_approx        | record           | func
 .
 <<<<< OUTPUT TRUNCATED>>>>>
 .
```

When the *pgstattuple* extension is created, it registers the extension in the current database by creating functions and objects in the public schema of the database. Also, the extension is specific to the database where it is installed, and all the functions provided by the *pgstattuple* module will be available for use by that database.

Now if we run the select on the *pgstatindex*, it will provide an output of the index statistics details. *pgstatindex* is a PostgreSQL extension that is part of the *pgstattuple* module that provides a method to analyze the index usage by collecting statistics.

CHAPTER 4 POSTGRESQL MANAGEMENT OF DATABASE SERVER

pgdb1=# \x
Expanded display is on.

pgdb1=# select * from pgstatindex('pgdb1sch1.s1tnewidx');
```
-[ RECORD 1 ]------+----------
version            | 4
tree_level         | 2
index_size         | 118497280
root_block_no      | 290
internal_pages     | 26
leaf_pages         | 5245
empty_pages        | 0
deleted_pages      | 9193
avg_leaf_density   | 58.97
leaf_fragmentation | 26.1
```

Perform the reindex operation on the index, *pgdb1sch1.s1tnewidx*, and check for the updated index stats.

pgdb1=# reindex index pgdb1sch1.s1tnewidx;
REINDEX

pgdb1=# select * from pgstatindex('pgdb1sch1.s1tnewidx');
```
-[ RECORD 1 ]------+----------
version            | 4
tree_level         | 2
index_size         | 27197440
root_block_no      | 209
internal_pages     | 14
leaf_pages         | 3305
empty_pages        | 0
deleted_pages      | 0
avg_leaf_density   | 89.96
leaf_fragmentation | 0
```

pg_stat_statements: The pg_stat_statements extension adds the capability to track the execution statistics of queries that are run in a database, including the number of calls, total execution time, the total number of returned rows, and internal information on memory and I/O access.

You can start by retrieving a list of the top ten most frequent queries:

In pg_server:

[postgres@pg_server ~]$ psql
psql (16.3)

postgres=# \c pgdb1
You are now connected to database "pgdb1" as user "postgres".

pgdb1=# select query from pg_stat_statements order by calls desc limit 10;
ERROR: relation "pg_stat_statements" does not exist
LINE 1: select query from pg_stat_statements order by calls desc lim...
                          ^

pgdb1=#

From the above output, we can see an error reported when trying to access pg_stat_statements, which does not exist.

Let's create the extension for this view.

pgdb1=# create extension pg_stat_statements;
CREATE EXTENSION

pgdb1=# \dx
```
                  List of installed extensions
        Name        | Version |   Schema   |           Description
--------------------+---------+------------+----------------------------------
 pg_stat_statements | 1.10    | public     | track planning and execution
                    |         |            | statistics of all SQL statements
                    |         |            | executed
 pgstattuple        | 1.5     | public     | show tuple-level statistics
 plpgsql            | 1.0     | pg_catalog | PL/pgSQL procedural language
(3 rows)
```

CHAPTER 4 POSTGRESQL MANAGEMENT OF DATABASE SERVER

```
pgdb1=# select * from pg_extension;
   oid  |      extname       | extowner | extnamespace | extversion
--------+--------------------+----------+--------------+------------
  14482 | plpgsql            |       10 |           11 | 1.0
 131266 | pgstattuple        |       10 |         2200 | 1.5
 131277 | pg_stat_statements |       10 |         2200 | 1.10
(3 rows)

pgdb1=# \dv public.*
                List of relations
 Schema |          Name           | Type |  Owner
--------+-------------------------+------+----------
 public | pg_stat_statements      | view | postgres
 public | pg_stat_statements_info | view | postgres
(2 rows)
```

When the *pg_stat_statements* extension is created, it registers the extension in the current database by creating functions and objects in the *public* schema of the database. Also, the extension is specific to the database where it is installed, and all the objects provided by the *pg_stat_statements* module will be available for use by that database.

Now a retry to access pg_stat_statements should be successful and provides an output.

```
pgdb1=# select query from pg_stat_statements order by calls desc limit 10;
                                 query
-------------------------------------------------------------------------------
 select * from information_schema.role_table_grants where grantee=$1
 SELECT r.rolname, r.rolsuper, r.rolinherit,                                  +
   r.rolcreaterole, r.rolcreatedb, r.rolcanlogin,                             +
   r.rolconnlimit, r.rolvaliduntil                                            +
 , r.rolreplication                                                           +
 , r.rolbypassrls                                                             +
 FROM pg_catalog.pg_roles r                                                   +
 WHERE r.rolname OPERATOR(pg_catalog.~) $1 COLLATE pg_catalog.default         +
 ORDER BY 1
 SELECT r.rolname, r.rolsuper, r.rolinherit,                                  +
   r.rolcreaterole, r.rolcreatedb, r.rolcanlogin,                             +
```

     r.rolconnlimit, r.rolvaliduntil   +
    , r.rolreplication   +
    , r.rolbypassrls   +
    FROM pg_catalog.pg_roles r   +
    WHERE r.rolname !~ $1   +
    ORDER BY 1
    .
    <<<<< OUTPUT TRUNCATED >>>>>
    .

This way we can work with several different extensions by installing and accessing the corresponding objects based on the need in the database.

Dropping Users in PostgreSQL

We can use the command below to drop a user in postgres from psql terminal.

Syntax:

DROP USER [IF EXISTS] name [, ...]

We have a user with name *appuser4*; we will use the above syntax to drop this user.

In pg_server:

[postgres@pg_server ~]$ psql
psql (16.3)

postgres=# \du
```
                         List of roles
 Role name |                        Attributes
-----------+------------------------------------------------------------
 appuser1  |
 appuser2  |
 appuser3  |
 appuser4  |
 grpaccnew | Create role, Create DB, Replication                        +
           | 1 connection                                               +
           | Password valid until 2024-12-31 00:00:00-06
 pguseradm |
 postgres  | Superuser, Create role, Create DB, Replication, Bypass RLS
```

postgres=# drop user appuser4;
DROP ROLE

postgres=# \du
                     List of roles
 Role name | Attributes
-----------+--
 appuser1 |
 appuser2 |
 appuser3 |
 grpaccnew | Create role, Create DB, Replication   +
           | 1 connection   +
           | Password valid until 2024-12-31 00:00:00-06
 pguseradm |
 postgres | Superuser, Create role, Create DB, Replication, Bypass RLS

Limitation: We cannot drop a user that has dependency, like database owner.

postgres=# drop user pguseradm;
ERROR: role "pguseradm" cannot be dropped because some objects depend on it
DETAIL: owner of database pgdbhrm
postgres=#

In postgres, role and user are interchangeable. Hence, when create or drop statement on a user or role is performed; the output will be create role and drop role.

Dropping a Schema in PostgreSQL

We can use the syntax below to drop a schema in PostgreSQL.
   Syntax:
   DROP SCHEMA [IF EXISTS] name [, ...] [CASCADE | RESTRICT]
   If the schema does not have any objects, we can just use "DROP SCHEMA name"; if the schema has objects, we need to drop all the dependent objects in the schema followed by dropping an empty schema or we can use CASCADE option, which will drop the schema along with the schema-owned objects. If we use RESTRICT, the command

refuses to drop the schema if it contains any objects. This is the default option the postgres uses internally whenever a drop schema command is issued.

We will now try to use these options to drop a schema that has objects. In this scenario, we will try drop schema with name *pgdb4sch5*, which owns one table in database *pgdb4*.

In pg_server:

[postgres@pg_server ~]$ psql
```
psql (16.3)
```

postgres=# \c pgdb4
```
You are now connected to database "pgdb4" as user "postgres".
```

pgdb4=# \dn
```
       List of schemas
    Name    |       Owner
------------+-------------------
 pgdb4sch4  | postgres
 pgdb4sch5  | postgres
 public     | pg_database_owner
(3 rows)
```

pgdb4=# \dt pgdb4*.*
```
          List of relations
  Schema   |  Name   | Type  |  Owner
-----------+---------+-------+----------
 pgdb4sch4 | db4s4t4 | table | postgres
 pgdb4sch5 | db4s5t5 | table | postgres
(2 rows)
```

We will try to use the "DROP SCHEMA" command without any options on first try.

pgdb4=# drop schema pgdb4sch5;
```
ERROR:  cannot drop schema pgdb4sch5 because other objects depend on it
DETAIL:  table pgdb4sch5.db4s5t5 depends on schema pgdb4sch5
HINT:  Use DROP ... CASCADE to drop the dependent objects too.
pgdb4=#
```

From the above output, we can observe that the drop schema reported an error due to dependent objects that exist in the schema. So drop all the dependent objects before reattempting the drop schema.

```
pgdb4=# drop table pgdb4sch5.db4s5t5;
DROP TABLE

pgdb4=# \dt pgdb4sch5.*
Did not find any relation named "pgdb4sch5.*".

pgdb4=# drop schema pgdb4sch5;
DROP SCHEMA

pgdb4=# \dn
        List of schemas
    Name    |      Owner
------------+-------------------
 pgdb4sch4  | postgres
 public     | pg_database_owner
(2 rows)
```

Let us try to drop a schema that has a dependent object using the CASCADE option.

```
pgdb4=# \dn
        List of schemas
    Name    |      Owner
------------+-------------------
 pgdb4sch4  | postgres
 public     | pg_database_owner
(2 rows)

pgdb4=# \dt pgdb4sch4.*
            List of relations
   Schema   |   Name   | Type  |  Owner
------------+----------+-------+----------
 pgdb4sch4  | db4s4t4  | table | postgres
(1 row)

pgdb4=# drop schema pgdb4sch4 cascade;
```

```
NOTICE:  drop cascades to table pgdb4sch4.db4s4t4
DROP SCHEMA
```

pgdb4=# \dn
```
      List of schemas
  Name  |       Owner
--------+-------------------
 public | pg_database_owner
(1 row)
```

So whenever a schema owns any object, we should use *CASCADE* option to drop the schema.

Dropping Database Using OS Command

As there are no more dependent objects and user-defined schemas in database *pgdb4*, let us drop the database using the dropdb os command.

In pg_server:

[postgres@pg_server ~]$ psql
```
psql (16.3)
```

postgres=# \l
```
                    List of databases
   Name    |  Owner   | Encoding |  Access privileges
-----------+----------+----------+-----------------------
 pgdb1     | postgres | UTF8     |
 pgdb2     | postgres | UTF8     |
 pgdb3     | postgres | UTF8     |
 pgdb4     | postgres | UTF8     |
 pgdbnew1  | postgres | UTF8     |
 postgres  | postgres | UTF8     |
 template0 | postgres | UTF8     | =c/postgres          +
           |          |          | postgres=CTc/postgres
 template1 | postgres | UTF8     | =c/postgres          +
           |          |          | postgres=CTc/postgres
(8 rows)
```

CHAPTER 4   POSTGRESQL MANAGEMENT OF DATABASE SERVER

postgres=# \c pgdb4
You are now connected to database "pgdb4" as user "postgres".

```
pgdb4=# \dn
      List of schemas
  Name   |       Owner
---------+-------------------
 public  | pg_database_owner
(1 row)

pgdb4=# exit
```

[postgres@pg_server ~]$ dropdb pgdb4
[postgres@pg_server ~]$
[postgres@pg_server ~]$ psql
psql (16.3)

postgres=# \l
```
              List of databases
   Name    |  Owner   | Encoding |   Access privileges
-----------+----------+----------+-----------------------
 pgdb1     | postgres | UTF8     |
 pgdb2     | postgres | UTF8     |
 pgdb3     | postgres | UTF8     |
 pgdbnew1  | postgres | UTF8     |
 postgres  | postgres | UTF8     |
 template0 | postgres | UTF8     | =c/postgres          +
           |          |          | postgres=CTc/postgres
 template1 | postgres | UTF8     | =c/postgres          +
           |          |          | postgres=CTc/postgres
(7 rows)
```

Summary

In this chapter, we have learned in detail about the management of schemas and users in a PostgreSQL database. The chapter also explained the authentication process involved in PostgreSQL in a server-client model stressing the importance of host-based authentication and other configuration files. An explanation about the roles and extensions in PostgreSQL gives a good understanding of a PostgreSQL cluster. The chapter is concluded with the details on how to create and drop a database using the OS command in the PostgreSQL database cluster.

CHAPTER 5

PostgreSQL Backup and Recovery

Introduction

In this chapter, we learn about the various backup and recovery methods essential to maintaining data integrity and availability. PostgreSQL offers a wide range of tools to perform backup and restore operations based on your requirements and data loss scenario.

We learn the following topics in this chapter:

- Importance of backing up data and real-world problem scenarios
- Type of backups in PostgreSQL
  - SQL Dump
  - File System-Level backup
  - Continuous archiving and point-in-time recovery (PITR)
  - Using external tools – *Barman* and *pgBackRest*
- Real-world practical backup and recovery use cases
  - Scenario 1: Backup and restore a single table
  - Scenario 2: Backup and restore a table structure without the data
  - Scenario 3: Backup and restore the table data without the structure
  - Scenario 4: Backup and restore multiple tables at a time
  - Scenario 5: Backup and restore a table in custom format

- Scenario 5a: Backup and restore a table using pg_dump in tar format
- Scenario 5b: Backup and restore a table using pg_dump in dir format
- Scenario 6: Backup multiple tables and restore one table in custom format
- Scenario 7: Backup and restore a schema within a database
- Scenario 8: Backup multiple schemas and restore a single schema within a database
- Scenario 9: Backup and restore an entire database
- Scenario 10: Restore a backup to a new database
- Scenario 11: Improve backup performance with parallel jobs
- Scenario 12: Restore a single table from a full database backup
- Scenario 13: Logical backup of a complete server and restore specific databases
- Scenario 14: Backup of global database objects
- Scenario 15: Physical backup of the complete server
- Scenario 15a: Verification of physical backups (pg_verifybackup) before restore
- Scenario 16: Restore a complete server from physical backup
- Scenario 16a: Restore to a new instance
- Scenario 16b: Restore to an existing instance
- Scenario 17: Perform a point-in-time recovery (PITR)
- Scenario 18: Backup and restore using **Barman**
- Scenario 19: Backup and restore using **pgBackRest**

Why Backup a Database?

Backup is an essential database operation. It is crucial for ensuring data security, business continuity, and protection against unforeseen events. Several real-world use cases prove that backups are vital for business operations.

Imagine the following situations within an enterprise for example:

- A hard drive or a storage area network (SAN) device has failed, with no immediate field service agent availability.

- A business user has accidentally deleted critical data or made an incorrect database update, causing data corruption.

- A system upgrade incorporating a software bug in the system, causing service disruption or incorrect functionality.

- A catastrophic event like fire, flood, or a cybersecurity incident causing extended downtime.

- A compliance or a regulatory audit compliance issue.

These situations in an enterprise not only result in critical data loss and cause service disruption, but most importantly, they also cause a loss of credibility and customer confidence in the company, which is what all huge enterprises strive for.

Backing up data provides the following key advantages:

- Data protection against loss

- Helps with disaster recovery

- Provides business continuity

- Provides data integrity and consistency

- Tracks changes over time, providing version control and historical reference

- Enables to meet compliance and legal requirements

- Protection against cyber-attacks through encrypted and historical backups

- Minimizes downtime and service disruption

- Helps with accelerated development of the product, where developers can use a copy of the production data for testing purposes without making changes to the actual production environment

- Increased recovery confidence through consistent backups

Importance of a Backup Strategy

While backing up a database is essential, it is also equally important to determine a backup strategy based on your business requirements. A backup strategy ensures that the backups are reliable, secure, and capable of meeting your business continuity and disaster recovery requirements.

Here are some key elements to consider when determining a backup strategy:

- **Backup frequency and schedule**

    It's very important to determine how often backups should be taken based on business operations, the rate at which business transactions occur, and during low-traffic volume times, minimizing system performance.

- **Backup type**

    The type of backup taken determines how quickly you can recover data. The backup and restore operations are usually system-intensive and time-consuming, so it is essential to decide whether you need a full backup, incremental backup, differential backup, replica, or a combination of these for optimal recovery to a point in time.

- **Backup storage location**

    The location of the backups determines how quickly we can recover and how durable they can be. For example, we can use onsite storage, off-site storage, cloud backup, or a combination of both onsite, off-site, or cloud backup. Each option has pros and cons and must be weighed when choosing a backup strategy.

- **Backup retention policy**

  This key element determines how long you would like to hold your backups. It all depends on the business requirements and other company-related regulatory requirements. An example of a retention policy would be weekly backups onsite and then archived into cloud storage or an offsite location, after which older backups can be deleted after a month.

- **Backup encryption and security**

  Determine whether the backups must be encrypted and the type of access control mechanisms to be defined to access them, including backup integrity checks to ensure they are not corrupted or tampered with using checksums and hash values.

- **Data recovery and restoration procedures**

  The Recovery Point Objective (RPO) and the Recovery Time Objective (RTO) determine the data recovery processing time and the needed granularity.

Combined, a comprehensive backup strategy ensures the data is easily recoverable, durable, and protected to meet business and legal requirements. It also ensures enterprises recover quickly from disasters or unforeseen events, avoiding costly downtime or data loss.

Backup Types in PostgreSQL

PostgreSQL offers different backup options, each suited to meet different needs in terms of granularity, complexity, and speed. Below are the most frequently used backup and restore methods in PostgreSQL:

- SQL Dump (*pg_dump* and *pg_restore*)
- File System-Level backup
- Continuous archiving and point-in-time recovery (PITR)
- Logical replication
- External tools (*pgBackRest* and *Barman*)

CHAPTER 5   POSTGRESQL BACKUP AND RECOVERY

SQL Dump

The SQL Dump method is most frequently used, especially for small and medium-scale databases. This method generates a file with a sequence of SQL commands created at the time of the dump and is equipped to recreate the database in the exact same state at the time of creating the dump. PostgreSQL provides the *pg_dump* utility to take a dump of the database.

To take a dump, issue the below command:

[postgres@pg_server ~]$ /usr/bin/pg_dump -U **username** -h **hostname** -p **port database_name** > **dump_file_name**

> where
> **-U** is the PostgreSQL username as which the backup is being taken
> **-h** is the host where the database resides
> **-p** is the port
> ***database_name*** is the database name for which the dump must be taken
> ***dump_file_name*** is the dump file's name

The ***dump_file_name*** is a plain-text file by default. The *pg_dump* can also create files in other formats, offering different granularity options with the restore process and restore performance with parallelism. It is a requirement that the user running the *pg_dump* utility has read access to all the tables that need to be backed up. So if we need to take a complete database backup, the user must be a superuser and have read access to all tables within the database.

The *pg_dump* utility has one specific advantage when compared to the other methods, and that is the flexibility and the compatibility it provides. For example, you are running on an older version of PostgreSQL and would want to migrate your database to a newer version of PostgreSQL. You can do that without any issues as the dumpfile is just a collection of standard SQL commands and is supported on any version. The other methods such as File System-Level backup and continuous archiving are server-version specific. The *pg_dump* utility will work if you want to migrate into another machine architecture, for example, from a 32-bit to a 64-bit server.

In addition to the *pg_dump* utility, PostgreSQL 16 offers another utility called *pg_dumpall*. The *pg_dumpall* utility is introduced to support dumping the entire database cluster contents. The *pg_dumpall* utility backs up all databases within a database cluster, as well as cluster-wide role definitions, tablespace definitions, and configuration settings that are shared across the PostgreSQL instance. The pg_dumpall output format is always SQL format, containing SQL commands to recreate all databases, roles, tablespaces, and other configuration settings.

To take a dump of the entire cluster, issue the below command:

```
[postgres@pg_server ~]$ /usr/bin/pg_dumpall -U username -h hostname -p port > dump_file_name.sql
```

where

-U is the PostgreSQL username as which the backup is being taken

-h is the host where the database resides

-p is the port

dump_file_name.sql is the SQL file name

File System-Level Backup

The File System-Level backup is a physical backup method where we copy the actual database files used by PostgreSQL using standard Linux operating system commands like *cp*, *mv*, etc. This method, although fast, comes with its own set of drawbacks. In this method, the PostgreSQL server must be shut down for data consistency, which incurs downtime. This option can be used even when the server runs using the continuous WAL archiving method, which we will learn about next. Still, additional steps need to be considered during the backup and restore process where we need to copy the WAL logs and apply them back on top of the base backup for the database to be current as part of the restore process.

Here is the syntax for backing up the default data directory (/var/lib/pgsql/16/data) to a backup location named pg_backup under the root directory. The backup location can typically be a local storage, an NFS mount, a third-party backup service, or even cloud storage.

```
[postgres@pg_server ~]# cp -r /var/lib/pgsql/16/data/ /pg_backup
```

You can also use the *tar* Linux command to create a tarball of all files you would want to include in your backup. For example:

```
[postgres@pg_server ~]# tar -cf pg_backup.tar /var/lib/pgsql/16/data/
```

where

tar is the Linux command we use to compress the files

-c creates a new archive

-f specifies the name of the archive file

pg_backup.tar is the name of the archive file

/var/lib/pgsql/16/data is the directory we want to copy and compress

Using this option can make consistent data backup challenging, especially if you don't shut down the PostgreSQL server; hence, it is not recommended. If physical backups are needed, it's best to rely on a third-party backup service that can effectively take a consistent snapshot of the PostgreSQL server at any point if this method is still preferred.

Continuous Archiving and Point-in-Time Recovery (PITR)

The continuous archiving method in PostgreSQL is an advanced backup method that continuously backs up *Write-Ahead Logs(WAL)* to maintain high data consistency and reliability. The *WAL* records every change made to the database files and protects them from system crashes, providing high data consistency. However, to restore a system to the last committed transaction, the continuous archiving method needs a base backup on top of which the *WAL* logs are replayed until the last committed transaction and to bring the system to the current state.

Compared to the other methods, this method is usually complex but provides the much-needed data consistency any system would require. This method only supports a full database cluster restore and does not provide the granularity of the logical backup methods *pg_dump* and *pg_dumpall*. The complexity usually arises in knowing which *WAL* to replay to get the database to the current state. In general, the PostgreSQL instance generates a lot of *WAL* records constantly when archiving is enabled.

For continuous archiving and point-in-time recovery (PITR), you must enable WAL logs archiving. To do so, in the *postgresql.conf* configuration file:

- Set *archive_mode* = *on* to enable WAL archiving

- Set *archive_command* parameter to the shell command used to copy completed WAL segments to an archive location

For example, in the *postgresql.conf*:

```
archive_mode = on
archive_command = 'cp %p /path_to_archive/%f'
```

where

%p is the path of the file to archive

%f is the file name

path_to_archive is the path to where you want to store the WAL logs

> **Note** For the changes to take effect, you must restart PostgreSQL.

```
# For systems using systemd
[postgres@pg_server ~]# sudo systemctl restart postgresql
```

Using External Tools

In addition to the above backup and restore methods, we also have a few external backup and recovery tools for PostgreSQL:

- Barman
- pgBackRest

Let us learn about each one of these tools.

Barman

This open source administration tool was developed using Python to perform backups of multiple PostgreSQL servers to a remote backup location. It is distributed under GNU GPL 3 and maintained by EnterpriseDB, a platinum sponsor of the open source PostgreSQL project.

Barman follows a typical client-server architecture. For example, a standard Barman architecture looks like the one below. The Barman server is where the Barman packages are installed, and PostgreSQL server 1, PostgreSQL server 2, and PostgreSQL server 3 represent the PostgreSQL servers configured to backup with Barman. Each of PostgreSQL servers 1, 2, and 3 establishes an SSH connection for base backup operations and WAL archiving, depending on the chosen backup method.

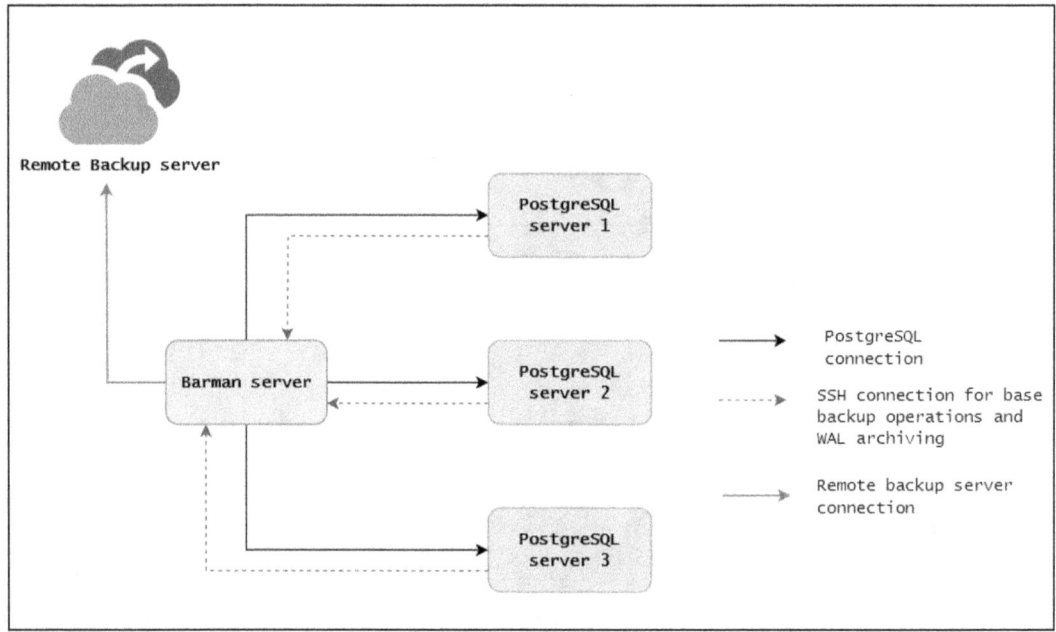

Figure 5-1. Sample Barman backup architecture

Barman supports many backup methods that rely on different PostgreSQL features. Each backup method can be specified using the *backup_method* parameter in the *postgresql.conf* configuration file. Table 5-1 shows a summary of the various backup methods supported by *Barman*.

CHAPTER 5   POSTGRESQL BACKUP AND RECOVERY

Table 5-1. Barman backup methods

Backup method	Information
Rsync backup	It uses *backup_method=rsync* combined with PostgreSQL low-level API to manually transfer cluster files over an SSH connection
Streaming backup	Uses *backup_method=postgres* combined with *pg_basebackup*
Snapshot backup	Uses *backup_method=snapshot* in combination with cloud CLI tools
File-level incremental backup	Can be used only when using *rsync* backups and uses features like deduplication including the filesystem hard links
Block-level incremental backup	Can be used only when using *streaming* backups. The block-level incremental backup uses a valid *backup_manifest* file for deduplication references
WAL archive backup	Used along with *rsync* backups to backup WAL files and is configured using the *archive_command* parameter
WAL streaming backup	Used along with *streaming* backups and uses the *pg_receivewal* utility to transfer the WAL files

Installing Barman

In this section, we will install *Barman* using *yum* installation.

1. Install and verify the PostgreSQL repository.

    On the server we want to use as a backup server, we can install the PostgreSQL repositories using the command below.

    Log in as **root** user and run the **yum** command.

    [root@pg_server ~]# **yum install -y** https://download.postgresql.org/pub/repos/yum/reporpms/EL-7-x86_64/pgdg-redhat-repo-latest.noarch.rpm

    Verify the repo using the command repolist.

    [root@pg_server ~]# **yum repolist**

CHAPTER 5   POSTGRESQL BACKUP AND RECOVERY

2. We need to install the recommended Extra Packages for Enterprise Linux (EPEL) repository configuration. We can install EPEL as shown below:

    `[root@pg_server ~]#` **`yum install epel-release`**

3. Install *Barman*.

    `[root@pg_server ~]#` **`yum install barman`**

As a part of *Barman* installation, a new user with name **barman** will be created. Check the user and change its password.

```
[root@pg_server ~]# id barman
uid=998(barman) gid=996(barman) groups=996(barman)
[root@pg_server ~]# passwd barman
Changing password for user barman.
New password:
BAD PASSWORD: The password is shorter than 8 characters
Retype new password:
passwd: all authentication tokens updated successfully.
[root@pg_server ~]#
```

To verify the installed barman version, run

```
[root@pg_server ~]# barman --version
3.7.0 Barman by EnterpriseDB (www.enterprisedb.com)
[root@pg_server ~]#
```

This completes the installation of *Barman* utility.

In the next section, we will configure *Barman* so that we can use it for backup and recovery operations.

Configuring Barman

To configure *Barman*, let us assume we have the following environment setup:

PostgreSQL database cluster server: *postgresql_db_server*

Barman backup server: *barman_host*

CHAPTER 5　POSTGRESQL BACKUP AND RECOVERY

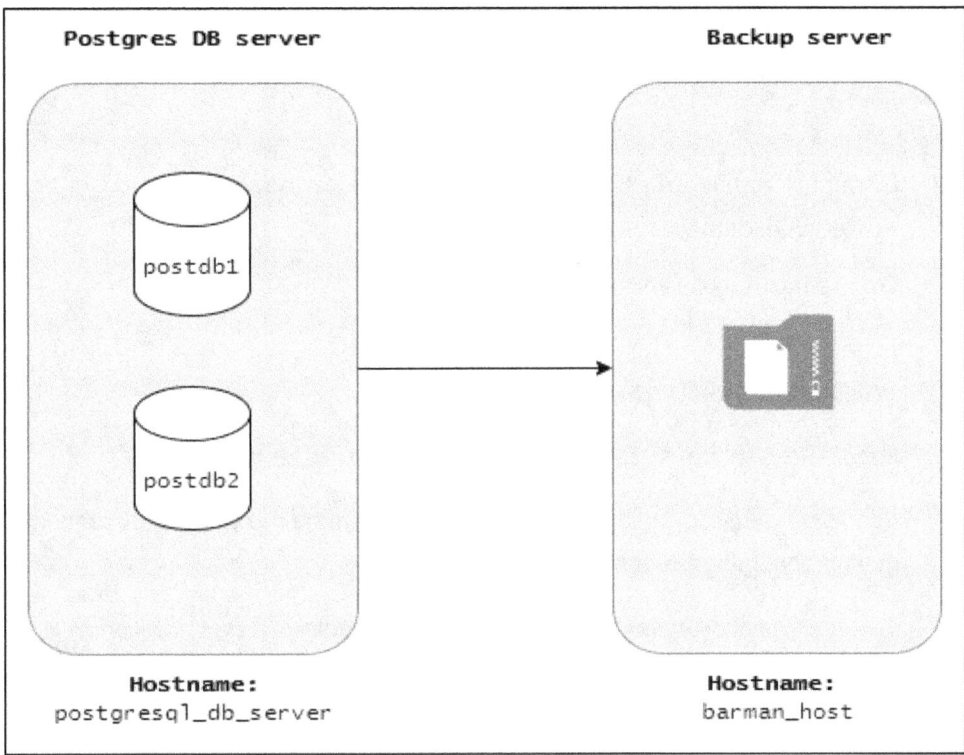

Figure 5-2. Sample Barman environment

Here are the steps that are required to configure *Barman* correctly.

1. As root user, add hostname and IPs of each server in the /etc/hosts file.

   [postgres@postgresql_db_server ~]$ **cat /etc/hosts**
   192.168.2.11 postgresql_db_server postgresql_db_server
   192.168.2.30 barman_host barman_host

   [root@barman_host ~]# **cat /etc/hosts**
   192.168.2.30 barman_host barman_host
   192.168.2.11 postgresql_db_server postgresql_db_server
   [root@barman_host ~]#

2. In the PostgreSQL database server, create a role with the name barman. This role will be used in the configuration file of the Barman server.

225

```
postgres=# create user barman superuser  password 'welcome';
CREATE ROLE
postgres=#
```

3. Configure passwordless authentication in the Barman server and PostgreSQL database server.

   On the Barman server:

   ```
   [root@pg_server ~]# su - barman
   [root@pg_server ~]# ssh-keygen -t rsa
   ```

   Copy the ssh keys to the PostgreSQL database server.

   ```
   [root@pg_server ~]# ssh-copy-id -i ~/.ssh/id_rsa.pub postgres@postgresql_db_server
   ```

   Test the passwordless connections from the backup server:

   ```
   -bash-4.2$ ssh 'postgres@postgresql_db_server'
   Last login: Sun Jul 30 10:32:15 2023 from barman_host
   [postgres@postgresql_db_server ~]$
   ```

   On PostgreSQL database server:

   As a *postgres* user.

   ssh-keygen -t rsa

   ```
   [postgres@postgresql_db_server ~]$ ssh-keygen -t rsa
   Generating public/private rsa key pair.
   Enter file in which to save the key (/home/postgres/.ssh/id_rsa):
   Enter passphrase (empty for no passphrase):
   Enter same passphrase again:
   Your identification has been saved in /home/postgres/.ssh/id_rsa.
   Your public key has been saved in /home/postgres/.ssh/id_rsa.pub.
   The key fingerprint is:
   SHA256:UgxniePxhAGFMXBdqsUMy1w+7YUnUisb7JH8sI5Ys4k postgres@postgresql_db_server
   The key's randomart image is:
   +---[RSA 2048]----+
   ```

```
|  ..**===.       |
|  +.@*Xoo        |
|   +.^=B o       |
|    +.&.+        |
|    + = S        |
|   + * .         |
|  E + .          |
|                 |
|                 |
+----[SHA256]-----+
[postgres@postgresql_db_server ~]$
```

Copy the ssh keys from PostgreSQL server to barman backup server

ssh-copy-id -i ~/.ssh/id_rsa.pub postgres@ postgresql_db_server

[postgres@postgresql_db_server ~]$ **ssh-copy-id -i ~/.ssh/id_rsa.pub barman@barman_host**
/usr/bin/ssh-copy-id: INFO: Source of key(s) to be installed: "/home/postgres/.ssh/id_rsa.pub"
The authenticity of host 'barman_host (192.168.2.30)' can't be established.
ECDSA key fingerprint is SHA256:YpDYEJtpp16FvKQ/X2muJuFwkOiL9YG2fRJWnQLaxGE.
ECDSA key fingerprint is MD5:77:b3:32:b9:5f:74:27:6d:df:1c:0f:c9:76:16:7c:cb.
Are you sure you want to continue connecting (yes/no)? yes
/usr/bin/ssh-copy-id: INFO: attempting to log in with the new key(s), to filter out any that are already installed
/usr/bin/ssh-copy-id: INFO: 1 key(s) remain to be installed -- if you are prompted now it is to install the new keys
barman@barman_host's password:

Number of key(s) added: 1

Now try logging into the machine, with: "ssh 'barman@barman_host'"
and check to make sure that only the key(s) you wanted were added.

```
[postgres@postgresql_db_server ~]$
```

Test the connection.

```
[postgres@postgresql_db_server ~]$ ssh 'barman@barman_host'
Last login: Sat Jul 29 15:51:46 2023 from 192.168.2.1
-bash-4.2$
```

4. Configure the Global Configuration File in the Barman server.

   The main configuration file in the Barman server is */etc/barman.conf*. This configuration file contains options as compression type, main directory, etc.

   Edit */etc/barman.conf* to set the global parameters suitable to the environment.

   As **root** user, for our setup, we will add the parameters below and save the file:

   ```
   [root@pg_server ~]# vi /etc/barman.conf
   compression = gzip
   immediate_checkpoint = true
   basebackup_retry_times = 3
   reuse_backup = link
   ```

   Number of retries of base backup copy, after an error. Used during both backup and recovery operations.

5. Configure the PostgreSQL server configuration files in the Barman server.

   In the Barman server, we must configure the server configuration files, one for each PostgreSQL server. These configuration files are located in the */etc/barman.d* directory and must have a .conf suffix. This configuration file will have the connection info of the database server and backup options.

   As **root** user, do the below steps:

   ```
   [root@barman_host etc]# cd /etc/barman.d/
   [root@barman_host barman.d]# ls -ltr
   ```

CHAPTER 5   POSTGRESQL BACKUP AND RECOVERY

```
total 16
-rw-r--r--. 1 root root 1500 Jul 25 08:50 streaming-server.
conf-template
-rw-r--r--. 1 root root 1546 Jul 25 08:50 ssh-server.conf-template
-rw-r--r--. 1 root root  950 Jul 25 08:50 passive-server.
conf-template
[root@barman_host barman.d]#
```

```
[root@barman_host barman.d]# vi postgresql_db_server.conf
[postgresql_db_server]
description =  "postgresql_db_server backup config"
ssh_command = ssh postgres@postgresql_db_server
conninfo = host=postgresql_db_server user=barman port=5432
dbname=postgres password=welcome
backup_options = concurrent_backup
backup_method = rsync
archiver = on
incoming_wals_directory=/u01/barman/backup/postgresql_db_
server/wallogs
[root@barman_host barman.d]#
```

Please note that we need to create a directory with name */u01/barman/backup/postgresql_db_server/wallogs* and change its permission to *0700 barman*.

6. Verify the configuration for the server setup in the Barman server.

   Log in as barman user on the backup server and run the below commands:

```
-bash-4.2$ barman list-server
postgresql_db_server - postgresql_db_server backup config
-bash-4.2$
```

```
-bash-4.2$ barman check postgresql_db_server
Server postgresql_db_server:
        WAL archive: FAILED (please make sure WAL shipping
        is setup)
        PostgreSQL: FAILED
```

229

CHAPTER 5 POSTGRESQL BACKUP AND RECOVERY

```
              superuser or standard user with backup privileges: OK
              wal_level: OK
              directories: OK
              retention policy settings: OK
              backup maximum age: OK (no last_backup_maximum_age
              provided)
              backup minimum size: OK (0 B)
              wal maximum age: OK (no last_wal_maximum_age provided)
              wal size: OK (0 B)
              compression settings: OK
              failed backups: OK (there are 0 failed backups)
              minimum redundancy requirements: OK (have 0 backups,
              expected at least 0)
              ssh: OK (PostgreSQL server)
              systemid coherence: OK (no system Id stored on disk)
              archive_mode: OK
              archive_command: OK
              continuous archiving: OK
              archiver errors: OK
-bash-4.2$
```

If you notice the above output, we see a couple of failed errors.

For "PostgreSQL: FAILED," we need to add the backup server information along with the *barman* username in the *pg_hba.conf* on the PostgreSQL server and restart the postgres service.

```
[postgres@postgresql_db_server data]$ cat pg_hba.conf |
grep barman
host    all             barman          192.168.2.30/32         trust
[postgres@postgresql_db_server data]$
```

For the WAL error:

WAL archive: FAILED (please make sure WAL shipping is setup)

In the PostgreSQL server, we need to configure the WAL parameters to correct one, as shown below:

CHAPTER 5   POSTGRESQL BACKUP AND RECOVERY

```
postgres=# alter system set archive_command='test ! -f barman@
barman_host:/var/lib/barman/postgresql_db_server/incoming/%f &&
rsync -a %p barman@barman_host:/var/lib/barman/postgresql_db_
server/incoming/%f';
ALTER SYSTEM
postgres=#
```

Please note that the location used in *archive_command* should match to the below parameter, which we did set in file *postgresql_db_server.conf*, which we added in step 4:

```
incoming_wals_directory=/u01/barman/backup/postgresql_db_
server/wallogs
```

Once you fix the above two errors, if you rerun the check command, it should come clean. Below is a sample output that showcases this.

```
-bash-4.2$ barman check postgresql_db_server
Server postgresql_db_server:
        PostgreSQL: OK
        superuser or standard user with backup privileges: OK
        wal_level: OK
        directories: OK
        retention policy settings: OK
        backup maximum age: OK (no last_backup_maximum_age provided)
        backup minimum size: OK (613.2 MiB)
        wal maximum age: OK (no last_wal_maximum_age provided)
        wal size: OK (86.2 KiB)
        compression settings: OK
        failed backups: OK (there are 0 failed backups)
        minimum redundancy requirements: OK (have 3 backups, expected at least 0)
        ssh: OK (PostgreSQL server)
        systemid coherence: OK
        archive_mode: OK
        archive_command: OK
        continuous archiving: OK
        archiver errors: OK
-bash-4.2$
```

From barman, do a force log switch for WAL.

```
-bash-4.2$ barman switch-xlog --force --archive postgresql_
db_server
The WAL file 000000010000000300000CD has been closed on server
'postgresql_db_server'
Waiting for the WAL file 000000010000000300000CD from server
'postgresql_db_server' (max: 30 seconds)
```

CHAPTER 5   POSTGRESQL BACKUP AND RECOVERY

```
Processing xlog segments from file archival for postgresql_
db_server
        000000010000000300000OCD
-bash-4.2$
```

7. Create a test schema and table in database postdb1:

```
postgres=# \c postdb1;
You are now connected to database "postdb1" as user "postgres".
postdb1=# create schema backuptest (name varchar);
ERROR:  syntax error at or near "("
LINE 1: create schema backuptest (name varchar);
                                 ^
postdb1=# create schema backuptest;
CREATE SCHEMA
postdb1=# create table backuptest.testtab (name varchar);
CREATE TABLE
postdb1=# insert into backuptest.testtab values ('Data_before_
level0_backup');
INSERT 0 1
postdb1=# select * from backuptest.testtab;
          name
---------------------------
 Data_before_level0_backup
(1 row)

postdb1=#
```

These steps ensure the *Barman* utility is configured correctly to perform successful and efficient backup and recovery operations. In the sections below, we will see a few practical examples of backup and restore operations using the *Barman* utility.

Given the extensive community involvement in improving the product, the *Barman* utility is a great external tool for managing PostgreSQL backups. Its comprehensive feature set, which supports full and incremental backups, point-in-time recovery, and the ability to manage remote backups, including cloud locations, makes it an excellent option for database administrators.

pgBackRest

pgBackRest is an open source backup and restore tool that we can use to create PostgreSQL physical backups. It is very easy to install/configure and use. It includes many features like parallel option for backups, local and remote backup/restore options, incremental and differential backup types, backup compression, and backup integrity check.

Here is how the different backup types – *Full, Incremental and Differential* – are supported using *pgBackRest*.

> **Full backup**: When performing a full backup, pgBackRest copies all the contents of the database cluster. The first backup of the database cluster is always a full backup, and when you use the full backup for restoration, you don't need to depend on any other backup files to get consistency.
>
> **Incremental backup**: When performing an incremental backup, pgBackRest copies only the contents that have changed since the last successful incremental, full, or differential backup.
>
> **Differential backup**: When performing a differential backup, pgBackRest backs up only the contents (database cluster files) that have been changed since the last full backup.

Before installing and configuring the pgBackRest backup tool, it is important to understand the concept of a ***stanza***. A *stanza* defines the backup configuration for a specific PostgreSQL server and includes details like the backup location, the backup method, archiving options, etc.

Installation and Configuration of pgBackRest Tool

In this demonstration, we will use pgBackRest to perform backup and recovery operations.

1. Install PostgreSQL database cluster.

    Install PostgreSQL version 16.3, and create a user-defined database with one schema and a few tables with data.

For 16.3 installation, we will use the steps below:

```
yum install -y https://download.postgresql.org/pub/repos/yum/
reporpms/EL-7-x86_64/pgdg-redhat-repo-latest.noarch.rpm
yum install epel-release
yum install -y postgresql15-server
yum install -y postgresql15-contrib
/usr/pgsql-15/bin/postgresql-15-setup initdb
systemctl enable postgresql-15
systemctl start postgresql-15

systemctl status postgresql-15
```

We can use the script below to create a new database and new schema with few tables:

```
Connect to the psql console and create database/schema/tables as shown below.

create database hrmdb;
\c hrmdb;

create schema hrm;

create table hrm.empinfo (ename varchar, empno integer, edept varchar, primary key (empno));
create index empno_udx on hrm.empinfo (edept);
insert into hrm.empinfo values ('Peter_J',1000,'Sales');
insert into hrm.empinfo values ('Robin_M',1001,'accounts');
insert into hrm.empinfo values ('David_S',1002,'Sales');
insert into hrm.empinfo values ('Stefeny',1003,'marketing');
insert into hrm.empinfo values ('Marshal',1004,'Sales');
insert into hrm.empinfo values ('Ross',1006,'5ccounts');
insert into hrm.empinfo values ('leanord',1200,'Sales');
insert into hrm.empinfo values ('Mark_W',1030,'Sales');
insert into hrm.empinfo values ('MarkK',1022,'marketing');
insert into hrm.empinfo values ('Raj_M',1094,'Sales');
insert into hrm.empinfo values ('Katy',1898,'accounts');
```

CHAPTER 5   POSTGRESQL BACKUP AND RECOVERY

```
create table hrm.deptinfo (dname varchar, deptno integer);

insert into hrm.deptinfo values ('sales',1111);
insert into hrm.deptinfo values ('accounts',1212);
insert into hrm.deptinfo values ('marketing',2312);

create table hrm.salinfo (ename varchar, salno integer);
insert into hrm.salinfo values ('sales',65000);
insert into hrm.salinfo values ('accounts',83000);
insert into hrm.salinfo values ('marketing',76000);

select * from   hrm.empinfo;
select * from   hrm.salinfo;
select * from   hrm.deptinfo;
```

Output for the above commands:

```
[postgres@pg_backuprst_01 ~]$ psql
psql (16.3)
Type "help" for help.

postgres=# create database hrmdb;
CREATE DATABASE
postgres-# \l
                    List of databases
 Name      | Owner    | Encoding | Collate     | Ctype       |
  ICU Locale | Locale Provider |   Access privileges
-----------+----------+----------+-------------+-------------+
------------+-----------------+-----------------------
 hrmdb     | postgres | UTF8     | en_US.UTF-8 | en_US.UTF-8 |
            | libc            |
 postgres  | postgres | UTF8     | en_US.UTF-8 | en_US.UTF-8 |
            | libc            |
 template0 | postgres | UTF8     | en_US.UTF-8 | en_US.UTF-8 |
            | libc            | c/postgres                  +
            |                 |             |               |             |
            |                 | postgres=CTc/postgres
```

235

CHAPTER 5 POSTGRESQL BACKUP AND RECOVERY

```
 template1 | postgres | UTF8     | en_US.UTF-8 | en_US.UTF-8 |
           | libc                | c/postgres                +
           |          |          |             |
|          |                     | postgres=CTc/postgres
(4 rows)

postgres-# \c hrmdb;
You are now connected to database "hrmdb" as user "postgres".
hrmdb-# create schema hrm;
CREATE SCHEMA
hrmdb=# create table hrm.empinfo (ename varchar, empno integer,
edept varchar, primary key (empno));
insert into hrm.empinfo values ('David_S',1002,'Sales');
insert into hrm.empinfo values ('Stefeny',1003,'marketing');
insert into hrm.empinfo values ('Marshal',1004,'Sales');
insert into hrm.empinfo values ('Ross',1006,'5ccounts');
insert into hrm.empinfo values ('leanord',1200,'Sales');
insert into hrm.empinfo values ('Mark_W',1030,'Sales');
insert into hrm.empinfo values ('MarkK',1022,'marketing');
insert into hrm.empinfo values ('Raj_M',1094,'Sales');
insert into hrm.empinfo values ('Katy',1898,'accounts');

create table hrm.deptinfo (dname varchar, deptno integer);

insert into hrm.deptinfo values ('sales',1111);
insert into hrm.deptinfo values ('accounts',1212);
insert into hrm.deptinfo values ('marketing',2312);
CREATE TABLE
hrmdb=# create index empno_udx on hrm.empinfo (edept);
CREATE INDEX
hrmdb=# insert into hrm.empinfo values ('Peter_J',1000,'Sales');
INSERT 0 1
hrmdb=# insert into hrm.empinfo values ('Robin_M',1001,'accounts');
INSERT 0 1
hrmdb=# insert into hrm.empinfo values ('David_S',1002,'Sales');
INSERT 0 1
```

```
hrmdb=# insert into hrm.empinfo values
('Stefeny',1003,'marketing');
INSERT 0 1
hrmdb=# insert into hrm.empinfo values ('Marshal',1004,'Sales');
INSERT 0 1
hrmdb=# insert into hrm.empinfo values ('Ross',1006,'5ccounts');
INSERT 0 1
hrmdb=# insert into hrm.empinfo values ('leanord',1200,'Sales');
INSERT 0 1
hrmdb=# insert into hrm.empinfo values ('Mark_W',1030,'Sales');
INSERT 0 1
hrmdb=# insert into hrm.empinfo values ('MarkK',1022,'marketing');
INSERT 0 1
hrmdb=# insert into hrm.empinfo values ('Raj_M',1094,'Sales');
INSERT 0 1
hrmdb=# insert into hrm.empinfo values ('Katy',1898,'accounts');
INSERT 0 1
hrmdb=#
hrmdb=#
hrmdb=# create table hrm.deptinfo (dname varchar, deptno integer);
CREATE TABLE
hrmdb=#
hrmdb=# insert into hrm.deptinfo values ('sales',1111);
INSERT 0 1
hrmdb=# insert into hrm.deptinfo values ('accounts',1212);
INSERT 0 1
hrmdb=# insert into hrm.deptinfo values ('marketing',2312);
INSERT 0 1
hrmdb=#

hrmdb=# \dn hrm*
 List of schemas
 Name |  Owner
------+----------
 hrm  | postgres
(1 row)
```

CHAPTER 5   POSTGRESQL BACKUP AND RECOVERY

```
hrmdb=# \dt hrm.*
          List of relations
 Schema |   Name   | Type  |  Owner
--------+----------+-------+----------
 hrm    | deptinfo | table | postgres
 hrm    | empinfo  | table | postgres
(2 rows)

hrmdb=#
```

2. Installation and configuration of *pgBackRest*.

   Log in as *root* user and run the below yum command to install the *pgBackRest* rpm:

   yum install pgbackrest

```
[root@pg_backuprst_01 ~]# yum install pgbackrest
Loaded plugins: fastestmirror
Loading mirror speeds from cached hostfile
 * base: tx-mirror.tier.net
 * epel: pubmirror2.math.uh.edu
 * extras: tx-mirror.tier.net
 * updates: abqix.mm.fcix.net
Resolving Dependencies
--> Running transaction check
---> Package pgbackrest.x86_64 0:2.47-1PGDG.rhel7 will be installed
--> Finished Dependency Resolution

Dependencies Resolved

================================================================
 Package        Arch      Version              Repository    Size
================================================================
Installing:
 pgbackrest    x86_64    2.47-1PGDG.rhel7     pgdg-common   389 k

Transaction Summary
================================================================
Install  1 Package
```

CHAPTER 5   POSTGRESQL BACKUP AND RECOVERY

```
Total download size: 389 k
Installed size: 944 k
Is this ok [y/d/N]: y
Downloading packages:
pgbackrest-2.47-1PGDG.rhel7.x86_64.rpm  | 389 kB   00:00:00
Running transaction check
Running transaction test
Transaction test succeeded
Running transaction
  Installing : pgbackrest-2.47-1PGDG.rhel7.x86_64    1/1
  Verifying  : pgbackrest-2.47-1PGDG.rhel7.x86_64    1/1
```

Installed:
  pgbackrest.x86_64 0:2.47-1PGDG.rhel7

```
Complete!
[root@pg_backuprst_01 ~]#
```

Verify if the pgBackRest is installed correctly.

```
[postgres@pg_backuprst_01 ~]$ pgbackrest
pgBackRest 2.47 - General help
```

```
Usage:
    pgbackrest [options] [command]

Commands:
    annotate        Add or modify backup annotation.
    archive-get     Get a WAL segment from the archive.
    archive-push    Push a WAL segment to the archive.
    backup          Backup a database cluster.
    check           Check the configuration.
    expire          Expire backups that exceed retention.
    help            Get help.
    info            Retrieve information about backups.
    repo-get        Get a file from a repository.
    repo-ls         List files in a repository.
    restore         Restore a database cluster.
```

```
server          pgBackRest server.
server-ping     Ping pgBackRest server.
stanza-create   Create the required stanza data.
stanza-delete   Delete a stanza.
stanza-upgrade  Upgrade a stanza.
start           Allow pgBackRest processes to run.
stop            Stop pgBackRest processes from running.
verify          Verify contents of the repository.
version         Get version.

Use 'pgbackrest help [command]' for more information.
[postgres@pg_backuprst_01 ~]$
```

Note Always make sure that after installing any tool, run the basic commands to ensure that the tool is returning expected values.

You can use the below command to check the version of the installed *pgBackRest*.

```
[postgres@pg_backuprst_01 ~]$ pgbackrest version
pgBackRest 2.47
[postgres@pg_backuprst_01 ~]$
```

We can also see that a configuration file with the name "*pgbackrest.conf*" will be created in the /etc/ directory.

```
[postgres@pg_backuprst_01 ~]$ cat /etc/pgbackrest.conf
[global]
repo1-path=/var/lib/pgbackrest

#[main]
#pg1-path=/var/lib/pgsql/10/data
[postgres@pg_backuprst_01 ~]$
```

CHAPTER 5   POSTGRESQL BACKUP AND RECOVERY

Location of the *pgBackRest* bin file:

```
[postgres@pg_backuprst_01 ~]$ which pgbackrest
/bin/pgbackrest
[postgres@pg_backuprst_01 ~]$
```

pgBackRest can be used from the command line or from the above location.

3. Add the below contents to the *.bash_profile* for the *postgres* user.

```
export PATH=$PATH:/usr/pgsql-15/bin
export PGDATA=/var/lib/pgsql/15/data/
export PGPORT=5432
```

4. Update the data directory in the pgBackRest configuration file.

   As root user, modify */etc/pgbackrest.conf* and include the data directory.

```
[root@pg_backuprst_01 ~]# cat /etc/pgbackrest.conf
[global]
repo1-path=/var/lib/pgbackrest

#[pg_backurst_01_bkp]
pg1-path=/var/lib/pgsql/15/data
pg1-port=5432
[root@pg_backuprst_01 ~]#
```

5. As root user, create the below directories for archive log location and for backups.

```
[root@pg_backuprst_01 ~]# mkdir -p /u01/postgres/archive
[root@pg_backuprst_01 ~]# mkdir -p /u02/pgBackRest/pg154_backups
[root@pg_backuprst_01 ~]# chown -rf postgres:postgres /u01/
[root@pg_backuprst_01 ~]# chown -rf postgres:postgres /u02/
[root@pg_backuprst_01 ~]# chmod -rf 777 /u01/
[root@pg_backuprst_01 ~]# chmod -rf 777 /u02
[root@pg_backuprst_01 ~]#
```

241

CHAPTER 5   POSTGRESQL BACKUP AND RECOVERY

6. Update the database cluster configuration file with the below changes.

```
listen_addresses = '*'
archive_command=on
archive_command = 'pgbackrest --stanza=prod_bkp archive-push %p'
```

[postgres@pg_backuprst_01 data]$ cat postgresql.conf | grep listen
listen_addresses = '*'   # what IP address(es) to listen on;
[postgres@pg_backuprst_01 data]$ cat postgresql.conf | grep archive_mode
archive_mode = on   # enables archiving; off, on, or always
[postgres@pg_backuprst_01 data]$ cat postgresql.conf | grep archive_command
                                  # (empty string indicates archive_command should
archive_command = 'pgbackrest --stanza=prod_bkp archive-push %p'   # command to use to archive a logfile segment
[postgres@pg_backuprst_01 data]$

Restart the postgres database cluster.

[root@pg_backuprst_01 ~]# systemctl stop postgresql-15
[root@pg_backuprst_01 ~]# systemctl start postgresql-15

7. Create a stanza.

Let us create the stanza for this scenario using the command below.

pgbackrest stanza-create --stanza=pg_backurst_01_bkp --log-level-console=info

[postgres@pg_backuprst_01 ~]$ pgbackrest stanza-create --stanza=pg_backurst_01_bkp --log-level-console=info
2023-08-29 11:44:05.619 P00   INFO: stanza-create command begin 2.47: --exec-id=2218-18e12ae8 --log-level-console=info --pg1-

CHAPTER 5   POSTGRESQL BACKUP AND RECOVERY

```
path=/var/lib/pgsql/15/data --pg1-port=5432 --repo1-path=/var/lib/
pgbackrest --stanza=pg_backurst_01_bkp
2023-08-29 11:44:06.233 P00   INFO: stanza-create for stanza 'pg_
backurst_01_bkp' on repo1
2023-08-29 11:44:06.267 P00   INFO: stanza-create command end:
completed successfully (650ms)
[postgres@pg_backuprst_01 ~]$
```

8. Run the *check* command to validate the configuration.

```
[postgres@pg_backuprst_01 data]$ pgbackrest --stanza=pg_
backurst_01_bkp check --log-level-console=info
2023-08-29 12:56:03.716 P00   INFO: check command begin 2.47:
--exec-id=3039-db4490b6 --log-level-console=info --pg1-path=/var/
lib/pgsql/15/data --pg1-port=5432 --repo1-path=/var/lib/pgbackrest
--stanza=pg_backurst_01_bkp
2023-08-29 12:56:04.325 P00   INFO: check repo1 configuration
(primary)
2023-08-29 12:56:05.131 P00   INFO: check repo1 archive for WAL
(primary)
2023-08-29 12:56:05.131 P00   INFO: WAL segment
000000010000000000000003 successfully archived
to '/var/lib/pgbackrest/archive/pg_backurst_01_
bkp/15-1/0000000100000000/000000010000000000000003-adba00d
31a22f0a3421483dd08780ac8dca99cbe.gz' on repo1
2023-08-29 12:56:05.131 P00   INFO: check command end: completed
successfully (1416ms)
[postgres@pg_backuprst_01 data]$
```

Once configured, the *pgBackRest* tool is ready to perform backup and recovery operations. It has a rich feature set to make these operations efficient and is known for its reliability and consistency. Support for full, incremental, and differential backups combined with WAL archiving provides a flexible and robust backup strategy and encryption support.

In the sections below, we will see practical examples of backup and recovery options using the *pgBackRest* utility.

Real-World Practical Backup and Recovery Scenarios

Let us look at a few backup and recovery scenarios with each one of the methods we learned so far.

Scenario 1: Backup and Restore a Single Table

In this test case, we will backup the table named *emp* of schema *s1* in the database *db1*.

```
[postgres@pg_server ~]$ pg_dump -d db1 -t db1_schema1.db1tb1 -f /u01/pgsql16/pgdata/backup/db1_schema1_db1tb1.sql
[postgres@pg_server ~]$
[postgres@pg_server ~]$ ls -lrt /u01/pgsql16/pgdata/backup/db1_schema1_db1tb1.sql
-rw-rw-r--. 1 postgres postgres 1444 May 30 23:38 /u01/pgsql16/pgdata/backup/db1_schema1_db1tb1.sql
[postgres@pg_server ~]$
```

The above command will create an SQL file with the data definition of the table *db1_schema1.db1tb1*, including the data.

```
[postgres@pg_server ~]$ cat /u01/pgsql16/pgdata/backup/db1_schema1_db1tb1.sql
--
-- PostgreSQL database dump
--

-- Dumped from database version 16.3
-- Dumped by pg_dump version 16.3

SET statement_timeout = 0;
SET lock_timeout = 0;
SET idle_in_transaction_session_timeout = 0;
SET client_encoding = 'UTF8';
SET standard_conforming_strings = on;
SELECT pg_catalog.set_config('search_path', '', false);
SET check_function_bodies = false;
```

CHAPTER 5 POSTGRESQL BACKUP AND RECOVERY

```
SET xmloption = content;
SET client_min_messages = warning;
SET row_security = off;

SET default_tablespace = '';

SET default_table_access_method = heap;

--
-- Name: db1tb1; Type: TABLE; Schema: db1_schema1; Owner: postgres
--

CREATE TABLE db1_schema1.db1tb1 (
    name character varying,
    id integer
);

ALTER TABLE db1_schema1.db1tb1 OWNER TO postgres;

--
-- Data for Name: db1tb1; Type: TABLE DATA; Schema: db1_schema1; Owner: postgres
--

COPY db1_schema1.db1tb1 (name, id) FROM stdin;
db1a    100
db1b    200
db1c    300
db1d    400
db1e    500
db1f    600
db1g    700
db1h    800
db1i    900
db1a    100
db1b    200
db1c    300
db1d    400
db1e    500
```

CHAPTER 5 POSTGRESQL BACKUP AND RECOVERY

```
db1f    600
db1g    700
db1h    800
db1i    900
\.

--
-- Name: db1_unq_idx; Type: INDEX; Schema: db1_schema1; Owner: postgres
--

CREATE INDEX db1_unq_idx ON db1_schema1.db1tb1 USING btree (name);


--
-- Name: TABLE db1tb1; Type: ACL; Schema: db1_schema1; Owner: postgres
--

GRANT SELECT,INSERT,DELETE,UPDATE ON TABLE db1_schema1.db1tb1 TO user1;
GRANT SELECT,INSERT,DELETE,UPDATE ON TABLE db1_schema1.db1tb1 TO db_user4;

--
-- PostgreSQL database dump complete
--

[postgres@pg_server ~]$
```

Now, let us **restore** the same table by simulating a scenario where the table is accidentally dropped. To do so, let us drop the table *db1_schema1.db1tb1* from database *db1* and restore it using the above backup.

```
postgres=# \c db1
You are now connected to database "db1" as user "postgres".
db1=#
db1=# select count(*) from db1_schema1.db1tb1;
 count
-------
    18
(1 row)

db1=#
db1=# drop table db1_schema1.db1tb1 cascade;
```

CHAPTER 5　POSTGRESQL BACKUP AND RECOVERY

```
NOTICE:  drop cascades to 2 other objects
DETAIL:  drop cascades to view db1_schema1.db1view1
drop cascades to materialized view db1_schema1.db1_mv
DROP TABLE
db1=#
```

Let us restore the table *db1_schema1.db1tb1* from the backup.

```
[postgres@pg_server ~]$ cd /u01/pgsql16/pgdata/backup/
[postgres@pg_server backup]$
[postgres@pg_server backup]$ psql -d db1 -f db1_schema1_db1tb1.sql -o db1tb1_restore.log
[postgres@pg_server backup]$
```

Review the log file

```
[postgres@pg_server backup]$ cat db1tb1_restore.log
SET
SET
SET
SET
SET
 set_config
------------

(1 row)

SET
SET
SET
SET
SET
SET
CREATE TABLE
ALTER TABLE
COPY 18
CREATE INDEX
```

CHAPTER 5 POSTGRESQL BACKUP AND RECOVERY

```
GRANT
GRANT
[postgres@pg_server backup]$
```

Let us now validate to ensure the table has been successfully restored.

```
[postgres@pg_server backup]$ psql -d db1
psql (16.3)
Type "help" for help.

db1=#
db1=# \dt db1_schema1.db1tb1
            List of relations
   Schema    | Name   | Type  | Owner
-------------+--------+-------+----------
 db1_schema1 | db1tb1 | table | postgres
(1 row)

db1=# select count(*) from db1_schema1.db1tb1;
 count
-------
    18
(1 row)

db1=# select * from db1_schema1.db1tb1;
 name | id
------+-----
 db1a | 100
 db1b | 200
 db1c | 300
 db1d | 400
 db1e | 500
 db1f | 600
 db1g | 700
 db1h | 800
 db1i | 900
 db1a | 100
 db1b | 200
```

```
db1c  |  300
db1d  |  400
db1e  |  500
db1f  |  600
db1g  |  700
db1h  |  800
db1i  |  900
(18 rows)

db1=#
```

As you can see, the table *db1_schema1.db1tb1* has been successfully restored from the backup taken earlier. This scenario is quite frequently encountered, where you will see several requests to restore a single table due to data corruption, accidental deletes, etc. Hence, it is very important to backup critical tables that are required for business operations separately outside of the standard backups to recover from failure faster.

Scenario 2: Backup and Restore a Table Structure Without the Data

To backup a table structure without the data, we use *pg_dump* with option *-s* to export the metadata of the database object.

For example, in our test case below, we are taking an export of the table structure for the table *db1tb1* that is under the schema *db1_schema1* in database *db1*.

```
[postgres@pg_server backup]$ pg_dump -d db1 -t db1_schema1.db1tb1 -s -f db1_schema1_db1tb1_structure.sql
[postgres@pg_server backup]$
[postgres@pg_server backup]$ ls -lrt db1_schema1_db1tb1_structure.sql
-rw-rw-r--. 1 postgres postgres 1142 May 30 23:54 db1_schema1_db1tb1_structure.sql
[postgres@pg_server backup]$
```

In the command above, all of the table structure is stored in the *db1_schema1_db1tb1_structure.sql* file. Let us examine the output file to confirm that the table structure has been exported successfully.

CHAPTER 5　POSTGRESQL BACKUP AND RECOVERY

```
[postgres@pg_server backup]$ cat db1_schema1_db1tb1_structure.sql
--
-- PostgreSQL database dump
--

-- Dumped from database version 16.3
-- Dumped by pg_dump version 16.3

SET statement_timeout = 0;
SET lock_timeout = 0;
SET idle_in_transaction_session_timeout = 0;
SET client_encoding = 'UTF8';
SET standard_conforming_strings = on;
SELECT pg_catalog.set_config('search_path', '', false);
SET check_function_bodies = false;
SET xmloption = content;
SET client_min_messages = warning;
SET row_security = off;

SET default_tablespace = '';

SET default_table_access_method = heap;

--
-- Name: db1tb1; Type: TABLE; Schema: db1_schema1; Owner: postgres
--

CREATE TABLE db1_schema1.db1tb1 (
    name character varying,
    id integer
);

ALTER TABLE db1_schema1.db1tb1 OWNER TO postgres;

--
-- Name: db1_unq_idx; Type: INDEX; Schema: db1_schema1; Owner: postgres
--

CREATE INDEX db1_unq_idx ON db1_schema1.db1tb1 USING btree (name);
```

```
--
-- Name: TABLE db1tb1; Type: ACL; Schema: db1_schema1; Owner: postgres
--

GRANT SELECT,INSERT,DELETE,UPDATE ON TABLE db1_schema1.db1tb1 TO db_user4;
GRANT SELECT,INSERT,DELETE,UPDATE ON TABLE db1_schema1.db1tb1 TO user1;

--
-- PostgreSQL database dump complete
--
[postgres@pg_server backup]$
```

To simulate a restore scenario, let us drop the table and try to restore it using the above backup. Please note that this just restores the table structure but not the data. To restore the data, you will need to use a backup file that also contains data from the table.

```
[postgres@pg_server backup]$ psql -d db1
psql (16.3)
Type "help" for help.

db1=#
db1=# select count(*) from db1_schema1.db1tb1;
 count
-------
    18
(1 row)

db1=# drop table db1_schema1.db1tb1;       <<<<<< DROP TABLE
DROP TABLE
db1=#
db1=# exit
```

Now, let us restore the table using the option *-f* and the *psql* command. In the command below:

> *-d: database name*
>
> *-f: backup file*
>
> *-o: restore log file*

CHAPTER 5   POSTGRESQL BACKUP AND RECOVERY

```
[postgres@pg_server backup]$ psql -d db1 -f db1_schema1_db1tb1_structure.sql -o db1tb1_structure_restore.log
[postgres@pg_server backup]$
[postgres@pg_server backup]$ cat db1tb1_structure_restore.log
SET
SET
SET
SET
SET
 set_config
------------

(1 row)

SET
SET
SET
SET
SET
SET
CREATE TABLE
ALTER TABLE
CREATE INDEX
GRANT
GRANT
[postgres@pg_server backup]$
[postgres@pg_server backup]$ psql -d db1
psql (16.3)
Type "help" for help.

db1=#
db1=# \dt db1_schema1.db1tb1
           List of relations
   Schema    |  Name  | Type  |  Owner
-------------+--------+-------+----------
 db1_schema1 | db1tb1 | table | postgres
(1 row)
```

252

CHAPTER 5   POSTGRESQL BACKUP AND RECOVERY

```
db1=#
db1=# select count(*) from db1_schema1.db1tb1;
 count
-------
     0
(1 row)

db1=#
```

Pro tip   Always ensure separate table backups, especially those critical for business operations, along with metadata, are scheduled daily to ensure data consistency in recovery.

Scenario 3: Backup and Restore the Table Data Without the Structure

In this scenario, we will do the following:

- Restore the *db1_schema1.db1tb1* table with data to ensure the environment is set up the way we wanted it to be.

- Backup the table with *-a* option to take the table data backup only without the structure.

- To fully recover the table, please note it is a two-step process.

  - First, restore the table structure using the appropriate backup file (*db1_schema1_db1tb1_structure.sql*).

  - Second, restore the table data using the appropriate backup file (*db1_schema1_db1tb1_data.sql*).

As a first step, let us restore the *db1_schema.db1tb1* table.

```
[postgres@pg_server backup]$ psql -d db1 -f db1_schema1_db1tb1.sql -o db1tb1_restore1.log
[postgres@pg_server backup]$
[postgres@pg_server backup]$ psql -d db1
```

253

CHAPTER 5   POSTGRESQL BACKUP AND RECOVERY

```
psql (16.3)
Type "help" for help.

db1=#
db1=# select count(*) from db1_schema1.db1tb1;
 count
-------
    18
(1 row)

db1=#
```

As a next step, take the table data backup using option *-a*.

```
[postgres@pg_server backup]$ pg_dump -d db1 -t db1_schema1.db1tb1 -a -f db1_schema1_db1tb1_data.sql -v
[postgres@pg_server backup]$
[postgres@pg_server backup]$ ls -lrt *sql
-rw-rw-r--. 1 postgres postgres 1444 May 30 23:38 db1_schema1_db1tb1.sql
-rw-rw-r--. 1 postgres postgres 1142 May 30 23:54 db1_schema1_db1tb1_structure.sql
-rw-rw-r--. 1 postgres postgres  930 May 31 00:04 db1_schema1_db1tb1_data.sql
[postgres@pg_server backup]$
```

To fully recover the table, let us follow the two-step process we learned earlier. First, use the *db1_schema1_db1tb1_structure.sql* to restore the table metadata and then use the *db1_schema1_db1tb1_data.sql* to import the data into it.

For the recovery scenario, let us drop the table *db1_schema1.db1tb1* from the db1 database.

```
[postgres@pg_server backup]$ psql -d db1
psql (16.3)
Type "help" for help.

db1=#
db1=# select count(*) from db1_schema1.db1tb1;
```

```
    count
-------
       18
(1 row)

db1=#
db1=# drop table db1_schema1.db1tb1;
DROP TABLE
db1=#
db1=# \dt db1_schema1.db1tb1
Did not find any relation named "db1_schema1.db1tb1".
db1=#
db1=# exit
```

Restore the table structure using the corresponding backup file.

```
[postgres@pg_server backup]$ psql -d db1 -f db1_schema1_db1tb1_structure.sql
SET
SET
SET
SET
SET
 set_config
------------

(1 row)

SET
SET
SET
SET
SET
SET
CREATE TABLE
ALTER TABLE
CREATE INDEX
GRANT
GRANT
```

CHAPTER 5   POSTGRESQL BACKUP AND RECOVERY

```
[postgres@pg_server backup]$
[postgres@pg_server backup]$
[postgres@pg_server backup]$ psql -d db1
psql (16.3)
Type "help" for help.

db1=#
db1=# \dt db1_schema1.db1tb1
            List of relations
   Schema    |  Name  | Type  |  Owner
-------------+--------+-------+----------
 db1_schema1 | db1tb1 | table | postgres
(1 row)

db1=#
db1=# select count(*) from db1_schema1.db1tb1;     <<<<< No data yet
 count
-------
     0
(1 row)

db1=#
```

Now, let us restore the table data using the corresponding backup file.

```
[postgres@pg_server backup]$ psql -d db1 -f db1_schema1_db1tb1_data.sql
SET
SET
SET
SET
SET
 set_config
------------

(1 row)

SET
SET
SET
```

CHAPTER 5   POSTGRESQL BACKUP AND RECOVERY

```
SET
COPY 18
[postgres@pg_server backup]$
```

This time, you can see the data as well.
```
[postgres@pg_server backup]$ psql -d db1
psql (16.3)
Type "help" for help.

db1=#
db1=# select count(*) from db1_schema1.db1tb1;
 count
-------
    18
(1 row)

db1=#
```

Scenario 4: Backup and Restore Multiple Tables at a Time

In this scenario, we will backup multiple tables – *db1_schema1.db1tb1*, *db1_schema1. db1new*, and *db1_schema1.all_test* – at the same time using the *pg_dump* utility.

First, let us observe the schema structure to list all the tables within the schema *db1_schema1*.

```
[postgres@pg_server ~]$ psql -d db1
psql (16.3)
Type "help" for help.

db1=#
db1=# \dt db1_schema1.*
            List of relations
   Schema    |   Name   | Type  |  Owner
-------------+----------+-------+----------
 db1_schema1 | all_test | table | postgres     <<< table included in backup
 db1_schema1 | db1new   | table | postgres     <<< table included in backup
 db1_schema1 | db1tb1   | table | postgres     <<< table included in backup
```

CHAPTER 5   POSTGRESQL BACKUP AND RECOVERY

```
 db1_schema1 | new_test | table | postgres
 db1_schema1 | test1    | table | user1
 db1_schema1 | test2    | table | postgres
 db1_schema1 | test3    | table | postgres
(7 rows)

db1=#
```

Now, let us export all the tables highlighted above using the *pg_dump* utility.

[postgres@pg_server backup]$ **pg_dump -d db1 -t db1_schema1.db1tb1 -t db1_schema1.db1new -t db1_schema1.all_test -f db1_schema1_multitab.sql**
[postgres@pg_server backup]$

Let us examine the backup file *db1_schema1_multitab.sql* to verify if it backed up all three tables: *db1_schema1.db1tb1*, *db1_schema1.db1new*, and *db1_schema1.all_test*.

[postgres@pg_server backup]$ **cat db1_schema1_multitab.sql**
--
-- PostgreSQL database dump
--

-- Dumped from database version 16.3
-- Dumped by pg_dump version 16.3

-- **Name: all_test; Type: TABLE; Schema: db1_schema1; Owner: postgres** <<<
--

CREATE TABLE db1_schema1.all_test (
    a integer,
    b text,
    c date
);

ALTER TABLE db1_schema1.all_test OWNER TO postgres;

--
-- **Name: db1new; Type: TABLE; Schema: db1_schema1; Owner: postgres** <<<
--

```
CREATE TABLE db1_schema1.db1new (
    a text,
    b integer
);

ALTER TABLE db1_schema1.db1new OWNER TO postgres;

--
-- Name: db1tb1; Type: TABLE; Schema: db1_schema1; Owner: postgres <<<
--

CREATE TABLE db1_schema1.db1tb1 (
    name character varying,
    id integer
);

ALTER TABLE db1_schema1.db1tb1 OWNER TO postgres;

--
-- Data for Name: all_test; Type: TABLE DATA; Schema: db1_schema1; Owner: postgres
--
```

Please note that multi-table backup has a downside. For example, if you would like to restore just one table out of all the three tables included in the backup file, you will not be able to, as the *psql* utility does not support it at this point. We can only perform a complete restore of all the tables included in the backup at once.

The other point to note is the truncating of data. When we restore the tables using the *psql* utility, it will not truncate the existing data; instead, it will append the data. So we must ensure the data is truncated within the table before restoring it.

For example, you can follow the below sequence of steps to perform a restore from a multi-table backup.

>> Login to *db1* database

```
[postgres@pg_server backup]$ psql -d db1
psql (16.3)
Type "help" for help.
```

CHAPTER 5   POSTGRESQL BACKUP AND RECOVERY

db1=#

>> Get the row count from each of the tables for validation post restore

db1=# **select count(*) from db1_schema1.db1tb1;**
 count

    18
(1 row)

db1=# **select count(*) from db1_schema1.db1new;**
 count

    18
(1 row)

db1=# **select count(*) from db1_schema1.all_test;**
  count

 1000002
(1 row)

>>> Truncate all the tables

```
db1=# truncate table db1_schema1.db1tb1;
TRUNCATE TABLE
db1=#
db1=# truncate table db1_schema1.db1new;
TRUNCATE TABLE
db1=#
db1=# truncate table db1_schema1.all_test;
TRUNCATE TABLE
db1=#
```

>>> Verify all the tables are truncated successfully

db1=# select count(*) from db1_schema1.db1tb1;

CHAPTER 5 POSTGRESQL BACKUP AND RECOVERY

```
 count
-------
     0
(1 row)

db1=# select count(*) from db1_schema1.db1new;
 count
-------
     0
(1 row)

db1=# select count(*) from db1_schema1.all_test;
 count
-------
     0
(1 row)

db1=#
db1=# exit
```

>>> Verify backup location

```
[postgres@pg_server backup]$ ls -lrt db1_schema1_multitab.sql
total 48436
-rw-rw-r--. 1 postgres postgres 24780417 May 31 07:21 db1_schema1_multitab.sql
[postgres@pg_server backup]$
```

>>> Restore from the backup

```
[postgres@pg_server backup]$ psql -d db1 -f db1_schema1_multitab.sql
SET
SET
SET
SET
SET
 set_config
------------

(1 row)
```

SET
SET
SET
SET
SET
SET
psql:db1_schema1_multitab.sql:31: ERROR: relation "all_test" already exists
ALTER TABLE
psql:db1_schema1_multitab.sql:43: ERROR: relation "db1new" already exists
ALTER TABLE
psql:db1_schema1_multitab.sql:55: ERROR: relation "db1tb1" already exists
ALTER TABLE
COPY 1000002
COPY 18
COPY 18
psql:db1_schema1_multitab.sql:1000126: ERROR: relation "db1_unq_idx" already exists
GRANT
GRANT
GRANT
GRANT
[postgres@pg_server backup]$

>>> **Login to the database and validate**

```
[postgres@pg_server backup]$ psql -d db1
psql (16.3)
Type "help" for help.

db1=#
db1=# select count(*) from db1_schema1.db1tb1;
 count
-------
    18
(1 row)
```

```
db1=# select count(*) from db1_schema1.db1new;
 count
-------
    18
(1 row)

db1=# select count(*) from db1_schema1.all_test;
  count
---------
 1000002
(1 row)

db1=#
```

Please note the errors above are because the metadata or the structure of those tables still exists and can be safely ignored.

Scenario 5: Backup and Restore a Table in Custom Format

In this scenario, we will backup the table *db1_schema1.db1tb1* using the *pg_dump* utility in *binary* format.

Here is the command we issue to take a backup of a table in binary format.

```
[postgres@pg_server backup]$ pg_dump -Fc -d db1 -t db1_schema1.db1tb1 -f db1_schema1_db1tb1.bin -v 2> db1_schema1_db1tb1_bin.log
[postgres@pg_server backup]$
[postgres@pg_server backup]$ ls -lrt db1_schema1_db1tb1.bin db1_schema1_db1tb1_bin.log
-rw-rw-r--. 1 postgres postgres 1954 May 31 08:46 db1_schema1_db1tb1_bin.log
-rw-rw-r--. 1 postgres postgres 1875 May 31 08:46 db1_schema1_db1tb1.bin
[postgres@pg_server backup]$
[postgres@pg_server backup]$ file db1_schema1_db1tb1.bin
db1_schema1_db1tb1.bin: PostgreSQL custom database dump - v1.15-0
[postgres@pg_server backup]$
```

CHAPTER 5   POSTGRESQL BACKUP AND RECOVERY

In the above command:

-F: Format

c: Custom

-v: Output in verbose

2: Verbose redirected to log

db1_schema1_db1tb1.bin: Name of the file with *.bin* extension

db1_schema1_db1tb1_bin.log: Name of the log file

You will also notice in the above command output, we can verify if the backup is taken in a custom format using the *file* command.

Now, let us create a recovery scenario by dropping the table *db1_schema1.db1tb1* so we can restore the table from the custom binary format backup file.

```
[postgres@pg_server backup]$ psql -d db1
psql (16.3)
Type "help" for help.

db1=#
db1=# select count(*) from db1_schema1.db1tb1;
 count
-------
    18
(1 row)

db1=# drop table db1_schema1.db1tb1;
DROP TABLE
db1=#
```

To restore the table from the backup, let us issue a *pg_restore* command like below:

```
[postgres@pg_server backup]$ pg_restore -Fc -d db1 -n db1_schema1 -t db1tb1
-c db1_schema1_db1tb1.bin -v 2> db1_schema1_db1tb1_bin_restore.log
[postgres@pg_server backup]$
```

Check the output of the log file.

```
[postgres@pg_server backup]$ cat db1_schema1_db1tb1_bin_restore.log
pg_restore: connecting to database for restore
pg_restore: dropping TABLE db1tb1
pg_restore: while PROCESSING TOC:
```

```
pg_restore: from TOC entry 231; 1259 41108 TABLE db1tb1 postgres
pg_restore: error: could not execute query: ERROR:  table "db1tb1" does
not exist
Command was: DROP TABLE db1_schema1.db1tb1;
pg_restore: creating TABLE "db1_schema1.db1tb1"
pg_restore: processing data for table "db1_schema1.db1tb1"
pg_restore: creating ACL "db1_schema1.TABLE db1tb1"
pg_restore: warning: errors ignored on restore: 1
[postgres@pg_server backup]$
```

Validation of the table:

```
[postgres@pg_server backup]$ psql -d db1
psql (16.3)
Type "help" for help.

db1=#
db1=# select count(*) from db1_schema1.db1tb1;
 count
-------
    18
(1 row)

db1=#
```

Scenario 5a: Backup and Restore a Table Using *pg_dump* in *tar* Format

In this scenario, let us take an export of the table *db1_schema1.db1tb1* using *pg_dump*.

```
[postgres@pg_server backup]$ pg_dump -Ft -d db1 -t db1_schema1.db1tb1 -f
db1_schema1_db1tb1.tar -v 2> db1_schema1_db1tb1_tar.log
[postgres@pg_server backup]$
[postgres@pg_server backup]$ ls -lrt *tar*
-rw-rw-r--. 1 postgres postgres 2210 May 31 09:00 db1_schema1_
db1tb1_tar.log
-rw-rw-r--. 1 postgres postgres 6656 May 31 09:00 db1_schema1_db1tb1.tar
[postgres@pg_server backup]$
```

CHAPTER 5 POSTGRESQL BACKUP AND RECOVERY

In the above command:

-Ft: Format

-d: Database_name

-f: File_name

c: Custom

-v: Output in verbose

2: Verbose redirected to log

db1_schema1_db1tb1.tar: Name of the file with *.tar* extension

db1_schema1_db1tb1_tar.log: Name of the log file

To restore the table from the dump, we use the option "*-c*" to clean up the table before performing the restore.

```
[postgres@pg_server backup]$ pg_restore -Ft -d db1 -t db1_schema1.db1tb1 -c db1_schema1_db1tb1.tar -v 2> db1_schema1_db1tb1_tar.log
[postgres@pg_server backup]$
```

To validate:

```
[postgres@pg_server backup]$ psql -d db1
psql (16.3)
Type "help" for help.

db1=#
db1=# select count(*) from db1_schema1.db1tb1;
 count
-------
    18
(1 row)

db1=#
```

Scenario 5b: Backup and Restore a Table Using *pg_dump* in *dir* Format

In this scenario, let us take an export of the table *db1_schema1.tb1* in *dir* format using *pg_dump*.

```
[postgres@pg_server backup]$
[postgres@pg_server backup]$ pg_dump -Fd -d db1 -t db1_schema1.db1tb1 -f
db1_schema1_db1tb1_dir -v 2> db1_schema1_db1tb1_dir.log
[postgres@pg_server backup]$
[postgres@pg_server backup]$ ls -ld db1_schema1_db1tb1_dir
drwx------. 2 postgres postgres 40 May 31 16:51 db1_schema1_db1tb1_dir
[postgres@pg_server backup]$
```

In the above command:

-Fd: dir format

-d: Database_name

-t: Table_name

-f: File_name

-v: Output in verbose

2: Verbose redirected to log

db1_schema1_db1tb1_dir: Name of the export backup file

db1_schema1_db1tb1_dir.log: Name of the log file

To simulate a recovery scenario, let us drop or truncate the table *db1_schema1_db1tb1* and restore the table.

```
[postgres@pg_server backup]$ psql -d db1
psql (16.3)
Type "help" for help.

db1=#
db1=# truncate table db1_schema1.db1tb1;  <<< truncating the table
TRUNCATE TABLE
db1=#
db1=# select count(*) from db1_schema1.db1tb1;  <<< validation
 count
-------
     0
(1 row)

db1=#
db1=# exit
```

Now, let us perform a restore using the *pg_restore* command.

```
[postgres@pg_server backup]$ pg_restore -Fd -d db1 -n db1_schema1 -t db1tb1
db1_schema1_db1tb1_dir -c -v 2> db1_schema1_db1tb1_dir_restore.log
[postgres@pg_server backup]$
[postgres@pg_server backup]$ psql -d db1
psql (16.3)
Type "help" for help.

db1=#
db1=# select count(*) from db1_schema1.db1tb1;
 count
-------
    18
(1 row)

db1=#
```

Scenario 6: Backup Multiple Tables and Restore One Table in Custom Format

In this scenario, let us backup multiple tables within the *db1_schema1* schema. To export the tables, we use *pg_dump* to initiate the export in *dir* format, which we use as the custom format in this scenario.

```
db1=# \dt db1_schema1.*            <<< To list the tables in db1_schema1
            List of relations
   Schema    |   Name   | Type  |  Owner
-------------+----------+-------+----------
 db1_schema1 | all_test | table | postgres
 db1_schema1 | db1new   | table | postgres
 db1_schema1 | db1tb1   | table | postgres
 db1_schema1 | new_test | table | postgres
 db1_schema1 | test1    | table | user1
 db1_schema1 | test2    | table | postgres
 db1_schema1 | test3    | table | postgres
```

(7 rows)
db1=# exit

>>> Backup the tables using *pg_dump*

[postgres@pg_server backup]$ **pg_dump -Fd -d db1 -t db1_schema1.db1tb1 -t db1_schema1.test1 -f db1_schema1_multitable -v 2> db1_schema1_multitable.log**
[postgres@pg_server backup]$
[postgres@pg_server backup]$ **ls -ld db1_schema1_multitable**
drwx------. 2 postgres postgres 59 May 31 16:44 db1_schema1_multitable
[postgres@pg_server backup]$
[postgres@pg_server backup]$ **ls -lrt db1_schema1_multitable**
total 4844
-rw-rw-r--. 1 postgres postgres   2395 May 31 16:44 **toc.dat**
-rw-rw-r--. 1 postgres postgres   77 May 31 16:44 **4319.dat.gz**
-rw-rw-r--. 1 postgres postgres 4950354 May 31 16:44 **4318.dat.gz**
[postgres@pg_server backup]$

Please note as we learned earlier, *pg_restore* provides us the flexibility to restore one single table from the backup unlike *psql*.

To create a recovery scenario, let us drop a single table *db1_schema1.db1tb1* and import from the above backup file.

To drop the table, perform the below steps:

[postgres@pg_server backup]$ **psql -d db1**
psql (16.3)
Type "help" for help.

db1=#
db1=# **drop table db1_schema1.db1tb1;**
DROP TABLE
db1=#
db1=# **\dt db1_schema1.db1tb1**
Did not find any relation named "db1_schema1.db1tb1".
db1=# exit

Restore the single table *db1_schema1.db1tb1* from the multi-table backup taken earlier. To restore, perform the steps below:

```
[postgres@pg_server backup]$ pg_restore -Fd -d db1 -n db1_schema1 -t db1tb1
db1_schema1_multitable -c -v 2> db1_schema1_multitable_restore.log
[postgres@pg_server backup]$
[postgres@pg_server backup]$ psql -d db1
psql (16.3)
Type "help" for help.

db1=#
db1=# \dt db1_schema1.db1tb1
          List of relations
   Schema    |  Name  | Type  |  Owner
-------------+--------+-------+----------
 db1_schema1 | db1tb1 | table | postgres
(1 row)

db1=# select count(*) from db1_schema1.db1tb1;
 count
-------
    18
(1 row)

db1=#
```

Scenario 7: Backup and Restore a Schema Within a Database

In this scenario, let us take a backup of the schema *db1_schema1* using *pg_dump*. To take the backup of the schema, let us issue the command below:

```
[postgres@pg_server backup]$ pg_dump -Fd -d db1 -n db1_schema1 -f db1_
schema1_bkp -v 2> db1_schema1_bkp.log
[postgres@pg_server backup]$
[postgres@pg_server backup]$ ls -ld db1_schema1_bkp
drwx------. 2 postgres postgres 154 May 31 17:03 db1_schema1_bkp
[postgres@pg_server backup]$
```

CHAPTER 5 POSTGRESQL BACKUP AND RECOVERY

```
[postgres@pg_server backup]$ ls -lrt db1_schema1_bkp
total 24196
-rw-rw-r--. 1 postgres postgres    5812 May 31 17:03 toc.dat
-rw-rw-r--. 1 postgres postgres      77 May 31 17:03 4329.dat.gz
-rw-rw-r--. 1 postgres postgres 4950354 May 31 17:03 4328.dat.gz
-rw-rw-r--. 1 postgres postgres      77 May 31 17:03 4330.dat.gz
-rw-rw-r--. 1 postgres postgres 4950354 May 31 17:03 4327.dat.gz
-rw-rw-r--. 1 postgres postgres 4950354 May 31 17:03 4324.dat.gz
-rw-rw-r--. 1 postgres postgres 4950354 May 31 17:03 4325.dat.gz
-rw-rw-r--. 1 postgres postgres 4950354 May 31 17:03 4326.dat.gz
[postgres@pg_server backup]$
```

-Fd: Output file format directory

-f: Output file or directory name

db1_schema1_bkp: Name of the backup file

To create a recovery scenario, let us drop the schema *db1_schema1* in database *db1*.

```
[postgres@pg_server backup]$ psql -d db1
psql (16.3)
Type "help" for help.

db1=#
db1=# drop schema db1_schema1 cascade;
NOTICE:  drop cascades to 7 other objects
DETAIL:  drop cascades to table db1_schema1.test1
drop cascades to table db1_schema1.test2
drop cascades to table db1_schema1.test3
drop cascades to table db1_schema1.new_test
drop cascades to table db1_schema1.all_test
drop cascades to table db1_schema1.db1new
drop cascades to table db1_schema1.db1tb1
DROP SCHEMA
db1=#
db1=# \dn db1_schema1
List of schemas
```

```
 Name | Owner
------+-------
(0 rows)

db1=#
```

To perform a restore, let us use *pg_restore* to recover the dropped schema *db1_schema1* from the backup file *db1_schema1_bkp*. *pg_restore* will drop the objects, creates the objects, and then loads the data. Let us verify the log file after restore to confirm the same as shown below.

[postgres@pg_server backup]$ **pg_restore -Fd -d db1 db1_schema1_bkp -v 2> db1_schema1_bkp_restore.log**
[postgres@pg_server backup]$

>>>> Check the log file

```
[postgres@pg_server backup]$ cat db1_schema1_bkp_restore.log
pg_restore: connecting to database for restore
pg_restore: creating SCHEMA "db1_schema1"
pg_restore: creating TABLE "db1_schema1.all_test"
pg_restore: creating TABLE "db1_schema1.db1new"
pg_restore: creating TABLE "db1_schema1.db1tb1"
pg_restore: creating TABLE "db1_schema1.new_test"
pg_restore: creating TABLE "db1_schema1.test1"
pg_restore: creating TABLE "db1_schema1.test2"
pg_restore: creating TABLE "db1_schema1.test3"
pg_restore: processing data for table "db1_schema1.all_test"
pg_restore: processing data for table "db1_schema1.db1new"
pg_restore: processing data for table "db1_schema1.db1tb1"
pg_restore: processing data for table "db1_schema1.new_test"
pg_restore: processing data for table "db1_schema1.test1"
pg_restore: processing data for table "db1_schema1.test2"
pg_restore: processing data for table "db1_schema1.test3"
pg_restore: creating ACL "SCHEMA db1_schema1"
pg_restore: creating ACL "db1_schema1.TABLE all_test"
pg_restore: creating ACL "db1_schema1.TABLE db1new"
```

CHAPTER 5   POSTGRESQL BACKUP AND RECOVERY

```
pg_restore: creating ACL "db1_schema1.TABLE db1tb1"
pg_restore: creating ACL "db1_schema1.TABLE test1"
pg_restore: creating ACL "db1_schema1.TABLE test2"
pg_restore: creating ACL "db1_schema1.TABLE test3"
pg_restore: creating DEFAULT ACL "db1_schema1.DEFAULT PRIVILEGES
FOR TABLES"
[postgres@pg_server backup]$
```

Let us log in to the database and validate to confirm if the schema and its objects have been successfully restored like below.

```
[postgres@pg_server backup]$ psql -d db1
psql (16.3)
Type "help" for help.

db1=#
db1=# \dn db1_schema1
    List of schemas
    Name     | Owner
-------------+-------
 db1_schema1 | user1
(1 row)

db1=# \dt db1_schema1.*
            List of relations
   Schema    |   Name   | Type  |  Owner
-------------+----------+-------+----------
 db1_schema1 | all_test | table | postgres
 db1_schema1 | db1new   | table | postgres
 db1_schema1 | db1tb1   | table | postgres
 db1_schema1 | new_test | table | postgres
 db1_schema1 | test1    | table | user1
 db1_schema1 | test2    | table | postgres
 db1_schema1 | test3    | table | postgres
(7 rows)

db1=# exit
[postgres@pg_server backup]$
```

273

Scenario 8: Backup Multiple Schemas and Restore a Single Schema Within a Database

In this scenario, we will backup multiple schemas *db1_schema1* and *db2_schema2* within the *db1* database and then restore *db2_schema2* from the backup.

To begin with, let us examine schemas *db1_schema1* and *db2_schema2* along with their objects so we can compare when we restore later.

```
[postgres@pg_server backup]$ psql -d db1
psql (16.3)
Type "help" for help.

db1=#
db1=# \dn
        List of schemas
    Name     |       Owner
-------------+--------------------
 db1_schema1 | user1
 db1_schema2 | user2
 public      | pg_database_owner
(3 rows)

db1=#
db1=# \dt db1_schema1.*
              List of relations
   Schema    |   Name   | Type  |  Owner
-------------+----------+-------+----------
 db1_schema1 | all_test | table | postgres
 db1_schema1 | db1new   | table | postgres
 db1_schema1 | db1tb1   | table | postgres
 db1_schema1 | new_test | table | postgres
 db1_schema1 | test1    | table | user1
 db1_schema1 | test2    | table | postgres
 db1_schema1 | test3    | table | postgres
(7 rows)

db1=#
```

```
db1=# \dt db1_schema2.*
            List of relations
   Schema    |    Name    | Type  |  Owner
-------------+------------+-------+----------
 db1_schema2 | index_test | table | postgres
 db1_schema2 | test2      | table | user2
 db1_schema2 | ts1        | table | postgres
 db1_schema2 | ts2        | table | postgres
(4 rows)

db1=#
```

>>> Get row counts to validate restore later

```
db1=# select count(*) from db1_schema2.index_test;
  count
----------
 20000000
(1 row)

db1=# select count(*) from db1_schema2.test2;
  count
---------
 1000001
(1 row)

db1=# select count(*) from db1_schema2.ts1;
 count
-------
     1
(1 row)

db1=# select count(*) from db1_schema2.ts2;
 count
-------
     0
(1 row)

db1=#
```

CHAPTER 5   POSTGRESQL BACKUP AND RECOVERY

Let us use *pg_dump* to backup schemas *db1_schema1* and *db2_schema2*.

```
[postgres@pg_server backup]$ pg_dump -Fd -d db1 -n db1_schema1 -n db1_schema2 -f db1_schema1_schema2_bkp -v 2> db1_schema1_schema2_bkp.log
[postgres@pg_server backup]$
[postgres@pg_server backup]$ ls -ld db1_schema1_schema2_bkp
drwx------. 2 postgres postgres 4096 May 31 17:18 db1_schema1_schema2_bkp
[postgres@pg_server backup]$
[postgres@pg_server backup]$ ls -lrt db1_schema1_schema2_bkp
total 49664
-rw-rw-r--. 1 postgres postgres     7894 May 31 17:17 toc.dat
-rw-rw-r--. 1 postgres postgres  4950354 May 31 17:17 4333.dat.gz
-rw-rw-r--. 1 postgres postgres       77 May 31 17:17 4334.dat.gz
-rw-rw-r--. 1 postgres postgres       77 May 31 17:17 4335.dat.gz
-rw-rw-r--. 1 postgres postgres  4950354 May 31 17:18 4336.dat.gz
-rw-rw-r--. 1 postgres postgres  4950354 May 31 17:18 4337.dat.gz
-rw-rw-r--. 1 postgres postgres  4950354 May 31 17:18 4338.dat.gz
-rw-rw-r--. 1 postgres postgres  4950354 May 31 17:18 4339.dat.gz
-rw-rw-r--. 1 postgres postgres 21116464 May 31 17:18 4330.dat.gz
-rw-rw-r--. 1 postgres postgres  4950341 May 31 17:18 4329.dat.gz
-rw-rw-r--. 1 postgres postgres       27 May 31 17:18 4331.dat.gz
-rw-rw-r--. 1 postgres postgres       25 May 31 17:18 4332.dat.gz
[postgres@pg_server backup]$
```

To create a recovery scenario to restore *db2_schema2*, let us truncate data from all the tables within *db2_schema2* and then perform a restore.

```
db1=# \dt db1_schema2.*
            List of relations
   Schema    |    Name    | Type  |  Owner
-------------+------------+-------+----------
 db1_schema2 | index_test | table | postgres
 db1_schema2 | test2      | table | user2
 db1_schema2 | ts1        | table | postgres
 db1_schema2 | ts2        | table | postgres
(4 rows)
```

```
db1=#
db1=#
db1=# truncate table db1_schema2.index_test;
TRUNCATE TABLE
db1=# truncate table db1_schema2.test2;
TRUNCATE TABLE
db1=#
db1=# truncate table db1_schema2.ts1;
TRUNCATE TABLE
db1=# truncate table db1_schema2.ts2;
TRUNCATE TABLE
db1=#
db1=# select count(*) from db1_schema2.index_test;
 count
-------
     0
(1 row)

db1=# select count(*) from db1_schema2.test2;
 count
-------
     0
(1 row)

db1=# select count(*) from db1_schema2.ts1;
 count
-------
     0
(1 row)
db1=# select count(*) from db1_schema2.ts2;
 count
-------
     0
(1 row)

db1=#
```

CHAPTER 5   POSTGRESQL BACKUP AND RECOVERY

To restore all the tables of *db2_schema2* from the backup file, let us issue a *pg_restore* command like below.

```
[postgres@pg_server backup]$ pg_restore -Fd -d db1 -n db1_schema2 db1_schema1_schema2_bkp -v 2> db1_schema2_restore.log
[postgres@pg_server backup]$
[postgres@pg_server backup]$ cat db1_schema2_restore.log
pg_restore: processing data for table "db1_schema2.index_test"
pg_restore: processing data for table "db1_schema2.test2"
pg_restore: processing data for table "db1_schema2.ts1"
pg_restore: processing data for table "db1_schema2.ts2"
pg_restore: creating INDEX "db1_schema2.fragmented_index"
```

Let us examine the schema to validate if the data has been restored successfully by comparing the row counts when we first examined the schemas earlier.

```
[postgres@pg_server backup]$ psql -d db1
psql (16.3)
Type "help" for help.

db1=#
db1=# select count(*) from db1_schema2.index_test;
  count
----------
 20000000
(1 row)

db1=# select count(*) from db1_schema2.test2;
  count
---------
 1000001
(1 row)

db1=# select count(*) from db1_schema2.ts1;
 count
-------
     1
(1 row)
```

```
db1=# select count(*) from db1_schema2.ts2;
 count
-------
     0
(1 row)

db1=#
```

As you can see, the row counts match with earlier, confirming a successful restore of all the tables within the schema *db2_schema2*.

Scenario 9: Backup and Restore an Entire Database

In this scenario, we will backup the entire database *db1* and restore it later.

Before taking the backup, let us examine the database server.

```
[postgres@pg_server backup]$ psql
psql (16.3)
Type "help" for help.

postgres=# \l
                    List of databases
    Name     |  Owner   | Encoding | Locale Provider |  Collate   |
    Ctype    | ICU Locale | ICU Rules |   Access privileges
-------------+----------+----------+-----------------+-------------+
-------------+------------+-----------+------------------------
 db1         | postgres | UTF8     | libc            | en_US.UTF-8 |
 en_US.UTF-8 |            |           |
 db1clone    | postgres | UTF8     | libc            | en_US.UTF-8 |
 en_US.UTF-8 |            |           |
 db2         | postgres | UTF8     | libc            | en_US.UTF-8 |
 en_US.UTF-8 |            |           |
 db3         | postgres | UTF8     | libc            | en_US.UTF-8 |
 en_US.UTF-8 |            |           |
 db4         | postgres | UTF8     | libc            | en_US.UTF-8 |
 en_US.UTF-8 |            |           |
 db5         | postgres | UTF8     | libc            | en_US.UTF-8 |
 en_US.UTF-8 |            |           |
```

```
 newdb     | postgres | UTF8     | libc              | en_US.UTF-8 |
en_US.UTF-8 |                   |                   |
 postgres  | postgres | UTF8     | libc              | en_US.UTF-8 |
en_US.UTF-8 |                   |                   |
 template0 | postgres | UTF8     | libc              | en_US.UTF-8 |
en_US.UTF-8 |                   | =c/postgres                    +
           |          |          |                   |
           |          |          | postgres=CTc/postgres
 template1 | postgres | UTF8     | libc              | en_US.UTF-8 |
en_US.UTF-8 |                   | =c/postgres                    +
           |          |          |                   |
           |          |          | postgres=CTc/postgres
(10 rows)

postgres=#
[postgres@pg_server backup]$ psql -d db1
psql (16.3)
Type "help" for help.

db1=#
db1=# \dn
         List of schemas
    Name     |       Owner
-------------+-------------------
 db1_schema1 | user1
 db1_schema2 | user2
 public      | pg_database_owner
(3 rows)

db1=#
```

To take the backup of the database, issue the command like below:

```
[postgres@pg_server backup]$ pg_dump -Ft -d db1 -f db1_backup.tar -v 2>
db1_backup_tar.log
[postgres@pg_server backup]$
[postgres@pg_server backup]$ ls -lrt *db1_backup*
-rw-rw-r--. 1 postgres postgres      4497 May 31 22:53 db1_backup_tar.log
```

CHAPTER 5   POSTGRESQL BACKUP AND RECOVERY

```
-rw-rw-r--. 1 postgres postgres 248696832 May 31 22:53 db1_backup.tar
[postgres@pg_server backup]$
```

The backup *db1_backup.tar* includes schemas *db1_schema1* and *db2_schema2* only. Now, let us create another schema, *db1_schema3*, after the backup is taken.

```
[postgres@pg_server backup]$ psql -d db1
psql (16.3)
Type "help" for help.

db1=#
db1=# create schema db1_schema3;
CREATE SCHEMA
db1=#
db1=# \dn
       List of schemas
    Name     |       Owner
-------------+-------------------
 db1_schema1 | user1
 db1_schema2 | user2
 db1_schema3 | postgres
 public      | pg_database_owner
(4 rows)

db1=#
db1=# create table db1_schema3.db1tb3 as select * from db1_schema1.db1tb1;
SELECT 18
db1=#
db1=# \dt db1_schema3.*
            List of relations
   Schema    | Name   | Type  | Owner
-------------+--------+-------+----------
 db1_schema3 | db1tb3 | table | postgres
(1 row)

db1=#
```

281

CHAPTER 5 POSTGRESQL BACKUP AND RECOVERY

To create a recovery scenario, let us now drop the complete database *db1*. Please note that the *db1* database now contains three schemas – *db1_schema1*, *db1_schema2*, and *db1_schema3* – and we did not take another backup upon creating the schema *db1_schema3*.

Now, if we perform a restore using the backup file *db1_backup.tar*, we can only restore *db1_schema1* and *db2_schema2* but not *db1_schema3*. Let us confirm the same.

```
postgres=# drop database db1;
DROP DATABASE
postgres=#

postgres=# \l
                                List of databases
   Name    |  Owner   | Encoding | Locale Provider |   Collate   |
   Ctype   | ICU Locale | ICU Rules |     Access privileges
-----------+----------+----------+-----------------+-------------+
-----------+------------+-----------+----------------------
 |
 db1clone  | postgres | UTF8     | libc            | en_US.UTF-8 |
 en_US.UTF-8 |          |           |
 db2       | postgres | UTF8     | libc            | en_US.UTF-8 |
 en_US.UTF-8 |          |           |
 db3       | postgres | UTF8     | libc            | en_US.UTF-8 |
 en_US.UTF-8 |          |           |
 db4       | postgres | UTF8     | libc            | en_US.UTF-8 |
 en_US.UTF-8 |          |           |
 db5       | postgres | UTF8     | libc            | en_US.UTF-8 |
 en_US.UTF-8 |          |           |
 newdb     | postgres | UTF8     | libc            | en_US.UTF-8 |
 en_US.UTF-8 |          |           |
 postgres  | postgres | UTF8     | libc            | en_US.UTF-8 |
 en_US.UTF-8 |          |           |
 template0 | postgres | UTF8     | libc            | en_US.UTF-8 |
 en_US.UTF-8 |          |           | =c/postgres            +
           |          |          |                 |             |
           |          |          | postgres=CTc/postgres
```

```
 template1 | postgres | UTF8      | libc              | en_US.UTF-8 |
en_US.UTF-8 |          |           | =c/postgres       +
            |          |           |                   |
            |          |           | postgres=CTc/postgres
(9 rows)

postgres=#
```

Let us perform the restore from the backup file *db1_backup.tar*.

```
[postgres@pg_server backup]$ pg_restore -Ft -d db1 -c db1_backup.tar -v 2>
db1_backup_restore.log
[postgres@pg_server backup]$

[postgres@pg_server backup]$ cat db1_backup_restore.log
pg_restore: connecting to database for restore
.
.
pg_restore: creating SCHEMA "db1_schema1"
pg_restore: creating SCHEMA "db1_schema2"
pg_restore: creating TABLE "db1_schema1.all_test"
pg_restore: creating TABLE "db1_schema1.db1new"
pg_restore: creating TABLE "db1_schema1.db1tb1"
.
.
pg_restore: creating TABLE "db1_schema2.test2"
pg_restore: creating TABLE "db1_schema2.ts1"
pg_restore: creating TABLE "db1_schema2.ts2"
pg_restore: processing data for table "db1_schema1.all_test"
pg_restore: processing data for table "db1_schema1.db1new"
.
.
pg_restore: processing data for table "db1_schema2.test2"
pg_restore: processing data for table "db1_schema2.ts1"
pg_restore: processing data for table "db1_schema2.ts2"
.
.
[postgres@pg_server backup]$
```

Now, if we validate, we should only see two schemas, *db1_schema1* and *db1_schema2*, within the *db1* database restored since the backup file does not contain a backup of the schema *db1_schema3*.

```
[postgres@pg_server backup]$ psql -d db1
psql (16.3)
Type "help" for help.

db1=#
db1=# \dn
        List of schemas
    Name     |       Owner
-------------+--------------------
 db1_schema1 | user1
 db1_schema2 | user2
 public      | pg_database_owner
(3 rows)

db1=#
```

Scenario 10: Restore a Backup to a New Database

In this scenario, let us restore the backup of the *db1* database from the earlier scenario and restore it to a new database named *newdb*. In order to do so, let us first create a new database named *newdb*.

```
postgres=# create database newdb;
CREATE DATABASE
postgres=#
postgres-# \c newdb
You are now connected to database "newdb" as user "postgres".
newdb-#
newdb-# \dn
```

```
       List of schemas
  Name   |      Owner
---------+-------------------
 public  | pg_database_owner
(1 row)

newdb-#
```

Now, let us restore the *db1* database using the backup file *db1_backup.tar* taken earlier.

```
[postgres@pg_server backup]$ pg_restore -Ft -d newdb -c db1_backup.tar -v
2> db1_newdb_restore.log
[postgres@pg_server backup]$

[postgres@pg_server backup]$ cat db1_newdb_restore.log
pg_restore: connecting to database for restore
.
pg_restore: creating SCHEMA "db1_schema1"
pg_restore: creating SCHEMA "db1_schema2"
.
.
pg_restore: creating TABLE "db1_schema1.all_test"
pg_restore: creating TABLE "db1_schema1.db1new"
.
.
pg_restore: processing data for table "db1_schema2.ts1"
pg_restore: processing data for table "db1_schema2.ts2".

[postgres@pg_server backup]$
[postgres@pg_server backup]$ psql -d newdb
psql (16.3)
Type "help" for help.

newdb=#
```

CHAPTER 5 POSTGRESQL BACKUP AND RECOVERY

```
newdb=# \dn                          <<<< List the schemas to validate
        List of schemas
    Name     |       Owner
-------------+--------------------
 db1_schema1 | user1
 db1_schema2 | user2
 public      | pg_database_owner
(3 rows)

newdb=#
newdb=# \dt db1_schema1.*
             List of relations
   Schema    |   Name   | Type  |  Owner
-------------+----------+-------+----------
 db1_schema1 | all_test | table | postgres
 db1_schema1 | db1new   | table | postgres
 db1_schema1 | db1tb1   | table | postgres
 db1_schema1 | new_test | table | postgres
 db1_schema1 | test1    | table | user1
 db1_schema1 | test2    | table | postgres
 db1_schema1 | test3    | table | postgres
(7 rows)

newdb=#
newdb=# \dt db1_schema2.*
              List of relations
   Schema    |    Name    | Type  |  Owner
-------------+------------+-------+----------
 db1_schema2 | index_test | table | postgres
 db1_schema2 | test2      | table | user2
 db1_schema2 | ts1        | table | postgres
 db1_schema2 | ts2        | table | postgres
(4 rows)

newdb=#
```

As you can see, schemas *db1_schema1* and *db1_schema2* from the backup file *db1_backup.tar* are successfully restored into the new database, *newdb*, we created.

Scenario 11: Improve Backup Performance with Parallel Jobs

In this scenario, let us see how to improve backup performance using parallel jobs in *pg_dump*. We can run the dump operation parallelly using the option *-j*. Please note while this option improves backup performance, it also increases the load on the database server. So it's important to initiate this operation during a low maintenance window.

In the example, we are taking a backup of the database *db1* in a standard way and then with *two* parallel jobs initiated using the option *-j*. We also use the *date* command to calculate the time it has taken with and without the parallel jobs to indicate there is an improvement.

```
[postgres@pg_server backup]$ date; pg_dump -Fd -d db1 -f db1_backup_up -v 2> db1_backup_up.log; date
Fri May 31 23:35:11 CDT 2024
Fri May 31 23:35:47 CDT 2024
[postgres@pg_server backup]$
[postgres@pg_server backup]$ date; pg_dump -Fd -d db1 -f db1_backup_parallel -j2 -v 2> db1_backup_parallel.log; date
Fri May 31 23:36:52 CDT 2024
Fri May 31 23:37:13 CDT 2024
[postgres@pg_server backup]$
```

In the above example, the standard backup took 36 seconds, and the backup with 2 parallel jobs took 21 seconds, showcasing an improvement in backup performance. As the data set gets huge, you will see a significant performance increase by running parallel jobs.

Scenario 12: Restore a Single Table from a Full Database Backup

In this scenario, we will restore a single table from a full database backup. In order to do so, please note the backup file has to be in *custom (tar, bin, or dir)* format.

To take an export of a database *db1*, issue the command below:

```
[postgres@pg_server backup]$ pg_dump -Ft -d db1 -f db1_bkp.tar -v 2> db1_bkp_tar.log
```

Now, let us restore the *db1_schema1.db1tb1* table using the full database backup from the backup file *db1_bkp.tar*. In the earlier scenarios, we have always created a recovery scenario by dropping the table prior to the restore operation. So what if we don't drop the table prior to the restore? The operation errors out saying the table *db1tb1* already exists.

To avoid the error, we can use *-c* option for a clean restore operation where *pg_restore* first drops the table and recreates the table before restoring the data.

```
[postgres@pg_server backup]$ pg_restore -Ft -d db1 -n db1_schema1 -t db1tb1
db1_bkp.tar -c -v
pg_restore: connecting to database for restore
pg_restore: dropping TABLE db1tb1
pg_restore: creating TABLE "db1_schema1.db1tb1"
pg_restore: processing data for table "db1_schema1.db1tb1"
pg_restore: creating ACL "db1_schema1.TABLE db1tb1"
[postgres@pg_server backup]$
```

Let us validate to ensure *db1_schema1.db1tb1* is restored successfully.

```
[postgres@pg_server backup]$ psql -d db1
psql (16.3)
Type "help" for help.

db1=#
db1=# \dn                        <<<< List the schemas to validate
        List of schemas
    Name     |       Owner
-------------+-------------------
 db1_schema1 | user1
 db1_schema2 | user2
 public      | pg_database_owner
(3 rows)

db1=#
db1=# \dt db1_schema1.*
```

```
                List of relations
   Schema    |    Name   | Type  | Owner
-------------+-----------+-------+----------
 db1_schema1 | all_test  | table | postgres
 db1_schema1 | db1new    | table | postgres
 db1_schema1 | db1tb1    | table | postgres    <<< table restored successfully
 db1_schema1 | new_test  | table | postgres
 db1_schema1 | test1     | table | user1
 db1_schema1 | test2     | table | postgres
 db1_schema1 | test3     | table | postgres
(7 rows)

db1=#
```

Scenario 13: Logical Backup of a Complete Server and Restore Specific Databases

In this scenario, we will take a logical backup of the complete server using *pg_dumpall*. Please note *pg_dumpall* supports only standard backup and does not support custom formats like *pg_dump*. The backup file for *pg_dumpall* is in *.sql format. The backup file can be opened with any editor, and you will notice it has the backup of all the databases, schemas, global users, global access, and user-defined tablespaces.

To take a logical backup of the complete server, issue the command below:

[postgres@pg_server backup]$ **pg_dumpall > postgres16_server_backup.sql**

To create a recovery scenario, let us drop databases *db1* and *db2* and then perform a full restore using the *psql* utility.

```
postgres=# drop database db1;
DROP DATABASE
postgres=#
postgres=# drop database db2;
DROP DATABASE
postgres=#
postgres=# \c db1
```

CHAPTER 5 POSTGRESQL BACKUP AND RECOVERY

```
connection to server on socket "/run/postgresql/.s.PGSQL.5432" failed:
FATAL:  database "db1" does not exist
Previous connection kept
postgres=#
postgres=# \c db2
connection to server on socket "/run/postgresql/.s.PGSQL.5432" failed:
FATAL:  database "db2" does not exist
Previous connection kept
postgres=#
```

Now that both databases *db1* and *db2* are dropped, let us perform a restore using the *psql* utility.

```
[postgres@pg_server backup]$ psql -f postgres16_server_backup.sql -o full_restore.log

[postgres@pg_server backup]$ psql
psql (16.3)
Type "help" for help.

postgres=# \l
                                                    List of databases
    Name      |   Owner  | Encoding | Locale Provider |   Collate   |    Ctype     | ICU Locale | ICU Rules |   Access privileges
--------------+----------+----------+-----------------+-------------+--------------+------------+-----------+------------------------
 db1          | postgres | UTF8     | libc            | en_US.UTF-8 | en_US.UTF-8 |            |           |
 db1clone     | postgres | UTF8     | libc            | en_US.UTF-8 | en_US.UTF-8 |            |           |
 db2          | postgres | UTF8     | libc            | en_US.UTF-8 | en_US.UTF-8 |            |           |
 db3          | postgres | UTF8     | libc            | en_US.UTF-8 | en_US.UTF-8 |            |           |
 db4          | postgres | UTF8     | libc            | en_US.UTF-8 | en_US.UTF-8 |            |           |
 db5          | postgres | UTF8     | libc            | en_US.UTF-8 | en_US.UTF-8 |            |           |
```

```
 newdb     | postgres | UTF8 | libc            | en_US.UTF-8 |
 en_US.UTF-8 |                |                |
 postgres  | postgres | UTF8 | libc            | en_US.UTF-8 |
 en_US.UTF-8 |                |                |
 template0 | postgres | UTF8 | libc            | en_US.UTF-8 |
 en_US.UTF-8 |                | =c/postgres                 +
           |          |      |                 |
           |          |      | postgres=CTc/postgres
 template1 | postgres | UTF8 | libc            | en_US.UTF-8 |
 en_US.UTF-8 |                | =c/postgres                 +
           |          |      |                 |
           |          |      | postgres=CTc/postgres
(10 rows)

postgres=#
postgres=# \c db1
You are now connected to database "db1" as user "postgres".
db1=#
db1=# \dn
         List of schemas
     Name     |       Owner
--------------+-------------------
 db1_schema1  | user1
 db1_schema2  | user2
 db1_schema3  | postgres
 public       | pg_database_owner
(4 rows)

db1=#
db1=# \c db2
You are now connected to database "db2" as user "postgres".
db2=#
db2=# \dn
```

```
          List of schemas
    Name     |       Owner
-------------+-------------------
 db2_schema2 | postgres
 public      | pg_database_owner
(2 rows)

db2=#
```

In addition to the validation above, you may also view the restore log file *full_restore. log* to confirm the restore.

Scenario 14: Backup of Global Database Objects

In this scenario, we will take a backup of all the global database objects using the *pg_dumpall* utility. Global database objects include users, user access rights, and tablespaces.

To take a backup of the global database objects, issue the command below:

```
[postgres@pg_server backup]$ pg_dumpall -f global_objects.sql -g -v
```

Scenario 15: Physical Backup of the Complete Server

In this scenario, we will physically backup the complete server using the *pg_basebackup* utility. To do so, pre-create a backup directory for the backup to be written in, as below:

```
[postgres@pg_server ~]$ mkdir -p /u01/pgsql16/physical_backup
[postgres@pg_server ~]$
[postgres@pg_server ~]$ pg_basebackup -D /u01/pgsql16/physical_backup
-Ft -z -P
16688000/16688000 kB (100%), 2/2 tableslespaceslespacesces
```

-Ft: output file format is tar
-P: Show the progress being made.
-z: to gzip the output

```
[postgres@pg_server ~]$ ls -lrt /u01/pgsql16/physical_backup
total 3077056
-rw-------. 1 postgres postgres  162022052 Jun  1 01:55 32891.tar.gz
-rw-------. 1 postgres postgres     617523 Jun  1 02:26 backup_manifest
```

```
-rw-------. 1 postgres postgres 2988240817 Jun  1 02:26 base.tar.gz
-rw-------. 1 postgres postgres      17097 Jun  1 02:26 pg_wal.tar.gz
[postgres@pg_server ~]$
```

To perform a physical backup, including WAL files upon the backup completion, use the command below:

```
[postgres@pg_server ~]$ mkdir -p /u01/pgsql16/physical_backup2
[postgres@pg_server ~]$
[postgres@pg_server ~]$ pg_basebackup -D /u01/pgsql16/physical_backup2 -X fetch -P -v
pg_basebackup: initiating base backup, waiting for checkpoint to complete
pg_basebackup: checkpoint completed
pg_basebackup: write-ahead log start point: 3/1D000028 on timeline 1
4733177/4733177 kB (100%), 1/1 tablespace
pg_basebackup: write-ahead log end point: 3/1D000138
pg_basebackup: syncing data to disk ...
pg_basebackup: renaming backup_manifest.tmp to backup_manifest
pg_basebackup: base backup completed
[postgres@pg_server ~]$
```

>>>>>>

'X: stands for method, and 'f' for fetch, which collects the WAL files after the backup has been completed.
-P: Show the progress being made.
-v: verbose

>>>>>>

```
[postgres@pg_server ~]$ ls -lrt /u01/pgsql16/physical_backup2
total 432
-rw-------. 1 postgres postgres    227 Jun  1 04:18 backup_label
drwx------. 2 postgres postgres      6 Jun  1 04:18 pg_notify
drwx------. 2 postgres postgres      6 Jun  1 04:18 pg_dynshmem
drwx------. 2 postgres postgres      6 Jun  1 04:18 pg_commit_ts
drwx------. 2 postgres postgres      6 Jun  1 04:18 pg_twophase
drwx------. 2 postgres postgres      6 Jun  1 04:18 pg_subtrans
drwx------. 2 postgres postgres      6 Jun  1 04:18 pg_snapshots
```

```
drwx------. 2 postgres postgres       6 Jun  1 04:18 pg_serial
drwx------. 4 postgres postgres      36 Jun  1 04:18 pg_multixact
drwx------. 8 postgres postgres      72 Jun  1 04:18 base
drwx------. 2 postgres postgres       6 Jun  1 04:18 pg_replslot
drwx------. 2 postgres postgres      18 Jun  1 04:18 pg_xact
drwx------. 2 postgres postgres       6 Jun  1 04:18 pg_tblspc
drwx------. 2 postgres postgres       6 Jun  1 04:18 pg_stat_tmp
drwx------. 2 postgres postgres       6 Jun  1 04:18 pg_stat
-rw-------. 1 postgres postgres       3 Jun  1 04:18 PG_VERSION
drwx------. 4 postgres postgres      68 Jun  1 04:18 pg_logical
-rw-------. 1 postgres postgres     168 Jun  1 04:18 postgresql.auto.conf
-rw-------. 1 postgres postgres    2640 Jun  1 04:18 pg_ident.conf
drwx------. 2 postgres postgres     136 Jun  1 04:18 log
-rw-------. 1 postgres postgres   29690 Jun  1 04:18 postgresql.conf_bkp
-rw-------. 1 postgres postgres    5499 Jun  1 04:18 pg_hba.conf_bkp
drwxrwxr-x. 2 postgres postgres   12288 Jun  1 04:19 archive
-rw-------. 1 postgres postgres    6240 Jun  1 04:19 pg_hba.conf
drwx------. 2 postgres postgres       6 Jun  1 04:19 tablespace1
-rw-------. 1 postgres postgres   29701 Jun  1 04:19 postgresql.conf
drwx------. 2 postgres postgres    4096 Jun  1 04:19 global
-rw-------. 1 postgres postgres      30 Jun  1 04:19 current_logfiles
drwx------. 3 postgres postgres      60 Jun  1 04:19 pg_wal
-rw-------. 1 postgres postgres  318238 Jun  1 04:19 backup_manifest
[postgres@pg_server ~]$
```

Scenario 15a: Verification of Physical Backups (pg_verifybackup) Before Restore

The pg_verifybackup command in PostgreSQL 16 is used to verify the integrity and completeness of a backup taken with pg_basebackup or other tools that produce a backup compatible with PostgreSQL's backup format.

Let's execute the pg_basebackup command again to check verification of the backup.

[postgres@pg_server physical_backup]$ **pg_basebackup -D /u01/pgsql16/ physical_backup -Fp -Xs -P -v**
pg_basebackup: initiating base backup, waiting for checkpoint to complete

CHAPTER 5 POSTGRESQL BACKUP AND RECOVERY

```
pg_basebackup: checkpoint completed
pg_basebackup: write-ahead log start point: 4/66000028 on timeline 1
pg_basebackup: starting background WAL receiver
pg_basebackup: created temporary replication slot "pg_basebackup_10588"
2702822/2702822 kB (100%), 5/5 tablespaces
pg_basebackup: write-ahead log end point: 4/66000138
pg_basebackup: waiting for background process to finish streaming ...
pg_basebackup: syncing data to disk ...
pg_basebackup: renaming backup_manifest.tmp to backup_manifest
pg_basebackup: base backup completed
[postgres@pg_server physical_backup]$

[postgres@pg_server physical_backup]$ ls -lrth /u01/pgsql16/physical_backup
total 456K
-rw-------. 1 postgres postgres  227 May 12 12:07 backup_label
drwx------. 3 postgres postgres   60 May 12 12:07 pg_wal
drwx------. 2 postgres postgres 8.0K May 12 12:07 archive
drwx------. 7 postgres postgres   59 May 12 12:07 base
drwx------. 2 postgres postgres  188 May 12 12:07 log
-rwx------. 1 postgres postgres 5.4K May 12 12:07 pg_hba.conf_bkp
drwx------. 2 postgres postgres    6 May 12 12:07 pg_dynshmem
drwx------. 2 postgres postgres    6 May 12 12:07 pg_commit_ts
drwx------. 4 postgres postgres   68 May 12 12:07 pg_logical
-rwx------. 1 postgres postgres 2.6K May 12 12:07 pg_ident.conf
drwx------. 2 postgres postgres    6 May 12 12:07 pg_notify
drwx------. 4 postgres postgres   36 May 12 12:07 pg_multixact
-rwx------. 1 postgres postgres    3 May 12 12:07 PG_VERSION
drwx------. 2 postgres postgres    6 May 12 12:07 pg_twophase
drwx------. 2 postgres postgres   60 May 12 12:07 pg_tblspc
drwx------. 2 postgres postgres    6 May 12 12:07 pg_subtrans
drwx------. 2 postgres postgres    6 May 12 12:07 pg_stat_tmp
drwx------. 2 postgres postgres    6 May 12 12:07 pg_stat
drwx------. 2 postgres postgres    6 May 12 12:07 pg_snapshots
drwx------. 2 postgres postgres    6 May 12 12:07 pg_serial
drwx------. 2 postgres postgres    6 May 12 12:07 pg_replslot
drwx------. 2 postgres postgres   18 May 12 12:07 pg_xact
```

```
drwx------.  2 postgres postgres     6 May 12 12:07 tablespace1
-rwx------.  1 postgres postgres   29K May 12 12:07 postgresql.conf_bkp
-rw-------.  1 postgres postgres   348 May 12 12:07 postgresql.auto.conf
-rwx------.  1 postgres postgres   30K May 12 12:07 postgresql.conf_bkp2
-rw-------.  1 postgres postgres   187 May 12 12:07 logfile
-rw-------.  1 postgres postgres   227 May 12 12:07 backup_label.old
-rw-------.  1 postgres postgres    38 May 12 12:07 tablespace_map.old
-rwx------.  1 postgres postgres   30K May 12 12:07 postgresql.conf_
                                                    bkp03172025
-rwx------.  1 postgres postgres   30K May 12 12:07 postgresql.conf
-rwx------.  1 postgres postgres  6.3K May 12 12:07 pg_hba.conf_new
-rwx------.  1 postgres postgres  6.1K May 12 12:07 pg_hba.conf_bkp122424
-rwx------.  1 postgres postgres  6.5K May 12 12:07 pg_hba.conf
drwx------.  2 postgres postgres  4.0K May 12 12:07 global
-rw-------.  1 postgres postgres    30 May 12 12:07 current_logfiles
-rw-------.  1 postgres postgres  248K May 12 12:07 backup_manifest
[postgres@pg_server physical_backup]$
```

Note: Options available with pg_verifybackup command.

[postgres@pg_server physical_backup]$ **pg_verifybackup --help**
pg_verifybackup verifies a backup against the backup manifest.

Usage:
  pg_verifybackup [OPTION]... BACKUPDIR

Options:
  -e, --exit-on-error   exit immediately on error
  -i, --ignore=RELATIVE_PATH ignore indicated path
  -m, --manifest-path=PATH   use specified path for manifest
  -n, --no-parse-wal   do not try to parse WAL files
  -P, --progress   show progress information
  -q, --quiet   do not print any output, except for errors
  -s, --skip-checksums   skip checksum verification
  -w, --wal-directory=PATH   use specified path for WAL files
  -V, --version   output version information, then exit
  -?, --help   show this help, then exit

Report bugs to <pgsql-bugs@lists.postgresql.org>.
PostgreSQL home page: <https://www.postgresql.org/>
[postgres@pg_server physical_backup]$

Let's do the verification of the backups executed through pg_basebackup command with different options.

- **Verifies the backup directory for completeness and correctness.**

[postgres@pg_server physical_backup]$ **pg_verifybackup /u01/pgsql16/physical_backup -P**
2701914/2701914 kB (100%) verified
backup successfully verified
[postgres@pg_server physical_backup]$

- **Ignores the file pg_control in global/ during verification**.

[postgres@pg_server physical_backup]$ **pg_verifybackup --ignore=global/pg_control /u01/pgsql16/physical_backup**
backup successfully verified
[postgres@pg_server physical_backup]$

- **Runs verification silently unless an error is encountered.**

[postgres@pg_server physical_backup]$ **pg_verifybackup --quiet /u01/pgsql16/physical_backup**
[postgres@pg_server physical_backup]$

- **Verifies backup without checking WAL files.**

[postgres@pg_server physical_backup]$ **pg_verifybackup --no-parse-wal /u01/pgsql16/physical_backup**
backup successfully verified
[postgres@pg_server physical_backup]$

Scenario 16: Restore Procedures

Scenario 16a: Restore to a New Instance

In this scenario, we will restore the physical backup from the previous scenario to a new server. To do so, we need to ensure the database and OS versions are the same as those on the backup server.

To restore the backup to a new server, please follow the below steps in order:

1. Validate the backup files in the backup directory.

   ```
   [postgres@pg_server ~]$ cd /u01/pgsql16/physical_backup2
   [postgres@pg_server physical_backup2]$ pwd
   /u01/pgsql16/physical_backup2
   [postgres@pg_server physical_backup2]$
   [postgres@pg_server physical_backup2]$ ls -lrt
   total 432
   -rw-------. 1 postgres postgres   227 Jun  1 04:18 backup_label
   drwx------. 2 postgres postgres     6 Jun  1 04:18 pg_notify
   drwx------. 2 postgres postgres     6 Jun  1 04:18 pg_dynshmem
   drwx------. 2 postgres postgres     6 Jun  1 04:18 pg_commit_ts
   drwx------. 2 postgres postgres     6 Jun  1 04:18 pg_twophase
   drwx------. 2 postgres postgres     6 Jun  1 04:18 pg_subtrans
   drwx------. 2 postgres postgres     6 Jun  1 04:18 pg_snapshots
   drwx------. 2 postgres postgres     6 Jun  1 04:18 pg_serial
   drwx------. 4 postgres postgres    36 Jun  1 04:18 pg_multixact
   drwx------. 8 postgres postgres    72 Jun  1 04:18 base
   drwx------. 2 postgres postgres     6 Jun  1 04:18 pg_replslot
   drwx------. 2 postgres postgres    18 Jun  1 04:18 pg_xact
   drwx------. 2 postgres postgres     6 Jun  1 04:18 pg_tblspc
   drwx------. 2 postgres postgres     6 Jun  1 04:18 pg_stat_tmp
   drwx------. 2 postgres postgres     6 Jun  1 04:18 pg_stat
   -rw-------. 1 postgres postgres     3 Jun  1 04:18 PG_VERSION
   drwx------. 4 postgres postgres    68 Jun  1 04:18 pg_logical
   -rw-------. 1 postgres postgres   168 Jun  1 04:18 postgresql.
                                                       auto.conf
   -rw-------. 1 postgres postgres  2640 Jun  1 04:18 pg_ident.conf
   ```

```
drwx------. 2 postgres postgres    136 Jun  1 04:18 log
-rw-------. 1 postgres postgres  29690 Jun  1 04:18 postgresql.
                                                    conf_bkp
-rw-------. 1 postgres postgres   5499 Jun  1 04:18 pg_hba.conf_bkp
drwxrwxr-x. 2 postgres postgres  12288 Jun  1 04:19 archive
-rw-------. 1 postgres postgres   6240 Jun  1 04:19 pg_hba.conf
drwx------. 2 postgres postgres      6 Jun  1 04:19 tablespace1
-rw-------. 1 postgres postgres  29701 Jun  1 04:19
                                                    postgresql.conf
drwx------. 2 postgres postgres   4096 Jun  1 04:19 global
-rw-------. 1 postgres postgres     30 Jun  1 04:19 current_
                                                    logfiles
drwx------. 3 postgres postgres     60 Jun  1 04:19 pg_wal
-rw-------. 1 postgres postgres 318238 Jun  1 04:19 backup_
                                                    manifest

[postgres@pg_server physical_backup2]$
```

2. Edit the *postgresql.conf* file and change the port information.

   ```
   [postgres@pg_server physical_backup2]$ vi postgresql.conf
   [postgres@pg_server physical_backup2]$ egrep -i 'cluster_name|port' postgresql.conf
   port = 5433                            # (change requires restart)
   cluster_name = 'backup_data'           # added to process titles
   if nonempty

   [postgres@pg_server physical_backup2]$
   ```

3. Change the permissions of the backup location to 700.

   ```
   [postgres@pg_server pgsql16]$ chmod -Rf 0700 physical_backup2
   ```

4. Start the *postgres* instance using the new backup location as the new data location.

   ```
   [postgres@pg_server ~]$ cd /u01/pgsql16/physical_backup2
   [postgres@pg_server physical_backup2]$ pwd
   ```

```
[postgres@pg_server physical_backup2]$
[postgres@pg_server physical_backup2]$ **pg_ctl start -D /u01/
pgsql16/physical_backup2 -l /tmp/backloc.log**
waiting for server to start........ done
**server started**
[postgres@pg_server physical_backup2]$

[postgres@pg_server physical_backup2]$ **ps -ef |grep -i postgres**
postgres    1145       1  0 May31 ?        00:00:05 /usr/pgsql-16/
bin/postgres -D **/var/lib/pgsql/16/data/   <<<< existing postgres
instance**
postgres    1230    1145  0 May31 ?        00:00:00
postgres: logger
postgres    1253    1145  0 May31 ?        00:00:07 postgres:
checkpointer
postgres    1254    1145  0 May31 ?        00:00:02 postgres:
background writer
postgres    3245    1145  0 May31 ?        00:00:10 postgres:
walwriter
postgres    3246    1145  0 May31 ?        00:00:01 postgres:
autovacuum launcher
postgres    3247    1145  0 May31 ?        00:00:00 postgres:
archiver last was 000000010000000300000001D.00000028.backup
postgres    3248    1145  0 May31 ?        00:00:00 postgres:
logical replication launcher

postgres    71037      1  0 04:29 ?        00:00:00 /usr/pgsql-16/
bin/postgres -D **/u01/pgsql16/physical_backup2 <<<< new postgres
instance**
postgres    71038  71037  0 04:29 ?        00:00:00 postgres:
backup_data: logger
postgres    71039  71037  0 04:29 ?        00:00:00 postgres:
backup_data: checkpointer
postgres    71040  71037  0 04:29 ?        00:00:00 postgres:
backup_data: background writer
postgres    71044  71037  0 04:29 ?        00:00:00 postgres:
backup_data: walwriter
```

CHAPTER 5   POSTGRESQL BACKUP AND RECOVERY

```
postgres   71045    71037   0 04:29 ?         00:00:00 postgres:
backup_data: autovacuum launcher
postgres   71046    71037   0 04:29 ?         00:00:00 postgres:
backup_data: archiver
postgres   71047    71037   0 04:29 ?         00:00:00 postgres:
backup_data: logical replication launcher
postgres   71070    65003   0 04:30 pts/0     00:00:00 ps -ef
postgres   71071    65003   0 04:30 pts/0     00:00:00 grep
--color=auto -i postgres
[postgres@pg_server physical_backup2]$
```

We can see that we now have two instances of the *postgres* server with two different data locations on the same server.

5. Connect to the new *postgres* instance using the newly configured port in step 2.

```
[postgres@pg_server ~]$ psql -p5433
psql (16.3)
Type "help" for help.

postgres=#
postgres=# show port;
 port
------
 5433
(1 row)

postgres=# show data_directory;
        data_directory
-------------------------------
 /u01/pgsql16/physical_backup2
(1 row)

postgres=#
postgres=# \l
```

301

```
    Name    |  Owner   | Encoding |
------------+----------+----------+
   db1      | postgres | UTF8     |
   db2      | postgres | UTF8     |
   db3      | postgres | UTF8     |
  postgres  | postgres | UTF8     |
  template0 | postgres | UTF8     |
            |          |          |
  template1 | postgres | UTF8     |
            |          |          |
(6 rows)

postgres=#
```

This way we can have a backup restored to a new instance on the same server and can have multiple instances of *postgres* running.

Scenario 16b: Restore to an Existing Instance

In this scenario, we will restore the physical backup taken from scenario 15 to the same instance. To do so, here is the sequence of steps to be followed:

1. Stop the *postgres* instance.

   ```
   [postgres@pg_server ~]$ pg_ctl status
   pg_ctl: server is running (PID: 1145)
   /usr/pgsql-16/bin/postgres "-D" "/var/lib/pgsql/16/data/"
   [postgres@pg_server ~]$
   [postgres@pg_server ~]$ pg_ctl stop
   waiting for server to shut down.... done
   server stopped
   [postgres@pg_server ~]$
   [postgres@pg_server ~]$ pg_ctl status
   pg_ctl: no server running
   [postgres@pg_server ~]$
   ```

CHAPTER 5 POSTGRESQL BACKUP AND RECOVERY

2. Rename the current data location.

   ```
   [postgres@pg_server ~]$
   [postgres@pg_server ~]$ mv /var/lib/pgsql/16/data /var/lib/
   pgsql/16/data_for_restore_test
   [postgres@pg_server ~]$
   [postgres@pg_server ~]$ ls -ld /var/lib/pgsql/16/data
   ls: cannot access '/var/lib/pgsql/16/data': No such file or
   directory
   [postgres@pg_server ~]$
   [postgres@pg_server ~]$ ls -ld /var/lib/pgsql/16/data_for_
   restore_test
   drwx------. 22 postgres postgres 4096 Jun  1 04:39 /var/lib/
   pgsql/16/data_for_restore_test
   [postgres@pg_server ~]$
   ```

3. Copy the backup data to the current data location.

   ```
   [postgres@pg_server ~]$ cd /var/lib/pgsql/16
   [postgres@pg_server 16]$
   [postgres@pg_server 16]$ ls -lrt
   total 8
   drwx------.  2 postgres postgres    6 May  8 04:30 backups
   -rw-------.  1 postgres postgres  923 May 23 10:28 initdb.log
   drwx------. 22 postgres postgres 4096 Jun  1 04:39 data_for_
   restore_test
   [postgres@pg_server 16]$
   [postgres@pg_server 16]$ mkdir data
   [postgres@pg_server 16]$
   [postgres@pg_server 16]$ cd data
   [postgres@pg_server data]$ pwd
   /var/lib/pgsql/16/data
   [postgres@pg_server data]$
   [postgres@pg_server data]$ cp -Rf /u01/pgsql16/physical_backup/* .
   [postgres@pg_server data]$
   [postgres@pg_server data]$ ls -lrt
   total 432
   ```

```
drwxrwxr-x. 2 postgres postgres  12288 Jun  1 04:43 archive
-rw-------. 1 postgres postgres    227 Jun  1 04:43 backup_label
-rw-------. 1 postgres postgres 318747 Jun  1 04:43 backup_
                                                    manifest
drwx------. 8 postgres postgres     72 Jun  1 04:43 base
-rw-------. 1 postgres postgres     30 Jun  1 04:43 current_
                                                    logfiles
drwx------. 2 postgres postgres   4096 Jun  1 04:43 global
drwx------. 2 postgres postgres      6 Jun  1 04:43 pg_dynshmem
drwx------. 2 postgres postgres      6 Jun  1 04:43 pg_commit_ts
drwx------. 2 postgres postgres    136 Jun  1 04:43 log
-rw-------. 1 postgres postgres   5499 Jun  1 04:43 pg_hba.
                                                    conf_bkp
-rw-------. 1 postgres postgres   6240 Jun  1 04:43 pg_hba.conf
-rw-------. 1 postgres postgres   2640 Jun  1 04:43 pg_ident.conf
drwx------. 4 postgres postgres     68 Jun  1 04:43 pg_logical
drwx------. 2 postgres postgres      6 Jun  1 04:43 pg_stat
drwx------. 2 postgres postgres      6 Jun  1 04:43 pg_snapshots
drwx------. 2 postgres postgres      6 Jun  1 04:43 pg_serial
drwx------. 2 postgres postgres      6 Jun  1 04:43 pg_replslot
drwx------. 2 postgres postgres      6 Jun  1 04:43 pg_notify
drwx------. 4 postgres postgres     36 Jun  1 04:43 pg_multixact
-rw-------. 1 postgres postgres      3 Jun  1 04:43 PG_VERSION
drwx------. 2 postgres postgres      6 Jun  1 04:43 pg_twophase
drwx------. 2 postgres postgres      6 Jun  1 04:43 pg_tblspc
drwx------. 2 postgres postgres      6 Jun  1 04:43 pg_subtrans
drwx------. 2 postgres postgres      6 Jun  1 04:43 pg_stat_tmp
drwx------. 2 postgres postgres     18 Jun  1 04:43 pg_xact
drwx------. 3 postgres postgres     60 Jun  1 04:43 pg_wal
-rw-------. 1 postgres postgres    168 Jun  1 04:43 postgresql.
                                                    auto.conf
-rw-------. 1 postgres postgres  29701 Jun  1 04:43 postgresql.conf
drwx------. 2 postgres postgres      6 Jun  1 04:43 tablespace1
-rw-------. 1 postgres postgres  29690 Jun  1 04:43 postgresql.
                                                    conf_bkp
```

```
[postgres@pg_server data]$
```

4. Start the instance with the copied data upon changing the permissions of the *data* directory to *0700*.

```
[postgres@pg_server data]$ cd ..
[postgres@pg_server 16]$ ls -ld
drwxrwxr-x. 22 postgres postgres 4096 Jun  1 04:43 data
[postgres@pg_server 16]$ chmod -Rf 0700 data
[postgres@pg_server 16]$
[postgres@pg_server 16]$ ls -ld data
drwx------. 22 postgres postgres 4096 Jun  1 04:46 data
[postgres@pg_server 16]$

[postgres@pg_server 16]$
[postgres@pg_server 16]$ pg_ctl start -D /var/lib/pgsql/16/data -l /tmp/newstartup.log
waiting for server to start....... done
server started

[postgres@pg_server 16]$
```

Scenario 17: Perform a Point-in-Time Recovery (PITR)

In this scenario, we will perform a point-in-time recovery (PITR) of the database cluster. In order to perform a PITR, we need to have a full base backup of the database server along with the backup of Write-Ahead Log (WAL) files.

Before proceeding with performing a PITR, let us check the current database server to compare upon the recovery operation.

List the databases, schemas, and corresponding tables, and archive log settings along with the table row counts.

Database list

CHAPTER 5 POSTGRESQL BACKUP AND RECOVERY

```
postgres=# \l
                              List of databases
   Name    |  Owner   | Encoding | Locale Provider |   Access privileges
-----------+----------+----------+-----------------+-----------------------
 db1       | postgres | UTF8     | libc            |
 postgres  | postgres | UTF8     | libc            |
 template0 | postgres | UTF8     | libc            | =c/postgres          +
           |          |          |                 | postgres=CTc/postgres
 template1 | postgres | UTF8     | libc            | =c/postgres          +
           |          |          |                 | postgres=CTc/postgres
(4 rows)

postgres=#
```

Schemas and its corresponding tables

```
postgres=# \c db1
You are now connected to database "db1" as user "postgres".
db1=#
db1=# \db
                    List of tablespaces
    Name    |  Owner   |          Location
------------+----------+---------------------------------
 db1_tbs1   | postgres | /u01/pgsql16/pgdata/tablespace1
 pg_default | postgres |
 pg_global  | postgres |
(3 rows)

db1=#
db1=# \dn
        List of schemas
    Name     |       Owner
-------------+-------------------
 db1_schema1 | postgres
 public      | pg_database_owner
(2 rows)

db1=#
```

```
db1=# \dt db1_schema1.*
            List of relations
   Schema    |  Name  | Type  |  Owner
-------------+--------+-------+----------
 db1_schema1 | db1tb1 | table | postgres
 db1_schema1 | db1tb2 | table | postgres
(2 rows)

db1=#
```

Archive log settings

```
db1=# select name,setting,unit from pg_settings where name in ('archive_mode','archive_command','archive_timeout');
      name       |                 setting                  | unit
-----------------+------------------------------------------+------
 archive_command | cp %p /var/lib/pgsql/16/data/archive/%f  |
 archive_mode    | on                                       |
 archive_timeout | 0                                        | s
(3 rows)
```

Table data

```
db1=# select * from db1_schema1.db1tb1;
 eno  |     ename     | esal | edno
------+---------------+------+------
 2940 | ROBIN TALES   | 5600 |  40
 1450 | PETE HILLS    | 8200 |  20
 1932 | BOB SMITH     | 3400 |  20
 3232 | ROSS MARSHAL  | 6750 |  10
 2121 | ANDREW MILLS  | 9900 |  40
 1212 | ROSE WINSLET  | 5450 |  30
 4455 | KATE FLOWER   | 7850 |  40
 5453 | ROB WILLS     | 4540 |  20
 3344 | JACK WOODS    | 5600 |  30
 2990 | MIKE TYLOR    | 7650 |  10
(10 rows)
```

CHAPTER 5 POSTGRESQL BACKUP AND RECOVERY

```
db1=#
db1=# select * from db1_schema1.db1tb2;
 dno |  dname
-----+----------
  10 | ACCOUNTS
  20 | FINANCE
  30 | HR
  40 | SALES
(4 rows)

db1=#
```

Here is the sequence of steps required to perform a PITR scenario:

1. Take a backup of the PostgreSQL cluster using *pg_basebackup*.

    ```
    [postgres@pg_server ~]$ pg_basebackup -D /u01/pgsql16/backups/base_backups/Full_backup_tar -Ft -z -Xs -P
    4750501/4750501 kB (100%), 2/2 tablespaces
    [postgres@pg_server ~]$
    [postgres@pg_server ~]$ ls -lrt /u01/pgsql16/backups/base_backups/Full_backup_tar
    total 844060
    -rw-------. 1 postgres postgres    1078542 Jun  6 17:31 65658.tar.gz
    -rw-------. 1 postgres postgres     239988 Jun  6 17:47 backup_
                                                                manifest
    -rw-------. 1 postgres postgres  862973903 Jun  6 17:47 base.tar.gz
    -rw-------. 1 postgres postgres      17099 Jun  6 17:47 pg_wal.tar.gz
    [postgres@pg_server ~]$
    ```

2. Get the current timestamp of the *db1* database and then drop the table *db1_schema1.db1tb2* and truncate data from the table *db1_schema1.db1tb1*.

    ```
    db1=# select now();
                  now
    -------------------------------
    ```

CHAPTER 5   POSTGRESQL BACKUP AND RECOVERY

```
  2024-06-06 17:49:16.455204-05          <<<< Current time stamp
(1 row)

db1=#
db1=#
db1=# drop table db1_schema1.db1tb2;
DROP TABLE
db1=#
db1=# delete from db1_schema1.db1tb1;
DELETE 10
db1=#
db1=# select now();                     <<<< Timestamp post table drop
and truncate
            now
-------------------------------
  2024-06-06 17:50:02.690654-05
(1 row)

db1=#
```

3. Clean up the current data directory.

   Before deleting the current data directory, please ensure the *postgres* instance is stopped to ensure data consistency and avoid data corruption.

   To stop the *postgres* instance, perform the following:

```
[postgres@pg_server ~]$ pg_ctl status
pg_ctl: server is running (PID: 1198)
/usr/pgsql-16/bin/postgres "-D" "/var/lib/pgsql/16/data/"
[postgres@pg_server ~]$ pg_ctl stop
waiting for server to shut down.... done
server stopped
[postgres@pg_server ~]$
[postgres@pg_server ~]$ pg_ctl status
pg_ctl: no server running
[postgres@pg_server ~]$
```

CHAPTER 5   POSTGRESQL BACKUP AND RECOVERY

Let us delete all the files in the data directory so we can simulate a recovery scenario. Please do the following to clean up the data directory:

```
[postgres@pg_server ~]$ cd /var/lib/pgsql/16/data/
[postgres@pg_server data]$ ls -lrt
total 440
-rwx------. 1 postgres postgres    227 Jun  1 04:43 backup_
                                                     label.old
-rwx------. 1 postgres postgres 318747 Jun  1 04:43 backup_
                                                     manifest
drwx------. 2 postgres postgres      6 Jun  1 04:43 pg_dynshmem
drwx------. 2 postgres postgres      6 Jun  1 04:43 pg_commit_ts
-rwx------. 1 postgres postgres   5499 Jun  1 04:43 pg_hba.conf_bkp
-rwx------. 1 postgres postgres   6240 Jun  1 04:43 pg_hba.conf
-rwx------. 1 postgres postgres   2640 Jun  1 04:43 pg_ident.conf
drwx------. 2 postgres postgres      6 Jun  1 04:43 pg_snapshots
drwx------. 2 postgres postgres      6 Jun  1 04:43 pg_serial
drwx------. 2 postgres postgres      6 Jun  1 04:43 pg_notify
drwx------. 4 postgres postgres     36 Jun  1 04:43 pg_multixact
-rwx------. 1 postgres postgres      3 Jun  1 04:43 PG_VERSION
drwx------. 2 postgres postgres      6 Jun  1 04:43 pg_twophase
drwx------. 2 postgres postgres     18 Jun  1 04:43 pg_xact
-rwx------. 1 postgres postgres    168 Jun  1 04:43 postgresql.
                                                     auto.conf
-rwx------. 1 postgres postgres  29701 Jun  1 04:43 postgresql.conf
drwx------. 2 postgres postgres      6 Jun  1 04:43 tablespace1
-rwx------. 1 postgres postgres  29690 Jun  1 04:43 postgresql.
                                                     conf_bkp
drwx------. 2 postgres postgres     18 Jun  1 04:46 pg_subtrans
drwx------. 2 postgres postgres    162 Jun  2 22:41 log
-rw-------. 1 postgres postgres     30 Jun  6 12:39 current_logfiles
-rw-------. 1 postgres postgres     58 Jun  6 12:39 
postmaster.opts
drwx------. 2 postgres postgres     19 Jun  6 13:08 pg_tblspc
drwx------. 2 postgres postgres   4096 Jun  6 13:10 global
drwx------. 6 postgres postgres     50 Jun  6 17:31 base
```

```
drwx------. 2 postgres postgres        6 Jun  6 17:47 pg_replslot
drwx------. 4 postgres postgres       68 Jun  6 17:50 pg_logical
drwx------. 2 postgres postgres    12288 Jun  6 17:50 archive
drwx------. 3 postgres postgres     4096 Jun  6 17:50 pg_wal
drwx------. 2 postgres postgres       56 Jun  6 17:50 pg_stat
drwx------. 2 postgres postgres        6 Jun  6 17:50 pg_stat_tmp
[postgres@pg_server data]$
[postgres@pg_server data]$ pwd
/var/lib/pgsql/16/data
[postgres@pg_server data]$
[postgres@pg_server data]$ rm -rf *
[postgres@pg_server data]$
[postgres@pg_server data]$ ls -lrt
total 0
[postgres@pg_server data]$
```

4. Restore the database using the backup taken in step 1 and recover the database using the timestamp taken in step 2.

   Before we perform a restore, let us examine the backup directory to understand the backup directory structure.

```
[postgres@pg_server data]$ cd /u01/pgsql16/backups/base_backups/Full_backup_tar
[postgres@pg_server Full_backup_tar]$ ls -lrt
total 844060
-rw-------. 1 postgres postgres    1078542 Jun  6 17:31 65658.tar.gz
-rw-------. 1 postgres postgres     239988 Jun  6 17:47 backup_
                                                         manifest
-rw-------. 1 postgres postgres  862973903 Jun  6 17:47 base.tar.gz
-rw-------. 1 postgres postgres      17099 Jun  6 17:47 pg_wal.tar.gz
[postgres@pg_server Full_backup_tar]$
[postgres@pg_server Full_backup_tar]$ cd /var/lib/pgsql/16/data
[postgres@pg_server data]$
```

In the backup directory */u01/pgsql16/backups/base_backups/Full_backup_tar*:

base.tar.gz: The backup of the base directory
65658.tar.gz: The backup of the tablespace
pg_wal.tar.gz: The backup of the WAL logs

To begin with the restore process, let us restore the base backup first.

```
[postgres@pg_server data]$ tar -xvf /u01/pgsql16/backups/base_backups/Full_backup_tar/base.tar.gz -C /var/lib/pgsql/16/data
backup_label
tablespace_map
archive/
.
base/
.
PG_VERSION
pg_wal/
./pg_wal/archive_status/
pg_xact/
pg_xact/0000
postgresql.auto.conf
postgresql.conf
postgresql.conf_bkp
tablespace1/
backup_label.old
current_logfiles
global/pg_control
[postgres@pg_server data]$
```

As a next step, restore the tablespaces.

```
[postgres@pg_server data]$ tar -xvf /u01/pgsql16/backups/base_backups/Full_backup_tar/65658.tar.gz -C /u01/pgsql16/pgdata/tablespace1
PG_16_202307071/
PG_16_202307071/49769/
```

CHAPTER 5   POSTGRESQL BACKUP AND RECOVERY

-
-

```
PG_16_202307071/49769/65668
[postgres@pg_server data]$
```

As a final step, restore the WAL logs.

```
[postgres@pg_server data]$ tar -xvf /u01/pgsql16/backups/
base_backups/Full_backup_tar/pg_wal.tar.gz -C /var/lib/pgsql/16/
data/pg_wal
000000010000000300000021
[postgres@pg_server data]$
```

5. To recover to the timestamp we noted earlier in step 2 before dropping and truncating a table from the *db1_schema1* schema, we need to modify the *postgresql.conf file* to include the *restore_command* and *recovery_target_time*.

```
[postgres@pg_server data]$ vi postgresql.conf
[postgres@pg_server data]$
[postgres@pg_server data]$ egrep -i 'restore_command|recovery_
target_time' postgresql.conf
restore_command = 'cp /var/lib/pgsql/16/data/archive/%f %p'
recovery_target_time = '2024-06-06 17:49:16.455204-05'

[postgres@pg_server data]$
```

By adding the *restore_command* parameter, we are telling the *postgres* service to fetch all the required WAL archived logs from the location that was originally set within the database.

And by adding the *recovery_target_time* parameter, we are telling the *postgres* service to recover to a specific point in time once the restoring of the logs is complete. For example, in the above configuration file, we set the *recovery_target_time* to a timestamp prior to dropping/truncating the tables from the schema.

313

6. Start the *postgres* database cluster.

   ```
   [postgres@pg_server data]$ pg_ctl -D /var/lib/pgsql/16/data -l logfile start
   waiting for server to start...... done
   server started
   [postgres@pg_server data]$
   [postgres@pg_server data]$ pg_ctl status
   pg_ctl: server is running (PID: 20680)
   /usr/pgsql-16/bin/postgres "-D" "/var/lib/pgsql/16/data"
   [postgres@pg_server data]$
   ```

   By default, the *postgres* database cluster starts with the *postgresql.conf* file, which is located in the default data directory */var/lib/pgsql/16/data* and has the parameters to restore the postgres database cluster from the backup and recover it to a specific point in time. Both operations are performed as part of the cluster startup process.

7. Validate the restore and recovery to point in time.

   Since we restored and recovered to the timestamp prior to dropping/truncating the tables in the schema, we should see tables *db1_schema1.db1tb2* and *db1_schema1.db1tb1* should have the same rows as before the drop/truncate action on these tables.

   ```
   [postgres@pg_server ~]$ psql
   psql (16.3)
   Type "help" for help.

   postgres=# \c db1
   You are now connected to database "db1" as user "postgres".
   db1=#
   db1=# \dn
           List of schemas
       Name     |     Owner
   -------------+----------------
    db1_schema1 | postgres
   ```

```
 public     | pg_database_owner
(2 rows)

db1=#
db1=# \dt db1_schema1.*
            List of relations
   Schema    | Name  | Type  |  Owner
-------------+-------+-------+----------
 db1_schema1 | db1tb1 | table | postgres
 db1_schema1 | db1tb2 | table | postgres
(2 rows)

db1=#
db1=# select * from db1_schema1.db1tb1;
 eno  |    ename      | esal | edno
------+---------------+------+------
 2940 | ROBIN TALES   | 5600 |   40
 1450 | PETE HILLS    | 8200 |   20
 1932 | BOB SMITH     | 3400 |   20
 3232 | ROSS MARSHAL  | 6750 |   10
 2121 | ANDREW MILLS  | 9900 |   40
 1212 | ROSE WINSLET  | 5450 |   30
 4455 | KATE FLOWER   | 7850 |   40
 5453 | ROB WILLS     | 4540 |   20
 3344 | JACK WOODS    | 5600 |   30
 2990 | MIKE TYLOR    | 7650 |   10
(10 rows)

db1=# select * from db1_schema1.db1tb2;
 dno |  dname
-----+----------
  10 | ACCOUNTS
  20 | FINANCE
  30 | HR
  40 | SALES
(4 rows)

db1=#
```

CHAPTER 5   POSTGRESQL BACKUP AND RECOVERY

This confirms that we could successfully perform a point-in-time recovery with continuous archiving. Please note that PITR can only be performed with File System-Level backups and not logical backups (*pg_dump* and *pg_dumpall*), as continuous archiving cannot be applied upon restoring a logical backup.

Scenario 18: Backup and Restore Using Barman

In this scenario, we will use an external tool named *Barman* to backup and recover a PostgreSQL database.

Before getting into the details, let us learn about **Barman** and its purpose. So what is Barman?

Barman (Backup and Recovery Manager) is an open source administration tool for backing up and recovering postgres databases. It allows users to configure full/incremental backups in postgres and perform point-in-time recovery.

Note 1 **PostgreSQL 17** introduces native Incremental Backup support, a significant enhancement that allows backing up only the data blocks that have changed since the last backup, rather than copying the entire data directory every time. This feature drastically reduces backup times, storage requirements, and network usage, making it ideal for large-scale databases and environments with frequent backup schedules. The implementation leverages block-level change tracking and backup manifests to ensure data consistency and integrates seamlessly with existing tools like pg_basebackup and WAL archiving for comprehensive disaster recovery solutions. We have shown practical scenarios in Chapter 10.

Note 2 While PostgreSQL 17 introduces powerful incremental backup capabilities, certain best practices and limitations remain. An initial full base backup is still mandatory before incremental backups can be utilized. WAL archiving continues to be essential for achieving point-in-time recovery (PITR), ensuring transaction consistency beyond backup snapshots. Additionally, backup and recovery tools must support backup manifests, which are critical for tracking file states and changes. It's important to note that incremental backups are physical backups, dealing with raw data files at the storage level, unlike pg_dump, which creates logical, schema-level backups suitable for individual database exports or migrations.

To get started, we need to install the *Barman* utility.

Installation of Barman

In this section, we will install Barman using yum installation.

Step 1: Install and verify the PostgreSQL repository.

On the server we want to use as a backup server, we can install the PostgreSQL repositories using the command below.

Log in as *root* user and run the *yum* command.

```
[root@centos7 ~]# yum install -y https://download.postgresql.org/pub/repos/yum/reporpms/EL-7-x86_64/pgdg-redhat-repo-latest.noarch.rpm
```

Verify the repo using the command repolist.

```
[root@centos7 ~]# yum repolist
```

Step 2: We must install the recommended Extra Packages for Enterprise Linux (EPEL) repository configuration. We can install EPEL as shown below:

```
[root@centos7 ~]# yum install epel-release
```

Step 3: Install the *Barman* utility.

```
[root@centos7 ~]# yum install barman
```

A new user named *barman* will be created as part of the **Barman** installation. Check the user and change its password.

```
[root@barman_host ~]# id barman
uid=998(barman) gid=996(barman) groups=996(barman)
[root@barman_host ~]# passwd barman
Changing password for user barman.
New password:
BAD PASSWORD: The password is shorter than 8 characters
```

```
Retype new password:
passwd: all authentication tokens updated successfully.
[root@barman_host ~]#
```

We can use the below command to verify the installed barman version.

```
[root@barman_host ~]# barman --version
3.7.0 Barman by EnterpriseDB (www.enterprisedb.com)
[root@barman_host ~]#
```

With this step, the installation of *Barman* is completed.

In the next section, we will see how to configure *Barman* and perform backup and recovery operations using it.

Configuring Barman

Below is our setup for this scenario.

postgres database cluster server: *postgresql_db_server*

Barman backup server: *barman_host*

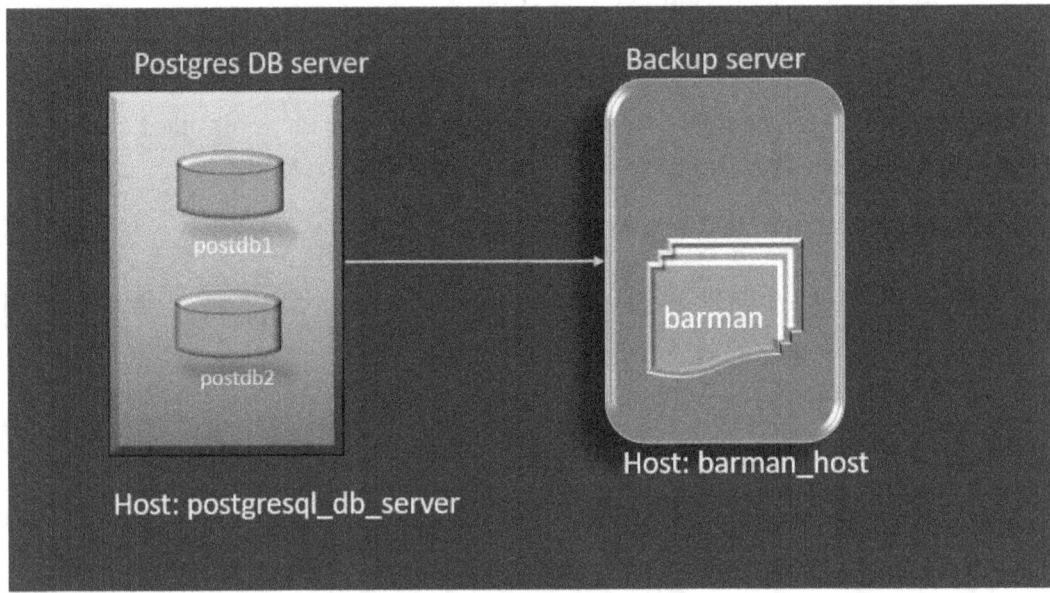

Figure 5-3. *PostgreSQL and Barman backup server*

Step 1: As the *root* user, add the *hostname* and *IP address* of each server to the */etc/hosts* file.

```
[root@barman_host ~]# cat /etc/hosts
```

192.168.2.30 barman_host **barman_host**
192.168.2.11 postgresql_db_server **postgresql_db_server**
[root@barman_host ~]#

Step 2: In the PostgreSQL database server, create a role with the name *barman*. This role will be used in the configuration file of the Barman server.

postgres=# **create user barman superuser password 'welcome';**
CREATE ROLE
postgres=#

Step 3: Configure passwordless authentication in the Barman server and PostgreSQL database server.

On the Barman server, perform the following:

[root@barman_host ~]# **su - barman**
[barman@barman_host ~]# **ssh-keygen -t rsa**

Copy the ssh keys to the PostgreSQL database server.

[barman@barman_host ~]# **ssh-copy-id -i ~/.ssh/id_rsa.pub postgres@postgresql_db_server**

Test the passwordless connections from the backup server.

-bash-4.2$ **ssh 'postgres@postgresql_db_server'**
Last login: Sun Jul 30 10:32:15 2023 from barman_host
[postgres@postgresql_db_server ~]$

On the PostgreSQL database server, issue the below command as *postgres* user to generate the SSH keys.

[postgres@postgresql_db_server ~]$ **ssh-keygen -t rsa**
Generating public/private rsa key pair.
Enter file in which to save the key (/home/postgres/.ssh/id_rsa):
Enter passphrase (empty for no passphrase):
Enter same passphrase again:
Your identification has been saved in /home/postgres/.ssh/id_rsa.
Your public key has been saved in /home/postgres/.ssh/id_rsa.pub.
The key fingerprint is:

CHAPTER 5   POSTGRESQL BACKUP AND RECOVERY

SHA256:UgxniePxhAGFMXBdqsUMy1w+7YUnUisb7JH8sI5Ys4k postgres@postgresql_db_server
The key's randomart image is:
```
+---[RSA 2048]----+
|  ..**===.       |
|   +.@*Xoo       |
|    +.^=B o      |
|     +.&.+       |
|     + = S       |
|    + * .        |
|   E + .         |
|                 |
|                 |
+----[SHA256]-----+
```
[postgres@postgresql_db_server ~]$

Copy the ssh keys from PostgreSQL server to barman backup server

[postgres@postgresql_db_server ~]$ **ssh-copy-id -i ~/.ssh/id_rsa.pub barman@barman_host**
/usr/bin/ssh-copy-id: INFO: Source of key(s) to be installed: "/home/postgres/.ssh/id_rsa.pub"
The authenticity of host 'barman_host (192.168.2.30)' can't be established.
ECDSA key fingerprint is SHA256:YpDYEJtpp16FvKQ/X2muJuFwkOiL9YG2fRJWnQLaxGE.
ECDSA key fingerprint is MD5:77:b3:32:b9:5f:74:27:6d:df:1c:0f:c9:76:16:7c:cb.
Are you sure you want to continue connecting (yes/no)? yes
/usr/bin/ssh-copy-id: INFO: attempting to log in with the new key(s), to filter out any that are already installed
/usr/bin/ssh-copy-id: INFO: 1 key(s) remain to be installed -- if you are prompted now it is to install the new keys
barman@barman_host's password:

Number of key(s) added: 1

CHAPTER 5 POSTGRESQL BACKUP AND RECOVERY

Now try logging into the machine, with: "ssh 'barman@barman_host'"
and check to make sure that only the key(s) you wanted were added.

[postgres@postgresql_db_server ~]$

Test the connection.

```
[postgres@postgresql_db_server ~]$ ssh 'barman@barman_host'
Last login: Sat Jul 29 15:51:46 2023 from 192.168.2.1
-bash-4.2$
```

Step 4: Configure the Global Configuration File in the Barman server.

The main configuration file in the Barman server is */etc/barman.conf*. This configuration file contains options such as compression type, main directory, etc.

Edit */etc/barman.conf* to set the global parameters that are suitable for the environment.

As *root* user, we will add the parameters below for our setup and save the file.

```
[root@barman_host ~]# vi /etc/barman.conf
compression = gzip
immediate_checkpoint = true
basebackup_retry_times = 3
reuse_backup = link
```

Step 5: Configure the PostgreSQL server configuration files in the Barman server.

We must configure the server configuration files on the Barman server, one for each PostgreSQL server. These configuration files are located in the */etc/barman.d* directory and must have a *.conf* suffix. The configuration file will contain the connection information of the database server and backup options.

As *root* user, execute the below steps.

```
[root@barman_host etc]# cd /etc/barman.d/
[root@barman_host barman.d]# ls -ltr
total 16
-rw-r--r--. 1 root root 1500 Jul 25 08:50 streaming-server.conf-template
-rw-r--r--. 1 root root 1546 Jul 25 08:50 ssh-server.conf-template
-rw-r--r--. 1 root root  950 Jul 25 08:50 passive-server.conf-template
[root@barman_host barman.d]#
```

CHAPTER 5   POSTGRESQL BACKUP AND RECOVERY

```
[root@barman_host barman.d]# vi postgresql_db_server.conf
[postgresql_db_server]
description = "postgresql_db_server backup config"
ssh_command = ssh postgres@postgresql_db_server
conninfo = host=postgresql_db_server user=barman port=5432 dbname=postgres
password=welcome
backup_options = concurrent_backup
backup_method = rsync
archiver = on
incoming_wals_directory=/u01/barman/backup/postgresql_db_server/wallogs
[root@barman_host barman.d]#
```

Please note that we need to create a directory with name */u01/barman/backup/postgresql_db_server/wallogs* and change its permission to *0700 barman*.

Step 6: Verify the configuration for the server setup in the Barman server.

Log in as a *barman* user on the backup server and run the below commands.

```
-bash-4.2$ barman list-server
postgresql_db_server - postgresql_db_server backup config
-bash-4.2$
```

```
-bash-4.2$ barman check postgresql_db_server
Server postgresql_db_server:
        WAL archive: FAILED (please make sure WAL shipping is setup)
        PostgreSQL: FAILED
        superuser or standard user with backup privileges: OK
        wal_level: OK
        directories: OK
        retention policy settings: OK
        backup maximum age: OK (no last_backup_maximum_age provided)
        backup minimum size: OK (0 B)
        wal maximum age: OK (no last_wal_maximum_age provided)
        wal size: OK (0 B)
        compression settings: OK
        failed backups: OK (there are 0 failed backups)
```

CHAPTER 5 POSTGRESQL BACKUP AND RECOVERY

```
        minimum redundancy requirements: OK (have 0 backups, expected at
        least 0)
        ssh: OK (PostgreSQL server)
        systemid coherence: OK (no system Id stored on disk)
        archive_mode: OK
        archive_command: OK
        continuous archiving: OK
        archiver errors: OK
-bash-4.2$
```

If you notice, we see a couple of errors. Let us see how to correct them.

For "PostgreSQL: FAILED," we need to add the backup server information along with the *barman* username in the *pg_hba.conf* on the PostgreSQL server and restart the *postgres* service.

```
[postgres@postgresql_db_server data]$ cat pg_hba.conf | grep barman
host    all            barman             192.168.2.30/32           trust
[postgres@postgresql_db_server data]$
```

For the WAL error, WAL archive: FAILED (please make sure WAL shipping is setup).

In the PostgreSQL server, we need to configure the WAL parameters to correct one as shown below:

```
postgres=# alter system set archive_command='test ! -f barman@barman_host:/
var/lib/barman/postgresql_db_server/incoming/%f && rsync -a %p barman@
barman_host:/var/lib/barman/postgresql_db_server/incoming/%f';
ALTER SYSTEM
postgres=# e
```

Please note that the location used in *archive_command* should match the parameter below, which we set in the file *postgresql_db_server.conf*, which we added in step 5.

```
incoming_wals_directory=/u01/barman/backup/postgresql_db_server/wallogs
```

Once you fix the above two errors, if you rerun the check command, it should come clean. Please refer to the screenshot below for a successful configuration check.

323

CHAPTER 5 POSTGRESQL BACKUP AND RECOVERY

```
-bash-4.2$ barman check postgresql_db_server
Server postgresql_db_server:
        PostgreSQL: OK
        superuser or standard user with backup privileges: OK
        wal_level: OK
        directories: OK
        retention policy settings: OK
        backup maximum age: OK (no last_backup_maximum_age provided)
        backup minimum size: OK (613.2 MiB)
        wal maximum age: OK (no last_wal_maximum_age provided)
        wal size: OK (86.2 KiB)
        compression settings: OK
        failed backups: OK (there are 0 failed backups)
        minimum redundancy requirements: OK (have 3 backups, expected at least 0)
        ssh: OK (PostgreSQL server)
        systemid coherence: OK
        archive_mode: OK
        archive_command: OK
        continuous archiving: OK
        archiver errors: OK
-bash-4.2$
```

Step 7: From the Barman host, do a force log switch for WAL.

```
-bash-4.2$ barman switch-xlog --force --archive postgresql_db_server
The WAL file 0000000100000003000000CD has been closed on server
'postgresql_db_server'
Waiting for the WAL file 0000000100000003000000CD from server 'postgresql_
db_server' (max: 30 seconds)
Processing xlog segments from file archival for postgresql_db_server
        0000000100000003000000CD
-bash-4.2$
```

Step 8: Create a test schema *backuptest* and table *testtab* in the database *postdb1*.

```
postgres=# \c postdb1;
You are now connected to database "postdb1" as user "postgres".
postdb1=# create schema backuptest (name varchar);
ERROR:  syntax error at or near "("
LINE 1: create schema backuptest (name varchar);
                                 ^
postdb1=# create schema backuptest;
CREATE SCHEMA
postdb1=# create table backuptest.testtab (name varchar);
CREATE TABLE
```

```
postdb1=# insert into backuptest.testtab values ('Data_before_level0_
backup');
INSERT 0 1
postdb1=# select * from backuptest.testtab;
          name
---------------------------
 Data_before_level0_backup
(1 row)

postdb1=#
```

Backup Using Barman

Step 9: Perform an incremental backup using the below barman command.

```
-bash-4.2$ barman backup --immediate-checkpoint --name level0 postgresql_
db_server --reuse-backup=link
Starting backup using rsync-concurrent method for server postgresql_db_
server in /var/lib/barman/postgresql_db_server/base/20230730T141028
Backup start at LSN: 3/DD000028 (000000010000003000000DD, 00000028)
This is the first backup for server postgresql_db_server
WAL segments preceding the current backup have been found:
Starting backup copy via rsync/SSH for 20230730T141028
Copy done (time: 7 seconds)
This is the first backup for server postgresql_db_server
Asking PostgreSQL server to finalize the backup.
Backup size: 613.2 MiB. Actual size on disk: 613.2 MiB (-0.00%
deduplication ratio).
Backup end at LSN: 3/DD000138 (000000010000003000000DD, 00000138)
Backup completed (start time: 2023-07-30 14:10:28.173156, elapsed time: 10
seconds)
Processing xlog segments from file archival for postgresql_db_server
        000000010000003000000DC
        000000010000003000000DD
        000000010000003000000DD.00000028.backup
-bash-4.2$
```

CHAPTER 5   POSTGRESQL BACKUP AND RECOVERY

To check the backup, use the below two commands:

```
-bash-4.2$ barman list-backup postgresql_db_server
postgresql_db_server 20230730T141028 'level0' - Sun Jul 30 14:10:35 2023 -
Size: 613.2 MiB - WAL Size: 0 B (tablespaces: tblspc_db1:/u01/pgdata/
postgres15/tablespace1)
-bash-4.2$
```

```
-bash-4.2$ barman show-backup postgresql_db_server   20230730T141028
Backup 20230730T141028:
  Backup Name            : level0
  Server Name            : postgresql_db_server
  System Id              : 7257293030347365311
  Status                 : DONE
  PostgreSQL Version     : 150003
  PGDATA directory       : /var/pgdata/postgres15/data

  Tablespaces:
    tblspc_db1           : /u01/pgdata/postgres15/tablespace1 (oid: 57423)

  Base backup information:
    Disk usage           : 613.2 MiB (613.2 MiB with WALs)
    Incremental size     : 613.2 MiB (-0.00%)
    Timeline             : 1
    Begin WAL            : 00000001000000030000000DD
    End WAL              : 00000001000000030000000DD
    WAL number           : 1
    WAL compression ratio: 99.90%
    Begin time           : 2023-07-30 14:10:27.488840-05:00
    End time             : 2023-07-30 14:10:35.639718-05:00
    Copy time            : 7 seconds
    Estimated throughput : 83.5 MiB/s
    Begin Offset         : 40
    End Offset           : 312
    Begin LSN            : 3/DD000028
    End LSN              : 3/DD000138

  WAL information:
```

```
       No of files          : 0
       Disk usage           : 0 B
       Last available       : 000000010000000300000000DD

    Catalog information:
       Retention Policy     : not enforced
       Previous Backup      : - (this is the oldest base backup)
       Next Backup          : - (this is the latest base backup)
-bash-4.2$
```

Step 10: In the PostgreSQL server, insert a new row in the schema *backuptest*.

```
postdb1=# insert into backuptest.testtab values ('Data_after_level0_
before_1st_level1');
INSERT 0 1
postdb1=# select pg_switch_wal();
 pg_switch_wal
---------------
 3/DE0001D8
(1 row)

postdb1=# select pg_switch_wal();
 pg_switch_wal
---------------
 3/DF000000
(1 row)

postdb1=# select * from backuptest.testtab;
               name
-------------------------------------
 Data_before_level0_backup
 Data_after_level0_before_1st_level1
(2 rows)

postdb1=#
```

Step 11: Perform a level 1 backup using the command below.

CHAPTER 5   POSTGRESQL BACKUP AND RECOVERY

```
-bash-4.2$ barman backup postgresql_db_server --reuse-backup=link --name firstINCR
Starting backup using rsync-concurrent method for server postgresql_db_server in /var/lib/barman/postgresql_db_server/base/20230730T141234
Backup start at LSN: 3/E0000028 (000000010000000300000E0, 00000028)
Starting backup copy via rsync/SSH for 20230730T141234
Copy done (time: less than one second)
Asking PostgreSQL server to finalize the backup.
Backup size: 613.2 MiB. Actual size on disk: 25.0 KiB (-100.00% deduplication ratio).
Backup end at LSN: 3/E0000100 (000000010000000300000E0, 00000100)
Backup completed (start time: 2023-07-30 14:12:34.878540, elapsed time: 3 seconds)
Processing xlog segments from file archival for postgresql_db_server
        000000010000000300000DE
        000000010000000300000DF
        000000010000000300000E0
        000000010000000300000E0.00000028.backup
-bash-4.2$
```

Step 12: In the PostgreSQL server, insert a new row in the *backuptest.testtab* table.

```
postdb1=# insert into backuptest.testtab values ('Data_after_first_INCR_before_2nd_INCR');
INSERT 0 1
postdb1=# select pg_switch_wal();
 pg_switch_wal
---------------
 3/E1000220
(1 row)

postdb1=# select pg_switch_wal();
 pg_switch_wal
---------------
 3/E2000078
```

(1 row)

```
postdb1=# select * from backuptest.testtab;
             name
---------------------------------------
 Data_before_level0_backup
 Data_after_level0_before_1st_level1
 Data_after_first_INCR_before_2nd_INCR
(3 rows)

postdb1=#
```

Step 13: Perform a second incremental backup using the command below.

```
-bash-4.2$ barman backup postgresql_db_server --reuse-backup=link --name secondINCR
Starting backup using rsync-concurrent method for server postgresql_db_server in /var/lib/barman/postgresql_db_server/base/20230730T141327
Backup start at LSN: 3/E3000028 (0000000100000003000000E3, 00000028)
Starting backup copy via rsync/SSH for 20230730T141327
Copy done (time: less than one second)
Asking PostgreSQL server to finalize the backup.
Backup size: 613.2 MiB. Actual size on disk: 25.0 KiB (-100.00% deduplication ratio).
Backup end at LSN: 3/E3000100 (0000000100000003000000E3, 00000100)
Backup completed (start time: 2023-07-30 14:13:27.789774, elapsed time: 3 seconds)
Processing xlog segments from file archival for postgresql_db_server
        0000000100000003000000E1
        0000000100000003000000E2
        0000000100000003000000E3
        0000000100000003000000E3.00000028.backup
-bash-4.2$
```

Step 14: Check the current backups.

```
-bash-4.2$ barman list-backup postgresql_db_server
```

CHAPTER 5   POSTGRESQL BACKUP AND RECOVERY

```
postgresql_db_server 20230730T141327 'secondINCR' - Sun Jul 30 14:13:28
2023 - Size: 613.2 MiB - WAL Size: 0 B (tablespaces: tblspc_db1:/u01/
pgdata/postgres15/tablespace1)
```
**postgresql_db_server 20230730T141234 'firstINCR' - Sun Jul 30 14:12:35
2023 - Size: 613.2 MiB - WAL Size: 48.4 KiB (tablespaces:** tblspc_db1:/u01/
pgdata/postgres15/tablespace1)
```
postgresql_db_server 20230730T141028 'level0' - Sun Jul 30 14:10:35 2023 -
Size: 613.2 MiB - WAL Size: 48.3 KiB (tablespaces: tblspc_db1:/u01/pgdata/
postgres15/tablespace1)
-bash-4.2$
```

Let us get the time of backup "firstINCR".

```
-bash-4.2$ barman show-backup postgresql_db_server 20230730T141234
Backup 20230730T141234:
  Backup Name            : firstINCR
  Server Name            : postgresql_db_server
  System Id              : 7257293030347365311
  Status                 : DONE
  PostgreSQL Version     : 150003
  PGDATA directory       : /var/pgdata/postgres15/data

  Tablespaces:
    tblspc_db1           : /u01/pgdata/postgres15/tablespace1 (oid: 57423)

  Base backup information:
    Disk usage             : 613.2 MiB (613.2 MiB with WALs)
    Incremental size       : 25.0 KiB (-100.00%)
    Timeline               : 1
    Begin WAL              : 000000010000000300000E0
    End WAL                : 000000010000000300000E0
    WAL number             : 1
    WAL compression ratio: 99.90%
    Begin time             : 2023-07-30 14:12:34.216495-05:00
    End time               : 2023-07-30 14:12:35.726610-05:00
    Copy time              : less than one second
    Estimated throughput : 37.4 KiB/s
```

```
      Begin Offset            : 40
      End Offset              : 256
      Begin LSN               : 3/E0000028
      End LSN                 : 3/E0000100

  WAL information:
      No of files             : 3
      Disk usage              : 48.4 KiB
      WAL rate                : 272.98/hour
      Compression ratio       : 99.90%
      Last available          : 000000010000000300000E3

  Catalog information:
      Retention Policy        : not enforced
      Previous Backup         : 20230730T141028
      Next Backup             : 20230730T141327
-bash-4.2$
```

We will try to do a recovery using the end backup time, using the backup piece 20230730T141234 and its end time, a few seconds over it, to be precise.

```
Begin time: 2023-07-30 14:12:34.216495-05:00
End time: 2023-07-30 14:12:35.726610-05:00
```

Performing Recovery Using Barman

We will try to do point-in-time recovery too little over time of end time.

Below is current data in the *backuptest.testtab* table.

```
postdb1=# select * from backuptest.testtab;
                name
----------------------------------------
 Data_before_level0_backup
 Data_after_level0_before_1st_level1
 Data_after_first_INCR_before_2nd_INCR
(3 rows)

postdb1=# exit
```

Chapter 5   POSTGRESQL BACKUP AND RECOVERY

Step 1: Stop the PostgreSQL service.

```
[postgres@postgresql_db_server data]$ pg_ctl stop
waiting for server to shut down.... done
server stopped
[postgres@postgresql_db_server data]$
```

Step 2: Perform the barman restore/recovery using the below command.

```
-bash-4.2$ barman recover --remote-ssh-command "ssh postgres@postgresql_
db_server" postgresql_db_server 20230730T141234 /var/pgdata/postgres15/
data  --target-time '2023-07-30 14:12:40'
Processing xlog segments from file archival for postgresql_db_server
        000000010000000300000E5
Starting remote restore for server postgresql_db_server using backup
20230730T141234
Destination directory: /var/pgdata/postgres15/data
Remote command: ssh postgres@postgresql_db_server
Doing PITR. Recovery target time: '2023-07-30 14:12:40-05:00'
        57423, tblspc_db1, /u01/pgdata/postgres15/tablespace1
Copying the base backup.
Copying required WAL segments.
Generating recovery configuration
Identify dangerous settings in destination directory.

IMPORTANT
These settings have been modified to prevent data losses

postgresql.auto.conf line 3: archive_command = false

Recovery completed (start time: 2023-07-30 14:22:21.223746-05:00, elapsed
time: 6 seconds)
Your PostgreSQL server has been successfully prepared for recovery!
-bash-4.2$
```

Step 3: Start the PostgreSQL service.

```
[postgres@postgresql_db_server barman_recover]$ pg_ctl start -D /var/
pgdata/postgres15/data -l /tmp/server.log
```

```
waiting for server to start.... stopped waiting
pg_ctl: could not start server
Examine the log output.
[postgres@postgresql_db_server barman_recover]$
```

Step 4: Perform a validation of the restore and recovery.

Connect to the *postdb1* database, and if you see the table *testtab*, it should NOT have a row that was inserted after **firstINCR** backup, i.e., it should not have the row '*Data_after_first_INCR_before_2nd_INCR*'.

```
[postgres@postgresql_db_server barman_recover]$ psql
psql (15.3)
Type "help" for help.

postgres=# \c postdb1;
You are now connected to database "postdb1" as user "postgres".
postdb1=# select * from backuptest.testtab;
              name
--------------------------------------
 Data_before_level0_backup
 Data_after_level0_before_1st_level1
(2 rows)

postdb1=#
```

As we can see, the database cluster did a point-in-time recovery using the Barman utility.

Scenario 19: Backup and Restore Using pgBackRest

In this scenario, we will use another external tool, ***pgBackRest***, to backup and restore PostgreSQL databases. ***pgBackRest*** is an open-source backup and restore tool that we can use to create physical backups. It is very easy to install/configure and use. It includes many features, such as a parallel backup option, a local and remote backup/restore option, support for full, incremental, and differential backup types, backup compression, and a backup integrity check.

CHAPTER 5 POSTGRESQL BACKUP AND RECOVERY

Step 1: Install a PostgreSQL database cluster.

As a first step for this scenario, we will install PostgreSQL version 16 and create a user-defined database with one schema with a few tables and some data in those tables.

To install PostgreSQL 16, perform the below steps.

```
[root@pg_backuprst_01 ~]$ yum install -y https://download.postgresql.org/pub/repos/yum/reporpms/EL-7-x86_64/pgdg-redhat-repo-latest.noarch.rpm

[root@pg_backuprst_01 ~]$ yum install epel-release
[root@pg_backuprst_01 ~]$ yum install -y postgresql16-server
[root@pg_backuprst_01 ~]$ yum install -y postgresql16-contrib
/usr/pgsql-16/bin/postgresql-16-setup initdb
[root@pg_backuprst_01 ~]$ systemctl enable postgresql-16
[root@pg_backuprst_01 ~]$ systemctl start postgresql-16
[root@pg_backuprst_01 ~]$ systemctl status postgresql-16
```

Let us use the script below to create a new database and new schema with few tables.

Connect to the psql console and create database/schema/tables as shown below.

```
create database hrmdb;
\c hrmdb;

create schema hrm;

create table hrm.empinfo (ename varchar, empno integer, edept varchar,
primary key (empno));
create index empno_udx on hrm.empinfo (edept);
insert into hrm.empinfo values ('Peter_J',1000,'Sales');
insert into hrm.empinfo values ('Robin_M',1001,'accounts');
insert into hrm.empinfo values ('David_S',1002,'Sales');
insert into hrm.empinfo values ('Stefeny',1003,'marketing');
insert into hrm.empinfo values ('Marshal',1004,'Sales');
insert into hrm.empinfo values ('Ross',1006,'5ccounts');
insert into hrm.empinfo values ('leanord',1200,'Sales');
insert into hrm.empinfo values ('Mark_W',1030,'Sales');
insert into hrm.empinfo values ('MarkK',1022,'marketing');
insert into hrm.empinfo values ('Raj_M',1094,'Sales');
```

```
insert into hrm.empinfo values ('Katy',1898,'accounts');

create table hrm.deptinfo (dname varchar, deptno integer);

insert into hrm.deptinfo values ('sales',1111);
insert into hrm.deptinfo values ('accounts',1212);
insert into hrm.deptinfo values ('marketing',2312);

create table hrm.salinfo (ename varchar, salno integer);
insert into hrm.salinfo values ('sales',65000);
insert into hrm.salinfo values ('accounts',83000);
insert into hrm.salinfo values ('marketing',76000);

select * from   hrm.empinfo;
select * from   hrm.salinfo;
select * from   hrm.deptinfo;
```

Please see below for the output of the above script.

```
[postgres@pg_backuprst_01 ~]$ psql
psql (16.3)
Type "help" for help.

postgres=# create database hrmdb;
CREATE DATABASE
postgres-# \l
                           List of databases
    Name    |  Owner   | Encoding |  Collate   |   Ctype    | ICU Locale |
 Locale Provider |   Access privileges
------------+----------+----------+------------+------------+------------+
-----------------+-----------------------
 hrmdb      | postgres | UTF8     | en_US.UTF-8 | en_US.UTF-8 |           |
 libc            |
 postgres   | postgres | UTF8     | en_US.UTF-8 | en_US.UTF-8 |           |
 libc            |
 template0  | postgres | UTF8     | en_US.UTF-8 | en_US.UTF-8 |           |
 libc            | =c/postgres           +
                 |                       |            |            |            |            |
                 | postgres=CTc/postgres
```

CHAPTER 5   POSTGRESQL BACKUP AND RECOVERY

```
 template1 | postgres | UTF8    | en_US.UTF-8 | en_US.UTF-8 |                |
 libc                | =c/postgres           +
                     |          |            |             |             |
                     | postgres=CTc/postgres
(4 rows)

postgres-# \c hrmdb;
You are now connected to database "hrmdb" as user "postgres".
hrmdb-# create schema hrm;
CREATE SCHEMA
hrmdb=# create table hrm.empinfo (ename varchar, empno integer, edept
varchar, primary key (empno));
insert into hrm.empinfo values ('David_S',1002,'Sales');
insert into hrm.empinfo values ('Stefeny',1003,'marketing');
insert into hrm.empinfo values ('Marshal',1004,'Sales');
insert into hrm.empinfo values ('Ross',1006,'5ccounts');
insert into hrm.empinfo values ('leanord',1200,'Sales');
insert into hrm.empinfo values ('Mark_W',1030,'Sales');
insert into hrm.empinfo values ('MarkK',1022,'marketing');
insert into hrm.empinfo values ('Raj_M',1094,'Sales');
insert into hrm.empinfo values ('Katy',1898,'accounts');

create table hrm.deptinfo (dname varchar, deptno integer);

insert into hrm.deptinfo values ('sales',1111);
insert into hrm.deptinfo values ('accounts',1212);
insert into hrm.deptinfo values ('marketing',2312);
CREATE TABLE
hrmdb=# create index empno_udx on hrm.empinfo (edept);
CREATE INDEX
hrmdb=# insert into hrm.empinfo values ('Peter_J',1000,'Sales');
INSERT 0 1
hrmdb=# insert into hrm.empinfo values ('Robin_M',1001,'accounts');
INSERT 0 1
hrmdb=# insert into hrm.empinfo values ('David_S',1002,'Sales');
INSERT 0 1
hrmdb=# insert into hrm.empinfo values ('Stefeny',1003,'marketing');
```

CHAPTER 5　POSTGRESQL BACKUP AND RECOVERY

```
INSERT 0 1
hrmdb=# insert into hrm.empinfo values ('Marshal',1004,'Sales');
INSERT 0 1
hrmdb=# insert into hrm.empinfo values ('Ross',1006,'5ccounts');
INSERT 0 1
hrmdb=# insert into hrm.empinfo values ('leanord',1200,'Sales');
INSERT 0 1
hrmdb=# insert into hrm.empinfo values ('Mark_W',1030,'Sales');
INSERT 0 1
hrmdb=# insert into hrm.empinfo values ('MarkK',1022,'marketing');
INSERT 0 1
hrmdb=# insert into hrm.empinfo values ('Raj_M',1094,'Sales');
INSERT 0 1
hrmdb=# insert into hrm.empinfo values ('Katy',1898,'accounts');
INSERT 0 1
hrmdb=#
hrmdb=#
hrmdb=# create table hrm.deptinfo (dname varchar, deptno integer);
CREATE TABLE
hrmdb=#
hrmdb=# insert into hrm.deptinfo values ('sales',1111);
INSERT 0 1
hrmdb=# insert into hrm.deptinfo values ('accounts',1212);
INSERT 0 1
hrmdb=# insert into hrm.deptinfo values ('marketing',2312);
INSERT 0 1
hrmdb=#
hrmdb=# **\dn hrm***
 **List of schemas**
 Name |  Owner
------+----------
 hrm  | postgres
(1 row)
```

CHAPTER 5　POSTGRESQL BACKUP AND RECOVERY

```
hrmdb=# \dt hrm.*
          List of relations
 Schema |   Name    | Type  |  Owner
--------+-----------+-------+----------
 hrm    | deptinfo  | table | postgres
 hrm    | empinfo   | table | postgres
(2 rows)

hrmdb=#
```

Step 2: Install and configure *pgBackRest*.

Log in as *root* user and run the below *yum* command to install the *pgBackRest* rpm.

```
[root@pg_backuprst_01 ~]# yum install pgbackrest
Loaded plugins: fastestmirror
Loading mirror speeds from cached hostfile
 * base: tx-mirror.tier.net
 * epel: pubmirror2.math.uh.edu
 * extras: tx-mirror.tier.net
 * updates: abqix.mm.fcix.net
Resolving Dependencies
--> Running transaction check
---> Package pgbackrest.x86_64 0:2.47-1PGDG.rhel7 will be installed
--> Finished Dependency Resolution

Dependencies Resolved

================================================================================
 Package         Arch         Version              Repository            Size
================================================================================
Installing:
 pgbackrest      x86_64       2.47-1PGDG.rhel7     pgdg-common          389 k

Transaction Summary
================================================================================
Install  1 Package
```

```
Total download size: 389 k
Installed size: 944 k
Is this ok [y/d/N]: y
Downloading packages:
pgbackrest-2.47-1PGDG.rhel7.x86_64.rpm  | 389 kB   00:00:00
Running transaction check
Running transaction test
Transaction test succeeded
Running transaction
  Installing : pgbackrest-2.47-1PGDG.rhel7.x86_64     1/1
  Verifying  : pgbackrest-2.47-1PGDG.rhel7.x86_64     1/1

Installed:
  pgbackrest.x86_64 0:2.47-1PGDG.rhel7

Complete!
[root@pg_backuprst_01 ~]#
```

Verify if the ***pgBackRest*** is installed correctly.

```
[postgres@pg_backuprst_01 ~]$ pgbackrest
pgBackRest 2.47 - General help

Usage:
    pgbackrest [options] [command]

Commands:
    annotate       Add or modify backup annotation.
    archive-get    Get a WAL segment from the archive.
    archive-push   Push a WAL segment to the archive.
    backup         Backup a database cluster.
    check          Check the configuration.
    expire         Expire backups that exceed retention.
    help           Get help.
    info           Retrieve information about backups.
    repo-get       Get a file from a repository.
    repo-ls        List files in a repository.
    restore        Restore a database cluster.
```

CHAPTER 5   POSTGRESQL BACKUP AND RECOVERY

```
    server           pgBackRest server.
    server-ping      Ping pgBackRest server.
    stanza-create    Create the required stanza data.
    stanza-delete    Delete a stanza.
    stanza-upgrade   Upgrade a stanza.
    start            Allow pgBackRest processes to run.
    stop             Stop pgBackRest processes from running.
    verify           Verify contents of the repository.
    version          Get version.

Use 'pgbackrest help [command]' for more information.
[postgres@pg_backuprst_01 ~]$
```

Check the version of the *pgBackRest* utility.

```
[postgres@pg_backuprst_01 ~]$ pgbackrest version
pgBackRest 2.47
[postgres@pg_backuprst_01 ~]$
```

Verify and examine the *pgbackrest.conf* configuration file in the */etc* directory and also the location of the binary file.

```
[postgres@pg_backuprst_01 ~]$ cat /etc/pgbackrest.conf
[global]
repo1-path=/var/lib/pgbackrest

#[main]
#pg1-path=/var/lib/pgsql/10/data
[postgres@pg_backuprst_01 ~]$

[postgres@pg_backuprst_01 ~]$ which pgbackrest
/bin/pgbackrest
[postgres@pg_backuprst_01 ~]$
```

Step 3: Update *.bash_profile* for the *postgres* user.

```
export PATH=$PATH:/usr/pgsql-16/bin
export PGDATA=/var/lib/pgsql/16/data/
export PGPORT=5432
```

CHAPTER 5   POSTGRESQL BACKUP AND RECOVERY

Step 4: Update the data directory in the *pgBackRest* configuration file.

As *root* user, modify */etc/pgbackrest.conf* and include the data directory.

```
[root@pg_backuprst_01 ~]# cat /etc/pgbackrest.conf
[global]
repo1-path=/var/lib/pgbackrest

#[pg_backurst_01_bkp]
pg1-path=/var/lib/pgsql/16/data
pg1-port=5432
[root@pg_backuprst_01 ~]#
```

Step 5: As *root* user, create the below directories for archive log location and for backups.

```
[root@pg_backuprst_01 ~]# mkdir -p /u01/postgres/archive
[root@pg_backuprst_01 ~]# mkdir -p /u02/pgBackRest/pg164_backups
[root@pg_backuprst_01 ~]# chown -Rf postgres:postgres /u01/
[root@pg_backuprst_01 ~]# chown -Rf postgres:postgres /u02/
[root@pg_backuprst_01 ~]# chmod -Rf 777 /u01/
[root@pg_backuprst_01 ~]# chmod -Rf 777 /u02
```

Step 6: Update the database cluster configuration file with below changes.

```
listen_addresses = '*'
archive_command=on
archive_command = 'pgbackrest --stanza=prod_bkp archive-push %p'

[postgres@pg_backuprst_01 data]$ cat postgresql.conf | grep listen
listen_addresses = '*'          # what IP address(es) to listen on;
[postgres@pg_backuprst_01 data]$ cat postgresql.conf | grep archive_mode
archive_mode = on               # enables archiving; off, on, or always
[postgres@pg_backuprst_01 data]$ cat postgresql.conf | grep archive_command
                                # (empty string indicates archive_
command should
archive_command = 'pgbackrest --stanza=prod_bkp archive-push
%p'                             # command to use to archive a logfile segment
[postgres@pg_backuprst_01 data]$
```

341

CHAPTER 5　POSTGRESQL BACKUP AND RECOVERY

Restart the postgres database cluster.

```
[root@pg_backuprst_01 ~]# systemctl stop postgresql-16
[root@pg_backuprst_01 ~]# systemctl start postgresql-16
```

Step 7: Create a stanza.

Before creating the stanza, let us see what does stanza means in pgBackRest.

A stanza defines the backup configuration for a specific PostgreSQL, including details like where it is located, how the database cluster will be backed up, the archiving options, etc.

Let us create the stanza for this scenario using the command below.

```
pgbackrest stanza-create --stanza=pg_backurst_01_bkp --log-level-console=info
```

```
[postgres@pg_backuprst_01 ~]$ pgbackrest stanza-create --stanza=pg_backurst_01_bkp --log-level-console=info
2023-08-29 11:44:05.619 P00   INFO: stanza-create command begin 2.47: --exec-id=2218-18e12ae8 --log-level-console=info --pg1-path=/var/lib/pgsql/16/data --pg1-port=5432 --repo1-path=/var/lib/pgbackrest --stanza=pg_backurst_01_bkp
2023-08-29 11:44:06.233 P00   INFO: stanza-create for stanza 'pg_backurst_01_bkp' on repo1
2023-08-29 11:44:06.267 P00   INFO: stanza-create command end: completed successfully (650ms)
[postgres@pg_backuprst_01 ~]$
```

Step 8: Run the *check* command to validate the configuration.

```
[postgres@pg_backuprst_01 data]$ pgbackrest --stanza=pg_backurst_01_bkp check --log-level-console=info
2023-08-29 12:56:03.716 P00   INFO: check command begin 2.47: --exec-id=3039-db4490b6 --log-level-console=info --pg1-path=/var/lib/pgsql/16/data --pg1-port=5432 --repo1-path=/var/lib/pgbackrest --stanza=pg_backurst_01_bkp
2023-08-29 12:56:04.325 P00   INFO: check repo1 configuration (primary)
2023-08-29 12:56:05.131 P00   INFO: check repo1 archive for WAL (primary)
```

CHAPTER 5   POSTGRESQL BACKUP AND RECOVERY

```
2023-08-29 12:56:05.131 P00    INFO: WAL segment 000000010000000000000003
successfully archived to '/var/lib/pgbackrest/archive/pg_backurst_01_
bkp/16-1/0000000100000000/000000010000000000000003-adba00d31a22f0a3421483dd
08780ac8dca99cbe.gz' on repo1
2023-08-29 12:56:05.131 P00    INFO: check command end: completed
successfully (1416ms)
[postgres@pg_backuprst_01 data]$
```

Step 9: Perform the *full database cluster backup* using the below command:

```
[postgres@pg_backuprst_01 data]$ pgbackrest --stanza=pg_backurst_01_bkp
--type=full backup --log-level-console=info
2023-08-29 13:16:03.011 P00    INFO: backup command begin 2.47: --exec-
id=3116-31b5775f --log-level-console=info --pg1-path=/var/lib/pgsql/16/data
--pg1-port=5432 --repo1-path=/var/lib/pgbackrest --stanza=pg_backurst_01_
bkp --type=full
WARN: option 'repo1-retention-full' is not set for 'repo1-retention-full-
type=count', the repository may run out of space
      HINT: to retain full backups indefinitely (without warning), set
option 'repo1-retention-full' to the maximum.
2023-08-29 13:16:03.728 P00    INFO: execute non-exclusive backup start:
backup begins after the next regular checkpoint completes
2023-08-29 13:16:04.838 P00    INFO: backup start archive =
000000010000000000000005, lsn = 0/5000060
2023-08-29 13:16:04.838 P00    INFO: check archive for prior segment
000000010000000000000004
2023-08-29 13:16:08.709 P00    INFO: execute non-exclusive backup stop and
wait for all WAL segments to archive
pgbackrest --stanza=pg_backurst_01_bkp --type=full backup --log-level-
console=info2023-08-29 13:16:09.213 P00    INFO: backup stop archive =
000000010000000000000005, lsn = 0/5000138
2023-08-29 13:16:09.219 P00    INFO: check archive for segment(s)
000000010000000000000005:000000010000000000000005
2023-08-29 13:16:09.248 P00    INFO: new backup label = 20230829-131603F
2023-08-29 13:16:09.325 P00    INFO: full backup size = 29.9MB, file
total = 1272
```

CHAPTER 5   POSTGRESQL BACKUP AND RECOVERY

```
2023-08-29 13:16:09.325 P00   INFO: backup command end: completed
successfully (6316ms)
2023-08-29 13:16:09.325 P00   INFO: expire command begin 2.47: --exec-
id=3116-31b5775f --log-level-console=info --repo1-path=/var/lib/pgbackrest
--stanza=pg_backurst_01_bkp
2023-08-29 13:16:09.333 P00   INFO: option 'repo1-retention-archive' is not
set - archive logs will not be expired
2023-08-29 13:16:09.333 P00   INFO: expire command end: completed
successfully (8ms)
[postgres@pg_backuprst_01 data]$
[postgres@pg_backuprst_01 data]$
[postgres@pg_backuprst_01 data]$
```

Step 10: Check the backup info in pgBackRest.

```
[postgres@pg_backuprst_01 data]$ pgbackrest info
stanza: pg_backurst_01_bkp
    status: ok
    cipher: none

    db (current)
        wal archive min/max (16): 000000010000000000000000
1/000000010000000000000005

        full backup: 20230829-131603F
            timestamp start/stop: 2023-08-29 13:16:03-05 / 2023-08-29
13:16:09-05
            wal start/stop: 000000010000000000000005 /
000000010000000000000005
            database size: 29.9MB, database backup size: 29.9MB
            repo1: backup set size: 4.0MB, backup size: 4.0MB
[postgres@pg_backuprst_01 data]$
```

Step 11: Create a new table in the *hrm* schema as shown below:

```
postgres=# \c hrmdb;
You are now connected to database "hrmdb" as user "postgres".
hrmdb=# create table hrm.pgbackrest_tab (name varchar(30));
```

CHAPTER 5   POSTGRESQL BACKUP AND RECOVERY

CREATE TABLE

```
hrmdb=# insert into hrm.pgbackrest_tab values ('After_full_
before_1st_incr');
INSERT 0 1
hrmdb=# select * from hrm.pgbackrest_tab;
          name
-----------------------------
 After_full_before_1st_incr
(1 row)

hrmdb=#
```

Step 12: Perform incremental backup using *pgBackRest*.

```
[postgres@pg_backuprst_01 data]$ pgbackrest --stanza=pg_backurst_01_bkp
--type=incr --log-level-console=info backup
2023-08-29 13:37:58.123 P00   INFO: backup command begin 2.47: --exec-
id=3201-56d253f6 --log-level-console=info --pg1-path=/var/lib/pgsql/16/data
--pg1-port=5432 --repo1-path=/var/lib/pgbackrest --stanza=pg_backurst_01_
bkp --type=incr
WARN: option 'repo1-retention-full' is not set for 'repo1-retention-full-
type=count', the repository may run out of space
      HINT: to retain full backups indefinitely (without warning), set
option 'repo1-retention-full' to the maximum.
2023-08-29 13:37:58.850 P00   INFO: last backup label = 20230829-131603F,
version = 2.47
2023-08-29 13:37:58.850 P00   INFO: execute non-exclusive backup start:
backup begins after the next regular checkpoint completes
2023-08-29 13:37:59.961 P00   INFO: backup start archive =
000000010000000000000007, lsn = 0/7000028
2023-08-29 13:37:59.961 P00   INFO: check archive for prior segment
000000010000000000000006
2023-08-29 13:38:00.642 P00   INFO: execute non-exclusive backup stop and
wait for all WAL segments to archive
```

```
2023-08-29 13:38:01.148 P00   INFO: backup stop archive =
000000010000000000000007, lsn = 0/7000100
2023-08-29 13:38:01.167 P00   INFO: check archive for segment(s)
000000010000000000000007:000000010000000000000007
2023-08-29 13:38:01.181 P00   INFO: new backup label =
20230829-131603F_20230829-133758I
2023-08-29 13:38:01.248 P00   INFO: incr backup size = 1.3MB, file
total = 1274
2023-08-29 13:38:01.248 P00   INFO: backup command end: completed
successfully (3125ms)
2023-08-29 13:38:01.248 P00   INFO: expire command begin 2.47: --exec-
id=3201-56d253f6 --log-level-console=info --repo1-path=/var/lib/pgbackrest
--stanza=pg_backurst_01_bkp
2023-08-29 13:38:01.257 P00   INFO: option 'repo1-retention-archive' is not
set - archive logs will not be expired
2023-08-29 13:38:01.257 P00   INFO: expire command end: completed
successfully (9ms)
[postgres@pg_backuprst_01 data]$
```

Step 13: Insert another row in in *hrm.pgbackrest_tab*.

```
[postgres@pg_backuprst_01 data]$ psql
psql (16.4)
Type "help" for help.

postgres=# \c hrmdb;
You are now connected to database "hrmdb" as user "postgres".
hrmdb=# insert into hrm.pgbackrest_tab values ('After_1st_incr_
before_2nd_incr');
INSERT 0 1
hrmdb=# select count(*) from hrm.pgbackrest_tab;
 count
-------
     2
(1 row)
```

CHAPTER 5 POSTGRESQL BACKUP AND RECOVERY

```
hrmdb=# select * from hrm.pgbackrest_tab;
              name
---------------------------------
 After_full_before_1st_incr
 After_1st_incr_before_2nd_incr
(2 rows)
```

Step 14: Perform another incremental backup using the below command:

```
[postgres@pg_backuprst_01 data]$ pgbackrest --stanza=pg_backurst_01_bkp --type=incr --log-level-console=info backup
2023-08-29 13:45:16.612 P00   INFO: backup command begin 2.47: --exec-id=3237-67313ccf --log-level-console=info --pg1-path=/var/lib/pgsql/16/data --pg1-port=5432 --repo1-path=/var/lib/pgbackrest --stanza=pg_backurst_01_bkp --type=incr
WARN: option 'repo1-retention-full' is not set for 'repo1-retention-full-type=count', the repository may run out of space
      HINT: to retain full backups indefinitely (without warning), set option 'repo1-retention-full' to the maximum.
2023-08-29 13:45:16.339 P00   INFO: last backup label = 20230829-131603F_20230829-133758I, version = 2.47
2023-08-29 13:45:16.339 P00   INFO: execute non-exclusive backup start: backup begins after the next regular checkpoint completes
2023-08-29 13:45:17.454 P00   INFO: backup start archive = 000000010000000000000009, lsn = 0/9000028
2023-08-29 13:45:17.454 P00   INFO: check archive for prior segment 000000010000000000000008
2023-08-29 13:45:18.560 P00   INFO: execute non-exclusive backup stop and wait for all WAL segments to archive
2023-08-29 13:45:19.080 P00   INFO: backup stop archive = 000000010000000000000009, lsn = 0/9000100
2023-08-29 13:45:19.085 P00   INFO: check archive for segment(s) 000000010000000000000009:000000010000000000000009
2023-08-29 13:45:19.114 P00   INFO: new backup label = 20230829-131603F_20230829-134516I
```

CHAPTER 5 POSTGRESQL BACKUP AND RECOVERY

```
2023-08-29 13:45:19.182 P00   INFO: incr backup size = 39KB, file
total = 1274
2023-08-29 13:45:19.182 P00   INFO: backup command end: completed
successfully (3571ms)
2023-08-29 13:45:19.182 P00   INFO: expire command begin 2.47: --exec-
id=3237-67313ccf --log-level-console=info --repo1-path=/var/lib/pgbackrest
--stanza=pg_backurst_01_bkp
2023-08-29 13:45:19.191 P00   INFO: option 'repo1-retention-archive' is not
set - archive logs will not be expired
2023-08-29 13:45:19.191 P00   INFO: expire command end: completed
successfully (9ms)
[postgres@pg_backuprst_01 data]$
```

Check the backup information using the *pgbackrest info* command.

```
[postgres@pg_backuprst_01 data]$ pgbackrest info
stanza: pg_backurst_01_bkp
    status: ok
    cipher: none

    db (current)
        wal archive min/max (16): 000000010000000000000000
1/000000010000000000000009

        full backup: 20230829-131603F
            timestamp start/stop: 2023-08-29 13:16:03-05 / 2023-08-29
            13:16:09-05
            wal start/stop: 000000010000000000000005 /
            000000010000000000000005
            database size: 29.9MB, database backup size: 29.9MB
            repo1: backup set size: 4.0MB, backup size: 4.0MB

        incr backup: 20230829-131603F_20230829-133758I
            timestamp start/stop: 2023-08-29 13:37:58-05 / 2023-08-29
            13:38:01-05
            wal start/stop: 000000010000000000000007 /
            000000010000000000000007
            database size: 29.9MB, database backup size: 1.3MB
```

CHAPTER 5 POSTGRESQL BACKUP AND RECOVERY

```
        repo1: backup set size: 4.0MB, backup size: 162.6KB
        backup reference list: 20230829-131603F

    incr backup: 20230829-131603F_20230829-134516I
        timestamp start/stop: 2023-08-29 13:45:16-05 / 2023-08-29
        13:45:18-05
        wal start/stop: 000000010000000000000009 /
        000000010000000000000009
        database size: 29.9MB, database backup size: 39KB
        repo1: backup set size: 4.0MB, backup size: 2.6KB
        backup reference list: 20230829-131603F, 20230829-131603F_20230
        829-133758I
[postgres@pg_backuprst_01 data]$
```

Step 15: Before trying the restore, let us see how we can perform the differential backup using *pgBackRest*.

```
[postgres@pg_backuprst_01 data]$ pgbackrest --stanza=pg_backurst_01_bkp
--type=diff --log-level-console=info backup
2023-08-29 13:47:33.786 P00   INFO: backup command begin 2.47: --exec-
id=3252-8ddb4d2b --log-level-console=info --pg1-path=/var/lib/pgsql/16/data
--pg1-port=5432 --repo1-path=/var/lib/pgbackrest --stanza=pg_backurst_01_
bkp --type=diff
WARN: option 'repo1-retention-full' is not set for 'repo1-retention-full-
type=count', the repository may run out of space
      HINT: to retain full backups indefinitely (without warning), set
option 'repo1-retention-full' to the maximum.
2023-08-29 13:47:34.520 P00   INFO: last backup label = 20230829-131603F,
version = 2.47
2023-08-29 13:47:34.520 P00   INFO: execute non-exclusive backup start:
backup begins after the next regular checkpoint completes
2023-08-29 13:47:35.638 P00   INFO: backup start archive =
00000001000000000000000B, lsn = 0/B000028
```

```
2023-08-29 13:47:35.638 P00   INFO: check archive for prior segment
000000010000000000000000A
2023-08-29 13:47:36.600 P00   INFO: execute non-exclusive backup stop and
wait for all WAL segments to archive
2023-08-29 13:47:37.405 P00   INFO: backup stop archive =
000000010000000000000000B, lsn = 0/B000100
2023-08-29 13:47:37.410 P00   INFO: check archive for segment(s)
000000010000000000000000B:000000010000000000000000B
2023-08-29 13:47:37.438 P00   INFO: new backup label =
20230829-131603F_20230829-134734D
2023-08-29 13:47:37.506 P00   INFO: diff backup size = 1.3MB, file
total = 1274
2023-08-29 13:47:37.506 P00   INFO: backup command end: completed
successfully (3720ms)
2023-08-29 13:47:37.506 P00   INFO: expire command begin 2.47: --exec-
id=3252-8ddb4d2b --log-level-console=info --repo1-path=/var/lib/pgbackrest
--stanza=pg_backurst_01_bkp
2023-08-29 13:47:37.516 P00   INFO: option 'repo1-retention-archive' is not
set - archive logs will not be expired
2023-08-29 13:47:37.516 P00   INFO: expire command end: completed
successfully (9ms)
[postgres@pg_backuprst_01 data]$
```

Check the backup information again.

```
[postgres@pg_backuprst_01 data]$ pgbackrest info
stanza: pg_backurst_01_bkp
    status: ok
    cipher: none

    db (current)
        wal archive min/max (16): 000000010000000000000000
        1/000000010000000000000000B

        full backup: 20230829-131603F
            timestamp start/stop: 2023-08-29 13:16:03-05 / 2023-08-29
            13:16:09-05
```

```
        wal start/stop: 000000010000000000000005 /
        000000010000000000000005
        database size: 29.9MB, database backup size: 29.9MB
        repo1: backup set size: 4.0MB, backup size: 4.0MB

    incr backup: 20230829-131603F_20230829-133758I
        timestamp start/stop: 2023-08-29 13:37:58-05 / 2023-08-29
        13:38:01-05
        wal start/stop: 000000010000000000000007 /
        000000010000000000000007
        database size: 29.9MB, database backup size: 1.3MB
        repo1: backup set size: 4.0MB, backup size: 162.6KB
        backup reference list: 20230829-131603F

    incr backup: 20230829-131603F_20230829-134516I
        timestamp start/stop: 2023-08-29 13:45:16-05 / 2023-08-29
        13:45:18-05
        wal start/stop: 000000010000000000000009 /
        000000010000000000000009
        database size: 29.9MB, database backup size: 39KB
        repo1: backup set size: 4.0MB, backup size: 2.6KB
        backup reference list: 20230829-131603F, 20230829-131603F_20230
        829-133758I

    diff backup: 20230829-131603F_20230829-134734D
        timestamp start/stop: 2023-08-29 13:47:34-05 / 2023-08-29
        13:47:37-05
        wal start/stop: 00000001000000000000000B /
        00000001000000000000000B
        database size: 29.9MB, database backup size: 1.3MB
        repo1: backup set size: 4.0MB, backup size: 162.7KB
        backup reference list: 20230829-131603F
[postgres@pg_backuprst_01 data]$
```

Step 16: Now let us drop the table, *hrm.pgbackrest_tab*.

```
[postgres@pg_backuprst_01 data]$ psql
psql (16.4)
```

CHAPTER 5   POSTGRESQL BACKUP AND RECOVERY

```
Type "help" for help.

postgres=# \c hrmdb;
You are now connected to database "hrmdb" as user "postgres".
hrmdb=# select * from hrm.pgbackrest_tab;
             name
---------------------------------
 After_full_before_1st_incr
 After_1st_incr_before_2nd_incr
(2 rows)

hrmdb=# drop table hrm.pgbackrest_tab;
DROP TABLE
hrmdb=# select * from hrm.pgbackrest_tab;
ERROR:  relation "hrm.pgbackrest_tab" does not exist
LINE 1: select * from hrm.pgbackrest_tab;
                      ^
hrmdb=#
```

Step 17: Let us see how we can perform a restore using the *pgBackRest* utility.

    a. Stop the PostgreSQL database cluster and remove the data directory.

```
[root@pg_backuprst_01 ~]# systemctl stop postgresql-16
[root@pg_backuprst_01 ~]# cd /var/lib/pgsql/16/
[root@pg_backuprst_01 16]# ls -ltr
total 8
drwx------. 2 postgres postgres    6 Aug 10 02:23 backups
-rw-------. 1 postgres postgres  923 Aug 29 10:47 initdb.log
drwx------. 20 postgres postgres 4096 Aug 29 14:04 data
[root@pg_backuprst_01 16]# rm -Rf data
[root@pg_backuprst_01 16]#
```

    b. Perform the point-in-time recovery.

```
[postgres@pg_backuprst_01 data]$ pgbackrest info
stanza: pg_backurst_01_bkp
```

CHAPTER 5   POSTGRESQL BACKUP AND RECOVERY

status: ok
cipher: none

db (current)
    wal archive min/max (16): 000000010000000000000001/000000010000000000000000C

    full backup: 20230829-131603F
        timestamp start/stop: 2023-08-29 13:16:03-05 / 2023-08-29 13:16:09-05
        wal start/stop: 000000010000000000000005 / 000000010000000000000005
        database size: 29.9MB, database backup size: 29.9MB
        repo1: backup set size: 4.0MB, backup size: 4.0MB

    incr backup: 20230829-131603F_20230829-133758I
        timestamp start/stop: 2023-08-29 13:37:58-05 / 2023-08-29 13:38:01-05
        wal start/stop: 000000010000000000000007 / 000000010000000000000007
        database size: 29.9MB, database backup size: 1.3MB
        repo1: backup set size: 4.0MB, backup size: 162.6KB
        backup reference list: 20230829-131603F

    incr backup: 20230829-131603F_20230829-134516I
        timestamp start/stop: 2023-08-29 13:45:16-05 / 2023-08-29 13:45:18-05
        wal start/stop: 000000010000000000000009 / 000000010000000000000009
        database size: 29.9MB, database backup size: 39KB
        repo1: backup set size: 4.0MB, backup size: 2.6KB
        backup reference list: 20230829-131603F, 20230829-131603F_20230829-133758I

    diff backup: 20230829-131603F_20230829-134734D
        timestamp start/stop: 2023-08-29 13:47:34-05 / 2023-08-29 13:47:37-05

CHAPTER 5   POSTGRESQL BACKUP AND RECOVERY

```
            wal start/stop: 000000010000000000000008 /
            000000010000000000000008
            database size: 29.9MB, database backup size: 1.3MB
            repo1: backup set size: 4.0MB, backup size: 162.7KB
            backup reference list: 20230829-131603F
            [postgres@pg_backuprst_01 data]$
```

Here is a pictorial representation of the backups taken above and the point at which we will perform the recovery.

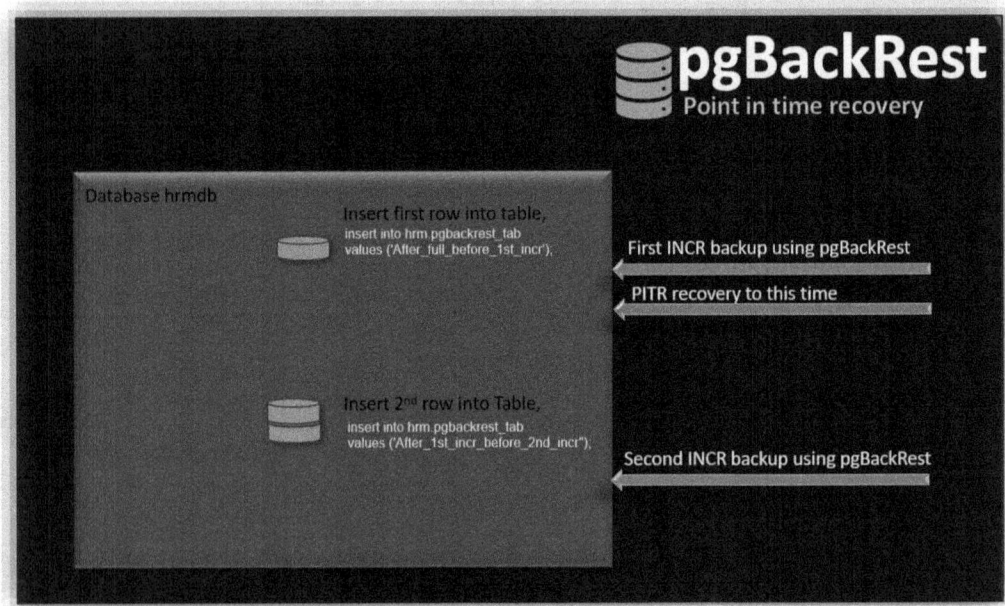

Figure 5-4. *pgBackRest architecture*

We will perform point-in-time recovery using the timestamp **2023-08-29 13:38:01-05** (from above), which is the end time of the first INCR backup taken using *pgBackRest*.

We will use the below command to perform PITR.

The time format is very important when using it in the restore command. We should add .00 at the end of the time which we get from the pgBackRest info command output.

```
[postgres@pg_backuprst_01 ~]$ pgbackrest --stanza=pg_backurst_01_bkp
--type=time --target="2023-08-29 13:38:01.00" restore
[postgres@pg_backuprst_01 ~]$
```

CHAPTER 5   POSTGRESQL BACKUP AND RECOVERY

Once the above restore command is completed, go to the data directory. We will see that the *pgBackRest* restore command has created two files:

> **recovery.signal**: This file tells PostgreSQL to enter normal archive recovery when it starts next time.
>
> **postgresql.auto.conf**: pgBackRest will add restore command and recovery target time details to this file so that whenever the database cluster starts, it will enter into the recovery mode and will apply the archives to bring the database to a consistent state as per the recovery time.

```
[postgres@pg_backuprst_01 data]$ cat postgresql.auto.conf
# Do not edit this file manually!
# It will be overwritten by the ALTER SYSTEM command.

# Recovery settings generated by pgBackRest restore on 2023-08-29 14:27:04
restore_command = 'pgbackrest --stanza=pg_backurst_01_bkp archive-get %f "%p"'
recovery_target_time = '2023-08-29 13:38:01.00'
[postgres@pg_backuprst_01 data]$
```

Once the recovery is complete, start the PostgreSQL database cluster.

```
[root@pg_backuprst_01 16]# systemctl start postgresql-16
```

When we start the database cluster, we can monitor the log file *(/var/lib/pgsql/16/data/log)* to see the recovery operation and its progress.

```
2023-08-29 14:28:23.850 CDT [3392] LOG:  listening on Unix socket "/tmp/.s.PGSQL.5432"
2023-08-29 14:28:23.853 CDT [3397] LOG:  database system was interrupted; last known up at 2023-08-29 13:16:04 CDT
2023-08-29 14:28:24.909 CDT [3397] LOG:  starting point-in-time recovery to 2023-08-29 13:38:01-05
2023-08-29 14:28:24.943 CDT [3397] LOG:  restored log file "000000010000000000000005" from archive
2023-08-29 14:28:24.972 CDT [3397] LOG:  redo starts at 0/5000060
```

355

```
2023-08-29 14:28:25.005 CDT [3397] LOG:  restored log file
"000000010000000000000006" from archive
2023-08-29 14:28:25.064 CDT [3397] LOG:  consistent recovery state reached
at 0/5000138
2023-08-29 14:28:25.065 CDT [3392] LOG:  database system is ready to accept
read-only connections
2023-08-29 14:28:25.105 CDT [3397] LOG:  restored log file
"000000010000000000000007" from archive
2023-08-29 14:28:25.208 CDT [3397] LOG:  restored log file
"000000010000000000000008" from archive
2023-08-29 14:28:25.289 CDT [3397] LOG:  restored log file
"000000010000000000000009" from archive
2023-08-29 14:28:25.370 CDT [3397] LOG:  restored log file
"00000001000000000000000A" from archive
2023-08-29 14:28:25.455 CDT [3397] LOG:  restored log file
"00000001000000000000000B" from archive
2023-08-29 14:28:25.661 CDT [3397] LOG:  restored log file
"00000001000000000000000C" from archive
2023-08-29 14:28:25.722 CDT [3397] LOG:  recovery stopping before commit of
transaction 755, time 2023-08-29 13:43:51.307043-05
2023-08-29 14:28:25.722 CDT [3397] LOG:  pausing at the end of recovery
2023-08-29 14:28:25.722 CDT [3397] HINT:  Execute pg_wal_replay_resume() to
promote.
2023-08-29 14:33:23.960 CDT [3395] LOG:  restartpoint starting: time
2023-08-29 14:33:25.944 CDT [3395] LOG:  restartpoint complete: wrote 21
buffers (0.1%); 0 WAL file(s) added, 3 removed, 0 recycled; write=1.946 s,
sync=0.020 s, total=1.984 s; sync files=17, longest=0.007 s, average=0.002
s; distance=49162 kB, estimate=49162 kB
2023-08-29 14:33:25.944 CDT [3395] LOG:  recovery restart point at
0/8000060
```

CHAPTER 5 POSTGRESQL BACKUP AND RECOVERY

```
2023-08-29 14:33:25.944 CDT [3395] DETAIL:  Last completed transaction was
at log time 2023-08-29 13:30:51.916179-05.
2023-08-29 14:56:01.205 CDT [3392] LOG:  received fast shutdown request
2023-08-29 14:56:01.208 CDT [3392] LOG:  aborting any active transactions
2023-08-29 14:56:01.843 CDT [3395] LOG:  shutting down
2023-08-29 14:56:01.846 CDT [3392] LOG:  database system is shut down
```

Once the database cluster is up, let us check the table to see if it has only one row in the table (which we inserted in step 11).

```
[postgres@pg_backuprst_01 data]$ psql
psql (16.4)
Type "help" for help.

postgres=# \l
                        List of databases
   Name    |  Owner   | Encoding |  Collate    |   Ctype     | ICU Locale |
 Locale Provider |   Access privileges
-----------+----------+----------+-------------+-------------+------------+
-----------------+----------------------
 hrmdb     | postgres | UTF8     | en_US.UTF-8 | en_US.UTF-8 |            |
 libc            |
 postgres  | postgres | UTF8     | en_US.UTF-8 | en_US.UTF-8 |            |
 libc            |
 template0 | postgres | UTF8     | en_US.UTF-8 | en_US.UTF-8 |            |
 libc            | =c/postgres         +
           |          |          |             |             |            |
                 | postgres=CTc/postgres
 template1 | postgres | UTF8     | en_US.UTF-8 | en_US.UTF-8 |            |
 libc            | =c/postgres         +
           |          |          |             |             |            |
                 | postgres=CTc/postgres
(4 rows)

postgres=# \c hrmdb;
You are now connected to database "hrmdb" as user "postgres".
hrmdb=# select * from hrm.pgbackrest_tab;
```

CHAPTER 5 POSTGRESQL BACKUP AND RECOVERY

```
            name
-----------------------------
 After_full_before_1st_incr
(1 row)

hrmdb=#
```

Once you have done all the required checks to ensure that the recovery has been performed as per the requirement, we can stop the PostgreSQL cluster once and remove the two files below that the pgBackRest restore command created.

Once you confirm, remove the two files so the PostgreSQL cluster will not perform the same PITR every time we restart it.

```
[postgres@pg_backuprst_01 data]$ rm postgresql.auto.conf recovery.signal
```

Stop and start the PostgreSQL database cluster.

```
[root@pg_backuprst_01 16]# systemctl stop postgresql-16
[root@pg_backuprst_01 16]# systemctl start postgresql-16
```

Summary

In this chapter, we explored the importance of backups, the various backup methods available, verification of physical backups, practical approaches to implementing them in real-world scenarios, and the step-by-step process required to perform a successful recovery operation.

CHAPTER 6

PostgreSQL Routine Maintenance

Introduction

In this chapter, we explore the routine maintenance tasks of PostgreSQL in depth, along with various other methods.

PostgreSQL provides some of the known maintenance options:

- Statistics/analyze
- Vacuum
- Vacuum all
- Routine reindexing
- Autovacuum
- vacuumdb
- Clearing WAL logs
- Log file maintenance

PostgreSQL routine maintenance is essential for ensuring database performance, stability, and efficient storage management. Key tasks include regularly running **vacuum** to remove dead tuples and avoid table bloat, **analyze** to keep planner statistics up to date for optimal query execution, and **REINDEX** to rebuild bloated or fragmented indexes. Additionally, monitoring disk usage with catalog functions like pg_table_size() and pg_total_relation_size() and scheduling periodic **backups** and **archiving** ensures

CHAPTER 6   POSTGRESQL ROUTINE MAINTENANCE

data durability and recovery readiness. Automated tools like **autovacuum** help manage these operations, but periodic manual checks are recommended for large or high-traffic databases.

Upon completing Chapter 6, readers will gain knowledge on routine maintenance tasks for PostgreSQL for lower and production environments.

In this chapter, the following topics are covered:

- Analyze commands for various objects
- Various methods of Vacuum
- Scenarios of reindex

Analyze

The analyze command in PostgreSQL updates table statistics to help the optimizer create more efficient execution plans. Important aspects of analyze include the following:

1. Up-to-date statistics enable the optimizer to choose the most efficient execution path.
2. Analyze does not lock the table, so it can be run at any time without interrupting other operations.
3. Running analyze does not require additional disk space.
4. The operation does not alter the table's actual data files; it only refreshes statistical metadata.

```
ANALYZE hrm.tab1;              Collects statistics for tab1 under
                               hrm schema.
ANALYZE VERBOSE hrm.tab1;      does exactly the same plus prints progress
                               messages.
ANALYZE hrm.tab1(id);          collects statistics for id column of tab1.
ANALYZE;                       collects statistics for all the
                               database tables
```

For instance, after creating a table, when we query the pg_stat_user_tables view, the last_analyzed field appears blank, indicating that no analysis has been performed yet.

CHAPTER 6 POSTGRESQL ROUTINE MAINTENANCE

Let's connect to the pgdb1 database and create a table (tab1) under hrm schema and perform some transactions.

postgres=# \c pgdb1
You are now connected to database "pgdb1" as user "postgres".

pgdb1=# create schema hrm;
CREATE SCHEMA

pgdb1=# create table hrm.tab1 (id INT);
CREATE TABLE

pgdb1=> insert into hrm.tab1 values (generate_series(1,100000));
INSERT 0 100000

pgdb1=> select count(*) from hrm.tab1;
```
 count
--------
 100000
(1 row)
```

pgdb1=> select schemaname, relname, n_tup_ins, n_dead_tup, n_live_tup, last_analyze, last_vacuum from pg_stat_user_tables where relname='tab1';
```
-[ RECORD 1 ]+-------
schemaname   | hrm
relname      | tab1
n_tup_ins    | 100000
n_dead_tup   | 0
n_live_tup   | 100000
last_analyze |
last_vacuum  |
```

pgdb1=# analyze verbose hrm.tab1;
INFO: analyzing "hrm.tab1"
INFO: "tab1": scanned 443 of 443 pages, containing 100000 live rows and 0 dead rows; 30000 rows in sample, 100000 estimated total rows
ANALYZE

361

CHAPTER 6   POSTGRESQL ROUTINE MAINTENANCE

```
pgdb1=# select schemaname, relname, n_tup_ins, n_dead_tup, n_live_tup,
last_analyze, last_vacuum from pg_stat_user_tables where relname='tab1';
[ RECORD 1 ]+------------------------------
schemaname   | hrm
relname      | tab1
n_tup_ins    | 100000
n_dead_tup   | 0
n_live_tup   | 100000
last_analyze | 2025-04-28 01:50:03.858832-05
last_vacuum  |
```

Running the analyze command for a specific column in tab2:

```
pgdb1=# create table hrm.tab2 (id INT, about TEXT, age INT);
CREATE TABLE

pgdb1=# insert into hrm.tab2 values (generate_series(1, 10000), repeat('A
Cool Player. ', 2) || 'My number is ' || trunc(random()*1000),
trunc(random()*10 * 2 + 10));
INSERT 0 10000
                            ^

pgdb1=# select count(*) from hrm.tab2;
[ RECORD 1 ]
count | 10000

pgdb1=# \dt+ hrm.tab2;
List of relations
[ RECORD 1 ]-+----------
Schema        | hrm
Name          | tab2
Type          | table
Owner         | postgres
Persistence   | permanent
Access method | heap
Size          | 872 kB
Description   |
```

CHAPTER 6   POSTGRESQL ROUTINE MAINTENANCE

pgdb1=# analyze verbose hrm.tab2(id);
INFO: analyzing "hrm.tab2"
INFO: "tab2": scanned 104 of 104 pages, containing 10000 live rows and 0 dead rows; 10000 rows in sample, 10000 estimated total rows
ANALYZE

pgdb1=# select schemaname, relname, n_tup_ins, n_dead_tup, n_live_tup, last_analyze, last_vacuum from pg_stat_user_tables where relname='tab2';
```
[ RECORD 1 ]+-----------------------------
schemaname   | hrm
relname      | tab2
n_tup_ins    | 10000
n_dead_tup   | 0
n_live_tup   | 10000
last_analyze | 2025-04-28 02:54:17.523985-05
last_vacuum  |
```

Running the analyze command for entire database:

pgdb1=# create table hrm.tab3 (id int);
CREATE TABLE

pgdb1=# insert into hrm.tab3 values (generate_series(1,2000));
INSERT 0 2000

pgdb1=# select schemaname, relname, n_tup_ins, n_dead_tup, n_live_tup, last_analyze, last_vacuum from pg_stat_user_tables where schemaname='hrm' order by relname;
```
[ RECORD 1 ]+-----------------------------
schemaname   | hrm
relname      | tab1
n_tup_ins    | 100000
n_dead_tup   | 0
n_live_tup   | 100000
last_analyze | 2025-04-28 01:50:03.858832-05
last_vacuum  |
[ RECORD 2 ]+-----------------------------
schemaname   | hrm
```

363

CHAPTER 6   POSTGRESQL ROUTINE MAINTENANCE

```
relname       | tab2
n_tup_ins     | 10000
n_dead_tup    | 0
n_live_tup    | 10000
last_analyze  | 2025-04-28 02:54:17.523985-05
last_vacuum   |
[ RECORD 3 ]+-----------------------------
schemaname    | hrm
relname       | tab3
n_tup_ins     | 2000
n_dead_tup    | 0
n_live_tup    | 2000
last_analyze  |
last_vacuum   |
```

pgdb1=# analyze;
ANALYZE

pgdb1=# select schemaname, relname, n_tup_ins, n_dead_tup, n_live_tup, last_analyze, last_vacuum from pg_stat_user_tables where schemaname='hrm' order by relname;

```
[ RECORD 1 ]+-----------------------------
schemaname    | hrm
relname       | tab1
n_tup_ins     | 100000
n_dead_tup    | 0
n_live_tup    | 100000
last_analyze  | 2025-04-28 02:58:59.057538-05
last_vacuum   |
[ RECORD 2 ]+-----------------------------
schemaname    | hrm
relname       | tab2
n_tup_ins     | 10000
n_dead_tup    | 0
n_live_tup    | 10000
```

```
last_analyze  | 2025-04-28 02:59:08.049454-05
last_vacuum   |
[ RECORD 3 ]+------------------------------
schemaname    | hrm
relname       | tab3
n_tup_ins     | 2000
n_dead_tup    | 0
n_live_tup    | 2000
last_analyze  | 2025-04-28 02:59:08.053361-05
last_vacuum   |
pgdb1=#
```

Vacuum in PostgreSQL

In PostgreSQL, vacuum is a crucial maintenance operation used to clean up dead tuples (obsolete row versions) left behind by updates and deletes. Since PostgreSQL uses a Multi-Version Concurrency Control (MVCC) model, old versions of rows are not immediately removed to maintain data consistency for concurrent transactions. Over time, these dead tuples accumulate, increasing table size and degrading performance.

Key Purposes of vacuum

- Reclaims storage occupied by dead tuples
- Marks space as available for future reuse without expanding the table file
- Helps prevent transaction ID wraparound issues (through a special "vacuum freeze" process)
- Updates table statistics related to visibility, which improves query planning

CHAPTER 6   POSTGRESQL ROUTINE MAINTENANCE

Types of vacuum

- Standard vacuum: Cleans dead rows but doesn't shrink the table for files
- VACUUM FULL: Compacts tables by rewriting them entirely, releasing unused disk space back to the operating system (but it locks the table)
- Autovacuum: A background daemon that automatically triggers vacuum operations based on activity thresholds, ensuring regular maintenance without manual intervention

For this demonstration, we will create a few tables and insert some data.

```
pgdb1=# create table hrm.tab4 (id int4);
CREATE TABLE

pgdb1=# create table hrm.tab5 (id int4);
CREATE TABLE

pgdb1=# insert into hrm.tab4 values (generate_series(1,100000));
INSERT 0 100000

pgdb1=# insert into hrm.tab5 values (generate_series(1,100000));
INSERT 0 100000
```

Create two indexes on the new tables on column id.

```
pgdb1=# create index idx4_tab4 on hrm.tab4 (id);
CREATE INDEX

pgdb1=# create index idx5_tab5 on hrm.tab5 (id);
CREATE INDEX
```

Create view, materialized view, and sequence as below.

```
pgdb1=# create view hrm.v1_tab1 as select * from hrm.tab1;
CREATE VIEW

pgdb1=# create materialized view hrm.mv1_tab1 as select * from hrm.tab1;
SELECT 100000
```

CHAPTER 6   POSTGRESQL ROUTINE MAINTENANCE

pgdb1=# create sequence hrm.seq1 start with 1 increment by 1 maxvalue 1000000;
CREATE SEQUENCE

Let's check the status details of tables tab1 and tab2, materialized view mv1_tab1.

pgdb1=# select schemaname, relname, n_tup_ins, n_dead_tup, n_live_tup, last_analyze, last_vacuum from pg_stat_user_tables where schemaname='hrm' order by relname;

```
[ RECORD 1 ]+------------------------------
schemaname   | hrm
relname      | mv1_tab1
n_tup_ins    | 100000
n_dead_tup   | 0
n_live_tup   | 100000
last_analyze |
last_vacuum  |
[ RECORD 2 ]+------------------------------
schemaname   | hrm
relname      | tab1
n_tup_ins    | 100000
n_dead_tup   | 0
n_live_tup   | 100000
last_analyze | 2025-04-28 02:58:59.057538-05
last_vacuum  |
[ RECORD 3 ]+------------------------------
schemaname   | hrm
relname      | tab2
n_tup_ins    | 10000
n_dead_tup   | 0
n_live_tup   | 10000
last_analyze | 2025-04-28 02:59:08.049454-05
last_vacuum  |
[ RECORD 4 ]+------------------------------
```

```
schemaname     | hrm
relname        | tab3
n_tup_ins      | 2000
n_dead_tup     | 0
n_live_tup     | 2000
last_analyze   | 2025-04-28 02:59:08.053361-05
last_vacuum    |
[ RECORD 5 ]+------------------------------
schemaname     | hrm
relname        | tab4
n_tup_ins      | 100000
n_dead_tup     | 0
n_live_tup     | 100000
last_analyze   |
last_vacuum    |
[ RECORD 6 ]+------------------------------
schemaname     | hrm
relname        | tab5
n_tup_ins      | 100000
n_dead_tup     | 0
n_live_tup     | 100000
last_analyze   |
last_vacuum    |
pgdb1=#
```

You can use the "explain" command to display the execution plan the PostgreSQL planner generates.

explain with index column

pgdb1=# explain select * from hrm.tab4;
```
[ RECORD 1 ]----------------------------------------------------------
QUERY PLAN | Seq Scan on tab4  (cost=0.00..1443.00 rows=100000 width=4)
```

pgdb1=# explain select * from hrm.tab5;
```
[ RECORD 1 ]----------------------------------------------------------
QUERY PLAN | Seq Scan on tab5  (cost=0.00..1443.00 rows=100000 width=4)
```

CHAPTER 6 POSTGRESQL ROUTINE MAINTENANCE

```
pgdb1=# explain select * from hrm.tab4 where id=999;
[ RECORD 1 ]---------------------------------------------------------
QUERY PLAN | Index Only Scan using idx4_tab4 on tab4  (cost=0.29..4.31
rows=1 width=4)
[ RECORD 2 ]---------------------------------------------------------
QUERY PLAN |   Index Cond: (id = 999)

pgdb1=# explain select * from hrm.tab5 where id=2345;
[ RECORD 1 ]---------------------------------------------------------
QUERY PLAN | Index Only Scan using idx5_tab5 on tab5  (cost=0.29..4.31
rows=1 width=4)
[ RECORD 2 ]---------------------------------------------------------
QUERY PLAN |   Index Cond: (id = 2345)
```

```
pgdb1=# \dt+ hrm.*
                              List of relations
 Schema | Name | Type  |  Owner   | Persistence | Access method | Size    | Description
--------+------+-------+----------+-------------+---------------+---------+-------------
 hrm    | tab1 | table | postgres | permanent   | heap          | 3576 kB |
 hrm    | tab2 | table | postgres | permanent   | heap          | 872 kB  |
 hrm    | tab3 | table | postgres | permanent   | heap          | 104 kB  |
 hrm    | tab4 | table | postgres | permanent   | heap          | 3576 kB |
 hrm    | tab5 | table | postgres | permanent   | heap          | 3576 kB |
(5 rows)
```

Figure 6-1. Information about the objects under hrm schema

```
pgdb1=# select schemaname, relname, n_tup_ins, n_dead_tup, n_live_tup, last_analyze, last_vacuum
pgdb1-# from pg_stat_user_tables
pgdb1-# where schemaname='hrm'
pgdb1-# order by relname;
 schemaname | relname  | n_tup_ins | n_dead_tup | n_live_tup |         last_analyze          | last_vacuum
------------+----------+-----------+------------+------------+-------------------------------+-------------
 hrm        | mv1_tab1 |    100000 |          0 |     100000 | 2025-04-28 03:27:53.896775-05 |
 hrm        | tab1     |    100000 |          0 |     100000 | 2025-04-28 03:27:51.623393-05 |
 hrm        | tab2     |     10000 |          0 |      10000 | 2025-04-28 03:27:53.853552-05 |
 hrm        | tab3     |      2000 |          0 |       2000 | 2025-04-28 03:27:53.856251-05 |
 hrm        | tab4     |    100000 |          0 |     100000 | 2025-04-28 03:27:53.870013-05 |
 hrm        | tab5     |    100000 |          0 |     100000 | 2025-04-28 03:27:53.883492-05 |
(6 rows)
```

Figure 6-2. Information about objects statistics

To check the size of the tables and indexes

```
pgdb1=# \dt+ hrm.tab4;
                              List of relations
 Schema | Name | Type  | Owner    | Persistence | Access method | Size    | Description
--------+------+-------+----------+-------------+---------------+---------+------------
 hrm    | tab4 | table | postgres | permanent   | heap          | 3576 kB |
(1 row)

pgdb1=# \dt+ hrm.tab5;
                              List of relations
 Schema | Name | Type  | Owner    | Persistence | Access method | Size    | Description
--------+------+-------+----------+-------------+---------------+---------+------------
 hrm    | tab5 | table | postgres | permanent   | heap          | 3576 kB |
(1 row)

pgdb1=# \di+ hrm.idx4_tab4;
                                    List of relations
 Schema | Name      | Type  | Owner    | Table | Persistence | Access method | Size    | Description
--------+-----------+-------+----------+-------+-------------+---------------+---------+------------
 hrm    | idx4_tab4 | index | postgres | tab4  | permanent   | btree         | 2208 kB |
(1 row)

pgdb1=# \di+ hrm.idx5_tab5;
                                    List of relations
 Schema | Name      | Type  | Owner    | Table | Persistence | Access method | Size    | Description
--------+-----------+-------+----------+-------+-------------+---------------+---------+------------
 hrm    | idx5_tab5 | index | postgres | tab5  | permanent   | btree         | 2208 kB |
(1 row)
```

Figure 6-3. *Displaying the size of the tables*

To check the path for the relations like tables and indexes

```
pgdb1=# select pg_relation_filepath('hrm.tab3');
 pg_relation_filepath
----------------------
 base/98428/164024
(1 row)

pgdb1=#
pgdb1=# select pg_relation_filepath('hrm.tab4');
 pg_relation_filepath
----------------------
 base/98428/164035
(1 row)

pgdb1=#
pgdb1=# select pg_relation_filepath('hrm.idx4_tab4');
 pg_relation_filepath
----------------------
 base/98428/164041
(1 row)

pgdb1=#
pgdb1=# select pg_relation_filepath('hrm.idx5_tab5');
 pg_relation_filepath
----------------------
 base/98428/164042
(1 row)
```

Figure 6-4. *Information of relation file path for tables and indexes under hrm schema*

CHAPTER 6 POSTGRESQL ROUTINE MAINTENANCE

Now, let's perform delete operations on these tables.

pgdb1=# delete from hrm.tab1 where id<10000;
DELETE 9999

pgdb1=# delete from hrm.tab2 where id<10000;
DELETE 9999

pgdb1=# delete from hrm.tab3 where id<10000;
DELETE 2000

pgdb1=# delete from hrm.tab4 where id<10000;
DELETE 9999

pgdb1=# delete from hrm.tab5 where id<10000;
DELETE 9999

pgdb1=# select schemaname, relname, n_tup_ins, n_dead_tup, n_live_tup, last_analyze, last_vacuum from pg_stat_user_tables where schemaname='hrm' order by relname;

```
schemaname | relname  | n_tup_ins | n_dead_tup | n_live_tup |
              last_analyze         | last_vacuum
-----------+----------+-----------+------------+-----------+
---------------------- hrm        | mv1_tab1 |    100000 |
        0 |    100000 | 2025-04-28 03:27:53.896775-05 |
hrm        | tab1     |    100000 |       9999 |     90001 |
 2025-04-28 03:27:51.623393-05 |
hrm        | tab2     |     10000 |          0 |         1 |
 2025-04-28 03:27:53.853552-05 |
hrm        | tab3     |      2000 |          0 |         0 |
 2025-04-28 03:27:53.856251-05 |
hrm        | tab4     |    100000 |       9999 |     90001 |
 2025-04-28 03:27:53.870013-05 |
hrm        | tab5     |    100000 |       9999 |     90001 |
 2025-04-28 03:27:53.883492-05 |
(6 rows)
```

> **Note** Please note the "n_dead_tup" column.

Now, if you check the size of the tables, you can see that the size of the table remains the same.

```
pgdb1=# \dt+ hrm.tab1
                                List of relations
 Schema | Name | Type  |  Owner   | Persistence | Access method |  Size   | Description
--------+------+-------+----------+-------------+---------------+---------+-------------
 hrm    | tab1 | table | postgres | permanent   | heap          | 3576 kB |
(1 row)

pgdb1=# \dt+ hrm.tab2
                                List of relations
 Schema | Name | Type  |  Owner   | Persistence | Access method |  Size   | Description
--------+------+-------+----------+-------------+---------------+---------+-------------
 hrm    | tab2 | table | postgres | permanent   | heap          | 872 kB  |
(1 row)

pgdb1=# \dt+ hrm.tab3
                                List of relations
 Schema | Name | Type  |  Owner   | Persistence | Access method |  Size   | Description
--------+------+-------+----------+-------------+---------------+---------+-------------
 hrm    | tab3 | table | postgres | permanent   | heap          | 16 kB   |
(1 row)

pgdb1=# \dt+ hrm.tab4
                                List of relations
 Schema | Name | Type  |  Owner   | Persistence | Access method |  Size   | Description
--------+------+-------+----------+-------------+---------------+---------+-------------
 hrm    | tab4 | table | postgres | permanent   | heap          | 3576 kB |
(1 row)
```

CHAPTER 6 POSTGRESQL ROUTINE MAINTENANCE

pgdb1=# \dt+ hrm.tab5

```
                                List of relations
 Schema | Name | Type  |  Owner   | Persistence | Access method |  Size   | Description
--------+------+-------+----------+-------------+---------------+---------+-------------
 hrm    | tab5 | table | postgres | permanent   | heap          | 3576 kB |
(1 row)
```

SQL Script to check bloat for the tables and indexes

```
pgdb1=# WITH constants AS (
pgdb1(#     -- define some constants for sizes of things
pgdb1(#     -- for reference down the query and easy maintenance
pgdb1(#     SELECT current_setting('block_size')::numeric AS bs, 23 AS
            hdr, 8 AS ma
pgdb1(# ),
pgdb1-# no_stats AS (
pgdb1(#     -- screen out table who have attributes
pgdb1(#     -- which dont have stats, such as JSON
pgdb1(#     SELECT table_schema, table_name,
pgdb1(#         n_live_tup::numeric as est_rows,
pgdb1(#         pg_table_size(relid)::numeric as table_size
pgdb1(#     FROM information_schema.columns
pgdb1(#         JOIN pg_stat_user_tables as psut
pgdb1(#            ON table_schema = psut.schemaname
pgdb1(#            AND table_name = psut.relname
pgdb1(#         LEFT OUTER JOIN pg_stats
pgdb1(#            ON table_schema = pg_stats.schemaname
pgdb1(#            AND table_name = pg_stats.tablename
pgdb1(#            AND column_name = attname
pgdb1(#     WHERE attname IS NULL
pgdb1(#         AND table_schema NOT IN ('pg_catalog', 'information_
            schema')
pgdb1(#     GROUP BY table_schema, table_name, relid, n_live_tup
pgdb1(# ),
pgdb1-# null_headers AS (
pgdb1(#     -- calculate null header sizes
```

CHAPTER 6 POSTGRESQL ROUTINE MAINTENANCE

```
pgdb1(#        -- omitting tables which dont have complete stats
pgdb1(#        -- and attributes which aren't visible
pgdb1(#        SELECT
pgdb1(#            hdr+1+(sum(case when null_frac <> 0 THEN 1 else 0 END)/8)
                   as nullhdr,
pgdb1(#            SUM((1-null_frac)*avg_width) as datawidth,
pgdb1(#            MAX(null_frac) as maxfracsum,
pgdb1(#            schemaname,
pgdb1(#            tablename,
pgdb1(#            hdr, ma, bs
pgdb1(#        FROM pg_stats CROSS JOIN constants
pgdb1(#            LEFT OUTER JOIN no_stats
pgdb1(#                ON schemaname = no_stats.table_schema
pgdb1(#                AND tablename = no_stats.table_name
pgdb1(#        WHERE schemaname NOT IN ('pg_catalog', 'information_schema')
pgdb1(#            AND no_stats.table_name IS NULL
pgdb1(#            AND EXISTS ( SELECT 1
pgdb1(#                FROM information_schema.columns
pgdb1(#                    WHERE schemaname = columns.table_schema
pgdb1(#                        AND tablename = columns.table_name )
pgdb1(#        GROUP BY schemaname, tablename, hdr, ma, bs
pgdb1(# ),
pgdb1-# data_headers AS (
pgdb1(#        -- estimate header and row size
pgdb1(#        SELECT
pgdb1(#            ma, bs, hdr, schemaname, tablename,
pgdb1(#            (datawidth+(hdr+ma-(case when hdr%ma=0 THEN ma ELSE
                   hdr%ma END)))::numeric AS datahdr,
pgdb1(#            (maxfracsum*(nullhdr+ma-(case when nullhdr%ma=0 THEN
                   ma ELSE nullhdr%ma END))) AS nullhdr2
pgdb1(#        FROM null_headers
pgdb1(# ),
pgdb1-# table_estimates AS (
pgdb1(#        -- make estimates of how large the table should be
pgdb1(#        -- based on row and page size
```

```
pgdb1(#       SELECT schemaname, tablename, bs,
pgdb1(#           reltuples::numeric as est_rows, relpages * bs as
                table_bytes,
pgdb1(#       CEIL((reltuples*
pgdb1(#               (datahdr + nullhdr2 + 4 + ma -
pgdb1(#                   (CASE WHEN datahdr%ma=0
pgdb1(#                       THEN ma ELSE datahdr%ma END)
pgdb1(#                )/(bs-20))) * bs AS expected_bytes,
pgdb1(#           reltoastrelid
pgdb1(#       FROM data_headers
pgdb1(#           JOIN pg_class ON tablename = relname
pgdb1(#           JOIN pg_namespace ON relnamespace = pg_namespace.oid
pgdb1(#               AND schemaname = nspname
pgdb1(#       WHERE pg_class.relkind = 'r'
pgdb1(# ),
pgdb1-# estimates_with_toast AS (
pgdb1(#     -- add in estimated TOAST table sizes
pgdb1(#     -- estimate based on 4 toast tuples per page because we
dont have
pgdb1(#     -- anything better.  also append the no_data tables
pgdb1(#     SELECT schemaname, tablename,
pgdb1(#         TRUE as can_estimate,
pgdb1(#         est_rows,
pgdb1(#         table_bytes + ( coalesce(toast.relpages, 0) * bs ) as
                table_bytes,
pgdb1(#         expected_bytes + ( ceil( coalesce(toast.reltuples, 0) / 4 )
                * bs ) as expected_bytes
pgdb1(#       FROM table_estimates LEFT OUTER JOIN pg_class as toast
pgdb1(#           ON table_estimates.reltoastrelid = toast.oid
pgdb1(#               AND toast.relkind = 't'
pgdb1(# ),
pgdb1-# table_estimates_plus AS (
pgdb1(# -- add some extra metadata to the table data
pgdb1(# -- and calculations to be reused
pgdb1(# -- including whether we cant estimate it
```

CHAPTER 6   POSTGRESQL ROUTINE MAINTENANCE

```
pgdb1(# -- or whether we think it might be compressed
pgdb1(#     SELECT current_database() as databasename,
pgdb1(#             schemaname, tablename, can_estimate,
pgdb1(#             est_rows,
pgdb1(#             CASE WHEN table_bytes > 0
pgdb1(#                 THEN table_bytes::NUMERIC
pgdb1(#                 ELSE NULL::NUMERIC END
pgdb1(#                 AS table_bytes,
pgdb1(#             CASE WHEN expected_bytes > 0
pgdb1(#                 THEN expected_bytes::NUMERIC
pgdb1(#                 ELSE NULL::NUMERIC END
pgdb1(#                     AS expected_bytes,
pgdb1(#             CASE WHEN expected_bytes > 0 AND table_bytes > 0
pgdb1(#                 AND expected_bytes <= table_bytes
pgdb1(#                 THEN (table_bytes - expected_bytes)::NUMERIC
pgdb1(#                 ELSE 0::NUMERIC END AS bloat_bytes
pgdb1(#     FROM estimates_with_toast
pgdb1(#     UNION ALL
pgdb1(#     SELECT current_database() as databasename,
pgdb1(#         table_schema, table_name, FALSE,
pgdb1(#         est_rows, table_size,
pgdb1(#         NULL::NUMERIC, NULL::NUMERIC
pgdb1(#     FROM no_stats
pgdb1(# ),
pgdb1-# bloat_data AS (
pgdb1(#     -- do final math calculations and formatting
pgdb1(#     select current_database() as databasename,
pgdb1(#         schemaname, tablename, can_estimate,
pgdb1(#         table_bytes, round(table_bytes/(1024^2)::NUMERIC,3) as
            table_mb,
pgdb1(#         expected_bytes, round(expected_bytes/(1024^2)::NUMERIC,3)
            as expected_mb,
pgdb1(#         round(bloat_bytes*100/table_bytes) as pct_bloat,
pgdb1(#         round(bloat_bytes/(1024::NUMERIC^2),2) as mb_bloat,
pgdb1(#         table_bytes, expected_bytes, est_rows
```

```
pgdb1(#        FROM table_estimates_plus
pgdb1(# )
pgdb1-# -- filter output for bloated tables
pgdb1-# SELECT databasename, schemaname, tablename,
pgdb1-#     can_estimate,
pgdb1-#     est_rows,
pgdb1-#     pct_bloat, mb_bloat,
pgdb1-#     table_mb
pgdb1-# FROM bloat_data;
```

databasename	schemaname	tablename	can_estimate	est_rows	pct_bloat	mb_bloat	table_mb
pgdb1	hrm	tab1	t	100000	0	0.02	3.461
pgdb1	hrm	tab2	t	1	99	0.80	0.813
pgdb1	hrm	tab3	t	0		0.00	
pgdb1	hrm	tab4	t	100000	0	0.02	3.461
pgdb1	hrm	tab5	t	100000	0	0.02	3.461
pgdb1	pgdb1sch1	db1s1t1	t	128	50	0.01	0.016
pgdb1	pgdb1sch1	db1s1t2	t	2	0	0.00	0.008
pgdb1	pgdb1sch1	db1s1t3	t	2	0	0.00	0.008
pgdb1	pgdb1sch1	db1s1tnew	t	1997420	75	202.66	271.414
pgdb1	public	db1t1	t	2	0	0.00	0.008
pgdb1	public	db1t2	t	2	0	0.00	0.008

(11 rows)

Figure 6-5. *Bloating information for tables*

Since you deleted some rows, run the analyze on those tables and check the stats again.

pgdb1=# analyze;
ANALYZE

pgdb1=# analyze verbose hrm.tab1;
INFO: analyzing "hrm.tab1"
INFO: "tab1": scanned 443 of 443 pages, containing 90001 live rows and
        9999 dead rows; 30000 rows in sample, 90001 estimated total rows
ANALYZE

pgdb1=# analyze verbose hrm.tab2;
INFO: analyzing "hrm.tab2"
INFO: "tab2": scanned 104 of 104 pages, containing 1 live rows and 0 dead
        rows; 1 rows in sample, 1 estimated total rows

CHAPTER 6 POSTGRESQL ROUTINE MAINTENANCE

ANALYZE

pgdb1=# analyze verbose hrm.tab3;
INFO: analyzing "hrm.tab3"
INFO: "tab3": scanned 0 of 0 pages, containing 0 live rows and 0 dead
       rows; 0 rows in sample, 0 estimated total rows
ANALYZE

pgdb1=# analyze verbose hrm.tab4;
INFO: analyzing "hrm.tab4"
INFO: "tab4": scanned 443 of 443 pages, containing 90001 live rows and
       9999 dead rows; 30000 rows in sample, 90001 estimated total rows
ANALYZE

pgdb1=# analyze verbose hrm.tab5;
INFO: analyzing "hrm.tab5"
INFO: "tab5": scanned 443 of 443 pages, containing 90001 live rows and
       9999 dead rows; 30000 rows in sample, 90001 estimated total rows
ANALYZE

Execute again the bloat SQL query to get the information.

```
pgdb1-# FROM bloat_data;
 databasename | schemaname | tablename  | can_estimate | est_rows | pct_bloat | mb_bloat | table_mb
--------------+------------+------------+--------------+----------+-----------+----------+----------
 pgdb1        | hrm        | tab1       | t            |    90001 |        10 |     0.36 |    3.461
 pgdb1        | hrm        | tab2       | t            |        1 |        99 |     0.80 |    0.813
 pgdb1        | hrm        | tab3       | t            |        0 |           |     0.00 |
 pgdb1        | hrm        | tab4       | t            |    90001 |        10 |     0.36 |    3.461
 pgdb1        | hrm        | tab5       | t            |    90001 |        10 |     0.36 |    3.461
 pgdb1        | pgdb1sch1  | db1s1t1    | t            |      128 |        50 |     0.01 |    0.016
 pgdb1        | pgdb1sch1  | db1s1t2    | t            |        2 |         0 |     0.00 |    0.008
 pgdb1        | pgdb1sch1  | db1s1t3    | t            |        2 |         0 |     0.00 |    0.008
 pgdb1        | pgdb1sch1  | db1s1tnew  | t            |  1987030 |        75 |   203.02 |  271.414
 pgdb1        | public     | db1t1      | t            |        2 |         0 |     0.00 |    0.008
 pgdb1        | public     | db1t2      | t            |        2 |         0 |     0.00 |    0.008
(11 rows)
```

Figure 6-6. *Bloating information for tables after the analyze command*

```
pgdb1=# select schemaname, relname, n_tup_ins, n_dead_tup, n_live_tup, last_analyze, last_vacuum
pgdb1-# from pg_stat_user_tables
pgdb1-# where schemaname='hrm'
pgdb1-# order by relname;
 schemaname | relname  | n_tup_ins | n_dead_tup | n_live_tup |         last_analyze          |         last_vacuum
------------+----------+-----------+------------+------------+-------------------------------+------------------------------
 hrm        | mv1_tab1 |    100000 |          0 |     100000 | 2025-04-28 04:43:50.500142-05 |
 hrm        | tab1     |    100000 |       9999 |      90001 | 2025-04-28 04:44:00.97481-05  |
 hrm        | tab2     |     10000 |          0 |          1 | 2025-04-28 04:44:07.79495-05  |
 hrm        | tab3     |      2000 |          0 |          0 | 2025-04-28 04:44:10.441813-05 |
 hrm        | tab4     |    100000 |       9999 |      90001 | 2025-04-28 04:44:12.682815-05 |
 hrm        | tab5     |    100000 |       9999 |      90001 | 2025-04-28 04:44:14.989505-05 |
(6 rows)
```

***Figure 6-7.** Information of the analyze command for tables*

Please note the dead tuples from the above output before we run the vacuum command. Now let's run the vacuum command on these tables as shown below:

pgdb1=# vacuum verbose hrm.tab1;
INFO: vacuuming "pgdb1.hrm.tab1"
INFO: finished vacuuming "pgdb1.hrm.tab1": index scans: 0
pages: 0 removed, 443 remain, 46 scanned (10.38% of total)
tuples: 9999 removed, 80935 remain, 0 are dead but not yet removable
removable cutoff: 2080, which was 0 XIDs old when operation ended
frozen: 1 pages from table (0.23% of total) had 171 tuples frozen
index scan not needed: 45 pages from table (10.16% of total) had 9999 dead item identifiers removed
avg read rate: 0.000 MB/s, avg write rate: 785.966 MB/s
buffer usage: 98 hits, 0 misses, 50 dirtied
WAL usage: 137 records, 47 full page images, 90706 bytes
system usage: CPU: user: 0.00 s, system: 0.00 s, elapsed: 0.00 s
VACUUM

pgdb1=# vacuum verbose hrm.tab2;
INFO: vacuuming "pgdb1.hrm.tab2"
INFO: finished vacuuming "pgdb1.hrm.tab2": index scans: 0
pages: 0 removed, 104 remain, 1 scanned (0.96% of total)
tuples: 0 removed, 1 remain, 0 are dead but not yet removable
removable cutoff: 2080, which was 0 XIDs old when operation ended
frozen: 0 pages from table (0.00% of total) had 0 tuples frozen
index scan not needed: 0 pages from table (0.00% of total) had 0 dead item identifiers removed
avg read rate: 0.000 MB/s, avg write rate: 0.000 MB/s

CHAPTER 6 POSTGRESQL ROUTINE MAINTENANCE

```
buffer usage: 7 hits, 0 misses, 0 dirtied
WAL usage: 0 records, 0 full page images, 0 bytes
system usage: CPU: user: 0.00 s, system: 0.00 s, elapsed: 0.00 s
INFO:   vacuuming "pgdb1.pg_toast.pg_toast_164019"
INFO:   finished vacuuming "pgdb1.pg_toast.pg_toast_164019": index scans: 0
pages: 0 removed, 0 remain, 0 scanned (100.00% of total)
tuples: 0 removed, 0 remain, 0 are dead but not yet removable
removable cutoff: 2080, which was 0 XIDs old when operation ended
new relfrozenxid: 2080, which is 187 XIDs ahead of previous value
frozen: 0 pages from table (100.00% of total) had 0 tuples frozen
index scan not needed: 0 pages from table (100.00% of total) had 0 dead
item identifiers removed
avg read rate: 67.349 MB/s, avg write rate: 67.349 MB/s
buffer usage: 1 hits, 1 misses, 1 dirtied
WAL usage: 1 records, 1 full page images, 3285 bytes
system usage: CPU: user: 0.00 s, system: 0.00 s, elapsed: 0.00 s
VACUUM
```

pgdb1=# vacuum verbose hrm.tab3;
```
INFO:   vacuuming "pgdb1.hrm.tab3"
INFO:   finished vacuuming "pgdb1.hrm.tab3": index scans: 0
pages: 0 removed, 0 remain, 0 scanned (100.00% of total)
tuples: 0 removed, 0 remain, 0 are dead but not yet removable
removable cutoff: 2080, which was 0 XIDs old when operation ended
new relfrozenxid: 2080, which is 58 XIDs ahead of previous value
frozen: 0 pages from table (100.00% of total) had 0 tuples frozen
index scan not needed: 0 pages from table (100.00% of total) had 0 dead
item identifiers removed
avg read rate: 0.000 MB/s, avg write rate: 0.000 MB/s
buffer usage: 1 hits, 0 misses, 0 dirtied
WAL usage: 1 records, 0 full page images, 188 bytes
system usage: CPU: user: 0.00 s, system: 0.00 s, elapsed: 0.00 s
VACUUM
```

pgdb1=# vacuum verbose hrm.tab4;
```
INFO:   vacuuming "pgdb1.hrm.tab4"
```

CHAPTER 6 POSTGRESQL ROUTINE MAINTENANCE

```
INFO:   finished vacuuming "pgdb1.hrm.tab4": index scans: 1
pages: 0 removed, 443 remain, 46 scanned (10.38% of total)
tuples: 9999 removed, 80935 remain, 0 are dead but not yet removable
removable cutoff: 2080, which was 0 XIDs old when operation ended
frozen: 1 pages from table (0.23% of total) had 171 tuples frozen
index scan needed: 45 pages from table (10.16% of total) had 9999 dead item
identifiers removed
index "idx4_tab4": pages: 276 in total, 27 newly deleted, 27 currently
deleted, 0 reusable
avg read rate: 628.886 MB/s, avg write rate: 204.516 MB/s
buffer usage: 310 hits, 246 misses, 80 dirtied
WAL usage: 220 records, 76 full page images, 318329 bytes
system usage: CPU: user: 0.00 s, system: 0.00 s, elapsed: 0.00 s
VACUUM
```

pgdb1=# vacuum verbose hrm.tab5;
```
INFO:   vacuuming "pgdb1.hrm.tab5"
INFO:   finished vacuuming "pgdb1.hrm.tab5": index scans: 1
pages: 0 removed, 443 remain, 46 scanned (10.38% of total)
tuples: 9999 removed, 80935 remain, 0 are dead but not yet removable
removable cutoff: 2080, which was 0 XIDs old when operation ended
frozen: 1 pages from table (0.23% of total) had 171 tuples frozen
index scan needed: 45 pages from table (10.16% of total) had 9999 dead item
identifiers removed
index "idx5_tab5": pages: 276 in total, 27 newly deleted, 27 currently
deleted, 0 reusable
avg read rate: 518.725 MB/s, avg write rate: 166.582 MB/s
buffer usage: 310 hits, 246 misses, 79 dirtied
WAL usage: 220 records, 75 full page images, 313660 bytes
system usage: CPU: user: 0.00 s, system: 0.00 s, elapsed: 0.00 s
VACUUM
```

Let's check the stats again.

```
pgdb1=# select schemaname, relname, n_tup_ins, n_dead_tup, n_live_tup, last_analyze, last_vacuum
pgdb1-# from pg_stat_user_tables
pgdb1-# where schemaname='hrm' order by relname;
 schemaname | relname  | n_tup_ins | n_dead_tup | n_live_tup |         last_analyze          |          last_vacuum
------------+----------+-----------+------------+------------+-------------------------------+-------------------------------
 hrm        | mv1_tab1 |    100000 |          0 |     100000 | 2025-04-28 04:43:50.500142-05 |
 hrm        | tab1     |    100000 |          0 |      80935 | 2025-04-28 04:44:00.97481-05  | 2025-04-28 04:49:24.476115-05
 hrm        | tab2     |     10000 |          0 |          1 | 2025-04-28 04:44:07.79495-05  | 2025-04-28 04:49:27.354682-05
 hrm        | tab3     |      2000 |          0 |          0 | 2025-04-28 04:44:10.441813-05 | 2025-04-28 04:49:30.25308-05
 hrm        | tab4     |    100000 |          0 |      80935 | 2025-04-28 04:44:12.682815-05 | 2025-04-28 04:49:32.93185-05
 hrm        | tab5     |    100000 |          0 |      80935 | 2025-04-28 04:44:14.989505-05 | 2025-04-28 04:49:35.123487-05
(6 rows)
```

Figure 6-8. *Information for tables after the vaccum command*

After executing the vacuum command, the dead tuples in the table are cleared, reducing their count to zero. vacuum works by scanning the table, identifying dead tuples, and marking their space as reusable for future operations. It's important to note that while vacuum reclaims space internally, it does not physically reduce the table size on disk. Additionally, it refreshes table statistics to help the optimizer generate better query plans.

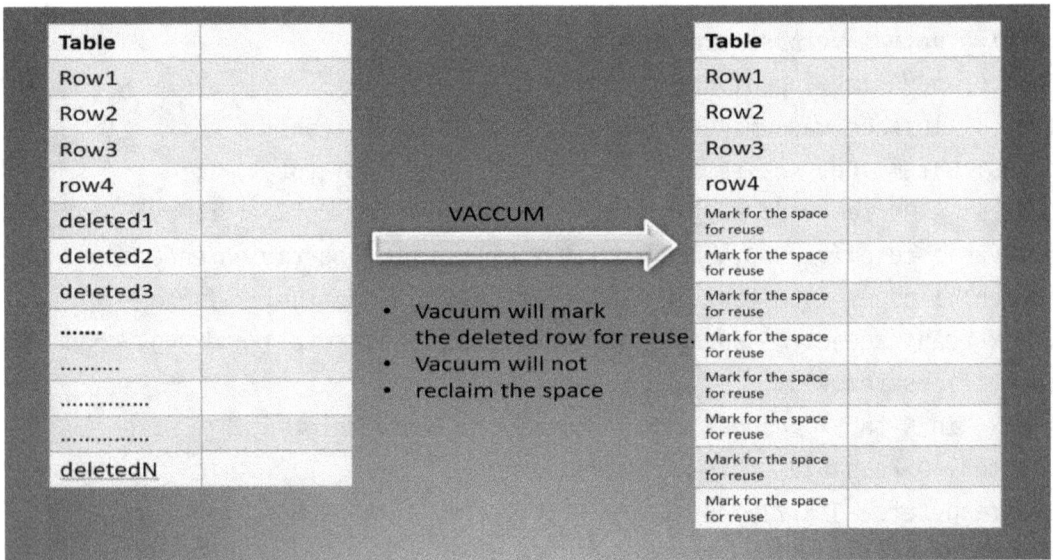

Figure 6-9. *Flow of the vaccum command*

So if you check the table size, the size will not decrease.

```
pgdb1-# \dt+ hrm.*
                                List of relations
 Schema | Name | Type  | Owner    | Persistence | Access method | Size    | Description
--------+------+-------+----------+-------------+---------------+---------+------------
 hrm    | tab1 | table | postgres | permanent   | heap          | 3576 kB |
 hrm    | tab2 | table | postgres | permanent   | heap          | 872 kB  |
 hrm    | tab3 | table | postgres | permanent   | heap          | 16 kB   |
 hrm    | tab4 | table | postgres | permanent   | heap          | 3576 kB |
 hrm    | tab5 | table | postgres | permanent   | heap          | 3576 kB |
(5 rows)

pgdb1-# \di+ hrm.*
                                       List of relations
 Schema |   Name    | Type  | Owner    | Table | Persistence | Access method | Size    | Description
--------+-----------+-------+----------+-------+-------------+---------------+---------+------------
 hrm    | idx4_tab4 | index | postgres | tab4  | permanent   | btree         | 2208 kB |
 hrm    | idx5_tab5 | index | postgres | tab5  | permanent   | btree         | 2208 kB |
(2 rows)
```

At this stage, even if you try to run the analyze command for the tables, the size will remain the same as before the delete operation was run.

VACUUM FULL in PostgreSQL

VACUUM FULL is a more aggressive version of the regular vacuum command in PostgreSQL. While a normal vacuum reclaims space by marking dead tuples for reuse, it does not physically reduce the table's on-disk size. In contrast, VACUUM FULL compacts tables and indexes by rewriting them entirely, releasing the unused space back to the operating system.

Key Points About VACUUM FULL

- Physically shrinks the table and index files, making them smaller on the disk

- Locks the table for the duration of the operation, blocking reads and writes

- Useful when a table has a large amount of dead space after heavy updates or deletes

- Helps in situations where you want to reclaim disk space and reduce storage costs

> **Note** Because VACUUM FULL rewrites the entire table, it can be a time-consuming and resource-intensive operation, especially for large tables. It should typically be scheduled during maintenance of windows to avoid impacting application performance.

```
pgdb1=# vacuum full verbose hrm.tab1;
INFO:  vacuuming "hrm.tab1"
INFO:  "hrm.tab1": found 0 removable, 90001 nonremovable row versions in 443 pages
DETAIL:  0 dead row versions cannot be removed yet.
CPU: user: 0.01 s, system: 0.00 s, elapsed: 0.04 s.
VACUUM

pgdb1=# vacuum full verbose hrm.tab4;
INFO:  vacuuming "hrm.tab4"
INFO:  "hrm.tab4": found 0 removable, 90001 nonremovable row versions in 443 pages
DETAIL:  0 dead row versions cannot be removed yet.
CPU: user: 0.01 s, system: 0.00 s, elapsed: 0.04 s.
VACUUM

pgdb1=# vacuum full verbose hrm.tab5;
INFO:  vacuuming "hrm.tab5"
INFO:  "hrm.tab5": found 0 removable, 90001 nonremovable row versions in
    443 pages
DETAIL:  0 dead row versions cannot be removed yet.
CPU: user: 0.00 s, system: 0.01 s, elapsed: 0.04 s.
VACUUM
```

CHAPTER 6 POSTGRESQL ROUTINE MAINTENANCE

Run the analyze command and check the stats and the size of the tables as well.

pgdb1=# analyze verbose hrm.tab1;
INFO: analyzing "hrm.tab1"
INFO: "tab1": scanned 399 of 399 pages, containing 90001 live rows and 0 dead rows; 30000 rows in sample, 90001 estimated total rows
ANALYZE

pgdb1=# analyze verbose hrm.tab4;
INFO: analyzing "hrm.tab4"
INFO: "tab4": scanned 399 of 399 pages, containing 90001 live rows and 0
       dead rows; 30000 rows in sample, 90001 estimated total rows
ANALYZE

pgdb1=# analyze verbose hrm.tab5;
INFO: analyzing "hrm.tab5"
INFO: "tab5": scanned 399 of 399 pages, containing 90001 live rows and 0
       dead rows; 30000 rows in sample, 90001 estimated total rows
ANALYZE

pgdb1=# select schemaname, relname, n_tup_ins, n_dead_tup, n_live_tup, last_analyze, last_vacuum
from pg_stat_user_tables
where schemaname='hrm'
order by relname;

schemaname	relname	n_tup_ins	n_dead_tup	n_live_tup	last_analyze	last_vacuum
hrm	mv1_tab1	100000	0	100000	2025-04-28 04:43:50.500142-05	
hrm	tab1	100000	0	90001	2025-04-28 07:50:23.390465-05	2025-04-28 04:49:24.476115-05
hrm	tab2	10000	0	1	2025-04-28 04:44:07.79495-05	2025-04-28 04:49:27.354682-05
hrm	tab3	2000	0	0	2025-04-28 04:44:10.441813-05	2025-04-28 04:49:30.25308-05
hrm	tab4	100000	0	90001	2025-04-28 07:50:36.955837-05	2025-04-28 04:49:32.93185-05
hrm	tab5	100000	0	90001	2025-04-28 07:50:40.625717-05	2025-04-28 04:49:35.123487-05

(6 rows)

Figure 6-10. Information about last_analyze and last_vaccum for tables in hrm schema

CHAPTER 6 POSTGRESQL ROUTINE MAINTENANCE

```
pgdb1=# \dt+ hrm.*
                                     List of relations
 Schema | Name | Type  |  Owner   | Persistence | Access method |  Size   | Description
--------+------+-------+----------+-------------+---------------+---------+------------
 hrm    | tab1 | table | postgres | permanent   | heap          | 3192 kB |
 hrm    | tab2 | table | postgres | permanent   | heap          | 16 kB   |
 hrm    | tab3 | table | postgres | permanent   | heap          | 0 bytes |
 hrm    | tab4 | table | postgres | permanent   | heap          | 3192 kB |
 hrm    | tab5 | table | postgres | permanent   | heap          | 3192 kB |
(5 rows)

pgdb1=# \di+ hrm.*
                                        List of relations
 Schema | Name      | Type  |  Owner   | Table | Persistence | Access method |  Size   | Description
--------+-----------+-------+----------+-------+-------------+---------------+---------+------------
 hrm    | idx4_tab4 | index | postgres | tab4  | permanent   | btree         | 1984 kB |
 hrm    | idx5_tab5 | index | postgres | tab5  | permanent   | btree         | 1984 kB |
(2 rows)
```

After running a VACUUM FULL, you can observe a reduction in the table size. Unlike a standard vacuum, which only marks dead tuples for reuse, VACUUM FULL reclaims the actual disk space. It does this by creating a temporary table, copying only the live data into it, and cleaning up the space left by deleted rows. This reclaimed space becomes available for the database to be used more efficiently.

CHAPTER 6 POSTGRESQL ROUTINE MAINTENANCE

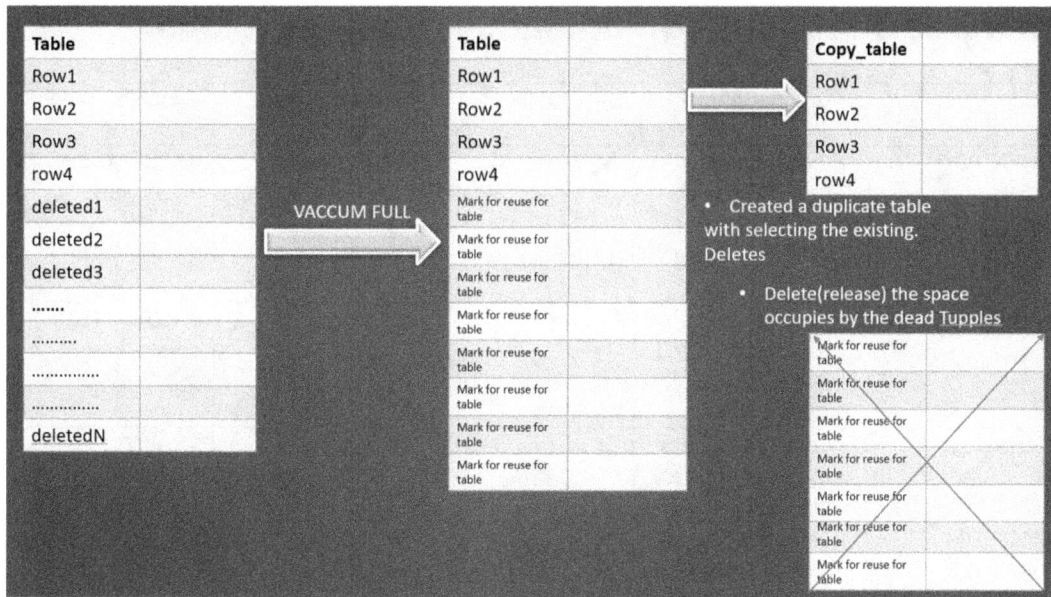

Figure 6-11. *Information of VACUUM FULL for tables under hrm schema*

```
 databasename | schemaname | tablename  | can_estimate | est_rows | pct_bloat | mb_bloat | table_mb
--------------+------------+------------+--------------+----------+-----------+----------+----------
 pgdb1        | hrm        | tab1       | t            |    90001 |         1 |     0.02 |    3.117
 pgdb1        | hrm        | tab2       | t            |        1 |         0 |     0.00 |    0.008
 pgdb1        | hrm        | tab3       | t            |        0 |           |     0.00 |
 pgdb1        | hrm        | tab4       | t            |    90001 |         1 |     0.02 |    3.117
 pgdb1        | hrm        | tab5       | t            |    90001 |         1 |     0.02 |    3.117
 pgdb1        | pgdb1sch1  | db1s1t1    | t            |      128 |        50 |     0.01 |    0.016
 pgdb1        | pgdb1sch1  | db1s1t2    | t            |        2 |         0 |     0.00 |    0.008
 pgdb1        | pgdb1sch1  | db1s1t3    | t            |        2 |         0 |     0.00 |    0.008
 pgdb1        | pgdb1sch1  | db1s1tnew  | t            |  1987030 |        75 |   203.02 |  271.414
 pgdb1        | public     | db1t1      | t            |        2 |         0 |     0.00 |    0.008
 pgdb1        | public     | db1t2      | t            |        2 |         0 |     0.00 |    0.008
(11 rows)
```

Figure 6-12. *Information of bloat for tables under hrm schema*

387

PostgreSQL vacuum Commands – Summary Table

Command	Description	Lock Tables	Reclaims Disk Space	Example Usage
VACCUM	Cleans dead tuples and makes space reusable within the table file.	✘ No	✘ No (space reused internally)	VACUUM employees;
VACUUM FULL	Rewrites the table to compact it and free up disk space.	☑ Yes	☑ Yes	VACUUM FULL employees;
ANALYZE	Collects statistics used by the query planner.	✘ No	✘ No	ANALYZE employees;
VACUUM ANALYZE	Performs cleanup and updates statistics in one command.	✘ No	✘ No	VACUUM ANALYZE employees;
Autovacuum	Background process that automatically runs VACUUM and ANALYZE.	✘ No	✘ No	(Runs automatically)

Figure 6-13. Summary of the vaccum command with example

Use VACUUM FULL only when necessary (e.g., after large deletions), as it locks the table.

- Monitor autovacuum using the pg_stat_user_tables view to ensure it's working properly.

Vacuum and Analyze Threshold Settings in postgresql.conf

PostgreSQL uses several configuration parameters to control when automatic vacuum and analyze operations are triggered. These settings help manage table bloat and keep query performance optimized without manual intervention.

CHAPTER 6 POSTGRESQL ROUTINE MAINTENANCE

```
#------------------------------------------------------------------------
# AUTOVACUUM
#------------------------------------------------------------------------

#autovacuum = on                        # Enable autovacuum subprocess? 'on'
                                        # requires track_counts to also be on.
#autovacuum_max_workers = 3             # max number of autovacuum subprocesses
                                        # (change requires restart)
#autovacuum_naptime = 1min              # time between autovacuum runs
#autovacuum_vacuum_threshold = 50       # min number of row updates before
                                        # vacuum
#autovacuum_vacuum_insert_threshold = 1000      # min number of row inserts
                                        # before vacuum; -1 disables insert
                                        # vacuums
#autovacuum_analyze_threshold = 50      # min number of row updates before
                                        # analyze
#autovacuum_vacuum_scale_factor = 0.2   # fraction of table size before vacuum
#autovacuum_vacuum_insert_scale_factor = 0.2    # fraction of inserts over table
                                        # size before insert vacuum
#autovacuum_analyze_scale_factor = 0.1  # fraction of table size before analyze
#autovacuum_freeze_max_age = 200000000  # maximum XID age before forced vacuum
                                        # (change requires restart)
#autovacuum_multixact_freeze_max_age = 400000000        # maximum multixact age
                                        # before forced vacuum
                                        # (change requires restart)
#autovacuum_vacuum_cost_delay = 2ms     # default vacuum cost delay for
                                        # autovacuum, in milliseconds;
                                        # -1 means use vacuum_cost_delay
#autovacuum_vacuum_cost_limit = -1      # default vacuum cost limit for
                                        # autovacuum, -1 means use
                                        # vacuum_cost_limit
```

Figure 6-14. *Information of the autovacuum command*

Calculation:

The formula to trigger vacuum or analyze for a table:

$$threshold = base\_threshold + (scale\_factor \times total\_rows)$$

Example:

If a table has 500,000 rows, with default settings:

- Vacuum triggers after $50 + (0.2 \times 500{,}000) = 100{,}050$ row changes.

- Analyze triggers after $50 + (0.1 \times 500{,}000) = 50{,}050$ row changes.

vacuumdb in PostgreSQL

In PostgreSQL, vacuumdb is a command-line utility used to perform maintenance operations on a database by cleaning up dead tuples and updating statistics, like the SQL-level vacuum and analyze commands.

```
pgdb1-# \dt+ hrm
Did not find any relation named "hrm".
pgdb1-# \dt+ hrm.*
                                List of relations
 Schema | Name | Type  |  Owner   | Persistence | Access method |  Size   | Description
--------+------+-------+----------+-------------+---------------+---------+-------------
 hrm    | tab1 | table | postgres | permanent   | heap          | 3192 kB |
 hrm    | tab2 | table | postgres | permanent   | heap          | 16 kB   |
 hrm    | tab3 | table | postgres | permanent   | heap          | 0 bytes |
 hrm    | tab4 | table | postgres | permanent   | heap          | 3192 kB |
 hrm    | tab5 | table | postgres | permanent   | heap          | 3192 kB |
(5 rows)
```

Figure 6-15. Information about objects statistics

vacuumdb Commands for Various Scenarios

Full vacuum on all databases:

postgres=# vacuumdb -all -full

Vacuum for complete database:

postgres-# vacuumdb -d pgdb1

Vacuum for multiple tables in the pgdb1 database:

postgres-# vacuumdb -d pgdb1 -t tab1 -t tab2

Vacuum + analyze for multiple tables in the pgdb1 database:

postgres-# vacuumdb -d pgdb1 -t tab1 -t tab2 -z

Only analyze for multiple tables in the pgdb1 database:

postgres-# vacuumdb -d pgdb1 -t tab1 -t tab2 -Z

Vacuum for multiple tables with parallel jobs in the pgdb1 database:

postgres-# vacuumdb -d pgdb1 -t tab1 -t tab2 -j 2

Forcing the vacuumdb command for the pgdb1 database:

postgres-# vacuumdb -d pgdb1 -f

Vacuum and analyze a specific table:

postgres-# vacuumdb -d mydatabase --table='hrm.tab4' -analyze

CHAPTER 6 POSTGRESQL ROUTINE MAINTENANCE

Check with the below command available options with the vacuumdb command:

[postgres@pg_server bin]$ ./vacuumdb --help
```
vacuumdb cleans and analyzes a PostgreSQL database.

Usage:
  vacuumdb [OPTION]... [DBNAME]

Options:
  -a, --all                       vacuum all databases
      --buffer-usage-limit=SIZE   size of ring buffer used for vacuum
  -d, --dbname=DBNAME             database to vacuum
      --disable-page-skipping     disable all page-skipping behavior
  -e, --echo                      show the commands being sent to
                                  the server
  -f, --full                      do full vacuuming
  -F, --freeze                    freeze row transaction information
      --force-index-cleanup       always remove index entries that point to
                                  dead tuples
  -j, --jobs=NUM                  use this many concurrent connections
                                  to vacuum
      --min-mxid-age=MXID_AGE     minimum multixact ID age of tables
                                  to vacuum
      --min-xid-age=XID_AGE       minimum transaction ID age of tables
                                  to vacuum
      --no-index-cleanup          don't remove index entries that point to
                                  dead tuples
      --no-process-main           skip the main relation
      --no-process-toast          skip the TOAST table associated with the
                                  table to vacuum
      --no-truncate               don't truncate empty pages at the end of
                                  the table
  -n, --schema=SCHEMA             vacuum tables in the specified
                                  schema(s) only
  -N, --exclude-schema=SCHEMA     do not vacuum tables in the specified
                                  schema(s)
```

```
-P, --parallel=PARALLEL_WORKERS use this many background workers for
vacuum, if available
-q, --quiet                     don't write any messages
    --skip-locked               skip relations that cannot be
                                immediately locked
-t, --table='TABLE[(COLUMNS)]'  vacuum specific table(s) only
-v, --verbose                   write a lot of output
-V, --version                   output version information, then exit
-z, --analyze                   update optimizer statistics
-Z, --analyze-only              only update optimizer statistics;
                                no vacuum
    --analyze-in-stages         only update optimizer statistics, in
                                multiple
                                stages for faster results; no vacuum
-?, --help                      show this help, then exit

Connection options:
  -h, --host=HOSTNAME       database server host or socket directory
  -p, --port=PORT           database server port
  -U, --username=USERNAME   user name to connect as
  -w, --no-password         never prompt for password
  -W, --password            force password prompt
  --maintenance-db=DBNAME   alternate maintenance database

Read the description of the SQL command VACUUM for details.

Report bugs to <pgsql-bugs@lists.postgresql.org>.
PostgreSQL home page: <https://www.postgresql.org/>
[postgres@pg_server bin]$
```

Reindexing in PostgreSQL

For this, we will create a new schema with the name hrm2 and create a new table as table1 and create an index on this table.

pgdb1=# create schema hrm2;
CREATE SCHEMA

CHAPTER 6 POSTGRESQL ROUTINE MAINTENANCE

```
pgdb1=# create table hrm2.table1 (id int4);
CREATE TABLE

pgdb1=# insert into hrm2.table1 select * from generate_series(1, 1000000);
INSERT 0 1000000

pgdb1=# create index idx1_table1 on hrm2.table1 (id);
CREATE INDEX

pgdb1=# select schemaname, relname, n_tup_ins, n_dead_tup, n_live_tup,
last_analyze, last_vacuum
from pg_stat_user_tables
where schemaname='hrm2' order by relname;

schemaname | relname | n_tup_ins | n_dead_tup | n_live_tup | last_analyze |
 last_vacuum
-----------+---------+-----------+------------+------------+--------------+--------------
 hrm2      | table1  |   1000000 |          0 |    1000000 |              |
(1 row)

pgdb1=# \dt+ hrm2.*
                        List of relations
Schema |  Name  | Type  |  Owner   | Persistence | Access method | Size  |
Description
-------+--------+-------+----------+-------------+---------------+-------+-
 hrm2  | table1 | table | postgres | permanent   | heap          | 35 MB |
(1 row)

pgdb1=# \di+ hrm2.*
                        List of relations
Schema |    Name     | Type  |  Owner   | Table  | Persistence |
Access method | Size  | Description
-------+-------------+-------+----------+--------+-------------+
---------------
 hrm2  | idx1_table1 | index | postgres | table1 | permanent   |
 btree         | 21 MB |
(1 row)
```

CHAPTER 6 POSTGRESQL ROUTINE MAINTENANCE

Check the path for this table and its index.

pgdb1=# select pg_relation_filepath('hrm2.table1');

```
pg_relation_filepath
-----------------------------
base/98428/164088
(1 row)
```

pgdb1=# select pg_relation_filepath('hrm2.idx1_table1');

```
pg_relation_filepath
-----------------------------
base/98428/164091
(1 row)
```

Note Take a note of the above file path.

Delete the data from table1 as shown below:

pgdb1=# delete from hrm2.table1 where id<100000;
```
DELETE 99999
```

pgdb1=# delete from hrm2.table1 where id<900000;
```
DELETE 800000
```

Check the stats and size of the table.

pgdb1=# select schemaname, relname, n_tup_ins, n_dead_tup, n_live_tup, last_analyze, last_vacuum
from pg_stat_user_tables
where schemaname='hrm2'
order by relname;

schemaname	relname	n_tup_ins	n_dead_tup	n_live_tup	last_analyze	last_vacuum
hrm2	table1	1000000	899999	100001		

(1 row)

CHAPTER 6   POSTGRESQL ROUTINE MAINTENANCE

```
pgdb1=# \dt+ hrm2.table1
                                List of relations
 Schema |  Name  | Type  |  Owner   | Persistence | Access method | Size  |
Description
--------+--------+-------+----------+-------------+---------------+-------+-
 hrm2   | table1 | table | postgres | permanent   | heap          | 35 MB |
(1 row)

pgdb1=# \di+ hrm2.idx1_table1
                                List of relations
 Schema |    Name     | Type  |  Owner   | Table  | Persistence |
Access method | Size  | Description
--------+-------------+-------+----------+--------+-------------+-------------
 hrm2   | idx1_table1 | index | postgres | table1 | permanent   |
 btree          | 21 MB |
(1 row)
```

Run the reindex on the table table1 (without mentioning the column name).

```
pgdb1=# reindex table hrm2.table1;
REINDEX

pgdb1=# \di+ hrm2.idx1_table1
                                List of relations
Schema |    Name     | Type  |  Owner   | Table  | Persistence |
Access method | Size    | Description
-------+-------------+-------+----------+--------+-------------+--------------
 hrm2  | idx1_table1 | index | postgres | table1 | permanent   |
 btree         | 2208 kB |
(1 row)

pgdb1=# \dt+ hrm2.table1
                                List of relations
 Schema | Name   | Type  |  Owner   | Persistence | Access method | Size  |
Description
-------+--------+-------+----------+-------------+---------------+-------+-
 hrm2  | table1 | table | postgres | permanent   | heap          | 35 MB |
(1 row)
```

```
pgdb1=# select pg_relation_filepath('hrm2.table1');
 pg_relation_filepath
-----------------------------
 base/98428/164088
(1 row)

pgdb1=# select pg_relation_filepath('hrm2.idx1_table1');
 pg_relation_filepath
-----------------------------
 base/98428/164092
(1 row)
```

After executing a REINDEX operation without specifying a particular column, you may notice a reduction in the index size, indicating that internal fragmentation or bloat has been cleaned up. Interestingly, the file path of the index remains the same before and after the operation, confirming that PostgreSQL rebuilt the index in place without changing its physical location on disk.

TIP: REINDEX TABLE <table_name>

- Table OID stays the same – the table structure is untouched.
- Index OIDs are regenerated – all associated indexes are dropped and rebuilt.
- Table size remains unchanged – no direct impact on the base table's storage.
- Index size is optimized – index bloat is removed during the rebuild process.
- Stale index entries (dead tuples) are cleared – resulting in better performance.
- Dead tuples in the table are not removed – since only the index is rebuilt, not the table data itself.

Note   REINDEX INDEX <index_name>

CHAPTER 6　POSTGRESQL ROUTINE MAINTENANCE

When reindexing an individual index, PostgreSQL creates a new physical file, which results in a different file path, indicating that a fresh copy of the index was built and swapped in.

In a different case, when reindexing a specific index using REINDEX INDEX <index_name>, PostgreSQL creates a new physical file for the index, leading to a **change in its file path**, which confirms that the original index file has been replaced with a newly generated one.

pgdb1=# select pg_relation_filepath('hrm2.table1');
pg_relation_filepath
----
 base/98428/164088
(1 row)

pgdb1=# select pg_relation_filepath('hrm2.idx1_table1');
pg_relation_filepath
----
 base/98428/164092
(1 row)

pgdb1=# insert into hrm2.table1 select * from generate_series(1, 1000000);
INSERT 0 1000000

pgdb1=# delete from hrm2.table1 where id<100000;
DELETE 99999

pgdb1=# reindex index hrm2.idx1_table1;
REINDEX

pgdb1=# select pg_relation_filepath('hrm2.table1');
pg_relation_filepath
----
base/98428/164088
(1 row)

pgdb1=# select pg_relation_filepath('hrm2.idx1_table1');
pg_relation_filepath
----
base/98428/164093
(1 row)

> **Note** Compare the index path before and after performing reindex operation on the index.

Reindexing in PostgreSQL – Key Options

- This command rebuilds the specified index without affecting others.

    Reindex a specific index: REINDEX INDEX index_name;

- Reconstructs all indexes associated with the given table.

    Reindex all indexes on a specific table: REINDEX TABLE table_name;

- Rebuilds every index in the specified schema.

    Reindex indexes within a schema: REINDEX SCHEMA schema_name;

- Recreates all indexes in the given database – useful after upgrades or corruption recovery.

    Reindex the entire database: REINDEX DATABASE database_name;

- Reconstructs indexes on system catalog tables for the specified database.

    Reindex system catalog indexes: REINDEX SYSTEM database_name;

PostgreSQL Catalog Views for Size Monitoring

- **pg_table_size()**: Returns the size of the actual table data only
- **pg_indexes_size()**: Gives the combined size of all indexes for a table
- **pg_total_relation_size()**: Sum of the table and all associated indexes

CHAPTER 6 POSTGRESQL ROUTINE MAINTENANCE

> **Note** Use pg_table_size() to assess data volume and pg_total_relation_size() for complete storage usage (data + indexes).

Finding the Largest Tables in the Database

With the query below, find the largest tables in the database and plan maintenance for day-to-day operations.

postgres=# \c pgdb1
You are now connected to database "pgdb1" as user "postgres".
pgdb1=# SELECT relname AS table_name,
pgdb1-# pg_size_pretty(pg_total_relation_size(relid)) AS total_size
pgdb1-# FROM pg_catalog.pg_statio_user_tables
pgdb1-# ORDER BY pg_total_relation_size(relid) DESC
pgdb1-# LIMIT 10;

table_name	total_size
table5	539 MB
db1s1tnew	297 MB
table1	115 MB
tab5	5176 kB
tab4	5176 kB
mv1_tab1	3616 kB
tab1	3192 kB
db1s1t1	56 kB
db1t1	24 kB
db1t2	24 kB

(10 rows)

CHAPTER 6   POSTGRESQL ROUTINE MAINTENANCE

Finding and Removing Unused Tables and Indexes

You can use PostgreSQL's statistical views, such as pg_stat_user_tables and pg_stat_user_indexes, to identify tables and indexes that show minimal or no activity. It's advisable to monitor these objects over a period to ensure they are truly unused. If they remain inactive, consider removing them to optimize storage and performance – but always take a full backup before dropping any objects to ensure data safety and rollback capability.

List unused tables in the database:

```
pgdb1=# SELECT relname, n_live_tup
pgdb1-# FROM pg_stat_user_tables
pgdb1-# ORDER BY n_live_tup DESC;
```

List unused indexes in the database:

```
pgdb1=# SELECT schemaname, relname, indexrelname, idx_scan
pgdb1-# FROM pg_stat_user_indexes
pgdb1-# WHERE idx_scan = 0;
```

Clear Write-Ahead Logging (WAL) Logs to Free Up Space in Database Server

If WAL (Write-Ahead Logging) files are consuming excessive disk space in PostgreSQL, they can be manually removed **with caution**, but it is strongly recommended to use supported tools and methods such as pg_archivecleanup or configuring proper archive_command and retention settings. Directly deleting WAL files without ensuring they are no longer needed by replication or recovery processes can lead to **data loss or corruption**.

```
[postgres@pg_server ~]$ du -sh /var/lib/pgsql/16/data/pg_wal
1.1G    /var/lib/pgsql/16/data/pg_wal
[postgres@pg_server ~]$ ls -lrth /var/lib/pgsql/16/data/pg_wal |less
total 1.0G
-rw-------. 1 postgres postgres 16M Apr 28 17:50 000000010000000400000006E
-rw-------. 1 postgres postgres 16M Apr 28 17:50 000000010000000400000006F
-rw-------. 1 postgres postgres 16M Apr 28 17:50 0000000100000004000000070
-rw-------. 1 postgres postgres 16M Apr 28 17:50 0000000100000004000000071
```

```
-rw-------. 1 postgres postgres 16M Apr 28 17:50 000000010000000400000063
-rw-------. 1 postgres postgres 16M Apr 28 17:50 000000010000000400000064
-rw-------. 1 postgres postgres 16M Apr 28 17:50 000000010000000400000065
-rw-------. 1 postgres postgres 16M Apr 28 17:50 000000010000000400000059
-rw-------. 1 postgres postgres 16M Apr 28 17:50 00000001000000040000005A
-rw-------. 1 postgres postgres 16M Apr 28 17:50 000000010000000400000066
-rw-------. 1 postgres postgres 16M Apr 28 17:50 000000010000000400000067
-rw-------. 1 postgres postgres 16M Apr 28 17:50 00000001000000040000005B
-rw-------. 1 postgres postgres 16M Apr 28 17:50 00000001000000040000005C
-rw-------. 1 postgres postgres 16M Apr 28 17:50 000000010000000400000068
```
<<<<< OUTPUT TRUNCATED >>>>>

Best Practices to Prevent Disk Space Issues in PostgreSQL Cluster

Apart from the above routine maintenance activities, below are best practices to implement in PostgreSQL cluster.

- **Enable autovacuum and auto reindexing**: Ensure that autovacuum is properly tuned to clean up dead tuples and avoid table/index bloat automatically.

- **Monitor WAL log growth**: Keep track of WAL activity using views like pg_stat_wal_receiver to detect unusual growth early.

- **Implement table partitioning**: Break large tables into smaller, manageable partitions to improve performance and reduce bloat.

- **Set up disk monitoring**: Use monitoring tools like Prometheus with Grafana dashboards to get real-time alerts on disk usage and trends.

- **Archive or move old data**: Periodically offload historical data to external or cheaper storage to free up space on the primary database.

Log File Maintenance in PostgreSQL

Storing PostgreSQL server logs in a consistent location is essential for effective troubleshooting and system monitoring. Avoid discarding logs using /dev/null, as they provide critical insights during error diagnosis and performance tuning. While you can redirect PostgreSQL's stderr output to a file, this method requires a full server restart to truncate or rotate the log file. A more robust and scalable approach is to integrate the server's log output with a log rotation tool, such as logrotate. This ensures logs are rotated, archived, and managed efficiently – without disrupting database operations.

```
pgdb1=# SELECT name, setting, short_desc
pgdb1-# FROM pg_settings
pgdb1-# WHERE name IN ('log_destination','logging_collector',
pgdb1(#                'log_directory','log_filename',
pgdb1(#                'log_file_mode','log_rotation_age',
pgdb1(#      'log_rotation_size','log_truncate_on_rotation');
[ RECORD 1 ]-----------------------------------------------
name       | log_destination
setting    | stderr
short_desc | Sets the destination for server log output.
[ RECORD 2 ]-----------------------------------------------
name       | log_directory
setting    | log
short_desc | Sets the destination directory for log files.
[ RECORD 3 ]-----------------------------------------------
name       | log_file_mode
setting    | 0600
short_desc | Sets the file permissions for log files.
[ RECORD 4 ]-----------------------------------------------
name       | log_filename
setting    | postgresql-%a.log
short_desc | Sets the file name pattern for log files.
[ RECORD 5 ]-----------------------------------------------
name       | log_rotation_age
setting    | 1440
```

```
short_desc | Sets the amount of time to wait before forcing log file
rotation.
[ RECORD 6 ]------------------------------------------------------------
name       | log_rotation_size
setting    | 1024
short_desc | Sets the maximum size a log file can reach before being
rotated.
[ RECORD 7 ]------------------------------------------------------------
name       | log_truncate_on_rotation
setting    | on
short_desc | Truncate existing log files of same name during log rotation.
[ RECORD 8 ]------------------------------------------------------------
name       | logging_collector
setting    | on
short_desc | Start a subprocess to capture stderr output and/or csvlogs
into log files.
```

Summary

This chapter provides a comprehensive overview of PostgreSQL's routine maintenance operations, including analyze, vacuum, VACUUMDB, VACUUM FULL, and REINDEX. We examined how each method functions and when to use them and demonstrated various practical scenarios to illustrate their role in maintaining database health, improving performance, and managing storage effectively.

CHAPTER 7

PostgreSQL Monitoring Using PgAdmin and Grafana

Introduction

Monitoring is one of the essential requirements for maintaining the stability, performance, and reliability of a PostgreSQL database. Along with the OS-level commands and database SQL statements, using PostgreSQL's built-in tools like pgAdmin and external tools like Grafana provides enhanced visibility, real-time metrics, alerting capabilities, and comprehensive dashboards. Together, these tools enable proactive identification of issues and better resource planning and maintain optimal database health.

Below are the key areas covered in this chapter:

- Monitoring system resources and OS-level metrics
- Understanding real-time system behavior
- Administering databases using **pgAdmin**
- Integrating PostgreSQL with monitoring solutions **(Grafana)**

Monitoring System Resources and OS-Level Metrics

System Activity Report (SAR)

SAR is a Linux command-line utility that provides information on CPU usage, memory usage, I/O operations, and network performance.

CHAPTER 7   POSTGRESQL MONITORING USING PGADMIN AND GRAFANA

To use the sar command, we must install sysstat rpm.

yum install -y sysstat

Once the sysstat rpm is installed, the sar command can be used to check the system activity.

sar -help: Provides the syntax and options to be used based on the monitoring requirements.

sar: Displays CPU usage at default ten-minute intervals.

sar -u 10 8: Reports CPU usage every ten seconds, eight times.

```
[postgres@pg_server ~]$ sar -u 10 8
Linux 5.15.0-3.60.5.1.el8uek.x86_64 (pg_server)    04/26/2025    _x86_64_    (4 CPU)

01:29:59 AM    CPU     %user    %nice    %system    %iowait    %steal    %idle
01:30:09 AM    all      0.23     0.00       0.30       0.01      0.00    99.46
01:30:19 AM    all      0.23     0.00       0.27       0.01      0.00    99.49
01:30:29 AM    all      0.33     0.00       0.31       0.01      0.00    99.36
01:30:39 AM    all      0.19     0.00       0.25       0.02      0.00    99.54
01:30:49 AM    all      0.25     0.00       0.28       0.02      0.00    99.45
01:30:59 AM    all      0.32     0.00       0.32       0.01      0.00    99.35
01:31:09 AM    all      0.22     0.00       0.27       0.01      0.00    99.50
01:31:19 AM    all      0.23     0.00       0.28       0.01      0.00    99.49
Average:       all      0.25     0.00       0.28       0.01      0.00    99.45
```

The output from the above command is explained as below:

- 10: Displays the number of seconds between sar readings

- 8: Indicates the number of times you want sar to run

    - %usr: % of CPU time spent on user processes (like PostgreSQL, applications)

    - %nice: % of CPU time spent on user processes with a "nice" priority (lower-priority tasks)

    - %system: % of CPU time spent on kernel/system processes (Linux kernel operations, drivers)

- %iowait: % of CPU time waiting for I/O operations (disk reads/writes) to complete

- %idle: % of CPU time the system was idle (not doing any work)

If any of the % values are abnormally high, then identifying the section contributing to the increased utilization helps narrow down the root cause and focus the troubleshooting efforts.

sar -r: Displays the memory usage statistics

```
[postgres@pg_server ~]$ sar -r
Linux 5.15.0-3.60.5.1.el8uek.x86_64 (pg_server) 04/27/2025 _x86_64_ (4 CPU)

12:00:15 AM kbmemfree kbavail kbmemused %memused kbbuffers kbcached kbcommit %commit kbactive kbinact kbdirty
12:10:15 AM    3269464 4626172    2503788
43.37       3352   1675608  2180188    18.19    784820 1319928        192
12:20:15 AM    3290940 4638260    2482312
43.00       3352   1666228  2176052    18.15    785160 1306332          4
12:30:15 AM    3288068 4639184    2485184
43.05       3352   1669984  2176216    18.15    785164 1310148          0
12:40:15 AM    3279948 4634808    2493304
43.19       3352   1673744  2175856    18.15    785168 1313876        128
12:50:15 AM    3280804 4639384    2492448
43.17       3352   1677492  2176476    18.16    785164 1317796          0
```

sar -d: Reports disk I/O statistics

```
[postgres@pg_server ~]$ sar -d
Linux 5.15.0-3.60.5.1.el8uek.x86_64 (pg_server) 04/27/2025 _x86_64_ (4 CPU)

12:00:15 AM       DEV  tps  rkB/s  wkB/s areq-sz aqu-sz await svctm %util
12:10:15 AM     dev8-0 0.40  0.01  17.01   42.38   0.00  1.10  0.57  0.02
12:10:15 AM    dev11-0 0.00  0.00   0.00    0.00   0.00  0.00  0.00  0.00
12:10:15 AM   dev252-0 0.46  0.01  17.01   36.60   0.00  1.20  0.49  0.02
12:10:15 AM   dev252-1 0.00  0.00   0.00    0.00   0.00  0.00  0.00  0.00
12:10:15 AM   dev252-2 0.00  0.00   0.00    0.00   0.00  0.00  0.00  0.00
```

CHAPTER 7   POSTGRESQL MONITORING USING PGADMIN AND GRAFANA

sar -n Dev: Displays network device statistics (packets received, transmitted, etc.)

```
[postgres@pg_server ~]$ sar -n DEV
Linux 5.15.0-3.60.5.1.el8uek.x86_64 (pg_server) 04/27/2025 _x86_64_ (4 CPU)

12:00:15 AM   IFACE  rxpck/s  txpck/s  rxkB/s  txkB/s  rxcmp/s  txcmp/s
rxmcst/s  %ifutil
12:10:15
AM     lo    0.25    0.25    0.01    0.01    0.00    0.00    0.00    0.00
12:10:15 AM enp0s3   0.01    0.01    0.00    0.00    0.00    0.00    0.00
0.00
12:10:15 AM enp0s8   0.01    0.00    0.00    0.00    0.00    0.00    0.00
0.00
12:10:15 AM virbr0   0.00    0.00    0.00    0.00    0.00    0.00    0.00
0.00
```

TOP: A real-time monitoring tool that shows a dynamic view of CPU and memory usage along with system processes

top -help: Provides syntax usage along with options to use

```
[postgres@pg_server ~]$ top
top - 01:37:14 up 6:39, 3 users,  load average: 0.05, 0.01, 0.00
Tasks: 275 total,   1 running, 274 sleeping,   0 stopped,   0 zombie
%Cpu(s): 0.9 us,  0.1 sy,  0.0 ni, 98.5 id,  0.0 wa,  0.2 hi,  0.2
si,  0.0 st
MiB Mem :   5637.9 total,    3168.0 free,     724.5 used,    1745.4 buff/cache
MiB Swap:   6068.0 total,    6068.0 free,       0.0 used.    4512.4 avail Mem

    PID USER       PR  NI    VIRT    RES    SHR S  %CPU  %MEM
    TIME+ COMMAND
   3018 gdm        20   0 3834316 257100 114208 S   1.0   4.5   0:07.63
    gnome-shell
  23047 postgres   20   0  508508  47684  44900 S   3.3   0.8   0:00.10
    postgres
  23308 postgres   20   0  507752  86956  84528 S   0.7   1.5   0:00.02
    postgres
   5037 postgres   20   0  503264  31552  30060 S   0.3   0.5   0:00.32
    postgres
```

CHAPTER 7   POSTGRESQL MONITORING USING PGADMIN AND GRAFANA

```
23327 postgres  20   0  264244   4532   3600 R   0.3   0.1   0:00.02 top
    1 root      20   0  241856  14540   8872
    S   0.0    0.3   0:01.65 systemd
    2 root      20   0       0      0      0 S   0.0   0.0   0:00.01
    kthreadd
    3 root       0 -20       0      0      0
    I   0.0    0.0   0:00.00 rcu_gp
    4 root       0 -20       0      0      0 I   0.0   0.0   0:00.00
    rcu_par_gp
    5 root       0 -20       0      0      0
    I   0.0    0.0   0:00.00 netns
   10 root       0 -20       0      0      0 I   0.0   0.0   0:00.00 mm_
    percpu_wq
   11 root      20   0       0      0      0 S   0.0   0.0   0:00.00 rcu_
    tasks_rude_
```

In case there is any high utilization of CPU or memory or load average, then the corresponding processes consuming high resources need to be investigated.

Along with the top command, the system load average can be viewed from the uptime command, which also provides the information about how long the system has been running.

[postgres@pg_server ~]$ uptime
15:20:25 up 31 days, 16:27, 1 user, load average: 0.15, 0.12, 0.09

Input/Output Statistics (IOSTAT)

IOSTAT provides information about CPU utilization and I/O statistics for devices.

iostat – help: Provides syntax and the options to use to get the resource statistics details

iostat: Provides details on transactions along with volume of data read and writes per second

[postgres@pg_server ~]$ iostat
Linux 5.15.0-3.60.5.1.el8uek.x86_64 (pg_server) 04/27/2025 _x86_64_ (4 CPU)

```
avg-cpu:   %user   %nice %system %iowait  %steal   %idle
            0.04    0.03    0.61    0.00    0.00   99.31
```

409

Device	tps	kB_read/s	kB_wrtn/s	kB_read	kB_wrtn
sda	0.71	12.63	33.51	872255	2314492
scd0	0.00	0.00	0.00	2	0
dm-0	0.80	11.75	33.45	811687	2310048
dm-1	0.00	0.03	0.00	2348	0
dm-2	0.00	0.08	0.03	5693	2375

iostat -d 5 5: Shows statistics for each device five times with an interval of five seconds

```
[postgres@pg_server ~]$ iostat -d 5 5
Linux 5.15.0-3.60.5.1.el8uek.x86_64 (pg_server)  04/27/2025  _x86_64_  (4 CPU)
```

Device	tps	kB_read/s	kB_wrtn/s	kB_read	kB_wrtn
sda	1.33	35.99	65.58	870675	1586511
scd0	0.00	0.00	0.00	2	0
dm-0	1.35	33.49	65.40	810107	1582067
dm-1	0.00	0.10	0.00	2348	0
dm-2	0.01	0.24	0.10	5693	2375
Device:	tps	kB_read/s	kB_wrtn/s	kB_read	kB_wrtn
sda	3.40	1.00	2.10	5	10
scd0	1.80	1.00	8.50	0	42
dm-0	0.40	0.00	6.40	0	32
dm-1	2.80	32.00	8.00	160	40
dm-2	3.40	1.00	2.10	5	10
Device:	tps	kB_read/s	kB_wrtn/s	kB_read	kB_wrtn
sda	3.20	1.00	1.30	5	6
scd0	1.40	0.00	4.50	0	22
dm-0	0.20	0.00	3.20	0	16
dm-1	1.00	9.60	4.00	48	20
dm-2	3.20	1.00	1.30	5	6
Device:	tps	kB_read/s	kB_wrtn/s	kB_read	kB_wrtn
sda	3.40	1.00	2.10	5	10
scd0	1.80	0.00	8.50	0	42

CHAPTER 7   POSTGRESQL MONITORING USING PGADMIN AND GRAFANA

dm-0	0.40	0.00	6.40	0	32
dm-1	4.80	64.00	8.00	320	40
dm-2	3.40	1.00	2.10	5	10
Device:	tps	kB_read/s	kB_wrtn/s	kB_read	kB_wrtn
sda	3.40	1.00	2.10	5	10
scd0	1.80	0.00	8.50	0	42
dm-0	0.40	0.00	6.40	0	32
dm-1	3.40	41.60	8.00	208	40
dm-2	3.40	1.00	2.10	5	10

iostat -x: Provides extended statistics for each device

```
[postgres@pg_server ~]$ iostat -x
Linux 5.15.0-3.60.5.1.el8uek.x86_64 (pg_server)   04/27/2025 _
x86_64_ (4 CPU)

avg-cpu:  %user   %nice %system %iowait  %steal   %idle
           0.04    0.03    0.61    0.00    0.00   99.31

Device    r/s  w/s rkB/s wkB/s rrqm/s wrqm/s %rrqm %wrqm r_await w_await
aqu-sz rareq-sz wareq-sz svctm %util
sda     0.25 0.46 12.63 33.51   0.00   0.12  0.08 20.89    0.59
0.97   0.00    51.22    72.21  0.55  0.04
scd0    0.00 0.00  0.00  0.00   0.00   0.00  0.00  0.00    0.10    0.00
0.00    0.20     0.00  0.70  0.00
dm-0    0.23 0.57 11.75
33.45   0.00    0.00  0.00  0.00     0.57    0.76  0.00   51.95
58.74  0.48     0.04
dm-1    0.00 0.00  0.03  0.00   0.00   0.00  0.00  0.00    0.22    0.00
0.00   23.72    0.00  0.22  0.00
dm-2    0.00 0.00  0.08  0.03   0.00   0.00  0.00  0.00    0.38    0.85
0.00   28.46   29.69  0.61  0.00
```

Virtual Memory Statistics (VMSTAT)

The vmstat command is used to report real-time performance statistics about processes, memory, paging, disk I/O, and CPU consumption.

vmstat -help: Provides syntax and options to capture the details as required

vmstat: Provides the output for memory and swap usage along with I/O and CPU stats

```
[postgres@pg_server ~]$ vmstat
procs -----------memory---------- ---swap-- -----io---- -system-- -----
-cpu-----
 r  b   swpd    free    buff    cache   si   so    bi   bo    in    cs us sy
 id wa st
 1  0      0 3160964    3352  1801464    0    0     3    8    48    50  0  1
 99 0  0
```

vmstat 5 5: Displays the performance metrics every five seconds for five times

```
[postgres@pg_server ~]$ vmstat 5 5
procs -----------memory---------- ---swap-- -----io---- -system-- -----
-cpu-----
 r  b   swpd    free    buff    cache   si   so    bi   bo    in    cs us sy
 id wa st
 1  0      0 3106964    3352  1857928    0    0     3    9     9    50  0  1
 99 0  0
 0  0      0 3106964    3352  1857968    0    0     0    0  1978   201  0  1
 99 0  0
 0  0      0 3106964    3352  1857968    0    0     0   13  1974   163  0  1
100 0  0
 0  0      0 3106460    3352  1858004    0    0     0    0  2050   199  0  0
 99 0  0
 0  0      0 3106460    3352  1858004    0    0     0    9  2028   160  0  1
 99 0  0
```

Network Statistics (NETSTAT)

The netstat command displays network connections, interface statistics and network protocol statistics.

In the below output of the netstat -i command, we can determine the number of packets a system transmits and receives on each network interface.

```
[postgres@pg_server ~]$ netstat -i
Kernel Interface table
```

Iface	MTU	RX-OK	RX-ERR	RX-DRP	RX-OVR	TX-OK	TX-ERR	TX-DRP	TX-OVR	Flg
enp0s3	9001	9162156156	0	0	0	15362910790	0	0	0	BMRU
enp0s8	9001	6789758130	0	0	0	975869449	0	0	0	BMRU
lo	65536	361516947	0	0	0	361516947	0	0	0	LRU

Understanding Real-Time System Behavior

The real-time system behavior of the PostgreSQL database can be checked using several SQL queries. The SQLs help to gather insights about system performance, query execution, database health, and resource utilization. Below are some common PostgreSQL SQL queries that help monitor and troubleshoot various aspects of the database in real time.

Identifying Sessions or Queries Running for Longer Duration
SQL:

```
SELECT pid, now() - pg_stat_activity.query_start AS duration, query, state
FROM pg_stat_activity
WHERE (now() - pg_stat_activity.query_start) > interval '5 minutes';
```

The query returns the process id, duration, query, and its state.

If the state is idle, you don't need to worry about it, but active queries may be the reason behind low performance on your database.

```
postgres=# SELECT pid, now() - pg_stat_activity.query_start AS duration,
query, state
FROM pg_stat_activity
WHERE (now() - pg_stat_activity.query_start) > interval '5 minutes';

[ RECORD 1 ]------------------------------------------------
pid      | 2083604
duration | 00:00:02.779112
query    | show server_version
state    | idle
[ RECORD 2 ]------------------------------------------------
pid      | 2083231
duration | 00:08:00
query    | SELECT pid, now() - pg_stat_activity.query_start A
```

```
state      | active
[ RECORD 3 ]-------------------------------------------------------
pid        | 2073607
duration   | -00:00:00.00141
query      |  SELECT * FROM hrmschema.teaminfo;
state      | idle in transaction
[ RECORD 4 ]-------------------------------------------------------
pid        | 2358207
duration   | 00:08:10.750826
query      | select count(*) from pgdb1sch1.db1s1tnew;
state      | active
```

Identifying the Current Session Count

One of the patterns of PostgreSQL DBs leading to high CPU utilization is a high number of active connections. The following SQL query lists the

   a. Total number of connections

   b. Number of non-idle connections

   c. Number of maximum available connections

   d. Connections utilization percentage.

SQL:

```
select A.total_connections, A.non_idle_connections,
B.max_connections,
round((100 * A.total_connections::numeric / B.max_connections::numeric), 2)
connections_utilization_pctg
from  (select count(1) as total_connections,
sum(case when state!='idle' then 1 else 0 end)
as non_idle_connections
from pg_stat_activity) A,
(select setting as max_connections
from pg_settings
where name='max_connections') B;
```

CHAPTER 7 POSTGRESQL MONITORING USING PGADMIN AND GRAFANA

```
postgres=# select A.total_connections, A.non_idle_connections,
B.max_connections, round((100 * A.total_connections::numeric / B.max_
connections::numeric), 2) connections_utilization_pctg
from  (select count(1) as total_connections, sum(case when state!='idle'
then 1 else 0 end) as non_idle_connections from pg_stat_activity) A,
(select setting as max_connections from pg_settings where name='max_
connections') B;

[ RECORD 1 ]----------------+-----
total_connections           | 43
non_idle_connections        | 5
max_connections             | 1024
connections_utilization_pctg | 4.20
```

Identifying the Parallel Session Count for Each Query

Check the distribution of non-idle connections per database and per query, sorted in descending order.

SQL:

```
select datname as db_name, substr(query,1,55), count(1) as num_non_idle_
connections
from pg_stat_activity
where state!='idle'
group by 1, 2 order by 3 desc;
```

**postgres=# select datname as db_name, substr(query,1,70) as query, count(1)
as num_non_idle_connections
from pg_stat_activity
where state!='idle'
group by 1, 2 order by 3 desc;**

```
[ RECORD 1 ]------------+-----------------------------------------------
db_name                 | pgdb1
query                   | select count(*) from pgdb1sch1.db1s1tnew;
num_non_idle_connections | 4
```

```
[ RECORD 2 ]------------+------------------------------------------
db_name                 | pgdb1
query                   | insert into pgdb1sch1.db1s1tnew values
(generate_series(1,1000000));
num_non_idle_connections | 2
[ RECORD 3 ]------------+------------------------------------------
db_name                 | pgdb1
query                   | reindex index pgdb1sch1.s1tnewidx;
num_non_idle_connections | 2
[ RECORD 4 ]------------+------------------------------------------
db_name                 | pgdb4
query                   | select * from pgdb4sch4.db4s4t4;
num_non_idle_connections | 1
[ RECORD 5 ]------------+------------------------------------------
db_name                 | pgdb1
query                   | update pgdb1sch1.db1s1tnew set id=9999
where id <
                          500000;
num_non_idle_connections | 1
```

Identifying Sessions Active for More Than Five Seconds:

List non-idle PostgreSQL sessions that take more than five seconds, sorted by the runtime in descending order.

SQL:

```
select now()-query_start as runtime, pid as process_id, datname as db_name,
client_addr, client_hostname,
query from pg_stat_activity
where state!='idle'and now() - query_start > '5 seconds'::interval
order by 1 desc;
```

```
postgres=# select now()-query_start as runtime, pid as process_id, datname
as db_name, client_addr, client_hostname, substr(query,1,55) as query
from pg_stat_activity
where state!='idle'and
now() - query_start > '5 seconds'::interval
order by 1 desc;
```

```
[ RECORD 1 ]----+--------------------------------------------------------
runtime         | 00:00:09.904854
process_id      | 2365212
db_name         | pgdb1
client_addr     | 192.168.2.30
client_hostname |
query           | insert into pgdb1sch1.db1s1tnew values (generate_
series(1,1000000));
[ RECORD 2 ]----+--------------------------------------------------------
runtime         | 00:00:08.586536
process_id      | 2365218
db_name         | pgdb1
client_addr     | 192.168.2.30
client_hostname |
query           | select count(*) from pgdb1sch1.db1s1tnew;
[ RECORD 3 ]----+--------------------------------------------------------
runtime         | 00:00:06.478641
process_id      | 2378155
db_name         | pgdb1
client_addr     | 192.168.2.30
client_hostname |
query           | update pgdb1sch1.db1s1tnew set id=9999 where id < 500000;
[ RECORD 4 ]----+--------------------------------------------------------
runtime         | 00:00:06.69462
process_id      | 2378204
db_name         | pgdb1
client_addr     | 192.168.2.30
client_hostname |
query           | select count(*) from pgdb1sch1.db1s1tnew;
```

Identifying Queries with High Execution Times per Second

The root cause of high CPU utilization in PostgreSQL databases may not be a necessary long-running query. Quick but too frequent queries running hundreds of times per second can cause high CPU utilization too.

To find the top frequent PostgreSQL queries, run the following SQL query as shown below.

CHAPTER 7   POSTGRESQL MONITORING USING PGADMIN AND GRAFANA

SQL:

```
with
a as (select dbid, queryid, query, calls s from pg_stat_statements),
b as (select dbid, queryid, query, calls s from pg_stat_statements,
pg_sleep(1))
select pd.datname as db_name,
substr(a.query, 1, 400) as the_query,
sum(b.s-a.s) as runs_per_second
from a, b, pg_database pd
where
a.dbid= b.dbid
and    a.queryid = b.queryid
and    pd.oid=a.dbid
group by 1, 2
order by 3 desc;
```

postgres=# with a as (select dbid, queryid, query, calls s from pg_stat_statements), b as (select dbid, queryid, query, calls s from pg_stat_statements, pg_sleep(1)) select pd.datname as db_name, substr(a.query, 1, 55) as the_query, sum(b.s-a.s) as runs_per_second
from a, b, pg_database pd
where a.dbid= b.dbid
and a.queryid = b.queryid
and pd.oid=a.dbid
group by 1, 2
order by 3 desc;

```
[ RECORD 1 ]----+------------------------------------------------
db_name         | pgdb1
the_query       | select count(*) from pgdb1sch1.db1s1tnew;
runs_per_second | 4
[ RECORD 2 ]----+------------------------------------------------
db_name         | pgdb4
the_query       | select * from pgdb4sch5.db4s5t5;
runs_per_second | 3
```

CHAPTER 7   POSTGRESQL MONITORING USING PGADMIN AND GRAFANA

```
[ RECORD 3 ]----+-----------------------------------------------------------
db_name          | pgdb4
the_query        | select * from pgdb4sch4.db4s4t4;
runs_per_second  | 3
[ RECORD 4 ]----+-----------------------------------------------------------
db_name          | pgdb2
the_query        | select * from pgdb2sch2.db2s2t2;
runs_per_second  | 2
```

Identifying CPU Consumption by Each Query

This query checks how much each query in each database uses the CPU. It provides a resultset sorted in descending order by the most CPU-intensive queries.

SQL:

```
SELECT pss.userid, pss.dbid,
pd.datname as db_name,
round((pss.total_exec_time + pss.total_plan_time)::numeric, 2) as
total_time,
pss.calls,
round((pss.mean_exec_time+pss.mean_plan_time)::numeric, 2) as mean,
round((100 * (pss.total_exec_time + pss.total_plan_time) / sum((pss.total_
exec_time + pss.total_plan_time)::numeric) OVER ())::numeric, 2)
as cpu_portion_pctg,
pss.queryFROM pg_stat_statements pss, pg_database pd
WHERE pd.oid=pss.dbidORDER BY (pss.total_exec_time + pss.total_plan_time)
DESC LIMIT 30;
```

```
postgres=# SELECT pss.userid, pss.dbid, pd.datname as db_name, round((pss.
total_exec_time + pss.total_plan_time)::numeric, 2) as total_time,
 pss.calls, round((pss.mean_exec_time+pss.mean_plan_time)::numeric, 2) as
mean, round((100 * (pss.total_exec_time + pss.total_plan_time) / sum((pss.
total_exec_time + pss.total_plan_time)::numeric) OVER ())::numeric, 2) as
cpu_portion_pctg, substr(pss.query, 1, 50) as the_query
FROM pg_stat_statements pss, pg_database pd
WHERE pd.oid=pss.dbid
ORDER BY (pss.total_exec_time + pss.total_plan_time)DESC LIMIT 30;
```

```
[ RECORD 1 ]-----+--------------------------------------------------
userid           | 10
dbid             | 98428
db_name          | pgdb1
total_time       | 1174.95
calls            | 1
mean             | 1174.95
cpu_portion_pctg | 50.54
the_query        | update pgdb1sch1.db1s1tpg set id=$1 where id<$2
[ RECORD 2 ]-----+--------------------------------------------------
userid           | 10
dbid             | 98428
db_name          | pgdb1
total_time       | 950.86
calls            | 1
mean             | 950.86
cpu_portion_pctg | 40.90
the_query        | create table pgdb1sch1.db1s1tpg as select * from p
[ RECORD 3 ]-----+--------------------------------------------------
userid           | 10
dbid             | 98428
db_name          | pgdb1
total_time       | 116.29
calls            | 1
mean             | 116.29
cpu_portion_pctg | 5.00
the_query        | select count(*) from pgdb1sch1.db1s1tnew
[ RECORD 4 ]-----+--------------------------------------------------
userid           | 10
dbid             | 98428
db_name          | pgdb1
total_time       | 50.96
calls            | 1
mean             | 50.96
cpu_portion_pctg | 2.19
the_query        | select count(*) from pgdb1sch1.db1s1tpg
```

Checking the Stats on the Tables

Outdated PostgreSQL statistics can be another root cause for high CPU utilization. When statistical data isn't updated, the PostgreSQL query planner may generate non-efficient execution plans for queries, which will lead to a bad performance of the entire PostgreSQL DB Server. To check the last date and time the statistics were updated for each table in the PostgreSQL DB Server for a specific DB, connect to the DB and run the following query:

SQL:

```
select schemaname, relname, date_trunc('minute', last_analyze) last_
analyze, date_trunc('minute', last_autoanalyze) last_autoanalyzer
from pg_stat_all_tables
order by last_analyze desc nulls first;
```

```
postgres=# select schemaname, relname, date_trunc('minute', last_analyze)
last_analyze, date_trunc('minute', last_autoanalyze) last_autoanalyzer
from pg_stat_all_tables
order by last_analyze desc nulls first;
```

schemaname	relname	last_analyze	last_autoanalyzer
pgdb1sch1	db1s1tnew		2025-04-19 00:47:00-05
public	db1t2		2025-04-19 00:33:00-05
public	db1t1_mv1		2025-04-20 18:51:00-05
public	public		2025-04-19 01:06:00-05
pgdb1sch1	db1s1t1		
pgdb1sch1	db1s1t3		
pgdb1sch1	db1s1t2		

Identify Dead Tuples in a Table

To check information about dead tuples, and when vacuum / autovacuum was run for each table in the PostgreSQL DB Server for a specific DB, connect to the DB and run the following query:

CHAPTER 7   POSTGRESQL MONITORING USING PGADMIN AND GRAFANA

SQL:

```
select schemaname, relname, n_tup_ins, n_tup_upd, n_tup_del, n_live_tup,
n_dead_tup, DATE_TRUNC('minute', last_vacuum) last_vacuum,
DATE_TRUNC('minute', last_autovacuum) last_autovacuum
from pg_stat_all_tables
order by n_dead_tup desc;
```

postgres=# select schemaname, relname, n_tup_ins, n_tup_upd, n_tup_del, n_live_tup, n_dead_tup, DATE_TRUNC('minute', last_vacuum) last_vacuum, DATE_TRUNC('minute', last_autovacuum) last_autovacuum
from pg_stat_all_tables
order by n_dead_tup desc;

```
[ RECORD 1 ]----+-------------------------
schemaname       | pgdb1sch1
relname          | db1s1tnew
n_tup_ins        | 0
n_tup_upd        | 999998
n_tup_del        | 0
n_live_tup       | 2000000
n_dead_tup       | 505
last_vacuum      |
last_autovacuum  | 2025-04-26 10:07:00-05
[ RECORD 2 ]----+-------------------------
schemaname       | pgdb1sch1
relname          | db1s1tpg
n_tup_ins        | 2000000
n_tup_upd        | 999998
n_tup_del        | 0
n_live_tup       | 2000000
n_dead_tup       | 180
last_vacuum      |
last_autovacuum  | 2025-04-26 21:29:00-05
[ RECORD 3 ]----+-------------------------
schemaname       | pgdb1sch1
relname          | db1s1t2
```

```
n_tup_ins        | 0
n_tup_upd        | 0
n_tup_del        | 0
n_live_tup       | 0
n_dead_tup       | 0
last_vacuum      |
last_autovacuum  |
[ RECORD 4 ]----+-------------------------
schemaname       | public
relname          | db1t1
n_tup_ins        | 0
n_tup_upd        | 0
n_tup_del        | 0
n_live_tup       | 0
n_dead_tup       | 0
last_vacuum      |
last_autovacuum  |
```

PostgreSQL System Views: Real-Time Insights, No Extra Setup

One of PostgreSQL's most underrated superpowers is its rich set of *system views* – predefined virtual tables that expose detailed metrics about the database's internal operations. Without any special configuration, these views are available by default, giving you immediate access to vital information for performance tuning, diagnostics, and capacity planning.

From lock monitoring to query analysis, these views allow you to see exactly what's happening under the hood. Whether you're trying to understand slow queries, investigate blocking sessions, or optimize I/O, these insights are invaluable.

Here are some of the key system views we regularly use to troubleshoot and optimize PostgreSQL databases:

- **pg_stat_activity**: Displays active sessions and queries
- The first system view that truly transformed how I manage PostgreSQL was **pg_stat_activity**.
    - Shows **all current sessions** and their **SQL activity**
    - Helps identify **long-running queries**, **idle connections**, and **blocking sessions**
    - Crucial for **real-time monitoring** and **troubleshooting**

```
postgres=# SELECT pid, usename, application_name, client_addr, state, query
FROM pg_stat_activity
WHERE state = 'active';
 pid  | usename  | application_name | client_addr | state  |                           query
------+----------+------------------+-------------+--------+------------------------------------------------------------
 7544 | postgres | psql             |             | active | SELECT pid, usename, application_name, client_addr, state, query+
      |          |                  |             |        | FROM pg_stat_activity                                      +
      |          |                  |             |        | WHERE state = 'active';
(1 row)
```

- **pg_locks**: Reveals lock contention and potential deadlocks

    This pg_locks view helps us to identify which locks were holding up transactions, allowing us to address the underlying issues and speed up PostgreSQL database performance.

```
postgres=# \d pg_locks;
                     View "pg_catalog.pg_locks"
      Column       |           Type           | Collation | Nullable | Default
-------------------+--------------------------+-----------+----------+---------
 locktype          | text                     |           |          |
 database          | oid                      |           |          |
 relation          | oid                      |           |          |
 page              | integer                  |           |          |
 tuple             | smallint                 |           |          |
 virtualxid        | text                     |           |          |
 transactionid     | xid                      |           |          |
 classid           | oid                      |           |          |
 objid             | oid                      |           |          |
 objsubid          | smallint                 |           |          |
 virtualtransaction| text                     |           |          |
 pid               | integer                  |           |          |
 mode              | text                     |           |          |
 granted           | boolean                  |           |          |
 fastpath          | boolean                  |           |          |
 waitstart         | timestamp with time zone |           |          |
```

- **pg_stat_user_tables**: Offers statistics on user-defined tables

    The **pg_stat_user_tables** view shows detailed statistics on table usage, including how many rows were read, updated, or deleted.

    ```
    db1=# SELECT relname, seq_scan, idx_scan, n_tup_ins, n_tup_upd, n_tup_del
    FROM pg_stat_user_tables;
         relname     | seq_scan | idx_scan | n_tup_ins | n_tup_upd | n_tup_del
    -----------------+----------+----------+-----------+-----------+-----------
     emp             |        2 |        0 |         0 |         0 |         0
     part_tab_p4     |        2 |          |         0 |         0 |         0
     part_tab_p5     |        2 |          |         0 |         0 |         0
     sales_data      |        0 |          |         0 |         0 |         0
     part_tab_p2     |        2 |          |         0 |         0 |         0
     part_tab_p6     |        2 |          |         0 |         0 |         0
     part_tab_p3     |        2 |          |         0 |         0 |         0
     part_tab        |        0 |          |         0 |         0 |         0
     part_tab_p1     |        2 |          |         0 |         0 |         0
     sales_data_2025 |        0 |          |         0 |         0 |         0
     sales_data_2024 |        0 |          |         0 |         0 |         0
    (11 rows)
    ```

- **pg_stat_statements**: Provides historical query performance metrics

    The pg_stat_statements view is one of PostgreSQL's most powerful extensions, and it tracks execution statistics for all SQL statements, helping DBAs and developers identify performance bottlenecks and tune queries effectively. Please refer to Chapter 4 for more details.

- **pg_stat_bgwriter**: Shows background writer and checkpoint activity

    The pg_stat_bgwriter view provides insights into how the background writer and checkpointer manage I/O and buffer flushing. This is crucial for understanding write performance, buffer cache efficiency, and checkpoint tuning.

    - This view will help us to identify I/O bottlenecks.
    - Tracks buffer flushing due to background writer vs. backends.
    - Shows critical information for high-write or OLTP workloads.

CHAPTER 7   POSTGRESQL MONITORING USING PGADMIN AND GRAFANA

```
postgres=# \d pg_stat_bgwriter;
                         View "pg_catalog.pg_stat_bgwriter"
      Column       |           Type           | Collation | Nullable | Default
-------------------+--------------------------+-----------+----------+---------
 buffers_clean     | bigint                   |           |          |
 maxwritten_clean  | bigint                   |           |          |
 buffers_alloc     | bigint                   |           |          |
 stats_reset       | timestamp with time zone |           |          |


postgres=# SELECT * FROM pg_stat_bgwriter;
 buffers_clean | maxwritten_clean | buffers_alloc |         stats_reset
---------------+------------------+---------------+-------------------------------
             0 |                0 |           555 | 2025-05-28 16:09:48.778301-05
(1 row)
```

- **pg_stat_database**: Database-wide performance metrics

    This pg_stat_database view shows general statistics for each database, such as the number of transactions, deadlocks, and I/O operations in a PostgreSQL cluster.

    ### Getting statistics for all the databases:

```
postgres=# SELECT datname, numbackends, xact_commit, xact_rollback, blks_hit, blks_read
FROM pg_stat_database;
  datname  | numbackends | xact_commit | xact_rollback | blks_hit | blks_read
-----------+-------------+-------------+---------------+----------+-----------
           |           0 |           0 |             0 |     7957 |        14
 postgres  |           1 |         485 |             6 |    21787 |       247
 db1       |           1 |         566 |             0 |    24048 |       292
 template1 |           0 |           0 |             0 |        0 |         0
 template0 |           0 |           0 |             0 |        0 |         0
(5 rows)
```

Getting cache hit ratios:

```
postgres=# SELECT datname, ROUND(100 * blks_hit::numeric / NULLIF(blks_hit + blks_read, 0), 2) AS cache_hit_ratio
FROM pg_stat_database;
  datname  | cache_hit_ratio
-----------+-----------------
           |           99.82
 postgres  |           98.88
 db1       |           98.80
 template1 |
 template0 |
(5 rows)
```

426

Getting deadlock and temp file monitoring:

```
postgres=# SELECT datname, deadlocks, temp_files, blk_read_time, blk_write_time
FROM pg_stat_database
ORDER BY deadlocks DESC, temp_files DESC;
  datname  | deadlocks | temp_files | blk_read_time | blk_write_time
-----------+-----------+------------+---------------+----------------
           |     0     |     0      |      0        |      0
 postgres  |     0     |     0      |      0        |      0
 db1       |     0     |     0      |      0        |      0
 template1 |     0     |     0      |      0        |      0
 template0 |     0     |     0      |      0        |      0
(5 rows)
```

Resetting the statistics:

postgres=# SELECT pg_stat_reset();

(OR)

postgres=#SELECT pg_stat_reset_single_table_counters('pg_stat_database');

- **pg_class**: Understanding database-wide objects

    This pg_class view will provide metadata about tables, views, and indexes – essential for anyone who needs to manage database objects in PostgreSQL.

```
postgres=# SELECT relname, relkind, relnamespace::regnamespace, relowner::regrole, reltuples, relpages
FROM pg_class;
          relname           | relkind |  relnamespace | relowner | reltuples | relpages
----------------------------+---------+---------------+----------+-----------+----------
 pg_statistic               |    r    |   pg_catalog  | postgres |    410    |    20
 pg_type                    |    r    |   pg_catalog  | postgres |    617    |    15
 pg_toast_1255              |    t    |   pg_toast    | postgres |     3     |     1
 pg_toast_1255_index        |    i    |   pg_toast    | postgres |     0     |     1
 pg_toast_1247              |    t    |   pg_toast    | postgres |     0     |     0
 pg_toast_1247_index        |    i    |   pg_toast    | postgres |     0     |     1
 pg_toast_2604              |    t    |   pg_toast    | postgres |     0     |     0
 pg_toast_2604_index        |    i    |   pg_toast    | postgres |     0     |     1
 pg_toast_2606              |    t    |   pg_toast    | postgres |     0     |     0
 pg_toast_2606_index        |    i    |   pg_toast    | postgres |     0     |     1
 pg_toast_2612              |    t    |   pg_toast    | postgres |     0     |     0
 pg_toast_2612_index        |    i    |   pg_toast    | postgres |     0     |     1
 pg_toast_2600              |    t    |   pg_toast    | postgres |     0     |     0
 pg_toast_2600_index        |    i    |   pg_toast    | postgres |     0     |     1
 pg_toast_2619              |    t    |   pg_toast    | postgres |    13     |     3
 pg_toast_2619_index        |    i    |   pg_toast    | postgres |     0     |     1
 pg_toast_3381              |    t    |   pg_toast    | postgres |     0     |     0
 pg_toast_3381_index        |    i    |   pg_toast    | postgres |     0     |     1
 pg_toast_3429              |    t    |   pg_toast    | postgres |     0     |     0
 pg_toast_3429_index        |    i    |   pg_toast    | postgres |     0     |     1
 pg_toast_2618              |    t    |   pg_toast    | postgres |    278    |    63
 pg_toast_2618_index        |    i    |   pg_toast    | postgres |     0     |     1
 pg_toast_2620              |    t    |   pg_toast    | postgres |     0     |     0
 pg_toast_2620_index        |    i    |   pg_toast    | postgres |     0     |     1
 pg_toast_3466              |    t    |   pg_toast    | postgres |     0     |     0
 pg_toast_3466_index        |    i    |   pg_toast    | postgres |     0     |     1
 pg_toast_2609              |    t    |   pg_toast    | postgres |     0     |     0
 pg_toast_2609_index        |    i    |   pg_toast    | postgres |     0     |     1
 pg_foreign_table           |    r    |   pg_catalog  | postgres |     0     |     0
```

Administering Databases Using pgAdmin

pgAdmin is one of the widely used and feature-rich open source administration and management tools for PostgreSQL database.

pgAdmin 4 is a modified version of pgAdmin built using Python, ReactJS, and JavaScript. This tool has a robust user-friendly graphical administration interface, an SQL query tool, etc., which help in performing day-to-day database management activities in PostgreSQL.

pgAdmin can be used on Linux, Unix, macOS, and Windows to manage PostgreSQL.

The following sections outline the steps involved in installation and configuration of pgAdmin, followed by the management of a PostgreSQL database using the pgAdmin console.

Installation and Configuration of pgAdmin

pgAdmin software for any platform can be downloaded from the URL provided below.

- Access the download page:

    https://www.pgadmin.org/download/

- On the download home page, select the download options:

    - Platform – Windows.
    - Platform selection will redirect to the versions page.

CHAPTER 7   POSTGRESQL MONITORING USING PGADMIN AND GRAFANA

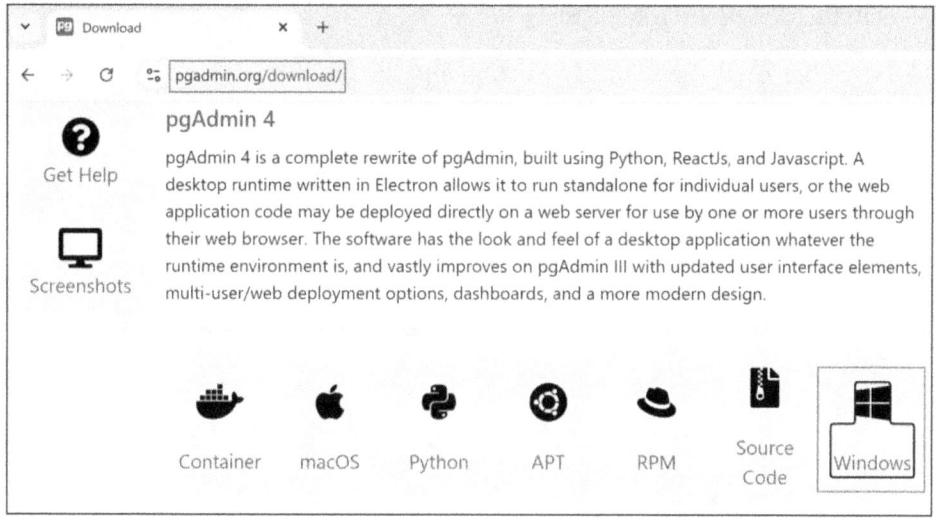

Figure 7-1. *pgAdmin download page*

- On the available versions page:

  - Select the latest version available, e.g., pgAdmin 4 v8.14.

  - Version selection will redirect to the downloadable page.

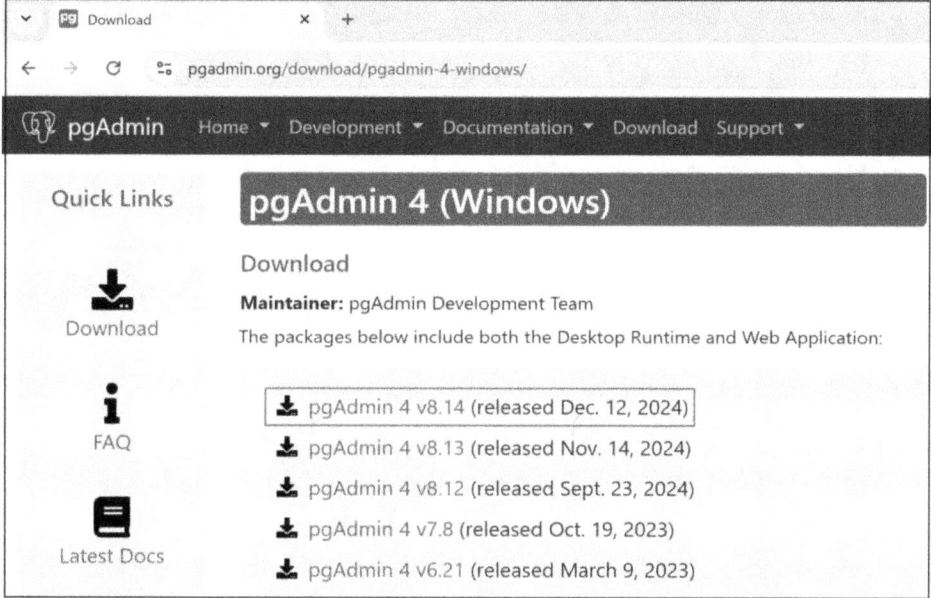

Figure 7-2. *pgAdmin version selection*

CHAPTER 7   POSTGRESQL MONITORING USING PGADMIN AND GRAFANA

- On the downloadable page:
  - Click on the executable file to begin the download.

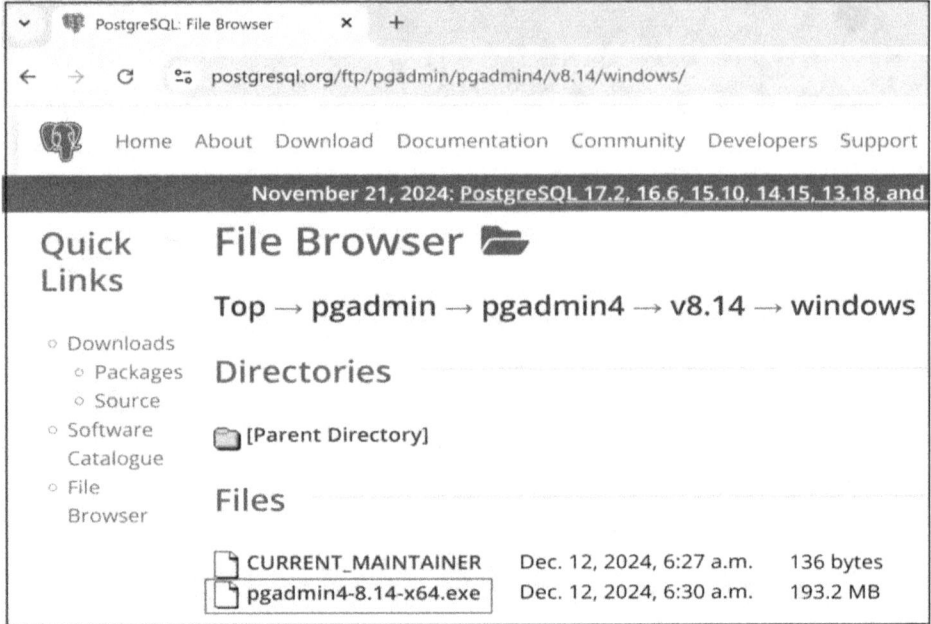

Figure 7-3. pgAdmin downloadable exe file

- Verify the executable is downloaded.

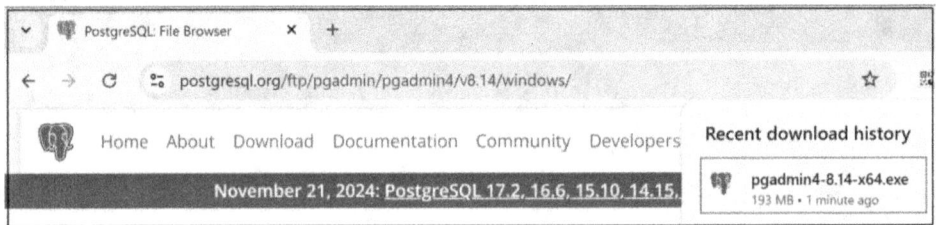

Figure 7-4. pgAdmin download status

- Once the download is complete, proceed with the installation.

CHAPTER 7   POSTGRESQL MONITORING USING PGADMIN AND GRAFANA

Installing pgAdmin 4 on Windows

- Run the downloaded executable to launch the installation wizard.
- On the installation setup wizard:
  - Verify the message and click "Next".

Figure 7-5. *pgAdmin setup wizard*

- Accept the license agreement and click "Next".

CHAPTER 7   POSTGRESQL MONITORING USING PGADMIN AND GRAFANA

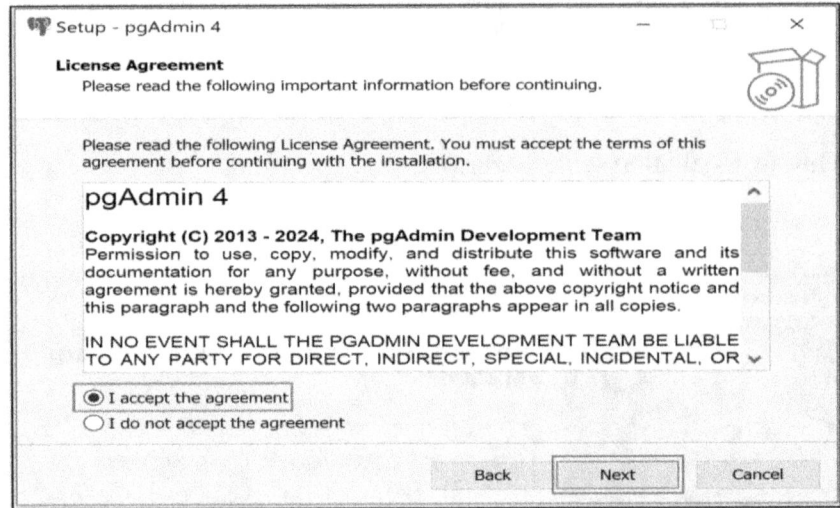

Figure 7-6. pgAdmin license agreement

- Choose the installation directory and click "Next".

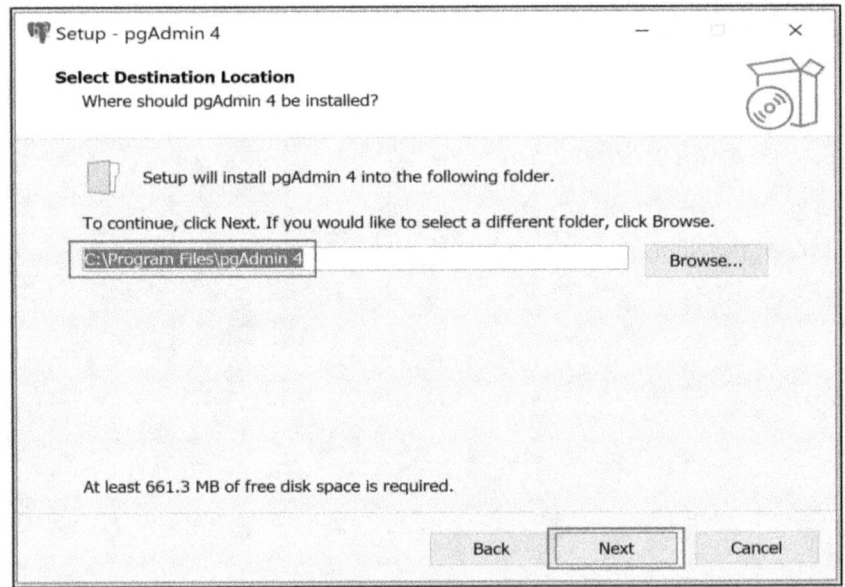

Figure 7-7. pgAdmin installation folder

- Verify the start menu folder name and click "Next".

CHAPTER 7   POSTGRESQL MONITORING USING PGADMIN AND GRAFANA

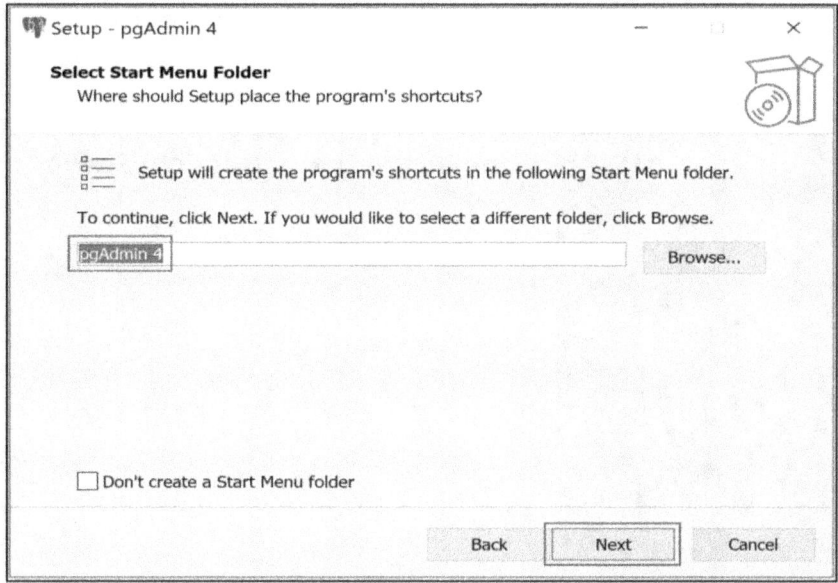

Figure 7-8.* pgAdmin shortcut name in the Start Menu folder*

- On the final screen, verify the details and click "Install".

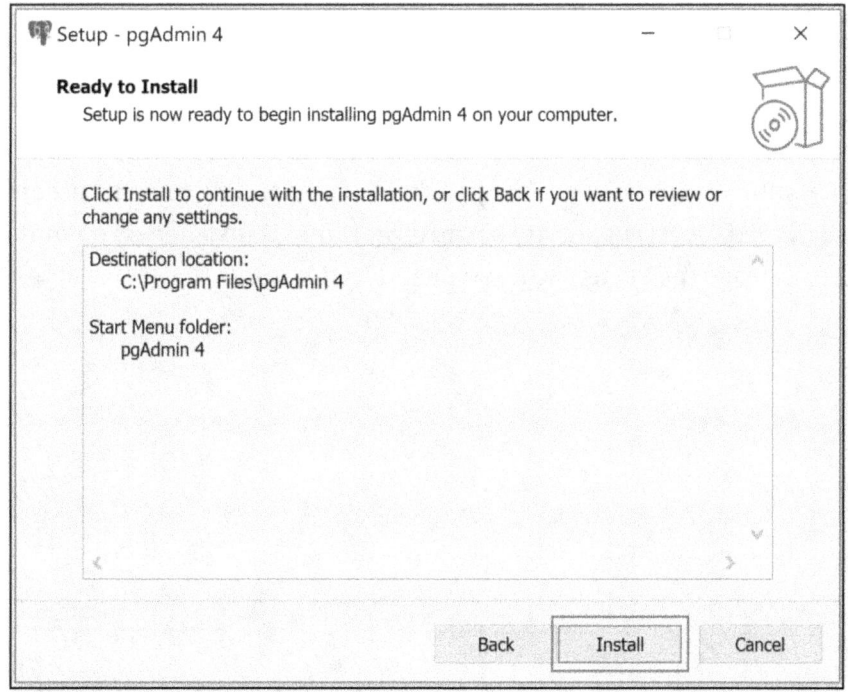

Figure 7-9.* pgAdmin install setup screen*

433

CHAPTER 7   POSTGRESQL MONITORING USING PGADMIN AND GRAFANA

- Once the installation is successfully complete, click "Finish".

Figure 7-10. pgAdmin installation complete

Connectivity Between pgAdmin and pg_server

To enable communication between the pgAdmin server and pg_server, authentication must be configured. This is necessary because pgAdmin is installed on a Windows server and needs to manage the PostgreSQL server and its databases.

CHAPTER 7   POSTGRESQL MONITORING USING PGADMIN AND GRAFANA

- On pg_server, modify pg_hba.conf and reload the configuration.

```
[postgres@pg_server ~]$ cd /var/lib/pgsql/16/data
[postgres@pg_server data]$ vi pg_hba.conf
[postgres@pg_server data]$ cat pg_hba.conf
# TYPE   DATABASE        USER            ADDRESS                 METHOD
# "local" is for Unix domain socket connections only
local    all             all                                     peer
# IPv4 local connections:
host     all             all             192.168.2.1/32          trust
[postgres@pg_server data]$ pg_ctl reload
server signaled
```

Registering PostgreSQL Server in pgAdmin

To perform administrative operations and monitor the PostgreSQL server, it needs to be registered in pgAdmin.

- Launch the pgAdmin 4 tool by searching for pgAdmin in the Start Menu (Windows).

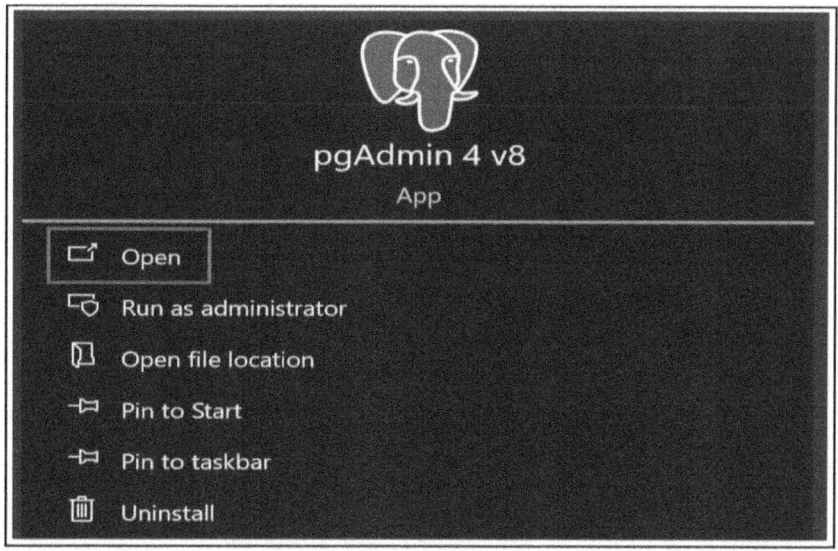

Figure 7-11. pgAdmin application location folder

435

CHAPTER 7   POSTGRESQL MONITORING USING PGADMIN AND GRAFANA

Figure 7-12. *pgAdmin application launching*

- Once the tool is launched, it opens the dashboard of servers.

Figure 7-13. *pgAdmin home screen*

CHAPTER 7   POSTGRESQL MONITORING USING PGADMIN AND GRAFANA

- On the Servers section, right-click.
  - Navigate to Register ➤ Server.

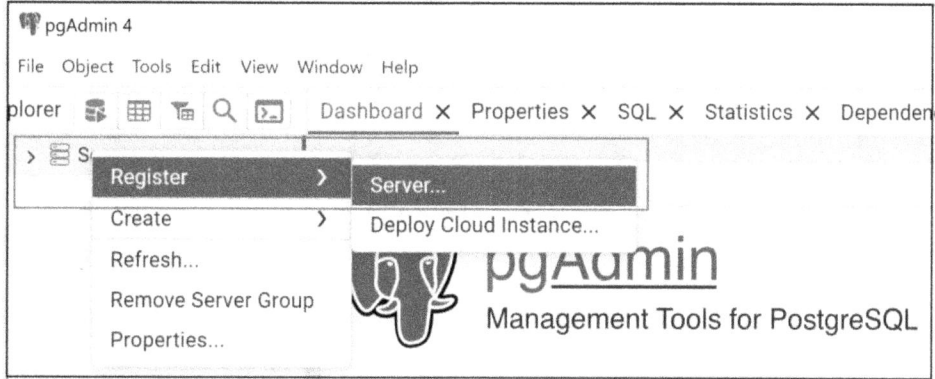

Figure 7-14. PostgreSQL server addition

- On the Register-Server page
  - Under the General section
    - Add Name – pg_server

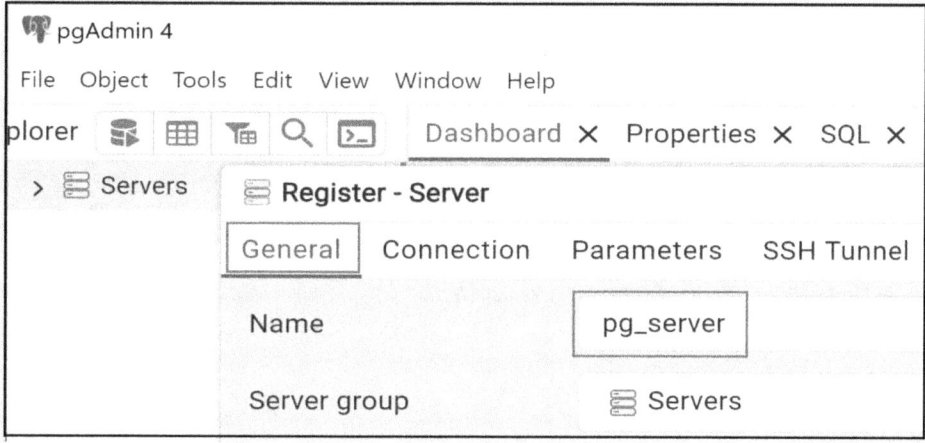

Figure 7-15. PostgreSQL server register screen

- Under the Connection section, add the values in respective fields:
  - Host name/address – 192.168.2.24
  - Port – 5432

437

CHAPTER 7 POSTGRESQL MONITORING USING PGADMIN AND GRAFANA

- Maintenance database – postgres
- Username – postgres
- Password – *******
- Save password – enable
- Click "Save", this will register the database.

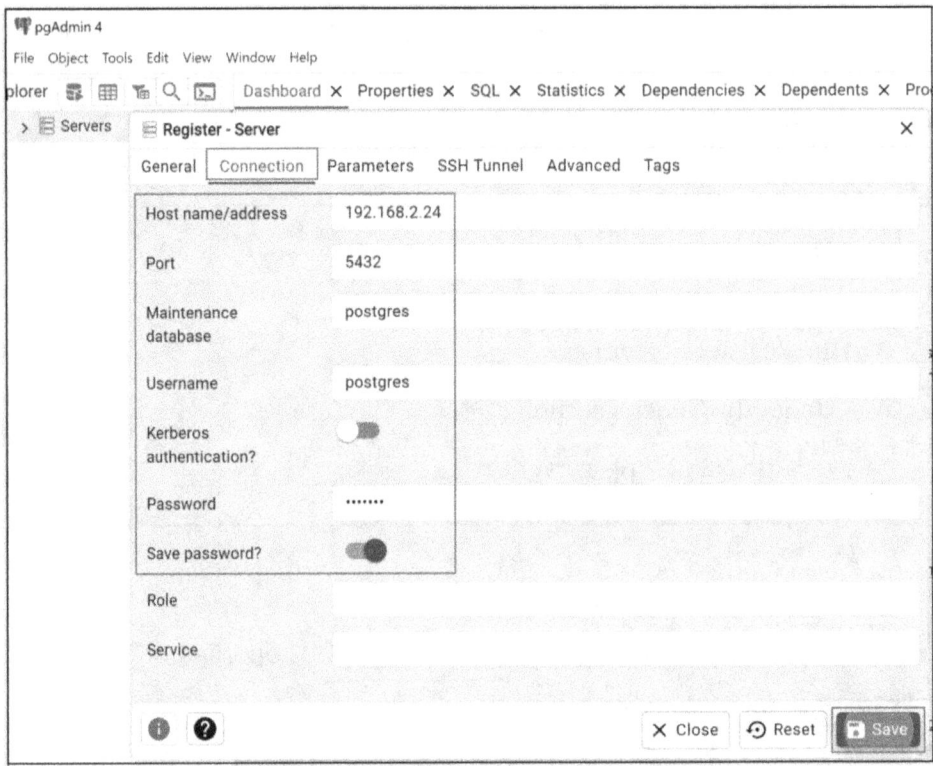

Figure 7-16. *PostgreSQL connection section*

Once the PostgreSQL server is added, the relevant databases and tablespaces become visible and accessible under the Servers section.

For each database, the dashboard provides a graphical representation of key performance metrics including database active sessions, transactions per second, DML operations, I/O statistics, etc.

Figure 7-17. Registered PostgreSQL dashboard

CHAPTER 7   POSTGRESQL MONITORING USING PGADMIN AND GRAFANA

- Database details can be seen under the Properties section as shown in Figure 7-18.

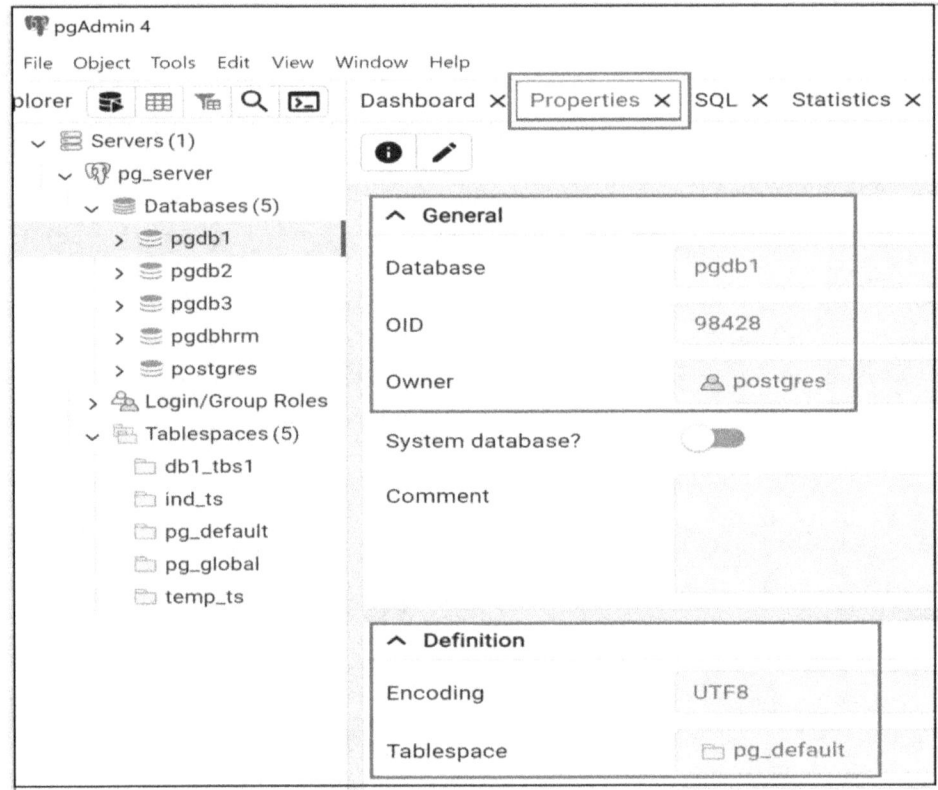

Figure 7-18. *PostgreSQL pgdb1 database properties*

- The DDL of the database can be seen under the SQL section as shown in Figure 7-19.

CHAPTER 7 POSTGRESQL MONITORING USING PGADMIN AND GRAFANA

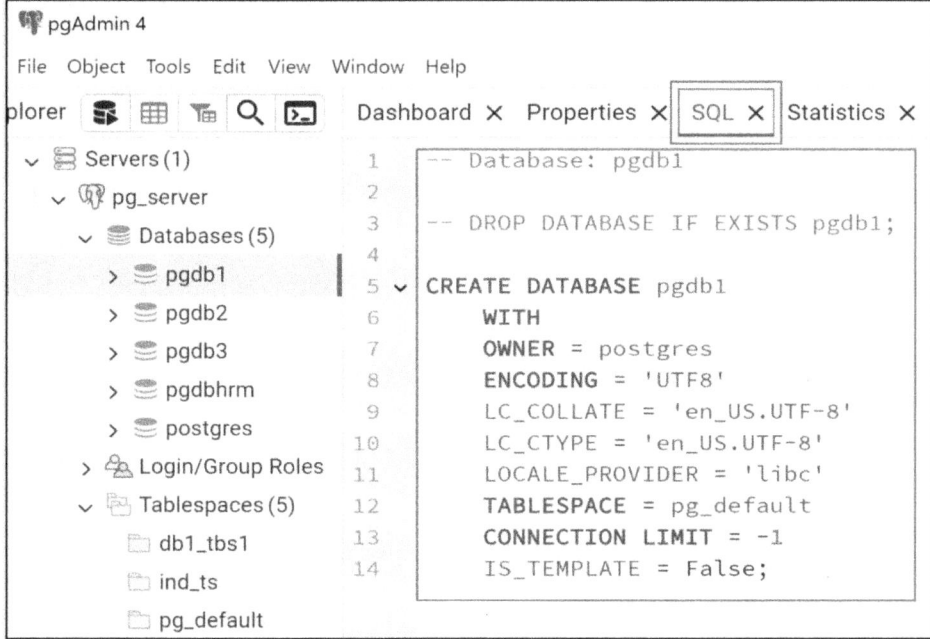

Figure 7-19. *PostgreSQL pgdb1 database DDL*

- The statistics of the database can be seen under the Statistics section as shown in Figure 7-20.

CHAPTER 7   POSTGRESQL MONITORING USING PGADMIN AND GRAFANA

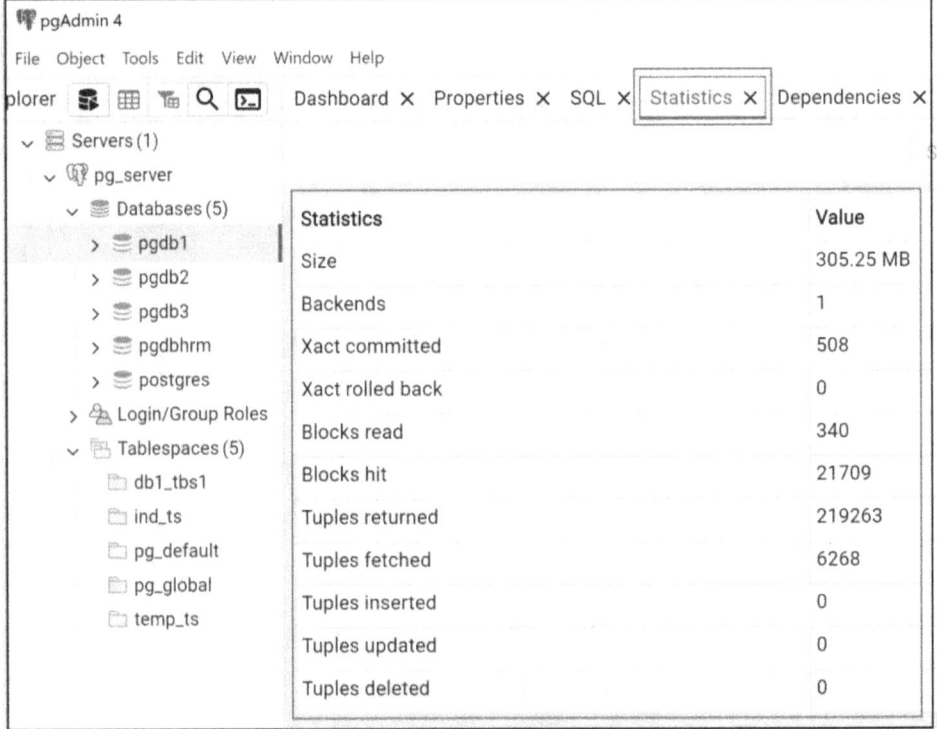

Figure 7-20. PostgreSQL pgdb1 database statistics

Now, let us try to perform some DML transactions in the database **pgdb1** and monitor the dashboard in pgAdmin.

- On server pg_client2:

    - Connect to the pgdb1 database as appuser1.

    - Perform an insert operation on table pgdb1sch1.db1s1t1.

        ```
        [postgres@pg_client2 ~]$ psql -d pgdb1 -U appuser1 -p 5432 -h 192.168.2.24
        Password for user appuser1:
        pgdb1=> \dt pgdb1sch1.*
        ```

442

CHAPTER 7   POSTGRESQL MONITORING USING PGADMIN AND GRAFANA

```
                List of relations
   Schema   |    Name    | Type  |  Owner
-----------+------------+-------+----------
 pgdb1sch1 | db1s1t1    | table | postgres
pgdb1=> insert into pgdb1sch1.db1s1t1 select * from pgdb1sch1.
db1s1t1;
INSERT 0 128
```

- The insert statement run from the command prompt can be monitored from the database's dashboard as shown in Figure 7-21.

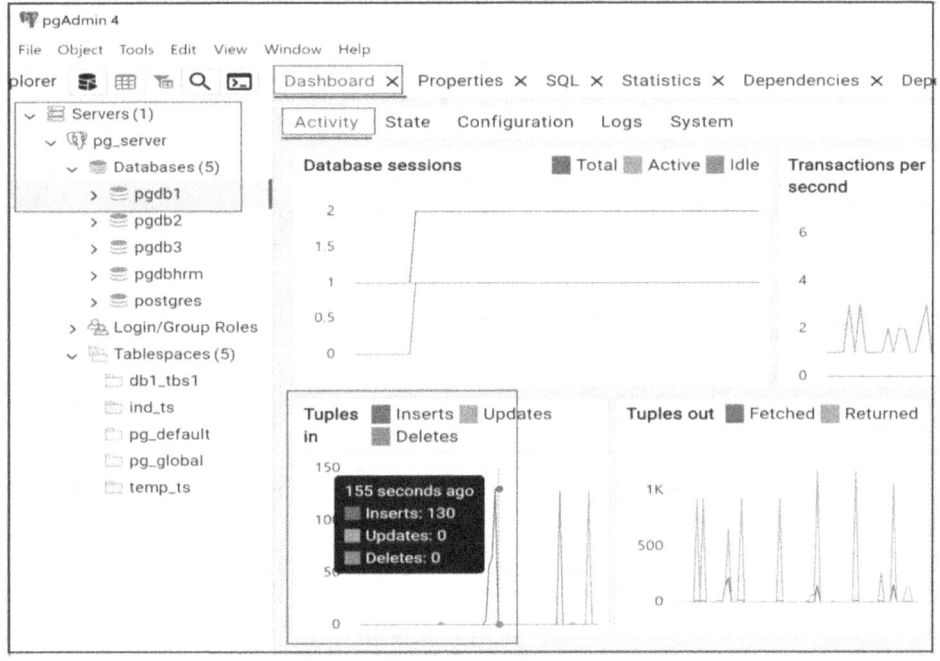

Figure 7-21. *PostgreSQL pgdb1 database insert activity*

- Perform a delete operation on table pgdb1sch1.db1s1t1.

  pgdb1=> delete from pgdb1sch1.db1s1t1 where id=2;

  DELETE 128

- The dashboard will show the DML operation and other details.

443

CHAPTER 7   POSTGRESQL MONITORING USING PGADMIN AND GRAFANA

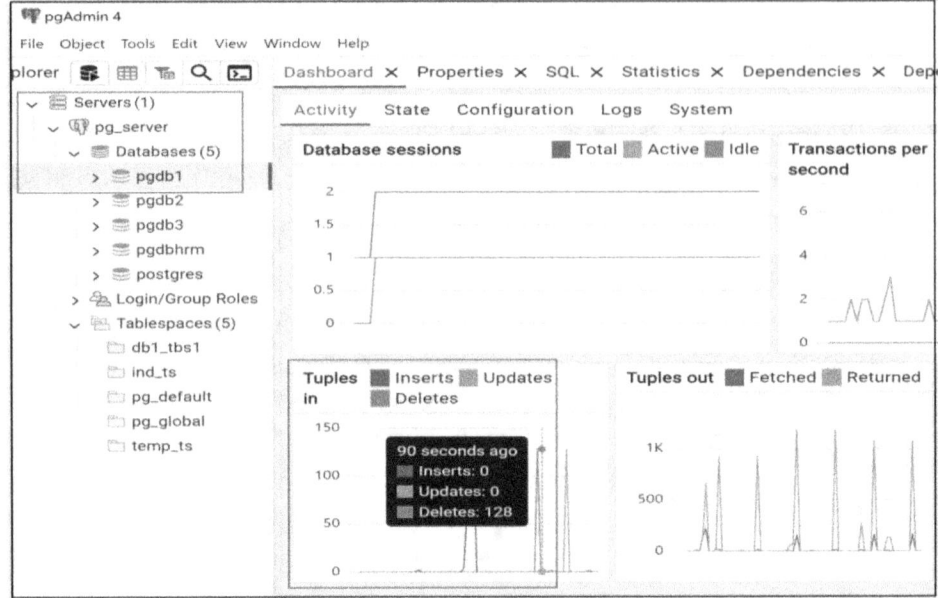

Figure 7-22. PostgreSQL pgdb1 database delete activity

Now let us perform some administrative tasks using pgAdmin console.

Create a Database

To create a database from pgAdmin console, perform the following:

- Navigate to Object ➤ Create ➤ Database.

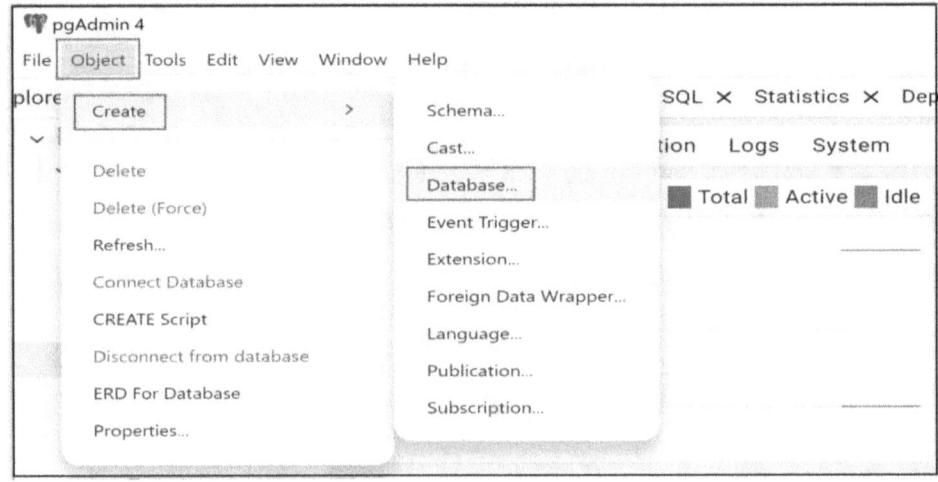

Figure 7-23. PostgreSQL new database creation

444

CHAPTER 7 POSTGRESQL MONITORING USING PGADMIN AND GRAFANA

- On the Create – Database screen, under the General section, add the below values:

  - Database – pga_db

  - Click "Save" and this will create the database

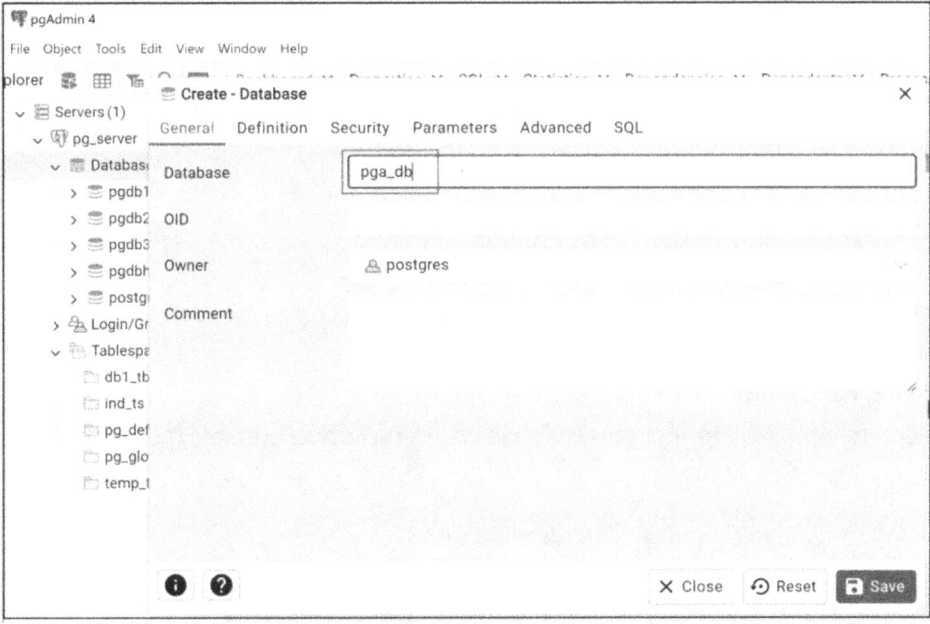

Figure 7-24. *PostgreSQL new database name*

The newly created database can be seen under Servers ➤ pg_server ➤ Databases.

CHAPTER 7   POSTGRESQL MONITORING USING PGADMIN AND GRAFANA

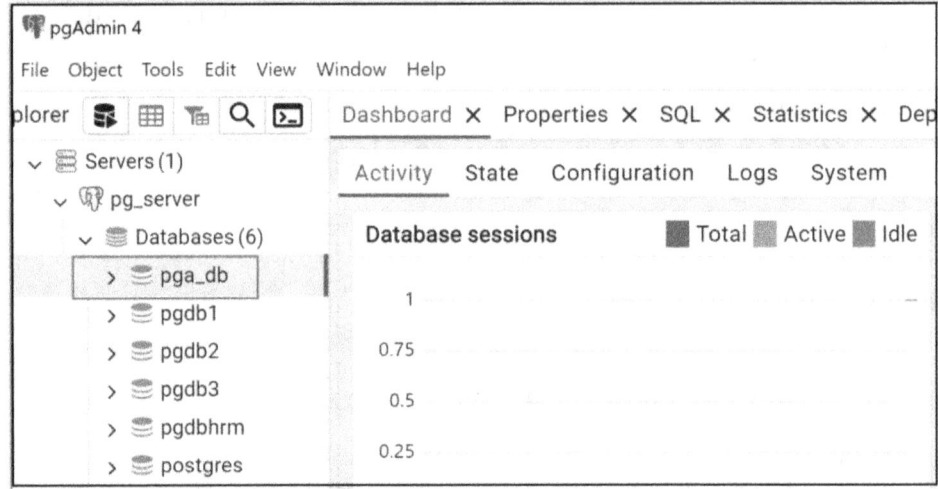

Figure 7-25. PostgreSQL new pga_db database dashboard

Create a Schema

To create a schema in postgres database from pgAdmin console, perform the following:

- Navigate to Object ➤ Create ➤ Schema.

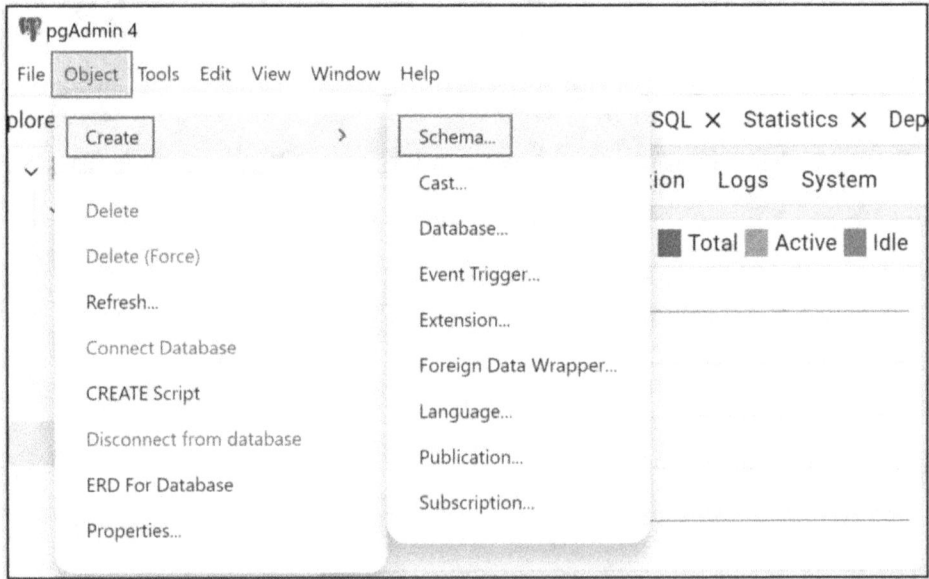

Figure 7-26. PostgreSQL schema creation

CHAPTER 7   POSTGRESQL MONITORING USING PGADMIN AND GRAFANA

- On the Create – Schema screen, under the General section, add the below values:

  - Name – pga_schema

  - Click "Save" and this will create a schema

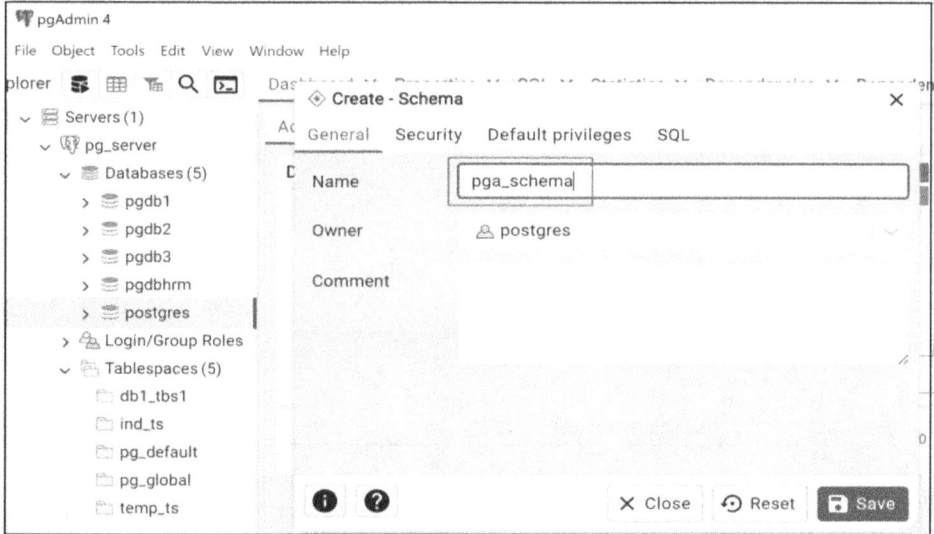

Figure 7-27. *PostgreSQL schema name*

The newly created schema can be seen under Servers ➤ pg_server ➤ Databases ➤ postgres.

Create a Table

- Navigate to postgres ➤ pga_schema.

  - Right-click on pga_schema.

  - Select Create ➤ Table.

CHAPTER 7   POSTGRESQL MONITORING USING PGADMIN AND GRAFANA

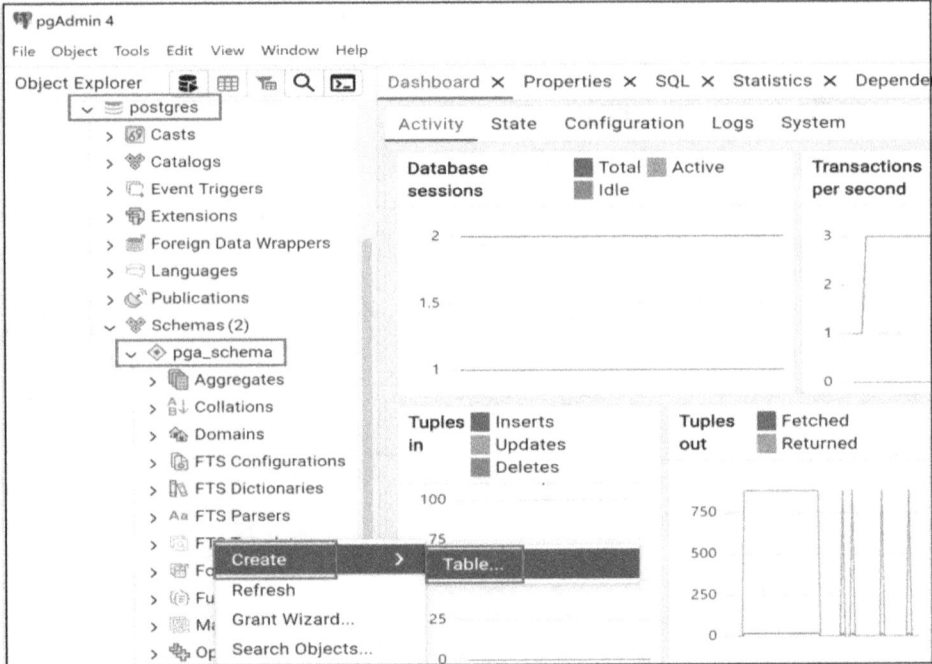

Figure 7-28. PostgreSQL table creation

- On the Create – Table screen, under the General section, add the below values:

    - Name – universities

CHAPTER 7   POSTGRESQL MONITORING USING PGADMIN AND GRAFANA

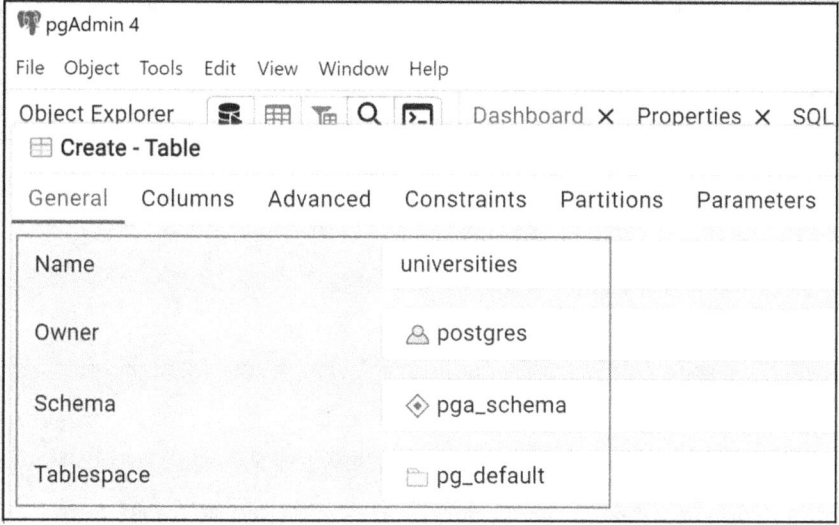

Figure 7-29. *PostgreSQL table and schema name*

- Under the Columns section:
  - Add the column names and respective data types as below.
  - Click "Save" and this will create the table.

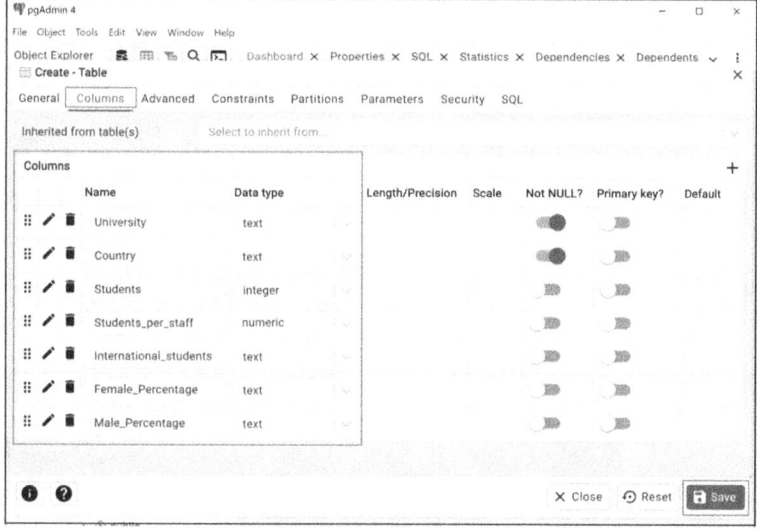

Figure 7-30. *PostgreSQL table columns definition*

449

CHAPTER 7   POSTGRESQL MONITORING USING PGADMIN AND GRAFANA

The newly created table can be seen under Servers ➤ pg_server ➤ Databases ➤ postgres ➤ pga_schema ➤ Tables.

Load data into the newly created table pga_schema.universities.

To load the data into the newly created table, sample data stored in a csv file is used.

- Navigate to postgres ➤ pga_schema ➤ Tables.

  - Right-click on table universities.

  - Select Import/Export Data.

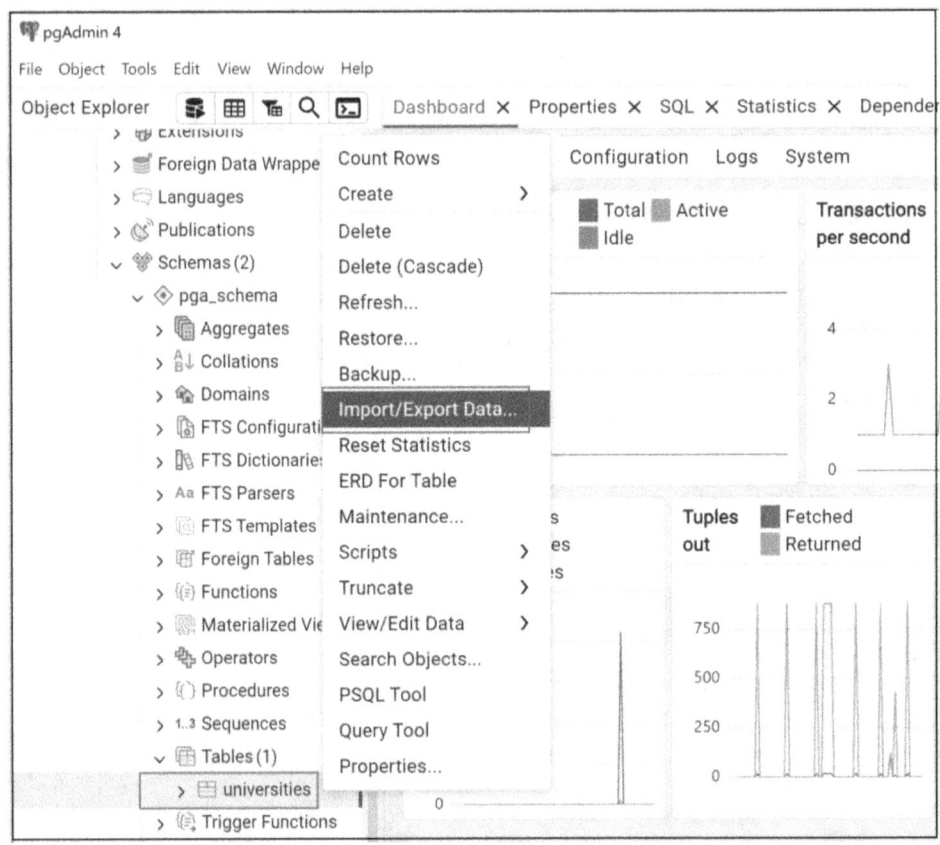

Figure 7-31. PostgreSQL table data import

450

CHAPTER 7   POSTGRESQL MONITORING USING PGADMIN AND GRAFANA

- On the Import/Export data – table 'universities' screen, select the following under the General section:

  - Import/Export – Import.

  - Filename – Browse the csv file having data to be loaded into the universities table.

  - Format – csv.

  - Click OK; this will load the data into the table from the csv file.

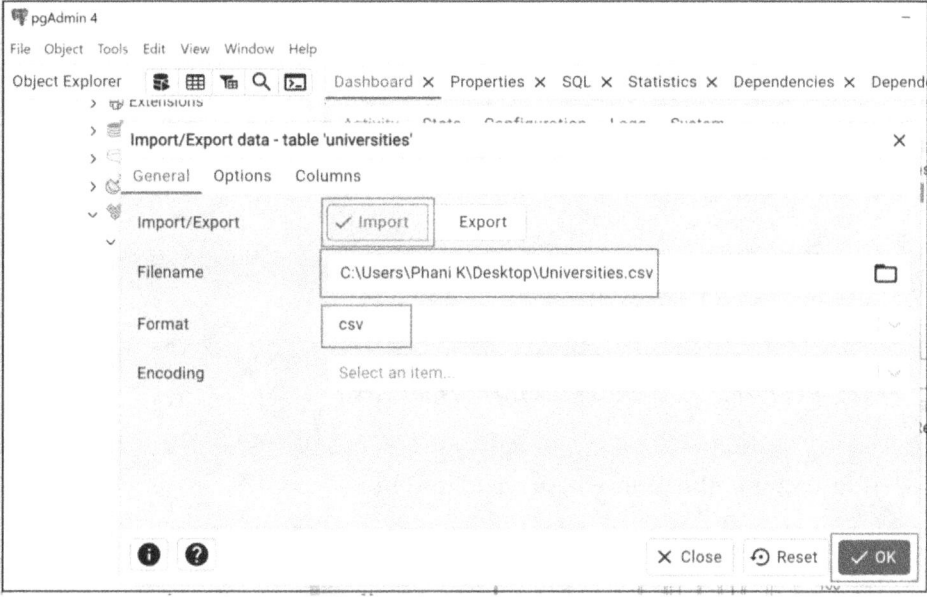

Figure 7-32. PostgreSQL table database import source file

- Data load status will be displayed as shown in Figure 7-33.

CHAPTER 7   POSTGRESQL MONITORING USING PGADMIN AND GRAFANA

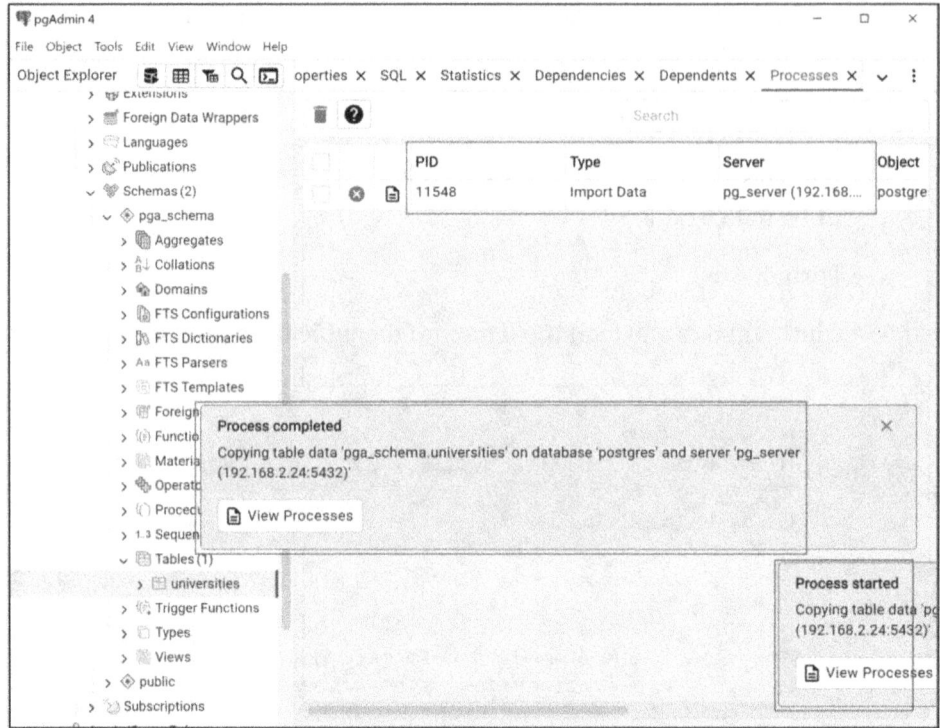

Figure 7-33. PostgreSQL table data import status

- Row count in the table can be validated by

    - Right-clicking on table universities

    - Selecting Count Rows

CHAPTER 7   POSTGRESQL MONITORING USING PGADMIN AND GRAFANA

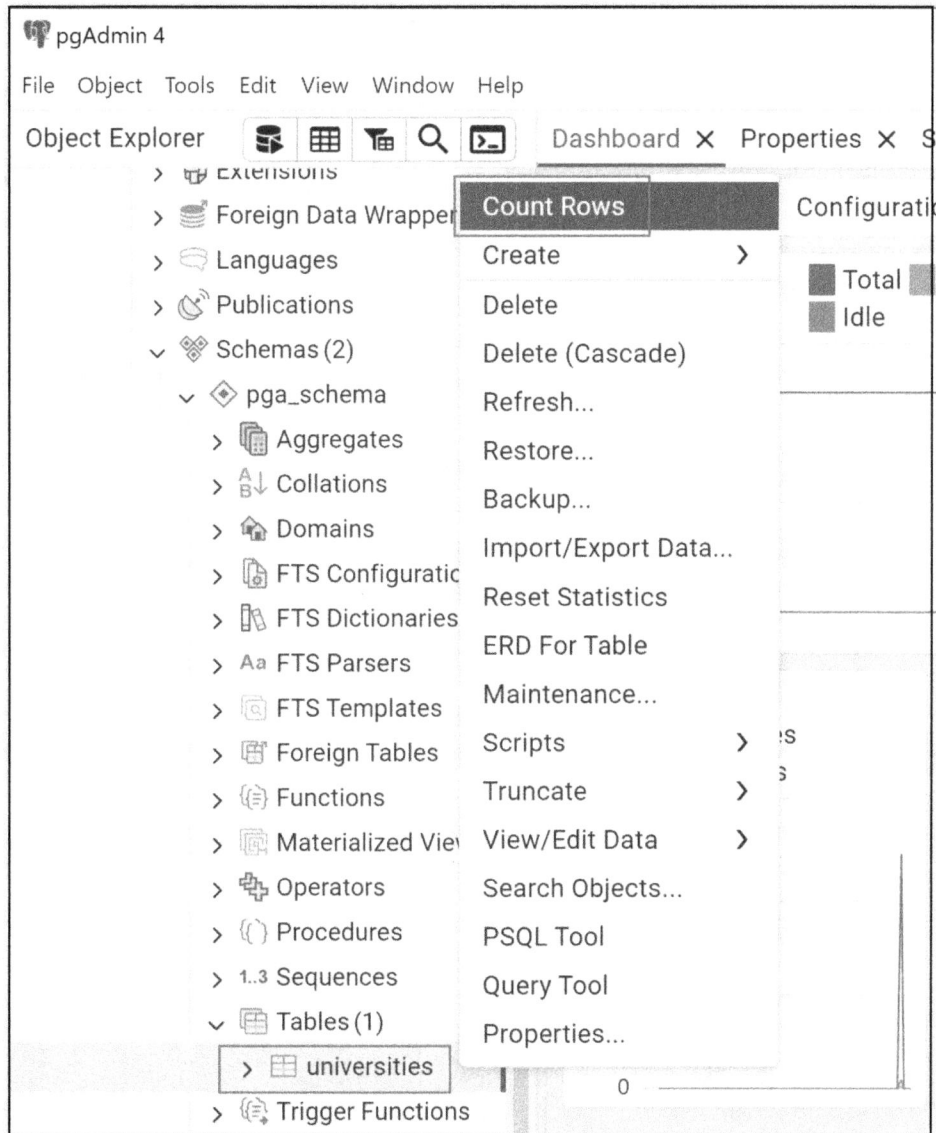

Figure 7-34. *PostgreSQL table row count validation*

CHAPTER 7   POSTGRESQL MONITORING USING PGADMIN AND GRAFANA

- Table row count will be displayed as shown in Figure 7-35.

Figure 7-35. PostgreSQL table row count

Create another table named University_H under pga_schema using the same process as above.

- Create table University_H in the pga_schema schema.

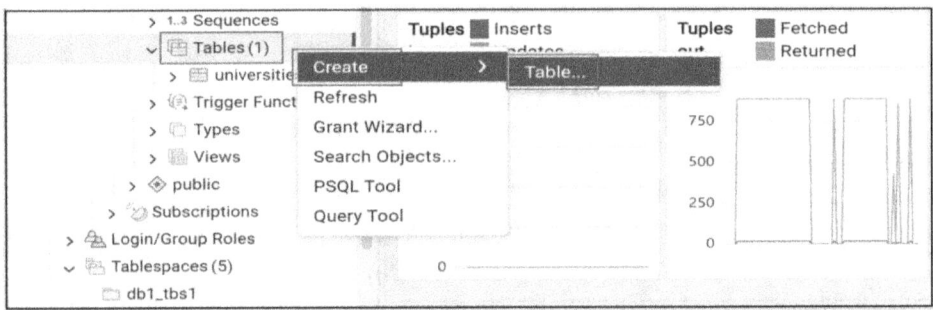

Figure 7-36. PostgreSQL create new table

- Add table name as University_H and validate the owner and schema.

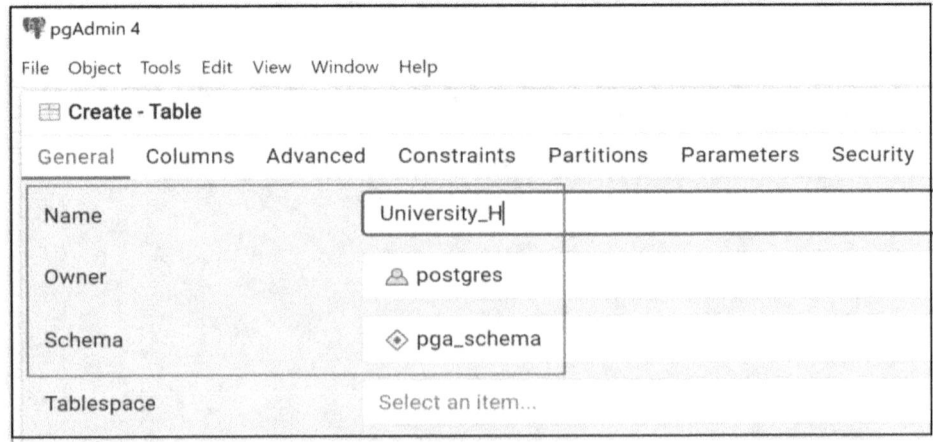

Figure 7-37. PostgreSQL table and schema name

CHAPTER 7   POSTGRESQL MONITORING USING PGADMIN AND GRAFANA

- Add column names and data type.

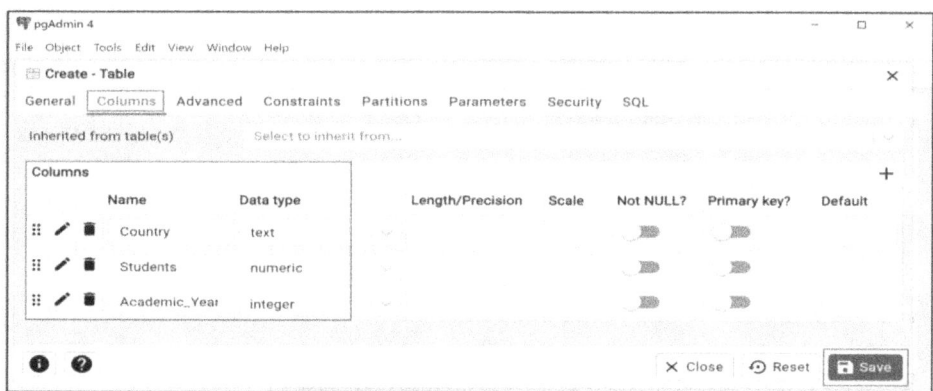

Figure 7-38. *PostgreSQL table columns definition*

- Import data into table pga_schema.University_H.
  - Right-click on table University_H.
  - Select Import/Export Data.

CHAPTER 7   POSTGRESQL MONITORING USING PGADMIN AND GRAFANA

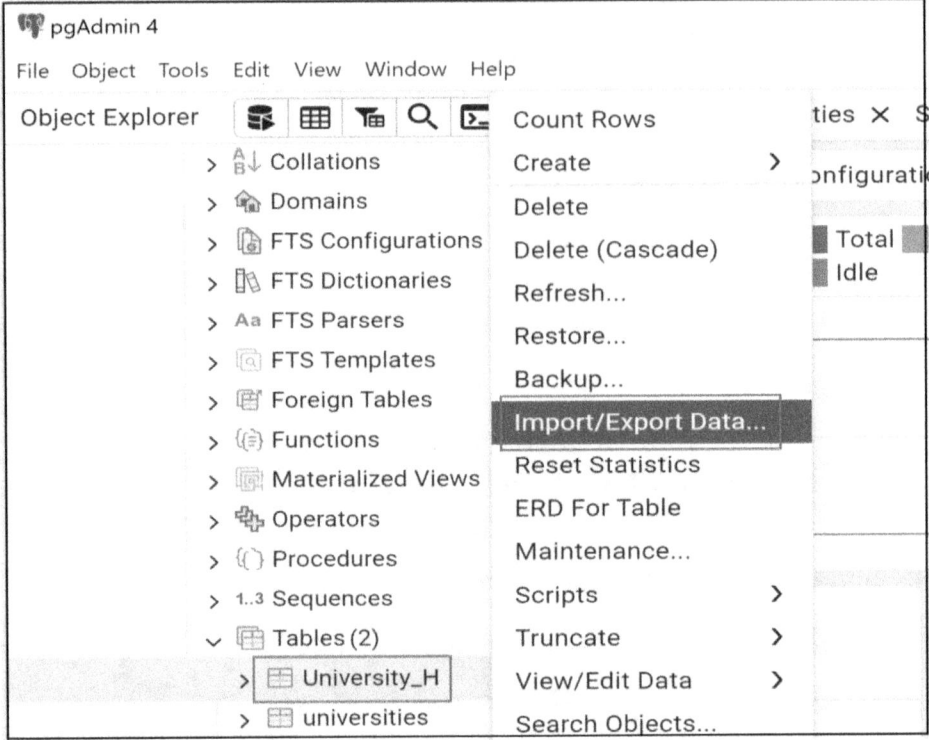

Figure 7-39. *PostgreSQL table data import*

- On the Import/Export data – table 'University_H' screen, select the following under the General section:

  - Import/Export – Import.

  - Filename – Browse the csv file having data to be loaded into the University_H table.

  - Format – csv.

  - Click OK; this will load the data into the table from the csv file.

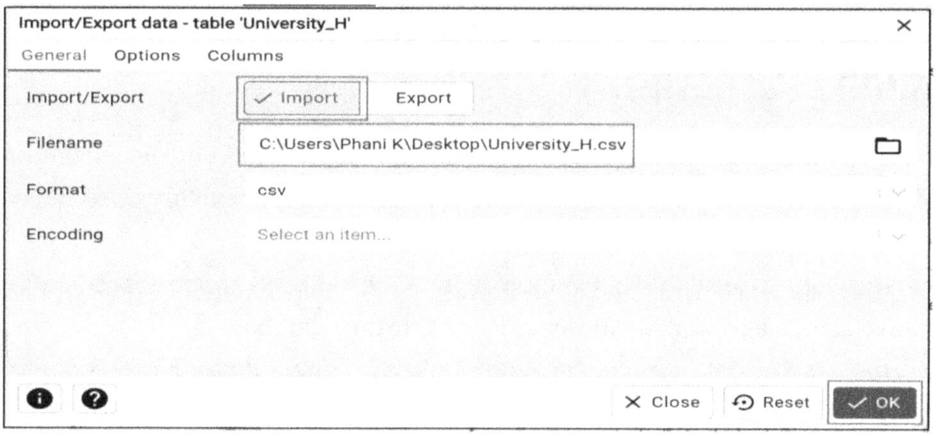

CHAPTER 7 POSTGRESQL MONITORING USING PGADMIN AND GRAFANA

Figure 7-40. PostgreSQL data import source file

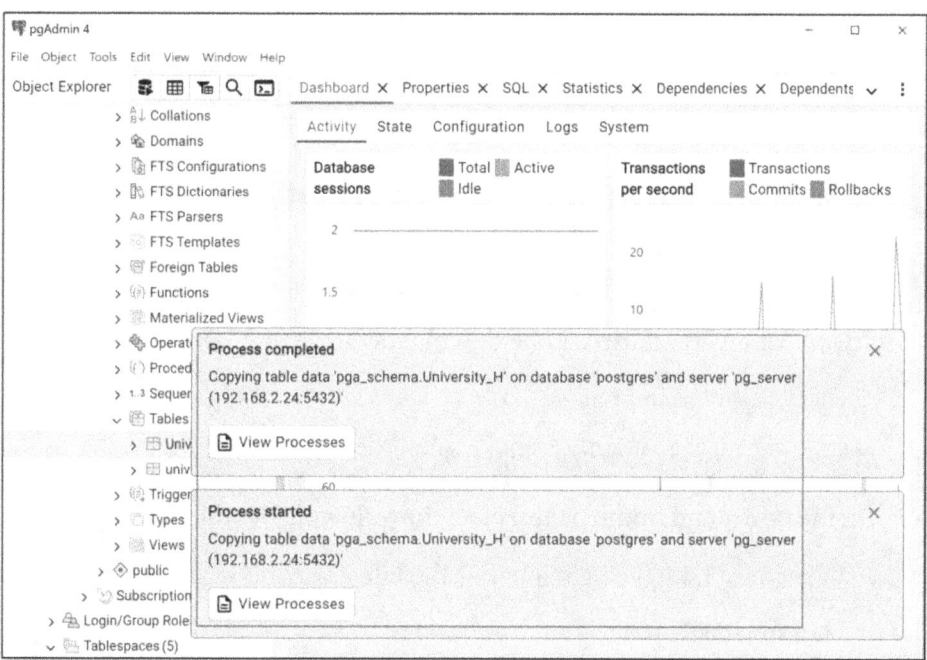

Figure 7-41. PostgreSQL data import status

The two tables, universities and University_H, created in previous sections will be used in generating graphs using Grafana.

Integrating PostgreSQL with Monitoring Solutions (Grafana)

Grafana Open Source (OSS) is open source software for analytics and visualization.

It provides various options to query, analyze, visualize, and explore the database metrics.

With the features available in Grafana, it gives the ability to create dashboards with informative graphs and visualizations using data from a database.

Also, the Grafana data source plug-ins enable us to query data sources including PostgreSQL databases.

Grafana Enterprise is Grafana's commercial version, which comes with extra functionality like exclusive data source plug-ins and features that are not available in the open source version.

Let us see the installation and usage of Grafana along with the creation of a dashboard and visualization graphs using the PostgreSQL tables created using pgAdmin.

Installation and Configuration of Grafana

Downloading Grafana on Windows

Grafana software for any platform can be downloaded from the URL provided below.

- Access the download page:

    https://grafana.com/grafana/download

- On the download home page, select the following download options:

    - Version: 11.4.0 (you can choose the latest version available)
    - Edition: OSS
    - Platform: Windows
    - Click "Download the installer"

CHAPTER 7   POSTGRESQL MONITORING USING PGADMIN AND GRAFANA

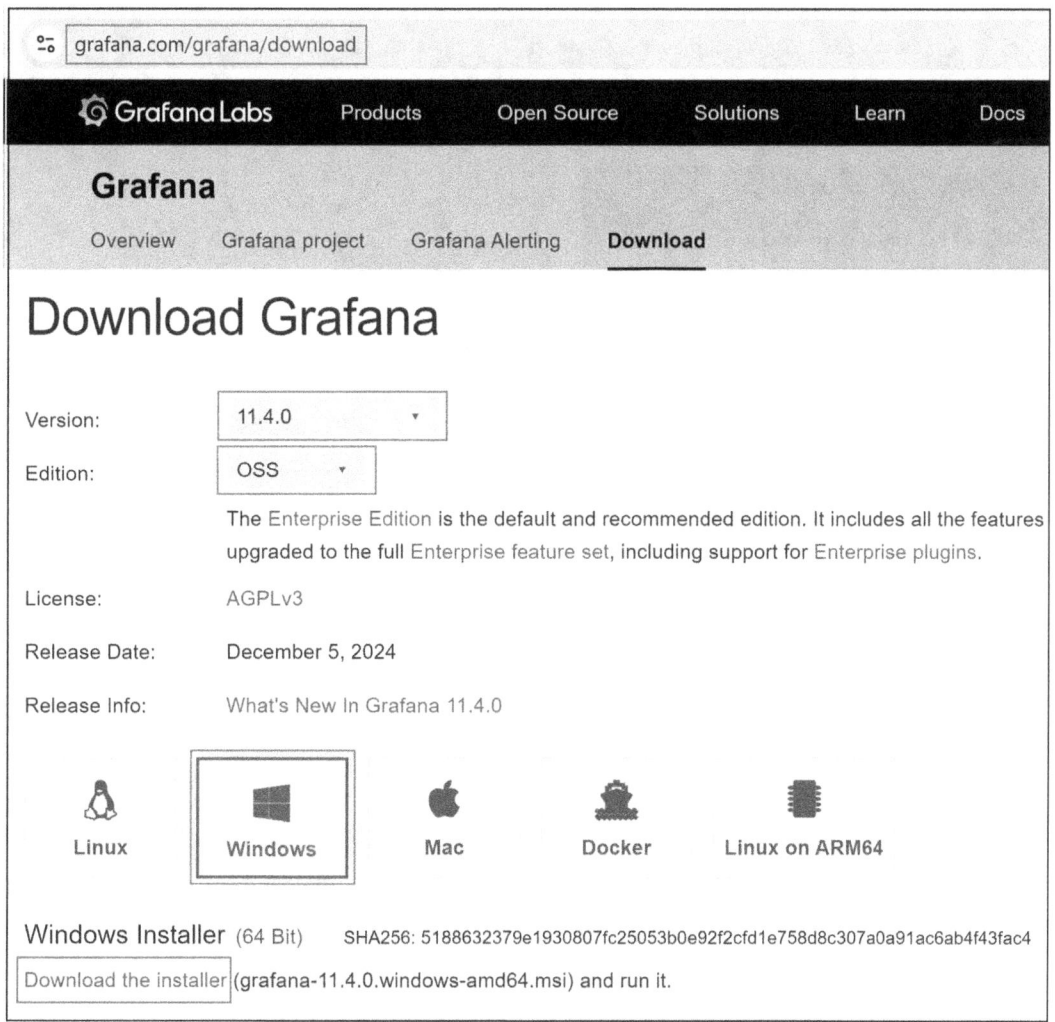

Figure 7-42. Grafana download screen

- Once the download is complete, proceed with the installation.

Installing Grafana on Windows

- Run the downloaded executable to launch the installation wizard.

CHAPTER 7   POSTGRESQL MONITORING USING PGADMIN AND GRAFANA

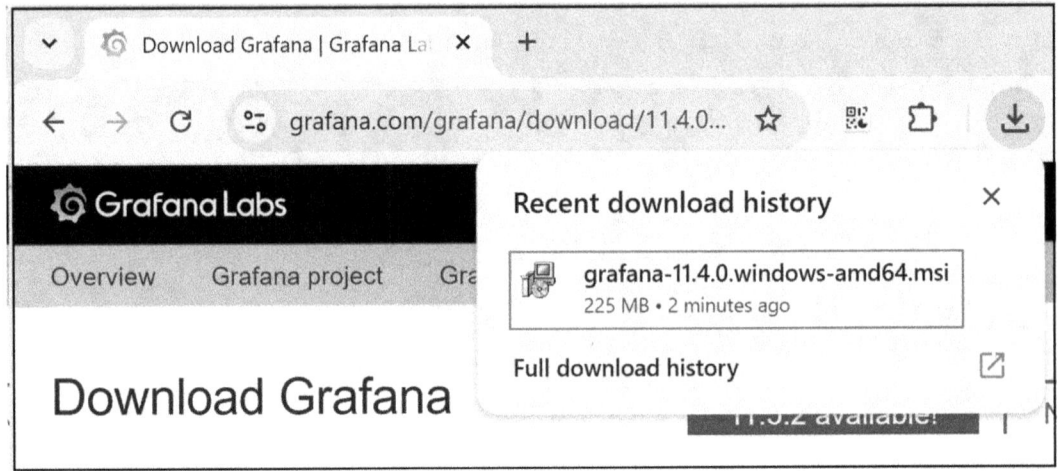

Figure 7-43. Grafana download status

- On the GrafanaOSS installation wizard welcome screen, click Next.

Figure 7-44. Grafana setup page

CHAPTER 7   POSTGRESQL MONITORING USING PGADMIN AND GRAFANA

- Accept the license agreement and click Next.

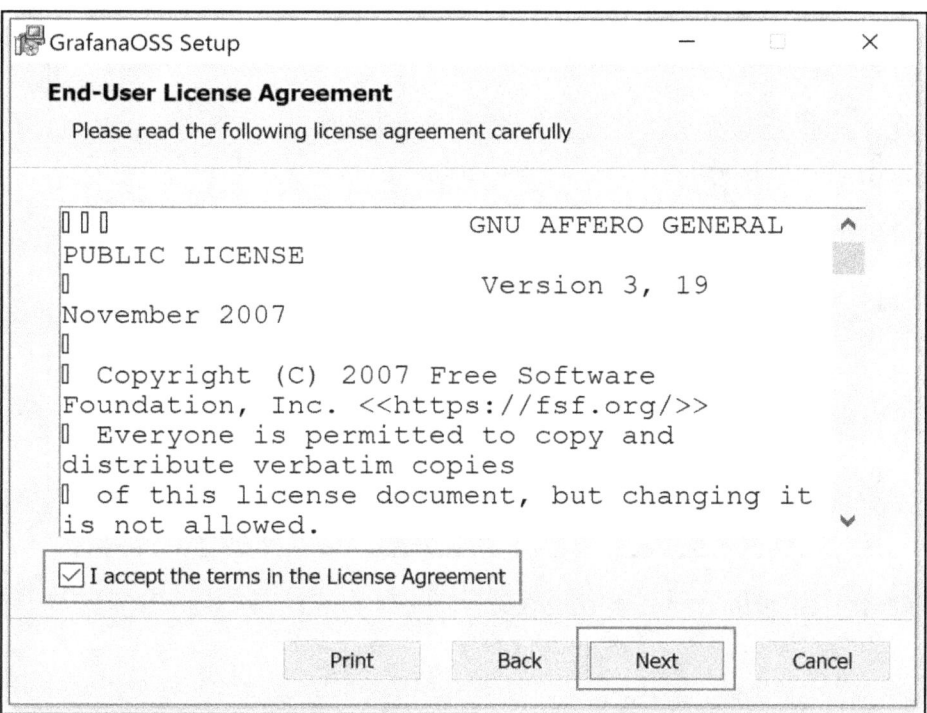

Figure 7-45. *Grafana license agreement*

- Choose the installation directory and verify the features to be installed and click Next.

CHAPTER 7 POSTGRESQL MONITORING USING PGADMIN AND GRAFANA

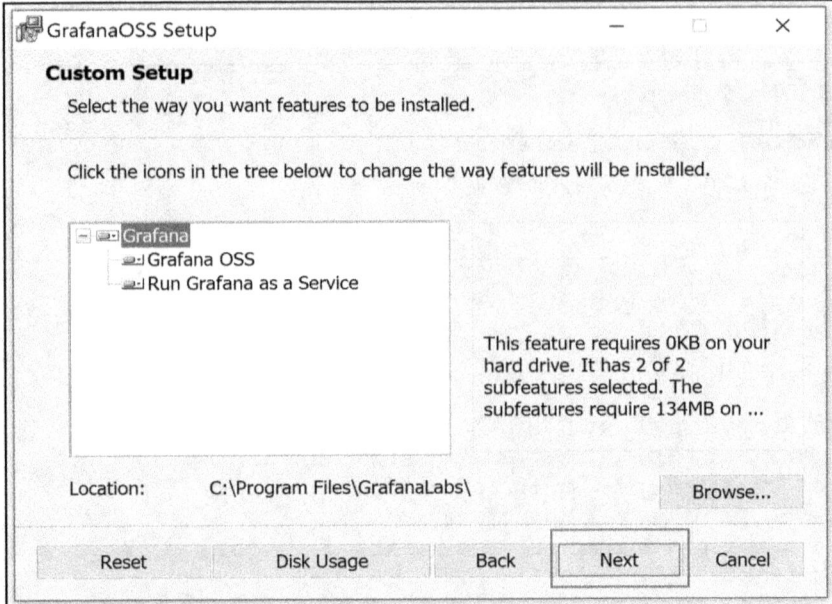

Figure 7-46. *Grafana features details*

- On the final screen, click Install to begin the process.

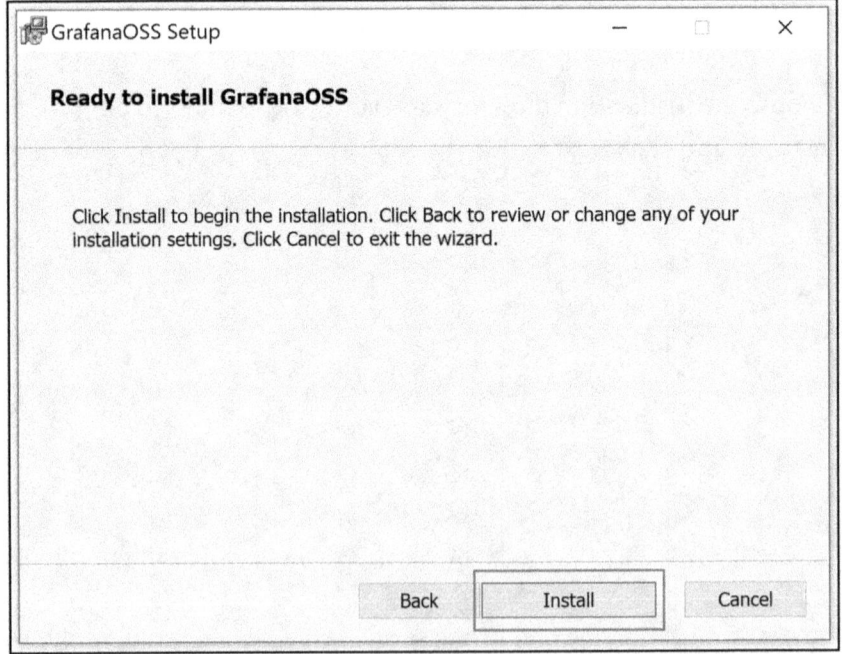

Figure 7-47. *Grafana install screen*

CHAPTER 7   POSTGRESQL MONITORING USING PGADMIN AND GRAFANA

- Verify the progress of the installation.

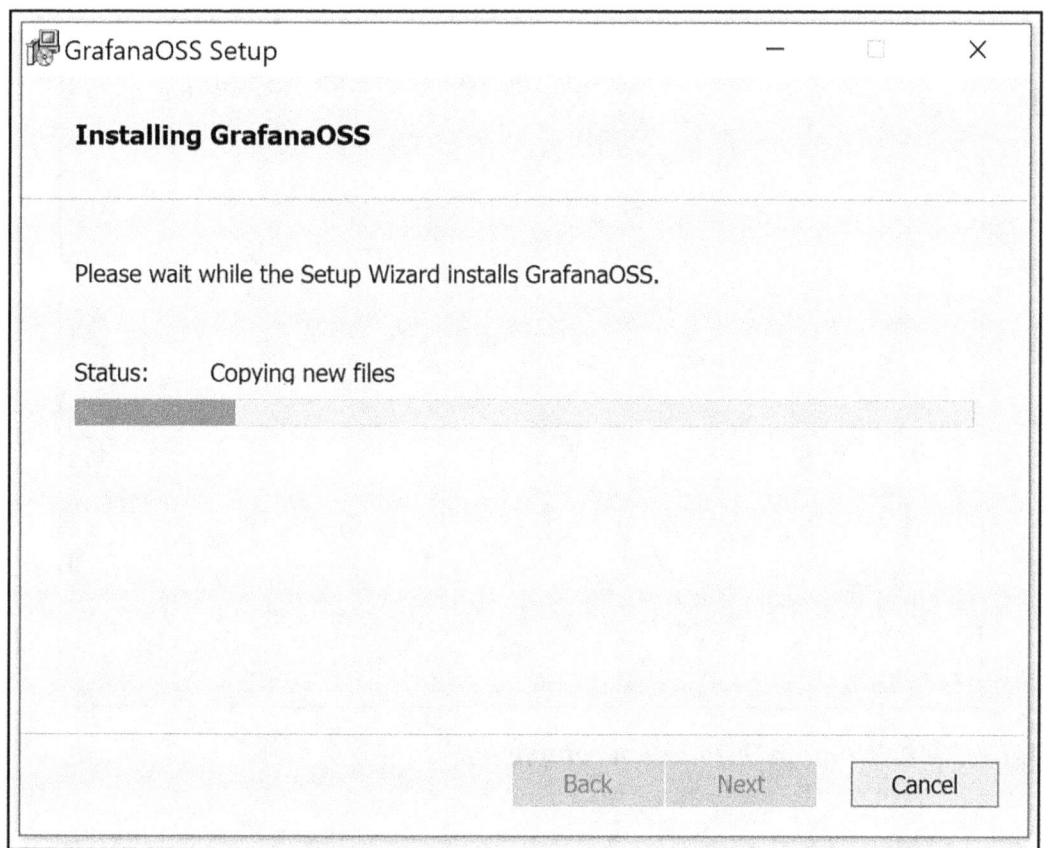

Figure 7-48. *Grafana installation progress*

- Once the installation is complete, click Finish.

CHAPTER 7   POSTGRESQL MONITORING USING PGADMIN AND GRAFANA

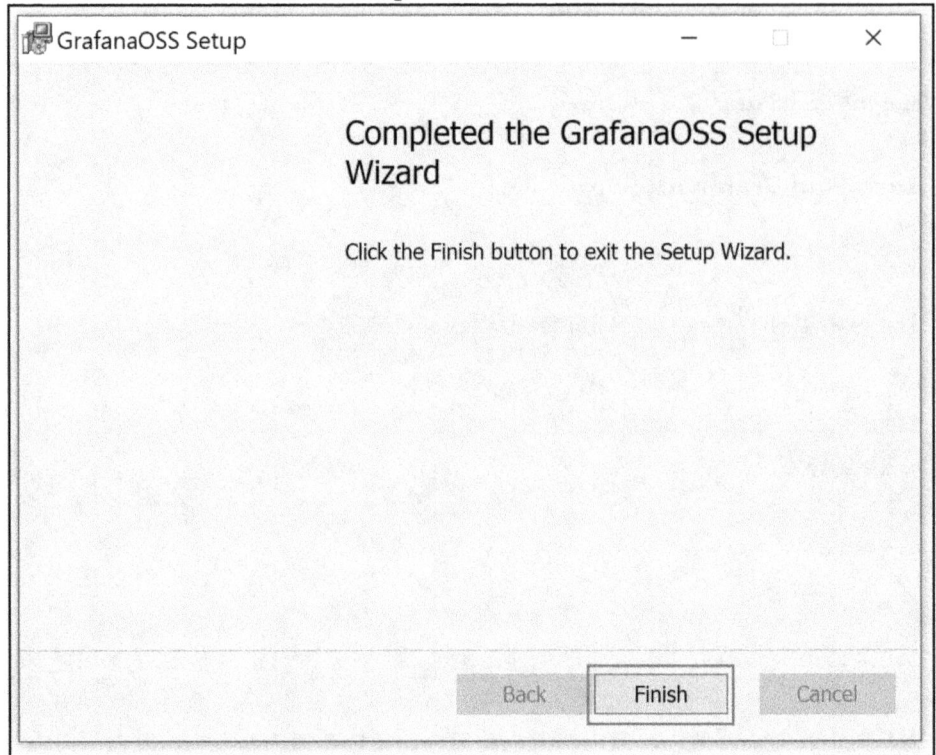

Figure 7-49. *Grafana installation completion*

Connecting to Grafana

Once the Grafana is installed, to log in to Grafana for the first time, open Grafana in the web browser using the following URL: https://localhost:3000/login.

By default, Grafana is set to use the localhost and port 3000, unless it is configured differently.

Use the default credentials to log in:

- Username – admin
- Password – admin

Change the default password upon first login (recommended).

CHAPTER 7   POSTGRESQL MONITORING USING PGADMIN AND GRAFANA

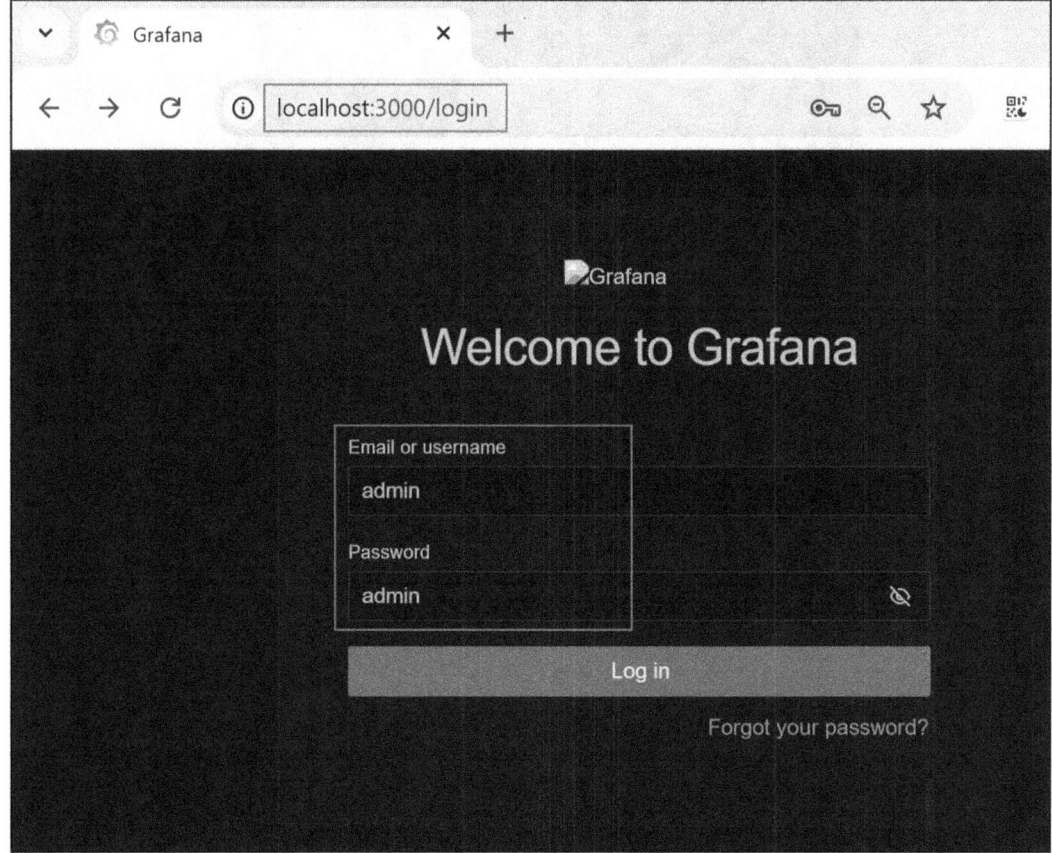

Figure 7-50. Grafana login page

Adding a PostgreSQL Data Source in Grafana

To connect PostgreSQL as a data source in Grafana:

- On the Grafana home page, navigate to Home ➤ Data sources.

CHAPTER 7 POSTGRESQL MONITORING USING PGADMIN AND GRAFANA

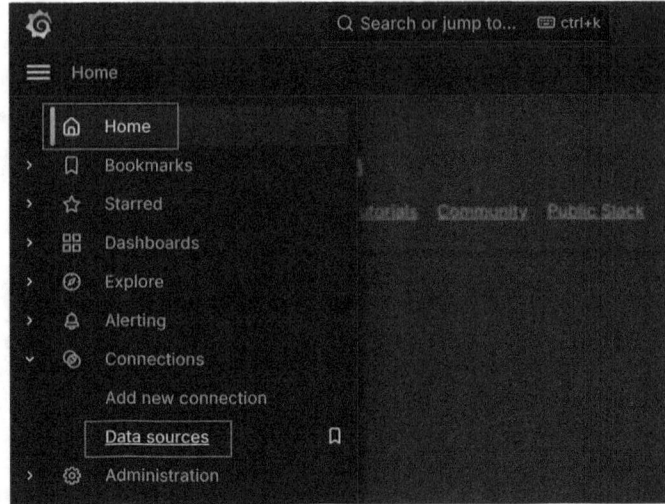

Figure 7-51. Grafana home screen

- On the Data sources page, click Add data source.

Figure 7-52. Grafana data source addition

CHAPTER 7   POSTGRESQL MONITORING USING PGADMIN AND GRAFANA

- Select the data source as PostgreSQL

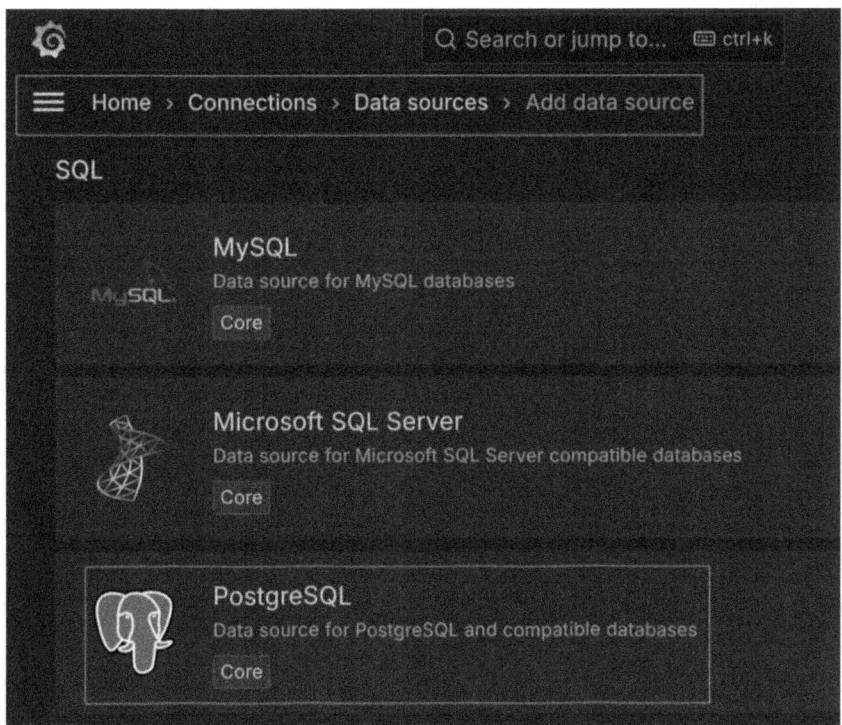

Figure 7-53. *Grafana data source selection*

- Provide the data source name as grafana-pg_server.

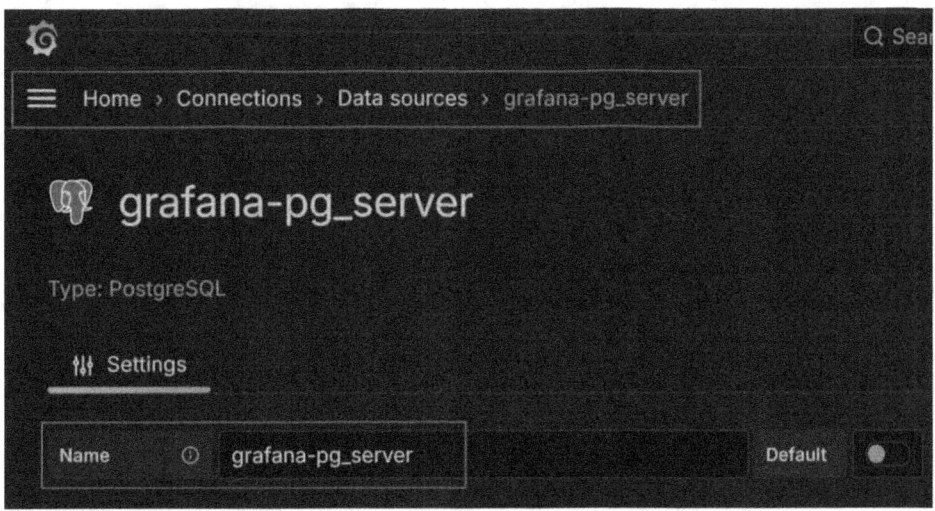

Figure 7-54. *Grafana PostgreSQL data source name specification*

CHAPTER 7   POSTGRESQL MONITORING USING PGADMIN AND GRAFANA

- Provide the connection and authentication details for the data source as below:

  - Host URL – 192.168.2.24:5432

    – This is the host IP of the PostgreSQL server and the default port 5432.

  - Database name – postgres
  - Username – postgres
  - Password – postgres

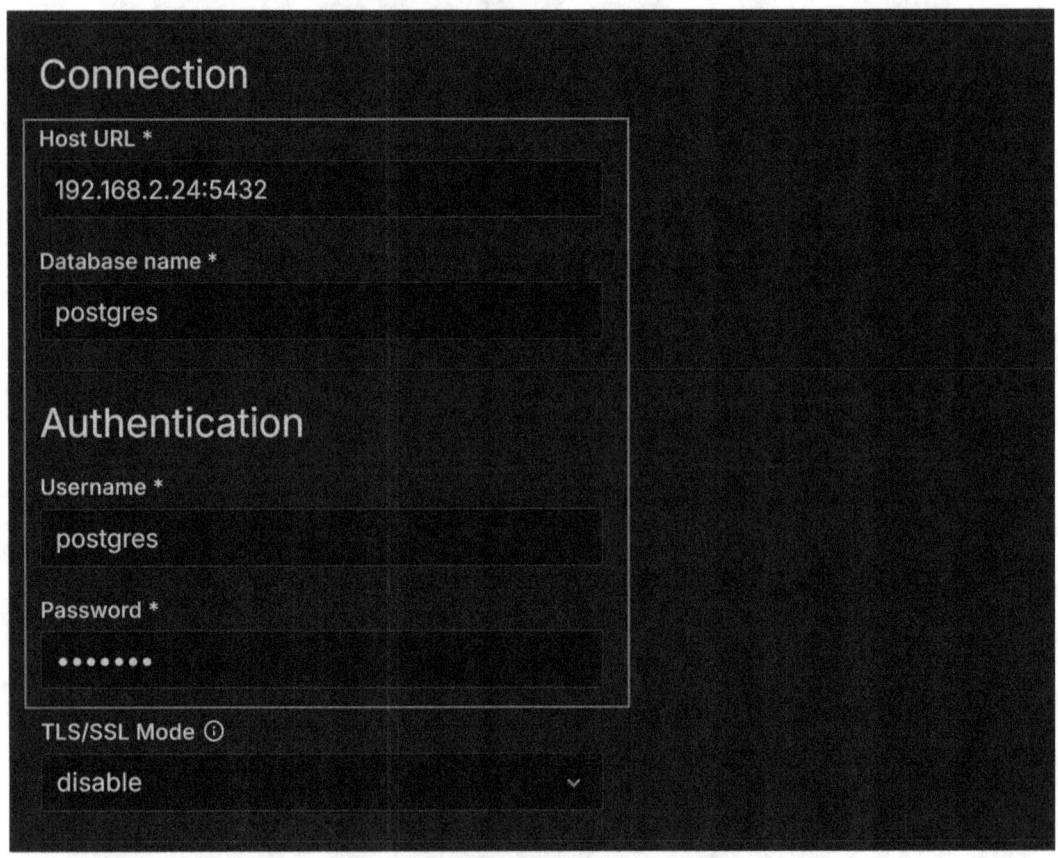

Figure 7-55. Grafana PostgreSQL connection details

- In additional settings, select version and click Save & test, which validates the data source connectivity.

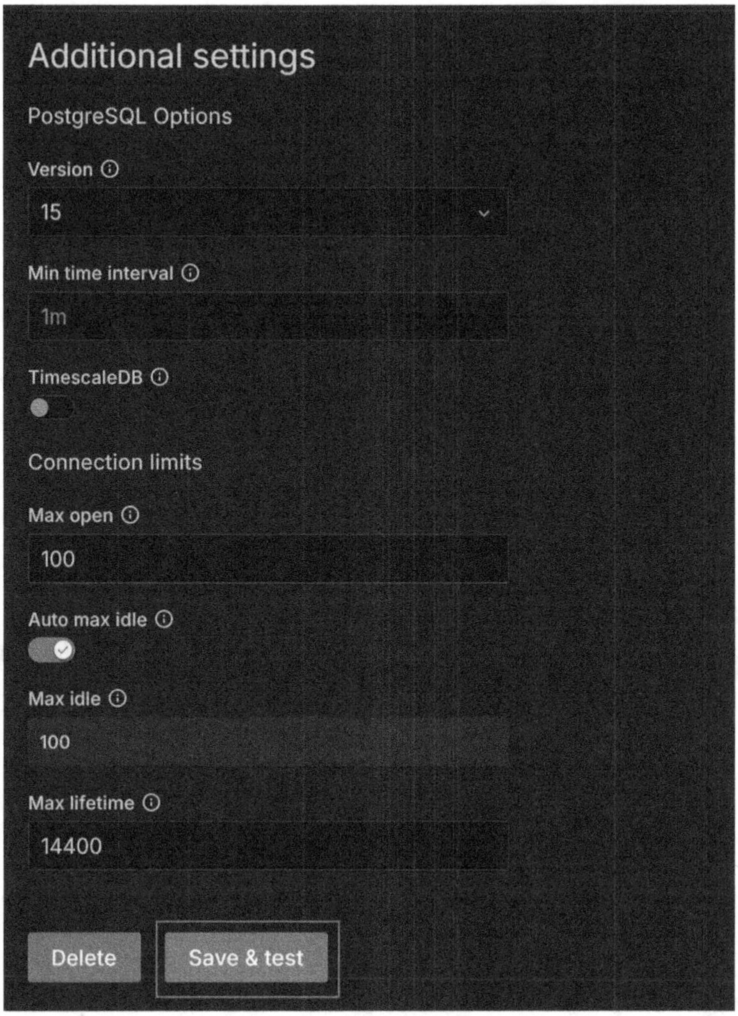

CHAPTER 7 POSTGRESQL MONITORING USING PGADMIN AND GRAFANA

Figure 7-56. Grafana PostgreSQL additionals

- If successful, the Database Connection OK message is displayed.

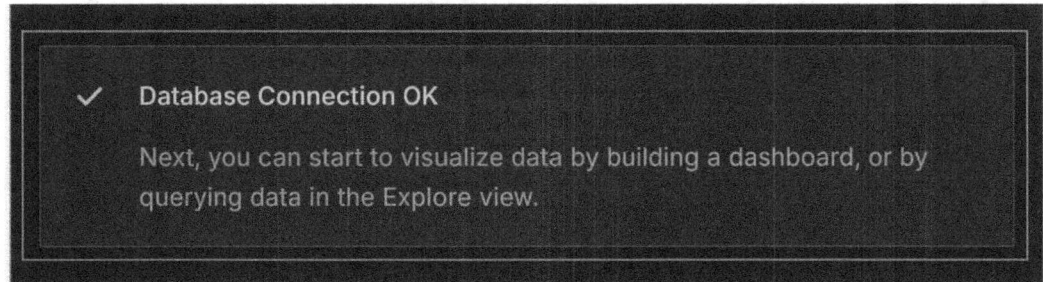

Figure 7-57. Grafana PostgreSQL database connection status

Building a Dashboard in Grafana

To create a dashboard for the PostgreSQL data source in Grafana:

- Navigate to Home ➤ Connections ➤ Data sources.
- Click "Build a dashboard" for the grafana-pg_server data source.

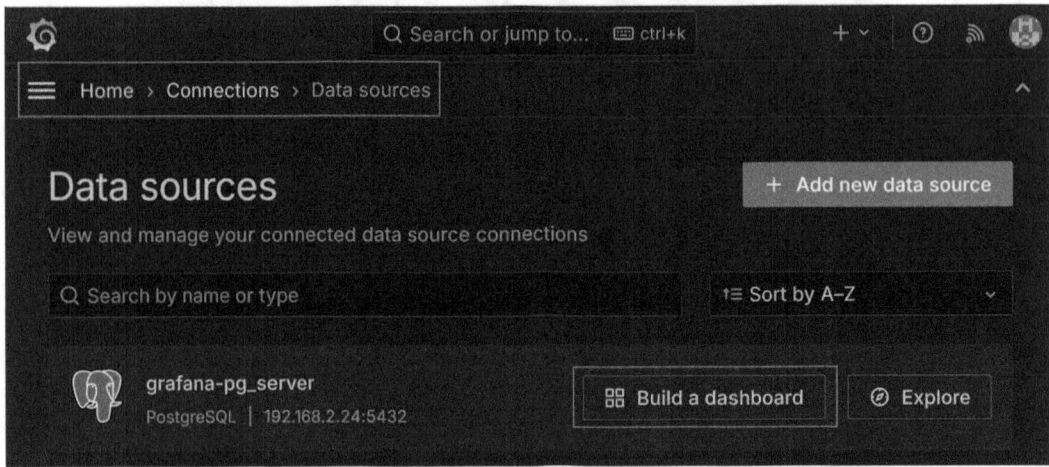

Figure 7-58. Grafana PostgreSQL dashboard build

- Select "+ Add visualization" for a visualization panel.

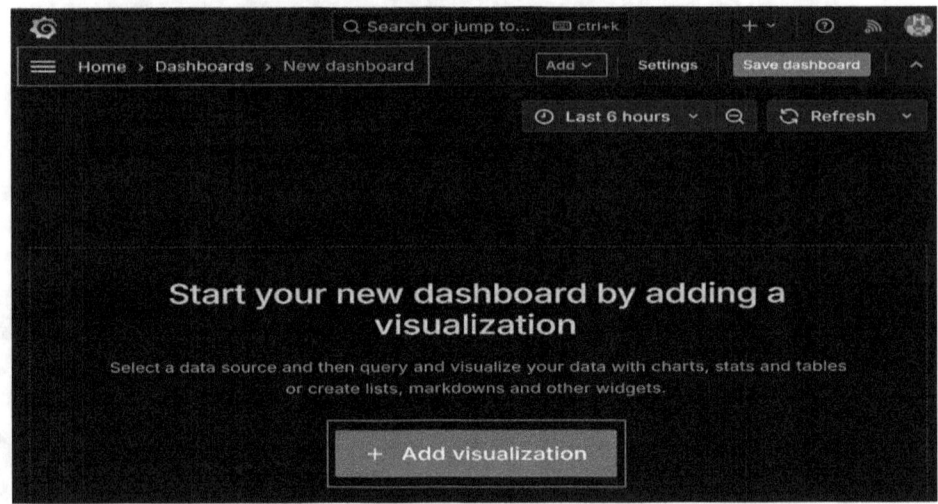

Figure 7-59. Grafana PostgreSQL dashboard visualization

- Select data source – grafana-pg_server.

CHAPTER 7   POSTGRESQL MONITORING USING PGADMIN AND GRAFANA

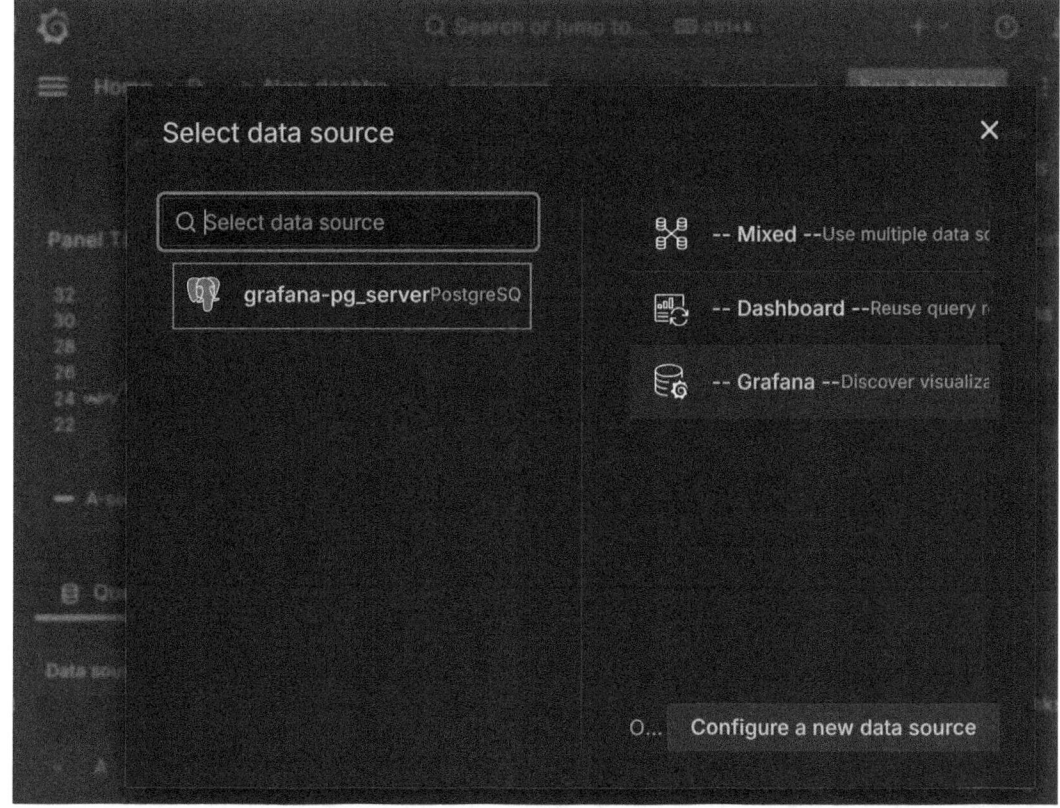

Figure 7-60. *Grafana data source selection*

In order to create the graphs in the dashboard, the tables universities and University_H, which were created in pga_schema using pgAdmin, are used.

Creating a Bar Chart in the Dashboard

In Grafana, a bar chart is a kind of visualization that uses rectangular bars to show category data. The length of each bar corresponds to the value it represents. This type of chart is helpful in visualizing and comparing several data categories.

To create a bar chart in the dashboard, perform the following:

- In the new dashboard panel:
  - Select "Bar chart"
  - Provide Title for the panel – University Students
  - Add the Description – Student count in universities per country

- Add Query under the Queries section

  ```
  select "Country", sum("Students") from pga_schema.universities group by "Country";
  ```

- Click "Run Query" to visualize the results

This will generate a bar chart displaying the total number of students in universities grouped by country.

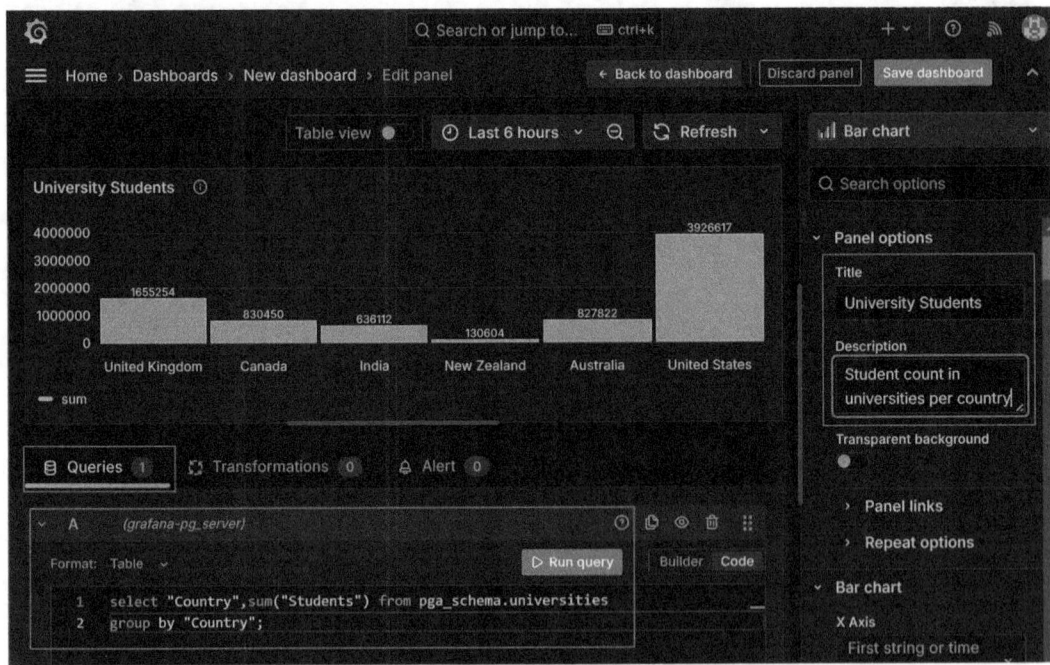

Figure 7-61. Grafana PostgreSQL bar graph student count per country

Review the bar chart graph and ensure that the data is correctly visualized as expected, i.e., student count per country, and if it is as expected and then save the dashboard by providing the details as below:

- Title – postgres.pga_schema
- Folder – Dashboards
- Click "Save"

CHAPTER 7　POSTGRESQL MONITORING USING PGADMIN AND GRAFANA

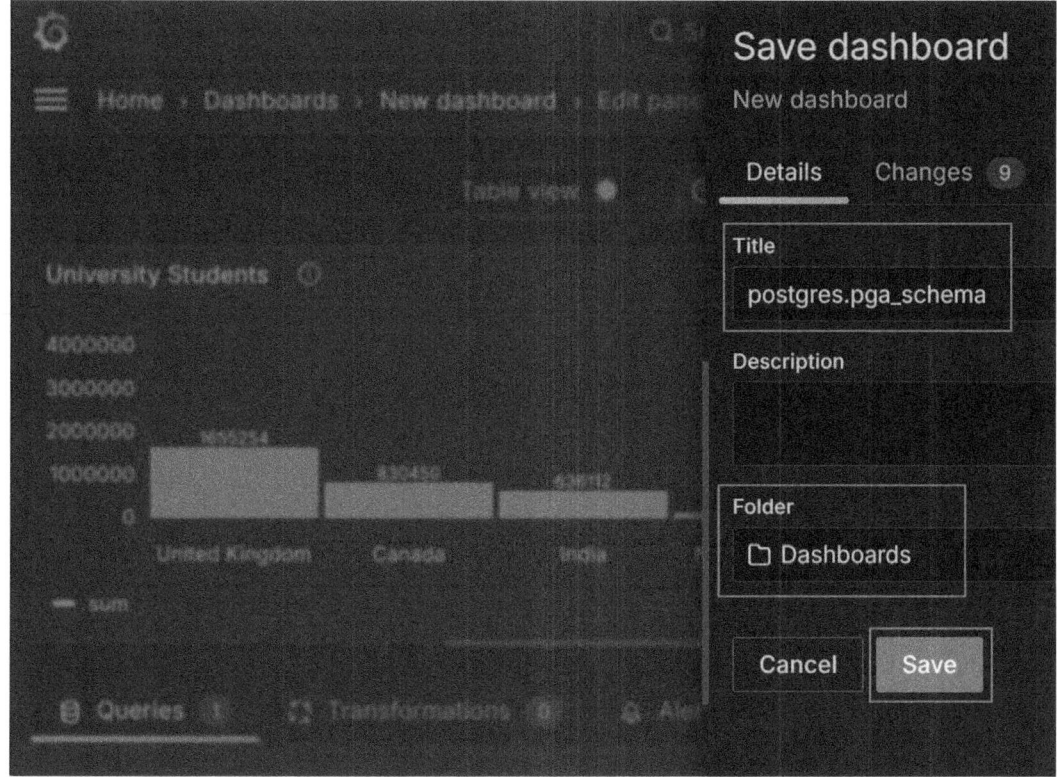

Figure 7-62. Grafana PostgreSQL dashboard saving

The dashboard is now stored and can be accessed later under the Dashboards section.

Adding a New Bar Chart Panel to the Existing Dashboard

To create a new panel in the existing dashboard:

- Navigate to Home ➤ Dashboards ➤ postgres.pga_schema
- Click "Add" and select Visualization from the drop-down menu

This will open a new panel where we can configure a new visualization.

CHAPTER 7   POSTGRESQL MONITORING USING PGADMIN AND GRAFANA

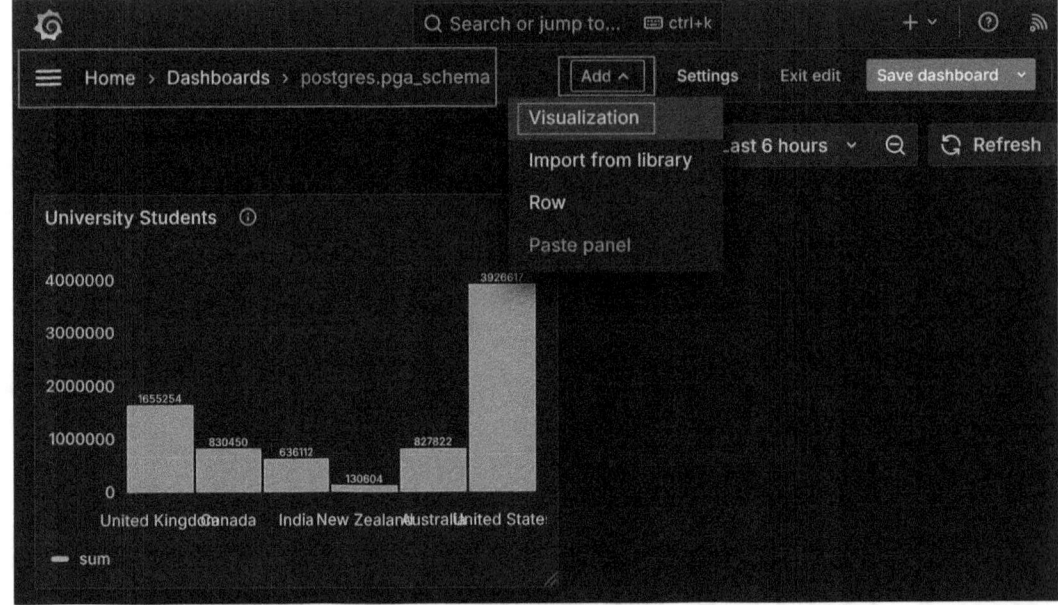

Figure 7-63. Grafana PostgreSQL adding new visualization

- In the new dashboard panel:
  - Select "Bar chart"
  - Provide Title for the panel – United States
  - Add the Description – Top 5 Universities with high volume of students
  - Add Query under the Queries section

    ```
    select "University", Students" from pga_schema.universities
    where "Country" = 'United States'
    order by 2 desc limit 5;
    ```
  - Click "Run Query" to visualize the results

This will generate a bar chart displaying the top five universities in the United States with the highest student population.

Review the bar chart graph and ensure that the data is correctly visualized as expected and click "Save dashboard".

CHAPTER 7   POSTGRESQL MONITORING USING PGADMIN AND GRAFANA

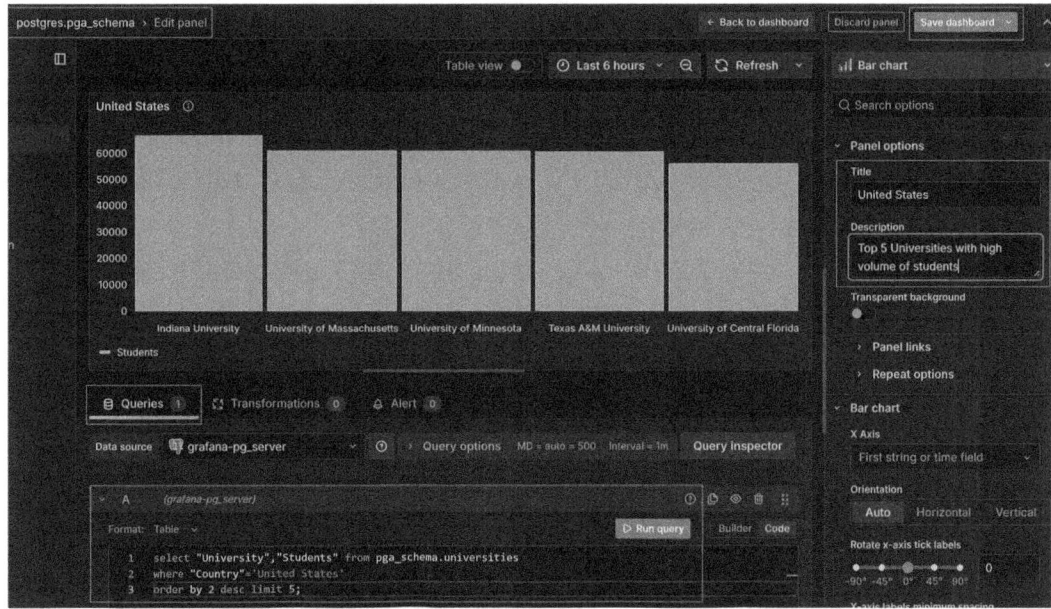

Figure 7-64. *Grafana PostgreSQL panel details*

Once the dashboard is saved, the new United States panel, along with the University Students panel, will be visible under the postgres.pga_schema dashboard.

Figure 7-65. *Grafana PostgreSQL multi-visualization*

CHAPTER 7 POSTGRESQL MONITORING USING PGADMIN AND GRAFANA

Adding a New XY Chart Panel to the Existing Dashboard

An XY Chart is a time series graph that visualizes relationships between variables over time.

In the chart, the X axis represents time (e.g., years) and the Y axis represents measured values (e.g., student count). Different datasets can be overlaid to create multiple series using distinct colors.

To create a new XY Chart panel in the existing dashboard, perform the following:

- Navigate to Home ➤ Dashboards ➤ postgres.pga_schema.
- Click "Add" and select Visualization from the drop-down menu.

This will open a new panel where we can configure an XY Chart.

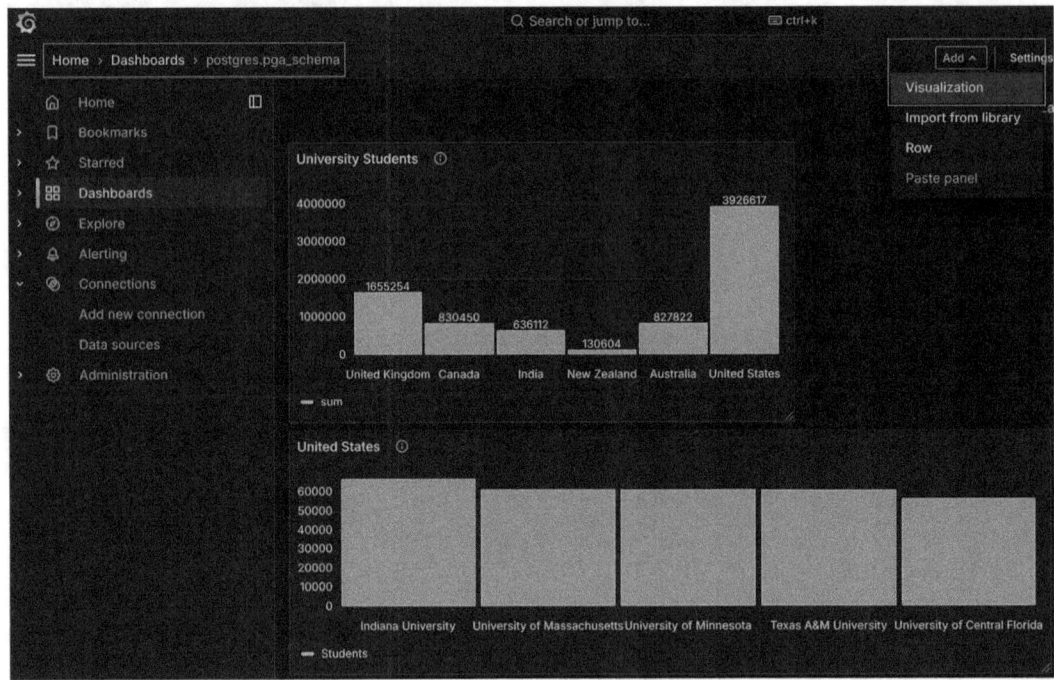

Figure 7-66. Grafana PostgreSQL adding new visualization

- In the XY Chart panel:
  - Select "XY Chart"
  - Provide Title for the panel – University Student Count

CHAPTER 7   POSTGRESQL MONITORING USING PGADMIN AND GRAFANA

- Add the Description – Country-wide universities student count for the last decade

- Add Query in Query Panel "A"

```
Select "Academic_Year", "Students"
from pga_schema."University_H"
where "Country" = "Australia";
```

- Click "Run Query" to visualize the results

This will generate a time series chart displaying the historical year-wise student count for the last ten years in Australia.

To add a series in the XY Chart, perform the following on the right side of the panel:

- Select Manual under Series Mapping

- Add Series Name – Australia

- Frame – Series (A)

- X field – Academic_Year (from table pga_schema.University_H)

- Y field – Students (from table pga_schema.University_H)

This will add a time series visualization with years on the X axis and student count on the Y axis, showing historical trends in Australian universities.

CHAPTER 7   POSTGRESQL MONITORING USING PGADMIN AND GRAFANA

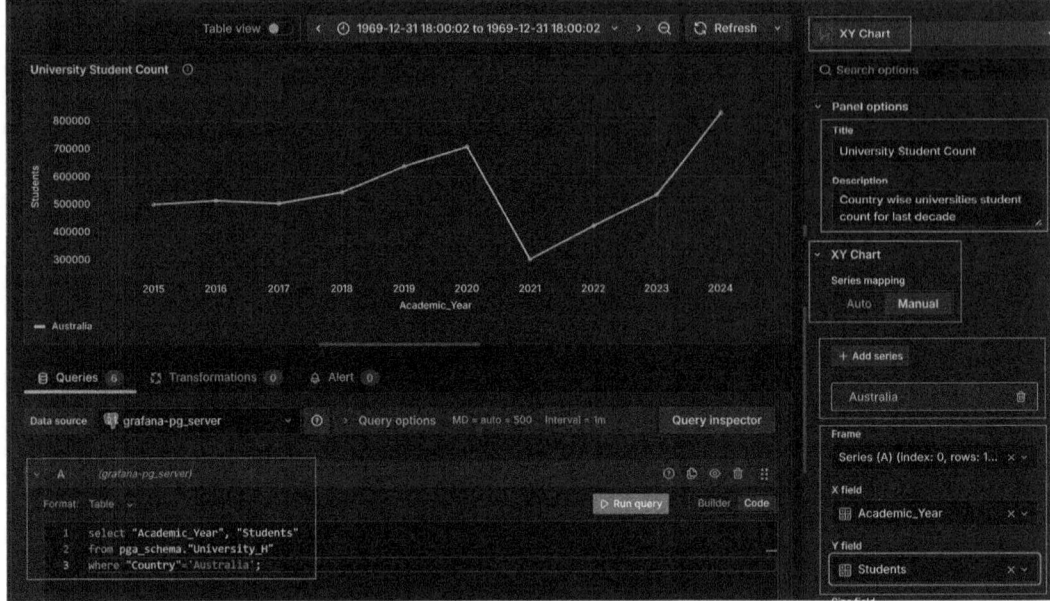

Figure 7-67. Grafana PostgreSQL XY Chart creation

Adding Multiple Series to the XY Chart

To compare multiple datasets (e.g., student counts across different countries), we can add multiple query sections and map them as separate series.

Add queries for multiple series as below:

- Query Panel "B"

  ```
  Select "Academic_Year", "Students"
  from pga_schema."University_H"
  where "Country" = "Canada";
  ```

- Query Panel "C"

  ```
  Select "Academic_Year", "Students"
  from pga_schema."University_H"
  where "Country" = "India";
  ```

- Query Panel "D"

  ```
  Select "Academic_Year", "Students"
  from pga_schema."University_H"
  where "Country" = "New Zealand";
  ```

- Query Panel "E"

  ```
  Select "Academic_Year", "Students"
  from pga_schema."University_H"
  where "Country" = "United Kingdom";
  ```

- Query Panel "F"

  ```
  Select "Academic_Year", "Students"
  from pga_schema."University_H"
  where "Country" = "United States";
  ```

- Click "Run Query" after adding query in each query panel to visualize the results

Mapping Series of Multi-country Visualization

To overlay each dataset as a separate series, perform the following under the Add series field:

For Canada

- Add Series Name – Canada
- Frame – Series (B)
- X field – Academic_Year
- Y field – Students

For India

- Add Series Name – India
- Frame – Series (C)
- X field – Academic_Year
- Y field – Students

CHAPTER 7 POSTGRESQL MONITORING USING PGADMIN AND GRAFANA

For New Zealand

- Add Series Name – New Zealand
- Frame – Series (D)
- X field – Academic_Year
- Y field – Students

For United Kingdom

- Add Series Name – United Kingdom
- Frame – Series (E)
- X field – Academic_Year
- Y field – Students

For United States

- Add Series Name – United States
- Frame – Series (F)
- X field – Academic_Year
- Y field – Students

This will generate a time series graph that overlays multiple datasets displaying trends over time to distinguish each country.

CHAPTER 7   POSTGRESQL MONITORING USING PGADMIN AND GRAFANA

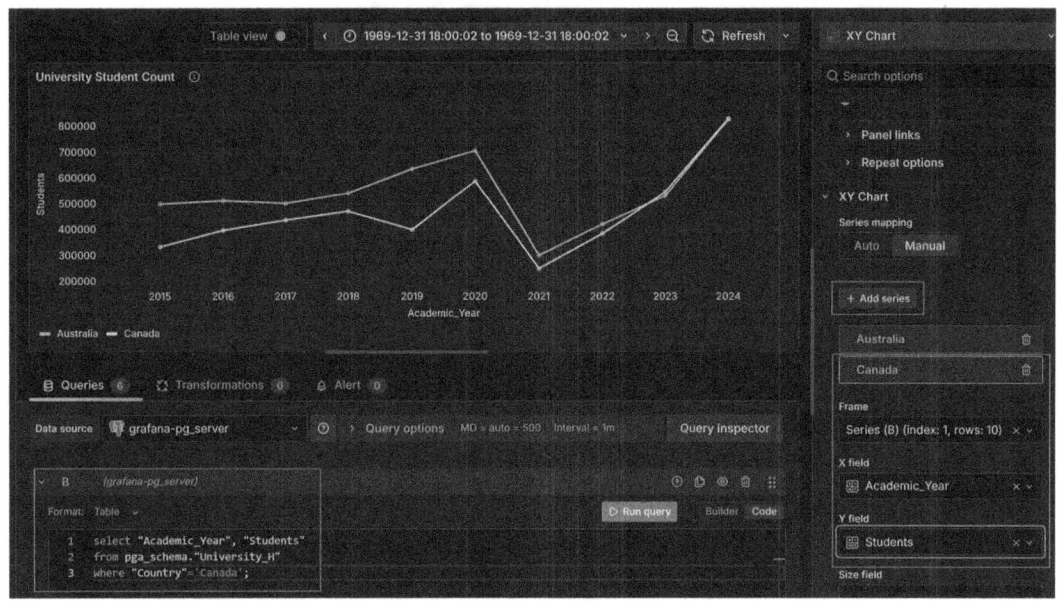

Figure 7-68.   Grafana PostgreSQL adding 2nd query for graph (dataset for Canada)

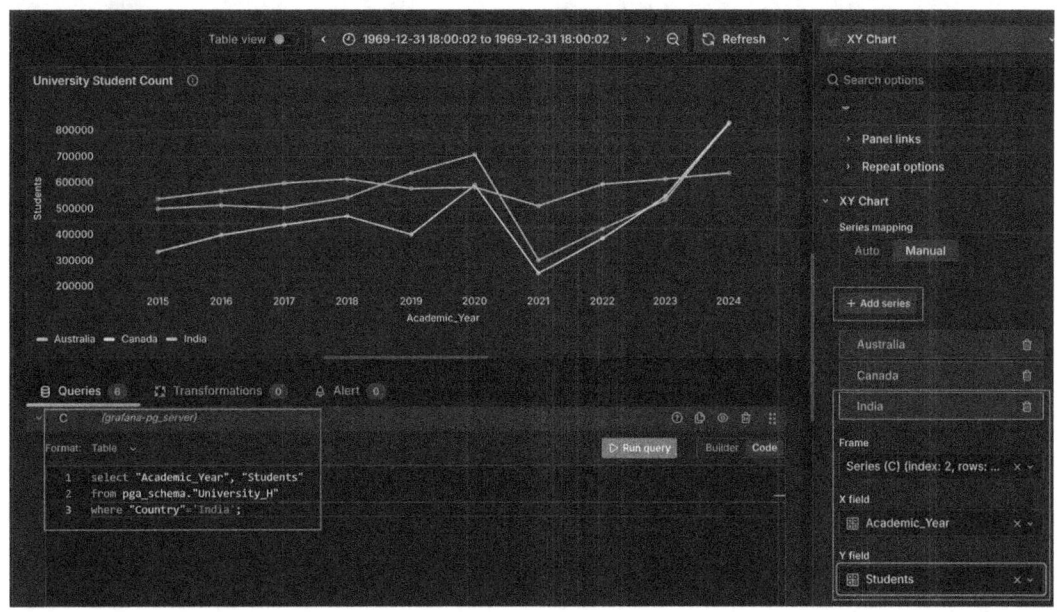

Figure 7-69.   Grafana PostgreSQL adding 3rd query for graph (dataset for India)

481

CHAPTER 7   POSTGRESQL MONITORING USING PGADMIN AND GRAFANA

Figure 7-70. *Grafana PostgreSQL adding 4th query for graph (dataset for New Zealand)*

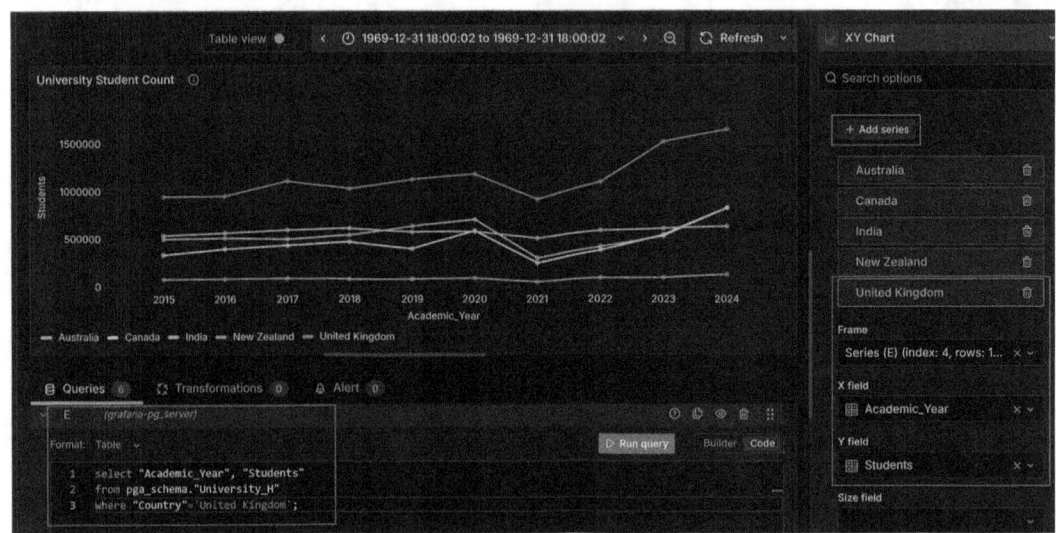

Figure 7-71. *Grafana PostgreSQL adding 5th query for graph (dataset for United Kingdom)*

CHAPTER 7　POSTGRESQL MONITORING USING PGADMIN AND GRAFANA

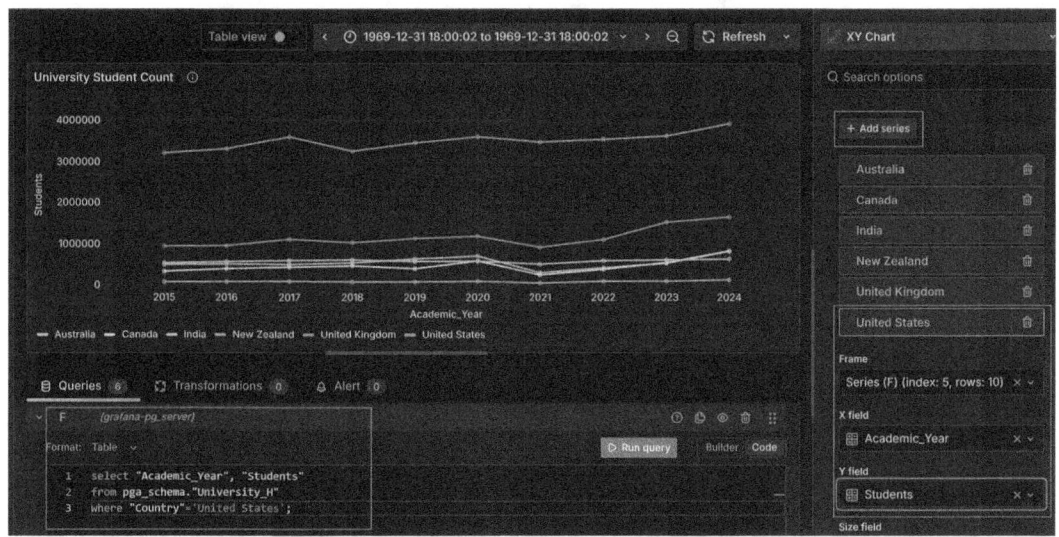

Figure 7-72. *Grafana PostgreSQL XY Chart (dataset for United States)*

Once the XY Chart panel is configured and the output is as expected, review the final output of all the graphs and click Save dashboard.

The dashboard is now updated, including XY Chart panel along with previously created bar graph panels, and is saved for future reference.

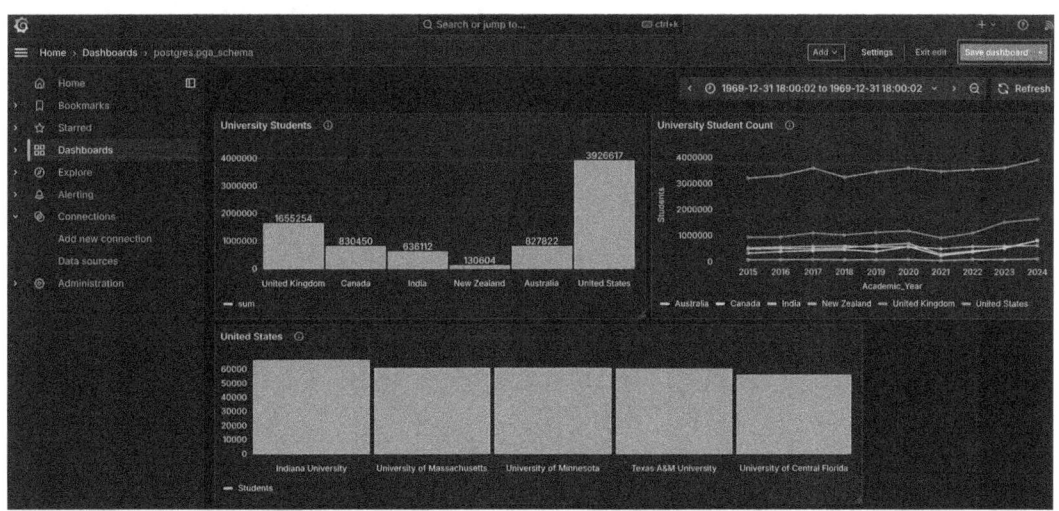

Figure 7-73. *Grafana PostgreSQL dashboard with multiple visualizations*

483

CHAPTER 7 POSTGRESQL MONITORING USING PGADMIN AND GRAFANA

Summary

This chapter covered the key aspects of monitoring and managing PostgreSQL environments. It explained how to use system resource monitoring tools like sar, top, uptime, iostat, vmstat, and netstat to assess OS-level performance. It also highlighted how to understand PostgreSQL's real-time behavior through built-in SQL queries and system views, helping to troubleshoot and optimize database operations. The chapter introduced pgAdmin as an intuitive GUI for database administration and demonstrated how integrating PostgreSQL with monitoring solutions like Grafana enables real-time metrics visualization.

CHAPTER 8

Data Migration from Oracle to PostgreSQL Using Ora2Pg

Introduction

This chapter explores the motives for migrating an Oracle database to a PostgreSQL database and explains the different migration methods and various tools available to migrate an Oracle database to a PostgreSQL database either within on-premises or to a cloud environment.

At the end of this chapter, one should be able to understand the reason and consider migrating to a PostgreSQL database, know migration tools and best practices to follow during migration, and perform migration of an Oracle database to PostgreSQL using the Ora2Pg migration tool.

Why Migrate to PostgreSQL

With a wide variety of options available for databases, organizations are increasingly adopting multi-database models for their applications due to the need to optimize costs, performance, and flexibility. A multi-database approach involves different types of databases supporting various applications and their functionality.

One such adoption and a strategic decision is moving from an Oracle database to a PostgreSQL database, one of the renowned RDBMS databases available, to benefit from various factors. One factor is cost since Oracle licensing cost is edition based per process cost, and in addition, there is support cost involved. Considering a production environment where primary and secondary databases exist, then the cost would become significantly higher, and this further increases with a greater number of servers within database estate hosting Oracle databases. On the other hand, PostgreSQL community edition comes with zero licensing fees, which eliminates the worry of per-core or per-processor cost. This free licensing gives organizations more options to run as many instances as needed and invest in commercial editions that offer advanced features.

With continuous improvements in architecture, performance, and other advanced features, PostgreSQL has transformed significantly from an open source relational database system to a robust, enterprise-grade solution capable of handling business-critical applications and enterprise workloads.

Also, since PostgreSQL is a community-driven database solution, organizations can avoid vendor lock-in dependencies.

PostgreSQL is also supported by major cloud vendors, which gives organizations varied choices to host their PostgreSQL database on suitable cloud. Also, choosing the cloud platform for a PostgreSQL database with applications already hosted on the same cloud platform reduces the latency between applications and database; this may benefit the performance. If choosing a cloud platform for PostgreSQL database different from applications hosted cloud platform, then choosing both the cloud regions within proximity will still benefit on performance, although there will be slight difference in latency compared to both hosted on same cloud platform.

Migration Tools

To migrate an Oracle database to a PostgreSQL database, whether it's between two on-premises environments or from an on-premises to a cloud environment or between different cloud platforms, there are several tools available to facilitate the migration process. Below is the list of some of the most popular tools for Oracle to PostgreSQL migration.

> **Ora2Pg:** This tool is one of the best tools available that is extensively used to migrate an on-premises or cloud-based Oracle database to an on-premises PostgreSQL database. This also supports the migration of an Oracle database to Azure Database for PostgreSQL.

EDB Migration Toolkit (MTK): In order to migrate an Oracle database to EDB postgres Advanced Server or PostgreSQL database, EDB MTK can be used. This is available to migrate to commercial/enterprise editions.

AWS Database Migration Service (DMS) and AWS Schema Conversion Tool (SCT): This tool is used to migrate an Oracle database to postgres (AWS RDS for postgres).

Google Database Migration Service (DMS): DMS service integrated with Ora2Pg is used to migrate an Oracle database to Cloud SQL for PostgreSQL.

Migration Best Practices

For complex cross-database migrations like Oracle to postgres, splitting the migration plan into multiple phases and sub-phases is always the best practice. This phased approach helps minimize the risks and provides the possibility of effective execution of tasks.

The complete migration plan can be divided into phases as below.

Pre-migration Phase

In the pre-migration phase, design the target PostgreSQL database considering factors like the existing Oracle database size, number of schemas to be migrated, capacity planning for future growth, workload type, etc.

To migrate an Oracle database to a PostgreSQL database using the Ora2Pg tool, we need to come up with a comprehensive plan for migration in the Pre-migration phase.

To build a comprehensive migration plan, a complete assessment needs to be performed in the environments planned for migration. There are many facets to be considered, like whether there are any code changes required for the application, any objects that need conversion, any table column data types that need conversion, re-designing object definitions, assessing the features compatibility, identifying unsupported data types if any, etc.

Migration Phase

In the migration phase, we can plan to perform a migration dry run to ensure a smooth actual migration or cutover. Perform the tasks defined in the comprehensive migration plan during dry run, i.e., in advance to actual cutover as this helps as below.

Identify potential risks or challenges: The issues or challenges that arise during dry run, fixing them prior to the actual cutover reduces the unwanted outage window and guarantees seamless migration.

Derive the time required for each step: Precise timelines assist to communicate with the business users and application owners about the actual downtime required for migration and validations. Also, it helps to coordinate and engage the right teams as necessary.

Testing application functionality: Thorough application testing can be done to ensure the data accessibility and functioning of all application modules on the migrated database.

Assessing performance: Running few application jobs or performing loads or generating reports to assess the performance, which can be compared against the source database.

In case during the execution of the first dry run, any issues or challenges with respect to data or conversions are encountered, address them and then initiate a second dry run and ensure this completes with no issues.

A clean migration dry run can be considered a critical milestone that provides necessary confidence to execute the final migration or cutover.

Post-migration Phase

After migration, the hyper-care period is considered very crucial to confirm that the migrated database and its associated application and application modules are functioning as expected and yield optimized results.

This chapter solely explains the process involved in migrating an Oracle database to a PostgreSQL database in an on-premises environment using the Ora2Pg tool.

Oracle to PostgreSQL Migration Using Ora2Pg

What Is Ora2Pg?

Ora2Pg is a renowned and free migration tool that is based on Perl DBI (Database Interface Module) and is extensively used to migrate an Oracle database to a PostgreSQL-compatible schema.

Ora2Pg is a combination of a Perl script (ora2pg) and a Perl module (Ora2Pg.pm); these two are loaded when Ora2Pg is installed in the system.

Ora2Pg can be downloaded from SourceForge or the Ora2Pg home page.

Download Ora2Pg from SourceForge:

- https://sourceforge.net/projects/ora2pg

Download Ora2Pg from the Ora2Pg site:

https://ora2pg.darold.net

The above link also provides more information on documentation along with download options.

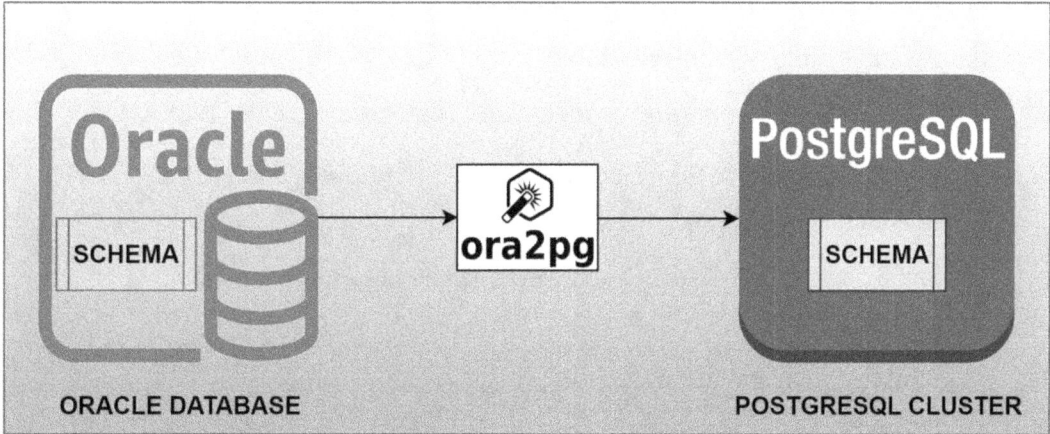

Figure 8-1. Ora2Pg tool for Oracle to PostgreSQL migration

Migration Approach

Based on the on-premises migration requirements, there are various options available to choose. The best option to choose is that it best fits the specific requirements of migration.

> **Option 1:** Consider migrating the database from Oracle to PostgreSQL on the same system where the source Oracle database is running.
>
> **Option 2:** Oracle database running on one system can be migrated to PostgreSQL on another system.

Chapter 8   Data Migration from Oracle to PostgreSQL using Ora2Pg

This chapter explains the migration process for *Option 1* where the existing server hosting the Oracle database has suitable configuration and resources that can host and run the PostgreSQL server with no additional hardware changes.

Migration Prerequisites

In the process of preparing the environment for migration, the below are the general requirements to use the Ora2Pg tool:

1. A valid Oracle installation.
2. A candidate Oracle database to migrate.
3. A valid PostgreSQL installation.
4. Perl version 5.6 or higher.
5. Perl DBI (Database Interface) and other Perl modules need to be installed and working.
6. Database Driver – DBD::Oracle Perl module needs to be installed and working.
7. Ora2Pg tool installation.

Let us now see various steps performed during the migration.

Prerequisites 1 and 2 are already assured as we are migrating an existing Oracle database; details are as described in Table 8-1.

Table 8-1. Details of the components used in migration

Component	Value
Server or host name	dbserver
Server or host IP	192.168.2.9
Database home path	/u01/app/oracle/product/19.3.0/dbhome_1
Database version	19.20.0.0.230718
Database name	orsrcdb
Schemas	HR, CO, SH

Pre-migration Phase: Prepare Environment for Migration

Install PostgreSQL and Initialize the Database Cluster

Since we are planning to migrate an Oracle database to a PostgreSQL database on the same system, install PostgreSQL and initialize the database cluster.

Refer to Chapter 2 for installation and initialization of PostgreSQL.

Validate Schemas and Listener in Source Database

- Connect to source Oracle database *orsrcdb*; validate the schemas identified for migration.

    In this scenario, schemas Human Resources (HR), Customer Orders (CO), and Sales History (SH) are being migrated.

    ```
    [oracle@dbserver ~]$ . oraenv
    ORACLE_SID = [orsrcdb] ?
    The Oracle base remains unchanged with value /u01/app/oracle

    [oracle@dbserver ~]$ sqlplus / as sysdba

    Connected to:
    Oracle Database 19c Enterprise Edition Release 19.0.0.0.0 -
    Production
    Version 19.20.0.0.0

    SQL> select name,db_unique_name,open_mode,database_role from
    gv$database;

    NAME       DB_UNIQUE_NAME           OPEN_MODE          DATABASE_ROLE
    ---------  ----------------------   -----------------  -------------
    ORSRCDB    orsrcdb                  READ WRITE         PRIMARY

    SQL> select owner, object_type, count(*) from dba_objects
    where owner in ('HR','CO','SH')
    group by owner, object_type
    order by owner, object_type;
    ```

CHAPTER 8   DATA MIGRATION FROM ORACLE TO POSTGRESQL USING ORA2PG

OWNER	OBJECT_TYPE	COUNT(*)
CO	INDEX	21
CO	LOB	3
CO	SEQUENCE	6
CO	TABLE	9
CO	VIEW	4
HR	INDEX	19
HR	PROCEDURE	2
HR	SEQUENCE	3
HR	TABLE	8
HR	TRIGGER	2
HR	VIEW	1
SH	DIMENSION	5
SH	INDEX	33
SH	INDEX PARTITION	115
SH	LOB	1
SH	MATERIALIZED VIEW	2
SH	TABLE	15
SH	TABLE PARTITION	35
SH	VIEW	1

SQL> select distinct owner,table_name,num_rows from dba_tab_statistics
where owner in ('HR','CO','SH') and num_rows > 0
order by owner,table_name;

OWNER	TABLE_NAME	NUM_ROWS
CO	CUSTOMERS	392
CO	INVENTORY	566
CO	ORDERS	1950
CO	ORDERS_H	27300
CO	ORDER_ITEMS	3914
CO	ORDER_ITEMS_H	15656
CO	PRODUCTS	46

CO	SHIPMENTS	1892
CO	STORES	23
HR	COUNTRIES	25
HR	DEPARTMENTS	27
HR	EMPLOYEES	107
HR	EMPLOYEES_H	366
HR	JOBS	19
HR	JOB_HISTORY	10
HR	LOCATIONS	23
HR	REGIONS	5
SH	CHANNELS	5
SH	COUNTRIES	35
SH	PRODUCTS	72

- Check the listener status. Listener should be running and ready to accept remote connections.

[oracle@dbserver ~]$ lsnrctl status

LSNRCTL for Linux: Version 19.0.0.0.0 - Production on 15-OCT-2024 14:51:50

Copyright (c) 1991, 2023, Oracle. All rights reserved.

Connecting to (DESCRIPTION=(ADDRESS=(PROTOCOL=TCP)(HOST=dbserver)(PORT=1521)))
STATUS of the LISTENER

Alias   LISTENER
Version   TNSLSNR for Linux: Version 19.0.0.0.0 - Production
Start Date   15-OCT-2024 14:47:14
Uptime   0 days 0 hr. 4 min. 36 sec
Trace Level   off
Security   ON: Local OS Authentication
SNMP   OFF

```
Listener Parameter File
/u01/app/oracle/product/19.3.0/dbhome_1/network/admin/listener.ora
Listener Log File  /u01/app/oracle/diag/tnslsnr/dbserver/listener/
alert/log.xml
Listening Endpoints Summary...
  (DESCRIPTION=(ADDRESS=(PROTOCOL=tcp)(HOST= dbserver)
  (PORT=1521)))
Services Summary...
Service "orsrcdb" has 1 instance(s).
  Instance "orsrcdb", status READY, has 1 handler(s) for this
  service...
Service "orsrcdbXDB" has 1 instance(s).
  Instance "orsrcdb", status READY, has 1 handler(s) for this
  service...
The command completed successfully
```

Install Perl Modules Required for DBD::Oracle and Ora2Pg

- Check the perl executable location and its version. Perl version required is 5.6 or higher.

  [root@dbserver ~]# find / -name perl
  /usr/bin/perl
  /usr/libexec/perf-core/scripts/perl
  /usr/src/kernels/4.18.0-80.el8.x86_64/tools/perf/scripts/perl
  /u01/app/oracle/product/19.3.0/dbhome_1/inventory/Templates/perl
  /u01/app/oracle/product/19.3.0/dbhome_1/perl
  /u01/app/oracle/product/19.3.0/dbhome_1/perl/bin/perl

  [root@dbserver ~]# which perl
  /usr/bin/perl

CHAPTER 8   DATA MIGRATION FROM ORACLE TO POSTGRESQL USING ORA2PG

[root@dbserver ~]# perl --version

This is perl 5, version 26, subversion 3 (v5.26.3) built for x86_64-linux-thread-multi

- Install Perl module perl-ExtUtils-MakeMaker.

  Perl-ExtUtils-MakeMaker is a Perl module that generates a standard Makefile file having a set of instructions that helps the make utility to build and install Perl modules.

  This is used during Ora2Pg installation.

[root@dbserver ~]# yum install perl-ExtUtils-MakeMaker

```
Oracle Linux 8 Application Stream (x86_64)          4.3 kB/s | 4.5
kB   00:01
Oracle Linux 8 BaseOS Latest (x86_64)               4.1 kB/s | 4.3
kB   00:01
PostgreSQL common RPMs for RHEL / Rocky 8 - x86_64 232  B/s | 659  B    00:02
PostgreSQL common RPMs for RHEL / Rocky 8 - x86_64 1.6 MB/s | 1.7
kB   00:00
PostgreSQL common RPMs for RHEL / Rocky 8 - x86_64 261  B/s | 659  B    00:02
Dependencies resolved.
================================================================================
 Package                      Arch    Version              Repository    Size
================================================================================
Installing:
 perl-ExtUtils-MakeMaker      noarch  1:7.34-1.el8         ol8_appstream 300 k
Installing dependencies:
 perl-CPAN-Meta-Requirements  noarch  2.140-396.el8        ol8_appstream  37 k
 perl-CPAN-Meta-YAML          noarch  0.018-397.el8        ol8_appstream  34 k
 perl-ExtUtils-Command        noarch  1:7.34-1.el8         ol8_appstream  19 k
 perl-ExtUtils-Install        noarch  2.14-4.el8           ol8_appstream  46 k
 perl-ExtUtils-Manifest       noarch  1.70-395.el8         ol8_appstream  36 k
 perl-ExtUtils-ParseXS        noarch  1:3.35-2.el8         ol8_appstream  83 k
 perl-JSON-PP                 noarch  1:2.97.001-3.el8     ol8_appstream  68 k
 perl-Test-Harness            noarch  1:3.42-1.el8         ol8_appstream 279 k
 perl-devel                   x86_64  4:5.26.3-416.el8     ol8_appstream 598 k
```

```
  systemtap-sdt-devel            x86_64 4.9-3.0.1.el8    ol8_appstream  88 k
Installing weak dependencies:
  perl-CPAN-Meta                 noarch 2.150010-396.el8 ol8_appstream 191 k

Transaction Summary
================================================================================
Install  12 Packages

Total download size: 1.7 M
Installed size: 6.0 M
Is this ok [y/N]: y
Downloading Packages:
(1/12): perl-CPAN-Meta-Requirements-2.140-396.el8.noarch.rpm   34 kB/s |  37 kB
                                                                        00:01
(2/12): perl-CPAN-Meta-YAML-0.018-397.el8.noarch.rpm     31 kB/s|  34 kB 00:01
(3/12): perl-ExtUtils-Command-7.34-1.el8.noarch.rpm     1.3 MB/s|  19 kB 00:00
(4/12): perl-CPAN-Meta-2.150010-396.el8.noarch.rpm      176 kB/s| 191 kB 00:01
(5/12): perl-ExtUtils-Install-2.14-4.el8.noarch.rpm     1.6 MB/s|  46 kB 00:00
(6/12): perl-ExtUtils-Manifest-1.70-395.el8.noarch.rpm  2.4 MB/s|  36 kB 00:00
(7/12): perl-ExtUtils-ParseXS-3.35-2.el8.noarch.rpm     4.0 MB/s|  83 kB 00:00
(8/12): perl-JSON-PP-2.97.001-3.el8.noarch.rpm          4.1 MB/s|  68 kB 00:00
(9/12): perl-ExtUtils-MakeMaker-7.34-1.el8.noarch.rpm   5.9 MB/s| 300 kB 00:00
(10/12): perl-Test-Harness-3.42-1.el8.noarch.rpm        8.9 MB/s| 279 kB 00:00
(11/12): systemtap-sdt-devel-4.9-3.0.1.el8.x86_64.rpm   4.4 MB/s|  88 kB 00:00
(12/12): perl-devel-5.26.3-416.el8.x86_64.rpm            12 MB/s| 598 kB 00:00
--------------------------------------------------------------------------------
Total                                                   1.5 MB/s| 1.7 MB 00:01
Running transaction check
Transaction check succeeded.
Running transaction test
Transaction test succeeded.
Running transaction  Preparing        :
  .
<<<<< OUTPUT TRUNCATED >>>>>
  .
```

CHAPTER 8 DATA MIGRATION FROM ORACLE TO POSTGRESQL USING ORA2PG

```
Installed:
  perl-ExtUtils-MakeMaker-1:7.34-1.el8.noarch
  perl-CPAN-Meta-2.150010-396.el8.noarch
  perl-CPAN-Meta-Requirements-2.140-396.el8.noarch
  perl-CPAN-Meta-YAML-0.018-397.el8.noarch
  perl-ExtUtils-Command-1:7.34-1.el8.noarch
  perl-ExtUtils-Install-2.14-4.el8.noarch
  perl-ExtUtils-Manifest-1.70-395.el8.noarch
  perl-ExtUtils-ParseXS-1:3.35-2.el8.noarch
  perl-JSON-PP-1:2.97.001-3.el8.noarch
  perl-Test-Harness-1:3.42-1.el8.noarch
  perl-devel-4:5.26.3-416.el8.x86_64
  systemtap-sdt-devel-4.9-3.0.1.el8.x86_64

Complete!
[root@dbserver ~]#
```

- Install Perl module perl-DBI.

    Perl-DBI (Database Interface) is a widely used Perl module that provides an interface for database management system (DBMS) interaction.

    This is internally called during the Ora2Pg usage for connections to Oracle database and PostgreSQL database.

    [root@dbserver ~]# yum install perl-DBI

    ```
    PostgreSQL common RPMs for RHEL / Rocky 8 - x86_64     309 B/s|659 B     00:02
    Last metadata expiration check: 0:01:25 ago on Tue 22 Oct 2024 08:26:39 PM EDT.
    Package perl-DBI-1.641-2.module+el8+5177+8fccb4aa.x86_64 is already installed.
    Dependencies resolved.
    ```

```
========================================================================
Package        Arch    Version                         Repository      Size
========================================================================
Upgrading:
 perl-DBI      x86_64  1.641-4.module+el8.6.0          ol8_appstream  740 k

Transaction Summary
========================================================================
Upgrade  1 Package

Total download size: 740 k
Is this ok [y/N]: y
Downloading Packages:
perl-DBI-1.641-4.module+el8.6.0.x86_64.rpm    632 kB/s|740 kB  00:01
------------------------------------------------------------------------
Total                                          630 kB/s|740 kB  00:01
Running transaction check
Transaction check succeeded.
Running transaction test
Transaction test succeeded.
Running transaction
  Preparing  :                                                         1/1
  Upgrading  : perl-DBI-1.641-4.module+el8.6.0+20590+70c0920f.
               x86_64      1/2
  Cleanup    : perl-DBI-1.641-2.module+el8+5177+8fccb4aa.
               x86_64           2/2
  Verifying  : perl-DBI-1.641-4.module+el8.6.0+20590+70c0920f.
               x86_64      1/2
  Verifying  : perl-DBI-1.641-2.module+el8+5177+8fccb4aa.
               x86_64           2/2
Upgraded:
  perl-DBI-1.641-4.module+el8.6.0+20590+70c0920f.x86_64

Complete!
[root@dbserver ~]#
```

CHAPTER 8   DATA MIGRATION FROM ORACLE TO POSTGRESQL USING ORA2PG

- Install Perl module perl-CPAN.

  Perl-CPAN (Comprehensive Perl Archive Network) is a Perl module that provides an interface to download, build, test, and install Perl modules from CPAN automatically.

  This is used during the installation of DBD::Oracle Perl module.

[root@dbserver ~]# yum install perl-CPAN

```
PostgreSQL common RPMs for RHEL / Rocky 8 - x86_64   1.6 MB/s| 1.7 kB
00:00
Last metadata expiration check: 0:04:49 ago on Tue 22 Oct 2024
08:26:39 PM EDT.
Dependencies resolved.
================================================================================
 Package                         Arch    Version           Repository      Size
================================================================================
Installing:
 perl-CPAN                       noarch  2.18-399.el8      ol8_appstream  553 k
Installing dependencies:
 perl                            x86_64  4:5.26.3-422.el8  ol8_appstream   73 k
.
<<<<< OUTPUT TRUNCATED >>>>>
.
 perl-utils                      noarch  5.26.3-422.el8    ol8_appstream  129 k

Transaction Summary
================================================================================
Install  71 Packages

Total download size: 6.4 M
Installed size: 17 M
Is this ok [y/N]: y
Downloading Packages:
(1/71):perl-Attribute-Handlers-0.99-422.el8.noarch.rpm   84 kB/s| 89 kB
                                                         00:01
(2/71): perl-5.26.3-422.el8.x86_64.rpm                   68 kB/s| 73 Kb
                                                         00:01
```
.

CHAPTER 8 DATA MIGRATION FROM ORACLE TO POSTGRESQL USING ORA2PG

<<<<< OUTPUT TRUNCATED >>>>>

.

```
(71/71): perl-utils-5.26.3-422.el8.noarch.rpm          5.3 MB/s|129 kB
                                                       00:00
--------------------------------------------------------------------------
Total                                                  3.9 MB/s|6.4 MB
                                                       00:01
Running transaction check
Transaction check succeeded.
Running transaction test
Transaction test succeeded.
Running transaction
  Preparing        :                                              1/1
  Installing       : perl-SelfLoader-1.23-422.el8.noarch         1/71
.
  Installing       : perl-utils-5.26.3-422.el8.noarch           26/71
  Installing       : perl-perlfaq-5.20180605-1.el8.noarch       27/71
.
  Installing       : perl-CPAN-2.18-399.el8.noarch              70/71
  Installing       : perl-4:5.26.3-422.el8.x86_64               71/71
.
```

<<<<< OUTPUT TRUNCATED >>>>>

.

```
Installed:
  perl-CPAN-2.18-399.el8.noarch
  perl-4:5.26.3-422.el8.x86_64
```

.

<<<<< OUTPUT TRUNCATED >>>>>

.

```
  perl-open-1.11-422.el8.noarch
  perl-perlfaq-5.20180605-1.el8.noarch
  perl-utils-5.26.3-422.el8.noarch

Complete!
[root@dbserver ~]#
```

- Install Perl module DBD::Oracle.

  DBD::Oracle is a Perl module that provides a Database Driver (DBD) for interacting with Oracle databases using the DBI (Database Interface) module.

  One of the prerequisites for this module installation is Oracle client binaries or Oracle server binaries to be installed or available on the system. Since this is a database server, Oracle server binaries are already available.

  Another prerequisite is to set environment variables like ORACLE_HOME, PATH, and LD_LIBRARY_PATH.

  As root user, set these environment variables.

  [root@ dbserver ~]# export ORACLE_HOME=/u01/app/oracle/product/19.3.0/dbhome_1

  [root@ dbserver ~]# export LD_LIBRARY_PATH=$ORACLE_HOME/lib:$LD_LIBRARY_PATH

  [root@ dbserver ~]# export PATH=$ORACLE_HOME/bin:$PATH

Install DBD::Oracle perl module

<<<<< OUTPUT TRUNCATED >>>>>

[root@dbserver ~]# perl -MCPAN -e 'install DBD::Oracle'

```
Reading '/root/.local/share/.cpan/Metadata'
  Database was generated on Fri, 15 Nov 2024 21:17:01 GMT
Running install for module 'DBD::Oracle'
Configuring DBD::Oracle for perl 5.026003 on linux (x86_64-linux-thread-multi)
Using Oracle in /u01/app/oracle/product/19.3.0/dbhome_1
DEFINE _SQLPLUS_RELEASE = "1920000000" (CHAR)
Oracle Version 19.20.0.0 (19.20)
Your LD_LIBRARY_PATH env var is set to '/u01/app/oracle/product/19.3.0/dbhome_1/lib:/u01/app/oracle/product/19.3.0/dbhome_1/lib:'
client_version=19.20
```

Using DBD::Oracle 1.90.
Using DBI 1.641 (for perl 5.026003 on x86_64-linux-thread-multi) installed in /usr/lib64/perl5/vendor_perl/auto/DBI/
Generating a Unix-style Makefile
Writing Makefile for DBD::Oracle
Running make test
"/usr/bin/perl" -MExtUtils::Command::MM -e 'cp_nonempty' -- Oracle.bs blib/arch/auto/DBD/Oracle/Oracle.bs 644
.

```
# === Configure Requires ===
#     Module              Want    Have
#     ------------------  -----   --------
#     DBI                 1.623   1.641
#     ExtUtils::MakeMaker any     7.34
#     perl                5.006   5.026003
#
# === Configure Suggests ===
#     Module      Want     Have
#     --------    -------  -------
#     JSON::PP    2.27300  2.97001
#
# === Build Requires ===
#     Module              Want    Have
#     ------------------  -----   --------
#     Config              any     5.026003
#     DBI                 1.623   1.641
#     ExtUtils::MakeMaker any     7.34
#
# === Test Requires ===
#     Module              Want    Have
#     ------------------  -----   --------
#     DBI                 1.623   1.641
#     Devel::Peek         any     1.26
#     ExtUtils::MakeMaker any     7.34
```

```
#      File::Spec            any      3.74
#      lib                   any      0.64
#      perl                  5.008    5.026003
#
# === Test Recommends ===
#      Module       Want           Have
#      ----------   --------       --------
#      CPAN::Meta   2.120900       2.150010
#
# === Runtime Requires ===
#      Module       Want     Have
#      ----------   -----    --------
#      DBI          1.623    1.641
#      perl         5.008    5.026003
All tests successful.
Files=45, Tests=21,  3 wallclock secs ( 0.06 usr  0.01 sys +  2.30
cusr   0.33 csys =  2.70 CPU)
Result: PASS
  ZARQUON/DBD-Oracle-1.90.tar.gz
  /usr/bin/make test -- OK
Running make install
"/usr/bin/perl" -MExtUtils::Command::MM -e 'cp_nonempty' -- Oracle.bs blib/
arch/auto/DBD/Oracle/Oracle.bs 644
Manifying 13 pod documents
Files found in blib/arch: installing files in blib/lib into architecture
dependent library tree
Appending installation info to /usr/lib64/perl5/perllocal.pod
  ZARQUON/DBD-Oracle-1.90.tar.gz
  /usr/bin/make install    -- OK
[root@dbserver ~]#
```

CHAPTER 8   DATA MIGRATION FROM ORACLE TO POSTGRESQL USING ORA2PG

Install Ora2Pg

If there are multiple db servers to migrate, installing Ora2Pg on each db server is a tedious task. Hence, it is recommended or considered to be the best practice to install Ora2Pg on a server other than the source Oracle db server or the target PostgreSQL db server. So install Ora2Pg only once on a separate server and use it to migrate multiple databases on various db servers.

Since we are moving only one database in this scenario, let us install Ora2Pg on the same db server where the Oracle database is running.

- Create directory for software download and other operations.

    [root@dbserver ~]# mkdir -p /var/lib/oracle

    [root@dbserver ~]# ls -ld /var/lib/oracle
    drwxr-xr-x 2 root root 6 Oct 22 20:18 /var/lib/oracle

- Download Ora2Pg.

    As mentioned in the previous section, Ora2Pg can be downloaded from SourceForge.

    [root@dbserver ~]# cd /var/lib/oracle

    [root@dbserver oracle]# wget https://sourceforge.net/projects/ora2pg/files/24.3/ora2pg-24.3.tar.gz

    --2024-11-16 00:16:38-- https://sourceforge.net/projects/ora2pg/files/24.3/ora2pg-24.3.tar.gz
    Resolving sourceforge.net (sourceforge.net)... 104.18.13.149, 104.18.12.149, 2606:4700::6812:d95, ...
    Connecting to sourceforge.net (sourceforge.net)|104.18.13.149|:443... connected.
    HTTP request sent, awaiting response... 301 Moved Permanently
    Location: https://sourceforge.net/projects/ora2pg/files/24.3/ora2pg-24.3.tar.gz/ [following]

    .

    <<<<< OUTPUT TRUNCATED >>>>>

    .

CHAPTER 8   DATA MIGRATION FROM ORACLE TO POSTGRESQL USING ORA2PG

```
HTTP request sent, awaiting response... 200 OK
Length: 577395 (564K) [application/x-gzip]
Saving to: 'ora2pg-24.3.tar.gz'

ora2pg-24.3.tar.gz  100%[====================>]
563.86K  3.15MB/s    in 0.2s

2024-11-16 00:16:40 (3.15 MB/s) - 'ora2pg-24.3.tar.gz' saved
[577395/577395]
```

[root@dbserver oracle]# ls -lrt
```
total 564
-rw-r--r-- 1 root root 577395 Mar 28  2024 ora2pg-24.3.tar.gz
```

- Uncompress the downloaded tarball of Ora2Pg.

[root@dbserver oracle]# tar -xvf ora2pg-24.3.tar.gz
```
ora2pg-24.3/
ora2pg-24.3/LICENSE
ora2pg-24.3/packaging/
ora2pg-24.3/packaging/debian/
ora2pg-24.3/packaging/debian/ora2pg/
.
```

<<<<< OUTPUT TRUNCATED >>>>>
```
.
ora2pg-24.3/lib/Ora2Pg.pm
ora2pg-24.3/doc/
ora2pg-24.3/doc/ora2pg.3
ora2pg-24.3/doc/Ora2Pg.pod
```

[root@dbserver oracle]# ls -lrt
```
total 564
drwxrwxr-x 6 admin admin    156 Mar 28  2024 ora2pg-24.3
-rw-r--r-- 1 root  root  577395 Mar 28  2024 ora2pg-24.3.tar.gz
[root@dbserver oracle]#
```

CHAPTER 8   DATA MIGRATION FROM ORACLE TO POSTGRESQL USING ORA2PG

- Install Ora2Pg.

    The actual installation of Ora2Pg involves execution of "makefile.pl" using perl followed by "make" and "make install" execution.

    [root@dbserver oracle]# cd ora2pg-24.3

    [root@dbserver ora2pg-24.3]# ls -lrt
    ```
    total 652
    drwxrwxr-x 2 admin admin       42 Mar 28  2024 scripts
    -rw-rw-r-- 1 admin admin   171271 Mar 28  2024 README
    drwxrwxr-x 5 admin admin       63 Mar 28  2024 packaging
    -rw-rw-r-- 1 admin admin      180 Mar 28  2024 MANIFEST
    -rw-rw-r-- 1 admin admin    75191 Mar 28  2024 Makefile.PL
    -rw-rw-r-- 1 admin admin    32472 Mar 28  2024 LICENSE
    drwxrwxr-x 3 admin admin       37 Mar 28  2024 lib
    -rw-rw-r-- 1 admin admin       21 Mar 28  2024 INSTALL
    drwxrwxr-x 2 admin admin       40 Mar 28  2024 doc
    -rw-rw-r-- 1 admin admin   374342 Mar 28  2024 changelog
    ```

    [root@dbserver ora2pg-24.3]# which perl
    /usr/bin/perl

    [root@dbserver ora2pg-24.3]# perl Makefile.PL
    ```
    Checking if your kit is complete...
    Looks good
    Generating a Unix-style Makefile
    Writing Makefile for Ora2Pg
    Writing MYMETA.yml and MYMETA.json
    Done...
    ------------------------------------------------------------------
    Please read documentation at http://ora2pg.darold.net/ before
    asking for help
    ------------------------------------------------------------------
    Now type: make && make install
    ```

[root@dbserver ora2pg-24.3]# make

```
cp lib/Ora2Pg/GEOM.pm blib/lib/Ora2Pg/GEOM.pm
cp lib/Ora2Pg/MySQL.pm blib/lib/Ora2Pg/MySQL.pm
cp lib/Ora2Pg.pm blib/lib/Ora2Pg.pm
cp lib/Ora2Pg/Oracle.pm blib/lib/Ora2Pg/Oracle.pm
cp lib/Ora2Pg/MSSQL.pm blib/lib/Ora2Pg/MSSQL.pm
cp lib/Ora2Pg/PLSQL.pm blib/lib/Ora2Pg/PLSQL.pm
cp scripts/ora2pg blib/script/ora2pg
"/usr/bin/perl" -MExtUtils::MY -e 'MY->fixin(shift)' -- blib/script/ora2pg
cp scripts/ora2pg_scanner blib/script/ora2pg_scanner
"/usr/bin/perl" -MExtUtils::MY -e 'MY->fixin(shift)' -- blib/script/ora2pg_scanner
Manifying 1 pod document
[root@dbserver ora2pg-24.3]#
```

[root@dbserver ora2pg-24.3]# make install

```
Manifying 1 pod document
Installing /usr/local/share/perl5/Ora2Pg.pm
Installing /usr/local/share/perl5/Ora2Pg/GEOM.pm
Installing /usr/local/share/perl5/Ora2Pg/MySQL.pm
Installing /usr/local/share/perl5/Ora2Pg/Oracle.pm
Installing /usr/local/share/perl5/Ora2Pg/MSSQL.pm
Installing /usr/local/share/perl5/Ora2Pg/PLSQL.pm
Installing /usr/local/share/man/man3/ora2pg.3
Installing /usr/local/bin/ora2pg
Installing /usr/local/bin/ora2pg_scanner
Installing default configuration file (ora2pg.conf.dist) to /etc/ora2pg
Appending installation info to /usr/lib64/perl5/perllocal.pod
[root@dbserver ora2pg-24.3]#
```

The make install command will perform the following operations:

- Install the Perl module Ora2Pg.pm in the Perl site repository.

- Add ora2pg executable binary in /usr/local/bin.
- Create a configuration file ora2pg.conf under /etc/ora2pg.

    [root@dbserver ora2pg-24.3]# ls -lrt /usr/local/share/perl5/Ora2Pg.pm
    -r--r--r-- 1 root root 725624 Mar 28 2024 /usr/local/share/perl5/Ora2Pg.pm

    [root@dbserver ora2pg-24.3]# ls -lrt /usr/local/bin/ora2pg
    -r-xr-xr-x 1 root root 47746 Nov 16 00:20 /usr/local/bin/ora2pg

    [root@dbserver ora2pg-24.3]# ls -lrt /etc/ora2pg/ora2pg.conf.dist
    -rw-r--r-- 1 root root 70673 Nov 16 00:20 /etc/ora2pg/ora2pg.conf.dist

    We can have the Ora2Pg configuration file ora2pg.conf in a different location other than its default location (/etc/ora2pg), because we will be specifying the absolute path of the file on the command prompt when we execute the Ora2Pg tool.

- Change ownership of executable and directories.

    Change ownership of ora2pg executable to oracle:oinstall.

    [root@dbserver ora2pg-24.3]# ls -lrt /usr/local/bin/ora2pg
    -r-xr-xr-x 1 root root 47746 Nov 16 00:20 /usr/local/bin/ora2pg

    [root@dbserver ora2pg-24.3]# chown oracle:oinstall /usr/local/bin/ora2pg

    [root@dbserver ora2pg-24.3]# ls -lrt /usr/local/bin/ora2pg
    -r-xr-xr-x 1 oracle oinstall 47746 Nov 16 00:20 /usr/local/bin/ora2pg

Change ownership of /etc/ora2pg to oracle:oinstall.

[root@dbserver ora2pg-24.3]# ls -ld /etc/ora2pg
drwxr-xr-x 2 root root 30 Nov 16 00:20 /etc/ora2pg

[root@dbserver ora2pg-24.3]# chown -R oracle:oinstall /etc/ora2pg

[root@dbserver ora2pg-24.3]# ls -ld /etc/ora2pg
drwxr-xr-x 2 oracle oinstall 30 Nov 16 00:20 /etc/ora2pg

[root@dbserver ora2pg-24.3]# ls -lrt /etc/ora2pg
total 72
-rw-r--r-- 1 oracle oinstall 70673 Nov 16 00:20 ora2pg.conf.dist

Migration Phase: Migrate Oracle Schemas to PostgreSQL Database

One of the key features of migration phase is the use of ora2pg.conf configuration file.

ora2pg.conf is a significant configuration file having key variables that are to be used as an input for the migration operation. Let us look at some of the important variables or directives handled in this migration.

One of the most obvious sections in the configuration file is the Oracle variables used for Oracle database connectivity. Table 8-2 explains the variables and their usage.

Table 8-2. *Variables used in the ora2pg.conf file*

Variable	Usage
ORACLE_HOME	This environment variable is set as path to the Oracle libraries required by DBD::Oracle Perl module
ORACLE_DSN	This variable is used to set the Data Source Name (DSN), which includes the source Oracle db host IP, instance name, port to connect, etc., in a standard format. Used for database connectivity
ORACLE_USER	This variable defines the username that will connect to the source Oracle database. The user can be superuser or with the equivalent privileges as superuser or a normal user
ORACLE_PWD	This variable defines the password of the user connecting to the source Oracle database
USER_GRANTS	This variable value tells the type of user used for connectivity 0 (default) – Indicates the user is superuser or a user with equivalent privileges as superuser 1 – Indicates the user connecting is a normal user and is not connecting as a sysdba or with superuser privileges. Allows the access of ALL_* tables instead of DBA_* tables

Another important section in the configuration file is directives related to Oracle schema, which is to migrate to PostgreSQL database and is described in Table 8-3.

Table 8-3. *Variables used in the ora2pg.conf file*

Variable	Usage
EXPORT_SCHEMA	This parameter basically says export the create schema command including the DDL of all the objects inside the schema The parameter value is set to 0 by default, i.e., false If the value is set to 1, this will direct Ora2pg to generate the DDL for creating the schema with objects in PostgreSQL database
SCHEMA	This parameter allows a value as a single schema name. The data from the schemas mentioned in this parameter will be exported when the Ora2Pg tool is run
CREATE_SCHEMA	This parameter is enabled by default, i.e., the value as 1 indicates the create schema DDL is exported to the output file and ensures the schema is created in PostgreSQL before the objects are created
COMPILE_SCHEMA	By default, Ora2Pg will export only valid PL/SQL objects in a schema; in case any invalid PL/SQL objects exist, forcing this parameter will make Oracle compile the invalid objects before Ora2Pg exports their DDL.

In support of previously mentioned parameters, there are other directives related to export/import operations, target PostgreSQL connectivity, etc., described in Table 8-4.

Table 8-4. Variables used in the ora2pg.conf file

Variable	Usage
TYPE	This is the primary variable that makes Ora2Pg export the DDL of the objects listed here
OUTPUT	This parameter allows a value to be specified for output file where Ora2Pg is going to dump all data read from source database Compression option is also allowed for the output file
OUTPUT_DIR	This parameter defines the directory path to have the output file
FDW_IMPORT_SCHEMA	This parameter has the default value as ora2pg_fdw_import, and this is a temporary schema used to dump data from foreign schema, i.e., Oracle schema
DROP_FOREIGN_SCHEMA	This parameter has the default value as 1, which indicates the temporary schema that stores the foreign schema data to be dropped before each new import
PG_NUMERIC_TYPE	This parameter, if set to 1, converts Oracle data type number with precision p and scale s into PostgreSQL data type real and float
PG_INTEGER_TYPE	This parameter, if set to 1, converts Oracle data type number to PostgreSQL data type smallint, integer, or bigint
PG_DSN	This variable is used to set the Data Source Name (DSN), which includes the target PostgreSQL database host IP, database name, port to connect, etc., in a standard format
PG_USER	This variable defines the target PostgreSQL user name
PG_PWD	This variable defines the password of PostgreSQL user

If PostgreSQL connection parameters are specified in the configuration file, then Ora2Pg by default connects to Oracle database to pull the data and then automatically connects to PostgreSQL memory and copies the data directly into the postgres database.

If PostgreSQL connection parameters are not set, i.e., the parameters are commented out, then the default behavior of Ora2Pg is to dump the statements from source Oracle database schema into a single or multiple flat files.

One of the limitations of Ora2Pg is it is designed to migrate a single schema at a time. Multiple schema migration is not allowed. Hence, to migrate multiple schemas, separate migration for each schema needs to be performed.

As stated in the previous sections, we have three Oracle schemas – Human Resources (HR), Customer Orders (CO), and Sales History (SH) – to migrate to PostgreSQL database.

Migrating HR Schema Using Direct Load Method

Objects in HR Schema: Table, Index, View, Sequence, Procedure, Trigger

- As Oracle user, update configuration file.

  [oracle@dbserver ~]$ cd /etc/ora2pg

  [oracle@dbserver ora2pg]$ ls -lrt
  total 144
  -rw-r--r-- 1 oracle oinstall 70673 Nov 16 00:20 ora2pg.conf.dist

  [oracle@dbserver ora2pg]$ cp ora2pg.conf.dist ora2pg.conf

  [oracle@dbserver ora2pg]$ vi ora2pg.conf

  Set the below parameters in the ora2pg.conf file.

  ```
  ORACLE_HOME      /u01/app/oracle/product/19.3.0/dbhome_1
  ORACLE_DSN       dbi:Oracle:host=192.168.2.9;sid=orsrcdb;port=1521
  ORACLE_USER      system
  ORACLE_PWD       manager
  USER_GRANTS      1
  EXPORT_SCHEMA    1
  SCHEMA           HR
  TYPE             TABLE PARTITION
  OUTPUT           ora2pg_mig_hr_output.sql
  OUTPUT_DIR       /tmp
  PG_DSN           dbi:Pg:dbname=postgres;host=192.168.2.9;port=5432
  PG_USER          postgres
  PG_PWD           postgres
  ```

Validate the below parameter that they have default values.

```
CREATE_SCHEMA           1
COMPILE_SCHEMA          1
FDW_IMPORT_SCHEMA       ora2pg_fdw_import
DROP_FOREIGN_SCHEMA     1
PG_NUMERIC_TYPE         1
PG_INTEGER_TYPE         1
```

- Validate ora2pg version, installation, and configuration.

  [oracle@dbserver ~]$ ora2pg --version
  Ora2Pg v24.3

  [oracle@dbserver ~]$ ora2pg -t SHOW_VERSION -c /etc/ora2pg/ora2pg.conf
  Oracle Database 19c Enterprise Edition Release 19.0.0.0.0

- Generate migration estimate cost for HR schema.

  **[oracle@dbserver ~]$ ora2pg -t SHOW_REPORT --estimate_cost **
  **> -c /etc/ora2pg/ora2pg.conf **
  > --dump_as_html > /tmp/ora2pg_hr_mig.html

  [2024-11-16 16:59:53] [==========================>] 8/8 tables (100.0%) end of scanning.
  [2024-11-16 16:59:58] [==========================>] 10/10 objects types (100.0%) end of objects auditing.

  ora2pg_hr_mig.html - HR Schema Database Migration Report

Ora2Pg - Database Migration Report

Version Oracle Database 19c Enterprise Edition Release 19.0.0.0.0
Schema HR
Size 77.06 MB

Object	Number	Invalid	Estimated cost	Details
INDEX	19	0	3.00	▼ See details 11 b-tree index(es)
PROCEDURE	2	0	8.20	▼ See details secure_dml: 3.2 add_job_history: 3
SEQUENCE	3	0	1.00	
TABLE	8	0	1.20	▼ See details Total number of rows: 582 Top 10 of tables sorted by number of rows: employees_h has 366 rows employees has 107 rows departments has 27 rows countries has 25 rows locations has 23 rows jobs has 19 rows job_history has 10 rows regions has 5 rows Top 10 of largest tables:
TRIGGER	2	0	8.00	▼ See details secure_employees: 3 update_job_history: 3
VIEW	1	0	1.00	
Total	35	0	22.40	

Figure 8-2. HR Schema Ora2Pg migration report

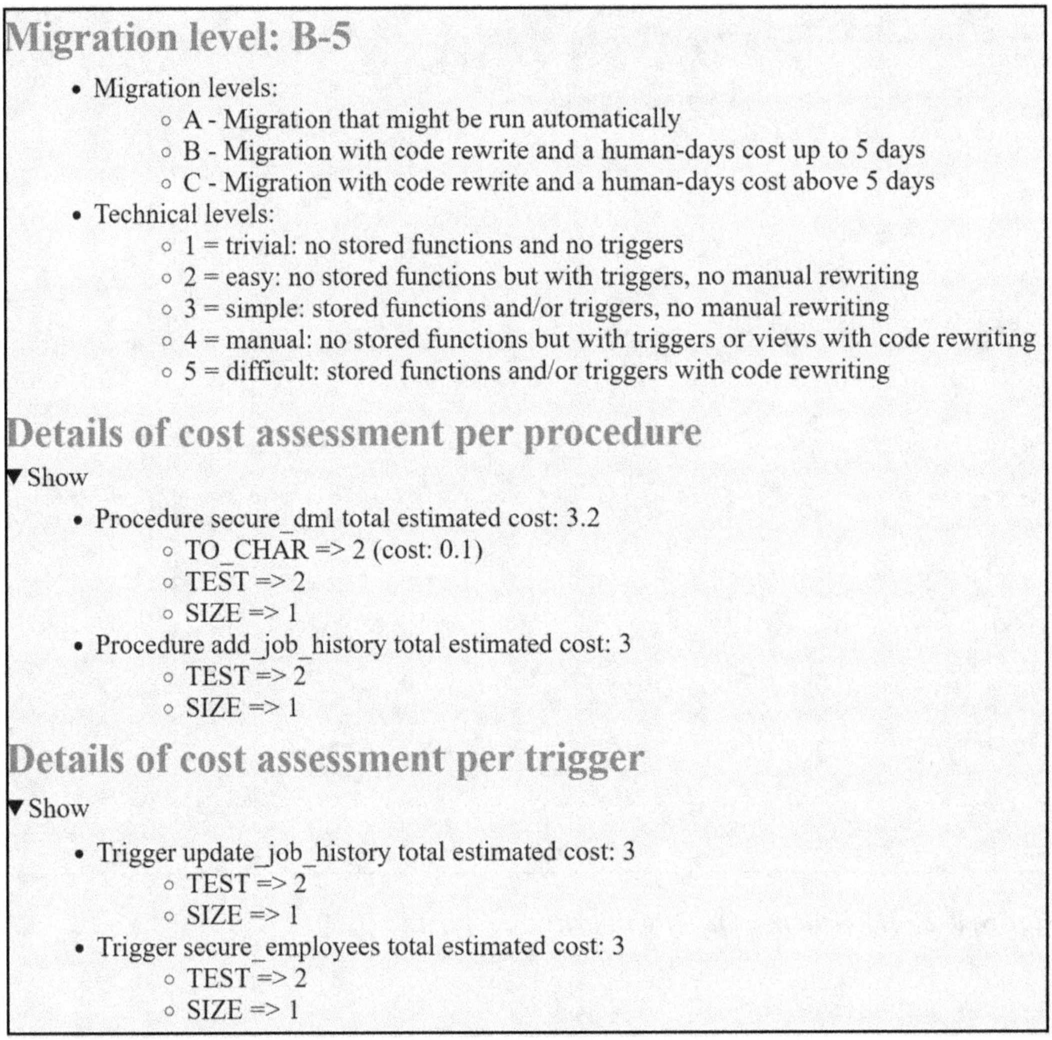

> **Migration level: B-5**
> - Migration levels:
>   - A - Migration that might be run automatically
>   - B - Migration with code rewrite and a human-days cost up to 5 days
>   - C - Migration with code rewrite and a human-days cost above 5 days
> - Technical levels:
>   - 1 = trivial: no stored functions and no triggers
>   - 2 = easy: no stored functions but with triggers, no manual rewriting
>   - 3 = simple: stored functions and/or triggers, no manual rewriting
>   - 4 = manual: no stored functions but with triggers or views with code rewriting
>   - 5 = difficult: stored functions and/or triggers with code rewriting
>
> **Details of cost assessment per procedure**
> ▼ Show
> - Procedure secure_dml total estimated cost: 3.2
>   - TO_CHAR => 2 (cost: 0.1)
>   - TEST => 2
>   - SIZE => 1
> - Procedure add_job_history total estimated cost: 3
>   - TEST => 2
>   - SIZE => 1
>
> **Details of cost assessment per trigger**
> ▼ Show
> - Trigger update_job_history total estimated cost: 3
>   - TEST => 2
>   - SIZE => 1
> - Trigger secure_employees total estimated cost: 3
>   - TEST => 2
>   - SIZE => 1

Figure 8-3. HR Schema Ora2Pg migration report

- Create a migration project.

    Ora2Pg migration project is a process of setting up a migration approach in a structured form of a project tree that creates subdirectories, configuration files, and scripts to perform export and import operations.

CHAPTER 8   DATA MIGRATION FROM ORACLE TO POSTGRESQL USING ORA2PG

Create a directory for migration and change ownership to Oracle.

[root@dbserver ~]# mkdir -p /var/lib/oracle/ora2pg_mig

[root@dbserver ~]# ls -ld /var/lib/oracle/ora2pg_mig
drwxr-xr-x 2 root root 6 Nov 16 17:22 /var/lib/oracle/ora2pg_mig

[root@dbserver ~]# chown -R oracle:oinstall /var/lib/oracle/ora2pg_mig

[root@dbserver ~]# ls -ld /var/lib/oracle/ora2pg_mig
drwxr-xr-x 2 oracle oinstall 6 Nov 16 17:22 /var/lib/oracle/ora2pg_mig

As Oracle user, create a migration project.

Since the ora2pg.conf file defined previously has SCHEMA directive value as HR, the project directory generated in this step will have specifications to perform migration operation of HR schema.

[oracle@dbserver ~]$ cd /var/lib/oracle/ora2pg_mig

[oracle@dbserver ora2pg_mig]$ which ora2pg
/usr/local/bin/ora2pg

**[oracle@dbserver ora2pg_mig]$ ora2pg --project_base /var/lib/oracle/ora2pg_mig **
**> --init_project hr_mig_proj **
> -c /etc/ora2pg/ora2pg.conf

```
Creating project hr_mig_proj.
/var/lib/oracle/ora2pg_mig/hr_mig_proj/
        schema/
                dblinks/
                directories/
                functions/
                grants/
                mviews/
                packages/
                partitions/
```

                    procedures/
                    sequences/
                    sequence_values/
                    synonyms/
                    tables/
                    tablespaces/
                    triggers/
                    types/
                    views/
            sources/
                    functions/
                    mviews/
                    packages/
                    partitions/
                    procedures/
                    triggers/
                    types/
                    views/
            data/
            config/
            reports/
Generating generic configuration file
Creating script export_schema.sh to automate all exports.
Creating script import_all.sh to automate all imports.

[oracle@dbserver ora2pg_mig]$ ls -lrt
total 0
drwxr-xr-x 7 oracle oinstall 121 Nov 16 17:27 hr_mig_proj

[oracle@dbserver ora2pg_mig]$ cd hr_mig_proj

[oracle@dbserver hr_mig_proj]$ ls -lrt
total 24
drwxr-xr-x 10 oracle oinstall 131 Nov 16 17:27 sources
drwxr-xr-x 18 oracle oinstall 268 Nov 16 17:27 schema
drwxr-xr-x 2 oracle oinstall   6 Nov 16 17:27 reports

```
-rwx------   1 oracle oinstall   2216 Nov 16 17:27 export_schema.sh
drwxr-xr-x   2 oracle oinstall      6 Nov 16 17:27 data
drwxr-xr-x   2 oracle oinstall     25 Nov 16 17:27 config
-rwx------   1 oracle oinstall  17175 Nov 16 17:27 import_all.sh
[oracle@dbserver hr_mig_proj]$
```

Review the content of the export_schema.sh script.

[oracle@dbserver hr_mig_proj]$ cat export_schema.sh

```
#!/bin/sh
#-------------------------------------------------------------------
#
# Generated by Ora2Pg, the Oracle database Schema converter, version 24.3
#
#-------------------------------------------------------------------
EXPORT_TYPE="SEQUENCE SEQUENCE_VALUES TABLE PACKAGE VIEW GRANT TRIGGER FUNCTION PROCEDURE TABLESPACE PARTITION TYPE MVIEW DBLINK SYNONYM DIRECTORY"
SOURCE_TYPE="PACKAGE VIEW TRIGGER FUNCTION PROCEDURE PARTITION TYPE MVIEW"
namespace="."
unit_cost=5

ora2pg -t SHOW_TABLE -c $namespace/config/ora2pg.conf > $namespace/reports/tables.txt
ora2pg -t SHOW_COLUMN -c $namespace/config/ora2pg.conf > $namespace/reports/columns.txt
ora2pg -t SHOW_REPORT -c $namespace/config/ora2pg.conf --dump_as_html --cost_unit_value $unit_cost --estimate_cost > $namespace/reports/report.html
```

<<<<< OUTPUT TRUNCATED >>>>>

CHAPTER 8   DATA MIGRATION FROM ORACLE TO POSTGRESQL USING ORA2PG

- Execute the export_schema script.

  This will export the DDL of all the various objects of HR schema from Oracle database *orsrcdb* to the respective object sql files under a subdirectory named schema.

  [oracle@dbserver hr_mig_proj]$ ./export_schema.sh

```
[2024-11-16] [>] 8/8 tables (100.0%) end of scanning.
[2024-11-16] [>] 10/10 objects types (100.0%) end of objects auditing.
Running: ora2pg -p -t SEQUENCE -o sequence.sql -b ./schema/sequences -c ./config/ora2pg.conf
[2024-11-16] [>] 3/3 sequences (100.0%) end of output.
Running: ora2pg -p -t SEQUENCE_VALUES -o sequence_value.sql -b ./schema/sequence_values -c ./config/ora2pg.conf
[2024-11-16] [>] 3/3 sequences (100.0%) end of output.
Running: ora2pg -p -t TABLE -o table.sql -b ./schema/tables -c ./config/ora2pg.conf
[2024-11-16] [>] 8/8 tables (100.0%) end of scanning.
[2024-11-16] [>] 8/8 tables (100.0%) end of table export.
Running: ora2pg -p -t VIEW -o view.sql -b ./schema/views -c ./config/ora2pg.conf
[2024-11-16] [>] 1/1 views (100.0%) end of output.
Running: ora2pg -p -t TRIGGER -o trigger.sql -b ./schema/triggers -c ./config/ora2pg.conf
[2024-11-16] [>] 2/2 triggers (100.0%) end of output.
Running: ora2pg -p -t PROCEDURE -o procedure.sql -b ./schema/procedures -c ./config/ora2pg.conf
[2024-11-16] [>] 2/2 procedures (100.0%) end of procedures export.
Running: ora2pg -t VIEW -o view.sql -b ./sources/views -c ./config/ora2pg.conf
[2024-11-16] [>] 1/1 views (100.0%) end of output.
Running: ora2pg -t TRIGGER -o trigger.sql -b ./sources/triggers -c ./config/ora2pg.conf
[2024-11-16] [>] 2/2 triggers (100.0%) end of output.
```

CHAPTER 8   DATA MIGRATION FROM ORACLE TO POSTGRESQL USING ORA2PG

```
Running: ora2pg -t PROCEDURE -o procedure.sql -b ./sources/
procedures -c ./config/ora2pg.conf
[2024-11-16] [>] 2/2 procedures (100.0%) end of procedures export.
```

To extract data use the following command:

```
ora2pg -t COPY -o data.sql -b ./data -c ./config/ora2pg.conf
```

```
[oracle@dbserver hr_mig_proj]$
```

- As postgres user, create a user named HR in postgres database. This is to avoid the errors related to grants while importing schema into PostgreSQL database.

  [root@dbserver ~]# sudo su - postgres

  [postgres@dbserver ~]$ psql
  psql (17.1)

  postgres=# create user hr;
  CREATE ROLE

  postgres=# \du
  ```
                              List of roles
   Role name |                       Attributes
  -----------+------------------------------------------------------
   hr        |
   postgres  | Superuser, Create role, Create DB, Replication,
             | Bypass RLS

  postgres=#
  ```

- PostgreSQL connection settings.

  Since the Ora2Pg tool will connect to postgres database, we need to update PostgreSQL configuration files to allow the remote connection to the database.

  As postgres user, update connection settings in pg_hba.conf.

521

CHAPTER 8 DATA MIGRATION FROM ORACLE TO POSTGRESQL USING ORA2PG

```
[postgres@dbserver ~]$ vi /var/lib/pgsql/17/data/pg_hba.conf
```

```
# "local" is for Unix domain socket connections only
local   all     all                             trust    <<< Change
keyword peer to trust

# IPv4 local connections:
host    all     all         192.168.2.9/32      trust    <<< Add
this line
host    all     postgres    192.168.2.9/32      trust    <<< Add
this line
```

Update postgresql.conf to include the IP address of host to allow incoming connection requests.

```
[postgres@dbserver ~]$ vi /var/lib/pgsql/17/data/postgresql.conf
```

```
listen_addresses = '192.168.2.9'     # what IP address(es) to
                                       listen on;
port = 5432                          # (change requires
                                       restart)
```

- As Oracle user, execute the import_all.sh script.

  The import_all.sh script will run in an interactive manner where it prompts for inputs for the operations to be performed.

  <<<<< OUTPUT TRUNCATED >>>>>

  ```
  [oracle@dbserver hr_mig_proj]$ ./import_all.sh -d postgres -o
  postgres -U postgres

  Database owner postgres already exists, skipping creation.
  Would you like to drop the database postgres before recreate it?
  [y/N/q] N
  Would you like to import SEQUENCE from ./schema/sequences/
  sequence.sql? [y/N/q] y
  Running: psql --single-transaction  -U postgres -d postgres -f
  ./schema/sequences/sequence.sql
  ```

Would you like to import SEQUENCE_VALUES from ./schema/sequence_values/sequence_value.sql? [y/N/q] **y**
Running: psql --single-transaction -U postgres -d postgres -f ./schema/sequence_values/sequence_value.sql
Would you like to import TABLE from ./schema/tables/table.sql? [y/N/q] **y**
Running: psql --single-transaction -U postgres -d postgres -f ./schema/tables/table.sql
psql:schema/tables/table.sql:9: NOTICE: schema "hr" already exists,
Would you like to import VIEW from ./schema/views/view.sql? [y/N/q] **y**
Running: psql --single-transaction -U postgres -d postgres -f ./schema/views/view.sql
Would you like to import TRIGGER from ./schema/triggers/trigger.sql? [y/N/q] **N**
Would you like to import PROCEDURE from ./schema/procedures/procedure.sql? [y/N/q] **y**
Running: psql --single-transaction -U postgres -d postgres -f ./schema/procedures/procedure.sql
psql:schema/procedures/procedure.sql:23: NOTICE: type reference job_history.employee_id%TYPE converted to integer
psql:schema/procedures/procedure.sql:23: NOTICE: type reference job_history.start_date%TYPE converted to timestamp without time zone
psql:schema/procedures/procedure.sql:23: NOTICE: type reference job_history.end_date%TYPE converted to timestamp without time zone
psql:schema/procedures/procedure.sql:23: NOTICE: type reference job_history.job_id%TYPE converted to character varying
psql:schema/procedures/procedure.sql:23: NOTICE: type reference job_history.department_id%TYPE converted to smallint
CREATE PROCEDURE
Would you like to process indexes and constraints before loading data? [y/N/q] **N**

CHAPTER 8   DATA MIGRATION FROM ORACLE TO POSTGRESQL USING ORA2PG

Would you like to import data from Oracle database directly into PostgreSQL? [y/N/q] y
Running: ora2pg -c config/ora2pg.conf -t COPY --pg_dsn "dbi:Pg:dbname=postgres;host=192.168.2.9;port=5432" --pg_user postgres
[2024-11-16] [>] 8/8 tables (100.0%) end of scanning.
.
[2024-11-16] [>] 25/25 rows (100.0%) Table COUNTRIES (25 recs/sec)
[2024-11-16] [>] 25/582 total rows (4.3%) - (0 sec., avg: 25 recs/sec).
[2024-11-16] [>] 25/582 rows (4.3%) on total estimated data
.
[2024-11-16] [>] 27/27 rows (100.0%) Table DEPARTMENTS (27 recs/sec)
[2024-11-16] [>] 52/582 total rows (8.9%) - (0 sec., avg: 52 recs/sec).
[2024-11-16] [>] 52/582 rows (8.9%) on total estimated data
.
[2024-11-16] [>] 107/107 rows (100.0%) Table EMPLOYEES (107 recs/sec)
[2024-11-16] [>] 159/582 total rows (27.3%) - (0 sec., avg: 159 recs/sec).
[2024-11-16] [>] 159/582 rows (27.3%) on total estimated data
.
[2024-11-16] [>] 366/366 rows (100.0%) Table EMPLOYEES_H (366 recs/sec)
[2024-11-16] [>] 525/582 total rows (90.2%) - (0 sec., avg: 525 recs/sec).
[2024-11-16] [>] 525/582 rows (90.2%) on total estimated data
.
[2024-11-16] [>] 19/19 rows (100.0%) Table JOBS (19 recs/sec)
[2024-11-16] [>] 544/582 total rows (93.5%) - (0 sec., avg: 544 recs/sec).
[2024-11-16] [>] 544/582 rows (93.5%) on total estimated data
.
[2024-11-16] [>] 10/10 rows (100.0%) Table JOB_HISTORY (10 recs/sec)

CHAPTER 8   DATA MIGRATION FROM ORACLE TO POSTGRESQL USING ORA2PG

```
[2024-11-16] [>] 554/582 total rows (95.2%) - (0 sec., avg: 554
recs/sec).
[2024-11-16] [>] 554/582 rows (95.2%) on total estimated data
.
[2024-11-16] [>] 23/23 rows (100.0%) Table LOCATIONS (23 recs/sec)
[2024-11-16] [>] 577/582 total rows (99.1%) - (0 sec., avg: 577
recs/sec).
[2024-11-16] [>] 577/582 rows (99.1%) on total estimated data
.
[2024-11-16] [>] 5/5 rows (100.0%) Table REGIONS (5 recs/sec)
[2024-11-16] [=====>] 582/582 total rows (100.0%) - (0 sec., avg:
582 recs/sec).
[2024-11-16] [>] 582/582 rows (100.0%) on total estimated data
Would you like to import TRIGGER from ./schema/triggers/trigger.
sql? [y/N/q] y
Running: psql --single-transaction  -U postgres -d postgres -f ./
schema/triggers/trigger.sql

[oracle@dbserver hr_mig_proj]$
```

Response as "y" to the below prompt confirms the data to be loaded directly from Oracle database into postgres schema. This uses the PG_DSN directive from ora2pg.conf.

```
Would you like to import data from Oracle database directly into
PostgreSQL? [y/N/q] y
```

Ora2Pg migrates object type triggers of Oracle database to PostgreSQL database by defining a separate function and then creating a trigger that calls this function. The same can be validated through DDL of trigger exported and converted to PostgreSQL-compatible syntax.

Snippet from file: /var/lib/oracle/ora2pg_mig/hr_mig_proj/schema/triggers/trigger.sql

```
CREATE OR REPLACE FUNCTION trigger_fct_secure_employees() RETURNS
trigger AS $BODY$
```

```
BEGIN
  CALL secure_dml();
IF TG_OP = 'DELETE' THEN
        RETURN OLD;
ELSE
        RETURN NEW;
END IF;
END
$BODY$
 LANGUAGE 'plpgsql' SECURITY DEFINER;

CREATE TRIGGER secure_employees
        BEFORE INSERT OR UPDATE OR DELETE ON employees FOR EACH
        STATEMENT
        EXECUTE PROCEDURE trigger_fct_secure_employees();
```

- Validation of imported data.

  Once the import is performed, we can validate the migration in two ways: one using the Ora2Pg tool itself and the other using manual validation.

  Ora2Pg provides an option called TEST, which performs the validation of number of objects in source Oracle HR schema and target PostgreSQL HR schema.

  In addition to the count of objects, we can even compare the number of rows in each table migrated from source to target using --count_rows along with option TEST.

  As Oracle user, generate a comparison report using Ora2Pg.

  [oracle@dbserver hr_mig_proj]$ ora2pg -c config/ora2pg. conf -t TEST --count_rows > ora2pg_test_hr_objects.log

  [oracle@dbserver hr_mig_proj]$ ls -lrt ora2pg_test_hr_ objects.log

  -rw-r--r-- 1 oracle oinstall 6648 Nov 16 20:35 ora2pg_test_hr_ objects.log

  [oracle@dbserver hr_mig_proj]$ cat ora2pg_test_hr_ objects.log

[TEST COLUMNS COUNT]
OK, Oracle and PostgreSQL have the same number of columns.
.

[TEST INDEXES COUNT]
OK, Oracle and PostgreSQL have the same number of indexes.
.

[TEST UNIQUE CONSTRAINTS COUNT]
OK, Oracle and PostgreSQL have the same number of unique constraints.
.

[TEST PRIMARY KEYS COUNT]
OK, Oracle and PostgreSQL have the same number of primary keys.
.

[TEST CHECK CONSTRAINTS COUNT]
OK, Oracle and PostgreSQL have the same number of check constraints.
.

[TEST NOT NULL CONSTRAINTS COUNT]
OK, Oracle and PostgreSQL have the same number of not null constraints.
.

[TEST FOREIGN KEYS COUNT]
OK, Oracle and PostgreSQL have the same number of foreign keys.
.

[TEST TABLE COUNT]
ORACLEDB:TABLE:8
POSTGRES:TABLE:8
OK, Oracle and PostgreSQL have the same number of TABLE.
.

[TEST TABLE TRIGGERS COUNT]
OK, Oracle and PostgreSQL have the same number of table triggers.
.

[TEST TRIGGER COUNT]
OK, Oracle and PostgreSQL have the same number of TRIGGER.
.

[TEST VIEW COUNT]
OK, Oracle and PostgreSQL have the same number of VIEW.
.
[TEST SEQUENCE COUNT]
OK, Oracle and PostgreSQL have the same number of SEQUENCE.
.
[TEST FUNCTION COUNT]
OK, Oracle and PostgreSQL have the same number of FUNCTION.
[TEST ROWS COUNT]
ORACLEDB:COUNTRIES:25
POSTGRES:hr.countries:25
ORACLEDB:DEPARTMENTS:27
POSTGRES:hr.departments:27
ORACLEDB:EMPLOYEES:107
POSTGRES:hr.employees:107
ORACLEDB:EMPLOYEES_H:366
POSTGRES:hr.employees_h:366
ORACLEDB:JOBS:19
POSTGRES:hr.jobs:19
ORACLEDB:JOB_HISTORY:10
POSTGRES:hr.job_history:10
ORACLEDB:LOCATIONS:23
POSTGRES:hr.locations:23
ORACLEDB:REGIONS:5
POSTGRES:hr.regions:5
[ERRORS ROWS COUNT]
OK, Oracle and PostgreSQL have the same number of rows.
[oracle@dbserver hr_mig_proj]$

Perform manual validation of schema objects and tables row count of PostgreSQL HR schema comparing with Oracle HR schema.

[postgres@dbserver ~]$ psql
psql (17.1)

postgres=# \dn
        List of schemas

```
 Name   | Owner
--------+-------------------
 hr     | hr
 public | pg_database_owner
(2 rows)

postgres=# SELECT relname AS object_name,
           CASE WHEN relkind='S' THEN 'sequence'
               WHEN relkind='i' THEN 'index'
               WHEN relkind='v' THEN 'view'
               ELSE 'table'
           END AS object_type
           FROM pg_class c JOIN pg_namespace n ON n.oid =
           c.relnamespace
           WHERE n.nspname = 'hr'
           ORDER BY object_type;

      object_name       | object_type
------------------------+-------------
 countries_pkey         | index
 departments_pkey       | index
 emp_department_ix      | index
 emp_job_ix             | index
 emp_manager_ix         | index
 emp_name_ix            | index
 employees_email_key    | index
 employees_pkey         | index
 loc_state_province_ix  | index
 jhist_department_ix    | index
 jhist_employee_ix      | index
 jhist_job_ix           | index
 job_history_pkey       | index
 locations_pkey         | index
 regions_pkey           | index
 loc_city_ix            | index
 loc_country_ix         | index
```

```
             jobs_pkey             | index
             dept_location_ix      | index
             departments_seq       | sequence
             employees_seq         | sequence
             locations_seq         | sequence
             employees_h           | table
             regions               | table
             countries             | table
             locations             | table
             departments           | table
             employees             | table
             jobs                  | table
             job_history           | table
             emp_details_view      | view
(31 rows)
```

```
postgres=# SELECT p.proname AS object_name,
           CASE WHEN p.prokind = 'p' THEN 'procedure'
               WHEN p.prokind = 'f' THEN 'function'
               ELSE 'unknown'
           END AS object_type
           FROM pg_proc p JOIN pg_namespace n ON n.oid =
           p.pronamespace
           WHERE n.nspname = 'hr';
```

```
  object_name                      | object_type
-----------------------------------+-------------
  add_job_history                  | procedure
  secure_dml                       | procedure
  trigger_fct_secure_employees     | function
  trigger_fct_update_job_history   | function
(4 rows)
```

```
postgres=# SELECT schemaname, relname AS table_name, n_live_tup AS
row_count
           FROM pg_stat_user_tables
           WHERE schemaname = 'hr'
```

ORDER BY n_live_tup;

```
 schemaname | table_name  | row_count
------------+-------------+-----------
 hr         | regions     |         5
 hr         | job_history |        10
 hr         | jobs        |        19
 hr         | locations   |        23
 hr         | countries   |        25
 hr         | departments |        27
 hr         | employees   |       107
 hr         | employees_h |       366
(8 rows)
```

The output details are compared to the details captured in Task 2, and since everything looks good, we conclude the successful migration of HR schema from Oracle to PostgreSQL.

Migrating CO Schema Using COPY (Bulk Load) Method

In COPY mode, Ora2Pg generates a COPY command that loads data in bulk manner from a file or standard input. This mode is highly efficient and significantly faster, especially for large datasets.

Objects in CO Schema: Table, Index, View, Sequence

- Update the below parameter values in the /etc/ora2pg/ora2pg. conf file.

    The same configuration file is used with few directive value changes.

    ```
    SCHEMA          CO
    OUTPUT          ora2pg_mig_co_output.sql
    ```

- Generate migration estimate cost for CO schema.

CHAPTER 8 DATA MIGRATION FROM ORACLE TO POSTGRESQL USING ORA2PG

```
[oracle@dbserver ~]$ ora2pg -t
SHOW_REPORT --estimate_cost \
> -c /etc/ora2pg/ora2pg.conf \
> --dump_as_html > /tmp/ora2pg_co_mig.html
```

[2024-11-16] [=========================>] 9/9 tables (100.0%) end of scanning.
[2024-11-16] [=========================>] 7/7 objects types (100.0%) end of objects auditing.
[oracle@dbserver ~]$

ora2pg_co_mig.html - CO Schema Database Migration Report

Ora2Pg - Database Migration Report

Version	Oracle Database 19c Enterprise Edition Release 19.0.0.0.0			
Schema	CO			
Size	77.06 MB			

Object	Number	Invalid	Estimated cost	Details
INDEX	18	0	2.50	▼ See details 7 b-tree index(es)
TABLE	9	0	1.40	▼ See details Total number of rows: 51739 Top 10 of tables sorted by number of rows: orders_h has 27300 rows order_items_h has 15656 rows order_items has 3914 rows orders has 1950 rows shipments has 1892 rows inventory has 566 rows customers has 392 rows products has 46 rows stores has 23 rows Top 10 of largest tables:
VIEW	4	3	1.00	
Total	31	3	4.90	

Migration level: A-1

- Migration levels:
  - A - Migration that might be run automatically

Figure 8-4. CO Schema Ora2Pg migration report

- As Oracle user, create a migration project.

CHAPTER 8 DATA MIGRATION FROM ORACLE TO POSTGRESQL USING ORA2PG

Since the ora2pg.conf file has SCHEMA directive value as CO, the project directory generated in this step will have specifications to perform migration operation of CO schema.

```
[oracle@dbserver ~]$ ora2pg --project_base /var/lib/oracle/ora2pg_mig \
> --init_project co_mig_proj \
> -c /etc/ora2pg/ora2pg.conf
Creating project co_mig_proj.
/var/lib/oracle/ora2pg_mig/co_mig_proj/
        schema/
                dblinks/
                directories/
                functions/
                grants/
                mviews/
                packages/
                partitions/
                procedures/
                sequences/
                sequence_values/
                synonyms/
                tables/
                tablespaces/
                triggers/
                types/
                views/
        sources/
                functions/
                mviews/
                packages/
                partitions/
                procedures/
                triggers/
                types/
```

CHAPTER 8   DATA MIGRATION FROM ORACLE TO POSTGRESQL USING ORA2PG

```
            views/
     data/
     config/
     reports/
```

```
Generating generic configuration file
Creating script export_schema.sh to automate all exports.
Creating script import_all.sh to automate all imports.
[oracle@dbserver ~]$
```

[oracle@dbserver ~]$ cd /var/lib/oracle/ora2pg_mig

[oracle@dbserver ora2pg_mig]$ ls -lrt
```
total 0
drwxr-xr-x 7 oracle oinstall 176 Nov 16 20:34 hr_mig_proj
drwxr-xr-x 7 oracle oinstall 121 Nov 17 11:52 co_mig_proj
```

[oracle@dbserver ora2pg_mig]$ cd co_mig_proj

[oracle@dbserver co_mig_proj]$ ls -lrt
```
total 24
drwxr-xr-x 10 oracle oinstall   131 Nov 17 11:52 sources
drwxr-xr-x 18 oracle oinstall   268 Nov 17 11:52 schema
drwxr-xr-x  2 oracle oinstall     6 Nov 17 11:52 reports
drwxr-xr-x  2 oracle oinstall     6 Nov 17 11:52 data
-rwx------  1 oracle oinstall 17175 Nov 17 11:52 import_all.sh
-rwx------  1 oracle oinstall  2216 Nov 17 11:52 export_schema.sh
drwxr-xr-x  2 oracle oinstall    25 Nov 17 11:52 config
[oracle@dbserver co_mig_proj]$
```

- Execute the export_schema script.

    This will export the DDL of all the various objects of CO schema from Oracle database orsrcdb to the respective object sql files under a subdirectory named schema.

    [oracle@dbserver co_mig_proj]$ ./export_schema.sh
    ```
    [2024-11-17] [>] 9/9 tables (100.0%) end of scanning.
    [2024-11-17] [>] 7/7 objects types (100.0%) end of objects auditing.
    ```

```
[2024-11-17] [>] 9/9 tables (100.0%) end of scanning.
[2024-11-17] [>] 9/9 tables (100.0%) end of table export.
Running: ora2pg -p -t VIEW -o view.sql -b ./schema/views -c ./
config/ora2pg.conf
[2024-11-17] [>] 4/4 views (100.0%) end of output.
Running: ora2pg -t VIEW -o view.sql -b ./sources/views -c ./
config/ora2pg.conf
[2024-11-17] [>] 4/4 views (100.0%) end of output.
```

To extract data use the following command:

ora2pg -t COPY -o data.sql -b ./data -c ./config/ora2pg.conf

```
[oracle@dbserver co_mig_proj]$
```

Please make a note of the ora2pg -t COPY command from the above output, as this will be used to load data in subsequent steps.

- As postgres user, create a user named CO in postgres database. This is to avoid the errors related to grants while importing schema into PostgreSQL database.

[postgres@dbserver ~]$ psql
```
psql (17.1)
```

postgres=# create user co;
```
CREATE ROLE
```

postgres=# \du
```
                          List of roles
  Role name |                     Attributes
 -----------+-----------------------------------------------------
  co        |
  hr        |
  postgres  | Superuser, Create role, Create DB, Replication,
            | Bypass RLS

postgres=#
```

- As Oracle user, execute the import_all.sh script.

CHAPTER 8   DATA MIGRATION FROM ORACLE TO POSTGRESQL USING ORA2PG

The import_all.sh script will execute in an interactive manner where it prompts for inputs for the operations to be performed.

<<<<< OUTPUT TRUNCATED >>>>>

[oracle@dbserver co_mig_proj]$ ./import_all.sh -d postgres -o postgres -U postgres

Database owner postgres already exists, skipping creation.
Would you like to drop the database postgres before recreate it? [y/N/q] **N**
Would you like to import SEQUENCE from ./schema/sequences/sequence.sql? [y/N/q] **y**
Running: psql --single-transaction -U postgres -d postgres -f ./schema/sequences/sequence.sql
Would you like to import SEQUENCE_VALUES from ./schema/sequence_values/sequence_value.sql? [y/N/q] **y**
Running: psql --single-transaction -U postgres -d postgres -f ./schema/sequence_values/sequence_value.sql
Would you like to import TABLE from ./schema/tables/table.sql? [y/N/q] **y**
Running: psql --single-transaction -U postgres -d postgres -f ./schema/tables/table.sql
psql:schema/tables/table.sql:9: NOTICE: schema "co" already exists, skipping
Would you like to import VIEW from ./schema/views/view.sql? [y/N/q] **y**
Running: psql --single-transaction -U postgres -d postgres -f ./schema/views/view.sql
Would you like to process indexes and constraints before loading data? [y/N/q] **y**
Would you like to import data from Oracle database directly into PostgreSQL? [y/N/q] N
[oracle@dbserver co_mig_proj]$

Response as "N" to this prompt will stop the data load into PostgreSQL database.

CHAPTER 8   DATA MIGRATION FROM ORACLE TO POSTGRESQL USING ORA2PG

Would you like to import data from Oracle database directly into PostgreSQL? [y/N/q] **N**

- Run the ora2pg COPY command copied from the output of the export_schema step previously.

<<<<< OUTPUT TRUNCATED >>>>>

[oracle@dbserver co_mig_proj]$ ora2pg -t COPY -o data.sql -b ./data -c ./config/ora2pg.conf

[2024-11-17] [>] 9/9 tables (100.0%) end of scanning.

[2024-11-17] [>] 392/392 rows (100.0%) Table CUSTOMERS (392 recs/sec)
[2024-11-17] [>] 392/51739 total rows (0.8%) - (1 sec., avg: 392 recs/sec).
[2024-11-17] [>] 392/51739 rows (0.8%) on total estimated data.

[2024-11-17] [>] 566/566 rows (100.0%) Table INVENTORY (566 recs/sec)
[2024-11-17] [>] 958/51739 total rows (1.9%) - (1 sec., avg: 958 recs/sec).
[2024-11-17] [>] 958/51739 rows (1.9%) on total estimated data.

[2024-11-17] [>] 1950/1950 rows (100.0%) Table ORDERS (1950 recs/sec)
[2024-11-17] [>] 2908/51739 total rows (5.6%) - (1 sec., avg: 2908 recs/sec).
[2024-11-17] [>] 2908/51739 rows (5.6%) on total estimated data.

[2024-11-17] [>] 27300/27300 rows (100.0%) Table ORDERS_H (27300 recs/sec)
[2024-11-17] [>] 30208/51739 total rows (58.4%) - (1 sec., avg: 30208 recs/sec).
[2024-11-17] [>] 30208/51739 rows (58.4%) on total estimated data.

```
[2024-11-17] [>] 3914/3914 rows (100.0%) Table ORDER_ITEMS (3914 recs/sec)
[2024-11-17] [>] 34122/51739 total rows (66.0%) - (1 sec., avg: 34122 recs/sec).
[2024-11-17] [>] 34122/51739 rows (66.0%) on total estimated data.
[2024-11-17] [>] 15656/15656 rows(100.0%) Table ORDER_ITEMS_H(15656 recs/sec)
[2024-11-17] [>] 49778/51739 total rows(96.2%)-(2 sec.,avg: 24889 recs/sec).
[2024-11-17] [>] 49778/51739 rows (96.2%) on total estimated data.
[2024-11-17] [>] 46/46 rows (100.0%) Table PRODUCTS (46 recs/sec)
[2024-11-17] [>] 49824/51739 total rows(96.3%)-(2 sec.,avg: 24912 recs/sec).
[2024-11-17] [>] 49824/51739 rows (96.3%) on total estimated data.
[2024-11-17] [>] 1892/1892 rows (100.0%) Table SHIPMENTS (1892 recs/sec)
[2024-11-17] [>] 51716/51739 total rows(100.0%) -(2 sec.,avg:25858 recs/sec).
[2024-11-17] [>] 51716/51739 rows (100.0%) on total estimated data.
[2024-11-17] [>] 23/23 rows (100.0%) Table STORES (23 recs/sec)
[2024-11-17] [>] 51739/51739 total rows(100.0%)-(2 sec.,avg: 25869 recs/sec).
[2024-11-17] [>] 51739/51739 rows (100.0%) on total estimated data
[oracle@dbserver co_mig_proj]$
```

- Validation of imported data

  As Oracle user, generate a comparison report.

  ```
  [oracle@dbserver co_mig_proj]$ ora2pg -c config/ora2pg.conf -t TEST --count_rows > ora2pg_test_co_objects.log
  [oracle@dbserver co_mig_proj]$ ls -lrt ora2pg_test_co_objects.log
  ```

```
-rw-r--r-- 1 oracle oinstall 6580 Nov 17 13:48 ora2pg_test_co_
objects.log
```

[oracle@dbserver co_mig_proj]$ cat ora2pg_test_co_objects.log
```
[TEST COLUMNS COUNT]
OK, Oracle and PostgreSQL have the same number of columns.
.
[TEST INDEXES COUNT]
OK, Oracle and PostgreSQL have the same number of indexes.
.
[TEST UNIQUE CONSTRAINTS COUNT]
OK, Oracle and PostgreSQL have the same number of unique
constraints.
.
[TEST PRIMARY KEYS COUNT]
OK, Oracle and PostgreSQL have the same number of primary keys.
.
[TEST CHECK CONSTRAINTS COUNT]
OK, Oracle and PostgreSQL have the same number of check
constraints.
.
[TEST NOT NULL CONSTRAINTS COUNT]
OK, Oracle and PostgreSQL have the same number of not null
constraints.
.
[TEST FOREIGN KEYS COUNT]
OK, Oracle and PostgreSQL have the same number of foreign keys.
.
[TEST TABLE COUNT]
ORACLEDB:TABLE:9
POSTGRES:TABLE:9
[ERRORS TABLE COUNT]
OK, Oracle and PostgreSQL have the same number of TABLE.
.
[TEST VIEW COUNT]
```

```
[ERRORS VIEW COUNT]
OK, Oracle and PostgreSQL have the same number of VIEW.
[TEST ROWS COUNT]
ORACLEDB:CUSTOMERS:392
POSTGRES:co.customers:392
ORACLEDB:INVENTORY:566
POSTGRES:co.inventory:566
ORACLEDB:ORDERS:1950
POSTGRES:co.orders:1950
ORACLEDB:ORDERS_H:27300
POSTGRES:co.orders_h:27300
ORACLEDB:ORDER_ITEMS:3914
POSTGRES:co.order_items:3914
ORACLEDB:ORDER_ITEMS_H:15656
POSTGRES:co.order_items_h:15656
ORACLEDB:PRODUCTS:46
POSTGRES:co.products:46
ORACLEDB:SHIPMENTS:1892
POSTGRES:co.shipments:1892
ORACLEDB:STORES:23
POSTGRES:co.stores:23
[ERRORS ROWS COUNT]
```
OK, Oracle and PostgreSQL have the same number of rows.
```
[oracle@dbserver co_mig_proj]$
```

Perform manual validation of schema objects and tables row count of PostgreSQL CO schema comparing with Oracle CO schema.

[postgres@dbserver ~]$ psql
```
psql (17.1)
```

postgres=# \dn
```
      List of schemas
```

```
  Name   |      Owner
---------+--------------------
 co      | co
 hr      | hr
 public  | pg_database_owner
(3 rows)

postgres=# SELECT relname AS object_name,
           CASE WHEN relkind='S' THEN 'sequence'
                WHEN relkind='i' THEN 'index'
                WHEN relkind='v' THEN 'view'
                ELSE 'table'
           END AS object_type
           FROM pg_class c JOIN pg_namespace n ON n.oid =
           c.relnamespace
           WHERE n.nspname = 'co'
           ORDER BY object_type;
```

object_name	object_type
products_pkey	index
customers_name_i	index
shipments_customer_id_i	index
shipments_store_id_i	index
shipments_pkey	index
inventory_product_id_i	index
inventory_store_id_product_id_key	index
inventory_pkey	index
customers_email_address_key	index
orders_customer_id_i	index
orders_store_id_i	index
orders_pkey	index
stores_pkey	index
order_items_shipment_id_i	index
order_items_pkey	index
order_items_product_id_order_id_key	index

```
 stores_store_name_key          | index
 customers_pkey                 | index
 customers_customer_id_seq      | sequence
 inventory_inventory_id_seq     | sequence
 orders_order_id_seq            | sequence
 products_product_id_seq        | sequence
 shipments_shipment_id_seq      | sequence
 stores_store_id_seq            | sequence
 order_items_h                  | table
 orders_h                       | table
 products                       | table
 inventory                      | table
 stores                         | table
 customers                      | table
 orders                         | table
 order_items                    | table
 shipments                      | table
 product_orders                 | view
 customer_order_products        | view
 product_reviews                | view
 store_orders                   | view
(37 rows)
```

```
postgres=# SELECT schemaname, relname AS table_name, n_live_tup AS row_count
            FROM pg_stat_user_tables
            WHERE schemaname = 'co'
            ORDER BY n_live_tup;
```

```
 schemaname | table_name  | row_count
------------+-------------+-----------
 co         | stores      |        23
 co         | products    |        46
 co         | customers   |       392
 co         | inventory   |       566
```

```
co         | shipments      |     1892
co         | orders         |     1950
co         | order_items    |     3914
co         | order_items_h  |    15656
co         | orders_h       |    27300
(9 rows)
```

The output details are compared to the details captured in Task 2, and since everything looks good, we conclude the successful migration of CO schema from Oracle to PostgreSQL.

Migrating SH Schema Using INSERT Method

In INSERT mode, Ora2Pg generates individual INSERT statements for each row of data from source Oracle tables to load into PostgreSQL tables. This method is slightly slower than COPY method due to the overhead of transaction management.

Objects in SH Schema: Table, Table Partition, Index, Index Partition, View, Materialized View

- Update the below parameter values in the /etc/ora2pg/ora2pg. conf file.

  The same configuration file is used with few directive value changes.

  ```
  SCHEMA           SH
  TYPE             TABLE PARTITION INSERT
  REPLACE_TABLES   TIMES:SALE_TIMES COSTS:SALE_COSTS
  OUTPUT           ora2pg_mig_hr_output.sql
  ```

  Ora2Pg provides a directive called REPLACE_TABLES, which allows us to rename table names in target postgres database during migration.

  In this scenario, table TIMES will be renamed SALE_TIMES, and COSTS will be renamed SALE_COSTS.

- Generate migration estimate cost for CO schema.

  ```
  [oracle@dbserver ~]$ ora2pg -t SHOW_REPORT
  --estimate_cost \
  ```

CHAPTER 8   DATA MIGRATION FROM ORACLE TO POSTGRESQL USING ORA2PG

> **-c /etc/ora2pg/ora2pg.conf **
> **--dump_as_html > /tmp/ora2pg_sh_mig.html**
[2024-11-18] [>] 9/9 tables (100.0%) end of scanning.
[2024-11-18] [>] 10/10 objects types (100.0%) end of objects auditing.
[oracle@dbserver ~]$

ora2pg_sh_mig.html - SH Schema Database Migration Report

Ora2Pg - Database Migration Report

Version: Oracle Database 19c Enterprise Edition Release 19.0.0.0.0
Schema: SH
Size: 77.06 MB

Object	Number	Invalid	Estimated cost	Details
INDEX	21	0	3.50	▼ See details 11 bitmap index(es) 1 domain index(es) 2 b-tree index(es)
INDEX PARTITION	115	0	0.00	
MATERIALIZED VIEW	2	0	6.00	
TABLE	9	0	1.00	▼ See details Total number of rows: 112 Top 10 of tables sorted by number of rows: products has 72 rows countries has 35 rows channels has 5 rows Top 10 of largest tables:
TABLE PARTITION	35	0	3.50	▼ See details RANGE
VIEW	1	0	1.00	
Total	183	0	15.00	

Migration level: A-1

- Migration levels:
  - A - Migration that might be run automatically

Figure 8-5. SH Schema Ora2Pg migration report

- As Oracle user, create a migration project.

Since the ora2pg.conf file defined previously has SCHEMA directive value as SH, the project directory generated in this step will have specifications to perform migration operation of SH schema.

```
[oracle@dbserver ~]$ ora2pg --project_base /var/lib/oracle/ora2pg_mig \
> --init_project sh_mig_proj \
> -c /etc/ora2pg/ora2pg.conf
Creating project sh_mig_proj.
/var/lib/oracle/ora2pg_mig/sh_mig_proj/
        schema/
                dblinks/
                directories/
                functions/
                grants/
                mviews/
                packages/
                partitions/
                procedures/
                sequences/
                sequence_values/
                synonyms/
                tables/
                tablespaces/
                triggers/
                types/
                views/
        sources/
                functions/
                mviews/
                packages/
                partitions/
                procedures/
                triggers/
                types/
```

CHAPTER 8   DATA MIGRATION FROM ORACLE TO POSTGRESQL USING ORA2PG

```
                    views/
           data/
           config/
           reports/
```

```
Generating generic configuration file
Creating script export_schema.sh to automate all exports.
Creating script import_all.sh to automate all imports.
[oracle@dbserver ~]$
```

[oracle@dbserver ~]$ cd /var/lib/oracle/ora2pg_mig

[oracle@dbserver ora2pg_mig]$ ls -lrt
```
total 0
drwxr-xr-x 7 oracle oinstall 176 Nov 16 20:34 hr_mig_proj
drwxr-xr-x 7 oracle oinstall 268 Nov 17 13:46 co_mig_proj
drwxr-xr-x 7 oracle oinstall 121 Nov 18 01:29 sh_mig_proj
```

[oracle@dbserver ora2pg_mig]$ cd sh_mig_proj

[oracle@dbserver sh_mig_proj]$ ls -lrt
```
total 24
drwxr-xr-x 10 oracle oinstall   131 Nov 18 01:29 sources
drwxr-xr-x 18 oracle oinstall   268 Nov 18 01:29 schema
drwxr-xr-x  2 oracle oinstall     6 Nov 18 01:29 reports
-rwx------  1 oracle oinstall 17175 Nov 18 01:29 import_all.sh
-rwx------  1 oracle oinstall  2216 Nov 18 01:29 export_schema.sh
drwxr-xr-x  2 oracle oinstall     6 Nov 18 01:29 data
drwxr-xr-x  2 oracle oinstall    25 Nov 18 01:29 config
[oracle@dbserver sh_mig_proj]$
```

- Execute the export_schema script.

    This will export the DDL of all the various objects of SH schema from Oracle database orsrcdb to the respective object sql files under a subdirectory named schema.

    [oracle@dbserver sh_mig_proj]$ ./export_schema.sh
    ```
    [2024-11-18] [>] 9/9 tables (100.0%) end of scanning.
    ```

[2024-11-18] [>] 10/10 objects types (100.0%) end of objects auditing.
.
Running: ora2pg -p -t TABLE -o table.sql -b ./schema/tables -c ./config/ora2pg.conf
[2024-11-18] [>] 9/9 tables (100.0%) end of scanning.
[2024-11-18] [>] 9/9 tables (100.0%) end of table export.
.
Running: ora2pg -p -t VIEW -o view.sql -b ./schema/views -c ./config/ora2pg.conf
[2024-11-18] [>] 1/1 views (100.0%) end of output.
.
Running: ora2pg -p -t PARTITION -o partition.sql -b ./schema/partitions -c ./config/ora2pg.conf
[2024-11-18] [>] 35/35 partitions (100.0%) end of output.
.
Running: ora2pg -p -t MVIEW -o mview.sql -b ./schema/mviews -c ./config/ora2pg.conf
[2024-11-18] [>] 2/2 materialized views (100.0%) end of output.
.
Running: ora2pg -t VIEW -o view.sql -b ./sources/views -c ./config/ora2pg.conf
[2024-11-18] [>] 1/1 views (100.0%) end of output.
.
Running: ora2pg -t PARTITION -o partition.sql -b ./sources/partitions -c ./config/ora2pg.conf
[2024-11-18] [>] 35/35 partitions (100.0%) end of output.
.
Running: ora2pg -t MVIEW -o mview.sql -b ./sources/mviews -c ./config/ora2pg.conf
[2024-11-18] [>] 2/2 materialized views (100.0%) end of output.

To extract data use the following command:

ora2pg -t INSERT -o data.sql -b ./data -c ./config/ora2pg.conf

[oracle@dbserver sh_mig_proj]$

CHAPTER 8   DATA MIGRATION FROM ORACLE TO POSTGRESQL USING ORA2PG

Please make a note of the ora2pg -t INSERT command from the above output, as this will be used to load data in subsequent steps.

- As postgres user, create a user named SH in postgres database. This is to avoid the errors related to grants while importing schema into PostgreSQL database.

[postgres@dbserver ~]$ psql
psql (17.1)

postgres=# create user sh;
CREATE ROLE

postgres=# \du
```
                           List of roles
  Role name  |                    Attributes
-------------+------------------------------------------------------
  co         |
  hr         |
  sh         |
  postgres   | Superuser, Create role, Create DB, Replication,
             | Bypass RLS

postgres=#
```

- As Oracle user, execute the import_all.sh script.

The import_all.sh script will execute in an interactive manner where it prompts for inputs for the operations to be performed.

<<<<< OUTPUT TRUNCATED >>>>>

[oracle@dbserver sh_mig_proj]$ ./import_all.sh -d postgres -o postgres -U postgres

Database owner postgres already exists, skipping creation.
Would you like to drop the database postgres before recreate it? [y/N/q] **N**
Would you like to import SEQUENCE from ./schema/sequences/sequence.sql? [y/N/q] **y**

CHAPTER 8　DATA MIGRATION FROM ORACLE TO POSTGRESQL USING ORA2PG

Running: psql --single-transaction -U postgres -d postgres -f ./schema/sequences/sequence.sql
Would you like to import SEQUENCE_VALUES from ./schema/sequence_values/sequence_value.sql? [y/N/q] **y**
Running: psql --single-transaction -U postgres -d postgres -f ./schema/sequence_values/sequence_value.sql
Would you like to import TABLE from ./schema/tables/table.sql? [y/N/q] **y**
Running: psql --single-transaction -U postgres -d postgres -f ./schema/tables/table.sql
psql:schema/tables/table.sql:9: NOTICE: schema "sh" already exists, skipping
Would you like to import VIEW from ./schema/views/view.sql? [y/N/q] **y**
Running: psql --single-transaction -U postgres -d postgres -f ./schema/views/view.sql
Would you like to import PARTITION from ./schema/partitions/partition.sql? [y/N/q] **y**
Running: psql --single-transaction -U postgres -d postgres -f ./schema/partitions/partition.sql
Would you like to import MVIEW from ./schema/mviews/mview.sql? [y/N/q] **y**
Running: psql --single-transaction -U postgres -d postgres -f ./schema/mviews/mview.sql
Would you like to process indexes and constraints before loading data? [y/N/q] **N**

Would you like to import data from Oracle database directly into PostgreSQL? [y/N/q] N

[oracle@dbserver sh_mig_proj]$

Response as "N" to the below prompt will stop the data load into PostgreSQL database.

CHAPTER 8   DATA MIGRATION FROM ORACLE TO POSTGRESQL USING ORA2PG

>   Would you like to import data from Oracle database directly into
>   PostgreSQL? [y/N/q] **N**

- Run the ora2pg INSERT command copied from the output of the export_schema step previously.

  <<<<< OUTPUT TRUNCATED >>>>>

  [oracle@dbserver sh_mig_proj]$ ora2pg -t INSERT -o data.sql -b ./ data -c ./config/ora2pg.conf

  ```
  [2024-11-18] [>] 9/9 tables (100.0%) end of scanning.
  [2024-11-18] [>] 5/5 rows (100.0%) Table CHANNELS (5 recs/sec)
  [2024-11-18] [>] 5/112 total rows (4.5%) - (0 sec., avg: 5 recs/sec).
  [2024-11-18] [>] 5/112 rows (4.5%) on total estimated data
  .
  [2024-11-18] [>] 35/35 rows (100.0%) Table COUNTRIES (35 recs/sec)
  [2024-11-18] [>] 40/112 total rows (35.7%) - (1 sec., avg: 40 recs/sec).
  [2024-11-18] [>] 40/112 rows (35.7%) on total estimated data
  .
  [2024-11-18] [>] 72/72 rows (100.0%) Table PRODUCTS (72 recs/sec)
  [2024-11-18] [>] 112/112 total rows (100.0%) - (1 sec., avg: 112 recs/sec).
  [2024-11-18] [>] 112/112 rows (100.0%) on total estimated data
  ```

  [oracle@dbserver sh_mig_proj]$

- Validation of imported data.

  As Oracle user, generate a comparison report.

  [oracle@dbserver sh_mig_proj]$ ora2pg -c config/ora2pg.conf -t TEST --count_rows > ora2pg_test_sh_objects.log
  [oracle@dbserver sh_mig_proj]$ ls -lrt ora2pg_test_sh_objects.log
  -rw-r--r-- 1 oracle oinstall 7313 Nov 18 03:07 ora2pg_test_sh_objects.log

CHAPTER 8　DATA MIGRATION FROM ORACLE TO POSTGRESQL USING ORA2PG

[oracle@dbserver sh_mig_proj]$ cat ora2pg_test_sh_objects.log
[TEST COLUMNS COUNT]
OK, Oracle and PostgreSQL have the same number of columns.

[TEST INDEXES COUNT]
OK, Oracle and PostgreSQL have the same number of indexes.
.
[TEST PRIMARY KEYS COUNT]
OK, Oracle and PostgreSQL have the same number of primary keys.
.
[TEST FOREIGN KEYS COUNT]
OK, Oracle and PostgreSQL have the same number of foreign keys.
.
[TEST PARTITION COUNT]
OK, Oracle and PostgreSQL have the same number of PARTITION.
.
[TEST TABLE COUNT]
ORACLEDB:TABLE:9
POSTGRES:TABLE:9
[ERRORS TABLE COUNT]
OK, Oracle and PostgreSQL have the same number of TABLE.
.
[TEST VIEW COUNT]
OK, Oracle and PostgreSQL have the same number of VIEW.
.
[TEST MVIEW COUNT]
OK, Oracle and PostgreSQL have the same number of MVIEW.
[TEST ROWS COUNT]
ORACLEDB:CHANNELS:5
POSTGRES:sh.channels:5
ORACLEDB:COSTS:0
POSTGRES:sh.sale_costs (origin: COSTS):0
ORACLEDB:COUNTRIES:35
POSTGRES:sh.countries:35
ORACLEDB:CUSTOMERS:0
POSTGRES:sh.customers:0

```
ORACLEDB:PRODUCTS:72
POSTGRES:sh.products:72
ORACLEDB:PROMOTIONS:0
POSTGRES:sh.promotions:0
ORACLEDB:SALES:0
POSTGRES:sh.sales:0
ORACLEDB:SUPPLEMENTARY_DEMOGRAPHICS:0
POSTGRES:sh.supplementary_demographics:0
ORACLEDB:TIMES:0
POSTGRES:sh.sale_times (origin: TIMES):0
[ERRORS ROWS COUNT]
```
OK, Oracle and PostgreSQL have the same number of rows.
```
[oracle@dbserver sh_mig_proj]$
```

Perform manual validation of schema objects and tables row count of PostgreSQL SH schema comparing with Oracle SH schema.

[postgres@dbserver ~]$ psql
```
psql (17.1)
```

postgres=# \dn
```
      List of schemas
  Name   |       Owner
---------+-------------------
 co      | co
 hr      | hr
 sh      | sh
 public  | pg_database_owner

(4 rows)
```

postgres=# SELECT schemaname, relname AS table_name, n_live_tup AS row_count
```
          FROM pg_stat_user_tables
          WHERE schemaname = 'sh'
          ORDER BY table_name,n_live_tup;
```

CHAPTER 8 DATA MIGRATION FROM ORACLE TO POSTGRESQL USING ORA2PG

```
schemaname | table_name  | row_count
-----------+-------------+----------
 sh        | channels    |         5
 sh        | countries   |        35
 sh        | products    |        72
 sh        | sale_costs  |         0
 sh        | sale_times  |         0

postgres=#
```

The output data is compared to the data captured in Task 2, and since everything looks good, we conclude the successful migration of SH schema from Oracle to PostgreSQL.

With the completion of this section, we have successfully migrated three Oracle database schemas to PostgreSQL-compatible schemas.

Migration Issues

During the migration of individual schemas from Oracle database to PostgreSQL database, there were a few different issues encountered. Migration was resumed and completed successfully after identifying the cause for each issue and providing a solution.

Given below are the references of issues along with cause and solution.

ISSUE 1: ERROR: cannot cast type bytea to json

- This error was reported during import of CO schema into postgres database when adding a check constraint on the *products* table.

    [oracle@dbserver co_mig_proj]$ ./import_all.sh -d postgres -o postgres -U postgres

    ```
    Database owner postgres already exists, skipping creation.
    Would you like to drop the database postgres before recreate it?
    [y/N/q] N
    Would you like to import SEQUENCE from ./schema/sequences/sequence.sql? [y/N/q] y
    Would you like to import SEQUENCE_VALUES from ./schema/sequence_values/sequence_value.sql? [y/N/q] y
    ```

Would you like to import TABLE from ./schema/tables/table.sql? [y/N/q] y
psql:schema/tables/table.sql:9: NOTICE: schema "co" already exists, skipping
ALTER TABLE
psql:schema/tables/table.sql:158: ERROR: cannot cast type bytea to json
ERROR: an error occurs when importing file ./schema/tables/table.sql.
[oracle@dbserver co_mig_proj]$

CAUSE

1. The CO.PRODUCTS.PRODUCT_ID column in Oracle database is of BLOB data type that got converted to bytea data type in PostgreSQL database.

Oracle database:

SQL> desc co.products

Name	Null?	Type
PRODUCT_DETAILS		**BLOB**

Import file: /var/lib/oracle/ora2pg_mig/co_mig_proj/schema/tables/table.sql

```
CREATE TABLE products (
        product_id bigint GENERATED BY DEFAULT AS IDENTITY (START
        WITH 47 INCREMENT BY 1 MAXVALUE 9223372036854775807
        MINVALUE 1 NO CYCLE CACHE 20 ),
        product_name varchar(255) NOT NULL,
        unit_price double precision,
        product_details bytea,
        product_image bytea,
        image_mime_type varchar(512),
```

```
        image_filename varchar(512),
        image_charset varchar(512),
        image_last_updated timestamp(0)
);
```

2. The CASE clause in ALTER TABLE tries to cast the product_details (bytea) column to json and perform a check.

   Import file: /var/lib/oracle/ora2pg_mig/co_mig_proj/schema/tables/table.sql

   ```
   152 COMMENT ON COLUMN products.product_details IS E'Further details of the product stored in JSON format';

   158 ALTER TABLE products ADD CONSTRAINT products_json_c CHECK
   ( (CASE WHEN product_details::json IS NULL THEN true ELSE true END));
   ```

SOLUTION

- Added the encode() function to the product_details column, which converts the column data to textual format and casts to json

  Import file: /var/lib/oracle/ora2pg_mig/co_mig_proj/schema/tables/table.sql

  ```
  158 ALTER TABLE products ADD CONSTRAINT products_json_c CHECK
  ( (CASE WHEN encode(product_details,'escape')::json IS NULL THEN true ELSE true END));
  ```

ISSUE 2: ERROR: foreign key constraint "inventory_product_id_fk" cannot be implemented

- This error was reported during import of CO schema into postgres database when adding a foreign key constraint to the *inventory* table.

  [oracle@dbserver co_mig_proj]$ ./import_all.sh -d postgres -o postgres -U postgres

  ```
  Database owner postgres already exists, skipping creation.
  ```

CHAPTER 8 DATA MIGRATION FROM ORACLE TO POSTGRESQL USING ORA2PG

```
Would you like to drop the database postgres before recreate it?
[y/N/q] N
Would you like to import SEQUENCE from ./schema/sequences/
sequence.sql? [y/N/q] y
Would you like to import SEQUENCE_VALUES from ./schema/sequence_
values/sequence_value.sql? [y/N/q] y
Would you like to import TABLE from ./schema/tables/table.sql?
[y/N/q] y
Running: psql --single-transaction  -U postgres -d postgres -f ./
schema/tables/table.sql
ALTER TABLE
```
**psql:schema/tables/table.sql:223: ERROR: foreign key constraint
"inventory_product_id_fk" cannot be implemented
DETAIL: Key columns "product_id" and "product_id" are of
incompatible types: numeric and bigint.
ERROR: an error occurs when importing file ./schema/tables/
table.sql.**
```
[oracle@dbserver co_mig_proj]$
```

CAUSE

- Data type mismatch found for column (product_id) of parent table (*products*) and child table (*inventory*). Hence, this reported an error when creating foreign key constraint on the *inventory* table.

Import file: /var/lib/oracle/ora2pg_mig/co_mig_proj/schema/tables/table.sql

```
32 CREATE TABLE inventory (
33         inventory_id bigint GENERATED BY DEFAULT AS
           IDENTITY (START WITH 567 INCREMENT BY 1 MAXVALUE
           9223372036854775807 MINVALUE 1 NO CYCLE CACHE 20 ),
34         store_id numeric(38) NOT NULL,
35         product_id numeric(38) NOT NULL,
36         product_inventory numeric(38) NOT NULL
37 ) ;

136 CREATE TABLE products (
```

CHAPTER 8   DATA MIGRATION FROM ORACLE TO POSTGRESQL USING ORA2PG

```
137        product_id bigint GENERATED BY DEFAULT AS
           IDENTITY (START WITH 47 INCREMENT BY 1 MAXVALUE
           9223372036854775807 MINVALUE 1 NO CYCLE CACHE 20 ),
138        product_name varchar(255) NOT NULL,
139        unit_price double precision,
140        product_details bytea,
141        product_image bytea,
142        image_mime_type varchar(512),
143        image_filename varchar(512),
144        image_charset varchar(512),
145        image_last_updated timestamp(0)
146 ) ;
```

223 ALTER TABLE inventory ADD CONSTRAINT inventory_product_id_fk FOREIGN KEY (product_id) REFERENCES products(product_id) ON DELETE NO ACTION DEFERRABLE INITIALLY IMMEDIATE;

SOLUTION

- Modified data type for column *inventory.product_id* in the table.
  sql file

Import file: /var/lib/oracle/ora2pg_mig/co_mig_proj/schema/tables/table.sql

```
32 CREATE TABLE inventory (
33        inventory_id bigint GENERATED BY DEFAULT AS
          IDENTITY (START WITH 567 INCREMENT BY 1 MAXVALUE
          9223372036854775807 MINVALUE 1 NO CYCLE CACHE 20 ),
34        store_id bigint NOT NULL,
35        product_id bigint NOT NULL,
36        product_inventory bigint NOT NULL
37 ) ;
```

ISSUE 3: ERROR: cannot cast type bytea to jsonb

- This error was reported during import of CO schema into postgres database when creating a view *product_reviews*.

557

CHAPTER 8   DATA MIGRATION FROM ORACLE TO POSTGRESQL USING ORA2PG

[oracle@dbserver co_mig_proj]$ ./import_all.sh -d postgres -o postgres -U postgres

Database owner postgres already exists, skipping creation.
Would you like to drop the database postgres before recreate it? [y/N/q] N
Would you like to import SEQUENCE from ./schema/sequences/sequence.sql? [y/N/q] y
Would you like to import SEQUENCE_VALUES from ./schema/sequence_values/sequence_value.sql? [y/N/q] y
Would you like to import TABLE from ./schema/tables/table.sql? [y/N/q] y
Would you like to import VIEW from ./schema/views/view.sql? [y/N/q] y
Running: psql --single-transaction -U postgres -d postgres -f ./schema/views/view.sql
CREATE VIEW
psql:schema/views/view.sql:71: ERROR: cannot cast type bytea to jsonb
LINE 11:   p.product_details, '$'
                       ^

ERROR: an error occurs when importing file ./schema/views/view.sql.
[oracle@dbserver co_mig_proj]$

CAUSE

- Column *products.product_details* with data type bytea is referred inside json_table in a view *product_reviews* definition.

Import file: /var/lib/oracle/ora2pg_mig/co_mig_proj/schema/views/view.sql

```
53 CREATE OR REPLACE VIEW product_reviews (product_name, rating,
    avg_rating, review) AS SELECT p.product_name, r.rating,
54       round((
55           AVG( r.rating ) over (
56               PARTITION BY product_name
```

```
57              ))::numeric,
58              2
59           ) avg_rating,
60           r.review
61    FROM   products p,
62           JSON_TABLE(
63             p.product_details, '$'
64             COLUMNS(
65               NESTED PATH '$.reviews[*]'
66               COLUMNS(
67                 rating INTEGER PATH '$.rating',
68                 review VARCHAR2(4000) PATH '$.review'
69               )
70             )
71           ) r;
```

SOLUTION

- Added the encode() function to the *product_details* column, which converts the binary data to textual format that can be used in a JSONB object.

Import file: /var/lib/oracle/ora2pg_mig/co_mig_proj/schema/views/view.sql

```
53 CREATE OR REPLACE VIEW product_reviews_n (product_name,
   rating, avg_rating, review) AS SELECT p.product_name,
   r.rating,
54           round((
55             AVG( r.rating ) over (
56               PARTITION BY product_name
57             ))::numeric,
58             2
59           ) avg_rating,
60           r.review
61    FROM   products p,
62           JSON_TABLE(
```

CHAPTER 8   DATA MIGRATION FROM ORACLE TO POSTGRESQL USING ORA2PG

```
63                encode(p.product_details,'base64'), '$'
64             COLUMNS(
65               NESTED PATH '$.reviews[*]'
66               COLUMNS(
67                 rating INTEGER PATH '$.rating',
68                 review VARCHAR2(4000) PATH '$.review'
69               )
70             )
71           ) r;
```

ISSUE 4: ERROR: type "varchar2" does not exist

- This error was reported during import of CO schema into postgres database when creating a view *product_reviews*.

[oracle@dbserver co_mig_proj]$ ./import_all.sh -d postgres -o postgres -U postgres

Database owner postgres already exists, skipping creation.
Would you like to drop the database postgres before recreate it? [y/N/q] N
Would you like to import SEQUENCE from ./schema/sequences/sequence.sql? [y/N/q] y
Would you like to import SEQUENCE_VALUES from ./schema/sequence_values/sequence_value.sql? [y/N/q] y
Would you like to import TABLE from ./schema/tables/table.sql? [y/N/q] y
Would you like to import VIEW from ./schema/views/view.sql? [y/N/q] y
Running: psql --single-transaction -U postgres -d postgres -f ./schema/views/view.sql
psql:schema/views/view.sql:71: ERROR: type "varchar2" does not exist
LINE 16:   review VARCHAR2(4000) PATH '$.review'
                                             ^
ERROR: an error occurs when importing file ./schema/views/view.sql.
[oracle@dbserver co_mig_proj]$

560

CHAPTER 8 DATA MIGRATION FROM ORACLE TO POSTGRESQL USING ORA2PG

CAUSE

- Data type conversion from varchar2 to varchar didn't happen during view *product_reviews* definition export.

  Import file: /var/lib/oracle/ora2pg_mig/co_mig_proj/ schema/views/view.sql

  ```
  53 CREATE OR REPLACE VIEW product_reviews (product_name, rating,
  avg_rating, review) AS SELECT p.product_name, r.rating,
  54          round((
  55             AVG( r.rating ) over (
  56                PARTITION BY product_name
  57             ))::numeric,
  58             2
  59          ) avg_rating,
  60          r.review
  61   FROM   products p,
  62          JSON_TABLE(
  63             p.product_details, '$'
  64             COLUMNS(
  65                NESTED PATH '$.reviews[*]'
  66                COLUMNS(
  67                   rating INTEGER PATH '$.rating',
  68                   review VARCHAR2(4000) PATH '$.review'
  69                )
  70             )
  71          ) r;
  ```

SOLUTION

- Modified data type from VARCHAR2 to VARCHAR in *product_reviews* view definition in file view.sql.

  Import file: /var/lib/oracle/ora2pg_mig/co_mig_proj/ schema/views/view.sql

  ```
  53 CREATE OR REPLACE VIEW product_reviews (product_name, rating,
       avg_rating, review) AS SELECT p.product_name, r.rating,
  ```

CHAPTER 8　DATA MIGRATION FROM ORACLE TO POSTGRESQL USING ORA2PG

```
54              round((
55                AVG( r.rating ) over (
56                  PARTITION BY product_name
57              ))::numeric,
58              2
59            ) avg_rating,
60            r.review
61     FROM   products p,
62            JSON_TABLE(
63              encode(p.product_details,'escape'), '$'
64              COLUMNS(
65                NESTED PATH '$.reviews[*]'
66                COLUMNS(
67                  rating INTEGER PATH '$.rating',
68                  review VARCHAR(4000) PATH '$.review'
69                )
70              )
71            ) r;
```

ISSUE 5: ERROR: function grouping_id(character varying, character varying) does not exist

- This error was reported during import of CO schema into postgres database when creating a view *store_orders*.

[oracle@dbserver co_mig_proj]$ ./import_all.sh -d postgres -o postgres -U postgres

Database owner postgres already exists, skipping creation.
Would you like to drop the database postgres before recreate it? [y/N/q] N
Would you like to import SEQUENCE from ./schema/sequences/sequence.sql? [y/N/q] y
Would you like to import SEQUENCE_VALUES from ./schema/sequence_values/sequence_value.sql? [y/N/q] y
Would you like to import TABLE from ./schema/tables/table.sql? [y/N/q] y

CHAPTER 8   DATA MIGRATION FROM ORACLE TO POSTGRESQL USING ORA2PG

Would you like to import VIEW from ./schema/views/view.sql?
[y/N/q] y
Running: psql --single-transaction -U postgres -d postgres -f
./schema/views/view.sql
CREATE VIEW
**psql:schema/views/view.sql:101: ERROR: function grouping_
id(character varying, character varying) does not exist
LINE 2:   grouping_id(store_name, order_status)
                    ^**

**HINT: No function matches the given name and argument types. You
might need to add explicit type casts.
ERROR: an error occurs when importing file ./schema/views/
view.sql.**
[oracle@dbserver co_mig_proj]$

CAUSE

- Oracle internal function grouping_id in view store_orders definition caused the issue as it is not supported in postgres.

Import file: /var/lib/oracle/ora2pg_mig/co_mig_proj/schema/views/view.sql

```
79 CREATE OR REPLACE VIEW store_orders (total, store_name,
   address, latitude, longitude, order_status, order_count, total_
   sales) AS SELECT CASE
   80          grouping_id( store_name, order_status )
   81            WHEN 1 THEN 'STORE TOTAL'
   82            WHEN 2 THEN 'STATUS TOTAL'
   83            WHEN 3 THEN 'GRAND TOTAL'
   84          END total,
   85          s.store_name,
   86          COALESCE( s.web_address, s.physical_address )
               address,
   87          s.latitude, s.longitude,
   88          o.order_status,
   89          COUNT( DISTINCT o.order_id ) order_count,
   90          SUM( oi.quantity * oi.unit_price ) total_sales
```

```
 91   FROM    stores s
 92   JOIN    orders o
 93   ON      s.store_id = o.store_id
 94   JOIN    order_items oi
 95   ON      o.order_id = oi.order_id
 96   GROUP BY GROUPING SETS (
 97     ( s.store_name, COALESCE( s.web_address, s.physical_address ), s.latitude, s.longitude ),
 98     ( s.store_name, COALESCE( s.web_address, s.physical_address ), s.latitude, s.longitude, o.order_status ),
 99     o.order_status,
100     ()
101   );
```

SOLUTION

- This required a manual intervention to change the definition of view store_orders as no automatic conversion happened.

  Replaced *grouping_id()* with the *grouping()* function in view *store_orders* definition.

  Import file: /var/lib/oracle/ora2pg_mig/co_mig_proj/schema/views/view.sql

```
79 CREATE OR REPLACE VIEW store_orders (total, store_name, address, latitude, longitude, order_status, order_count, total_sales) AS SELECT CASE
80          grouping( store_name, order_status )
81            WHEN 1 THEN 'STORE TOTAL'
82            WHEN 2 THEN 'STATUS TOTAL'
83            WHEN 3 THEN 'GRAND TOTAL'
84          END total,
85          s.store_name,
86          COALESCE( s.web_address, s.physical_address ) address,
87          s.latitude, s.longitude,
88          o.order_status,
```

```
 89           COUNT( DISTINCT o.order_id ) order_count,
 90           SUM( oi.quantity * oi.unit_price ) total_sales
 91    FROM   stores s
 92    JOIN   orders o
 93    ON     s.store_id = o.store_id
 94    JOIN   order_items oi
 95    ON     o.order_id = oi.order_id
 96    GROUP  BY GROUPING SETS (
 97      ( s.store_name, COALESCE( s.web_address, s.physical_
         address ), s.latitude, s.longitude ),
 98      ( s.store_name, COALESCE( s.web_address, s.physical_
         address ), s.latitude, s.longitude, o.order_status ),
 99      o.order_status,
100      ()
101    );
```

ISSUE 6: ERROR: insert or update on table "inventory" violates foreign key constraint "inventory_product_id_fk"

This error was reported during the data load into postgres CO schema for table inventory.

[oracle@dbserver co_mig_proj]$ ora2pg -t COPY -o data.sql -b ./data -c ./config/ora2pg.conf

[2024-11-17] [>] 9/9 tables (100.0%) end of scanning.
[2024-11-17] [>] 392/392 rows (100.0%) Table CUSTOMERS (392 recs/sec)
[2024-11-17] [>] 392/51739 total rows (0.8%) - (0 sec., avg: 392 recs/sec).
[2024-11-17] [>] 392/51739 rows (0.8%) on total estimated data

FATAL: ERROR: insert or update on table "inventory" violates foreign key constraint "inventory_product_id_fk"
DETAIL: Key (product_id)=(19) is not present in table "products".
Aborting export...
[oracle@dbserver co_mig_proj]$

CHAPTER 8   DATA MIGRATION FROM ORACLE TO POSTGRESQL USING ORA2PG

CAUSE

1. No implicit parent-child table relation maintained by Ora2Pg during data load.

2. Foreign key constraint restricted the data insertion into inventory table due to missing rows in parent table products.

SOLUTION

- Disabled triggers on table *inventory* that deferred the constraints. Then loaded the data and re-enabled the triggers after data load.

   postgres database:

   postgres=# alter table co.inventory disable trigger all;
   ALTER TABLE

   postgres=# \d co.inventory
   ```
                                 Table "co.inventory"
        Column       |  Type  | Nullable | Default
   ------------------+--------+----------+----------------------------
    inventory_id     | bigint | not null | generated by default as
                                           identity
    store_id         | bigint | not null |
    product_id       | bigint | not null |
    product_inventory| bigint | not null |
   Indexes:
       "inventory_pkey" PRIMARY KEY, btree (inventory_id)
       "inventory_product_id_i" btree (product_id)
       "inventory_store_id_product_id_key" UNIQUE CONSTRAINT, btree
       (store_id, product_id)
   Foreign-key constraints:
       "inventory_product_id_fk" FOREIGN KEY (product_id) REFERENCES
       co.products(product_id) DEFERRABLE
       "inventory_store_id_fk" FOREIGN KEY (store_id) REFERENCES
       co.stores(store_id) DEFERRABLE
   ```
   Disabled internal triggers:

CHAPTER 8   DATA MIGRATION FROM ORACLE TO POSTGRESQL USING ORA2PG

```
"RI_ConstraintTrigger_c_20523" AFTER INSERT ON co.inventory
FROM co.products DEFERRABLE INITIALLY IMMEDIATE FOR EACH ROW
EXECUTE FUNCTION "RI_FKey_check_ins"()
"RI_ConstraintTrigger_c_20524" AFTER UPDATE ON co.inventory
FROM co.products DEFERRABLE INITIALLY IMMEDIATE FOR EACH ROW
EXECUTE FUNCTION "RI_FKey_check_upd"()
"RI_ConstraintTrigger_c_20528" AFTER INSERT ON co.inventory
FROM co.stores DEFERRABLE INITIALLY IMMEDIATE FOR EACH ROW
EXECUTE FUNCTION "RI_FKey_check_ins"()
"RI_ConstraintTrigger_c_20529" AFTER UPDATE ON co.inventory
FROM co.stores DEFERRABLE INITIALLY IMMEDIATE FOR EACH ROW
EXECUTE FUNCTION "RI_FKey_check_upd"()
```

<< Executed ora2pg -t COPY -o data.sql -b ./data -c ./config/ora2pg.conf >>

postgres=# alter table co.inventory enable trigger all;
```
ALTER TABLE
```

postgres=# \d co.inventory
```
                          Table "co.inventory"
      Column       | Type   | Nullable | Default
-------------------+--------+----------+--------------------------
 inventory_id      | bigint | not null | generated by default as
                                         identity
 store_id          | bigint | not null |
 product_id        | bigint | not null |
 product_inventory | bigint | not null |
Indexes:
    "inventory_pkey" PRIMARY KEY, btree (inventory_id)
    "inventory_product_id_i" btree (product_id)
    "inventory_store_id_product_id_key" UNIQUE CONSTRAINT, btree
    (store_id, product_id)
Foreign-key constraints:
    "inventory_product_id_fk" FOREIGN KEY (product_id) REFERENCES
    co.products(product_id) DEFERRABLE
```

CHAPTER 8   DATA MIGRATION FROM ORACLE TO POSTGRESQL USING ORA2PG

```
            "inventory_store_id_fk" FOREIGN KEY (store_id) REFERENCES
            co.stores(store_id) DEFERRABLE
```

ISSUE 7: ERROR: data type bigint has no default operator class for access method "gin"

- This error was reported during import of SH schema into postgres database when creating an index costs_prod_bix on table sale_costs.

[oracle@dbserver sh_mig_proj]$ ./import_all.sh -d postgres -o postgres -U postgres

```
Database owner postgres already exists, skipping creation.
Would you like to drop the database postgres before recreate it?
[y/N/q] N
Would you like to import SEQUENCE from ./schema/sequences/
sequence.sql? [y/N/q] y
Would you like to import SEQUENCE_VALUES from ./schema/sequence_
values/sequence_value.sql? [y/N/q] y
Would you like to import TABLE from ./schema/tables/table.sql?
[y/N/q] y
Running: psql --single-transaction  -U postgres -d postgres -f
./schema/tables/table.sql
```
psql:schema/tables/table.sql:44: ERROR: data type bigint has no default operator class for access method "gin"
HINT: You must specify an operator class for the index or define a default operator class for the data type.
ERROR: an error occurs when importing file ./schema/tables/table.sql.
[oracle@dbserver sh_mig_proj]$

CAUSE

1. The BITMAP index *costs_prod_bix* of Oracle is converted into BTREE_GIN (Generalized Inverted Index) in PostgreSQL.

2. The index creation failed due to no default operator class is specified for the bigint data type column *sale_costs.prod_id*.

Oracle index definition:

CHAPTER 8   DATA MIGRATION FROM ORACLE TO POSTGRESQL USING ORA2PG

SQL> select owner,table_name,index_name,index_type from dba_indexes where owner='SH' and table_name='COSTS';

```
OWNER           TABLE_NAME        INDEX_NAME          INDEX_TYPE
-------------   ---------------   -----------------   --------------
SH              COSTS             COSTS_PROD_BIX      BITMAP
```

DBMS_METADATA.GET_DDL('INDEX','COSTS_PROD_BIX','SH')

```
  CREATE BITMAP INDEX "SH"."COSTS_PROD_BIX" ON "SH"."COSTS"
  ("PROD_ID")
  PCTFREE 10 INITRANS 2 MAXTRANS 255  NOLOGGING
  STORAGE(
  BUFFER_POOL DEFAULT FLASH_CACHE DEFAULT CELL_FLASH_CACHE
  DEFAULT) LOCAL
 (PARTITION "COSTS_Q1_2019" NOCOMPRESS
  PCTFREE 10 INITRANS 2 MAXTRANS 255 NOLOGGING
  .
  PARTITION "COSTS_Q4_2023" NOCOMPRESS
  PCTFREE 10 INITRANS 2 MAXTRANS 255 NOLOGGING
  STORAGE(
  BUFFER_POOL DEFAULT FLASH_CACHE DEFAULT CELL_FLASH_CACHE
  DEFAULT)
  TABLESPACE "USERS" )
```

Import file: /var/lib/oracle/ora2pg_mig/sh_mig_proj/schema/tables/table.sql

```
36 CREATE TABLE sale_costs (
37      prod_id bigint NOT NULL,
38      time_id timestamp(0) NOT NULL,
39      promo_id bigint NOT NULL,
40      channel_id bigint NOT NULL,
41      unit_cost double precision NOT NULL,
42      unit_price double precision NOT NULL
43 ) PARTITION BY RANGE (time_id) ;
44 CREATE INDEX costs_prod_bix ON sale_costs USING gin(prod_id);
```

CHAPTER 8 DATA MIGRATION FROM ORACLE TO POSTGRESQL USING ORA2PG

SOLUTION

- There is an extension named *btree_gin* available in PostgreSQL that allows the use of GIN indexes with B-tree operators.

    Created and enabled the extension *btree_gin*.

    Index *costs_prod_bix* successfully created after this solution.

    postgres database:

    postgres=# SELECT * FROM pg_available_extensions;

    ```
                default_ installed_
    name       | version | version  | comment
    -----------+---------+----------+---------------------------------
    btree_gin  | 1.3     |          | support for indexing common
                                      datatypes in GIN
    ```

    postgres=# select * from pg_extension where extname='btree_gin';

    ```
     oid | extname | extowner | extnamespace | extversion
    -----+---------+----------+--------------+------------
    (0 rows)
    ```

    postgres=# CREATE EXTENSION IF NOT EXISTS btree_gin;
    CREATE EXTENSION

    postgres=# select * from pg_extension where extname='btree_gin';

    ```
      oid  | extname   | extowner | extnamespace | extversion
    -------+-----------+----------+--------------+------------
     20627 | btree_gin | 10       | 2200         | 1.3
    (1 row)
    ```

    postgres=# select * from pg_available_extensions order by name;

    ```
                default_ installed_
    name       | version | version   | comment
    -----------+---------+-----------+---------------------------------
    btree_gin  | 1.3     | 1.3       | support for indexing common
                                       datatypes in GIN
    ```

CHAPTER 8   DATA MIGRATION FROM ORACLE TO POSTGRESQL USING ORA2PG

ISSUE 8: ERROR: relation "costs" does not exist

- This error was reported during import of SH schema into postgres database when creating a view *profits*.

```
[oracle@dbserver sh_mig_proj]$ ./import_all.sh -d
postgres -o postgres -U postgres
```

```
Database owner postgres already exists, skipping creation.
Would you like to drop the database postgres before recreate it?
[y/N/q] N
Would you like to import SEQUENCE from ./schema/sequences/
sequence.sql? [y/N/q] y
Would you like to import SEQUENCE_VALUES from ./schema/sequence_
values/sequence_value.sql? [y/N/q] y
Would you like to import TABLE from ./schema/tables/table.sql?
[y/N/q] y
Would you like to import VIEW from ./schema/views/view.sql?
[y/N/q] y
Running: psql --single-transaction  -U postgres -d postgres -f
./schema/views/view.sql
psql:schema/views/view.sql:26: ERROR:  relation "costs" does
not exist
LINE 13:    costs c, sales s
            ^
ERROR: an error occurs when importing file ./schema/views/
view.sql.
[oracle@dbserver sh_mig_proj]$
```

CAUSE

- Table *costs* has been renamed to *sale_costs* during the migration, and since the dependent object view *profits* definition still has old name, the view creation got failed.

  ```
  Import file: /var/lib/oracle/ora2pg_mig/sh_mig_proj/
  schema/views/view.sql
  ```

571

CHAPTER 8 DATA MIGRATION FROM ORACLE TO POSTGRESQL USING ORA2PG

```
10 CREATE OR REPLACE VIEW profits (channel_id, cust_id, prod_
    id, promo_id, time_id, unit_cost, unit_price, amount_sold,
    quantity_sold, total_cost) AS SELECT
11    s.channel_id,
12    s.cust_id,
13    s.prod_id,
14    s.promo_id,
15    s.time_id,
16    c.unit_cost,
17    c.unit_price,
18    s.amount_sold,
19    s.quantity_sold,
20    c.unit_cost * s.quantity_sold TOTAL_COST
21 FROM
22    costs c, sales s
23 WHERE c.prod_id = s.prod_id
24    AND c.time_id = s.time_id
25    AND c.channel_id = s.channel_id
26    AND c.promo_id = s.promo_id;
```

SOLUTION

- Modified view *profits* definition to use new renamed table name *sale_costs* in view.sql

Import file: /var/lib/oracle/ora2pg_mig/sh_mig_proj/schema/views/view.sql

```
10 CREATE OR REPLACE VIEW profits (channel_id, cust_id, prod_id,
    promo_id, time_id, unit_cost, unit_price, amount_sold, quantity_
    sold, total_cost) AS SELECT
11    s.channel_id,
12    s.cust_id,
13    s.prod_id,
14    s.promo_id,
15    s.time_id,
16    c.unit_cost,
17    c.unit_price,
```

```
18    s.amount_sold,
19    s.quantity_sold,
20    c.unit_cost * s.quantity_sold TOTAL_COST
21  FROM
22    sale_costs c, sales s
23  WHERE c.prod_id = s.prod_id
24    AND c.time_id = s.time_id
25    AND c.channel_id = s.channel_id
26    AND c.promo_id = s.promo_id;
```

As mentioned earlier, a migration dry run would help us identify all the aforementioned issues and handle them in advance to the actual cutover, directing us toward a seamless migration.

Summary

In this chapter, we explored reasons for migrating an Oracle database to PostgreSQL along with the tools available for migration. We have seen the migration planning and the benefits of doing migration in phases. We have practically seen the installation of various Perl modules and the Ora2Pg tool. We extensively performed migration of multiple Oracle database schemas to PostgreSQL database using different possible methods and learned various issues along with solutions.

CHAPTER 9

Data Replication from Oracle to PostgreSQL Using Oracle GoldenGate

Introduction

Oracle GoldenGate is a comprehensive software application that offers various solutions like data replication, data integration, data transformation, data streaming, data high availability, real-time data transactions and analytics, transactional change data capture, etc., for the enterprise systems.

One of the best features of Oracle GoldenGate is the data replication between homogeneous and heterogeneous systems and environments by enabling the exchange and manipulation of data at the transaction level.

With enterprise data often distributed across various heterogeneous databases, the data between different data sources can be seamlessly exchanged using Oracle GoldenGate replication feature. This capability provides an organization with flexibility to use different databases for both transactional operations and real-time analytics.

Using the Oracle GoldenGate, we can replicate data between heterogeneous database environments like Oracle and PostgreSQL. Also, using replication, we can migrate a database from one RDBMS to another like from Oracle to PostgreSQL. There are various replication topologies supported by GoldenGate including unidirectional replication (i.e., the data replication flows only one way from source database to target database) and bidirectional replication (i.e., the data is replicated from source database to target database and vice versa).

CHAPTER 9 DATA REPLICATION FROM ORACLE TO POSTGRESQL USING ORACLE GOLDENGATE

Oracle GoldenGate functions through classic architecture via GGSCI, a command-line interface (CLI) and microservices architecture using both adminclient CLI and GUI console, i.e., REST-enabled services and APIs. This chapter emphasizes unidirectional data replication from Oracle database to PostgreSQL database using Oracle GoldenGate Microservices and Hub configuration.

Figure 9-1 shows the data replication flow from Oracle database to PostgreSQL database using Oracle GoldenGate Hub.

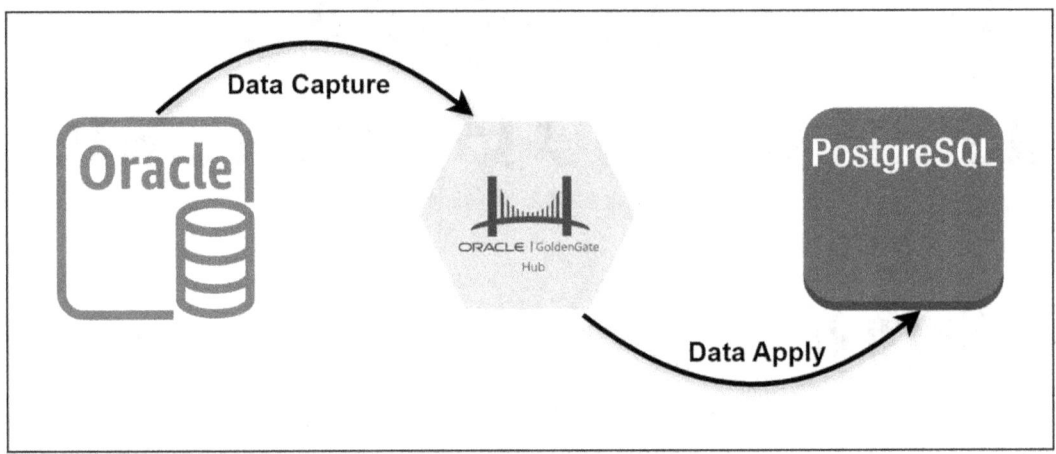

Figure 9-1. *GoldenGate replication between Oracle and PostgreSQL*

In this chapter, the following configuration tasks that are part of data replication are explained:

- GoldenGate replication configuration prerequisites
  - Configure source database ready for replication.
  - Configure target database ready for replication.
- GoldenGate Hub configuration
  - Install Oracle Client.
  - Install GoldenGate Software for Oracle and PostgreSQL.
  - Create the deployments for Source and Target environments.
- GoldenGate configuration in Source Oracle database
  - Create capture and distribution processes.

CHAPTER 9   DATA REPLICATION FROM ORACLE TO POSTGRESQL USING ORACLE GOLDENGATE

- GoldenGate configuration in Target PostgreSQL database
  - Create apply process; validate receiver process.
- Transaction replication from Oracle to PostgreSQL

Tables 9-1 to 9-6 show the details of the servers and environment used in the GoldenGate replication configuration.

Source:

Table 9-1. Server details of source environment

Server name	Machine type	IP address	OS and version
ora_serv	Source Oracle database server	192.168.2.9	Oracle Linux Server 8.10

Table 9-2. Database details of source environment

RDBMS	RDBMS version	Database name
Oracle	Oracle Database 19c	SRCDB

Target:

Table 9-3. Server details of target environment

Server name	Machine type	IP address	OS and version
pg_serv	Target PostgreSQL database server	192.168.2.24	Oracle Linux Server 8.7

Table 9-4. Database details of target environment

RDBMS	RDBMS version	Database name
PostgreSQL	PostgreSQL 16.3	postgres

CHAPTER 9 DATA REPLICATION FROM ORACLE TO POSTGRESQL USING ORACLE GOLDENGATE

Goldengate Hub:

Table 9-5. Server details of hub environment

Server name	Machine type	IP address	OS and version
ogg_hub	GoldenGate Hub Server for Replication	192.168.2.99	Oracle Linux Server 8.10

Table 9-6. Software component details on hub environment

Software	Version
Oracle Client	19c
Oracle GoldenGate for Oracle	23ai
Oracle GoldenGate for PostgreSQL	23ai

Now, let us see various steps involved in the replication configuration for a successful data replication from Oracle database to PostgreSQL database.

GoldenGate Replication Configuration Prerequisites
Configure Source Database (Oracle) Ready for Replication

On Source Server ora_serv:

- As root user, update the /etc/hosts file to include *ora_hub* server IP and hostname. This will allow communication between source server and hub server.

    [root@ora_serv ~]# vi /etc/hosts

    [root@ora_serv ~]# cat /etc/hosts
    ```
    192.168.2.9     ora_serv.localdomain        ora_serv
    192.168.2.99    ogg_hub.localdomain         ogg_hub        <<< Add
    this line
    ```

CHAPTER 9   DATA REPLICATION FROM ORACLE TO POSTGRESQL USING ORACLE GOLDENGATE

- As Oracle user, check listener status. This is to ensure the database service is registered and accepts the remote connections.

[oracle@ora_serv ~]$ lsnrctl status LISTENER

LSNRCTL for Linux: Version 19.0.0.0.0 - Production on 02-DEC-2024 17:45:02

Copyright (c) 1991, 2023, Oracle. All rights reserved.

Connecting to (DESCRIPTION=(ADDRESS=(PROTOCOL=TCP)(HOST=ora_serv)(PORT=1521)))
STATUS of the LISTENER

```
Alias                     LISTENER
Version                   TNSLSNR for Linux: Version 19.0.0.0.0 -
Production
Start Date                01-DEC-2024 20:07:06
Uptime                    0 days 21 hr. 37 min. 56 sec
Trace Level               off
Security                  ON: Local OS Authentication
SNMP                      OFF
Listener Parameter File   /u01/app/oracle/product/19.3.0/dbhome_1/
                          network/admin/listener.ora
Listener Log File         /u01/app/oracle/diag/tnslsnr/ora_serv/
                          listener/alert/log.xml
```
Listening Endpoints Summary...
  (DESCRIPTION=(ADDRESS=(PROTOCOL=tcp)(HOST=ora_serv.localdomain)(PORT=1521)))
Services Summary...
Service "srcdb" has 1 instance(s).
  Instance "srcdb", status READY, has 1 handler(s) for this service...
Service "srcdbXDB" has 1 instance(s).
  Instance "srcdb", status READY, has 1 handler(s) for this service...
The command completed successfully
[oracle@ora_serv ~]$

CHAPTER 9   DATA REPLICATION FROM ORACLE TO POSTGRESQL USING ORACLE GOLDENGATE

- As Oracle user, in database srcdb, verify whether the below features are enabled in database. If not enabled, enable them.

  - **Archivelog mode:** Allows data to be read from archivelog files for long-running transactions.

  - **Force logging:** Forces the logging of all transactions and data loads and ensures no data in source gets missed

  - **Supplemental logging:** Enables unconditional supplemental logging of all the columns in a table, for all the tables in a schema

    [oracle@ora_serv ~]$ sqlplus

    Enter user-name: / as sysdba

    Connected to:
    Oracle Database 19c Enterprise Edition Release 19.0.0.0.0 - Production
    Version 19.20.0.0.0

    SQL> select name,log_mode,force_logging from v$database;

    ```
    NAME          LOG_MODE        FORCE_LOGGING
    ----------    ------------    ---------------
    SRCDB         ARCHIVELOG      YES
    ```

    SQL> ALTER DATABASE ADD SUPPLEMENTAL LOG DATA (ALL) COLUMNS;

    Database altered.

    SQL> select name,supplemental_log_data_min,supplemental_log_data_all from v$database;

    ```
    NAME         SUPPLEMENTAL_LOG_DATA_MIN  SUPPLEMENTAL_LOG_DATA_ALL
    ---------   -------------------------  -------------------------
    SRCDB        YES                        YES
    ```

CHAPTER 9 DATA REPLICATION FROM ORACLE TO POSTGRESQL USING ORACLE GOLDENGATE

- In database srcdb, enable Oracle GoldenGate replication by setting the following initialization parameter.

    SQL> select name,display_value from v$parameter where name='enable_goldengate_replication';

    ```
    NAME                            VALUE
    ------------------------------  ------------
    enable_goldengate_replication   FALSE
    ```

    SQL> alter system set enable_goldengate_replication ='TRUE';

    System altered.

    SQL> select name,display_value from v$parameter where name='enable_goldengate_replication';

    ```
    NAME                            DISPLAY_VALUE
    ------------------------------  ------------------------------
    enable_goldengate_replication   TRUE
    ```

- In database srcdb, create a schema user named ora_rep_user and grant the necessary privileges.

    SQL> grant connect, resource to ora_rep_user identified by ora_rep_user;

    Grant succeeded.

    SQL> grant unlimited tablespace to ora_rep_user;

    Grant succeeded.

- In database srcdb, connect as ora_rep_user and create a table named ggtest in ora_rep_user schema. This is the schema table we will be replicating from source database to PostgreSQL database. The data in this table will be loaded in the later steps.

    [oracle@ora_serv ~]$ sqlplus

    Enter user-name: ora_rep_user/ora_rep_user
    Last Successful login time: Tue Dec 03 2024 01:09:04 -05:00

581

```
Connected to:
Oracle Database 19c Enterprise Edition Release 19.0.0.0.0 -
Production
Version 19.20.0.0.0

SQL> create table ggtest (id number, name varchar2(20));

Table created.

SQL> alter table ggtest add primary key (id);

Table altered.
```

- In database srcdb, create a replication administrator user ggadmin and grant appropriate privileges. This administrator account will be used in the replication process that connects to srcdb and captures the data changes.

```
SQL> CREATE USER ggadmin IDENTIFIED BY ggadmin;

User created.

SQL> GRANT CONNECT, RESOURCE, CREATE SESSION, CREATE VIEW, ALTER
SYSTEM, ALTER USER TO ggadmin;

Grant succeeded.

SQL> GRANT INSERT ANY TABLE, UPDATE ANY TABLE, DELETE ANY TABLE TO
ggadmin;

Grant succeeded.

SQL> GRANT SELECT ANY DICTIONARY TO ggadmin;

Grant succeeded.

SQL> GRANT SELECT ANY TRANSACTION TO ggadmin;

Grant succeeded.

SQL> GRANT UNLIMITED TABLESPACE TO GGADMIN;

Grant succeeded.
```

CHAPTER 9   DATA REPLICATION FROM ORACLE TO POSTGRESQL USING ORACLE GOLDENGATE

SQL> GRANT EXECUTE ON DBMS_FLASHBACK TO GGADMIN;

Grant succeeded.

SQL> EXEC DBMS_GOLDENGATE_AUTH.GRANT_ADMIN_PRIVILEGE ('GGADMIN');

PL/SQL procedure successfully completed.

Configure Target Database (PostgreSQL) Ready for Replication

On Target Server pg_serv:

- As root user, update the /etc/hosts file to include *ora_hub* server IP and hostname. This will allow communication between source server and hub server.

   [root@pg_serv ~]# vi /etc/hosts

   [root@pg_serv ~]# cat /etc/hosts
   ```
   192.168.2.24     pg_serv.localdomain      pg_serv
   192.168.2.99     ogg_hub.localdomain      ogg_hub        <<< Add this line
   ```

- As root user, validate the PostgreSQL contrib package is installed on the database server.

Note This package is required only if PostgreSQL database is considered for data capture as part of bidirectional replication.

   [root@pg_serv ~]# rpm -qa postgres*contrib
   postgresql16-contrib-16.3-1PGDG.rhel8.x86_64

- As postgres user, update the pg_hba.conf configuration file to include the entry of ogg_hub server. This entry is to authenticate the remote connectivity from ogg_hub server to postgres database on pg_serv server.

CHAPTER 9   DATA REPLICATION FROM ORACLE TO POSTGRESQL USING ORACLE GOLDENGATE

```
[postgres@pg_serv ~]$ cd /var/lib/pgsql/16/data
[postgres@pg_serv data]$ vi pg_hba.conf
# TYPE   DATABASE   USER     ADDRESS              METHOD
# "local" is for Unix domain socket connections only
local    all        all                           peer
# IPv4 local connections:
host     postgres   gguser   192.168.2.99/32      trust        <<< Add this line

[postgres@pg_serv data]$ pg_ctl reload
server signaled
```

- As postgres user, validate the port and listen_address parameters in configuration file postgresql.conf. Port and listen address will allow the communications between pg_serv and ogg_hub servers.

```
[postgres@pg_serv data]$ grep -i port postgresql.conf
port = 5432                          # (change requires restart)

[postgres@pg_serv data]$ grep -i listen postgresql.conf
listen_addresses = '*'               # what IP address(es) to listen on;
```

- In database *postgres,* create a table named ggtest (same as in source src database) under public schema.

```
[postgres@pg_serv ~]$ psql
psql (16.3)

postgres=# create table ggtest (id int, name varchar);
CREATE TABLE

postgres=# \dt public.*
         List of relations
 Schema |  Name  | Type  |  Owner
--------+--------+-------+----------
 public | ggtest | table | postgres
(1 row)
```

```
postgres=# select * from public.ggtest;
 id | name
----+------
(0 rows)
```

- In database postgres, create a replication administrator user gguser and grant necessary privileges. This administrator account will be used in the replication process that connects to postgres database and applies the data received from source database srcdb.

```
postgres=# create user gguser password 'gguser';
CREATE ROLE

postgres=# grant connect on database postgres to gguser;
GRANT

postgres=# grant create on database postgres to gguser;
GRANT

postgres=# grant create, usage on schema public to gguser;
GRANT

postgres=# grant select on all tables in schema public to gguser;
GRANT

postgres=# grant all on all tables in schema public to gguser;
GRANT

postgres=# alter user gguser with superuser;
ALTER ROLE

postgres=# \du
                          List of roles
 Role name |                     Attributes
-----------+------------------------------------------------------
 gguser    | Superuser
 postgres  | Superuser, Create role, Create DB, Replication,
           | Bypass RLS
```

- In database postgres, create a schema gguser and assign user gguser as owner to the schema. The schema is required as the administrator user gguser would create GoldenGate internal tables like checkpoint, heartbeat, etc., used for replication management.

```
postgres=# CREATE SCHEMA AUTHORIZATION gguser;
CREATE SCHEMA

postgres=# \dn
        List of schemas
   Name   |       Owner
----------+-------------------
 gguser   | gguser
 public   | pg_database_owner
(2 rows)
```

Configure Oracle GoldenGate Hub

What Is Oracle GoldenGate Hub?

In general, for the data replication configuration, the Oracle GoldenGate software is installed individually on both the source Oracle server and target PostgreSQL server. Since the GoldenGate processes runs on the individual database servers, there will be little overhead on resource utilization on the database servers. If there are multiple source or target systems, installing and managing Oracle GoldenGate on each server is quite challenging.

Alternatively, the GoldenGate software for both source and target databases can be installed on a separate server, i.e., a different host than the database servers. This architectural concept is called Oracle GoldenGate Hub. One of the advantages of Oracle GoldenGate Hub is the isolation of resource utilization on database servers since the GoldenGate processes runs on hub server instead of the source and target database servers. Another advantage is that the hub server can be used for any source and target environments by installing respective GoldenGate software. So the hub server works as a centralized environment to configure and manage multiple configurations within the estate.

In this scenario, the Oracle GoldenGate for both source Oracle and target PostgreSQL databases is installed in the GoldenGate hub server.

Install Oracle Client

One of the prerequisites of the GoldenGate hub server is the installation of Oracle Client software since one of the databases involved in replication configuration is Oracle database. Oracle Client is required for the database remote connectivity from ogg_hub to Oracle database srcdb running in source server ora_serv.

- Download Oracle Database 19c Client binaries from the following URL: https://www.oracle.com/database/technologies/oracle19c-linux-downloads.html.

    Please ensure to review the downloadable file that corresponds to the operating system being used.

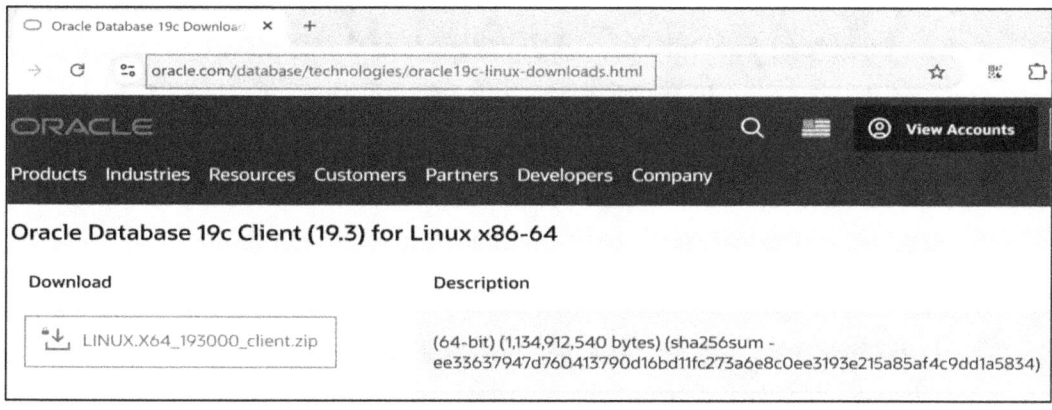

Figure 9-2. Oracle Database 19c Client Download page

On GoldenGate Hub Server ogg_hub:

- As root user, update the /etc/hosts file to include ora_serv and pg_serv server IP and hostnames. This will allow communication between hub server and source and target database servers.

    [root@ogg_hub ~]# vi /etc/hosts

    [root@ogg_hub ~]# cat /etc/hosts
    ```
    192.168.2.99    ogg_hub.localdomain     ogg_hub
    192.168.2.9     ora_serv.localdomain    ora_serv    <<< Add this line
    192.168.2.24    pg_serv.localdomain     pg_serv     <<< Add this line
    ```

- As root user, perform the below steps:
  - Create staging directory – A directory path to place the downloaded software files
  - Create install directory – A directory path to install Oracle 19c client binaries
  - Change the directories' ownership to Oracle user and oinstall group.

    [root@ogg_hub ~]# mkdir -p /u01/stage

    [root@ogg_hub ~]# mkdir -p /u01/app/oracle/19client

    [root@ogg_hub ~]# chown -R oracle:oinstall /u01

    [root@ogg_hub ~]# ls -ld /u01/app/oracle/19client
    drwxr-xr-x 2 oracle oinstall 6 Dec 1 21:09 /u01/app/oracle/19client

- As root user, upload and stage the downloaded software file to the staging directory created in the previous step. Also, change the ownership of the software file to Oracle.

  [root@ogg_hub ~]# ls -lrt LINUX.X64_193000_client.zip
  total 2192584
  -rw-r--r-- 1 root root 1134912540 Dec 1 21:17 LINUX.X64_193000_client.zip

  [root@ogg_hub ~]# cp LINUX.X64_193000_client.zip /u01/stage/

  [root@ogg_hub ~]# cd /u01/stage

  [root@ogg_hub stage]# chown oracle:oinstall LINUX.X64_193000_client.zip

- As Oracle user, uncompress the staged software file.

  [root@ogg_hub ~]# sudo su - oracle

  [oracle@ogg_hub ~]$ cd /u01/stage

CHAPTER 9   DATA REPLICATION FROM ORACLE TO POSTGRESQL USING ORACLE GOLDENGATE

```
[oracle@ogg_hub stage]$ ls -lrt
total 1108320
-rw-r--r-- 1 oracle oinstall 1134912540 Dec  1 21:20 LINUX.
X64_193000_client.zip

[oracle@ogg_hub stage]$ unzip LINUX.X64_193000_client.zip
Archive:  LINUX.X64_193000_client.zip
   creating: client/
  inflating: client/install/runInstaller.sh
.
<<<<< OUTPUT TRUNCATED >>>>>
.
  inflating: client/stage/globalvariables/variable.properties
  inflating: client/welcome.html
[oracle@ogg_hub stage]$

[oracle@ogg_hub stage]$ ls -lrt
total 1108320
drwxr-xr-x 5 oracle oinstall         90 Apr 17 2019 client
-rw-r--r-- 1 root     root     1134912540 Dec  1 21:20 LINUX.
X64_193000_client.zip

[oracle@ogg_hub stage]$ cd client
[oracle@ogg_hub client]$ ls
install  response  runInstaller  stage  welcome.html
```

- As Oracle user, run the runInstaller executable to launch the Graphical User Interface (GUI) installer tool to install the Oracle 19c client binaries.

```
[oracle@ogg_hub client]$ ./runInstaller
Starting Oracle Universal Installer...

Checking Temp space: must be greater than 415 MB.
Actual 11795 MB    Passed
Checking swap space: must be greater than 150 MB.
Actual 7394 MB    Passed
Checking monitor: must be configured to display at least 256
colors.    Actual 16777216    Passed
```

CHAPTER 9 DATA REPLICATION FROM ORACLE TO POSTGRESQL USING ORACLE GOLDENGATE

```
Preparing to launch Oracle Universal Installer from /tmp/
OraInstall2024-12-01_09-22-17PM. Please wait ...[oracle@ogg_hub
client]$ The response file for this session can be found at:
 /u01/app/oracle/19client/install/response/
 client_2024-12-01_09-22-17PM.rsp
You can find the log of this install session at:
 /u01/app/oraInventory/logs/installActions2024-12-01_09-
 22-17PM.log
```

Figures 9-3 through 9-7 show steps involved in Oracle 19c client installation.

- In step 1, select Installation Type – Administrator.

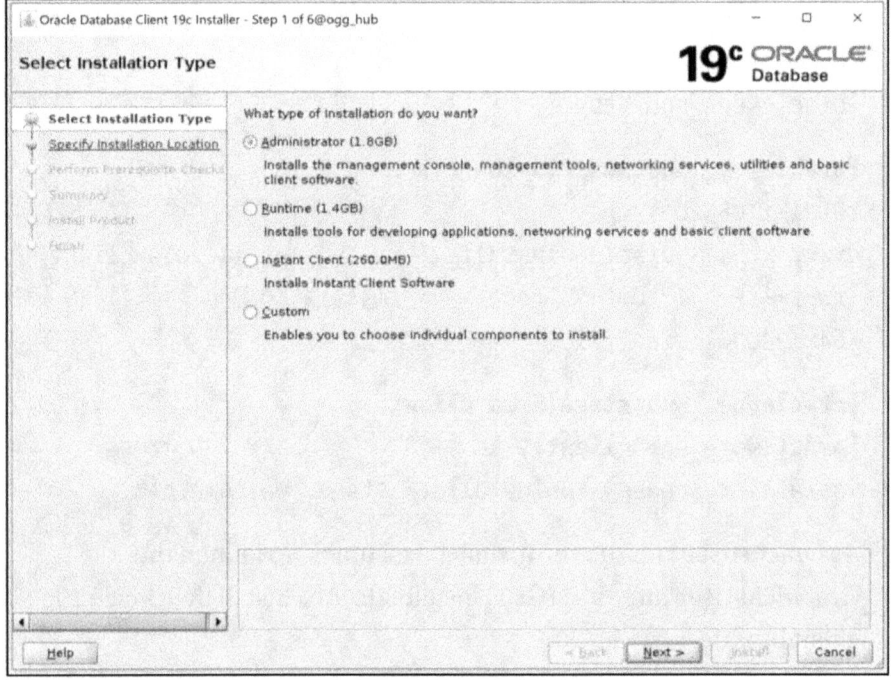

Figure 9-3. *Oracle 19c client installation – step 1*

- In step 2, specify Installation Location; set values as below and proceed with Next.
    - Oracle base – /u01/app/oracle
    - Software location – /u01/app/oracle/19client

CHAPTER 9 DATA REPLICATION FROM ORACLE TO POSTGRESQL USING ORACLE GOLDENGATE

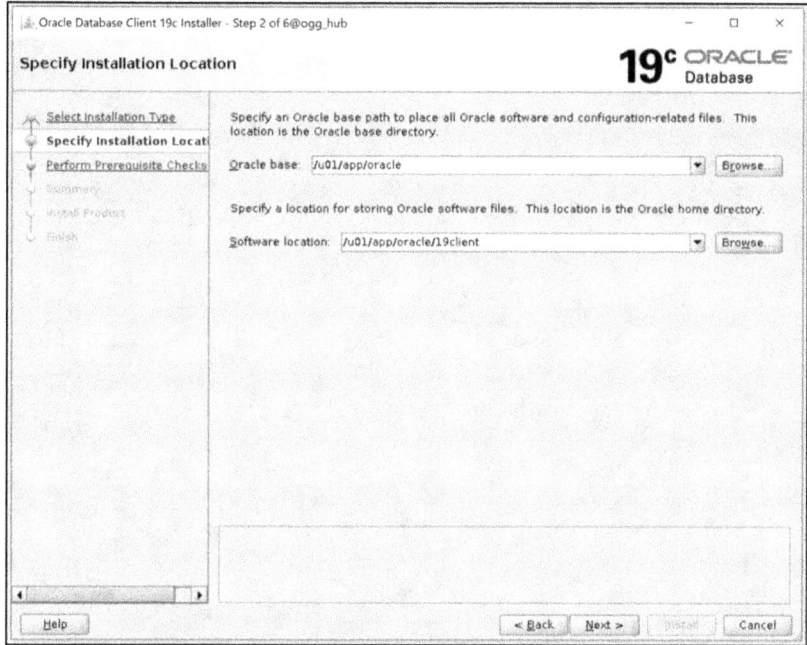

Figure 9-4. *Oracle 19c client installation – step 2*

- In step 3, review the summary and proceed with Install.

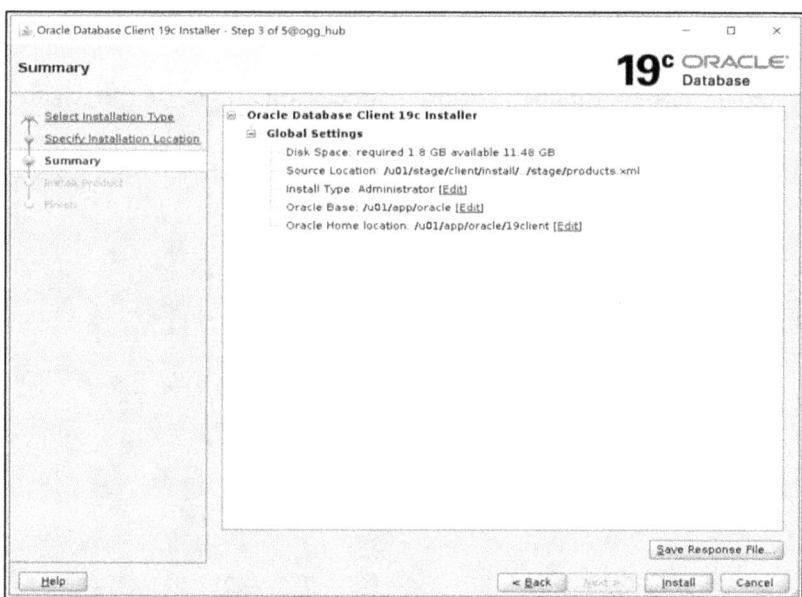

Figure 9-5. *Oracle 19c client installation – step 3*

CHAPTER 9　DATA REPLICATION FROM ORACLE TO POSTGRESQL USING ORACLE GOLDENGATE

- In step 4, monitor the progress of the product installation.

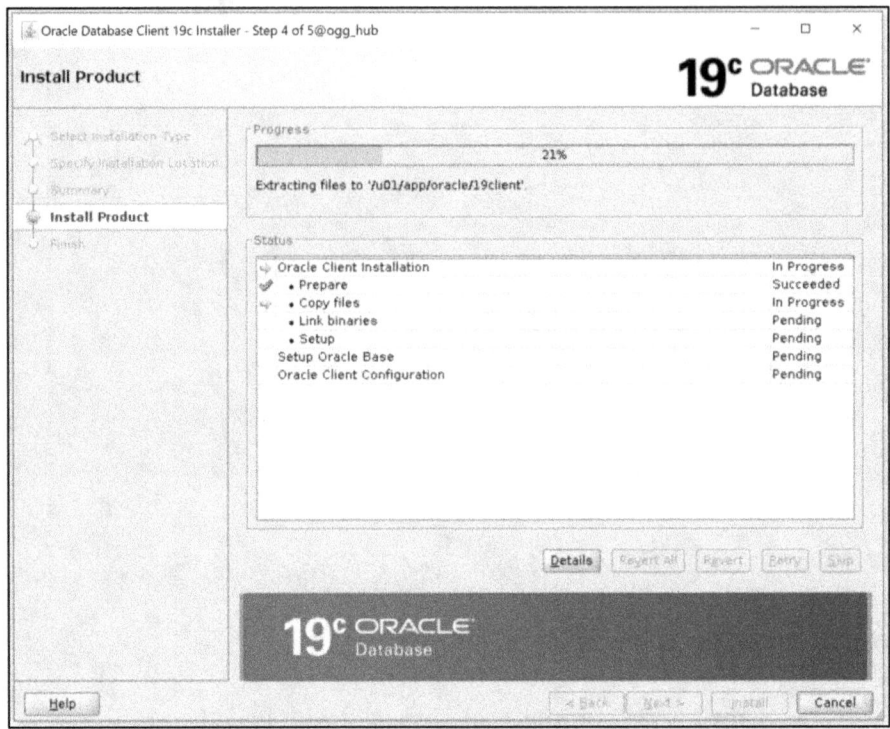

Figure 9-6. *Oracle 19c client installation – step 4*

- In step 5, validate the installation is successful and close the wizard.

CHAPTER 9 DATA REPLICATION FROM ORACLE TO POSTGRESQL USING ORACLE GOLDENGATE

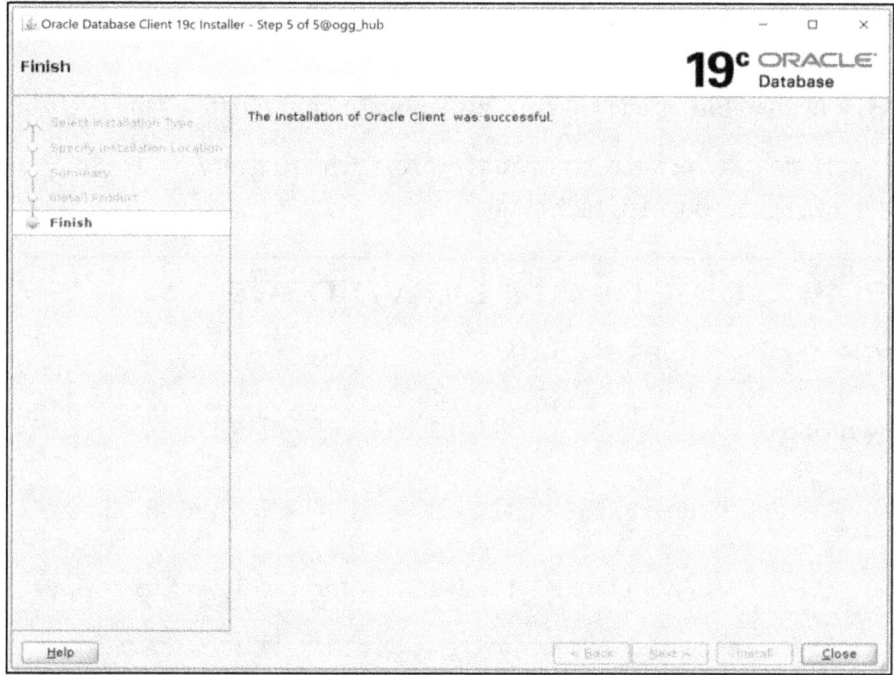

Figure 9-7. *Oracle 19c client installation – step 5*

- Once the Oracle Client installation is successful, verify the installation by reviewing the binary home directory.

```
[oracle@ogg_hub client]$ cd /u01/app/oracle/19client/
[oracle@ogg_hub 19client]$ ls
assistants    clone      cv          diagnostics  has
instantclient
jdbc          jpub       network     olap         oracore    oss
perl          OOpatch    relnotes    sdk          sqlj       suptools
utl           bin        crs         dbjava       dmu        hs
inventory     jdk        ldap        nls          OPatch
oraInst.loc
oui           plsql      racg        root.sh      slax       sqlplus
ucp           wwg        cfgtoollogs css          deinstall  env.ora
install       javavm     jlib        lib          odbc       opmn
ord           owm        precomp     rdbms        runInstaller
sqldeveloper  srvm       usm         xdk
```

593

CHAPTER 9 DATA REPLICATION FROM ORACLE TO POSTGRESQL USING ORACLE GOLDENGATE

Install GoldenGate Software

- Download the Oracle GoldenGate software from the following URL:

  https://www.oracle.com/middleware/technologies/goldengate-downloads.html#

> **Oracle GoldenGate Downloads**
>
> **Oracle GoldenGate 23ai**
>
> Download
>
> ⬇ Oracle GoldenGate 23.4.1.24.05 on Linux x86-64 for Oracle
>
> ⬇ Oracle GoldenGate 23.4.0.24.05 on Linux x86-64 for PostgreSQL

Figure 9-8. Oracle GoldenGate Downloads page

- As root user, perform the following:
  - Create staging subdirectory – To place downloaded software files.
  - Copy the downloaded GoldenGate software files to the stage directory.

  ```
  [root@ogg_hub ~]# mkdir -p /u01/stage/oggsw
  ```

  ```
  [root@ogg_hub ~]# cp V1041909-01.zip V1042871-01.zip /u01/stage/oggsw
  ```

  ```
  [root@ogg_hub ~]# ls -lrt /u01/stage/oggsw
  total 1010872
  -rw-r--r-- 1 oracle oinstall 517595181 Dec  1 19:28 V1041909-01.zip
  -rw-r--r-- 1 oracle oinstall 517531573 Dec  1 19:28 V1042871-01.zip
  ```

CHAPTER 9   DATA REPLICATION FROM ORACLE TO POSTGRESQL USING ORACLE GOLDENGATE

Install Oracle GoldenGate for Oracle Database

- As Oracle user, perform the following:
    - Create software home directory – to install GoldenGate for Oracle binaries.
    - Uncompress the software file in staging subdirectory.

    [oracle@ogg_hub ~]$ mkdir -p /u01/app/ogg/oragg

    [oracle@ogg_hub ~]$ cd /u01/stage/oggsw

    [oracle@ogg_hub oggsw]$ ls -lrt
    ```
    total 1010872
    -rw-r--r-- 1 oracle oinstall 517595181 Dec  1 19:28
    V1041909-01.zip
    -rw-r--r-- 1 oracle oinstall 517531573 Dec  1 19:28
    V1042871-01.zip

     'Archive:  V1042871-01.zip
       inflating: META-INF/MANIFEST.MF
         creating: fbo_ggs_Linux_x64_Oracle_services_shiphome/Disk1/
     .
    ```

    <<<<< OUTPUT TRUNCATED >>>>>
    ```
     .
       creating: fbo_ggs_Linux_x64_Oracle_services_shiphome/Disk1/
       response/
       inflating: fbo_ggs_Linux_x64_Oracle_services_shiphome/Disk1/
       response/oggcore.rsp
       inflating: fbo_ggs_Linux_x64_Oracle_services_shiphome/Disk1/
       runInstaller
       inflating: OGGCORE_Release_Notes_23.4.1.24.05.pdf
       inflating: OGG-23ai-README.txt
    ```

    [oracle@ogg_hub oggsw]$ ls -lrt
    ```
    total 1011156
    -rw-r--r-- 1 oracle oinstall      3092 Apr 29  2024 OGG-23ai-
    README.txt
    ```

CHAPTER 9   DATA REPLICATION FROM ORACLE TO POSTGRESQL USING ORACLE GOLDENGATE

```
drwxr-xr-x 3 oracle oinstall          19 May 29  2024 fbo_ggs_
Linux_x64_Oracle_services_shiphome
-rw-r--r-- 1 oracle oinstall      285705 May 31  2024 OGGCORE_
Release_Notes_23.4.1.24.05.pdf
-rw-r--r-- 1 oracle oinstall 517595181 Dec   1 19:28
V1041909-01.zip
-rw-r--r-- 1 oracle oinstall 517531573 Dec   1 19:28
V1042871-01.zip
drwxr-xr-x 2 oracle oinstall          64 Dec   1 19:29 META-INF
[oracle@ogg_hub oggsw]$
```

- As Oracle user, run the runInstaller executable to launch the Graphical User Interface (GUI) installer tool to install the Oracle GoldenGate for Oracle.

[oracle@ogg_hub oggsw]$ cd fbo_ggs_Linux_x64_Oracle_services_shiphome/Disk1/
[oracle@ogg_hub Disk1]$ ls -lrt
```
total 8
drwxr-xr-x  4 oracle oinstall  187 May 29  2024 install
drwxr-xr-x 12 oracle oinstall 4096 May 29  2024 stage
-rwxr-xr-x  1 oracle oinstall  918 May 29  2024 runInstaller
drwxrwxr-x  2 oracle oinstall   25 May 29  2024 response

[oracle@ogg_hub Disk1]$ ./runInstaller
Starting Oracle Universal Installer...

Checking Temp space: must be greater than 120 MB. Actual 15900 MB
                                                           Passed
Checking swap space: must be greater than 150 MB. Actual 7403 MB
                                                           Passed
Checking monitor: must be configured to display at least 256
colors.    Actual 16777216    Passed
Preparing to launch Oracle Universal Installer from /tmp/
OraInstall2024-12-01_07-33-22PM. Please wait ...[oracle@ogg_hub
Disk1]$ You can find the log of this install session at:
 /u01/app/oraInventory/logs/installActions2024-12-01_07-
33-22PM.log
```

CHAPTER 9 DATA REPLICATION FROM ORACLE TO POSTGRESQL USING ORACLE GOLDENGATE

Figures 9-9 through 9-13 show steps involved in Oracle GoldenGate for Oracle 23ai installation.

- In step 1, select Installation Option - Oracle GoldenGate for Oracle Database, by default.

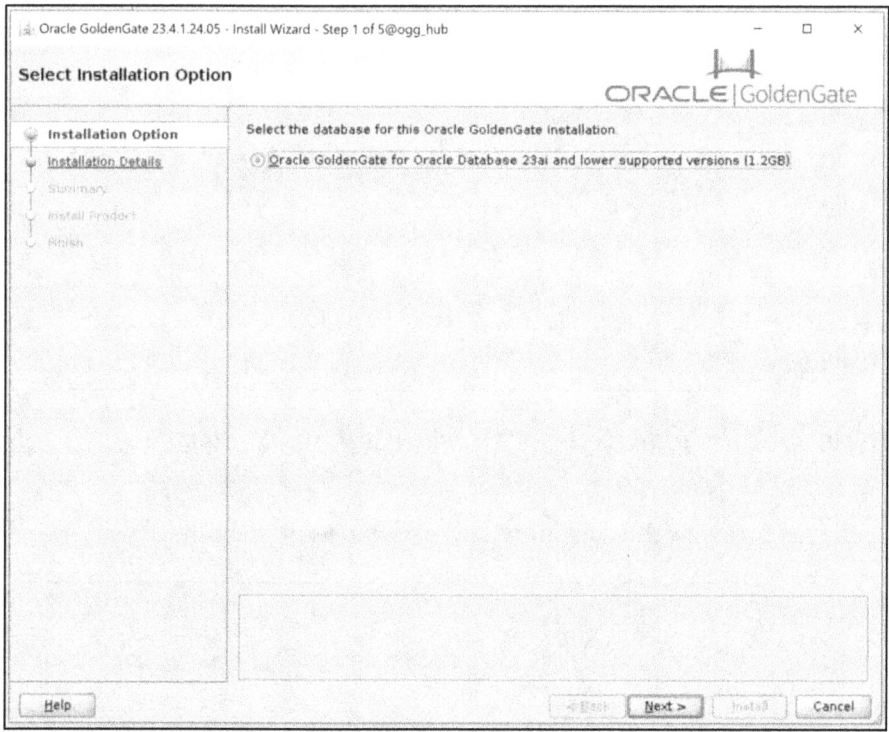

Figure 9-9. *Oracle GoldenGate for Oracle installation – step 1*

- In step 2, specify Installation Details.
    - Software Location – /u01/app/ogg/oragg

CHAPTER 9 DATA REPLICATION FROM ORACLE TO POSTGRESQL USING ORACLE GOLDENGATE

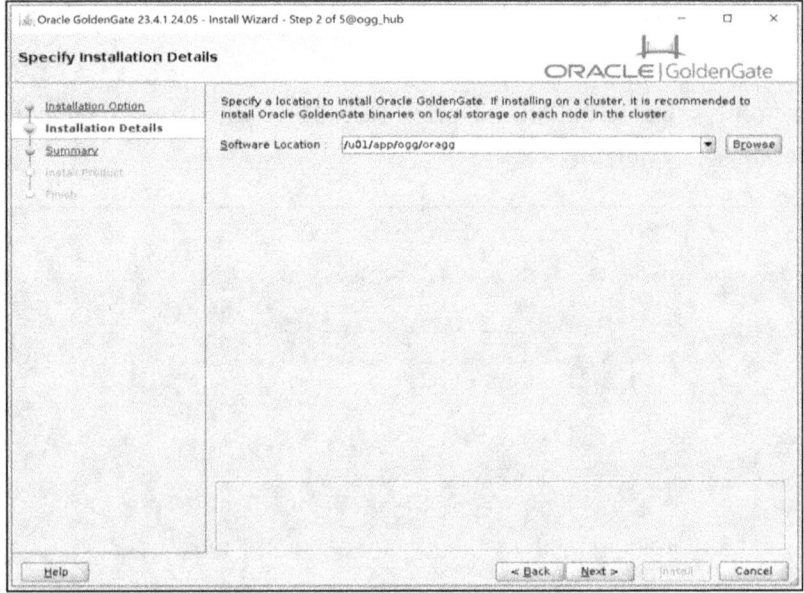

Figure 9-10. *Oracle GoldenGate for Oracle installation – step 2*

- In step 3, review the summary and proceed with Install.

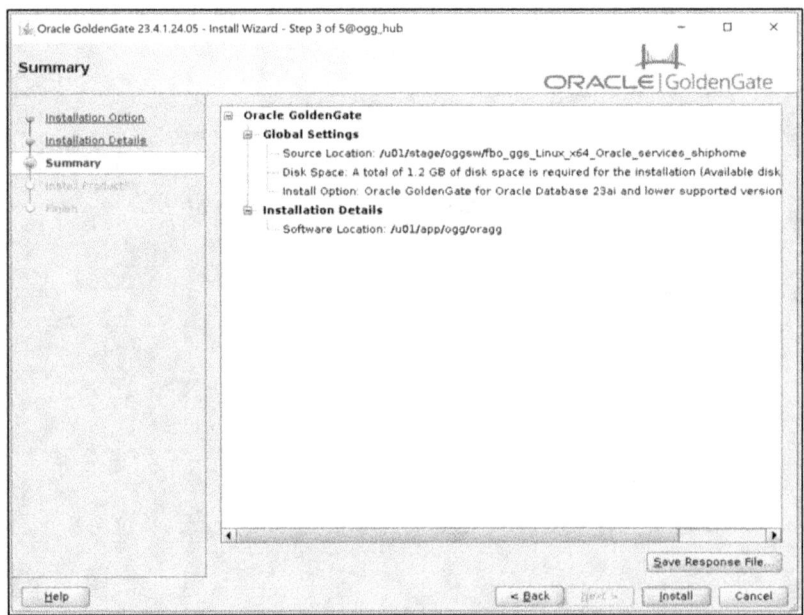

Figure 9-11. *Oracle GoldenGate for Oracle installation – step 3*

CHAPTER 9   DATA REPLICATION FROM ORACLE TO POSTGRESQL USING ORACLE GOLDENGATE

- In step 4, monitor the progress of the product installation.

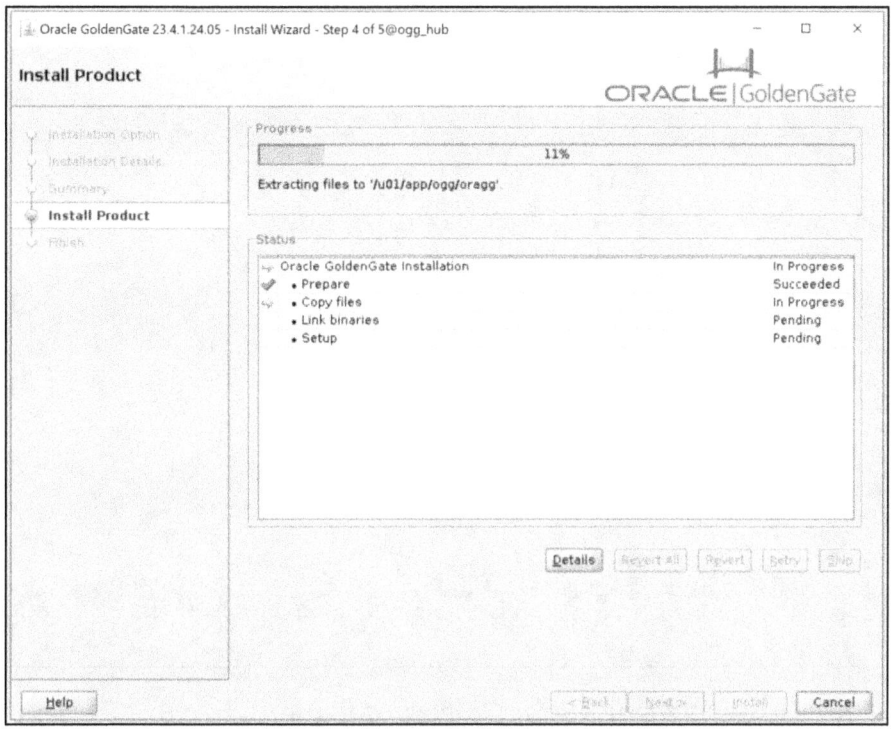

Figure 9-12. *Oracle GoldenGate for Oracle installation – step 4*

- In step 5, validate the installation is successful and close the wizard.

CHAPTER 9   DATA REPLICATION FROM ORACLE TO POSTGRESQL USING ORACLE GOLDENGATE

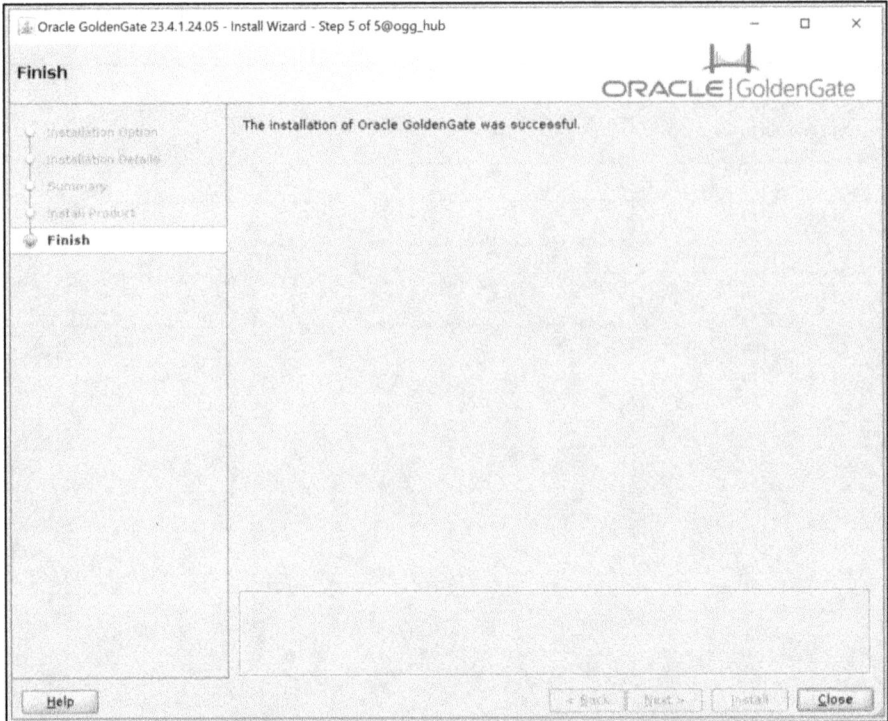

Figure 9-13. *Oracle GoldenGate for Oracle installation – step 5*

- Once the Oracle GoldenGate for Oracle Database installation is successful, verify the installation by reviewing the binaries installed in the home directory.

```
[oracle@ogg_hub Disk1]$ cd /u01/app/ogg/oragg
[oracle@ogg_hub oragg]$ ls -lrt
total 24
-rw-r-----   1 oracle oinstall   56 Aug 26  2022 oraInst.loc
drwxr-xr-x   7 oracle oinstall 4096 Dec   1 19:37 lib
drwxr-xr-x  13 oracle oinstall 4096 Dec   1 19:37 OPatch
 .
<<<<< OUTPUT TRUNCATED >>>>>
 .
drwxr-xr-x   2 oracle oinstall 4096 Dec   1 19:37 bin
drwxr-x---  13 oracle oinstall 4096 Dec   1 19:37 inventory
drwxr-xr-x   3 oracle oinstall   28 Dec   1 19:37 install
```

CHAPTER 9   DATA REPLICATION FROM ORACLE TO POSTGRESQL USING ORACLE GOLDENGATE

Install Oracle GoldenGate for PostgreSQL

- As Oracle user, perform the following:

  - Create software home directory – To install GoldenGate for PostgreSQL binaries.

  - Uncompress the software file in stage directory.

    [oracle@ogg_hub ~]$ mkdir -p /u01/app/ogg/pggg

    [oracle@ogg_hub ~]$ cd /u01/stage/oggsw/

    [oracle@ogg_hub oggsw]$ ls -lrt
    ```
    total 1011156
    -rw-r--r-- 1 oracle oinstall       3092 Apr 29  2024 OGG-23ai-README.txt
    drwxr-xr-x 3 oracle oinstall         19 May 29  2024 fbo_ggs_Linux_x64_Oracle_services_shiphome
    -rw-r--r-- 1 oracle oinstall     285705 May 31  2024 OGGCORE_Release_Notes_23.4.1.24.05.pdf
    -rw-r--r-- 1 oracle oinstall  517595181 Dec  1 19:28 V1041909-01.zip
    -rw-r--r-- 1 oracle oinstall  517531573 Dec  1 19:28 V1042871-01.zip
    drwxr-xr-x 2 oracle oinstall         64 Dec  1 19:29 META-INF
    [oracle@ogg_hub oggsw]$
    ```

    [oracle@ogg_hub oggsw]$ unzip V1041909-01.zip
    ```
    Archive:  V1041909-01.zip
      inflating: META-INF/MANIFEST.MF
      inflating: META-INF/ORACLE_C.SF
       creating: ggs_Linux_x64_PostgreSQL_services_shiphome/Disk1/
    ```
    .

    <<<<< OUTPUT TRUNCATED >>>>>
    .

    ```
       creating: ggs_Linux_x64_PostgreSQL_services_shiphome/Disk1/response/
    ```

CHAPTER 9   DATA REPLICATION FROM ORACLE TO POSTGRESQL USING ORACLE GOLDENGATE

```
       inflating: ggs_Linux_x64_PostgreSQL_services_shiphome/Disk1/
       runInstaller
       inflating: OGGCORE_Release_Notes_23ai.pdf
```

[oracle@ogg_hub oggsw]$ ls -lrt *PostgreSQL*
```
total 1011436
drwxr-xr-x 3 oracle oinstall          19 Apr 27  2024 ggs_Linux_
x64_PostgreSQL_services_shiphome
```

- As Oracle user, run the runInstaller executable to launch the Graphical User Interface (GUI) installer tool to install the Oracle GoldenGate for PostgreSQL.

[oracle@ogg_hub oggsw]$ cd ggs_Linux_x64_PostgreSQL_services_shiphome/Disk1

[oracle@ogg_hub Disk1]$ ls -lrt
```
total 8
drwxr-xr-x  4 oracle oinstall  187 Apr 27  2024 install
drwxr-xr-x 12 oracle oinstall 4096 Apr 27  2024 stage
-rwxr-xr-x  1 oracle oinstall  918 Apr 27  2024 runInstaller
drwxrwxr-x  2 oracle oinstall   25 Apr 27  2024 response
```

[oracle@ogg_hub Disk1]$ ./runInstaller
```
Starting Oracle Universal Installer...

Checking Temp space: must be greater than 120 MB.  Actual 14036
                                                   MB    Passed
Checking swap space: must be greater than 150 MB.  Actual 7401
                                                   MB    Passed
Checking monitor: must be configured to display at least 256
colors.   Actual 16777216      Passed
Preparing to launch Oracle Universal Installer from /tmp/
OraInstall2024-12-01_07-43-24PM. Please wait ...[oracle@ogg_hub
Disk1]$ You can find the log of this install session at:
 /u01/app/oraInventory/logs/installActions2024-12-01_07-
43-24PM.log
```

CHAPTER 9 DATA REPLICATION FROM ORACLE TO POSTGRESQL USING ORACLE GOLDENGATE

Figures 9-14 through 9-18 show steps involved in Oracle GoldenGate for PostgreSQL 23ai installation.

- In step 1, select Installation Option – Oracle GoldenGate for PostgreSQL, by default.

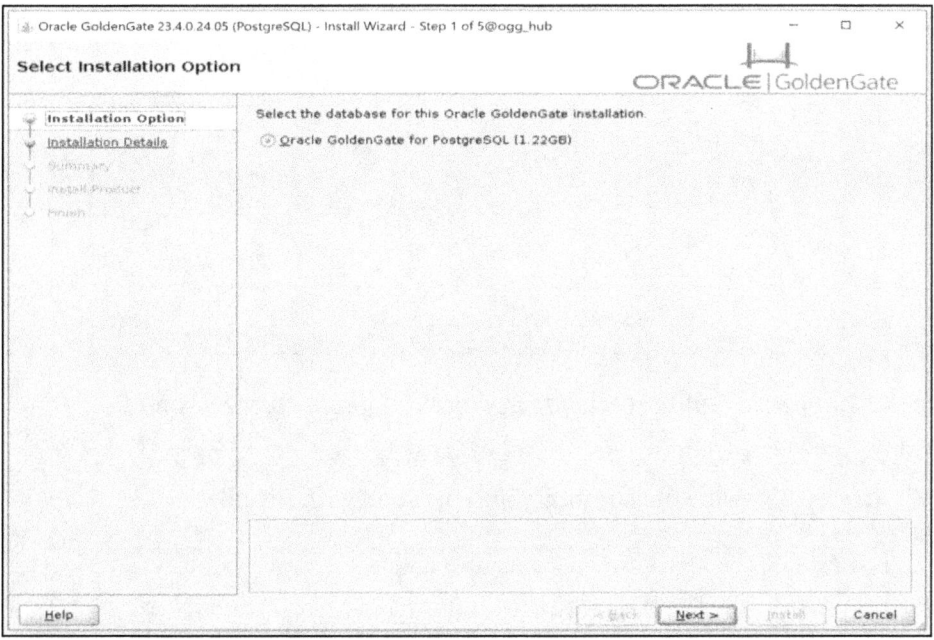

Figure 9-14. *Oracle GoldenGate for PostgreSQL installation – step 1*

- In step 2, specify Installation Details.
    - Software Location – /u01/app/ogg/pggg

CHAPTER 9 DATA REPLICATION FROM ORACLE TO POSTGRESQL USING ORACLE GOLDENGATE

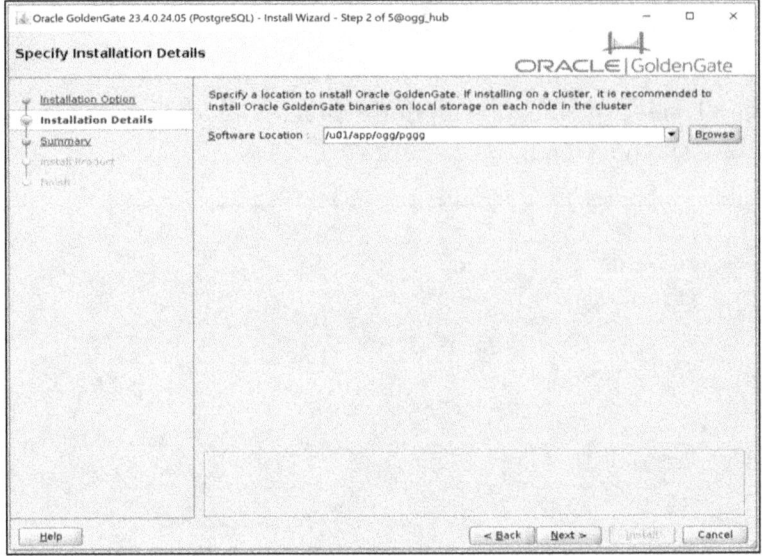

Figure 9-15. Oracle GoldenGate for PostgreSQL installation – step 2

- In step 3, review the summary and proceed with Install.

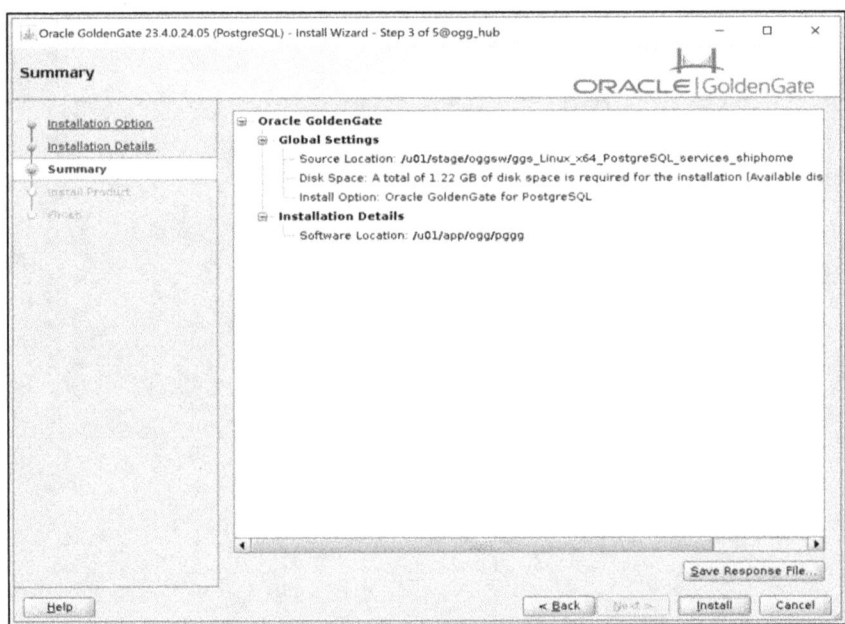

Figure 9-16. Oracle GoldenGate for PostgreSQL installation – step 3

CHAPTER 9   DATA REPLICATION FROM ORACLE TO POSTGRESQL USING ORACLE GOLDENGATE

- In step 4, monitor the progress of the product installation.

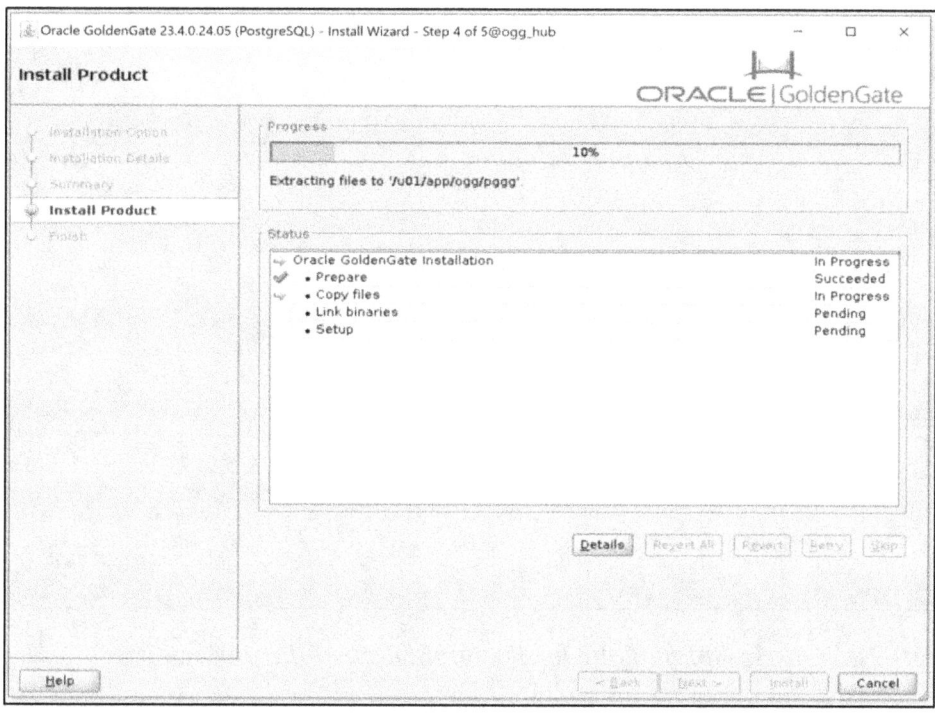

Figure 9-17. *Oracle GoldenGate for PostgreSQL installation – step 4*

- In step 5, validate the installation is successful.

CHAPTER 9 DATA REPLICATION FROM ORACLE TO POSTGRESQL USING ORACLE GOLDENGATE

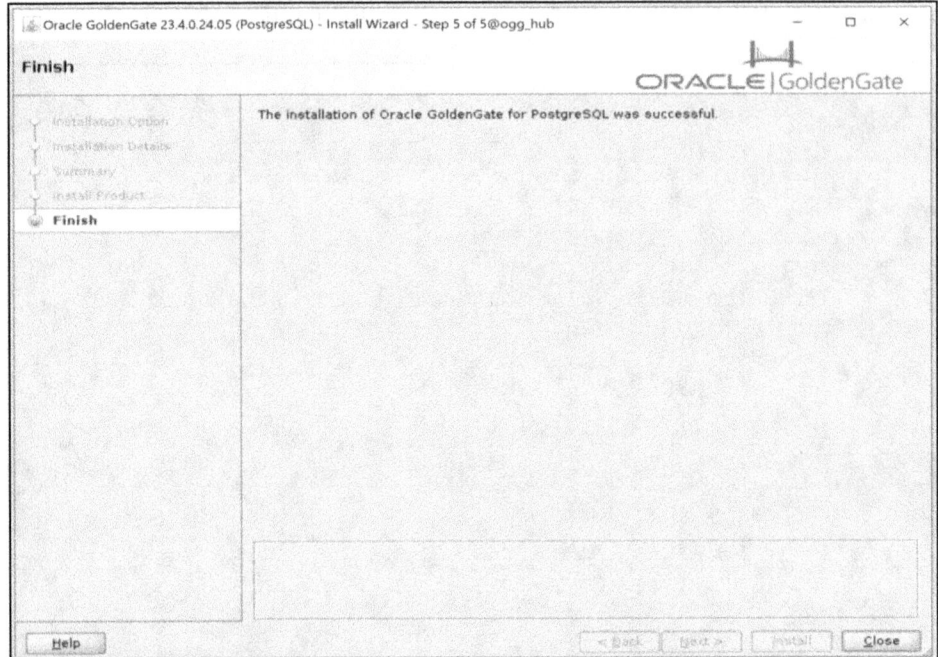

Figure 9-18. *Oracle GoldenGate for PostgreSQL installation – step 5*

- Once the Oracle GoldenGate for PostgreSQL installation is successful, verify the installation by reviewing the binaries installed in the home directory

[oracle@ogg_hub Disk1]$ cd /u01/app/ogg/pggg/

[oracle@ogg_hub pggg]$ ls -lrt
```
total 24
-rw-r-----  1 oracle oinstall   56 Aug 26  2022 oraInst.loc
drwxr-xr-x  3 oracle oinstall   20 Dec  1 19:45 diagnostics
drwxr-xr-x  3 oracle oinstall   19 Dec  1 19:45 srvm
drwxr-xr-x  2 oracle oinstall   26 Dec  1 19:45 deinstall
drwxr-xr-x  4 oracle oinstall   67 Dec  1 19:45 datadirect
drwxr-xr-x  2 oracle oinstall   63 Dec  1 19:45 include
drwxr-xr-x  2 oracle oinstall   85 Dec  1 19:45 jlib
drwxr-xr-x  6 oracle oinstall 4096 Dec  1 19:45 lib
drwxr-xr-x  8 oracle oinstall  115 Dec  1 19:45 jdk
drwxr-xr-x 13 oracle oinstall 4096 Dec  1 19:45 OPatch
```

```
drwxr-xr-x   2 oracle oinstall 4096 Dec  1 19:45 bin
drwxr-xr-x   8 oracle oinstall 4096 Dec  1 19:45 oui
drwxr-x---  13 oracle oinstall 4096 Dec  1 19:45 inventory
drwxr-xr-x   3 oracle oinstall   28 Dec  1 19:45 install
drwxr-xr-x   3 oracle oinstall   17 Dec  1 19:46 cfgtoollogs
[oracle@ogg_hub pggg]$
```

Create the Deployments

Create Deployment for Source Oracle Database

- As Oracle user, create directories for the following:

    - **Service manager deployment home:** For a new Service Manager deployment that stores Service Manager files

    - **User deployment home:** Stores the deployment configuration files, trail files, wallet files, log files, etc.

    - **Data store home:** Stores the Performance Metrics data

        [oracle@ogg_hub ~]$ mkdir -p /u01/app/ogg/o_smd

        [oracle@ogg_hub ~]$ mkdir -p /u01/app/ogg/o_udh

        [oracle@ogg_hub ~]$ mkdir -p /u01/app/ogg/o_dsh

- As Oracle user, from Oracle OGG_HOME/bin, run Configuration Assistant (oggca) to create the deployment.

    [oracle@ogg_hub ~]$ cd /u01/app/ogg/oragg/bin/

    [oracle@ogg_hub bin]$ ./oggca.sh

Figures 9-19 through 9-27 show steps involved in Oracle GoldenGate Service Manager Deployment for Oracle.

- In step 1, Service Manager Deployment, set values as below and proceed with Next.

    - Software Home – /u01/app/ogg/oragg

    - Deployment Home – /u01/app/ogg/o_smd

CHAPTER 9   DATA REPLICATION FROM ORACLE TO POSTGRESQL USING ORACLE GOLDENGATE

- Hostname/IP Address – localhost
- Port – 9100
- Register as a service/system daemon – Check this box so that the service manager will be registered as a system daemon that can be managed using the systemctl command

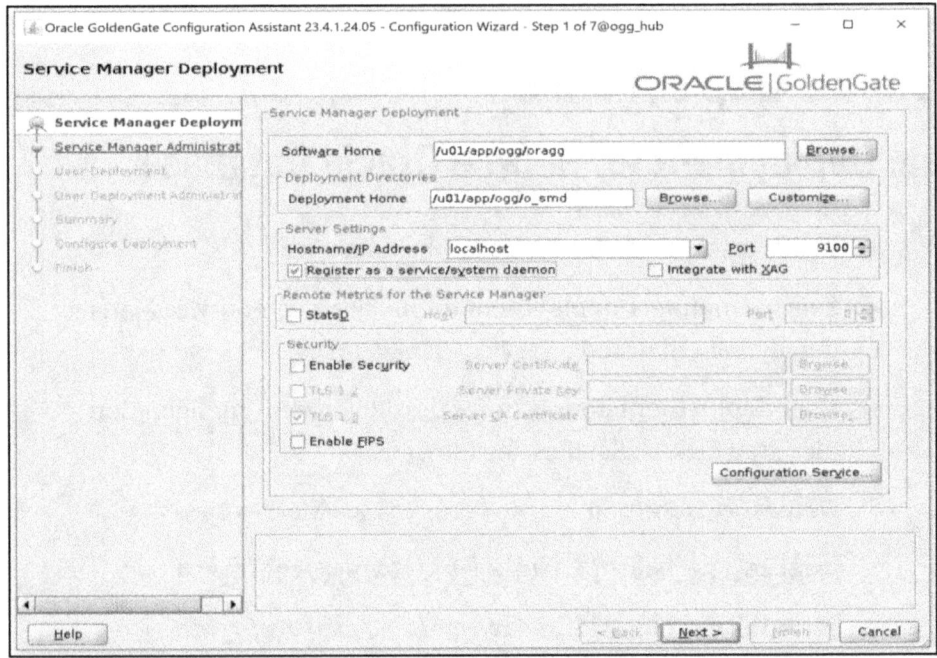

Figure 9-19.   GG Oracle Service Manager Deployment – step 1

- In step 2, Service Manager Administrator, set values as below and proceed with Next.
  - Username – admin
  - Password/Confirm Password – ********

This credential will be used to log in to Service Manager Console.

CHAPTER 9   DATA REPLICATION FROM ORACLE TO POSTGRESQL USING ORACLE GOLDENGATE

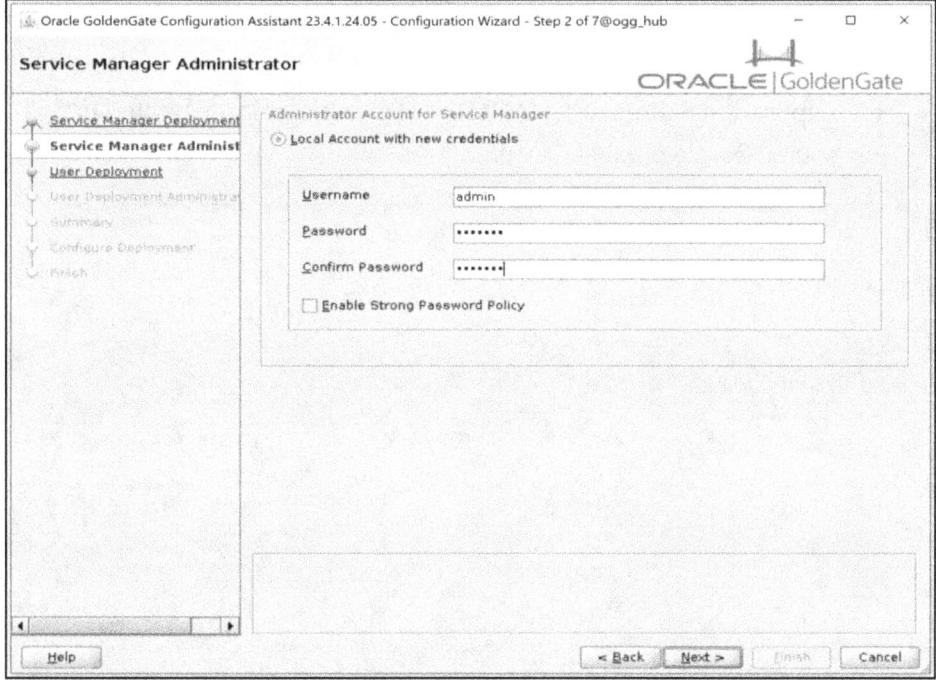

Figure 9-20. GG Oracle Service Manager Deployment – step 2

- In step 3, User Deployment, set values as below and proceed with Next.
    - Deployment Name – ora_source
    - Deployment Home – /u01/app/ogg/o_udh
    - Port numbers for services
        - Administration Service – 9101
        - Distribution Service – 9102
        - Receiver Service – 9103
    - Performance Metrics Service – 9104
    - Data Store Type – BDB
    - Data Store Home – /u01/app/ogg/o_dsh

- TNS_ADMIN – /u01/app/oracle/19client/network/admin – This path is from the installed Oracle 19c Client Home

- Replication Schema – GGADMIN – This was the user created in source Oracle database srcdb

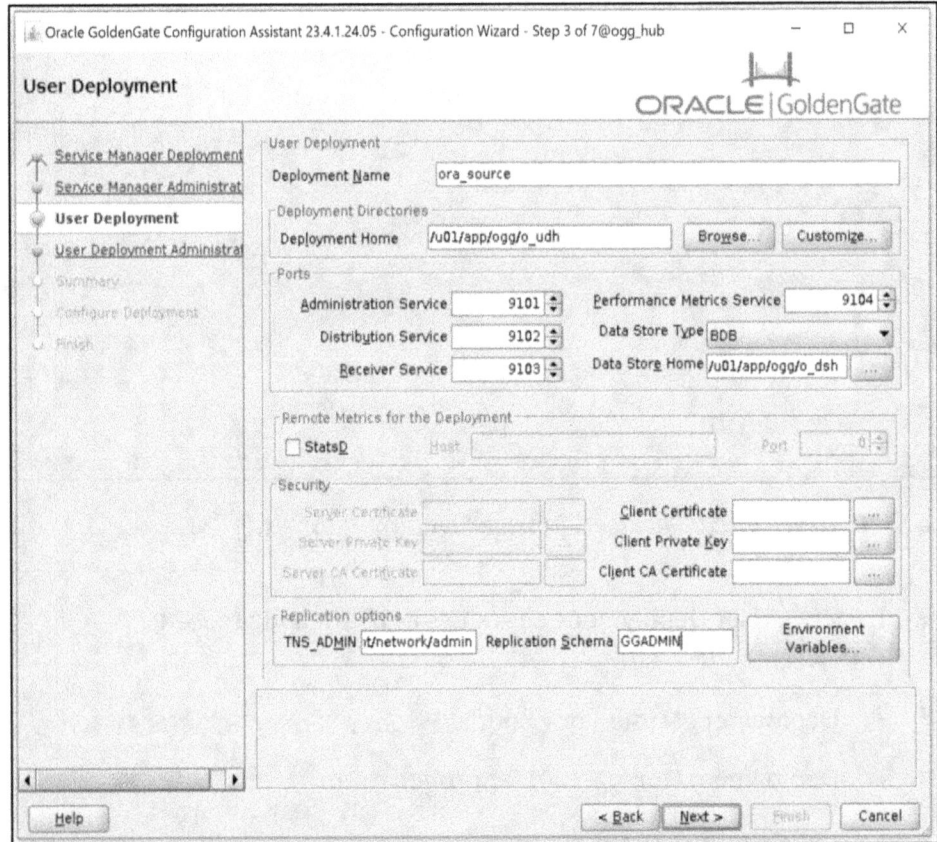

Figure 9-21. GG Oracle Service Manager Deployment – step 3

- In step 4, User Deployment Administrator, check and proceed with Next.
  - Same as Service Manager Administrator credentials.

  This allows to use the same username and password set in step 2.

CHAPTER 9　DATA REPLICATION FROM ORACLE TO POSTGRESQL USING ORACLE GOLDENGATE

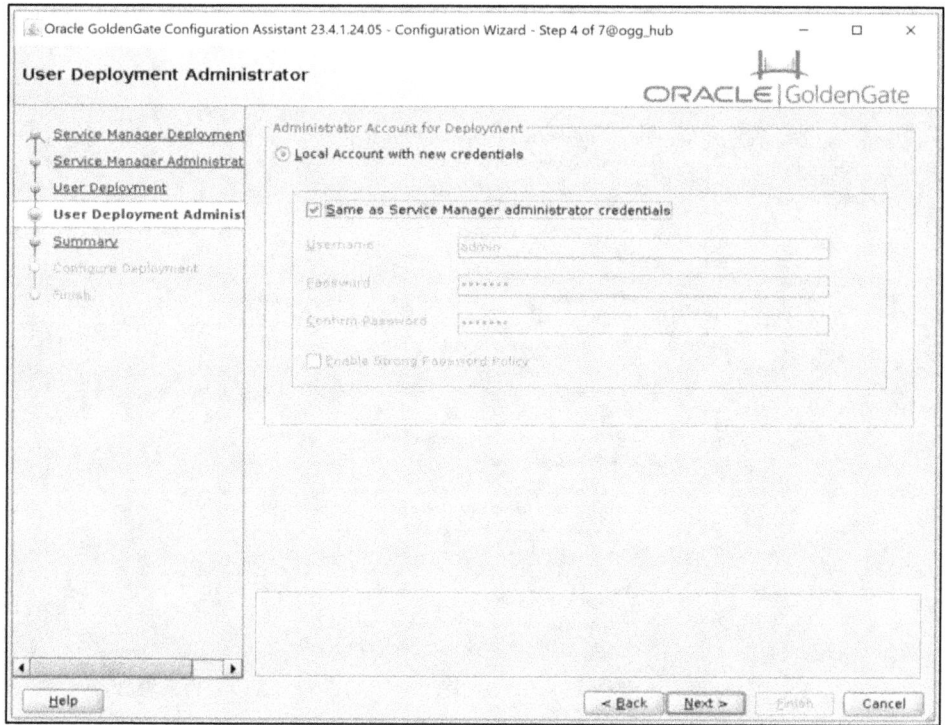

Figure 9-22. *GG Oracle Service Manager Deployment – step 4*

- In step 5, review the summary and click Finish.

CHAPTER 9   DATA REPLICATION FROM ORACLE TO POSTGRESQL USING ORACLE GOLDENGATE

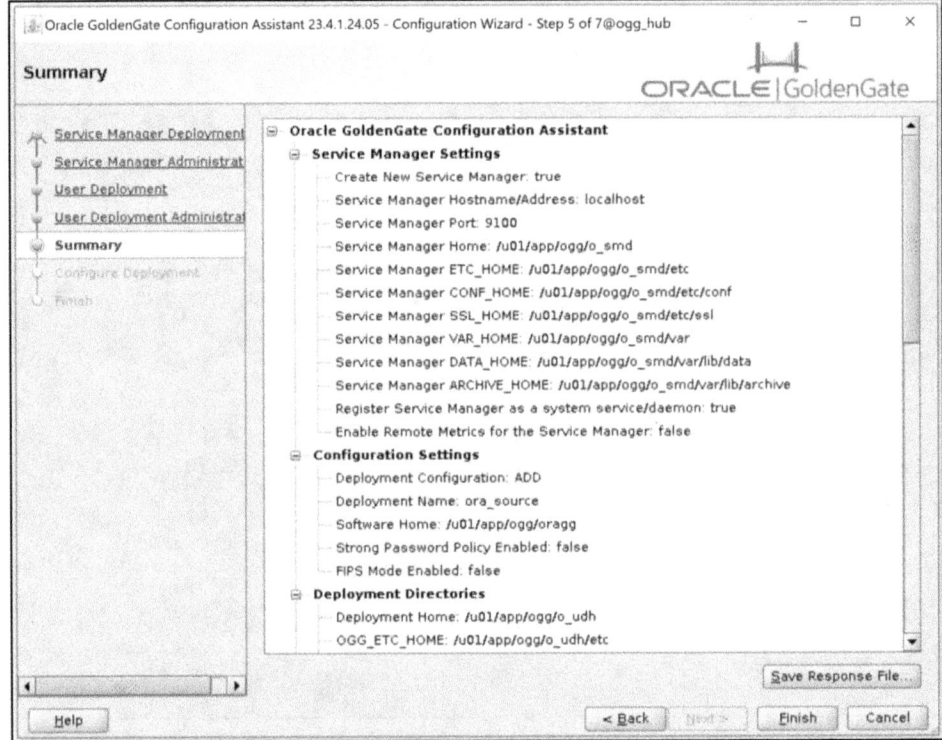

Figure 9-23. *GG Oracle Service Manager Deployment – step 5*

- In step 6, monitor the progress of the deployment configuration.

CHAPTER 9 DATA REPLICATION FROM ORACLE TO POSTGRESQL USING ORACLE GOLDENGATE

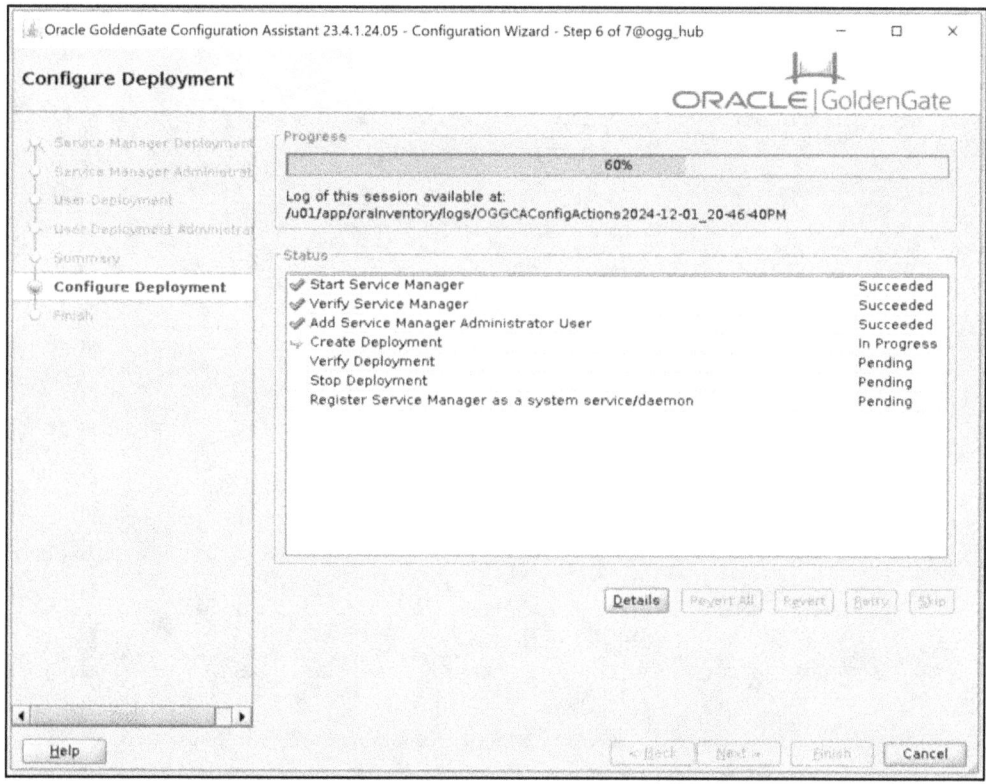

Figure 9-24. *GG Oracle Service Manager Deployment – step 6a*

CHAPTER 9 DATA REPLICATION FROM ORACLE TO POSTGRESQL USING ORACLE GOLDENGATE

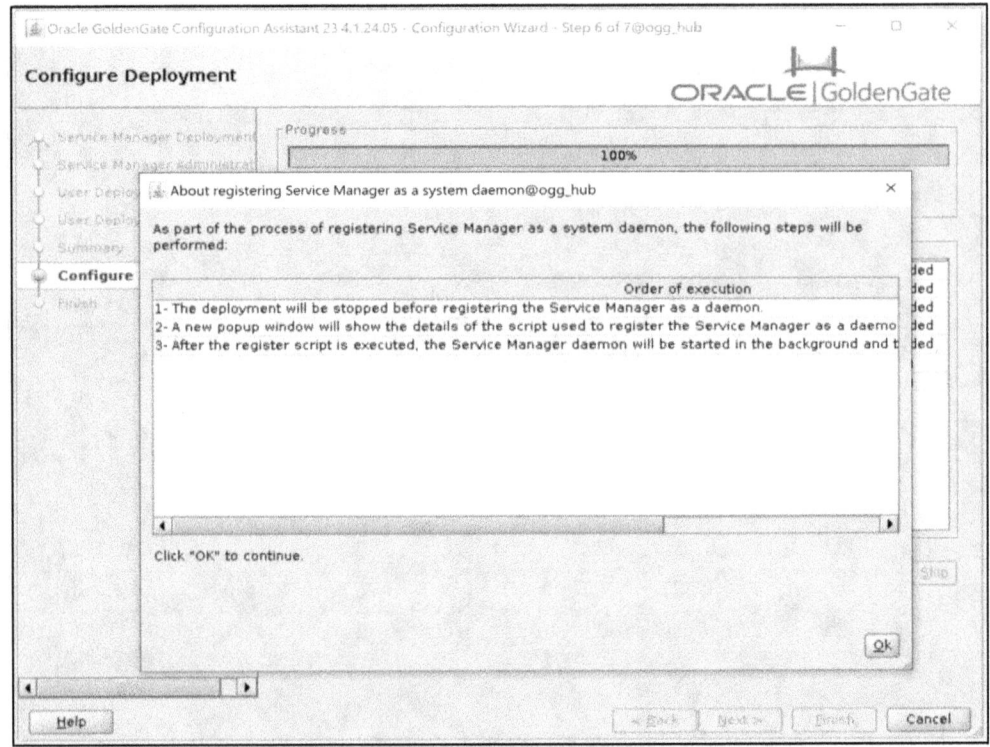

Figure 9-25. *GG Oracle Service Manager Deployment – step 6b*

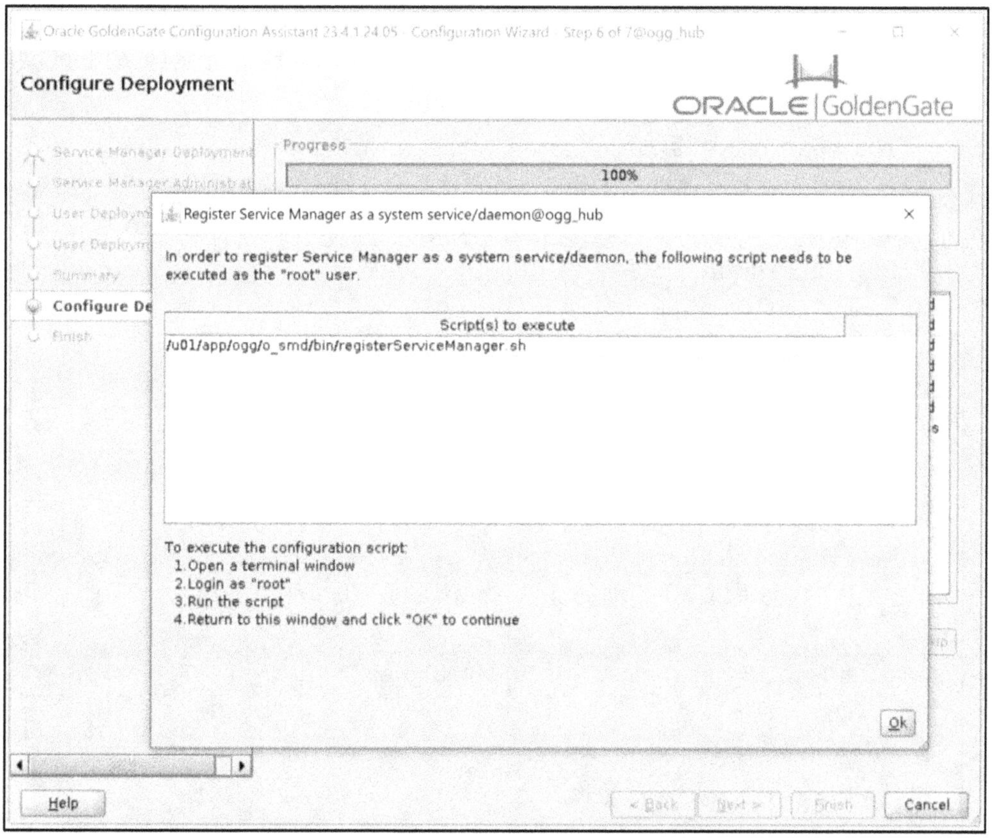

CHAPTER 9 DATA REPLICATION FROM ORACLE TO POSTGRESQL USING ORACLE GOLDENGATE

Figure 9-26. GG Oracle Service Manager Deployment – step 6c

- As recommended in the figure, as root user, execute the command to register the service manager as a system service/daemon.

[root@ogg_hub ~]# /u01/app/ogg/o_smd/bin/registerServiceManager.sh
Copyright (c) 2017, 2024, Oracle and/or its affiliates. All rights reserved.

      Oracle GoldenGate Install As Service Script

OGG_HOME=/u01/app/ogg/oragg
OGG_CONF_HOME=/u01/app/ogg/o_smd/etc/conf
OGG_VAR_HOME=/u01/app/ogg/o_smd/var
OGG_USER=oracle
Running OracleGoldenGateInstall.sh...

CHAPTER 9 DATA REPLICATION FROM ORACLE TO POSTGRESQL USING ORACLE GOLDENGATE

```
Created symlink /etc/systemd/system/multi-user.target.wants/
OracleGoldenGate.service → /etc/systemd/system/OracleGoldenGate.
service.
[root@ogg_hub ~]#
```

- In step 7, validate the deployment configuration is successful and close the wizard.

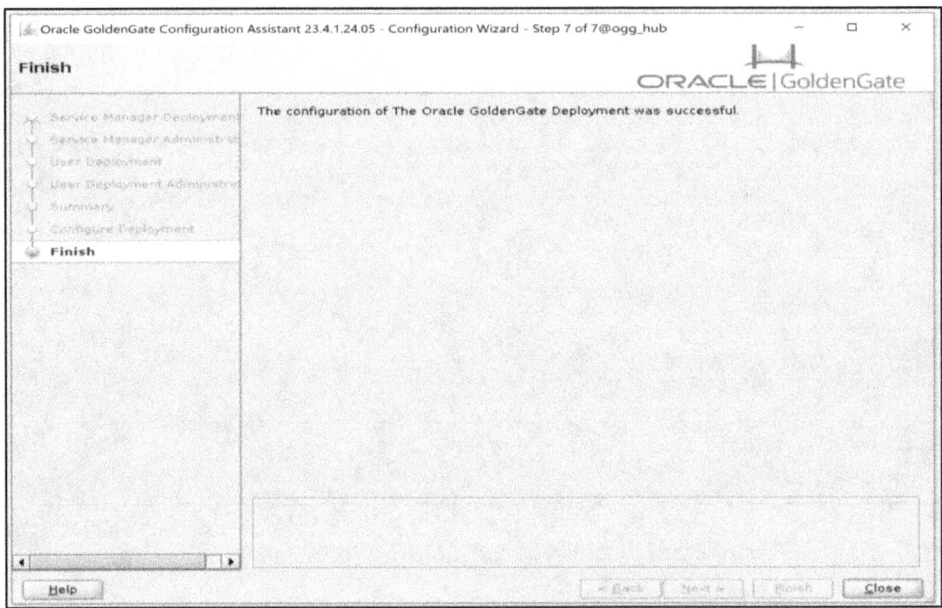

Figure 9-27. *GG Oracle Service Manager Deployment – step 7*

- Once the deployment for source Oracle is created, check the service manager processes.

  The service manager along with the deployment services can be seen running.

  [oracle@ogg_hub bin]$ ps -ef |grep -i service
  oracle   85842   1 0 21:39 ?   00:00:00 /u01/app/ogg/oragg/bin/ServiceManager --inventory '/u01/app/ogg/o_smd/etc/conf'

  [oracle@ogg_hub bin]$ ps -ef |grep -i gg

616

CHAPTER 9   DATA REPLICATION FROM ORACLE TO POSTGRESQL USING ORACLE GOLDENGATE

```
oracle     85842      1  0 21:39 ?        00:00:00 /u01/app/ogg/
oragg/bin/ServiceManager --inventory '/u01/app/ogg/o_smd/etc/conf'
oracle     85921  85842  0 21:39 ?        00:00:00 /u01/app/
ogg/oragg/bin/adminsrvr --config /u01/app/ogg/o_smd/var/run/ora_
source-adminsrvr-config.dat
oracle     85923  85842  0 21:39 ?        00:00:00 /u01/app/ogg/
oragg/bin/distsrvr --config /u01/app/ogg/o_smd/var/run/ora_source-
distsrvr-config.dat
oracle     85925  85842  0 21:39 ?        00:00:00 /u01/app/ogg/
oragg/bin/pmsrvr --config /u01/app/ogg/o_smd/var/run/ora_source-
pmsrvr-config.dat
oracle     85927  85842  0 21:39 ?        00:00:00 /u01/app/ogg/
oragg/bin/recvsrvr --config /u01/app/ogg/o_smd/var/run/ora_source-
recvsrvr-config.dat
```

- The service manager and deployment status can be verified by connecting to the Oracle service manager's console.

  Use the following URL: http://192.168.2.99:9100.

  - 192.168.2.99 – This is the ogg_hub server IP.

  - 9100 – This is the service manager port for ora_source deployment.

  Use credentials as admin/<password> set during step 2 in Figure 9-20.

617

CHAPTER 9   DATA REPLICATION FROM ORACLE TO POSTGRESQL USING ORACLE GOLDENGATE

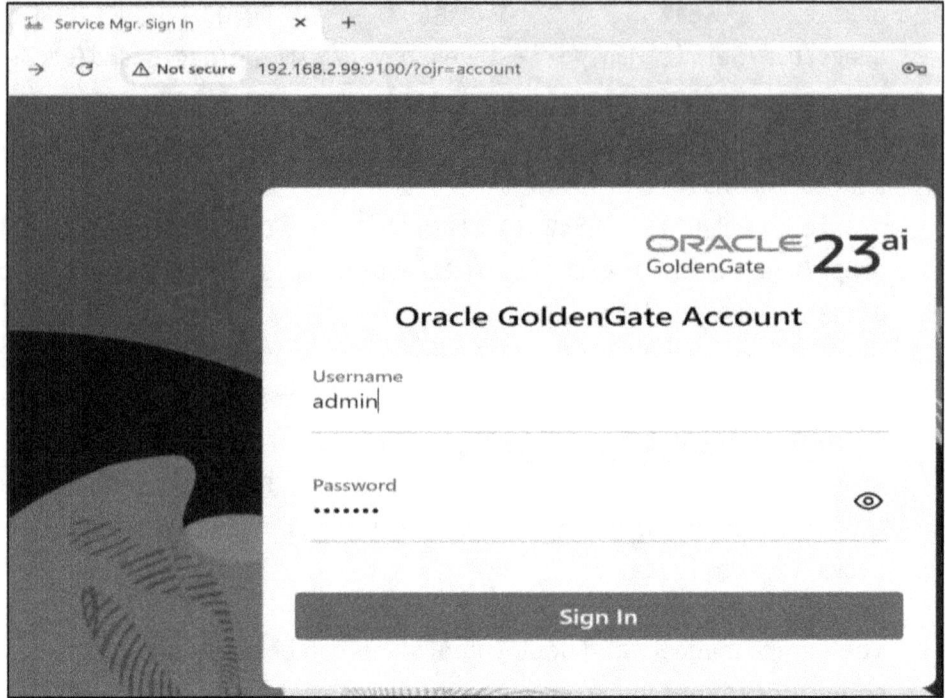

Figure 9-28. *Oracle GoldenGate Service Manager Login page*

- Once logged into Service Manager Console, on the home page, we can see the deployment details along with status of services.

Figure 9-29. *Oracle GoldenGate Service Manager home page*

CHAPTER 9   DATA REPLICATION FROM ORACLE TO POSTGRESQL USING ORACLE GOLDENGATE

- Navigate to Deployments ➤ ora_source ➤ Configuration, to check the environment variable TNS_ADMIN set during deployment creation.

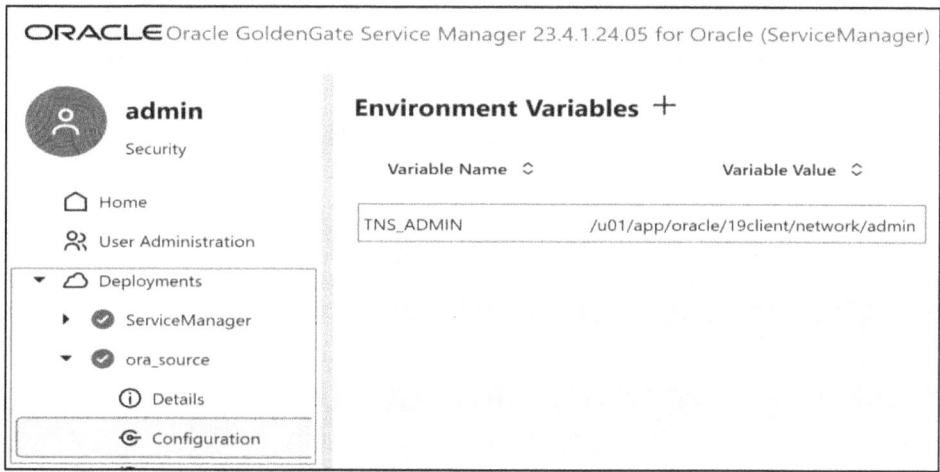

Figure 9-30. ora_source deployment environment variables

Create Deployment for Target PostgreSQL Database

- As Oracle user, create directories for the following:

  - **Service manager deployment home:** For a new Service Manager deployment that stores Service Manager files

  - **User deployment home:** Stores the deployment configuration files, trail files, wallet files, log files, etc.

  - **Data store home:** Stores the Performance Metrics data

    [oracle@ogg_hub ~]$ mkdir -p /u01/app/ogg/p_smd

    [oracle@ogg_hub ~]$ mkdir -p /u01/app/ogg/p_udh

    [oracle@ogg_hub ~]$ mkdir -p /u01/app/ogg/p_dsh

- As Oracle user, from PostgreSQL OGG_HOME/bin, run Configuration Assistant (oggca) to create the deployment for target.

  [oracle@ogg_hub ~]$ cd /u01/app/ogg/pggg/bin

  [oracle@ogg_hub bin]$ ./oggca.sh

CHAPTER 9   DATA REPLICATION FROM ORACLE TO POSTGRESQL USING ORACLE GOLDENGATE

Figures 9-31 through 9-37 show steps involved in Oracle GoldenGate Service Manager Deployment for PostgreSQL.

- In step 1, Service Manager Deployment, set values as below and proceed with Next.

    - Software Home – /u01/app/ogg/pggg
    - Deployment Home – /u01/app/ogg/p_smd
    - Hostname/IP Address – localhost
    - Port – 9200

Note Since Oracle Service Manager is already registered as service daemon, the Service Manager creating for PostgreSQL cannot be registered because two service managers cannot be registered with same name.

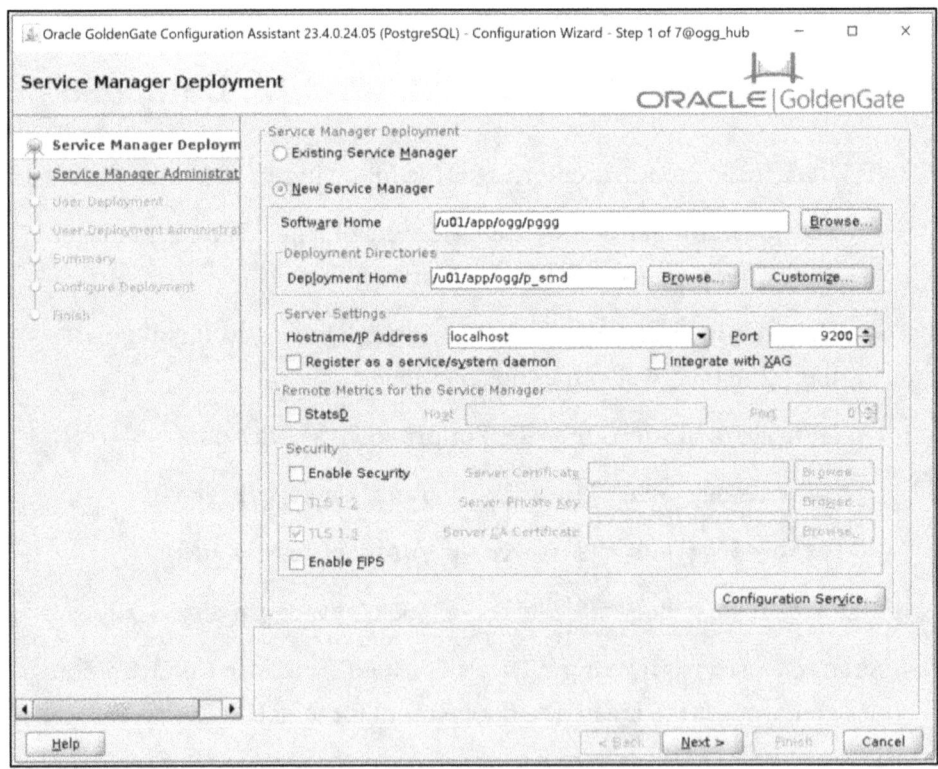

Figure 9-31. *GG PostgreSQL Service Manager Deployment – step 1*

CHAPTER 9   DATA REPLICATION FROM ORACLE TO POSTGRESQL USING ORACLE GOLDENGATE

- In step 2, Service Manager Administrator, set values as below and proceed with Next.

  - Username – admin

  - Password/Confirm Password – ********

  This credential will be used to log in to Service Manager Console.

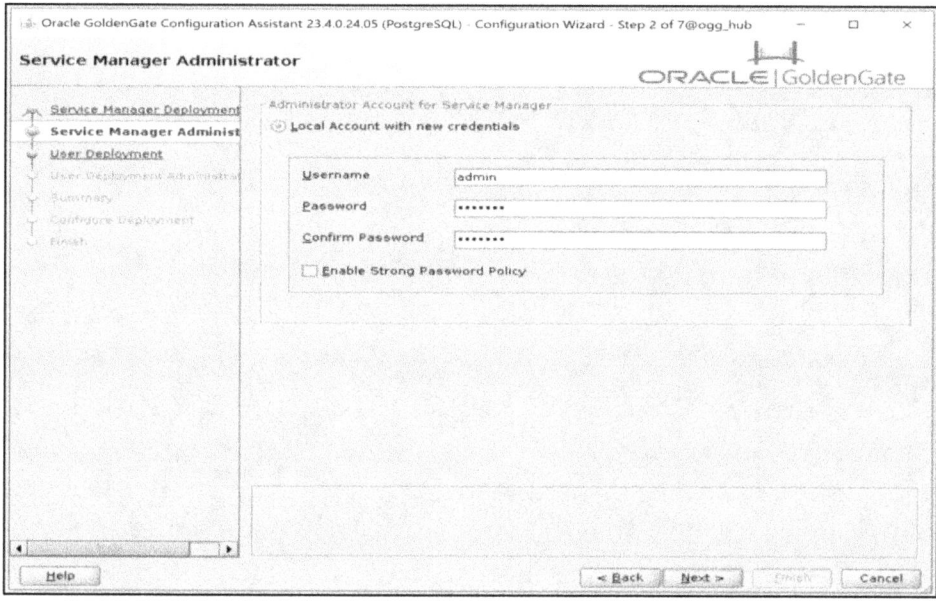

Figure 9-32. GG PostgreSQL Service Manager Deployment – step 2

In step 3, User Deployment, set values as below and proceed with Next.

- Deployment Name – pg_target

- Deployment Home – /u01/app/ogg/p_udh

- Port numbers for services

- Administration Service – 9201

- Distribution Service – 9202

- Receiver Service – 9203

- Performance Metrics Service – 9204

CHAPTER 9　DATA REPLICATION FROM ORACLE TO POSTGRESQL USING ORACLE GOLDENGATE

- Data Store Type – BDB

- Data Store Home – /u01/app/ogg/p_dsh

- Replication Schema – gguser – This was the user created in target PostgreSQL database postgres

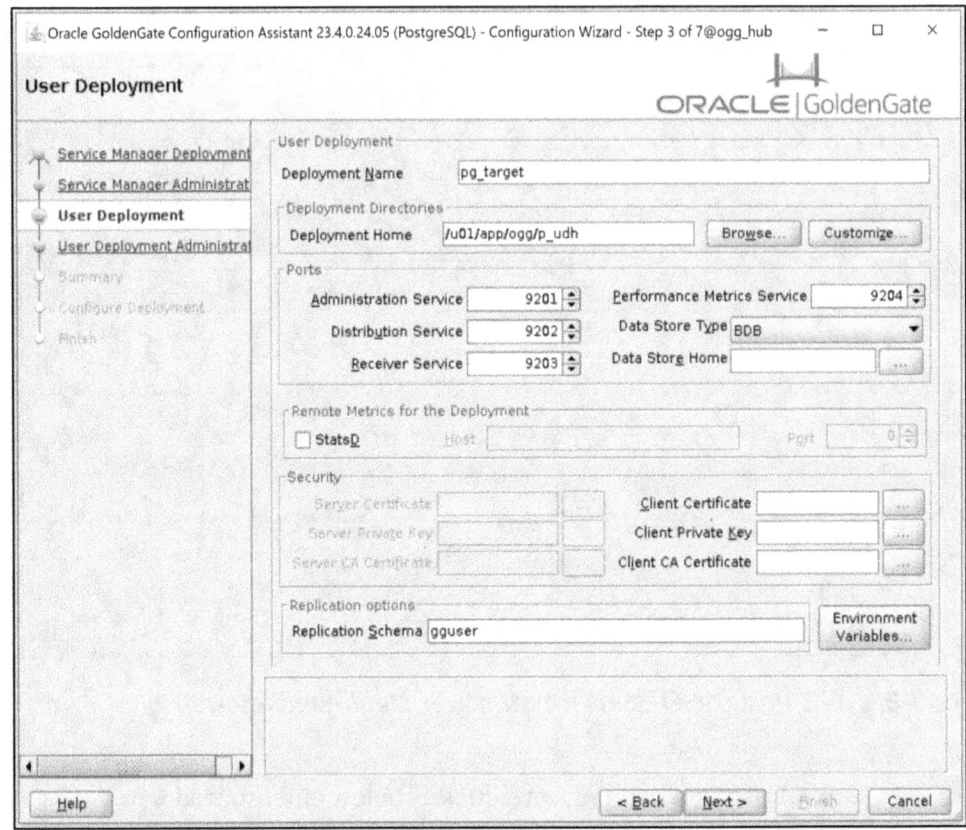

Figure 9-33. *GG PostgreSQL Service Manager Deployment – step 3*

CHAPTER 9   DATA REPLICATION FROM ORACLE TO POSTGRESQL USING ORACLE GOLDENGATE

- In step 4, User Deployment Administrator, check and proceed with Next.

  - Same as Service Manager Administrator credentials

  This allows to use the same username and password set in step 2.

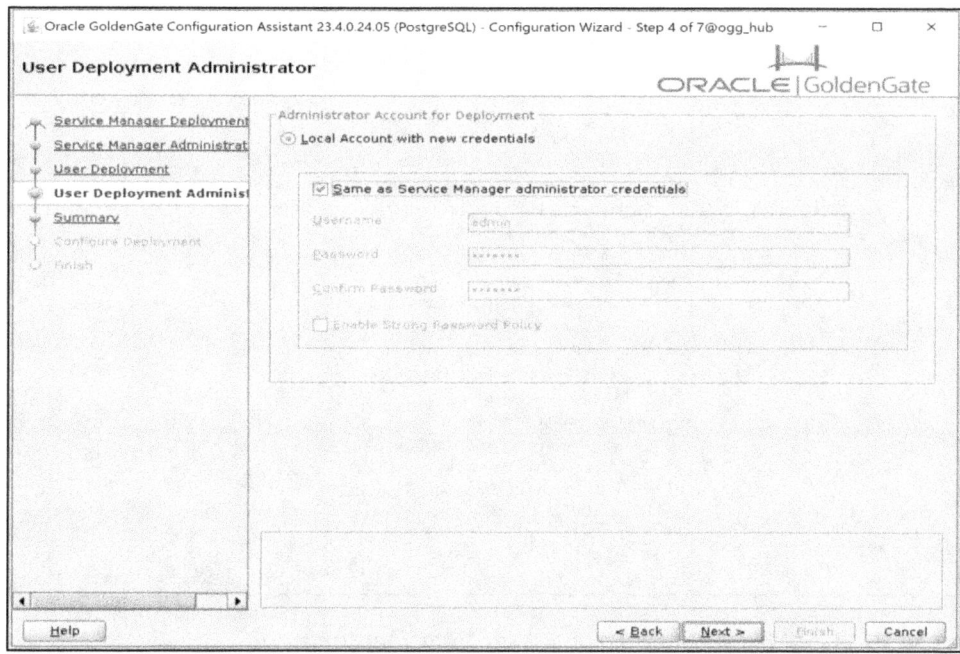

Figure 9-34. *GG PostgreSQL Service Manager Deployment – step 4*

CHAPTER 9 DATA REPLICATION FROM ORACLE TO POSTGRESQL USING ORACLE GOLDENGATE

- In step 5, review the summary and click Finish.

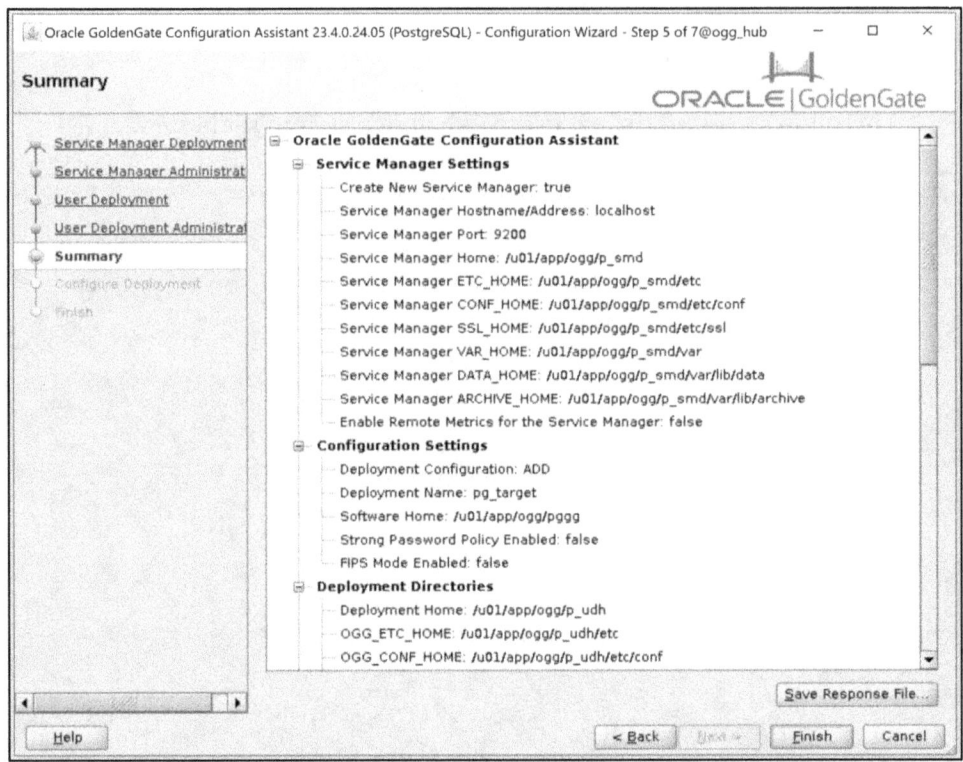

Figure 9-35. GG PostgreSQL Service Manager Deployment – step 5

- In step 6, monitor the progress of the deployment configuration.

CHAPTER 9   DATA REPLICATION FROM ORACLE TO POSTGRESQL USING ORACLE GOLDENGATE

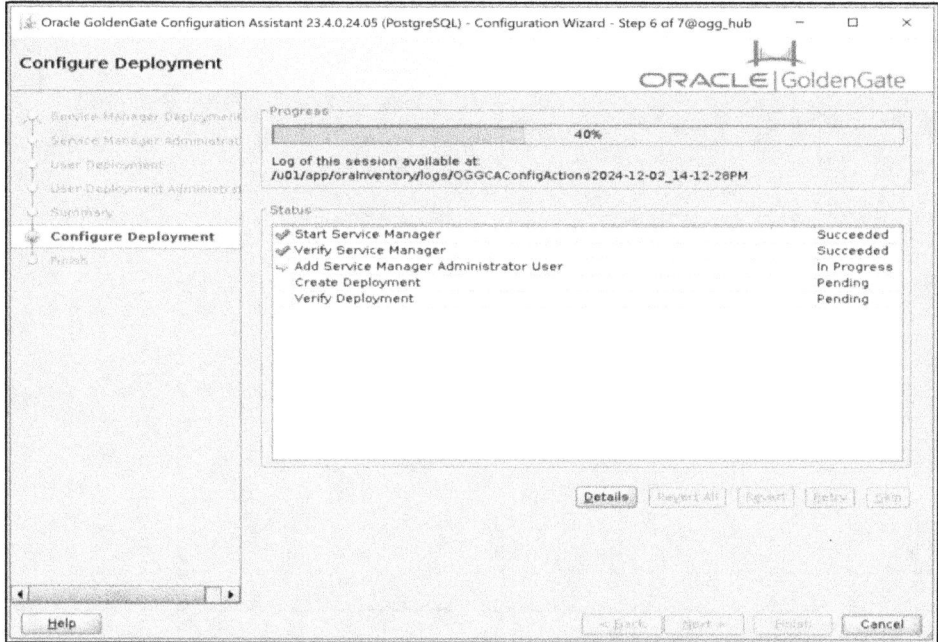

Figure 9-36. *GG PostgreSQL Service Manager Deployment – step 6*

- In step 7, validate the deployment configuration is successful and close the wizard.

CHAPTER 9   DATA REPLICATION FROM ORACLE TO POSTGRESQL USING ORACLE GOLDENGATE

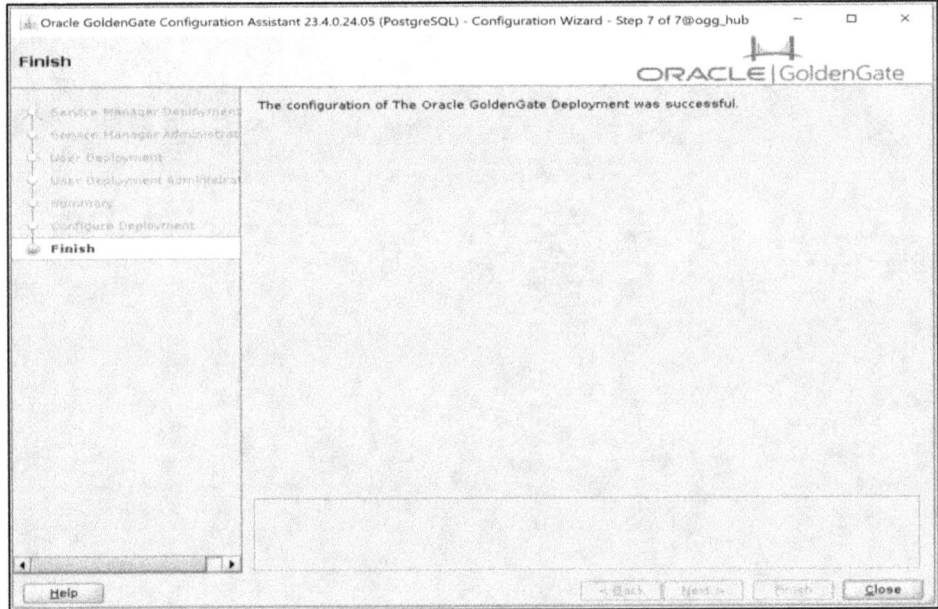

Figure 9-37. GG PostgreSQL Service Manager Deployment – step 7

- Once the deployment for target PostgreSQL is created, check the service manager processes.

The service manager along with the deployment services for target postgres can be seen running.

[oracle@ogg_hub bin]$ ps -ef |grep -i service
oracle   85842   1 0 Dec01 ?   00:00:40 /u01/app/ogg/oragg/bin/ServiceManager --inventory '/u01/app/ogg/o_smd/etc/conf'
oracle   130975   1 0 15:18 ?   00:00:00 /u01/app/ogg/pggg/bin/ServiceManager

[oracle@ogg_hub bin]$ ps -ef |grep -i gg |grep -i pgg
oracle   130975   1 0 15:18 ?   00:00:00 /u01/app/ogg/pggg/bin/ServiceManager
oracle   131054 130975 0 15:18 ?   00:00:00 /u01/app/ogg/pggg/bin/adminsrvr --config /u01/app/ogg/p_smd/var/run/pg_target-adminsrvr-config.dat

CHAPTER 9   DATA REPLICATION FROM ORACLE TO POSTGRESQL USING ORACLE GOLDENGATE

```
oracle    131059    130975   0 15:18 ?         00:00:01 /u01/app/ogg/
pggg/bin/distsrvr --config /u01/app/ogg/p_smd/var/run/pg_target-
distsrvr-config.dat
oracle    131072    130975   0 15:18 ?         00:00:00 /u01/app/ogg/
pggg/bin/recvsrvr --config /u01/app/ogg/p_smd/var/run/pg_target-
recvsrvr-config.dat
oracle    131101    130975   0 15:18 ?         00:00:01 /u01/app/ogg/
pggg/bin/pmsrvr
oracle    131267    11059    0 15:23 pts/0     00:00:00
grep --color=auto -i pgg
```

- The service manager and deployment status can be verified by connecting to PostgreSQL service manager's console.

- Use the URL http://192.168.2.99:9200 and credentials as admin/<password> set during step 2 in Figure 9-32.

    - 192.168.2.99 – This is the ogg_hub server IP.

    - 9200 – This is the service manager port for pg_target deployment.

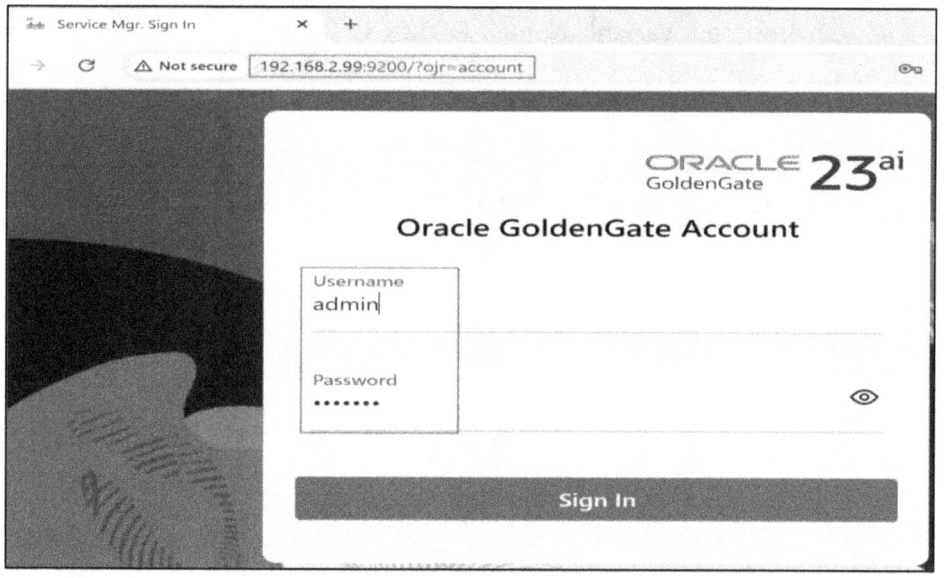

Figure 9-38. *PostgreSQL Goldengate Service Manager Login page*

CHAPTER 9   DATA REPLICATION FROM ORACLE TO POSTGRESQL USING ORACLE GOLDENGATE

- To add a new Environment Variable:
- Navigate to Deployments ➤ pg_target ➤ Configuration
- Click "+"

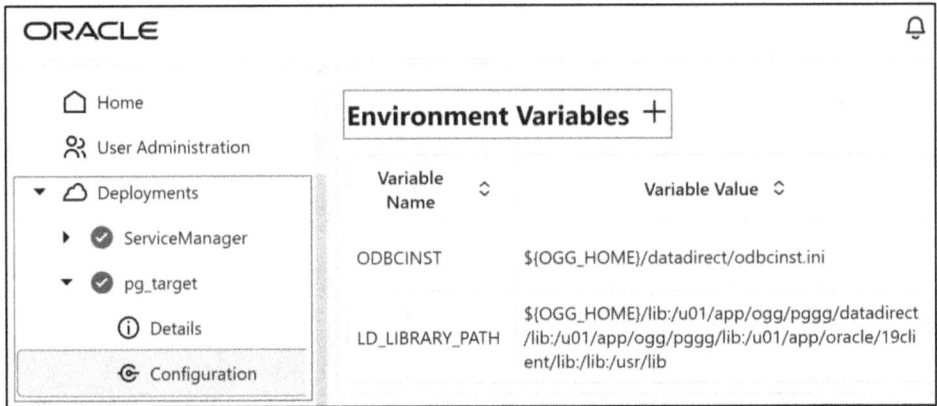

Figure 9-39. *pg_target deployment environment variables page*

- On the Add Environment screen, set variables and submit:
  - Environment Variable Name – ODBCINI
  - Environment Variable Value – /u01/app/ogg/pggg/datadirect/odbc.ini

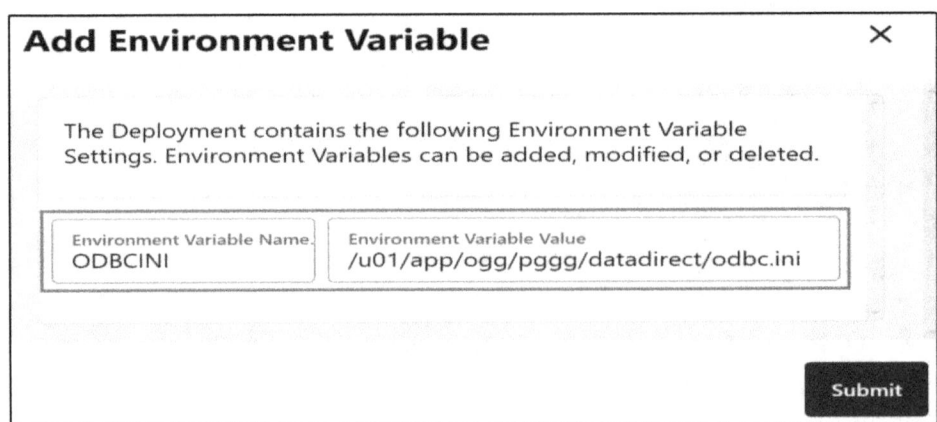

Figure 9-40. *pg_target deployment adding environment variable*

- The newly added environment variable can be seen.

CHAPTER 9   DATA REPLICATION FROM ORACLE TO POSTGRESQL USING ORACLE GOLDENGATE

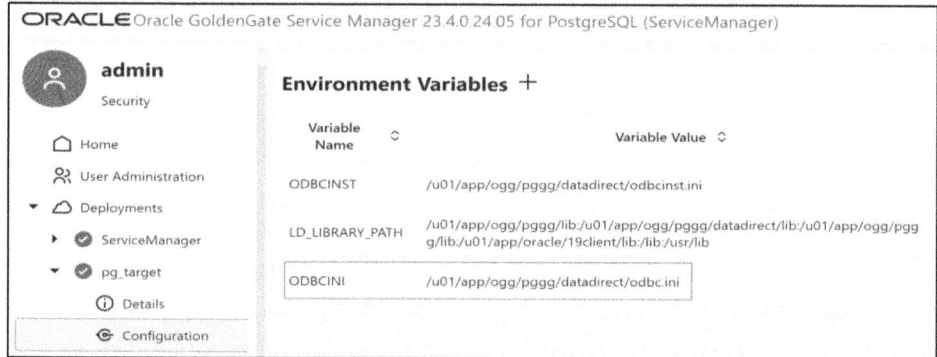

Figure 9-41. *pg_target deployment environment variables page*

Configure GoldenGate on Source Deployment
Add TNS Alias

- In ogg_hub server, as Oracle user, add TNS Alias in tnsnames.ora located in Oracle 19c client home $ORACLE_HOME/network/admin directory.

[oracle@ogg_hub ~]$ cd /u01/app/oracle/19client/network/admin/

[oracle@ogg_hub admin]$ vi tnsnames.ora

[oracle@ogg_hub admin]$ cat tnsnames.ora
```
ORSRCDB =
  (DESCRIPTION =
    (ADDRESS_LIST =
      (ADDRESS = (PROTOCOL = TCP)(HOST = ora_serv)(PORT = 1521))
    )
    (CONNECT_DATA =
      (SERVICE_NAME = srcdb)
    )
  )
```

CHAPTER 9   DATA REPLICATION FROM ORACLE TO POSTGRESQL USING ORACLE GOLDENGATE

- Verify the database remote connectivity to source Oracle database srcdb from ogg_hub server using TNS Alias added in the previous step.

[oracle@ogg_hub admin]$ export ORACLE_HOME=/u01/app/oracle/19client

[oracle@ogg_hub admin]$ export PATH=$PATH:$ORACLE_HOME/bin:$ORACLE_HOME/lib

[oracle@ogg_hub ~]$ sqlplus

```
SQL*Plus: Release 19.0.0.0.0 - Production on Mon Dec 2 18:55:52 2024
Version 19.3.0.0.0
Copyright (c) 1982, 2019, Oracle.  All rights reserved.
```

Enter user-name: ggadmin/ggadmin@orsrcdb

```
Connected to:
Oracle Database 19c Enterprise Edition Release 19.0.0.0.0
```

SQL> show user
```
USER is "GGADMIN"
```

Configure Source Database for GoldenGate

- Connect to Oracle administration service console at http://192.168.2.99:9101.

CHAPTER 9   DATA REPLICATION FROM ORACLE TO POSTGRESQL USING ORACLE GOLDENGATE

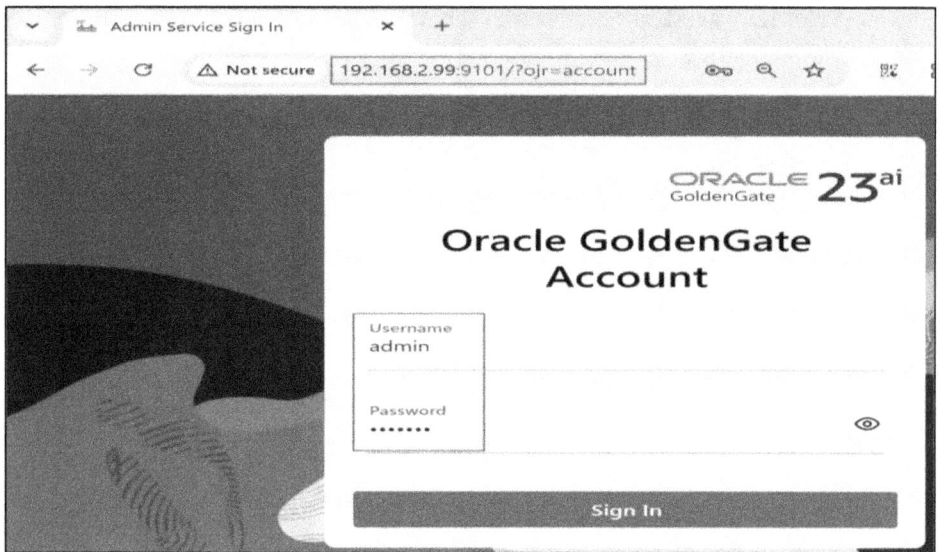

Figure 9-42. ora_source deployment administration service login page

- Add the database credential.
  - Navigate to Administration Service ➤ DB Connections. Click "+".

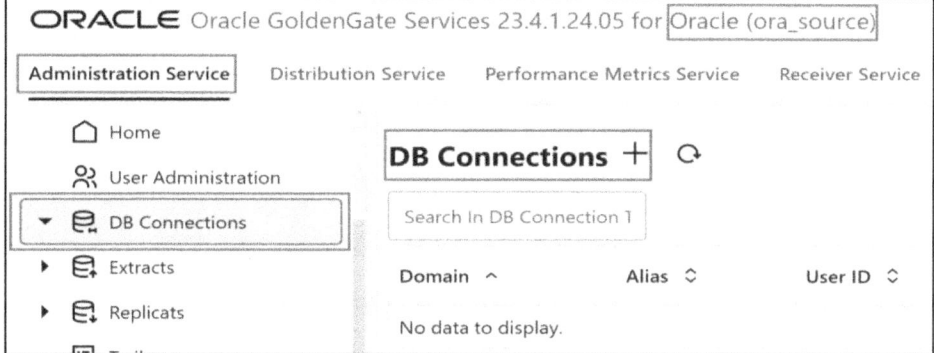

Figure 9-43. ora_source administration service DB connections page

- In the Credentials screen, add the values as below and submit:
  - Credential Domain – OracleGoldenGate
  - Credential Alias – ora_srcdb

CHAPTER 9   DATA REPLICATION FROM ORACLE TO POSTGRESQL USING ORACLE GOLDENGATE

- User ID – ggadmin@orsrcdb – This user and tnsalias are used for database remote connectivity

- Password and Verify Password – Password of ggadmin user from srcdb

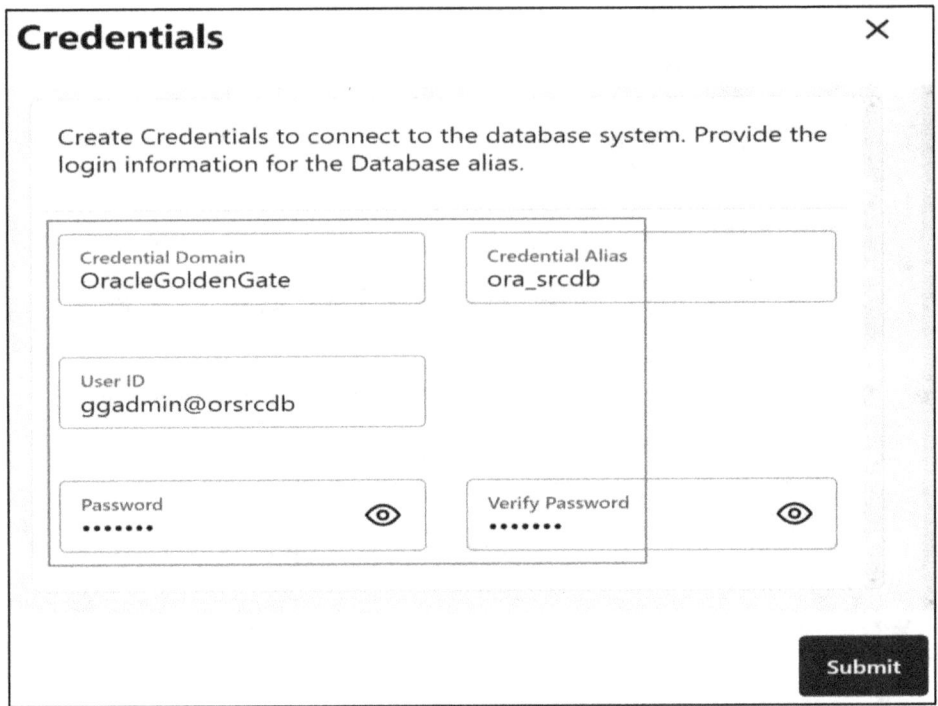

Figure 9-44. DB Credentials addition page

- We can see the newly created DB Connection.
  - Click on the icon under the Actions field to make the remote connection to the source database srcdb.

CHAPTER 9   DATA REPLICATION FROM ORACLE TO POSTGRESQL USING ORACLE GOLDENGATE

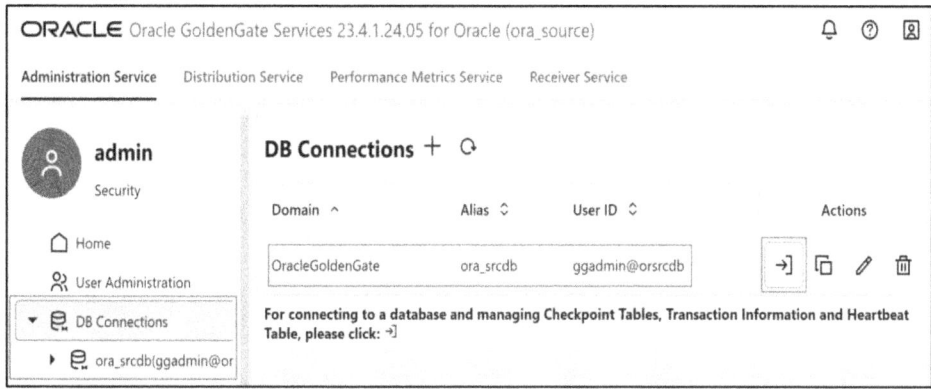

Figure 9-45. ora_source newly added DB connection page

- Create a checkpoint table. Once the DB connection to source database srcdb is established:
    - Navigate to Administration Service ➤ DB Connections ➤ ora_srcdb(ggadmin@orsrc) ➤ Checkpoint
- Click "+"

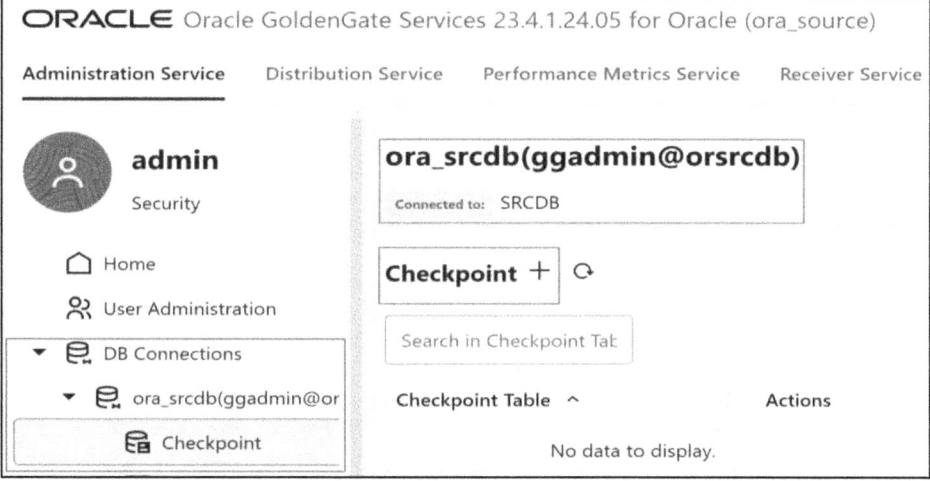

Figure 9-46. DB checkpoint creation page

- On the Checkpoint Table window, add Checkpoint Table as ggadmin. orackpt and submit.

CHAPTER 9   DATA REPLICATION FROM ORACLE TO POSTGRESQL USING ORACLE GOLDENGATE

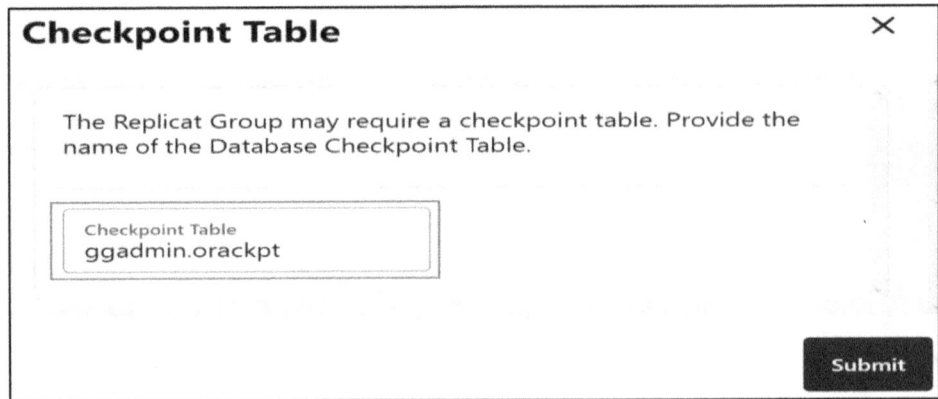

Figure 9-47. DB checkpoint table name

- Verify the Checkpoint table created.

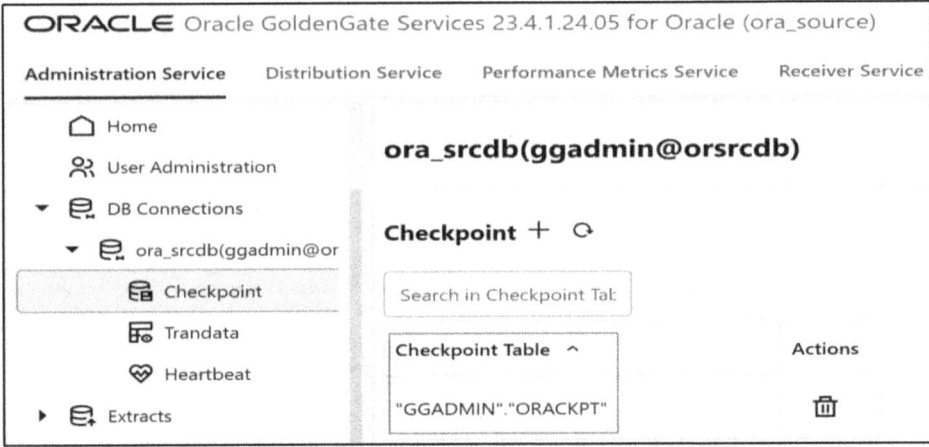

Figure 9-48. DB checkpoint table created

- Add trandata for schema ora_rep_user.
    - Navigate to Administration Service ➤ DB Connections ➤ ora_srcdb(ggadmin@orsrc) ➤ Trandata.
    - Select the Schema option and click "+".

CHAPTER 9   DATA REPLICATION FROM ORACLE TO POSTGRESQL USING ORACLE GOLDENGATE

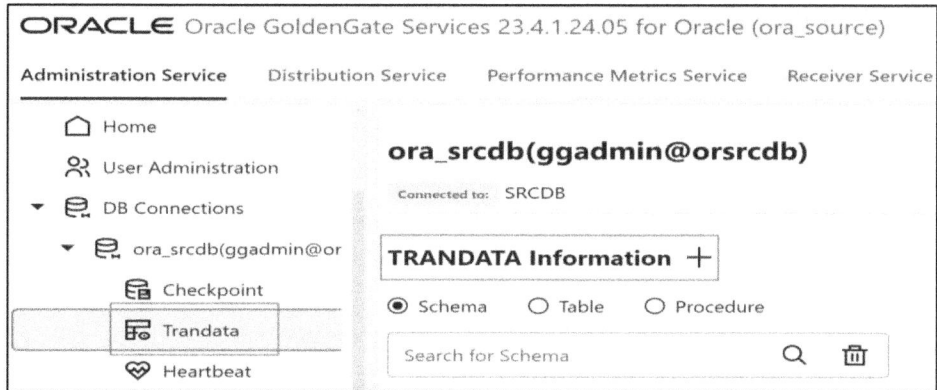

Figure 9-49.   DB trandata addition page

- On the Trandata window, add values as below and submit:
  - Schema Name – ora_rep_user
  - Check the All Columns option

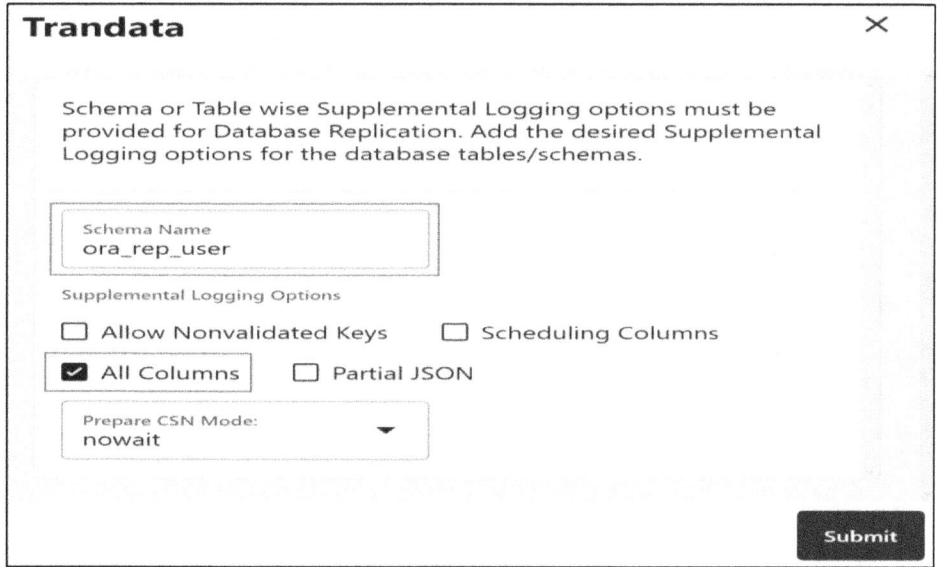

Figure 9-50.   DB trandata addition for schema

- Verify the schema trandata by searching with schema name.

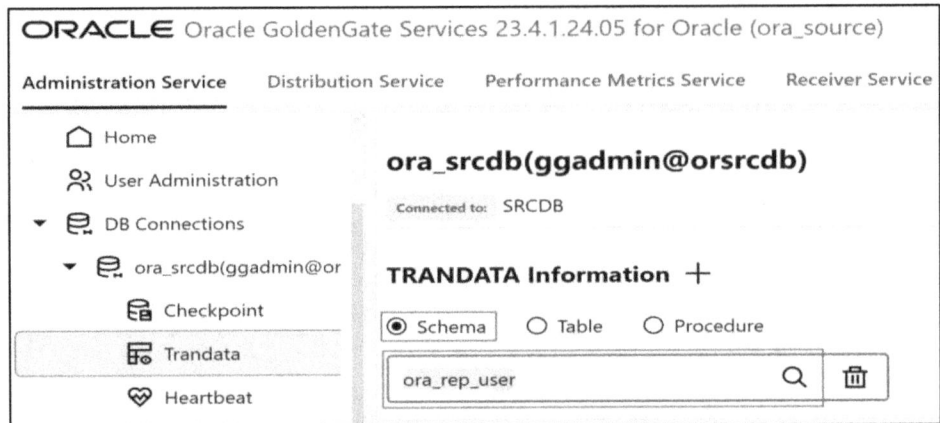

Figure 9-51. *DB trandata for schema search option*

Figure 9-52. *DB trandata for schema details*

- Add trandata for table ora_rep_user.ggtest.
  - Select the Table option and click "+".

CHAPTER 9   DATA REPLICATION FROM ORACLE TO POSTGRESQL USING ORACLE GOLDENGATE

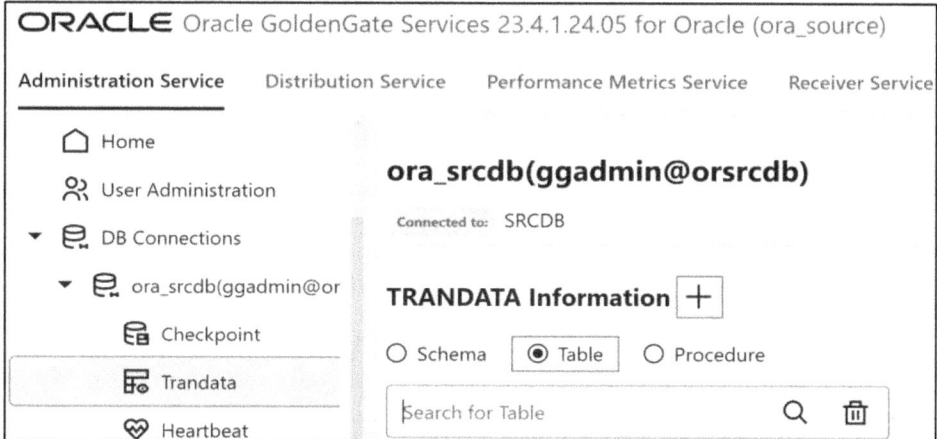

Figure 9-53. DB trandata for table addition page

- On the Trandata window, add values as below and submit:
  - Table Name – ora_rep_user.ggtest
  - Select Scheduling Columns and All Columns options

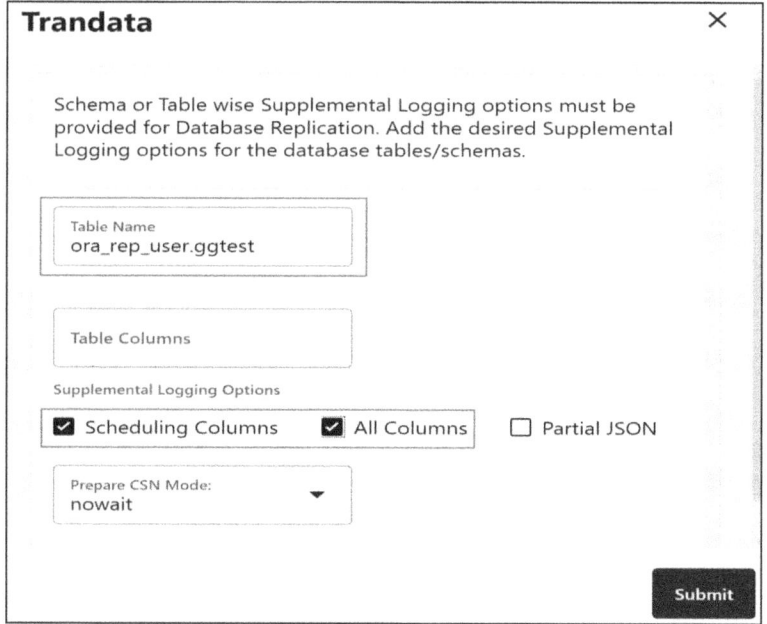

Figure 9-54. DB trandata creation for table

- Verify the table trandata by searching with table name.

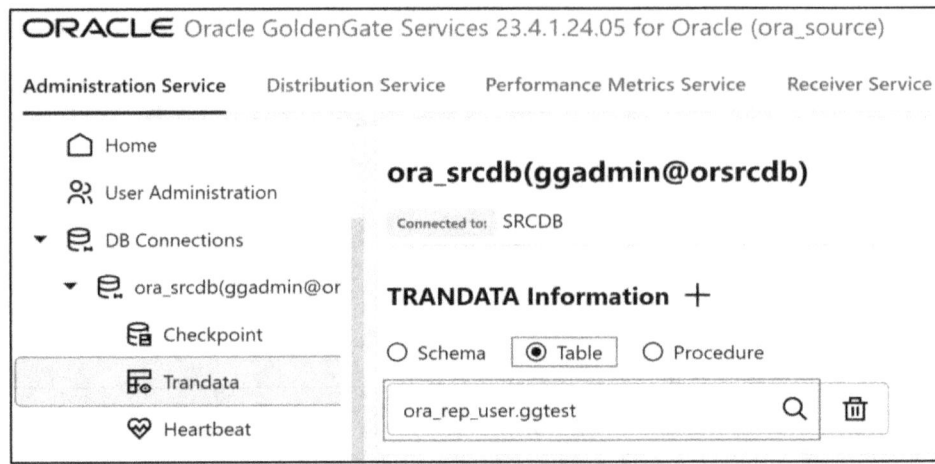

Figure 9-55. DB trandata for table search option

Figure 9-56. DB trandata for table details

- Add a Heartbeat table.

  - Navigate to Administration Service ➤ DB Connections ➤ ora_srcdb(ggadmin@orsrc) ➤ Heartbeat.

  - Click "+" followed by submit with default values.

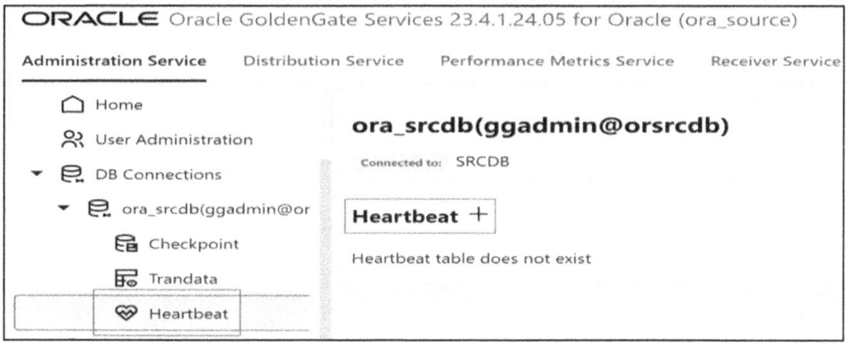

Figure 9-57. DB heartbeat table addition page

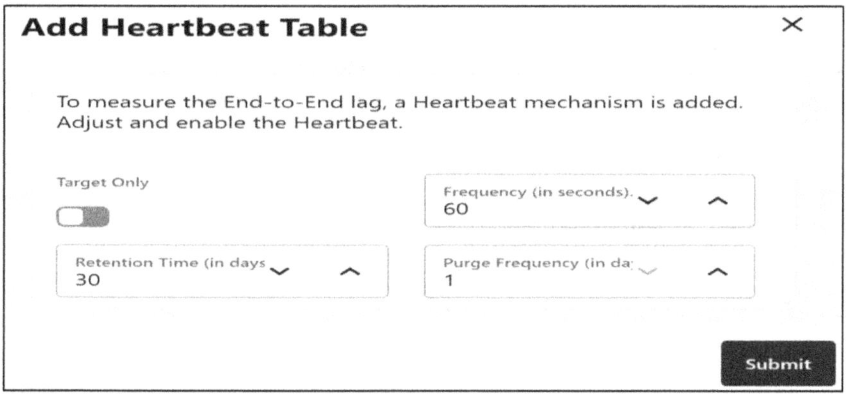

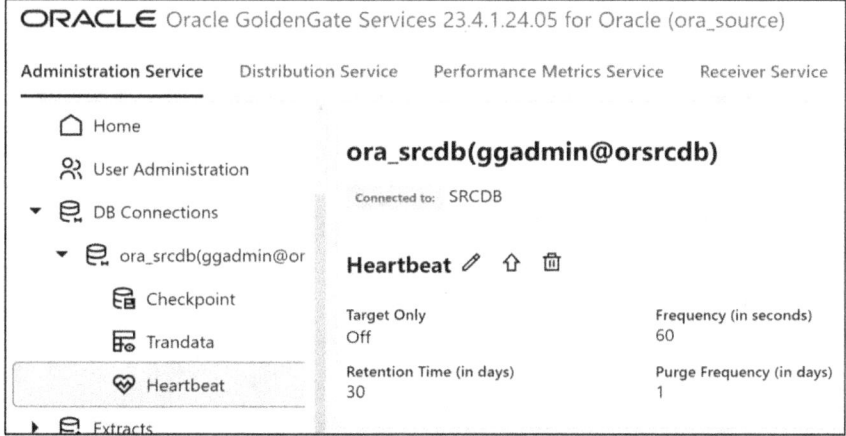

Figure 9-58. DB heartbeat table addition

Figure 9-59. DB heartbeat table details

CHAPTER 9   DATA REPLICATION FROM ORACLE TO POSTGRESQL USING ORACLE GOLDENGATE

Replication Configuration – Create Extract Process

Figures 9-60 through 9-65 show steps involved in Oracle Extract creation.

- Navigate to Administration Service ➤ Home.
  - Click "+".

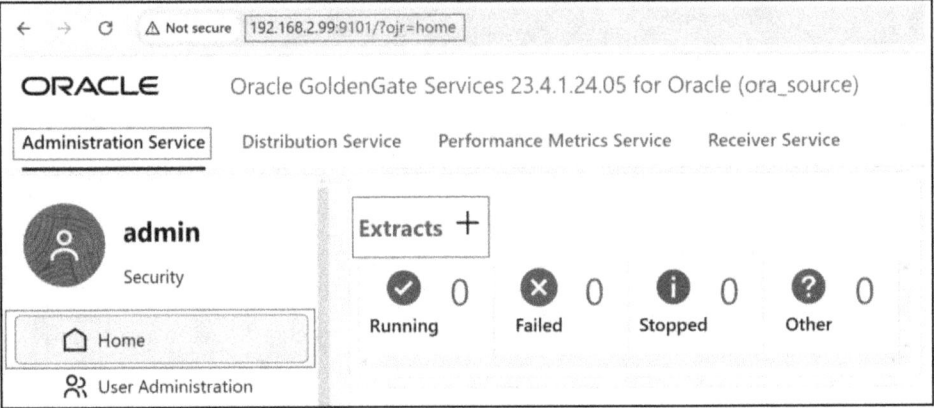

Figure 9-60. *Oracle administration service extract home page*

- In step 1, Add Extract ➤ Extract Information, add/select values as below and proceed with Next.
  - Extract Type – Integrated Extract
  - Process Name – EXTORA
  - Description – Extract for ora_rep_user

CHAPTER 9   DATA REPLICATION FROM ORACLE TO POSTGRESQL USING ORACLE GOLDENGATE

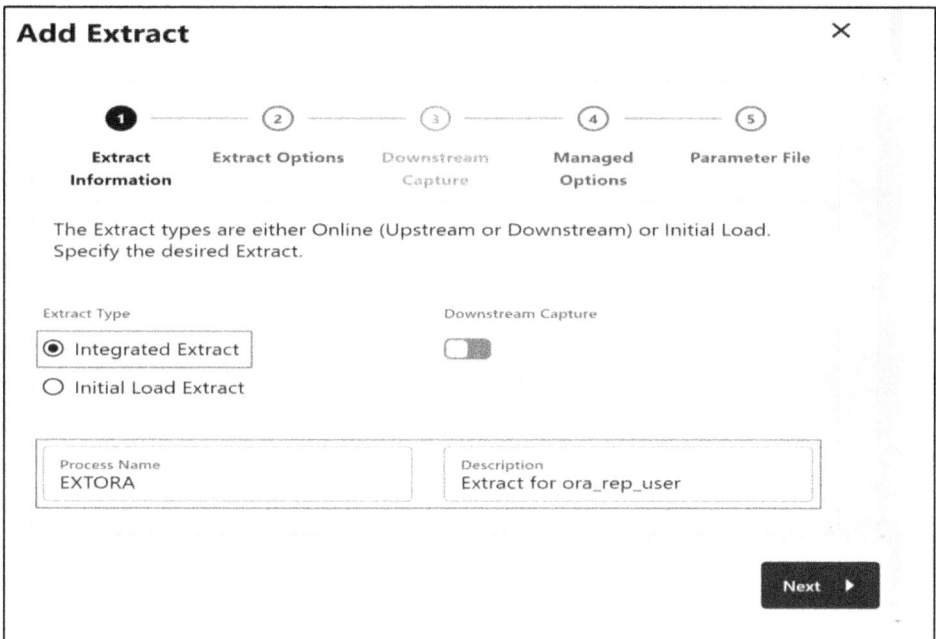

Figure 9-61. *Oracle add extract – extract information page*

- In step 2, Extract Options, add/select values as below and proceed with Next.

    - Source Credentials Domain – OracleGoldenGate
    - Alias – ora_srcdb
    - Extract Trail – eo
    - Subdirectory – oratrail

CHAPTER 9 DATA REPLICATION FROM ORACLE TO POSTGRESQL USING ORACLE GOLDENGATE

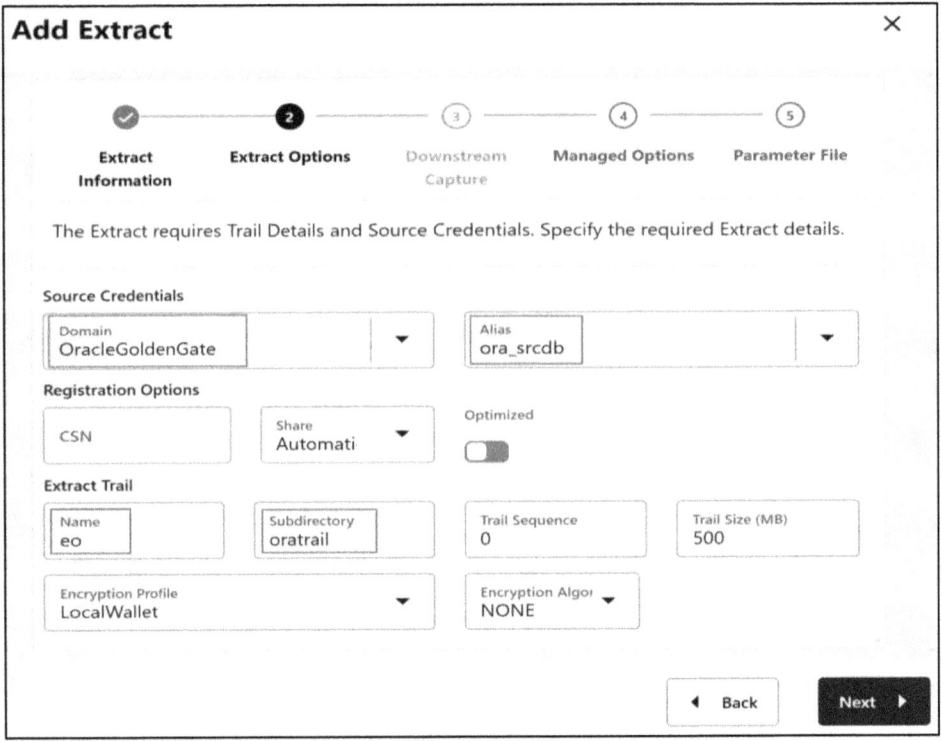

Figure 9-62. *Oracle add extract – extract options page*

- Step 3, Downstream Capture, is skipped since we have not enabled the Downstream Capture option in step 1.

- In step 4, Managed Options – leave default values and proceed with Next.

CHAPTER 9   DATA REPLICATION FROM ORACLE TO POSTGRESQL USING ORACLE GOLDENGATE

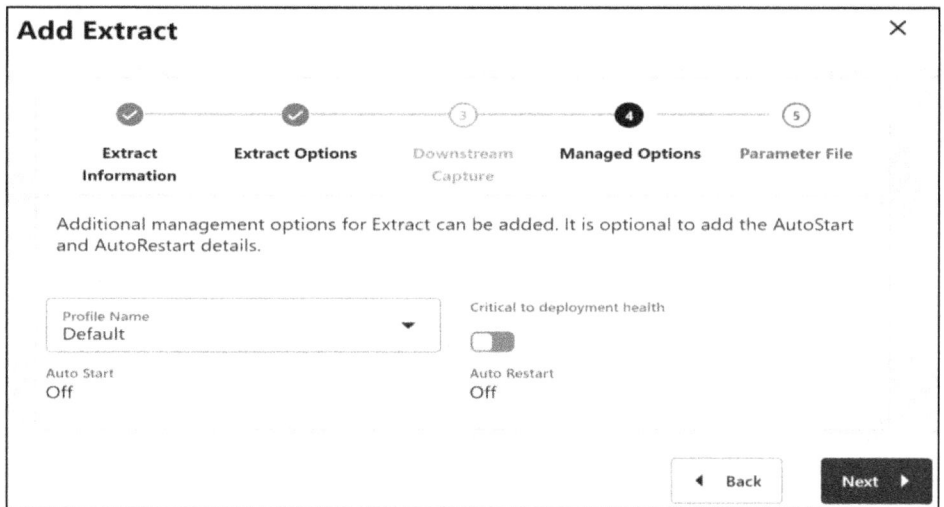

Figure 9-63. *Oracle add extract – managed options page*

- In step 5, Parameter File, add the below lines in addition to existing lines and proceed with Create and Run.

    - TABLE ora_rep_user.*;

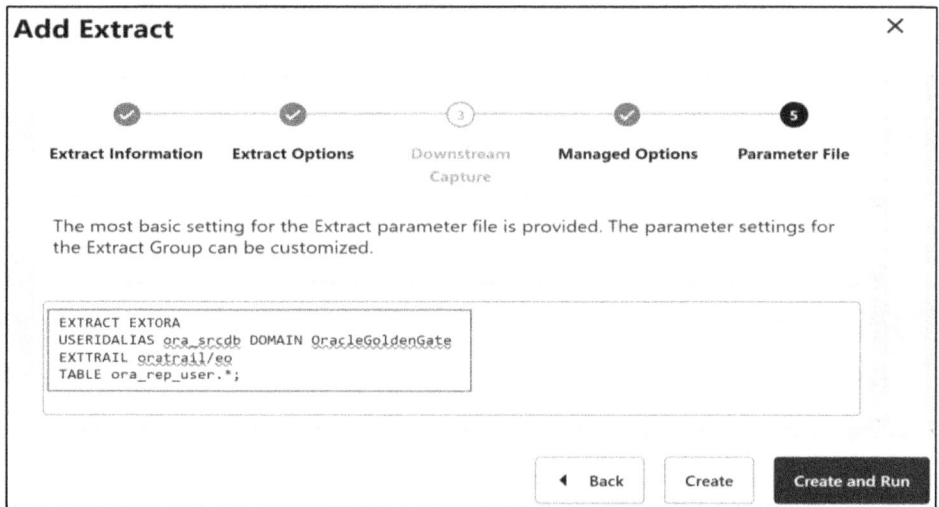

Figure 9-64. *Oracle add extract – parafile file page*

- The new extract is created and running.

    - Navigate to Administration Service ➤ Extracts.

CHAPTER 9   DATA REPLICATION FROM ORACLE TO POSTGRESQL USING ORACLE GOLDENGATE

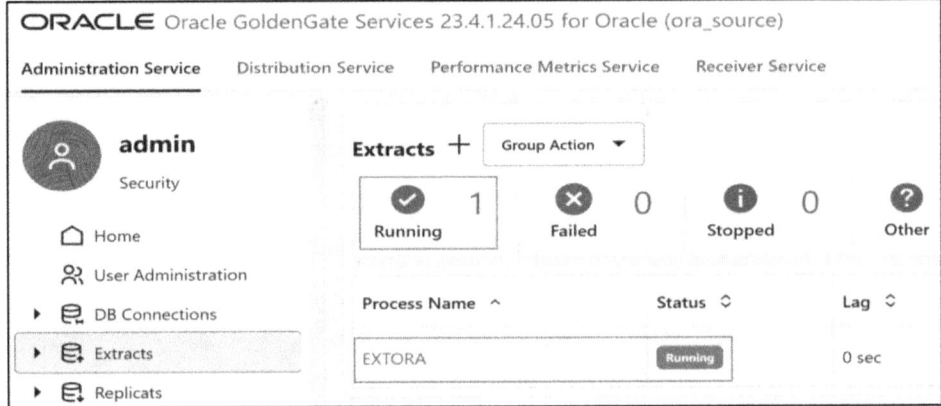

Figure 9-65. *Oracle newly created extract details*

- Extract status can be validated from command line using the adminclient utility as below:

[oracle@ogg_hub ~]$ /u01/app/ogg/oragg/bin/adminclient
Oracle GoldenGate Administration Client for Oracle
Version 23.4.1.24.05 OGGCORE_23.4.0.0.00GGR_LINUX.
X64_240529.0500_FBO

Copyright (C) 1995, 2024, Oracle and/or its affiliates. All rights reserved.

Linux, x64, 64bit (optimized) on May 29 2024 09:21:59
Operating system character set identified as UTF-8.

OGG (not connected) 1> connect http://192.168.2.99:9100 deployment ora_source as admin password welcome

OGG (http://192.168.2.99:9100 ora_source) 2> info credentialstore

Default domain: OracleGoldenGate

　Alias: ora_srcdb
　Userid: ggadmin@orsrcdb

OGG (http://192.168.2.99:9100 ora_source) 3> info all
Program   Status   Group   Type   Lag at Chkpt   Time Since Chkpt

644

ADMINSRVR	RUNNING			
DISTSRVR	RUNNING			
PMSRVR	RUNNING			
RECVSRVR	RUNNING			
EXTRACT	RUNNING	EXTORA	INTEGRATED	00:00:03 00:00:06

OGG (http://192.168.2.99:9100 ora_source) 5> info extract EXTORA

```
Extract     EXTORA    Last Started 2024-12-03 01:14    Status RUNNING
Description             Extract for ora_rep_user
Checkpoint Lag          00:00:03 (updated 00:00:05 ago)
Process ID              158410
Log Read Checkpoint     Oracle Integrated Redo Logs
                        2024-12-03 01:16:22
                        SCN 0.6475905 (6475905)
Settings Profile        ogg:managedProcessSettings:Default
Encryption Profile      LocalWallet
```

OGG (http://192.168.2.99:9100 ora_source as ora_srcdb@SRCDB) 15> INFO EXTTRAIL eo

```
          Local Trail: oratrail/eo
        Seqno Length: 9
   Flip Seqno Length: no
              Extract: EXTORA
                Seqno: 0
                  RBA: 11693
            File Size: 500M
```

[oracle@ogg_hub ~]$ cd /u01/app/ogg/o_udh/var/lib/data/oratrail
[oracle@ogg_hub oratrail]$ ls -lrt
total 16
-rw-r----- 1 oracle oinstall 13017 Dec 3 01:21 eo000000000

CHAPTER 9 DATA REPLICATION FROM ORACLE TO POSTGRESQL USING ORACLE GOLDENGATE

Configure GoldenGate on Target Deployment

Configure Network Connectivity for PostgreSQL

- In ogg_hub server, create the network configuration file odbc.ini and update the connectivity details.

    [oracle@ogg_hub ~]$ cd /u01/app/ogg/pggg/datadirect

    [oracle@ogg_hub datadirect]$ ls
    DDgg.LIC lib locale odbcinst.ini

    [oracle@ogg_hub datadirect]$ cp odbcinst.ini odbc.ini

    [oracle@ogg_hub datadirect]$ vi odbc.ini

    [oracle@ogg_hub datadirect]$ cat odbc.ini
    [ODBC Drivers]
    Oracle GoldenGate PostgreSQL Wire Protocol=Installed

    [ODBC]
    InstallDir=/u01/app/ogg/pggg/datadirect
    TraceDll=/u01/app/ogg/pggg/datadirect/lib/ggtrc25.so
    IANAAppCodePage=4

    [Oracle GoldenGate PostgreSQL Wire Protocol]

    Driver=./lib/ggpsql25.so

    [PG_tgt]

    Driver=/u01/app/ogg/pggg/datadirect/lib/ggpsql25.so
    Description=Oracle GoldenGate PostgreSQL Wire Protocol
    Database=postgres
    Hostname=pg_serv
    PortNumber=5432

Configure Target Database for GoldenGate

- Connect to PostgreSQL administration service console at http://192.168.2.99:9201 using admin user and password.

CHAPTER 9   DATA REPLICATION FROM ORACLE TO POSTGRESQL USING ORACLE GOLDENGATE

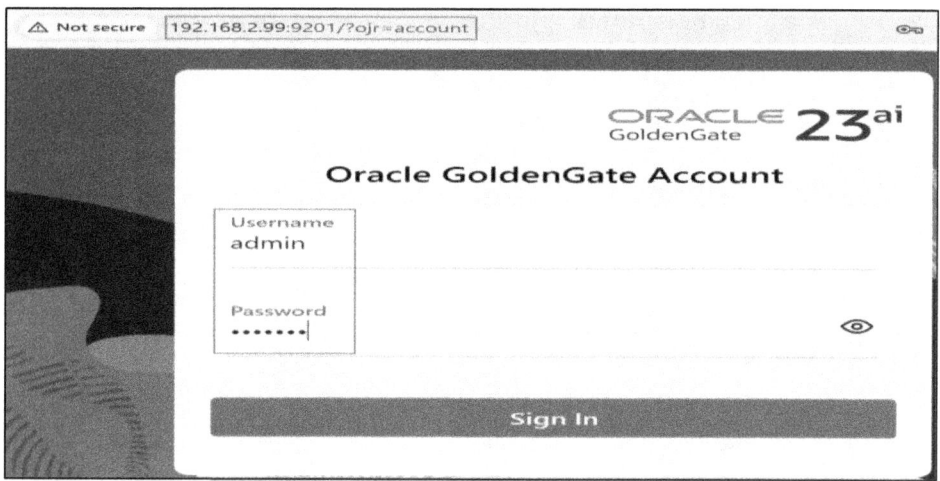

Figure 9-66. *pg_target deployment administration service login page*

- Add the database credential.

  - Navigate to Administration Service ➤ DB Connections. Click "+".

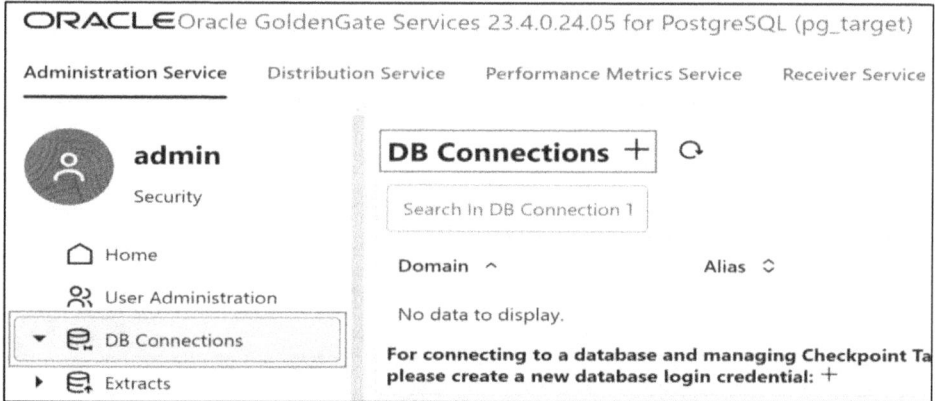

Figure 9-67. *pg_target administration service DB connections page*

- In the Credentials screen, add the values as below and submit:

  - Credential Domain – OracleGoldenGate

  - Credential Alias – pg_tgtdb

  - Connection Type – Data Source Name (DSN)

CHAPTER 9 DATA REPLICATION FROM ORACLE TO POSTGRESQL USING ORACLE GOLDENGATE

- Data Source Name (DSN) – PG_tgt – This was from odbc.ini created in an earlier step

- Database Name – postgres

- User ID – gguser

- Password and Verify Password – Password of gguser user from postgres database

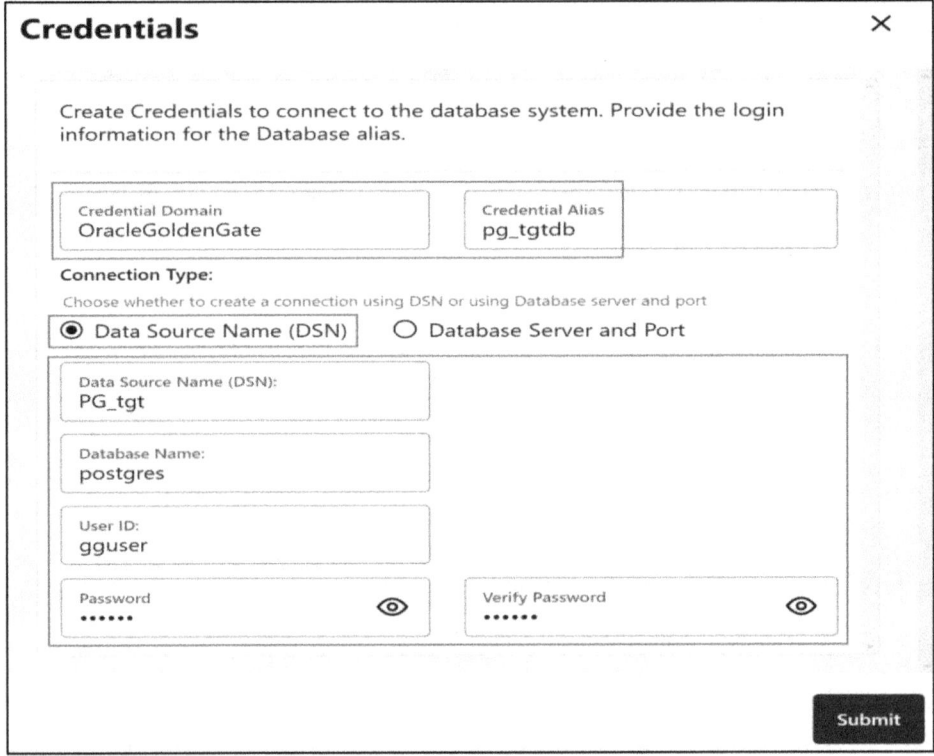

Figure 9-68. PostgreSQL DB credentials addition page

- We can see the newly created DB connection.
    - Click on the icon under the Actions field to make the remote connection to the target database postgres.

CHAPTER 9   DATA REPLICATION FROM ORACLE TO POSTGRESQL USING ORACLE GOLDENGATE

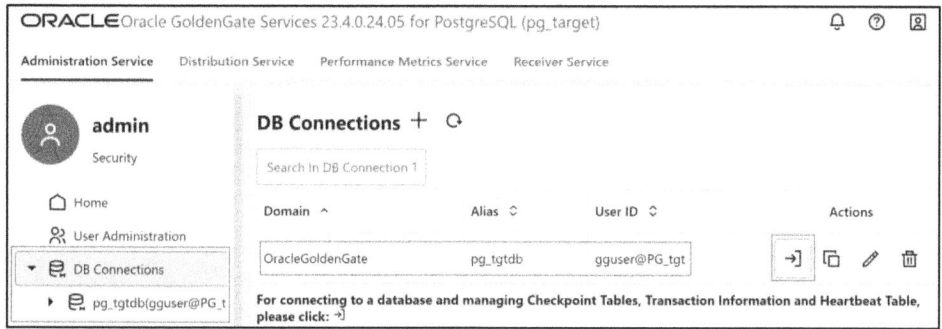

Figure 9-69. pg_target newly added DB connection

- Create a checkpoint table. Once the DB connection to target database postgres is established:

    - Navigate to Administration Service ➤ DB Connections ➤ pg_tgtdb(gguser@PG_tgt) ➤ Checkpoint

    - Click "+"

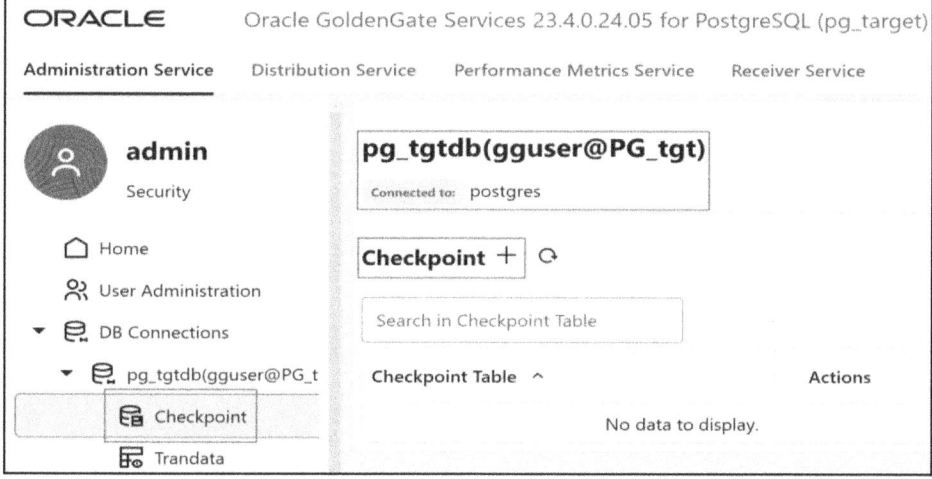

Figure 9-70. PostgreSQL DB checkpoint table addition page

- On the Checkpoint Table window, add Checkpoint Table as gguser. pgckpt and submit.

CHAPTER 9   DATA REPLICATION FROM ORACLE TO POSTGRESQL USING ORACLE GOLDENGATE

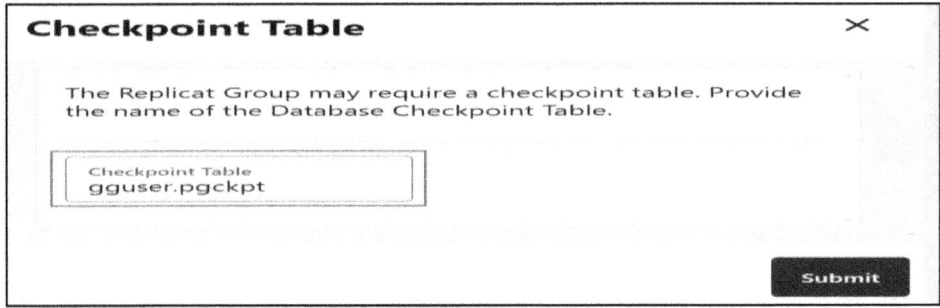

Figure 9-71. *PostgreSQL DB checkpoint table name*

- Add Heartbeat table.
  - Navigate to Administration Service ➤ DB Connections ➤ pg_tgtdb(gguser@PG_tgt) ➤ Heartbeat.
  - Click "+" followed by Submit with default values.

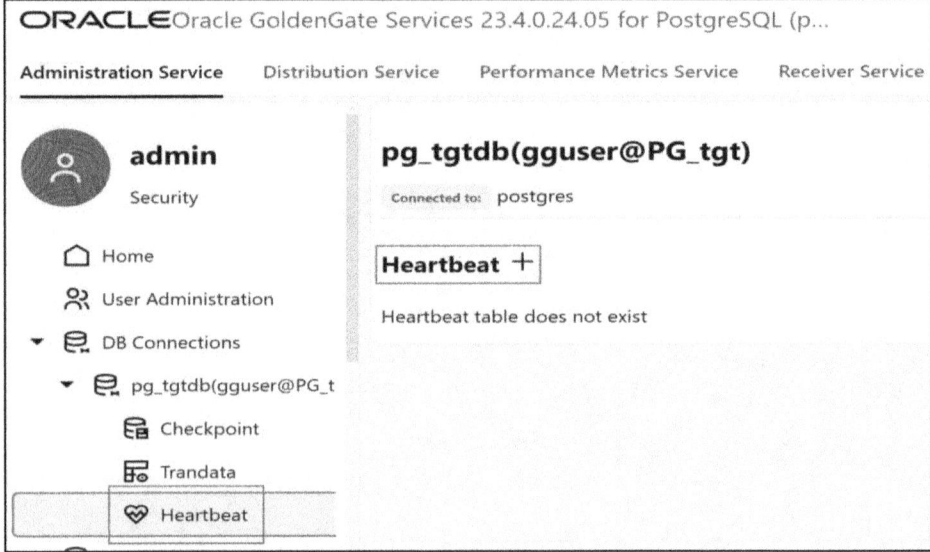

Figure 9-72. *PostgreSQL DB heartbeat table addition page*

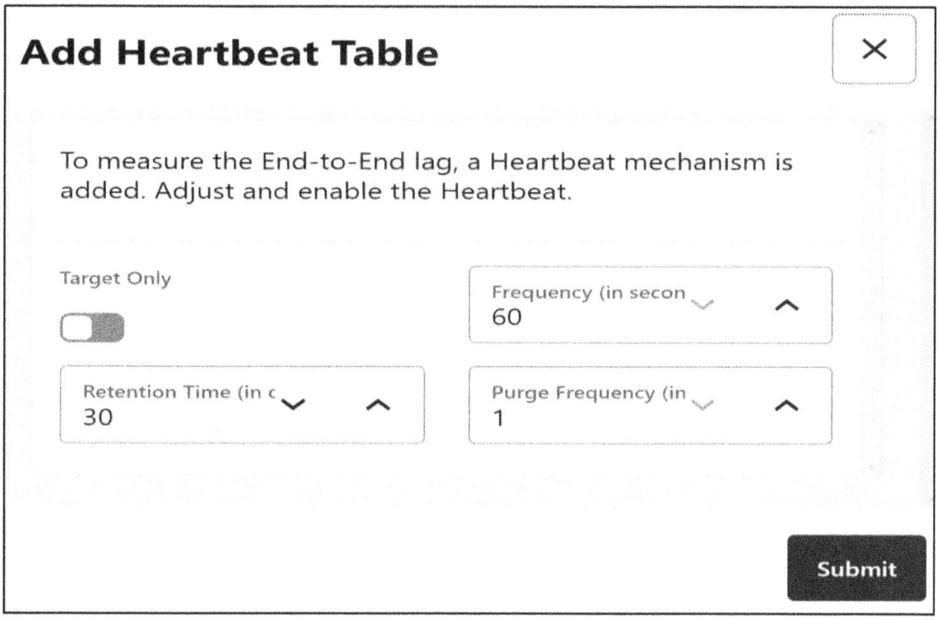

CHAPTER 9   DATA REPLICATION FROM ORACLE TO POSTGRESQL USING ORACLE GOLDENGATE

Figure 9-73.   PostgreSQL DB heartbeat table addition

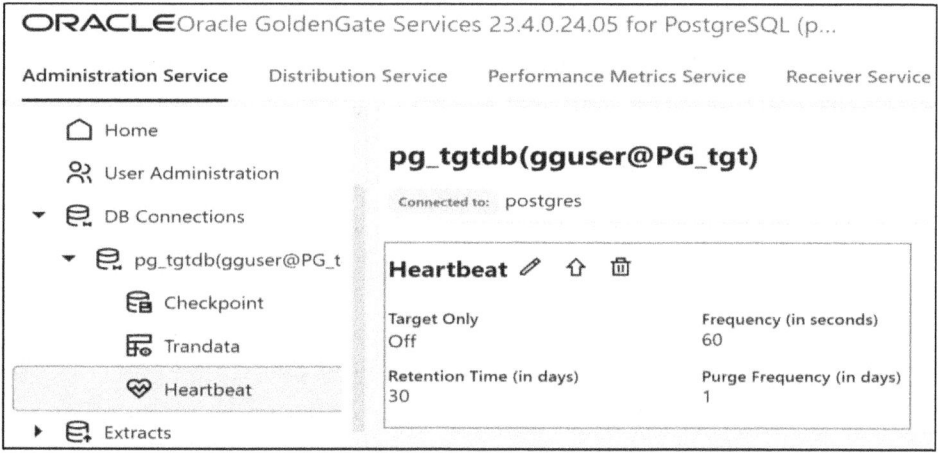

Figure 9-74.   PostgreSQL heartbeat table details

CHAPTER 9   DATA REPLICATION FROM ORACLE TO POSTGRESQL USING ORACLE GOLDENGATE

Replication Configuration – Create Replicat Process

Figures 9-75 through 9-81 show steps involved in PostgreSQL Replicat creation.

- Navigate to Administration Service ➤ Replicats.
  - Click "+".

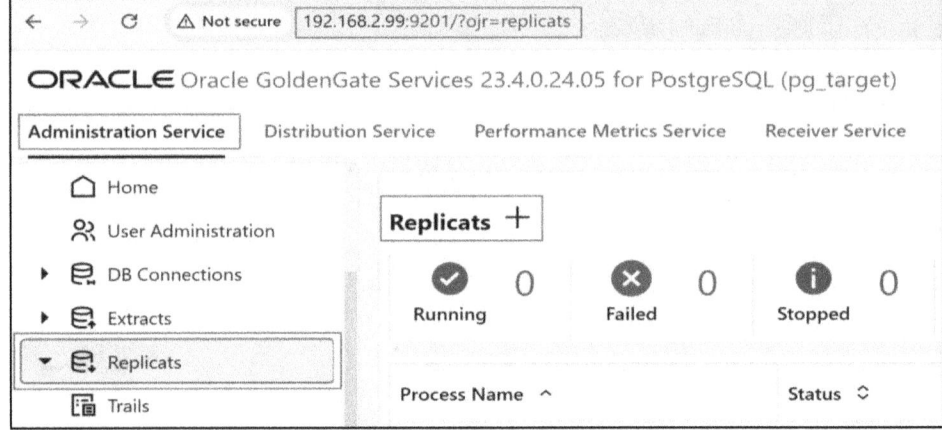

Figure 9-75. pg_target deployment Replicat Creation page

- In step 1, Add Replicat ➤ Replicat Information, add/select values as below and proceed with Next.
  - Replicat Type – Parallel Replicat
  - Process Name – REPPG
  - Description – Replicat for postgres db

CHAPTER 9   DATA REPLICATION FROM ORACLE TO POSTGRESQL USING ORACLE GOLDENGATE

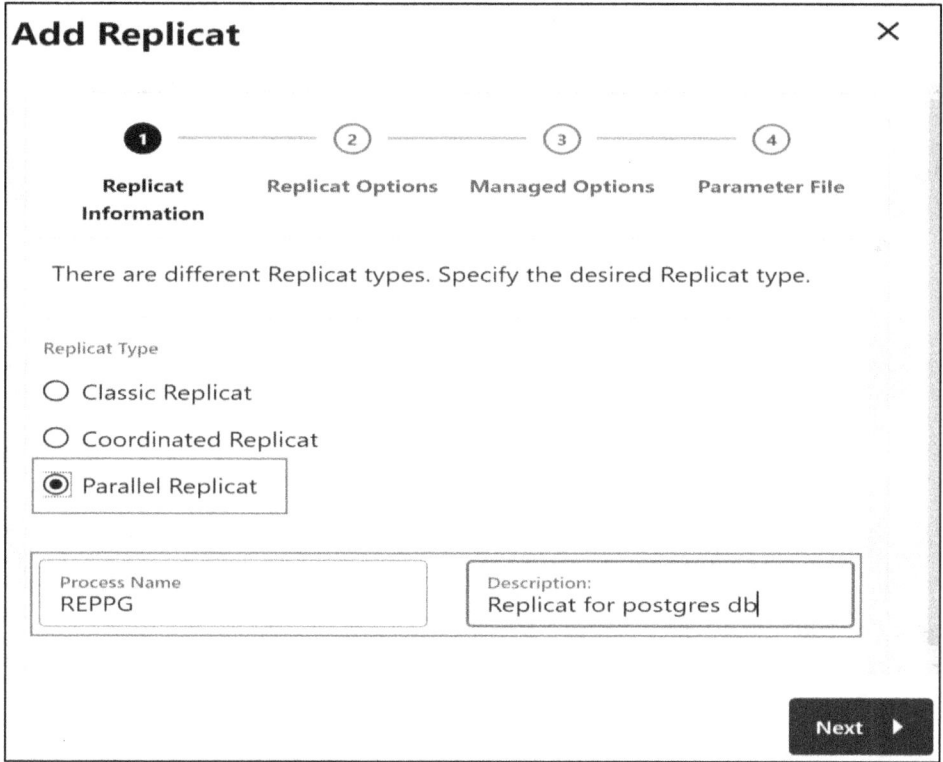

Figure 9-76. *pg_target deployment Replicat Information page*

- In step 2, Replicat Options, add/select values as below and proceed with Next.
    - Replicat Trail Name – rt
    - Replicat Trail Subdirectory – pgtrail
    - Target Credentials Domain – OracleGoldenGate
    - Target Credentials Alias – pg_tgtdb
    - Checkpoint Table – gguser.pgckpt

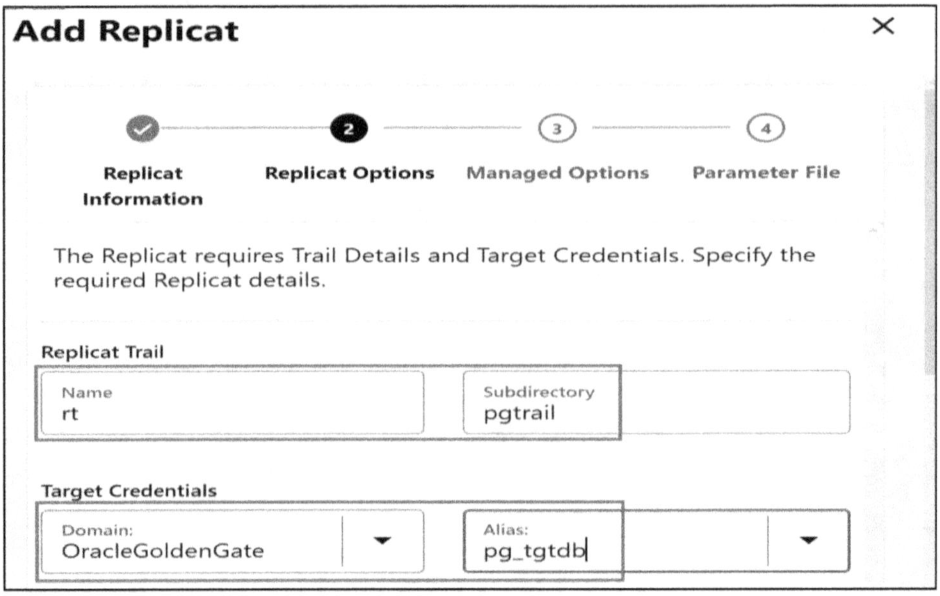

CHAPTER 9 DATA REPLICATION FROM ORACLE TO POSTGRESQL USING ORACLE GOLDENGATE

Figure 9-77. *pg_target deployment Replicat Options page*

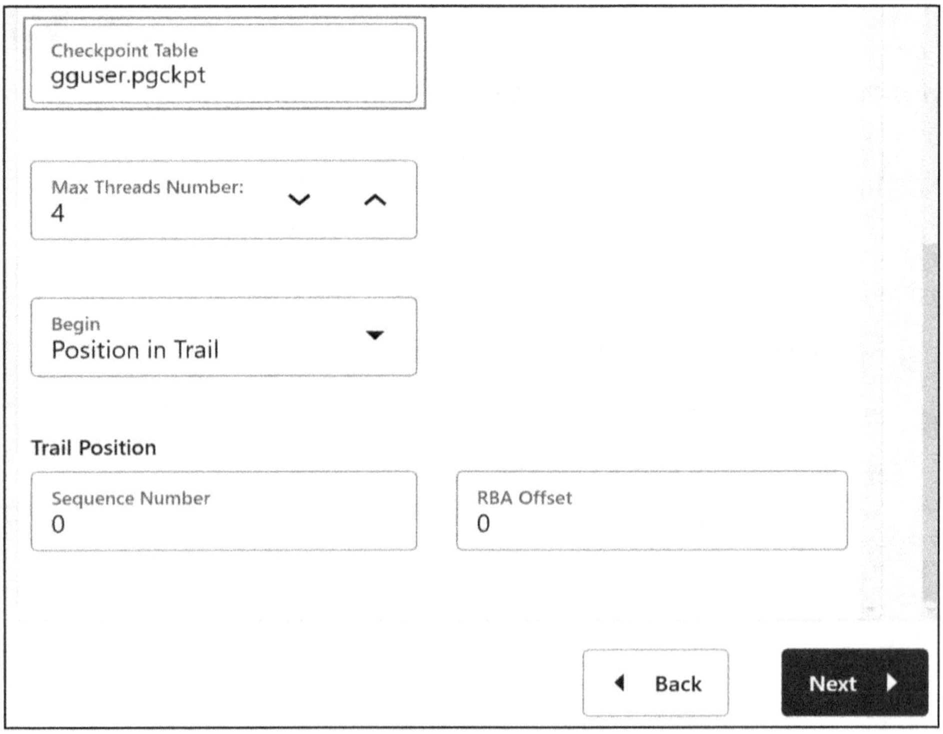

Figure 9-78. *pg_target deployment Replicat Options page*

CHAPTER 9   DATA REPLICATION FROM ORACLE TO POSTGRESQL USING ORACLE GOLDENGATE

- In step 3, Managed Options, leave the values as default and click Next.

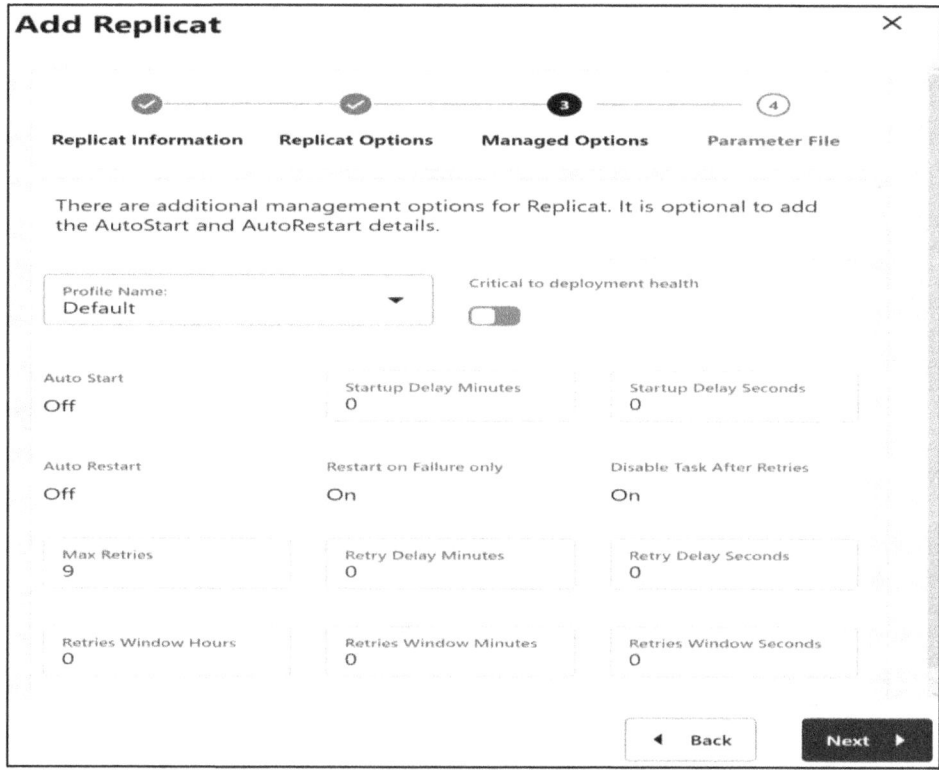

Figure 9-79. pg_target deployment Managed Options page

- In step 4, Parameter File, add the below line in addition to existing lines and proceed with Create and Run.
- MAP ora_rep_user.*, TARGET public.*;

CHAPTER 9   DATA REPLICATION FROM ORACLE TO POSTGRESQL USING ORACLE GOLDENGATE

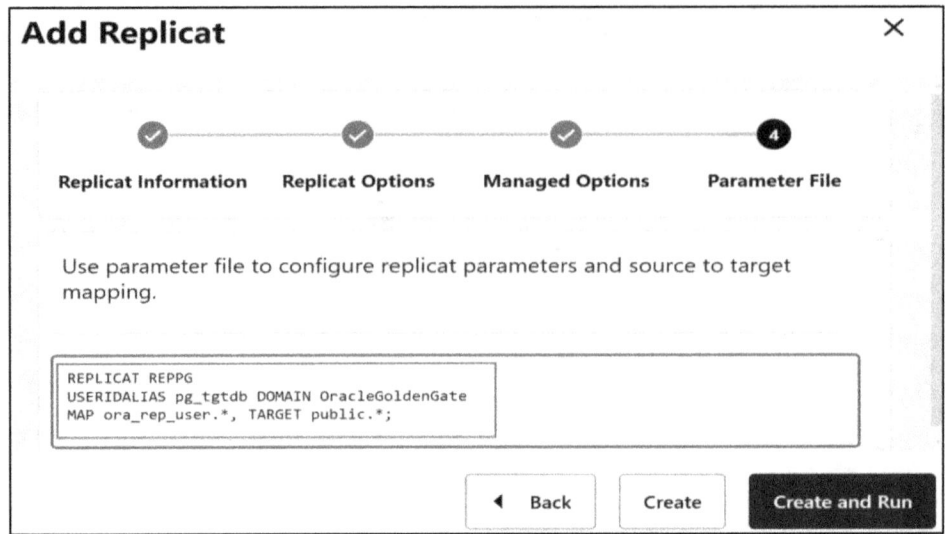

Figure 9-80.   pg_target deployment Parameter File page

- The new replicat is created and running.
  - Navigate to Administration Service ➤ Replicats.

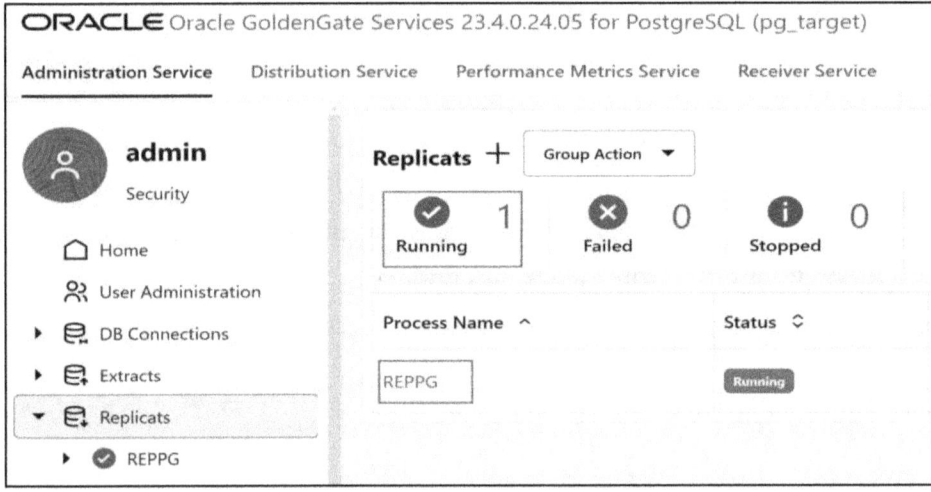

Figure 9-81.   pg_target deployment Replicat home page

- Replicat status can be validated from command line using the adminclient utility as below:

[oracle@ogg_hub ~]$ /u01/app/ogg/pggg/bin/adminclient
Oracle GoldenGate Administration Client for PostgreSQL
Version 23.4.0.24.05 OGGCORE_23.0.0.0.0_LINUX.X64_240426.1726

Copyright (C) 1995, 2024, Oracle and/or its affiliates. All rights reserved.

Linux, x64, 64bit (optimized) on Apr 26 2024 21:04:28
Operating system character set identified as UTF-8.

OGG (not connected) 1> connect http://192.168.2.99:9200 deployment pg_target as admin password welcome

OGG (http://192.168.2.99:9200 pg_target) 2> info all
```
Program      Status     Group     Type              Lag at Chkpt    Time Since Chkpt

ADMINSRVR    RUNNING
DISTSRVR     RUNNING
PMSRVR       RUNNING
RECVSRVR     RUNNING
REPLICAT     RUNNING    REPPG     PARALLEL NONINT   00:00:00        00:00:06
```

OGG (http://192.168.2.99:9200 pg_target) 3> info REPPG

```
Replicat    REPPG      Last Started 2024-12-03 01:44    Status RUNNING
Description                Replicat for postgres db
Parallel
Checkpoint Lag             00:00:00 (updated 00:00:04 ago)
Process ID                 159710
Log Read Checkpoint        File pgtrail/rt000000000
                           2024-12-03 23:08:54.768316   RBA 1802365
Settings Profile           ogg:managedProcessSettings:Default
Encryption Profile         LocalWallet
```

CHAPTER 9   DATA REPLICATION FROM ORACLE TO POSTGRESQL USING ORACLE GOLDENGATE

Replication Configuration – Create Dist Path in Source Deployment

Figures 9-82 through 9-92 show steps involved in Oracle Distribution Path creation.

- Connect to Oracle distribution service at http://192.168.2.99:9102.

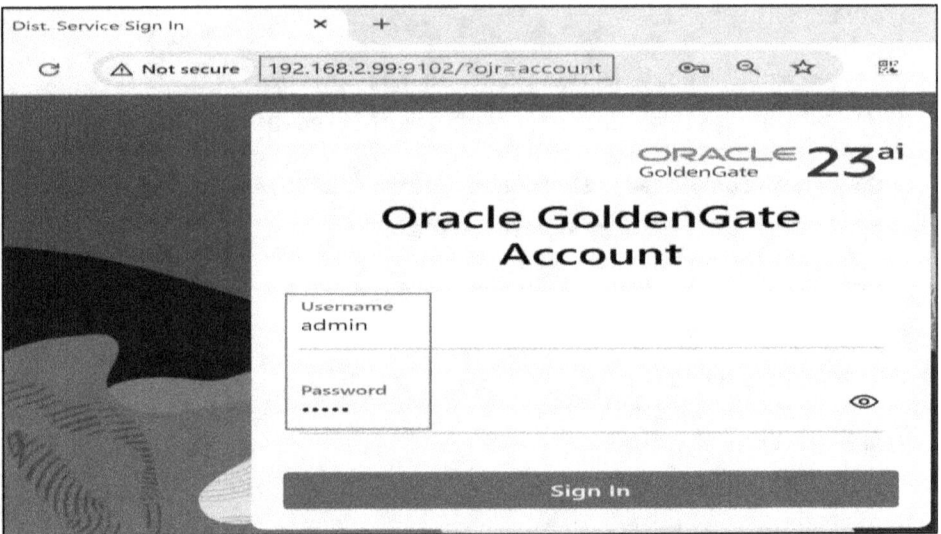

Figure 9-82. ora_source deployment Distribution Service Login page

- Create Distribution Path.
- Navigate to Distribution Service ➤ Home. Click "+".

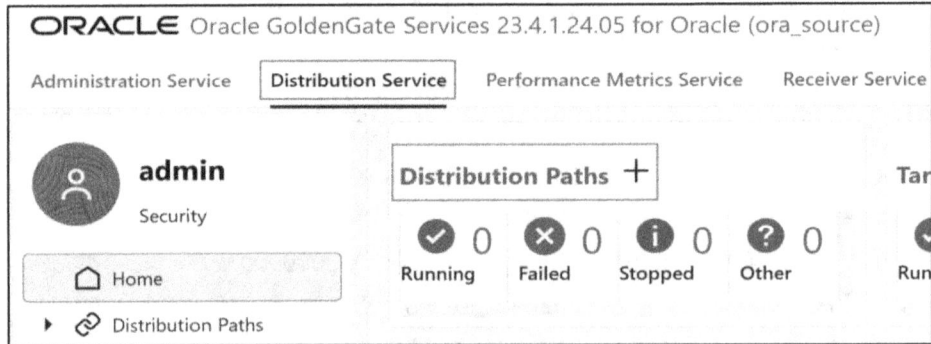

Figure 9-83. ora_source deployment Distribution Path creation

658

CHAPTER 9   DATA REPLICATION FROM ORACLE TO POSTGRESQL USING ORACLE GOLDENGATE

- In step 1, Add Path ➤ Path Information, add values as below and proceed with Next.
    - Path Name – DORA2PG
    - Description – Dist path for ora_rep_user

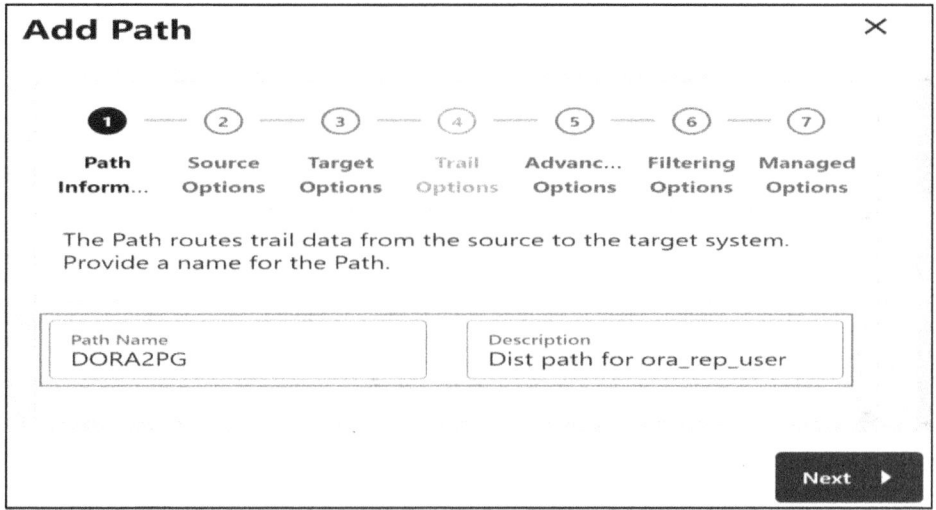

Figure 9-84. ora_source deployment Add Path page

- In step 2, Source Options, add/select values as below and proceed with Next.
    - Source Extract Name – EXTORA
    - Trail Name – eo
    - Subdirectory – oratrail

CHAPTER 9   DATA REPLICATION FROM ORACLE TO POSTGRESQL USING ORACLE GOLDENGATE

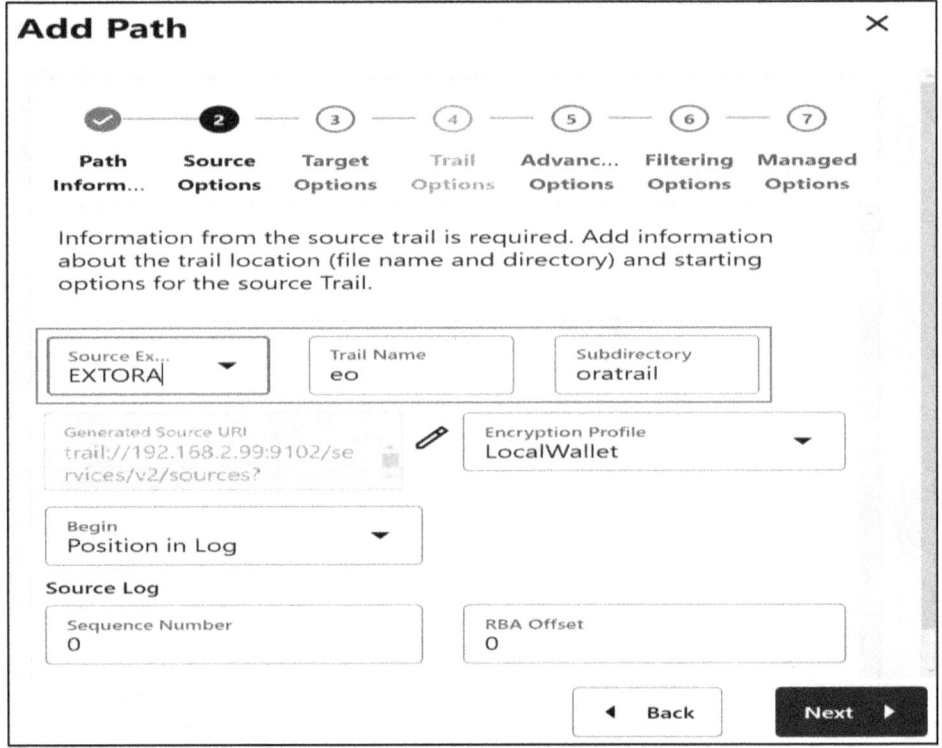

Figure 9-85. *ora_source deployment Source Options page*

- In step 3, Target Options, add/select values as below and proceed with Next.

    - Target Protocol – ogg

    - Target Type – Receiver Service

    - Target Host – 192.168.2.99

    - Port Number – 9203

    - Trail Name – rt

    - Subdirectory – pgtrail

    - Target Type – GGFormat

CHAPTER 9 DATA REPLICATION FROM ORACLE TO POSTGRESQL USING ORACLE GOLDENGATE

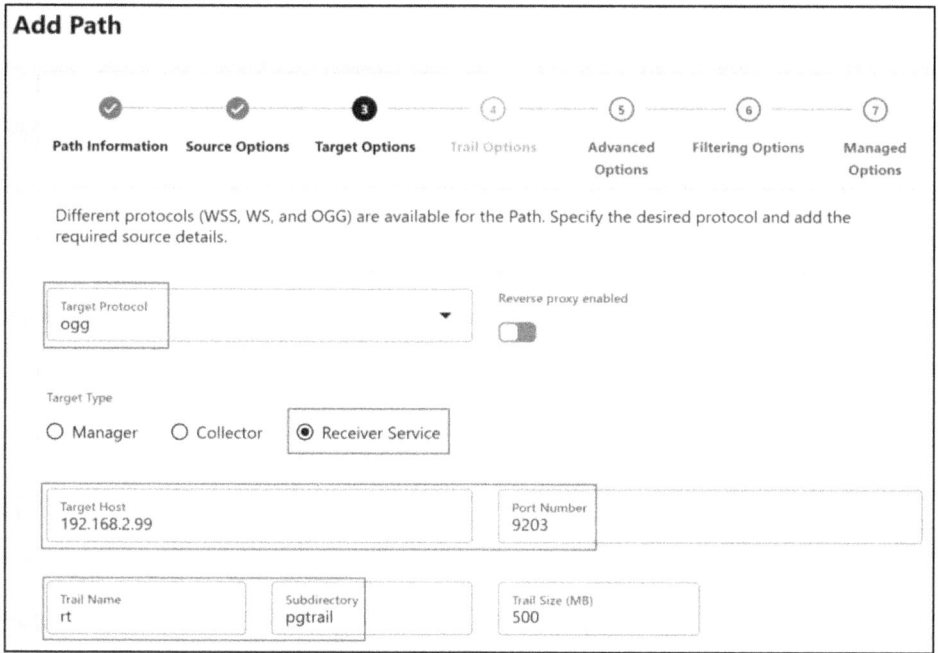

Figure 9-86. *ora_source deployment Target Options page*

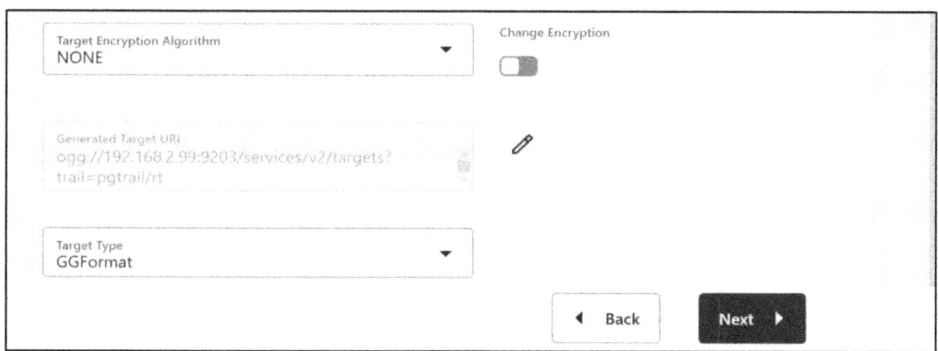

Figure 9-87. *ora_source deployment Target Options page*

- In step 5, Advanced Options, leave the default values and proceed with Next.

CHAPTER 9 DATA REPLICATION FROM ORACLE TO POSTGRESQL USING ORACLE GOLDENGATE

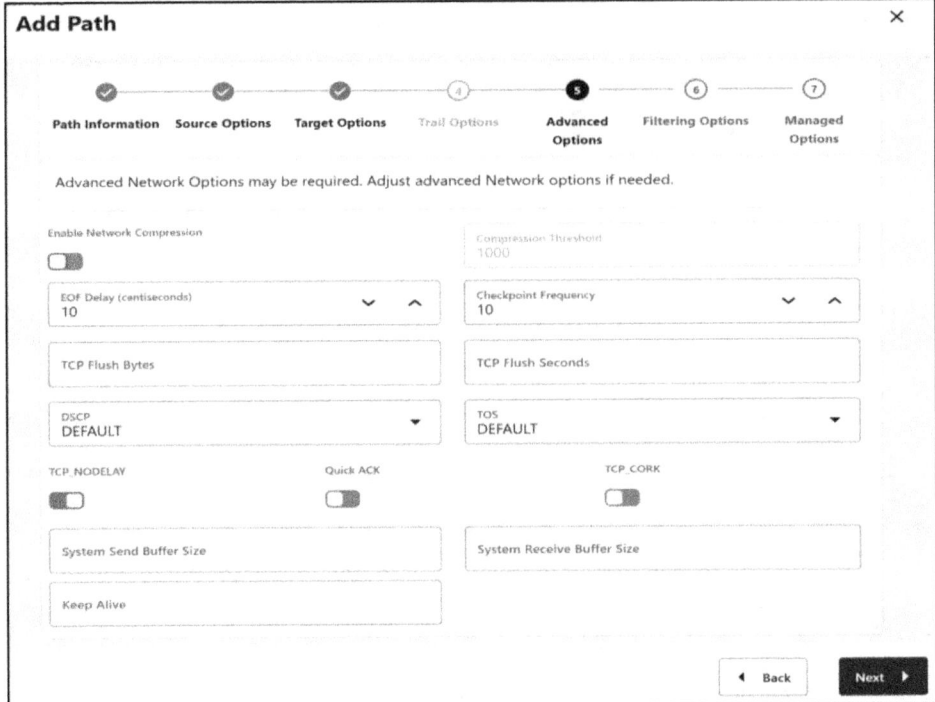

Figure 9-88. *ora_source deployment Advanced Options page*

- In step 6, Filtering Options, leave the default values and proceed with Next.

CHAPTER 9 DATA REPLICATION FROM ORACLE TO POSTGRESQL USING ORACLE GOLDENGATE

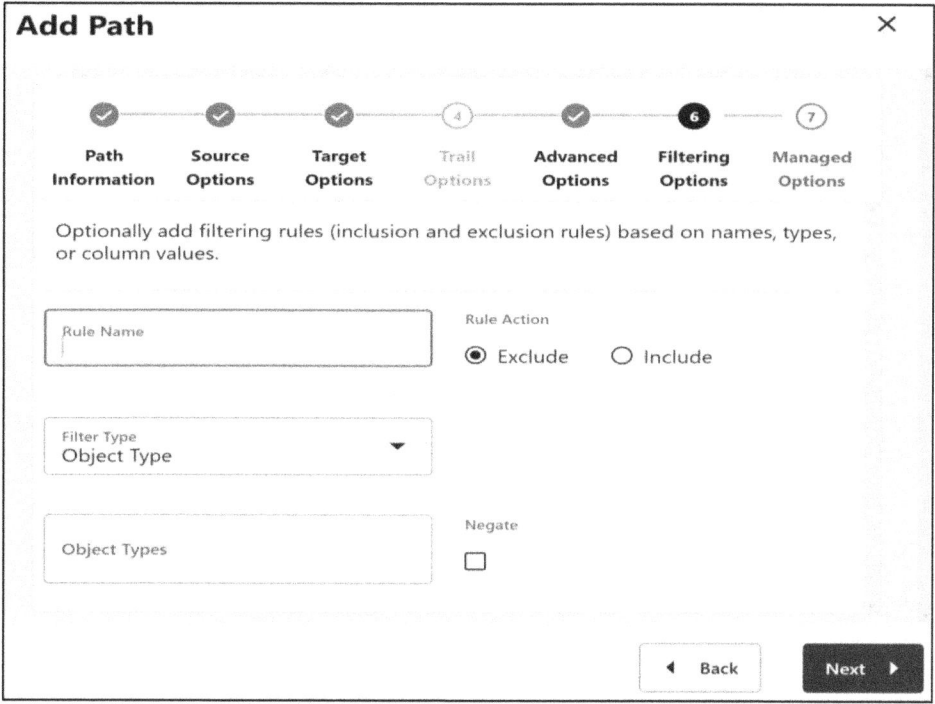

Figure 9-89. *ora_source deployment Filtering Options page*

- In step 7, Managed Options, leave the default values and proceed with Create Path and Run.

CHAPTER 9   DATA REPLICATION FROM ORACLE TO POSTGRESQL USING ORACLE GOLDENGATE

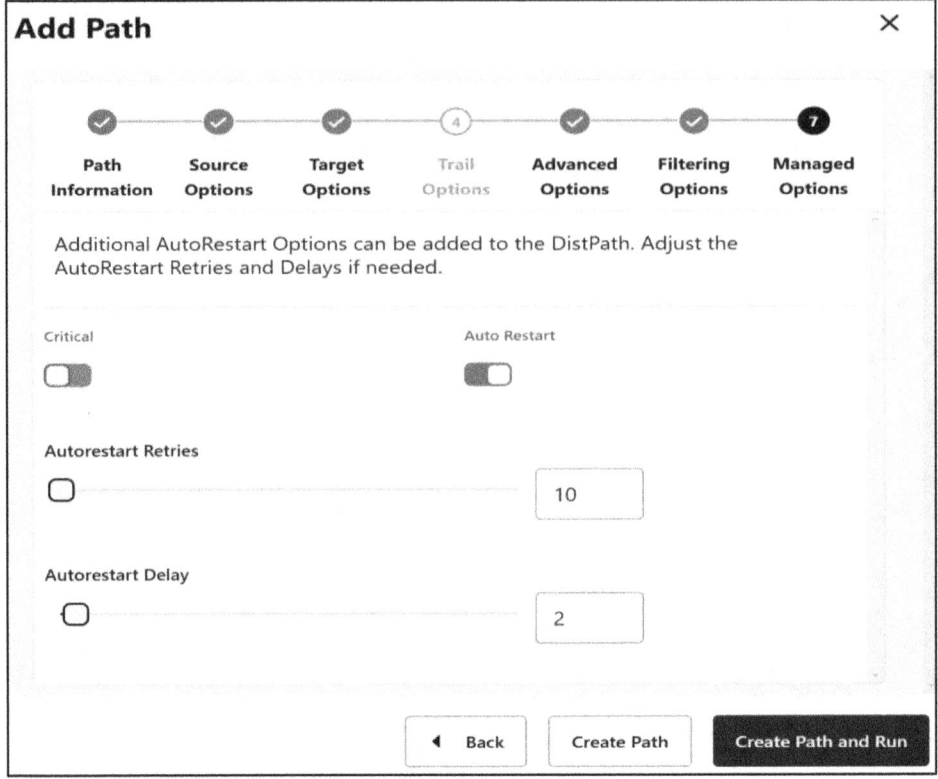

Figure 9-90. ora_source deployment Managed Options page

- The new Dist Path is created and running.
    - Navigate to Distribution Service ➤ Distribution Paths.

CHAPTER 9   DATA REPLICATION FROM ORACLE TO POSTGRESQL USING ORACLE GOLDENGATE

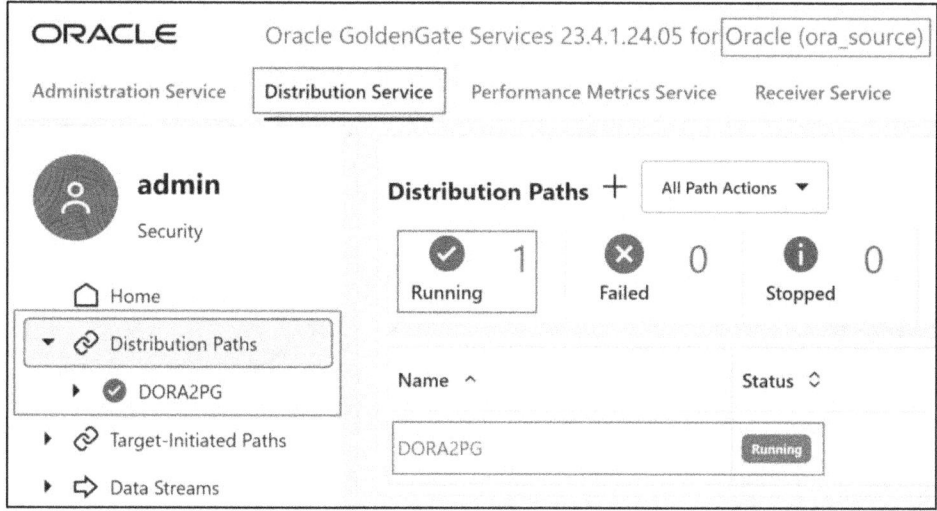

Figure 9-91. *ora_source deployment Distribution Service Path*

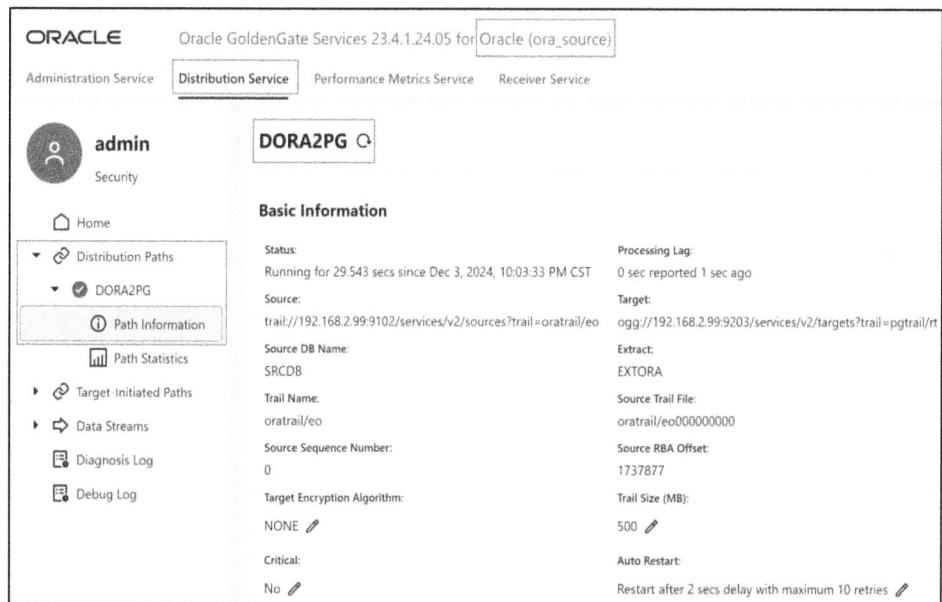

Figure 9-92. *ora_source deployment Distribution Service Path Information*

Check the Receiver Server on Target Deployment

- Connect to PostgreSQL receiver service using the URL `http://192.168.2.99:9203`.

CHAPTER 9   DATA REPLICATION FROM ORACLE TO POSTGRESQL USING ORACLE GOLDENGATE

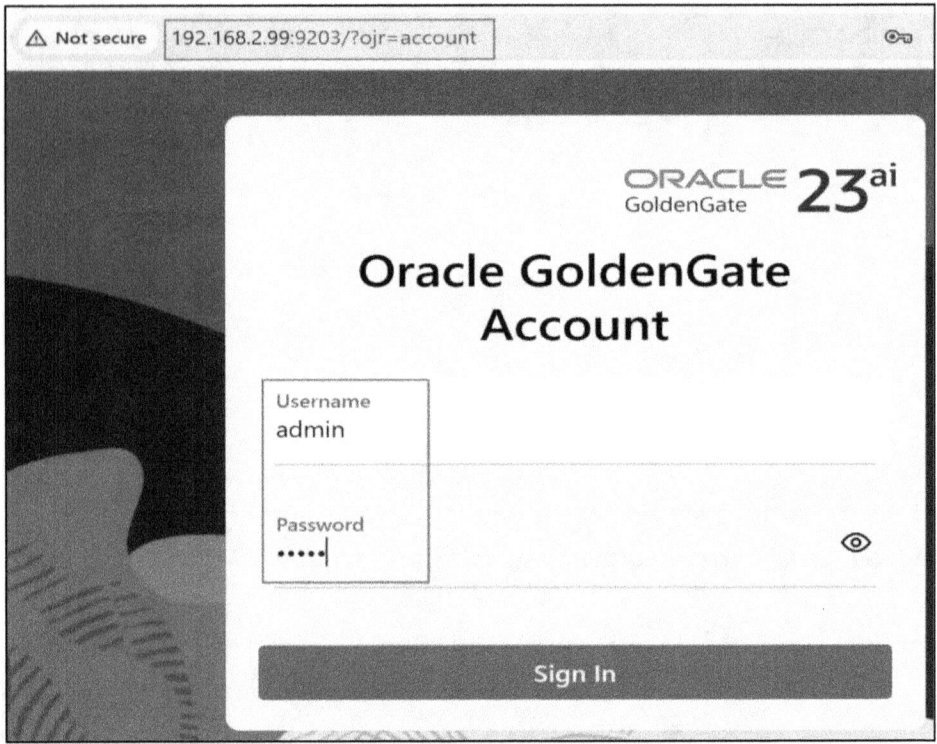

Figure 9-93. pg_target deployment Receiver Service login page

- Check the distribution path.
  - Navigate to Receiver Service ➤ Distribution Paths.

Figure 9-94. pg_target deployment Receiver Service Path

666

CHAPTER 9   DATA REPLICATION FROM ORACLE TO POSTGRESQL USING ORACLE GOLDENGATE

The configuration that is added till now can be seen in Figure 9-95. It shows the end-to-end replication flow from Oracle database to PostgreSQL database using GoldenGate Hub and multiple processes involved in data capture and apply.

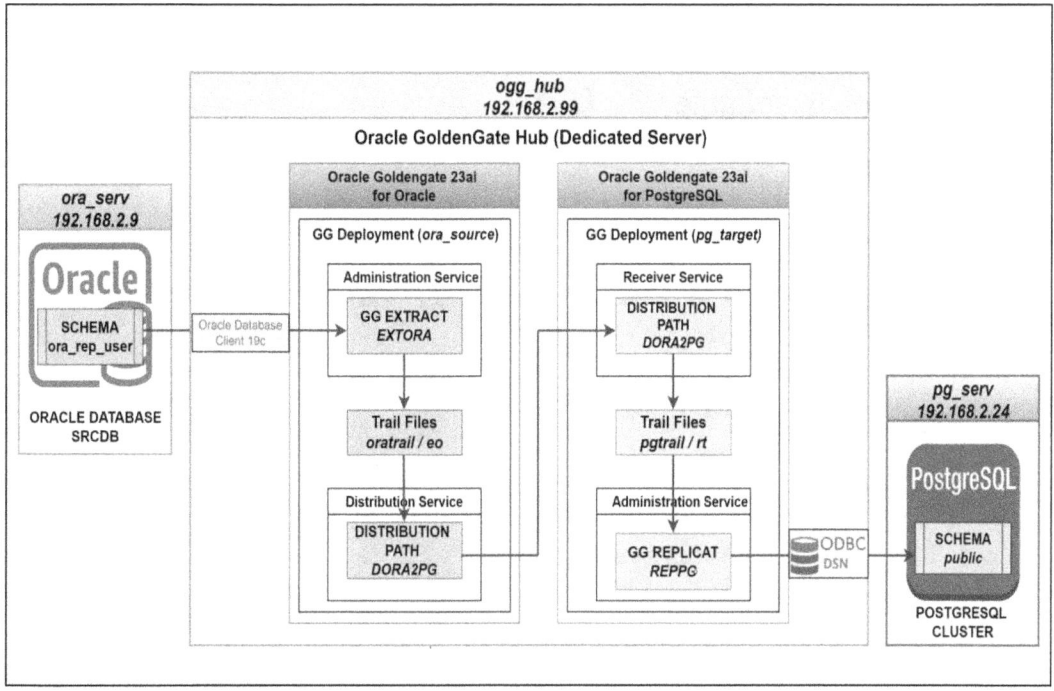

Figure 9-95.   *Oracle GoldenGate End-to-End Replication between Oracle and PostgreSQL*

Transaction Replication from Oracle to PostgreSQL

- In ora_serv server, connect to database srcdb as user ora_rep_user and perform a transaction.

[oracle@ora_serv ~]$ sqlplus

SQL*Plus: Release 19.0.0.0.0 - Production on Tue Dec 3 23:11:04 2024
Version 19.20.0.0.0

Copyright (c) 1982, 2022, Oracle. All rights reserved.

Enter user-name: ora_rep_user/ora_rep_user
Last Successful login time: Tue Dec 03 2024 23:09:22 -05:00

Connected to:
Oracle Database 19c Enterprise Edition Release 19.0.0.0.0 - Production
Version 19.20.0.0.0

SQL> select * from ggtest;

no rows selected

SQL> insert into ggtest values (1001, 'GGTEST1');

1 row created.

SQL> commit;

Commit complete.

SQL> select * from ggtest;

```
        ID NAME
---------- --------------------
      1001 GGTEST1
```

Oracle GoldenGate captures the committed transactions from Oracle redolog files and replicates it to the target PostgreSQL system by maintaining transaction integrity with sub-second latency. GoldenGate uses its own Commit Sequence Number (CSN) to identify a transaction that is based on Oracle Database SCN (System Change Number) to capture it for the replication.

- Check the distribution path metrics in source deployment.

CHAPTER 9 DATA REPLICATION FROM ORACLE TO POSTGRESQL USING ORACLE GOLDENGATE

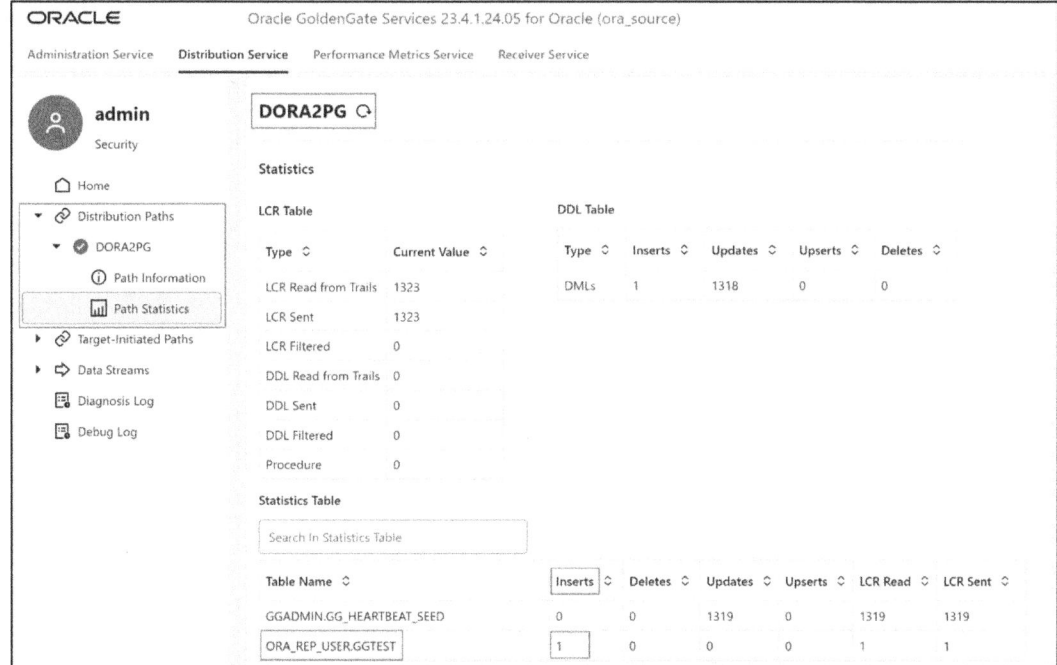

Figure 9-96. *ora_source deployment Distribution Service Path Statistics*

- In ogg_hub server, check the source trail file and we can observe an increase in its size.

[oracle@ogg_hub ~]$ ls -lrt /u01/app/ogg/o_udh/var/lib/data/oratrail
```
total 3712
-rw-r----- 1 oracle oinstall 1727280 Dec  3 22:55 eo000000000
```

- In pg_serv server, validate the transaction in target database postgres.

[postgres@pg_serv ~]$ psql
```
psql (16.3)
```

postgres=# \dt public.*
```
        List of relations
 Schema |  Name  | Type  |  Owner
--------+--------+-------+----------
 public | ggtest | table | postgres
(1 row)
```

669

CHAPTER 9   DATA REPLICATION FROM ORACLE TO POSTGRESQL USING ORACLE GOLDENGATE

```
postgres=# select * from public.ggtest;
  id  |  name
------+---------
 1001 | GGTEST1
(1 row)
```

- In ora_serv server, connect to database srcdb as user ora_rep_user and perform additional transactions.

[oracle@ora_serv ~]$ sqlplus

```
SQL*Plus: Release 19.0.0.0.0 - Production on Tue Dec 3 23:11:04 2024
Version 19.20.0.0.0

Copyright (c) 1982, 2022, Oracle.  All rights reserved.
```

Enter user-name: ora_rep_user/ora_rep_user
```
Last Successful login time: Tue Dec 03 2024 23:09:22 -05:00

Connected to:
Oracle Database 19c Enterprise Edition Release 19.0.0.0.0 - Production
Version 19.20.0.0.0
```

SQL> select * from ggtest;
```
        ID NAME
---------- --------------------
      1001 GGTEST1
```

SQL> insert into ggtest values (2002, 'GGTEST2');

1 row created.

SQL> insert into ggtest values (2003, 'GGTEST3');

1 row created.

SQL> update ggtest set id=2001 where id=1001;

1 row updated.

CHAPTER 9   DATA REPLICATION FROM ORACLE TO POSTGRESQL USING ORACLE GOLDENGATE

SQL> commit;

Commit complete.

SQL> select * from ggtest;

```
      ID NAME
---------- --------------------
    2001 GGTEST1
    2002 GGTEST2
    2003 GGTEST3
```

- Check again the distribution path metrics in source deployment. The new transaction with two insert and one update operation is shown in the metrics.

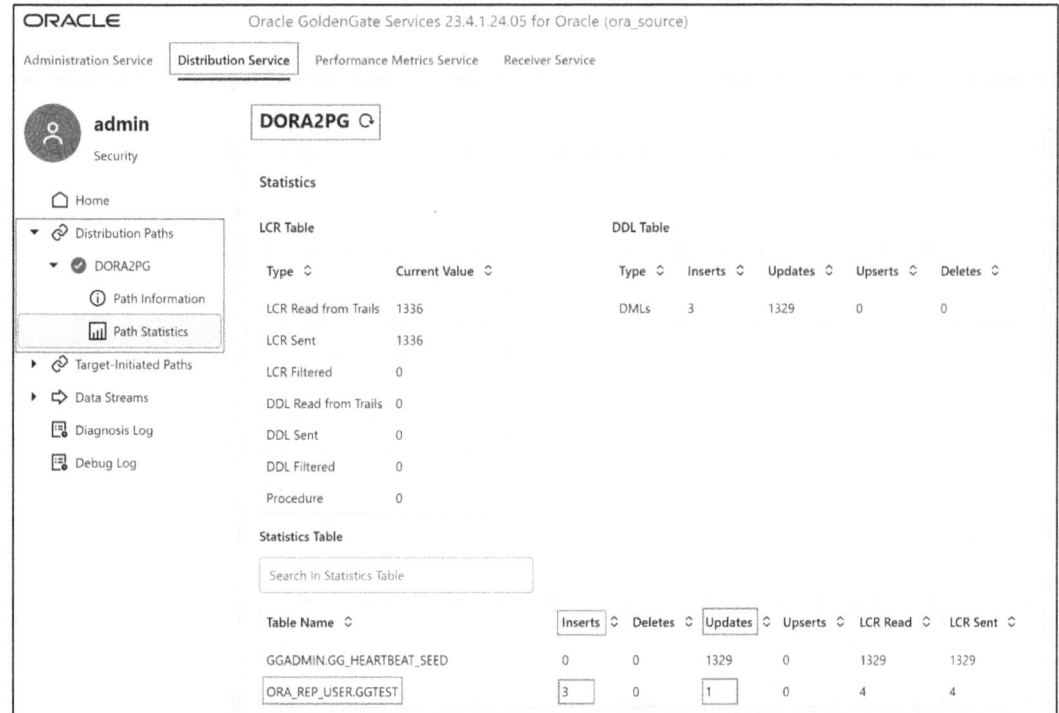

Figure 9-97. ora_source deployment Distribution Service Path Statistics

- In pg_serv server, validate the new transaction in target database postgres.

```
postgres=# select * from public.ggtest;
  id  |  name
------+---------
 2002 | GGTEST2
 2003 | GGTEST3
 2001 | GGTEST1
(3 rows)
```

From the above output, it can be clearly observed that when a transaction is performed and committed on source database srcdb, it will be captured and replicated through Oracle GoldenGate Hub to the target postgres database.

Summary

In this chapter, we explored data replication configuration using Oracle GoldenGate Hub. This involved installing essential software such as Oracle 19c Client and Oracle GoldenGate 23ai for both Oracle and PostgreSQL environments. Deployments were created for the source and target environments within the Oracle GoldenGate Hub, facilitating the setup of capture and replicat processes to enable seamless data replication between Oracle database and PostgreSQL database.

CHAPTER 10

New Features of PostgreSQL 17

Introduction

In this chapter, we explore the new features of PostgreSQL 17 in depth, along with the steps for configuring, installing, and initializing the database cluster. PostgreSQL 17 is compatible with a wide range of operating systems and can be installed using either precompiled binary packages (RPMs) or by building it from source code.

Upon completing Chapter 10, readers will gain the knowledge to install the latest version of PostgreSQL using binary packages (RPMs) and successfully initialize database clusters and also a couple of new features from PostgreSQL 17.

In this chapter, the following topics are covered:

- Installing required RPMs for PostgreSQL 17
- Environment details and how to download PostgreSQL
- Learn how to install PostgreSQL using RPMs
- Learn about additional packages required for PostgreSQL 17
- How to initialize a database cluster
- Connecting to PostgreSQL using the psql utility
- Incremental backups using PostgreSQL 17
- Logical Replication from Standby Servers
- Combining I/Os in PostgreSQL 17
- Query planner improvements in PostgreSQL 17
- Split and Merge partitions in PostgreSQL 17

CHAPTER 10   NEW FEATURES OF POSTGRESQL 17

Downloading PostgreSQL 17 Software Binaries

PostgreSQL offers several ways to download and install binaries. We will discuss the most used approach for installing PostgreSQL.

- Installing PostgreSQL using binary packages (RPMs)

Installing PostgreSQL Using Binary Packages (RPMs)

This installation method focuses on using binary packages to install PostgreSQL 17. PostgreSQL provides precompiled RPM packages for various versions, ensuring compatibility with the most widely used operating systems. The appropriate RPM package for the specific operating system is selected and then used to complete the PostgreSQL installation.

In this section, we will go over the step-by-step process of installing PostgreSQL 17.4 using the RPMs.

Step 1: Browse the PostgreSQL website, which is the source for multiple releases of PostgreSQL: www.postgresql.org/downloads.

Step 2: On the Downloads page, select the operating system as **Linux**.

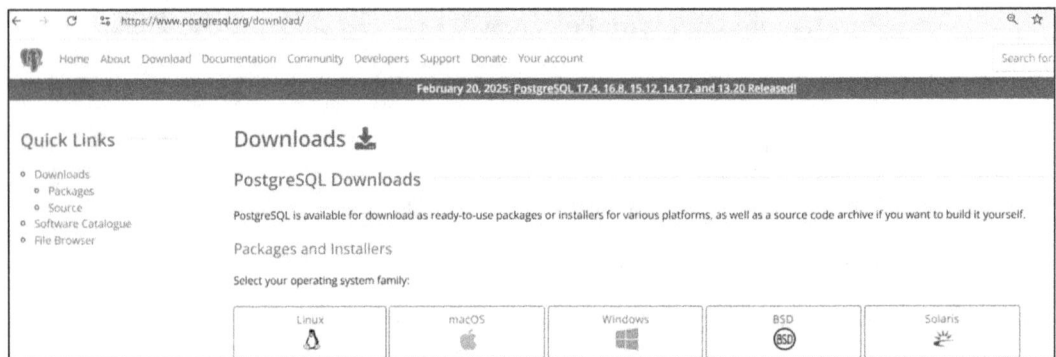

Figure 10-1. Operating system family selection

Once the Linux option is selected, a list will expand to choose the required Linux distribution.

Step 3: Select appropriate Linux Distribution (in this case, choose **Red Hat/Rocky/AlmaLinux**).

CHAPTER 10   NEW FEATURES OF POSTGRESQL 17

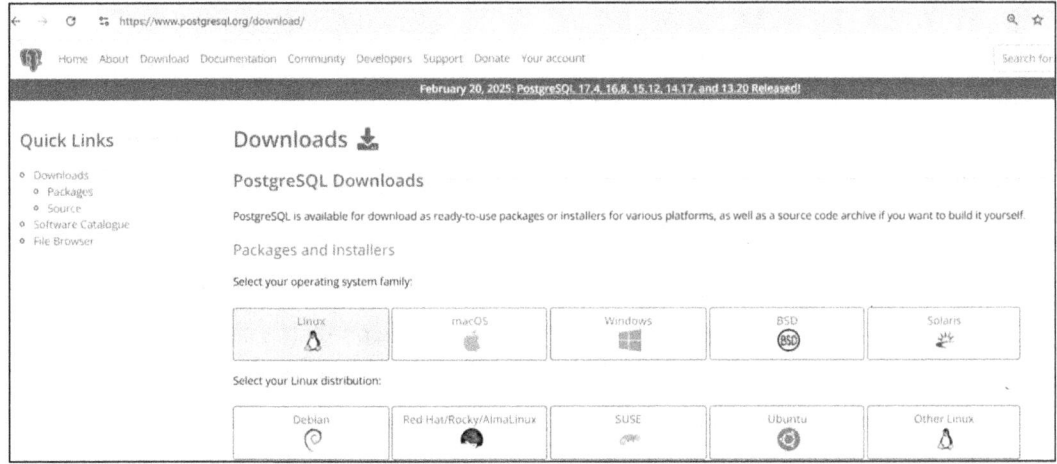

Figure 10-2. Linux distribution selection

Selection of the *Red Hat/Rocky/AlmaLinux* option will redirect to PostgreSQL Yum Repository.

Step 4: In the PostgreSQL Yum Repository section, select

Version-**17**

Platform - **Red at Enterprise, Rocky, AlmaLinux or Oracle version 9**

Architecture - **x86_64**

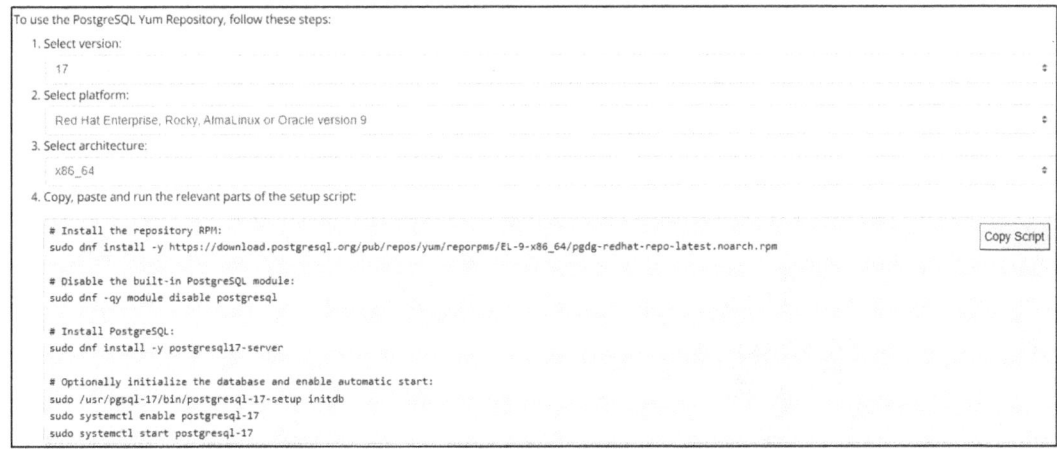

Figure 10-3. PostgreSQL version, OS platform, and architecture selection

Once version, platform, and architecture are selected, a setup script will be displayed, which can be copied and used in subsequent tasks.

The setup script has four sections, and each plays its part in installing PostgreSQL.

675

Note To install RPMs, either YUM (Yellowdog Updater, Modified) or DNF (Dandified Yum) can be used. YUM is used in our case.

The first section has the command to download and install the RPM repository.

Install the repository RPM:

```
[root@pg17 ~]# yum install -y https://download.postgresql.org/pub/repos/yum/reporpms/EL-9-x86_64/pgdg-redhat-repo-latest.noarch.rpm
Last metadata expiration check: 0:23:19 ago on Sun 20 May 1525 10:20:24 AM CDT.
pgdg-redhat-repo-latest.noarch.rpm
                                                       17 kB/s |  12 kB     00:00
Dependencies resolved.
================================================================================
 Package              Architecture   Version          Repository        Size
================================================================================
Installing:
 pgdg-redhat-repo     noarch         42.0-50PGDG      @commandline      12 k

Transaction Summary
================================================================================
Install  1 Package

Total size: 12 k
Installed size: 15 k
Downloading Packages:
Running transaction check
Transaction check succeeded.
Running transaction test
Transaction test succeeded.
Running transaction
  Preparing  :                                                           1/1
  Installing : pgdg-redhat-repo-42.0-50PGDG.noarch                       1/1
  Verifying  : pgdg-redhat-repo-42.0-50PGDG.noarch                       1/1
```

```
Installed:
  pgdg-redhat-repo-42.0-50PGDG.noarch

Complete!
[root@pg17 ~]#
```

The second section has a command to disable the built-in PostgreSQL module.

Disable the built-in PostgreSQL module:

Red Hat Linux 9, CentOS 9, and Oracle Linux 9 ship with the default PostgreSQL module, which may conflict with the new installation. Hence, disable the built-in PostgreSQL module to prevent conflicts.

[root@pg17 ~]# yum -qy module disable postgresql

If we want to install the previous versions of the RPMs, we can search below, and as the root user, locate the downloaded PostgreSQL repository package RPM.

https://download.postgresql.org/pub/repos/yum/reporpms/

In the below command, we are installing the latest RPMs (pgdg-redhat-repo-latest. noarch.rpm).

Once we download the required RPM package, we can install the repository package as root user as below:

[root@pg17 ~]# yum localinstall pgdg-redhat-repo-latest.noarch.rpm -y
```
PostgreSQL common RPMs for RHEL / Rocky / AlmaLinux 9 - x86_64    1.7 kB/s |
659  B     00:00
PostgreSQL common RPMs for RHEL / Rocky / AlmaLinux 9 - x86_64    2.4 MB/s |
2.4 kB     00:00
Importing GPG key 0x08B40D20:
 Userid     : "PostgreSQL RPM Repository <pgsql-pkg-yum@lists.
postgresql.org>"
 Fingerprint: D4BF 08AE 67A0 B4C7 A1DB CCD2 40BC A2B4 08B4 0D20
 From       : /etc/pki/rpm-gpg/PGDG-RPM-GPG-KEY-RHEL
PostgreSQL common RPMs for RHEL / Rocky / AlmaLinux 9 - x86_64    762 kB/s
| 476 kB     00:00
PostgreSQL 17 for RHEL / Rocky / AlmaLinux 9 - x86_64    1.9 kB/s |
659  B     00:00
PostgreSQL 17 for RHEL / Rocky / AlmaLinux 9 - x86_64    2.4 MB/s | 2.4
kB         00:00
```

```
Importing GPG key 0x08B40D20:
 Userid     : "PostgreSQL RPM Repository <pgsql-pkg-yum@lists.
 postgresql.org>"
 Fingerprint: D4BF 08AE 67A0 B4C7 A1DB CCD2 40BC A2B4 08B4 0D20
 From       : /etc/pki/rpm-gpg/PGDG-RPM-GPG-KEY-RHEL
PostgreSQL 17 for RHEL / Rocky / AlmaLinux 9 - x86_64     167 kB/s | 391
kB    00:02
PostgreSQL 16 for RHEL / Rocky / AlmaLinux 9 - x86_64     1.9 kB/s |
659 B    00:00
PostgreSQL 16 for RHEL / Rocky / AlmaLinux 9 - x86_64     2.4 MB/s | 2.4
kB    00:00
Importing GPG key 0x08B40D20:
 Userid     : "PostgreSQL RPM Repository <pgsql-pkg-yum@lists.
 postgresql.org>"
 Fingerprint: D4BF 08AE 67A0 B4C7 A1DB CCD2 40BC A2B4 08B4 0D20
 From       : /etc/pki/rpm-gpg/PGDG-RPM-GPG-KEY-RHEL
PostgreSQL 16 for RHEL / Rocky / AlmaLinux 9 - x86_64     916 kB/s | 610
kB    00:00
PostgreSQL 15 for RHEL / Rocky / AlmaLinux 9 - x86_64     1.9 kB/s |
659 B    00:00
PostgreSQL 15 for RHEL / Rocky / AlmaLinux 9 - x86_64     2.4 MB/s | 2.4
kB    00:00
Importing GPG key 0x08B40D20:
 Userid     : "PostgreSQL RPM Repository <pgsql-pkg-yum@lists.
 postgresql.org>"
 Fingerprint: D4BF 08AE 67A0 B4C7 A1DB CCD2 40BC A2B4 08B4 0D20
 From       : /etc/pki/rpm-gpg/PGDG-RPM-GPG-KEY-RHEL
PostgreSQL 15 for RHEL / Rocky / AlmaLinux 9 - x86_64     1.3 MB/s | 845
kB    00:00
PostgreSQL 14 for RHEL / Rocky / AlmaLinux 9 - x86_64     1.9 kB/s |
659 B    00:00
PostgreSQL 14 for RHEL / Rocky / AlmaLinux 9 - x86_64     2.4 MB/s | 2.4
kB    00:00
Importing GPG key 0x08B40D20:
```

```
Userid      : "PostgreSQL RPM Repository <pgsql-pkg-yum@lists.
postgresql.org>"
Fingerprint: D4BF 08AE 67A0 B4C7 A1DB CCD2 40BC A2B4 08B4 0D20
From        : /etc/pki/rpm-gpg/PGDG-RPM-GPG-KEY-RHEL
PostgreSQL 14 for RHEL / Rocky / AlmaLinux 9 - x86_64    1.6 MB/s | 1.1
MB    00:00
PostgreSQL 13 for RHEL / Rocky / AlmaLinux 9 - x86_64    1.8 kB/s |
659 B    00:00
PostgreSQL 13 for RHEL / Rocky / AlmaLinux 9 - x86_64    2.4 MB/s | 2.4
kB    00:00
Importing GPG key 0x08B40D20:
Userid      : "PostgreSQL RPM Repository <pgsql-pkg-yum@lists.
postgresql.org>"
Fingerprint: D4BF 08AE 67A0 B4C7 A1DB CCD2 40BC A2B4 08B4 0D20
From        : /etc/pki/rpm-gpg/PGDG-RPM-GPG-KEY-RHEL
[root@pg17 ~]#
```

For PostgreSQL 17, we need to install the recommended Extra Packages for Enterprise Linux (EPEL) repository configuration. We can install EPEL as shown below:

[root@pg17 ~]# yum install epel-release
```
Last metadata expiration check: 0:00:21 ago on Sun 20 May 1525
10:44:44 AM CDT.
Dependencies resolved.
================================================================================
Package                    Architecture   Version      Repository        Size
================================================================================
Installing:
 epel-release              noarch         9-7.el9      extras-common     19 k
Installing weak dependencies:
 epel-next-release         noarch         9-7.el9      extras-common     8.1 k

Transaction Summary
================================================================================
Install 2 Packages
```

```
Total download size: 27 k
Installed size: 29 k
Is this ok [y/N]: y
Downloading Packages:
(1/2): epel-next-release-9-7.el9.noarch.rpm
                                            34 kB/s |  8.1 kB     00:00
(2/2): epel-release-9-7.el9.noarch.rpm
                                            65 kB/s |   19 kB     00:00
--------------------------------------------------------------------------
--Total
                                            30 kB/s |   27 kB     00:00
CentOS Stream 9 - Extras packages
                                           2.1 MB/s |  2.1 kB     00:00
Importing GPG key 0x1D997668:
 Userid     : "CentOS Extras SIG (https://wiki.centos.org/
SpecialInterestGroup) <security@centos.org>"
 Fingerprint: 363F C097 2F64 B699 AED3 968E 1FF6 A217 1D99 7668
 From       : /etc/pki/rpm-gpg/RPM-GPG-KEY-CentOS-SIG-Extras-SHA512
Is this ok [y/N]: y
Key imported successfully
Running transaction check
Transaction check succeeded.
Running transaction test
Transaction test succeeded.
Running transaction
  Preparing        :                                           1/1
  Installing       : epel-release-9-7.el9.noarch              1/2
  Running scriptlet: epel-release-9-7.el9.noarch              1/2
Many EPEL packages require the CodeReady Builder (CRB) repository.
It is recommended that you run /usr/bin/crb enable to enable the CRB
repository.

  Installing       : epel-next-release-9-7.el9.noarch         2/2
  Running scriptlet: epel-next-release-9-7.el9.noarch         2/2
```

CHAPTER 10 NEW FEATURES OF POSTGRESQL 17

```
Verifying          : epel-next-release-9-7.el9.noarch     1/2
Verifying          : epel-release-9-7.el9.noarch          2/2

Installed:
  epel-next-release-9-7.el9.
noarch                                                  epel-release-9-7.
el9.noarch

Complete!
[root@pg17 ~]#
```

The third section has the command that it will actually install the PostgreSQL server binaries.

Installing PostgreSQL 17:

Install PostgreSQL 17 server binaries using yum. When yum is run, the pgdg-redhat-all.repo file will be referred for download and install recommendations for PostgreSQL 17 and the required dependencies for CentOS 9.

[root@pg17 ~]# yum install -y postgresql17-server

```
Extra Packages for Enterprise Linux 9 - x86_64     7.3 MB/s |  23
MB     00:03
Extra Packages for Enterprise Linux 9 openh264 (From Cisco) - x86_64
                                                   1.5 kB/s | 2.5
kB     00:01
Extra Packages for Enterprise Linux 9 - Next - x86_64 7.9 kB/s | 612
kB 01:16
Dependencies resolved.
================================================================
Package                         Architecture
Version                         Repository                       Size
Installing:
 postgresql17-
server                          x86_64                     17.4-1PGDG.rhel9
pgdg17                          6.9 M
Installing dependencies:
```

```
  postgresql17                              x86_64
17.4-1PGDG.rhel9
pgdg17                         1.9 M
  postgresql17-libs                         x86_64
17.4-1PGDG.rhel9
pgdg17                         342 k

Transaction Summary

Install  3 Packages

Total download size: 9.2 M
Installed size: 42 M
Downloading Packages:
(1/3): postgresql17-libs-17.4-1PGDG.rhel9.x86_64.rpm     588 kB/s |  342
kB     00:00
(2/3): postgresql17-17.4-1PGDG.rhel9.x86_64.rpm          2.5 MB/s |  1.9
MB     00:00
(3/3): postgresql17-server-17.4-1PGDG.rhel9.x86_64.rpm   6.4 MB/s |  6.9
MB     00:01
-------------------------------------------------------------------------
Total                                                    8.4 MB/s |  9.2
MB     00:01
PostgreSQL 17 for RHEL / Rocky / AlmaLinux 9 - x86_64    2.4 MB/s |  2.4
kB     00:00
Importing GPG key 0x08B40D20:
 Userid     : "PostgreSQL RPM Repository <pgsql-pkg-yum@lists.
postgresql.org>"
 Fingerprint: D4BF 08AE 67A0 B4C7 A1DB CCD2 40BC A2B4 08B4 0D20
 From       : /etc/pki/rpm-gpg/PGDG-RPM-GPG-KEY-RHEL
Key imported successfully
Running transaction check
Transaction check succeeded.
Running transaction test
Transaction test succeeded.
Running transaction
  Preparing        :                                                  1/1
```

```
Installing        : postgresql17-libs-17.4-1PGDG.rhel9.x86_64      1/3
Running scriptlet: postgresql17-libs-17.4-1PGDG.rhel9.x86_64       1/3
Installing        : postgresql17-17.4-1PGDG.rhel9.x86_64           2/3
Running scriptlet: postgresql17-17.4-1PGDG.rhel9.x86_64            2/3
Running scriptlet: postgresql17-server-17.4-1PGDG.rhel9.x86_64     3/3
Installing        : postgresql17-server-17.4-1PGDG.rhel9.x86_64    3/3
Running scriptlet: postgresql17-server-17.4-1PGDG.rhel9.x86_64     3/3
Verifying         : postgresql17-17.4-1PGDG.rhel9.x86_64           1/3
Verifying         : postgresql17-libs-17.4-1PGDG.rhel9.x86_64      2/3
Verifying         : postgresql17-server-17.4-1PGDG.rhel9.x86_64    3/3
```

Installed:
postgresql17-17.4-1PGDG.rhel9.x86_64
postgresql17-libs-17.4-1PGDG.rhel9.x86_64
postgresql17-server-17.4-1PGDG.rhel9.x86_64

Complete!
[root@pg17 ~]#

Installing the contrib Package of PostgreSQL 17

We can install the PostgreSQL 17-contrib package that contains a few additional various extension modules that are included in the PostgreSQL distribution.

[root@pg17 ~]# yum install -y postgresql17-contrib

Last metadata expiration check: 0:32:50 ago on Sun 20 May 1525 10:47:29 AM CDT. Dependencies resolved.

Package	Architecture	Version	Repository	Size
Installing:				
postgresql17-contrib	x86_64	17.4-1PGDG.rhel9	pgdg17	730 k

Transaction Summary
===
Install 1 Package

Total download size: 730 k
Installed size: 2.7 M

CHAPTER 10   NEW FEATURES OF POSTGRESQL 17

```
Downloading Packages:
postgresql17-contrib-17.4-1PGDG.rhel9.x86_64.rpm
950 kB/s | 730 kB     00:00
--------------------------------------------------------------------
Total
942 kB/s | 730 kB     00:00
Running transaction check
Transaction check succeeded.
Running transaction test
Transaction test succeeded.
Running transaction
  Preparing        :                                                   1/1
  Installing       : postgresql17-contrib-17.4-1PGDG.rhel9.x86_64      1/1
  Running scriptlet: postgresql17-contrib-17.4-1PGDG.rhel9.x86_64      1/1
  Verifying        : postgresql17-contrib-17.4-1PGDG.rhel9.x86_64      1/1

Installed:
  postgresql17-contrib-17.4-1PGDG.rhel9.x86_64

Complete!
[root@pg17 ~]#
```

We can now check the installed PostgreSQL 17–related packages using the "rpm -qa" command.

```
[root@pg17 ~]# rpm -qa |grep -i postgres
pcp-pmda-postgresql-6.3.2-3.el9.x86_64
postgresql17-libs-17.4-1PGDG.rhel9.x86_64
postgresql17-17.4-1PGDG.rhel9.x86_64
postgresql17-server-17.4-1PGDG.rhel9.x86_64
postgresql17-contrib-17.4-1PGDG.rhel9.x86_64
[root@pg17 ~]#
```

CHAPTER 10 NEW FEATURES OF POSTGRESQL 17

We can check the installed binaries in the bin location of /usr/pgsql-17.

[root@pg17 ~]# ls -lrt /usr/pgsql-17/bin
```
total 14460
-rwxr-xr-x. 1 root root        9617 Feb 18 04:17 postgresql-17-setup
-rwxr-xr-x. 1 root root        2167 Feb 18 04:17 postgresql-17-check-db-dir
-rwxr-xr-x. 1 root root       41400 Feb 18 04:17 vacuumlo
-rwxr-xr-x. 1 root root       88520 Feb 18 04:17 vacuumdb
-rwxr-xr-x. 1 root root       83992 Feb 18 04:17 reindexdb
-rwxr-xr-x. 1 root root      729544 Feb 18 04:17 psql
-rwxr-xr-x. 1 root root       96176 Feb 18 04:17 pg_waldump
-rwxr-xr-x. 1 root root       32816 Feb 18 04:17 pg_test_timing
-rwxr-xr-x. 1 root root       41304 Feb 18 04:17 pg_test_fsync
-rwxr-xr-x. 1 root root      108768 Feb 18 04:17 pg_rewind
-rwxr-xr-x. 1 root root      194624 Feb 18 04:17 pg_restore
-rwxr-xr-x. 1 root root       54000 Feb 18 04:17 pg_resetwal
-rwxr-xr-x. 1 root root       92192 Feb 18 04:17 pg_receivewal
-rwxr-xr-x. 1 root root       37144 Feb 18 04:17 pg_isready
-rwxr-xr-x. 1 root root      443320 Feb 18 04:17 pg_dump
-rwxr-xr-x. 1 root root       62496 Feb 18 04:17 pg_ctl
-rwxr-xr-x. 1 root root       70960 Feb 18 04:17 pg_createsubscriber
-rwxr-xr-x. 1 root root       45184 Feb 18 04:17 pg_controldata
-rwxr-xr-x. 1 root root       36824 Feb 18 04:17 pg_config
-rwxr-xr-x. 1 root root       49832 Feb 18 04:17 pg_checksums
-rwxr-xr-x. 1 root root      163168 Feb 18 04:17 pgbench
-rwxr-xr-x. 1 root root       97024 Feb 18 04:17 pg_amcheck
-rwxr-xr-x. 1 root root       66760 Feb 18 04:17 dropuser
-rwxr-xr-x. 1 root root       66824 Feb 18 04:17 dropdb
-rwxr-xr-x. 1 root root       75824 Feb 18 04:17 createuser
-rwxr-xr-x. 1 root root       75440 Feb 18 04:17 createdb
-rwxr-xr-x. 1 root root       71256 Feb 18 04:17 clusterdb
-rwxr-xr-x. 1 root root    10839464 Feb 18 04:17 postgres
-rwxr-xr-x. 1 root root       41368 Feb 18 04:17 pg_walsummary
-rwxr-xr-x. 1 root root       96112 Feb 18 04:17 pg_verifybackup
-rwxr-xr-x. 1 root root      167952 Feb 18 04:17 pg_upgrade
-rwxr-xr-x. 1 root root       54736 Feb 18 04:17 pg_recvlogical
```

```
-rwxr-xr-x. 1 root root    117816 Feb 18 04:17 pg_dumpall
-rwxr-xr-x. 1 root root    117040 Feb 18 04:17 pg_combinebackup
-rwxr-xr-x. 1 root root    143096 Feb 18 04:17 pg_basebackup
-rwxr-xr-x. 1 root root     41240 Feb 18 04:17 pg_archivecleanup
-rwxr-xr-x. 1 root root     41592 Feb 18 04:17 oid2name
-rwxr-xr-x. 1 root root    113464 Feb 18 04:17 initdb
[root@pg17 ~]#
```

The fourth section has three separate commands.

Optionally initialize the database and enable automatic start:

This command will initialize the storage area and create data directories.

[root@pg17 ~]# /usr/pgsql-17/bin/postgresql-17-setup initdb
```
Initializing database ... OK
```

[root@pg17 ~]# ls -lrth /var/lib/pgsql/17/data
```
total 56K
-rw-------. 1 postgres postgres    3 May 15 11:21 PG_VERSION
drwx------. 2 postgres postgres    6 May 15 11:21 pg_twophase
drwx------. 2 postgres postgres    6 May 15 11:21 pg_tblspc
drwx------. 2 postgres postgres    6 May 15 11:21 pg_stat_tmp
drwx------. 2 postgres postgres    6 May 15 11:21 pg_snapshots
drwx------. 2 postgres postgres    6 May 15 11:21 pg_serial
drwx------. 2 postgres postgres    6 May 15 11:21 pg_replslot
drwx------. 2 postgres postgres    6 May 15 11:21 pg_notify
drwx------. 4 postgres postgres   36 May 15 11:21 pg_multixact
drwx------. 2 postgres postgres    6 May 15 11:21 pg_dynshmem
drwx------. 2 postgres postgres    6 May 15 11:21 pg_commit_ts
-rw-------. 1 postgres postgres  30K May 15 11:21 postgresql.conf
-rw-------. 1 postgres postgres   88 May 15 11:21 postgresql.auto.conf
-rw-------. 1 postgres postgres 2.6K May 15 11:21 pg_ident.conf
-rw-------. 1 postgres postgres 5.4K May 15 11:21 pg_hba.conf
drwx------. 2 postgres postgres   18 May 15 11:21 pg_xact
drwx------. 4 postgres postgres   77 May 15 11:21 pg_wal
drwx------. 2 postgres postgres   18 May 15 11:21 pg_subtrans
drwx------. 2 postgres postgres 4.0K May 15 11:21 global
drwx------. 5 postgres postgres   33 May 15 11:21 base
```

CHAPTER 10   NEW FEATURES OF POSTGRESQL 17

```
drwx------. 2 postgres postgres   25 May 15 11:21 pg_stat
drwx------. 4 postgres postgres   68 May 15 11:21 pg_logical
drwx------. 2 postgres postgres    6 May 15 11:21 log
[root@pg17 ~]#
```

This command enables the auto start of the PostgreSQL server every time the system restarts.

```
[root@pg17 ~]# systemctl enable postgresql-17
Created symlink /etc/systemd/system/multi-user.target.wants/postgresql-17.
service → /usr/lib/systemd/system/postgresql-17.service.
[root@pg17 ~]#
```

The below commands use start/stop/status of PostgreSQL server.

[root@pg17 ~]# systemctl start postgresql-17

[root@pg17 ~]# systemctl status postgresql-17
- postgresql-17.service - PostgreSQL 17 database server
     Loaded: loaded (/usr/lib/systemd/system/postgresql-17.service;
     enabled; preset: disabled)
     Active: active (running) since Sun 2025-04-20 11:22:30 CDT; 5s ago
       Docs: https://www.postgresql.org/docs/17/static/
    Process: 14270 ExecStartPre=/usr/pgsql-17/bin/postgresql-17-check-db-
    dir ${PGDATA} (code=exited, status=0/SUCCESS)
   Main PID: 14275 (postgres)
      Tasks: 7 (limit: 35850)
     Memory: 17.7M
        CPU: 71ms
     CGroup: /system.slice/postgresql-17.service
             ├─14275 /usr/pgsql-17/bin/postgres -D /var/lib/pgsql/17/data/
             ├─14276 "postgres: logger "
             ├─14277 "postgres: checkpointer "
             ├─14278 "postgres: background writer "
             ├─14280 "postgres: walwriter "
             ├─14281 "postgres: autovacuum launcher "
             └─14282 "postgres: logical replication launcher "

May 15 11:22:30 pg17 systemd[1]: Starting PostgreSQL 17 database server...
May 15 11:22:30 pg17 postgres[14275]: 2025-04-20 11:22:30.342 CDT [14275]
LOG: redirecting log output to logging collector process
May 15 11:22:30 pg17 postgres[14275]: 2025-04-20 11:22:30.342 CDT [14275]
HINT: Future log output will appear in directory "log".
May 15 11:22:30 pg17 systemd[1]: Started PostgreSQL 17 database server.
[root@pg17 ~]#
[root@pg17 ~]# systemctl stop postgresql-17
[root@pg17 ~]#
[root@pg17 ~]# systemctl status postgresql-17
○ postgresql-17.service - PostgreSQL 17 database server
     Loaded: loaded (/usr/lib/systemd/system/postgresql-17.service;
   enabled; preset: disabled)
     Active: inactive (dead) since Sun 2025-04-20 11:22:45 CDT; 2s ago
   Duration: 14.930s
       Docs: https://www.postgresql.org/docs/17/static/
    Process: 14270 ExecStartPre=/usr/pgsql-17/bin/postgresql-17-check-db-
   dir ${PGDATA} (code=exited, status=0/SUCCESS)
    Process: 14275 ExecStart=/usr/pgsql-17/bin/postgres -D ${PGDATA}
   (code=exited, status=0/SUCCESS)
   Main PID: 14275 (code=exited, status=0/SUCCESS)
        CPU: 101ms

May 15 11:22:30 pg17 systemd[1]: Starting PostgreSQL 17 database server...
May 15 11:22:30 pg17 postgres[14275]: 2025-04-20 11:22:30.342 CDT [14275]
LOG: redirecting log output to logging collector process
May 15 11:22:30 pg17 postgres[14275]: 2025-04-20 11:22:30.342 CDT [14275]
HINT: Future log output will appear in directory "log".
May 15 11:22:30 pg17 systemd[1]: Started PostgreSQL 17 database server.
May 15 11:22:45 pg17 systemd[1]: Stopping PostgreSQL 17 database server...
May 15 11:22:45 pg17 systemd[1]: postgresql-17.service: Deactivated
successfully.
May 15 11:22:45 pg17 systemd[1]: Stopped PostgreSQL 17 database server.
[root@pg17 ~]#
[root@pg17 ~]# systemctl start postgresql-17
[root@pg17 ~]#

CHAPTER 10   NEW FEATURES OF POSTGRESQL 17

[root@pg17 ~]# systemctl status postgresql-17
* postgresql-17.service - PostgreSQL 17 database server
    Loaded: loaded (/usr/lib/systemd/system/postgresql-17.service;
    enabled; preset: disabled)
    Active: active (running) since Sun 2025-04-20 11:22:51 CDT; 1s ago
      Docs: https://www.postgresql.org/docs/17/static/
   Process: 14300 ExecStartPre=/usr/pgsql-17/bin/postgresql-17-check-db-
   dir ${PGDATA} (code=exited, status=0/SUCCESS)
  Main PID: 14305 (postgres)
     Tasks: 7 (limit: 35850)
    Memory: 17.7M
       CPU: 55ms
    CGroup: /system.slice/postgresql-17.service
            ├─14305 /usr/pgsql-17/bin/postgres -D /var/lib/pgsql/17/data/
            ├─14306 "postgres: logger "
            ├─14307 "postgres: checkpointer "
            ├─14308 "postgres: background writer "
            ├─14310 "postgres: walwriter "
            ├─14311 "postgres: autovacuum launcher "
            └─14312 "postgres: logical replication launcher "

May 15 11:22:51 pg17 systemd[1]: Starting PostgreSQL 17 database server...
May 15 11:22:51 pg17 postgres[14305]: 2025-04-20 11:22:51.660 CDT [14305]
LOG: redirecting log output to logging collector process
May 15 11:22:51 pg17 postgres[14305]: 2025-04-20 11:22:51.660 CDT [14305]
HINT: Future log output will appear in directory "log".
May 15 11:22:51 pg17 systemd[1]: Started PostgreSQL 17 database server.
[root@pg17 ~]#

Check the status of PostgreSQL 17 using the following:

[root@pg17 ~]# ps -ef |grep -i postgres
```
postgres    14305       1  0 11:22 ?        00:00:00 /usr/pgsql-17/bin/
postgres -D /var/lib/pgsql/17/data/
postgres    14306   14305  0 11:22 ?        00:00:00 postgres: logger
postgres    14307   14305  0 11:22 ?        00:00:00 postgres: checkpointer
```

CHAPTER 10 NEW FEATURES OF POSTGRESQL 17

```
postgres    14308    14305   0 11:22 ?        00:00:00 postgres:
                                                       background writer
postgres    14310    14305   0 11:22 ?        00:00:00 postgres: walwriter
postgres    14311    14305   0 11:22 ?        00:00:00 postgres: autovacuum
launcher
postgres    14312    14305   0 11:22 ?        00:00:00 postgres: logical
replication launcher
root        14338     6688   0 11:23 pts/1    00:00:00 grep --color=auto -i
postgres
[root@pg17 ~]#
```

Log in as "postgres" user using the "psql" utility and check the list of databases (\l).

```
[postgres@pg17 ~]$ psql
psql (17.4)
Type "help" for help.

postgres=# \l
                                               List of databases
   Name    |  Owner   | Encoding | Locale Provider |  Collate   |   Ctype    | Locale | ICU Rules |   Access privileges
-----------+----------+----------+-----------------+------------+------------+--------+-----------+-----------------------
 postgres  | postgres | UTF8     | libc            | en_US.UTF-8| en_US.UTF-8|        |           |
 template0 | postgres | UTF8     | libc            | en_US.UTF-8| en_US.UTF-8|        |           | =c/postgres          +
           |          |          |                 |            |            |        |           | postgres=CTc/postgres
 template1 | postgres | UTF8     | libc            | en_US.UTF-8| en_US.UTF-8|        |           | =c/postgres          +
           |          |          |                 |            |            |        |           | postgres=CTc/postgres
(3 rows)
```

Figure 10-4. Login to PostgreSQL and displaying databases

postgres=# select setting from pg_settings where name='data_directory';

setting

\---------------------------

 /var/lib/pgsql/17/data
(1 row)
postgres=#

postgres=# select version();

version

\---PostgreSQL
17.4 on x86_64-pc-linux-gnu, compiled by gcc (GCC) 11.5.0 20240719
(Red Hat 11.5.0-5), 64-bit
(1 row)
postgres=#

CHAPTER 10   NEW FEATURES OF POSTGRESQL 17

As part of creating a database cluster, the above command will create three default databases: postgres, template1, and template0.

- The database named *postgres* is a default database meant for use by users, utilities, and third-party applications.

- The two databases named *template1* and *template0* are meant as source databases to be copied by later CREATE DATABASE commands.

Also, as part of database cluster creation, data directories will get created; these are the directories that will be used by the database to save the data. Check the data directories with the below command:

postgres=# show data_directory;
```
    data_directory
-------------------------
 /var/lib/pgsql/17/data

(1 row)

postgres=#
```

CHAPTER 10 NEW FEATURES OF POSTGRESQL 17

```
[postgres@pg17 ~]$ ls -lrth /var/lib/pgsql/17/data
total 68K
-rw-------. 1 postgres postgres    3 Apr 20 11:21 PG_VERSION
drwx------. 2 postgres postgres    6 Apr 20 11:21 pg_twophase
drwx------. 2 postgres postgres    6 Apr 20 11:21 pg_tblspc
drwx------. 2 postgres postgres    6 Apr 20 11:21 pg_stat_tmp
drwx------. 2 postgres postgres    6 Apr 20 11:21 pg_snapshots
drwx------. 2 postgres postgres    6 Apr 20 11:21 pg_serial
drwx------. 2 postgres postgres    6 Apr 20 11:21 pg_replslot
drwx------. 2 postgres postgres    6 Apr 20 11:21 pg_notify
drwx------. 4 postgres postgres   36 Apr 20 11:21 pg_multixact
drwx------. 2 postgres postgres    6 Apr 20 11:21 pg_dynshmem
drwx------. 2 postgres postgres    6 Apr 20 11:21 pg_commit_ts
-rw-------. 1 postgres postgres  30K Apr 20 11:21 postgresql.conf
-rw-------. 1 postgres postgres   88 Apr 20 11:21 postgresql.auto.conf
-rw-------. 1 postgres postgres 2.6K Apr 20 11:21 pg_ident.conf
-rw-------. 1 postgres postgres 5.4K Apr 20 11:21 pg_hba.conf
drwx------. 2 postgres postgres   18 Apr 20 11:21 pg_xact
drwx------. 4 postgres postgres   77 Apr 20 11:21 pg_wal
drwx------. 2 postgres postgres   18 Apr 20 11:21 pg_subtrans
drwx------. 5 postgres postgres   33 Apr 20 11:21 base
drwx------. 2 postgres postgres   32 Apr 20 11:22 log
drwx------. 4 postgres postgres   68 Apr 20 11:22 pg_logical
-rw-------. 1 postgres postgres   30 Apr 20 11:22 current_logfiles
-rw-------. 1 postgres postgres   58 Apr 20 11:22 postmaster.opts
drwx------. 2 postgres postgres    6 Apr 20 11:22 pg_stat
-rw-------. 1 postgres postgres  100 Apr 20 11:22 postmaster.pid
drwx------. 2 postgres postgres 4.0K Apr 20 11:23 global
[postgres@pg17 ~]$
```

Figure 10-5. *Data directories created during database creation*

We can check the installed binaries using the following command:

```
[postgres@pg17 ~]$ pg_config --bindir
/usr/pgsql-17/bin
[postgres@pg17 ~]$
```

```
[postgres@pg17 ~]$ cd /usr/pgsql-17/bin
[postgres@pg17 bin]$ ls -lrth
total 15M
-rwxr-xr-x. 1 root root 9.4K Feb 18 04:17 postgresql-17-setup
-rwxr-xr-x. 1 root root 2.2K Feb 18 04:17 postgresql-17-check-db-dir
-rwxr-xr-x. 1 root root  41K Feb 18 04:17 vacuumlo
-rwxr-xr-x. 1 root root  87K Feb 18 04:17 vacuumdb
-rwxr-xr-x. 1 root root  83K Feb 18 04:17 reindexdb
-rwxr-xr-x. 1 root root 713K Feb 18 04:17 psql
-rwxr-xr-x. 1 root root  94K Feb 18 04:17 pg_waldump
-rwxr-xr-x. 1 root root  33K Feb 18 04:17 pg_test_timing
-rwxr-xr-x. 1 root root  41K Feb 18 04:17 pg_test_fsync
-rwxr-xr-x. 1 root root 107K Feb 18 04:17 pg_rewind
-rwxr-xr-x. 1 root root 191K Feb 18 04:17 pg_restore
-rwxr-xr-x. 1 root root  53K Feb 18 04:17 pg_resetwal
-rwxr-xr-x. 1 root root  91K Feb 18 04:17 pg_receivewal
-rwxr-xr-x. 1 root root  37K Feb 18 04:17 pg_isready
-rwxr-xr-x. 1 root root 433K Feb 18 04:17 pg_dump
-rwxr-xr-x. 1 root root  62K Feb 18 04:17 pg_ctl
-rwxr-xr-x. 1 root root  70K Feb 18 04:17 pg_createsubscriber
-rwxr-xr-x. 1 root root  45K Feb 18 04:17 pg_controldata
-rwxr-xr-x. 1 root root  36K Feb 18 04:17 pg_config
-rwxr-xr-x. 1 root root  49K Feb 18 04:17 pg_checksums
-rwxr-xr-x. 1 root root 160K Feb 18 04:17 pgbench
-rwxr-xr-x. 1 root root  95K Feb 18 04:17 pg_amcheck
-rwxr-xr-x. 1 root root  66K Feb 18 04:17 dropuser
-rwxr-xr-x. 1 root root  66K Feb 18 04:17 dropdb
-rwxr-xr-x. 1 root root  75K Feb 18 04:17 createuser
-rwxr-xr-x. 1 root root  74K Feb 18 04:17 createdb
-rwxr-xr-x. 1 root root  70K Feb 18 04:17 clusterdb
-rwxr-xr-x. 1 root root  11M Feb 18 04:17 postgres
-rwxr-xr-x. 1 root root  41K Feb 18 04:17 pg_walsummary
-rwxr-xr-x. 1 root root  94K Feb 18 04:17 pg_verifybackup
-rwxr-xr-x. 1 root root 165K Feb 18 04:17 pg_upgrade
-rwxr-xr-x. 1 root root  54K Feb 18 04:17 pg_recvlogical
-rwxr-xr-x. 1 root root 116K Feb 18 04:17 pg_dumpall
-rwxr-xr-x. 1 root root 115K Feb 18 04:17 pg_combinebackup
-rwxr-xr-x. 1 root root 140K Feb 18 04:17 pg_basebackup
-rwxr-xr-x. 1 root root  41K Feb 18 04:17 pg_archivecleanup
-rwxr-xr-x. 1 root root  41K Feb 18 04:17 oid2name
-rwxr-xr-x. 1 root root 111K Feb 18 04:17 initdb
[postgres@pg17 bin]$ pwd
/usr/pgsql-17/bin
```

Figure 10-6. Binaries related to PostgreSQL 17

This command below reads and outputs control information from the pg_control file located inside the PostgreSQL data directory. It includes details like

- PostgreSQL version
- System identifier
- Checkpoint information
- WAL (Write-Ahead Logging) information
- Last modification timestamps
- Data alignment and block sizes
- Timeline ID

[postgres@pg17 bin]$ /usr/pgsql-17/bin/pg_controldata -D /var/lib/pgsql/17/data

```
pg_control version number:            1700
Catalog version number:               202406281
Database system identifier:           7495431247654111083
Database cluster state:               in production
pg_control last modified:             Sun 20 May 1525 11:27:56 AM CDT
Latest checkpoint location:           0/1587090
Latest checkpoint's REDO location:    0/1587000
Latest checkpoint's REDO WAL file:    000000010000000000000001
Latest checkpoint's TimeLineID:       1
Latest checkpoint's PrevTimeLineID:   1
Latest checkpoint's full_page_writes: on
Latest checkpoint's NextXID:          0:749
Latest checkpoint's NextOID:          24576
Latest checkpoint's NextMultiXactId:  1
Latest checkpoint's NextMultiOffset:  0
Latest checkpoint's oldestXID:        730
Latest checkpoint's oldestXID's DB:   1
Latest checkpoint's oldestActiveXID:  749
Latest checkpoint's oldestMultiXid:   1
Latest checkpoint's oldestMulti's DB: 1
Latest checkpoint's oldestCommitTsXid:0
```

```
Latest checkpoint's newestCommitTsXid:0
Time of latest checkpoint:               Sun 20 May 1525 11:27:51 AM CDT
Fake LSN counter for unlogged rels:      0/3E8
Minimum recovery ending location:        0/0
Min recovery ending loc's timeline:      0
Backup start location:                   0/0
Backup end location:                     0/0
End-of-backup record required:           no
wal_level setting:                       replica
wal_log_hints setting:                   off
max_connections setting:                 100
max_worker_processes setting:            8
max_wal_senders setting:                 10
max_prepared_xacts setting:              0
max_locks_per_xact setting:              64
track_commit_timestamp setting:          off
Maximum data alignment:                  8
Database block size:                     8192
Blocks per segment of large relation:    131072
WAL block size:                          8192
Bytes per WAL segment:                   16777216
Maximum length of identifiers:           64
Maximum columns in an index:             32
Maximum size of a TOAST chunk:           1996
Size of a large-object chunk:            2048
Date/time type storage:                  64-bit integers
Float8 argument passing:                 by value
Data page checksum version:              0
Mock authentication nonce:               d5d45cf6cddd7a76b37bf0b7ad3a2277bca
                                         09c1cc519b4b740a5d4d05d191fe1
[postgres@pg17 bin]$
```

Log in as postgres user and configure the *.bash_profile file*.

[postgres@pg17 ~]$ vi .bash_profile
[postgres@pg17 ~]$ . ./.bash_profile

```
[postgres@pg17 ~]$ cat .bash_profile
# .bash_profile

# Get the aliases and functions
if [ -f ~/.bashrc ]; then
        . ~/.bashrc
fi
```
export PATH=$PATH:/usr/pgsql-17/bin
export PGDATA=/var/lib/pgsql/17/data/
```
# User specific environment and startup programs
[postgres@pg17 ~]$
```

pg_ctl is a PostgreSQL utility to initialize, start, stop, reload, or check the status of a PostgreSQL server (postgres process). It's often used by administrators to control the database instance.

Check the status of the PostgreSQL server with the following:

```
[postgres@pg17 ~]$ pg_ctl status
pg_ctl: server is running (PID: 14305)
/usr/pgsql-17/bin/postgres "-D" "/var/lib/pgsql/17/data/"
[postgres@pg17 ~]$
```

Stop the PostgreSQL server.

```
[postgres@pg17 ~]$ pg_ctl stop
waiting for server to shut down.... done
server stopped
[postgres@pg17 ~]$
```

Restart the PostgreSQL server.

```
[postgres@pg17 ~]$ pg_ctl start
waiting for server to start....2025-04-20 11:53:09.116 CDT [16192]
LOG:  redirecting log output to logging collector process
2025-04-20 11:53:09.116 CDT [16192] HINT:  Future log output will appear in directory "log".
 done
server started
```

[postgres@pg17 ~]$

[postgres@pg17 ~]$ pg_ctl status
pg_ctl: server is running (PID: 16192)
/usr/pgsql-17/bin/postgres
[postgres@pg17 ~]$

Reload the configuration files of the PostgreSQL server.

[postgres@pg17 ~]$ pg_ctl reload
server signaled
[postgres@pg17 ~]$

Creating Database in PostgreSQL

You can create a new database in PostgreSQL using the createdb command-line utility.

```
[postgres@pg17 ~]$ createdb db1
[postgres@pg17 ~]$
[postgres@pg17 ~]$ psql
psql (17.4)
Type "help" for help.

postgres=# \l
                                                List of databases
   Name    |  Owner   | Encoding | Locale Provider |   Collate   |   Ctype     | Locale | ICU Rules |   Access privileges
-----------+----------+----------+-----------------+-------------+-------------+--------+-----------+-----------------------
 db1       | postgres | UTF8     | libc            | en_US.UTF-8 | en_US.UTF-8 |        |           |
 postgres  | postgres | UTF8     | libc            | en_US.UTF-8 | en_US.UTF-8 |        |           |
 template0 | postgres | UTF8     | libc            | en_US.UTF-8 | en_US.UTF-8 |        |           | =c/postgres          +
           |          |          |                 |             |             |        |           | postgres=CTc/postgres
 template1 | postgres | UTF8     | libc            | en_US.UTF-8 | en_US.UTF-8 |        |           | =c/postgres          +
           |          |          |                 |             |             |        |           | postgres=CTc/postgres
(4 rows)
```

Figure 10-7. New database creation using the "createdb" command

New Features: Incremental Backups in PostgreSQL 17

PostgreSQL 17 brings a game-changing enhancement for database administrators support for incremental backups using pg_basebackup. This long-awaited feature streamlines backup operations, particularly for large-scale databases where taking full backups regularly can be resource-intensive. In this guide, we will explore how to set up and use incremental backups alongside full backups and how to restore your data efficiently using the latest PostgreSQL 17 capabilities.

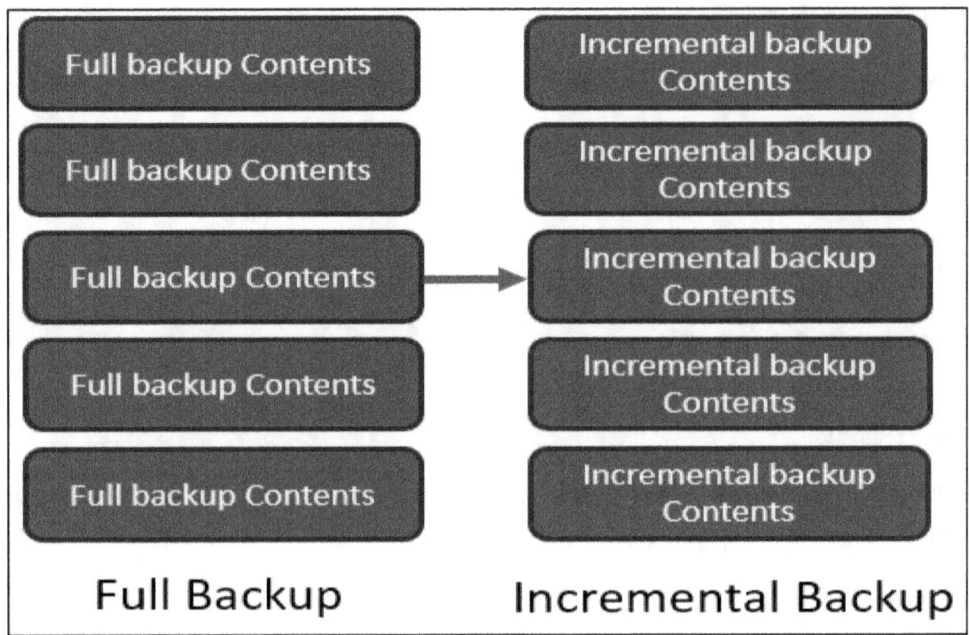

Figure 10-8. Full backups vs. incremental backups in PostgreSQL 17

PostgreSQL 17 adds support for incremental backups using "pg_basebackup" and the new "pg_combinebackup" tools. This feature allows for more efficient backup processes by only saving changes since the last backup performed through "pg_basebackup".

pg_basebackup can do full backup or incremental backup. Incremental backups store only changed blocks, not whole data files, in a PostgreSQL database cluster. Added new background process called "WAL Summarizer" and must be enabled using the parameter "summarize_wal".

Check the following parameters in PostgreSQL database cluster.

```
postgres=# show summarize_wal;
postgres=# show wal_summary_keep_time;
postgres=#
```

Note The parameter "wal_summary_keep_time" will retain summaries for ten days.

Once the parameter "*summarize_wal*" is ON, then we can see the background process with the command shown in Figure 10-9.

```
[postgres@pg17 ~]$ ps -ef |grep postgres
postgres    1257     1  0 10:16 ?        00:00:00 /usr/pgsql-17/bin/postgres -D /var/lib/pgsql/17/data/
postgres    1313  1257  0 10:16 ?        00:00:00 postgres: logger
postgres    1317  1257  0 10:16 ?        00:00:00 postgres: checkpointer
postgres    1319  1257  0 10:16 ?        00:00:00 postgres: background writer
postgres    1655  1257  0 10:16 ?        00:00:00 postgres: walwriter
postgres    1656  1257  0 10:16 ?        00:00:00 postgres: walsummarizer
postgres    1657  1257  0 10:16 ?        00:00:00 postgres: autovacuum launcher
postgres    1658  1257  0 10:16 ?        00:00:00 postgres: logical replication launcher
root        6482  6408  0 10:26 pts/0    00:00:00 su - postgres
postgres    6483  6482  0 10:26 pts/0    00:00:00 -bash
postgres    7070  6483  0 10:45 pts/0    00:00:00 ps -ef
postgres    7071  6483  0 10:45 pts/0    00:00:00 grep --color=auto postgres
[postgres@pg17 ~]$
```

Figure 10-9. *New background process – walsummarizer*

Let's get into small demonstration on incremental backups using pg_basebackup and pg_combinebackup commands.

1. Create the following directories under /home/postgres for our demonstration:

   [postgres@pg17 ~]$cd /home/postgres/backups
   [postgres@pg17 ~]$mkdir -p fullbackup incrementalbackup combinebackup

   [postgres@pg17 backups]$ ls -lrth /home/postgres/backups
   total 0
   drwxr-xr-x. 2 postgres postgres 6 May 15 16:03 fullbackup
   drwxr-xr-x. 2 postgres postgres 6 May 15 16:04 incrementalbackup
   drwxr-xr-x. 2 postgres postgres 6 May 15 16:04 combinebackup

2. Connect to "db1" database and create table "emp" and insert rows for full backup.

   postgres=# \c db1
   You are now connected to database "db1" as user "postgres".
   db1=#
   db1=# CREATE TABLE emp (
   emp_no   SERIAL PRIMARY KEY,
   emp_fname   VARCHAR(50),
   emp_lname   VARCHAR(50),

CHAPTER 10 NEW FEATURES OF POSTGRESQL 17

```
    emp_email               VARCHAR(100),
    emp_sal                 NUMERIC
);
CREATE TABLE
db1=#

db1=# select * from emp;
 emp_no | emp_fname | emp_lname | emp_email | emp_sal
--------+-----------+-----------+-----------+---------(0 rows)

db1=# insert into emp (emp_fname, emp_lname, emp_email, emp_sal)
values ('john','peter','john@gmail.com',1000);
INSERT 0 1

db1=# insert into emp (emp_fname, emp_lname, emp_email, emp_sal)
values ('sam','curran','sam@gmail.com',2000);
INSERT 0 1

db1=# insert into emp (emp_fname, emp_lname, emp_email, emp_sal)
values ('bills','roger','bills@gmail.com',3000);
INSERT 0 1

db1=# insert into emp (emp_fname, emp_lname, emp_email, emp_sal)
values ('lawrence','larry','larry@gmail.com',4000);
INSERT 0 1

db1=# insert into emp (emp_fname, emp_lname, emp_email, emp_sal)
values ('peter','larry','peter@gmail.com',5000);
INSERT 0 1
```

db1=# select * from emp;
```
 emp_no | emp_fname | emp_lname |    emp_email      | emp_sal
--------+-----------+-----------+-------------------+---------
      1 | john      | peter     | john@gmail.com    |    1000
      2 | sam       | curran    | sam@gmail.com     |    2000
      3 | bills     | roger     | bills@gmail.com   |    3000
      4 | lawrence  | larry     | larry@gmail.com   |    4000
      5 | peter     | larry     | peter@gmail.com   |    5000
```

CHAPTER 10 NEW FEATURES OF POSTGRESQL 17

(5 rows)
db1=# \q

You can see the utilities pg_basebackup and pg_combinebackup in the following directory:

[postgres@pg17 ~]$ ls -lrth /usr/pgsql-17/bin/
total 15M
-rwxr-xr-x. 1 root root 9.4K Feb 18 04:17 postgresql-17-setup
-rwxr-xr-x. 1 root root 2.2K Feb 18 04:17 postgresql-17-check-db-dir
-rwxr-xr-x. 1 root root 41K Feb 18 04:17 vacuumlo
-rwxr-xr-x. 1 root root 87K Feb 18 04:17 vacuumdb
-rwxr-xr-x. 1 root root 83K Feb 18 04:17 reindexdb
-rwxr-xr-x. 1 root root 713K Feb 18 04:17 psql
-rwxr-xr-x. 1 root root 94K Feb 18 04:17 pg_waldump
-rwxr-xr-x. 1 root root 33K Feb 18 04:17 pg_test_timing
-rwxr-xr-x. 1 root root 41K Feb 18 04:17 pg_test_fsync
-rwxr-xr-x. 1 root root 107K Feb 18 04:17 pg_rewind
-rwxr-xr-x. 1 root root 191K Feb 18 04:17 pg_restore
-rwxr-xr-x. 1 root root 53K Feb 18 04:17 pg_resetwal
-rwxr-xr-x. 1 root root 91K Feb 18 04:17 pg_receivewal
-rwxr-xr-x. 1 root root 37K Feb 18 04:17 pg_isready
-rwxr-xr-x. 1 root root 433K Feb 18 04:17 pg_dump
-rwxr-xr-x. 1 root root 62K Feb 18 04:17 pg_ctl
-rwxr-xr-x. 1 root root 70K Feb 18 04:17 pg_createsubscriber
-rwxr-xr-x. 1 root root 45K Feb 18 04:17 pg_controldata
-rwxr-xr-x. 1 root root 36K Feb 18 04:17 pg_config
-rwxr-xr-x. 1 root root 49K Feb 18 04:17 pg_checksums
-rwxr-xr-x. 1 root root 160K Feb 18 04:17 pgbench
-rwxr-xr-x. 1 root root 95K Feb 18 04:17 pg_amcheck
-rwxr-xr-x. 1 root root 66K Feb 18 04:17 dropuser
-rwxr-xr-x. 1 root root 66K Feb 18 04:17 dropdb
-rwxr-xr-x. 1 root root 75K Feb 18 04:17 createuser
-rwxr-xr-x. 1 root root 74K Feb 18 04:17 createdb

```
-rwxr-xr-x. 1 root root   70K Feb 18 04:17 clusterdb
-rwxr-xr-x. 1 root root   11M Feb 18 04:17 postgres
-rwxr-xr-x. 1 root root   41K Feb 18 04:17 pg_walsummary
-rwxr-xr-x. 1 root root   94K Feb 18 04:17 pg_verifybackup
-rwxr-xr-x. 1 root root  165K Feb 18 04:17 pg_upgrade
-rwxr-xr-x. 1 root root   54K Feb 18 04:17 pg_recvlogical
-rwxr-xr-x. 1 root root  116K Feb 18 04:17 pg_dumpall
```
-rwxr-xr-x. 1 root root 115K Feb 18 04:17 pg_combinebackup
-rwxr-xr-x. 1 root root 140K Feb 18 04:17 pg_basebackup
```
-rwxr-xr-x. 1 root root   41K Feb 18 04:17 pg_archivecleanup
-rwxr-xr-x. 1 root root   41K Feb 18 04:17 oid2name
-rwxr-xr-x. 1 root root  111K Feb 18 04:17 initdb
[postgres@pg17 bin]$
```

Perform full backup using pg_basebackup under the "/home/postgres/backups/fullbackups" directory.

[postgres@pg17 backups]$ /usr/pgsql-17/bin/pg_basebackup -D /home/postgres/backups/fullbackup -v

```
pg_basebackup: initiating base backup, waiting for checkpoint to complete
pg_basebackup: checkpoint completed
pg_basebackup: write-ahead log start point: 0/B000028 on timeline 1
pg_basebackup: starting background WAL receiver
pg_basebackup: created temporary replication slot "pg_basebackup_7587"
pg_basebackup: write-ahead log end point: 0/B000120
pg_basebackup: waiting for background process to finish streaming ...
pg_basebackup: syncing data to disk ...
pg_basebackup: renaming backup_manifest.tmp to backup_manifest
pg_basebackup: base backup completed
[postgres@pg17 backups]$
```

[postgres@pg17 backups]$ ls -lrth /home/postgres/backups/fullbackup
```
total 248K
drwx------. 4 postgres postgres  77 May 15 16:44 pg_wal
-rw-------. 1 postgres postgres 225 May 15 16:44 backup_label
drwx------. 2 postgres postgres   6 May 15 16:44 pg_twophase
drwx------. 2 postgres postgres   6 May 15 16:44 pg_subtrans
```

```
drwx------. 2 postgres postgres    6 May 15 16:44 pg_snapshots
drwx------. 2 postgres postgres    6 May 15 16:44 pg_serial
drwx------. 2 postgres postgres    6 May 15 16:44 pg_notify
drwx------. 2 postgres postgres    6 May 15 16:44 pg_dynshmem
drwx------. 2 postgres postgres    6 May 15 16:44 pg_commit_ts
drwx------. 4 postgres postgres   36 May 15 16:44 pg_multixact
drwx------. 6 postgres postgres   46 May 15 16:44 base
drwx------. 2 postgres postgres   18 May 15 16:44 pg_xact
drwx------. 2 postgres postgres    6 May 15 16:44 pg_tblspc
drwx------. 2 postgres postgres    6 May 15 16:44 pg_stat_tmp
drwx------. 2 postgres postgres    6 May 15 16:44 pg_stat
drwx------. 2 postgres postgres    6 May 15 16:44 pg_replslot
drwx------. 4 postgres postgres   68 May 15 16:44 pg_logical
-rw-------. 1 postgres postgres  30K May 15 16:44 postgresql.conf
-rw-------. 1 postgres postgres  109 May 15 16:44 postgresql.auto.conf
-rw-------. 1 postgres postgres    3 May 15 16:44 PG_VERSION
-rw-------. 1 postgres postgres 2.6K May 15 16:44 pg_ident.conf
-rw-------. 1 postgres postgres 5.4K May 15 16:44 pg_hba.conf
drwx------. 2 postgres postgres  188 May 15 16:44 log
drwx------. 2 postgres postgres 4.0K May 15 16:44 global
-rw-------. 1 postgres postgres   30 May 15 16:44 current_logfiles
-rw-------. 1 postgres postgres 183K May 15 16:44 backup_manifest
[postgres@pg17 backups]$
```

Backups contain the "backup_manifest" file with metadata. Check the contents of the "backup_manifest" file.

[postgres@pg17 backups]$ cat /home/postgres/backups/fullbackup/backup_manifest

```
{ "PostgreSQL-Backup-Manifest-Version": 2,
"System-Identifier": 7495431247654111083,
"Files": [
{ "Path": "backup_label", "Size": 225, "Last-Modified": "2025-05-15
21:44:55 GMT", "Checksum-Algorithm": "CRC32C", "Checksum": "7e92f880" },
{ "Path": "global/1262", "Size": 8192, "Last-Modified": "2025-04-20
17:15:05 GMT", "Checksum-Algorithm": "CRC32C", "Checksum": "9eb2dc4d" },
```

{ "Path": "global/2964", "Size": 0, "Last-Modified": "2025-04-20 16:21:21 GMT", "Checksum-Algorithm": "CRC32C", "Checksum": "00000000" },
{ "Path": "global/1213", "Size": 8192, "Last-Modified": "2025-04-20 16:21:22 GMT", "Checksum-Algorithm": "CRC32C", "Checksum": "860d02d5" },
{ "Path": "global/1260", "Size": 8192, "Last-Modified": "2025-04-20 16:21:22 GMT", "Checksum-Algorithm": "CRC32C", "Checksum": "c8d4de5c" },
{ "Path": "global/1261", "Size": 8192, "Last-Modified": "2025-04-20 16:21:22 GMT", "Checksum-Algorithm": "CRC32C", "Checksum": "49cc473e" },
{ "Path": "global/1214", "Size": 0, "Last-Modified": "2025-04-20 16:21:21 GMT", "Checksum-Algorithm": "CRC32C", "Checksum": "00000000" },
{ "Path": "global/2396", "Size": 8192, "Last-Modified": "2025-04-27 18:59:09 GMT", "Checksum-Algorithm": "CRC32C", "Checksum": "55c36962" },
{ "Path": "global/6000", "Size": 0, "Last-Modified": "2025-04-20 16:21:21 GMT", "Checksum-Algorithm": "CRC32C", "Checksum": "00000000" },
{ "Path": "global/3592", "Size": 0, "Last-Modified": "2025-04-20 16:21:21 GMT", "Checksum-Algorithm": "CRC32C", "Checksum": "00000000" },
{ "Path": "global/6243", "Size": 0, "Last-Modified": "2025-04-20 16:21:21 GMT", "Checksum-Algorithm": "CRC32C", "Checksum": "00000000" },
{ "Path": "global/6100", "Size": 0, "Last-Modified": "2025-04-20 16:21:21 GMT", "Checksum-Algorithm": "CRC32C", "Checksum": "00000000" },
{ "Path": "global/4177", "Size": 0, "Last-Modified": "2025-04-20 16:21:21 GMT", "Checksum-Algorithm": "CRC32C", "Checksum": "00000000" },
{ "Path": "global/4178", "Size": 8192, "Last-Modified": "2025-04-20 16:21:21 GMT", "Checksum-Algorithm": "CRC32C", "Checksum": "0dea818e" },
{ "Path": "global/2966", "Size": 0, "Last-Modified": "2025-04-20 16:21:21 GMT", "Checksum-Algorithm": "CRC32C", "Checksum": "00000000" },
{ "Path": "global/2967", "Size": 8192, "Last-Modified": "2025-04-20 16:21:21 GMT", "Checksum-Algorithm": "CRC32C", "Checksum": "b18bfaec" },
{ "Path": "global/4185", "Size": 0, "Last-Modified": "2025-04-20 16:21:21 GMT", "Checksum-Algorithm": "CRC32C", "Checksum": "00000000" },
{ "Path": "global/4186", "Size": 8192, "Last-Modified": "2025-04-20 16:21:21 GMT", "Checksum-Algorithm": "CRC32C", "Checksum": "1282df7d" },
{ "Path": "global/4175", "Size": 0, "Last-Modified": "2025-04-20 16:21:21 GMT", "Checksum-Algorithm": "CRC32C", "Checksum": "00000000" },

{ "Path": "global/4176", "Size": 8192, "Last-Modified": "2025-04-20 16:21:21 GMT", "Checksum-Algorithm": "CRC32C", "Checksum": "7b15d9f9" },
{ "Path": "global/2846", "Size": 0, "Last-Modified": "2025-04-20 16:21:21 GMT", "Checksum-Algorithm": "CRC32C", "Checksum": "00000000" },
{ "Path": "global/2847", "Size": 8192, "Last-Modified": "2025-04-20 16:21:21 GMT", "Checksum-Algorithm": "CRC32C", "Checksum": "0c1a8002" },
{ "Path": "global/4181", "Size": 0, "Last-Modified": "2025-04-20 16:21:21 GMT", "Checksum-Algorithm": "CRC32C", "Checksum": "00000000" },
{ "Path": "global/4182", "Size": 8192, "Last-Modified": "2025-04-20 16:21:21 GMT", "Checksum-Algorithm": "CRC32C", "Checksum": "24610e56" },
{ "Path": "global/4060", "Size": 0, "Last-Modified": "2025-04-20 16:21:21 GMT", "Checksum-Algorithm": "CRC32C", "Checksum": "00000000" },
{ "Path": "global/4061", "Size": 8192, "Last-Modified": "2025-04-20 16:21:21 GMT", "Checksum-Algorithm": "CRC32C", "Checksum": "ebc75eb5" },
{ "Path": "global/6244", "Size": 0, "Last-Modified": "2025-04-20 16:21:21 GMT", "Checksum-Algorithm": "CRC32C", "Checksum": "00000000" },
{ "Path": "global/6245", "Size": 8192, "Last-Modified": "2025-04-20 16:21:21 GMT", "Checksum-Algorithm": "CRC32C", "Checksum": "21597da0" },
{ "Path": "global/4183", "Size": 0, "Last-Modified": "2025-04-20 16:21:21 GMT", "Checksum-Algorithm": "CRC32C", "Checksum": "00000000" },
{ "Path": "global/4184", "Size": 8192, "Last-Modified": "2025-04-20 16:21:21 GMT", "Checksum-Algorithm": "CRC32C", "Checksum": "e5fbf006" },
{ "Path": "global/2671", "Size": 16384, "Last-Modified": "2025-04-20 17:15:05 GMT", "Checksum-Algorithm": "CRC32C", "Checksum": "b00c8207" },
{ "Path": "global/2672", "Size": 16384, "Last-Modified": "2025-04-20 17:15:05 GMT", "Checksum-Algorithm": "CRC32C", "Checksum": "f170282f" },
{ "Path": "global/2965", "Size": 8192, "Last-Modified": "2025-04-20 16:21:21 GMT", "Checksum-Algorithm": "CRC32C", "Checksum": "4c8835cc" },
{ "Path": "global/2697", "Size": 16384, "Last-Modified": "2025-04-20 16:21:21 GMT", "Checksum-Algorithm": "CRC32C", "Checksum": "41fd1807" },
{ "Path": "global/2698", "Size": 16384, "Last-Modified": "2025-04-20 16:21:21 GMT", "Checksum-Algorithm": "CRC32C", "Checksum": "bbf3e291" },
{ "Path": "global/2676", "Size": 16384, "Last-Modified": "2025-04-20 16:21:21 GMT", "Checksum-Algorithm": "CRC32C", "Checksum": "0abfa2c3" },

{ "Path": "global/2677", "Size": 16384, "Last-Modified": "2025-04-20 16:21:21 GMT", "Checksum-Algorithm": "CRC32C", "Checksum": "87ceec4a" },
{ "Path": "global/6303", "Size": 16384, "Last-Modified": "2025-04-20 16:21:22 GMT", "Checksum-Algorithm": "CRC32C", "Checksum": "081acdc5" },
{ "Path": "global/2694", "Size": 16384, "Last-Modified": "2025-04-20 16:21:22 GMT", "Checksum-Algorithm": "CRC32C", "Checksum": "e50fdd17" },
<<<<< OUTPUT TRUNCATED >>>>>

Log in to the "db1" database and insert some more transactions for incremental backups.

```
[postgres@pg17 backups]$ psql
psql (17.4)
Type "help" for help.

postgres=# \c db1
You are now connected to database "db1" as user "postgres".
db1=#

db1=# select * from emp;
 emp_no | emp_fname | emp_lname |    emp_email     | emp_sal
--------+-----------+-----------+------------------+---------
      1 | john      | peter     | john@gmail.com   |    1000
      2 | sam       | curran    | sam@gmail.com    |    2000
      3 | bills     | roger     | bills@gmail.com  |    3000
      4 | lawrence  | larry     | larry@gmail.com  |    4000
      5 | peter     | larry     | peter@gmail.com  |    5000
(5 rows)

db1=#

db1=# insert into emp (emp_fname, emp_lname, emp_email, emp_sal) values ('maxwell','john','maxwell2gmail.com',6000);
INSERT 0 1
db1=#

db1=# select * from emp;
```

```
 emp_no | emp_fname | emp_lname |     emp_email      | emp_sal
--------+-----------+-----------+--------------------+---------
      1 | john      | peter     | john@gmail.com     |    1000
      2 | sam       | curran    | sam@gmail.com      |    2000
      3 | bills     | roger     | bills@gmail.com    |    3000
      4 | lawrence  | larry     | larry@gmail.com    |    4000
      5 | peter     | larry     | peter@gmail.com    |    5000
      6 | maxwell   | john      | maxwell2gmail.com  |    6000
(6 rows)

db1=#
```

> **Note** When you execute the following command to take incremental backups, you will get an error because the **summarize_wal** parameter is "OFF".

```
[postgres@pg17 ~]$ /usr/pgsql-17/bin/pg_basebackup --incremental=/home/postgres/backups/fullbackup/backup_manifest --pgdata /home/postgres/backups/incrementalbackup/
pg_basebackup: error: could not initiate base backup: ERROR:  incremental backups cannot be taken unless WAL summarization is enabled
pg_basebackup: removing contents of data directory "/home/postgres/backups/incrementalbackup/"
[postgres@pg17 ~]$
```

In **PostgreSQL 17**, the *summarize_wal* functionality refers to a **new feature introduced** to help you understand and analyze Write-Ahead Logging (WAL) activity **without needing external tools or complex setup**.

summarize_wal is a built-in SQL-accessible function that allows you to summarize WAL activity over a period of time directly from WAL files. It gives insights into

- Number of WAL records
- Types of operations (INSERT, UPDATE, etc.)
- WAL volume per relation or database
- Resource managers involved
- Blocks changed

```
[postgres@pg17 ~]$ psql
psql (17.4)
Type "help" for help.

postgres=#alter system set summarize_wal=on;
ALTER SYSTEM
postgres=#

postgres=# show summarize_wal;
 summarize_wal
---------------
 off
(1 row)
postgres=# \q

[postgres@pg17 ~]$ pg_ctl restart
waiting for server to shut down.... done
server stopped
waiting for server to start....2025-04-20 16:22:17.472 CDT [16041] LOG:  redirecting log output to logging collector process
2025-04-20 16:22:17.472 CDT [16041] HINT:  Future log output will appear in directory "log".
 done
server started

[postgres@pg17 ~]$ psql
psql (17.4)
Type "help" for help.

postgres=# show summarize_wal;
 summarize_wal
---------------------
 on
(1 row)
postgres=# \q
```

CHAPTER 10　NEW FEATURES OF POSTGRESQL 17

　　Perform incremental backup using pg_basebackup under the "/home/postgres/backups/incrementalbackup/" directory.

[postgres@pg17 backups]$ /usr/pgsql-17/bin/pg_basebackup --incremental=/home/postgres/backups/fullbackup/backup_manifest --pgdata /home/postgres/backups/incrementalbackup/ -v

```
pg_basebackup: initiating base backup, waiting for checkpoint to complete
pg_basebackup: checkpoint completed
pg_basebackup: write-ahead log start point: 0/D000028 on timeline 1
pg_basebackup: starting background WAL receiver
pg_basebackup: created temporary replication slot "pg_basebackup_7659"
pg_basebackup: write-ahead log end point: 0/D000120
pg_basebackup: waiting for background process to finish streaming ...
pg_basebackup: syncing data to disk ...
pg_basebackup: renaming backup_manifest.tmp to backup_manifest
pg_basebackup: base backup completed
[postgres@pg17 backups]$
```

**[postgres@pg17 backups]$ ls -lrth /home/postgres/backups/incrementalbackup/
total 256K**

```
drwx------. 4 postgres postgres    77 May 15 16:47 pg_wal
-rw-------. 1 postgres postgres   281 May 15 16:47 backup_label
drwx------. 2 postgres postgres     6 May 15 16:47 pg_twophase
drwx------. 2 postgres postgres     6 May 15 16:47 pg_subtrans
drwx------. 2 postgres postgres     6 May 15 16:47 pg_snapshots
drwx------. 2 postgres postgres     6 May 15 16:47 pg_serial
drwx------. 2 postgres postgres     6 May 15 16:47 pg_notify
drwx------. 4 postgres postgres    36 May 15 16:47 pg_multixact
drwx------. 2 postgres postgres     6 May 15 16:47 pg_dynshmem
drwx------. 2 postgres postgres     6 May 15 16:47 pg_commit_ts
drwx------. 6 postgres postgres    46 May 15 16:47 base
drwx------. 2 postgres postgres     6 May 15 16:47 pg_tblspc
drwx------. 2 postgres postgres     6 May 15 16:47 pg_stat_tmp
drwx------. 2 postgres postgres     6 May 15 16:47 pg_stat
drwx------. 2 postgres postgres     6 May 15 16:47 pg_replslot
-rw-------. 1 postgres postgres   30K May 15 16:47 postgresql.conf
```

CHAPTER 10 NEW FEATURES OF POSTGRESQL 17

```
-rw-------. 1 postgres postgres  109 May 15 16:47 postgresql.auto.conf
drwx------. 2 postgres postgres   18 May 15 16:47 pg_xact
-rw-------. 1 postgres postgres    3 May 15 16:47 PG_VERSION
drwx------. 4 postgres postgres   68 May 15 16:47 pg_logical
-rw-------. 1 postgres postgres 2.6K May 15 16:47 pg_ident.conf
-rw-------. 1 postgres postgres 5.4K May 15 16:47 pg_hba.conf
drwx------. 2 postgres postgres  188 May 15 16:47 log
drwx------. 2 postgres postgres 4.0K May 15 16:47 global
-rw-------. 1 postgres postgres   30 May 15 16:47 current_logfiles
-rw-------. 1 postgres postgres 192K May 15 16:47 backup_manifest
[postgres@pg17 backups]$
```

pg_walsummary is a utility that summarizes the contents of PostgreSQL WAL segment files (.wal or .log files) by scanning them at the file system level.

```
[postgres@pg17 backups]$ ls -lrth /var/lib/pgsql/17/data/pg_wal/summaries
total 56K
-rw-------. 1 postgres postgres   32 May  7 17:14 000000010000000008002
CA00000000008002D50.summary
-rw-------. 1 postgres postgres   32 May  7 21:07 00000001000000000800
2D500000000008002E00.summary
-rw-------. 1 postgres postgres   32 May 11 12:16 00000001000000000800
2E000000000008002EB0.summary
-rw-------. 1 postgres postgres   32 May 12 10:06 000000010000000008002
EB00000000008002F60.summary
-rw-------. 1 postgres postgres   32 May 14 18:26 00000001000000000800
2F600000000008003010.summary
-rw-------. 1 postgres postgres  460 May 14 18:51
00000001000000000800301000000000080169C8.summary
-rw-------. 1 postgres postgres 1.2K May 14 18:56 000000010000000008016
9C800000000080A7178.summary
-rw-------. 1 postgres postgres  704 May 14 21:46 000000010000000008
0A717800000000080C1D68.summary
-rw-------. 1 postgres postgres  812 May 14 21:51 000000010000000080C
1D6800000000080E4C20.summary
```

```
-rw-------. 1 postgres postgres     32 May 15 10:16 
0000000100000000080E4C2000000000080E4D60.summary
-rw-------. 1 postgres postgres     32 May 15 15:47 0000000100000000080E
4D6000000000080E4E10.summary
-rw-------. 1 postgres postgres     32 May 15 16:43 0000000100000000080E
4E10000000009000028.summary
-rw-------. 1 postgres postgres     32 May 15 16:44 
00000001000000009000028000000000B000028.summary
-rw-------. 1 postgres postgres    116 May 15 16:47 0000000100000000
0B000028000000000D000028.summary
[postgres@pg17 backups]$
```

Using the pg_walsummary command, you can grep for our table before that find out pg_relation_filepath for the rable.

[postgres@pg17 backups]$ psql
```
psql (17.4)
Type "help" for help.
```

postgres=# \c db1
```
You are now connected to database "db1" as user "postgres".
db1=#
```

db1=# select pg_relation_filepath('emp');
```
 pg_relation_filepath
----------------------
 base/16388/16390
(1 row)
db1=# exit
```
[postgres@pg17 summaries]$ pwd
```
/var/lib/pgsql/17/data/pg_wal/summaries
[postgres@pg17 summaries]$
```

[postgres@pg17 summaries]$ pg_walsummary 00000001000000000B0000280000000
```
0D000028.summary |grep 16390
TS 1663, DB 16388, REL 16390, FORK main: block 0
[postgres@pg17 summaries]$
```

Chapter 10 New Features of PostgreSQL 17

To check the current state of walsummarizer, execute the below command:

```
postgres=# SELECT * FROM pg_get_wal_summarizer_state();
 summarized_tli | summarized_lsn | pending_lsn | summarizer_pid
----------------+----------------+-------------+----------------
              1 | 0/80E4D60      | 0/80E4E10   |           1656
(1 row)
```

***Figure 10-10.** Getting walsummarizer state*

List available WAL summary files along with their timeline IDs and LSN ranges.

```
postgres=# select * from pg_available_wal_summaries();
 tli | start_lsn  |  end_lsn
-----+------------+-----------
   1 | 0/7000028  | 0/8000060
   1 | 0/8000060  | 0/8000110
   1 | 0/8000110  | 0/8000218
   1 | 0/8000218  | 0/8002B98
   1 | 0/8002B98  | 0/8002CA0
   1 | 0/8002CA0  | 0/8002D50
   1 | 0/8002D50  | 0/8002E00
   1 | 0/8002E00  | 0/8002EB0
   1 | 0/8002EB0  | 0/8002F60
   1 | 0/8002F60  | 0/8003010
   1 | 0/8003010  | 0/80169C8
   1 | 0/80169C8  | 0/80A7178
   1 | 0/80A7178  | 0/80C1D68
   1 | 0/80C1D68  | 0/80E4C20
   1 | 0/80E4C20  | 0/80E4D60
(15 rows)

postgres=#
```

***Figure 10-11.** Getting available walsummaries*

The ***pg_wal_summary_contents*** function will give us some insights into contents of the summary. Execute the following command:

```
postgres=# select * from pg_wal_summary_contents ( 1, '0/80A7178', '0/80C1D68');
 relfilenode | reltablespace | reldatabase | relforknumber | relblocknumber | is_limit_block
-------------+---------------+-------------+---------------+----------------+----------------
        1247 |          1663 |       16388 |             0 |             14 | f
        1249 |          1663 |       16388 |             0 |             56 | f
        1249 |          1663 |       16388 |             0 |             57 | f
        1259 |          1663 |       16388 |             0 |              1 | f
        2224 |          1663 |       16388 |             0 |              0 | f
        2604 |          1663 |       16388 |             0 |              0 | f
        2608 |          1663 |       16388 |             0 |             13 | f
        2656 |          1663 |       16388 |             0 |              1 | f
        2657 |          1663 |       16388 |             0 |              1 | f
        2658 |          1663 |       16388 |             0 |             15 | f
        2659 |          1663 |       16388 |             0 |             10 | f
        2662 |          1663 |       16388 |             0 |              2 | f
        2663 |          1663 |       16388 |             0 |              2 | f
        2673 |          1663 |       16388 |             0 |              9 | f
        2673 |          1663 |       16388 |             0 |              4 | f
        2674 |          1663 |       16388 |             0 |              7 | f
        2674 |          1663 |       16388 |             0 |              5 | f
        2703 |          1663 |       16388 |             0 |              2 | f
        2704 |          1663 |       16388 |             0 |              2 | f
        2704 |          1663 |       16388 |             0 |              4 | f
        3350 |          1663 |       16388 |             0 |              0 | f
        3351 |          1663 |       16388 |             0 |              1 | f
        3455 |          1663 |       16388 |             0 |              1 | f
        5002 |          1663 |       16388 |             0 |              1 | f
       16431 |          1663 |       16388 |             0 |              0 | t
       16431 |          1663 |       16388 |             0 |              0 | f
       16431 |          1663 |       16388 |             2 |              0 | t
       16431 |          1663 |       16388 |             3 |              0 | t
       16436 |          1663 |       16388 |             0 |              0 | t
       16436 |          1663 |       16388 |             0 |              0 | f
(30 rows)

postgres=#
```

Figure 10-12. Getting contents from walsummaries

PostgreSQL 17 offers the pg_combinebackup tool, which enables you to merge a full backup and subsequent incremental backups into a single, ready-to-restore backup set. This streamlined approach simplifies backup management and recovery. The following steps demonstrate how to combine the backups:

The below command:

- /home/postgres/backups/fullbackup/ is the directory containing the full backup.

- /home/postgres/backups/incrementalbackup/ is the first incremental backup directory.

- -o specifies the output directory where the combined backup will be stored.

CHAPTER 10   NEW FEATURES OF POSTGRESQL 17

```
[postgres@pg17 ~]$ /usr/pgsql-17/bin/pg_combinebackup /home/postgres/
backups/fullbackup/ /home/postgres/backups/incrementalbackup/ -o /home/
postgres/backups/combinebackup/

[postgres@pg17 ~]$ ls -lrth /home/postgres/backups/combinebackup/
total 244K
drwxr-x---. 4 postgres postgres   77 May 15 16:50 pg_wal
-rw-r-----. 1 postgres postgres  225 May 15 16:50 backup_label
drwxr-x---. 2 postgres postgres    6 May 15 16:50 pg_commit_ts
drwxr-x---. 2 postgres postgres 4.0K May 15 16:50 global
drwxr-x---. 2 postgres postgres    6 May 15 16:50 pg_twophase
drwxr-x---. 2 postgres postgres    6 May 15 16:50 pg_subtrans
drwxr-x---. 2 postgres postgres    6 May 15 16:50 pg_snapshots
drwxr-x---. 2 postgres postgres    6 May 15 16:50 pg_serial
drwxr-x---. 2 postgres postgres    6 May 15 16:50 pg_notify
drwxr-x---. 4 postgres postgres   36 May 15 16:50 pg_multixact
drwxr-x---. 2 postgres postgres    6 May 15 16:50 pg_dynshmem
drwxr-x---. 6 postgres postgres   46 May 15 16:50 base
drwxr-x---. 2 postgres postgres   18 May 15 16:50 pg_xact
drwxr-x---. 2 postgres postgres    6 May 15 16:50 pg_tblspc
drwxr-x---. 2 postgres postgres    6 May 15 16:50 pg_stat_tmp
drwxr-x---. 2 postgres postgres    6 May 15 16:50 pg_stat
drwxr-x---. 2 postgres postgres    6 May 15 16:50 pg_replslot
-rw-r-----. 1 postgres postgres  30K May 15 16:50 postgresql.conf
-rw-r-----. 1 postgres postgres  109 May 15 16:50 postgresql.auto.conf
-rw-r-----. 1 postgres postgres    3 May 15 16:50 PG_VERSION
drwxr-x---. 4 postgres postgres   68 May 15 16:50 pg_logical
-rw-r-----. 1 postgres postgres 2.6K May 15 16:50 pg_ident.conf
-rw-r-----. 1 postgres postgres 5.4K May 15 16:50 pg_hba.conf
drwxr-x---. 2 postgres postgres   32 May 15 16:50 log
-rw-r-----. 1 postgres postgres   30 May 15 16:50 current_logfiles
-rw-r-----. 1 postgres postgres 178K May 15 16:50 backup_manifest
[postgres@pg17 ~]$
```

CHAPTER 10   NEW FEATURES OF POSTGRESQL 17

Stop the PostgreSQL service and start to reflect the changes.

```
[postgres@pg17 ~]$ /usr/pgsql-17/bin/pg_ctl -D /var/lib/pgsql/17/data/ -l
logfile stop
waiting for server to shut down.... done
server stopped
[postgres@pg17 ~]$
```

To verify that your database is up and running, connect to PostgreSQL and check the data directory and the number of records in the "emp" table.

```
[postgres@pg17 ~]$ /usr/pgsql-17/bin/pg_ctl -D /home/postgres/backups/
combinebackup/ -l /home/postgres/backups/combinebackup/logfile start
waiting for server to start....... done
server started
[postgres@pg17 ~]$
```

```
[postgres@pg17 ~]$ psql
psql (17.4)
Type "help" for help.
```

```
postgres=# show data_directory;
       data_directory
-----------------------------------
 /home/postgres/backups/combinebackup
(1 row)
postgres=#
```

```
postgres=# \c db1
You are now connected to database "db1" as user "postgres".
db1=#
```

```
db1=# select * from emp;
 emp_no | emp_fname | emp_lname |    emp_email      | emp_sal
--------+-----------+-----------+-------------------+---------
      1 | john      | peter     | john@gmail.com    |    1000
      2 | sam       | curran    | sam@gmail.com     |    2000
      3 | bills     | roger     | bills@gmail.com   |    3000
      4 | lawrence  | larry     | larry@gmail.com   |    4000
```

```
    5 | peter    | larry   | peter@gmail.com    |    5000
    6 | maxwell  | john    | maxwell2gmail.com  |    6000
(6 rows)

db1=#
```

New Features: Logical Replication from Standby Servers in PostgreSQL 17

A new feature in PostgreSQL 17 allows you to replicate data not only from primary servers but also from standby servers. This feature reduces the load from the primary servers.

The pg_createsubscriber utility can be used to create a logical replica directly from a physical standby server.

PostgreSQL 17 has made it easier to upgrade between major versions with logical replication by eliminating the need to remove replication slots during the upgrade process. It also introduces failover control for logical replication and provides the new pg_createsubscriber tool to convert physical replicas into logical replicas.

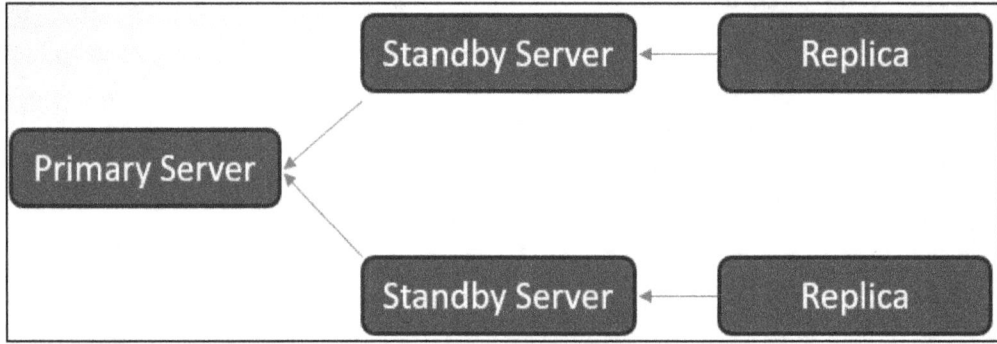

Figure 10-13. Logical replication from standby servers

CHAPTER 10 NEW FEATURES OF POSTGRESQL 17

New Features: Combining I/Os in PostgreSQL 17

In PostgreSQL 16, each page read involved a separate pread syscall, introducing some overhead. In PostgreSQL 17, sequential page reads are combined into fewer vectorized syscalls (configurable), reducing overhead and improving performance. Figures 10-13 and 10-14 explain the flow.

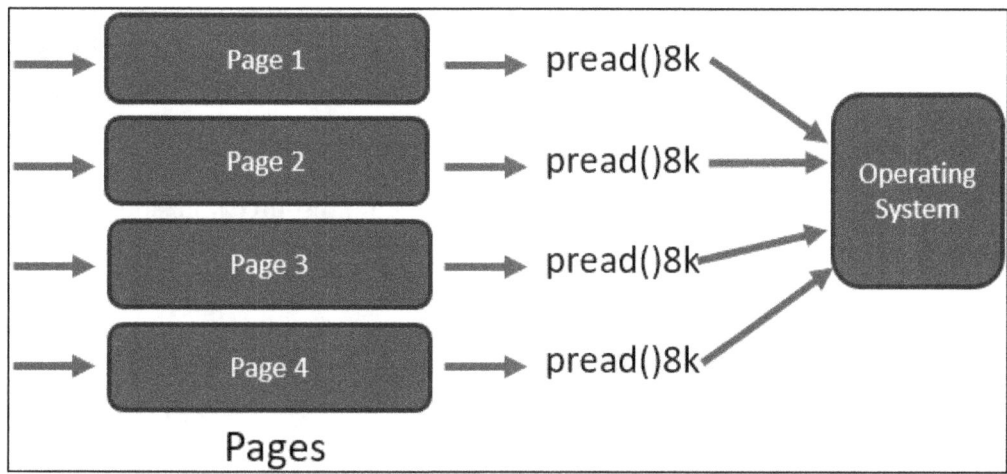

Figure 10-14. *In PostgreSQL 16*

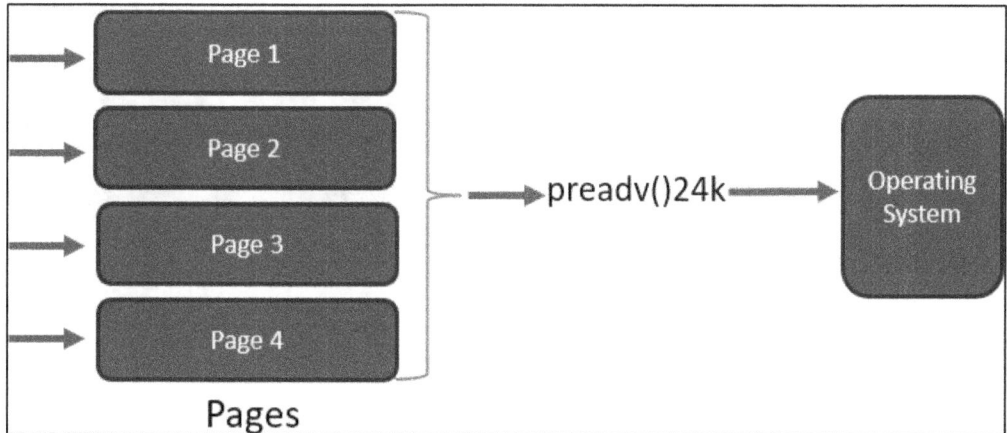

Figure 10-15. *In PostgreSQL 17*

CHAPTER 10 NEW FEATURES OF POSTGRESQL 17

New Features: Query Planner Improvements in PostgreSQL 17

PostgreSQL introduces several core improvements that enhance performance and efficiency.

Key enhancements in PostgreSQL 17

- Optimized Common Table Expression (CTE) usage
- Enhanced evaluation of IS NOT NULL conditions
- Improved parallel query handling

The above enhancements lead to faster queries, better resource utilization, and a reduced need for manual query tuning.

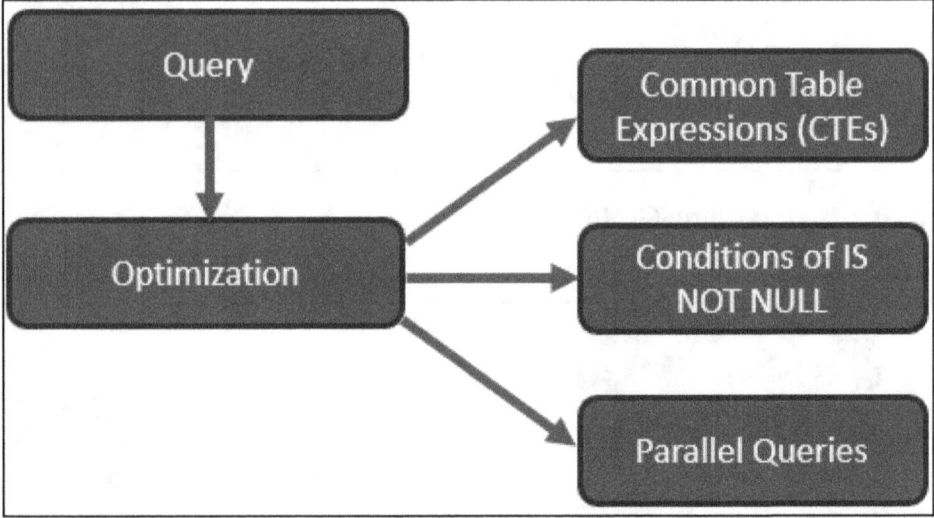

Figure 10-16. Query planner improvements in PostgreSQL 17

CHAPTER 10   NEW FEATURES OF POSTGRESQL 17

New Features: Introducing Split and Merge Partitions in PostgreSQL 17

With PostgreSQL 17, partition management becomes more flexible and efficient through the new **MERGE PARTITIONS** and **SPLIT PARTITION** commands. These features streamline common maintenance tasks, enabling easy reorganization of partitioned tables without downtime or manual intervention, ultimately reducing administrative overhead.

Summary

In this chapter, we discussed the installation of PostgreSQL 17 using RPMs and examined the new incremental backup feature introduced in PostgreSQL 17, configuring logical replication from standby servers, combining I/Os to the operating system, and query planner improvements.

Index

A

Analyze command, 360, 362, 363, 378, 379, 389
Architecture, PostgreSQL
    client and server, 1
    components, 1, 2
        memory, 5
        physical files, 8
        server process, 2, 3
        utility process, 3
    features, 1
    flow, 16, 17
    server process tree, 14
archive_command, 220, 231, 323, 400
Authentication methods
    appuser3, 190
    database connectivity, 190
    host-based authentication, 173, 211
    password-based authentication, 189
    pg_hba.conf file, 189
    process, 191
    reject authentication, 190
    sample output, 191
    trust authentication, 190
Autovacuum, 4, 5, 360, 366, 388, 389, 401
AWS Database Migration Service (DMS), 487
AWS Schema Conversion Tool (SCT), 487

B

Backup, 215
    advantages, 215
    key elements, 216, 217
    types, 217
        continuous archiving method, 220
        external tools, 221
        file system-level backup, 219, 220
        PITR, 220, 221
        SQL Dump method, 218
Backup and Recovery Manager (Barman)
    architecture, 221, 222
    backup methods, 222, 223
    configuration
        database server, 225
        environment setup, 224
        global configuration file, 228
        passwordless authentication, 226, 228
        PostgreSQL server configuration files, 228, 229
        root user, hostname and IPs, 225
        schema and table, 232
        server setup, 229, 231
    installation, 223, 224
    Its comprehensive feature set, 232
    Python, 221
Backup and restore
    Barman
        backup server, 318
        backuptest.testtab table, 324, 328

INDEX

Back up and restore (*cont.*)
    command, 332
    configuration, 318
    create role, 319
    current backups, 329, 330
    definition, 316
    global configuration file, 321
    hostname and IP address, 318
    incremental backup, 325–327, 329
    insert row, 327
    installation, 317, 318
    level 1 backup, 327, 328
    log switch, WAL, 324
    passwordless authentication, 319, 320
    PostgreSQL server configuration files, 321, 322
    PostgreSQL service, 332
    server setup, 322, 323
    validation, 333
    complete server, specific databases, 289–291
    database
        command, 280
        database server, 279, 280
        db1_backup.tar, 282, 283
        db1 schemas, 281, 282, 284
        newdb, 284–286
    global database objects, 292
    multiple tables
        custom format, 268–270
        db1_schema1_multitab.sql, 258, 259
        pg_dump utility, 258
        psql utility, 259
        schema structure, 257, 258
        steps, 259–262
        truncating data, 259
    performance, parallel jobs, 287

pgBackRest
    architecture, 354
    backup info, 344
    check command, 342
    create table, 344
    database cluster, 355, 356
    database cluster configuration file, 341
    data directory, 341
    differential backup, 349–351
    directories, 341
    drop table, 351
    files, 355
    full database cluster backup, 343, 344
    incremental backup, 345–347, 349
    insert row, 346
    installation and configuration, 338–340
    performance, 352, 353
    PITR, 354, 358
    PostgreSQL database cluster, 334–337
    stanza, 342
    table, 357
    time format, 354
pg_basebackup
    complete server, 292, 294
    verification, 294–297
restore procedures
    existing instance, 302, 303, 305
    new instance, 298, 300–302
schemas, database
    command, 270, 271
    db1_schema1, 270, 271
    db2_schema2/db1_schema1, 274, 275
    pg_dump, 276

pg_restore, 272, 278
truncate data, 276, 277
validation, 273, 278, 279
single table, 244–249
full database backup, 287, 288
table
custom format, 263–265
pg_dump, dir format, 266–268
pg_dump, tar format, 265, 266
table data, without structure, 253
-a option, 254
backup file, 255–257
db1_schema.db1tb1, 253
drop table, 254, 255
two-step process, 254
table structure, without data
db1_schema1_db1tb1_structure.sql file, 249, 251
db1tb1, 249
drop table, 251
f option/psql command, 251–253

C

Cloud platform, 20, 486
Continuous archiving method, 220, 221
CO Schema database migration
execute export_schema script, 534
execute import_all.sh script, 535
migration project, 532
migration report, 532
objects, 531
ora2pg-t COPY command, 535
PostgreSQL CO schema, 540
validation, imported data, 538
current_database(), 141

D

Database
creation, OS command
createdb command, 138
pgdbhrm, 139
syntax, 138
users/roles, 139
dropping, 209, 210
pgdbhrm, 143
schemas, 140
Database cluster, 76
object hierarchy, 76
tablespaces, 76
Database local connectivity
authentication, 154
grpaccount user, 157
pg_ctl reload/systemctl stop/start, 155
pgdbhrm database, 155, 157
pg_hba.conf file, 155
postgres, 157
psql utility, 154
Database postgres, 584–586, 622, 648, 649, 669, 672
Database remote connectivity
authentication, 165
create users, 170
pg_client1, 173
pg_server, 165, 166
psql utility, 172
scenarios, 171
schema, databases, 166, 167
server and client machine details, 165
table, databases, 168–170
Databases, 88
directories, 94
layout, 91, 92
object layout, 96, 99
pgdb1 and pgdb2, 94

INDEX

Databases (*cont.*)
    PostgreSQL, 89, 90
    srcdb, 580–582, 585, 587, 610, 630, 632, 633, 667, 670, 672
    software installation, 19
Data page, 110
    header, 111
    layout, 111
DBD::Oracle, 499, 501, 510
Directory structure
    authentication method, 83
    command-line option, 87
    configuration file, 85
    configuration parameters, 84
    database cluster, 80
    file contents, 80
    hba, 80
    layout, 79
    md5, 82
    path, 77
    pg_ident.conf, 83
    pictorial representation, 78
    postgresql.conf, 83
    subdirectories, 88
    trust, 82
    USER field, 82
Dropping default databases, 135
Dynamic parameter, 125

E

EDB Migration Toolkit (MTK), 487
Enterprise, situations, 215
Execution plan, 112–114, 368, 421
Extensions, 197
    pg_server, 197
    pg_stat_statements, 203
        creation, 203
        database, 204
        output, 204
        queries, 203
    pgstattuple, 198
        creation, 200, 201
        database, 201
        index, 199, 200
        pgdb1sch1.s1tnewidx, 202
        pgstatindex, 201, 202
        SQL, 200
        table, 198
Extra Packages for Enterprise Linux (EPEL), 29, 224, 317, 679

F

File system-level backup, 217–220, 316

G

GoldenGate replication configuration, 577
    source database (Oracle) for replication, 578–583
    target database (PostgreSQL) for replication, 583–586
Google Database Migration Service (DMS), 487
Grafana, 405, 458
    bar chart, 471
        creation, 472
        dashboard panel, 471, 474
        dashboard saving, 472, 473
        multi-visualization, 475
        panel creation, 473
        panel details, 475
        student count per country, 472
        visualization, 473
    data source addition, 466

data source selection, 466, 467, 470, 471
download, 458, 459
download status, 459
features, 461, 462
home page, 465
installation, 459, 462–464
license agreement, 460, 461
log in page, 464, 465
multi-country visualization, 479
    Canada, 479, 481
    dashboard, 483
    India, 479, 481
    New Zealand, 480, 482
    United Kingdom, 480, 482
    United States, 480, 483
PostgreSQL
    additional settings, 468, 469
    connection/authentication details, 468
    dashboard, 469
    dashboard visualization, 470
    database connection status, 469
    data source name specification, 467
setup page, 460
URL, 464
XY chart, 476
    add query, 477
    add series, 477
    creation, 476, 478
    multiple series, 478, 479
    visualization, 476
Grafana Enterprise, 458

H

Host-based authentication, 80, 173, 211
HR Schema database migration
    create migration project, 516
    execute export_schema script, 520
    import_all.sh script, 522
    manual validation, schema objects, 528
    migration report, 514–516
    objects, 513
    object type triggers, 525
    postgres database, 521
    PostgreSQL connection settings, 521
    validation, imported data, 526

I, J, K

import_all.sh script, 522, 535, 536, 548
Input/Output Statistics (IOSTAT), 409

L

Linux distribution, 23, 36, 674, 675
Linux option, 23, 674
Logrotate, 402

M

Migration issues
    cannot cast type bytea to json, 553–555
    cannot cast type bytea to jsonb, 557–559
    data type bigint, 568–570
    foreign key constraint "inventory_product_id_fk" cannot be implemented, 555–557
    function grouping_id(character varying, character varying) does not exist, 562–564
    insert/update on table "inventory", 565, 566
    relation "costs" does not exist, 571–573
    type "varchar2" does not exist, 560, 561

INDEX

Migration phase, 487, 509–513
Migration plan
    migration phase, 487, 488
    post-migration phase, 488
    pre-migration phase, 487
Migration tools, 486
    DMS, 487
    MTK, 487
    Ora2Pg, 486
    SCT, 487
Monitoring, 398, 401, 405, 423, 458, 484
Multi-database models, 485
Multi-Version Concurrency Control (MVCC), 365

N

Network Statistics (NETSTAT), 412

O

Open source software (OSS), 458
Ora2Pg, 486, 488, 489
    components used in migration, 490
    general requirements for migration, 490
    home page, 489
    installation, 504, 506–508
    install Perl modules for DBD::Oracle and Ora2Pg, 494
    install Perl module DBD::Oracle, 501
    install Perl module perl-CPAN, 499
    install Perl module perl-DBI, 497
    Perl-ExtUtils-MakeMaker, 495
    migration approach, 489, 490
    migration project, 516
    for Oracle to PostgreSQL migration, 489
    pre-migration phase, 491, 493

ora2pg.conf configuration file, 509
    variables, 510–512
Oracle database connectivity, 509
Oracle Enterprise Linux (OEL) system, 74
Oracle GoldenGate, 575
    configure GoldenGate on target deployment
        configure target database for GoldenGate, 646–651
        network connectivity for PostgreSQL, 646
        replication configuration, create Replicat process, 652–656
    configure Oracle GoldenGate Hub (*see* Oracle GoldenGate Hub)
    create deployment for Source Oracle Database
        data store home, 607
        Oracle GoldenGate Service Manager Deployment, 607–617
        Oracle GoldenGate Service Manager home page, 618
        Oracle GoldenGate Service Manager login, 618
        ora_source deployment environment variables, 619
        Service manager deployment home, 607
        user deployment home, 607
    create deployment for Target PostgreSQL Database
        add TNS Alias in tnsnames.ora, 629, 630
        configure Source Database for GoldenGate, 630–639
        data store home, 619
        Oracle Extract creation, 640–644
        Oracle GoldenGate Service Manager Deployment, 620–626

pg_target deployment adding environment variable, 628
pg_target deployment environment variables page, 628, 629
PostgreSQL Goldengate Service Manager Login page, 627
service manager and deployment status, 627
Service manager deployment home, 619
user deployment home, 619
create dist path in source deployment
  check receiver server on target deployment, 665–667, 669, 671
  Oracle Distribution Path creation, 658, 660–665
data replication, 575
replication between Oracle and PostgreSQL, 576
REST-enabled services and APIs, 576
Oracle GoldenGate Hub, 586
  advantage, 586
  install Oracle Client
    GUI installer tool, 589
    ogg_hub to Oracle database srcdb, 587
    Oracle 19c client installation, steps, 590–593
    Oracle Database 19c Client, 587
    ora_serv and pg_serv server IP, 587
    staging directory, 588
    steps, 588
  install Oracle GoldenGate for Oracle Database, 595
    GUI installer tool, 596
    Oracle 23ai installation, 597–600
  install Oracle GoldenGate for PostgreSQL, 601
    GUI installer tool, 602
    PostgreSQL 23ai installation, 603–606
  install Oracle GoldenGate software, 594
  Oracle GoldenGate Service Manager Deployment, 607, 620

P

Page Header, 110, 111, 114, 115
Parser stage, 113
Perl-CPAN (Comprehensive Perl Archive Network), 499
Perl-DBI (Database Interface), 497
Perl-ExtUtils-MakeMaker, 495
pgAdmin, 4, 405, 428
  connection section, 437, 438
  download, 428, 429
  downloadable exe file, 430
  download status, 430
  home screen, 436
  installation
    completion, 434
    directory, 432
    folder name, 432, 433
    license agreement, 431, 432
    setup screen, 433
    setup wizard, 431
  launching, 436
  location folder, 435
  and pg_server, 434, 435
  PostgreSQL
    column names, 455
    dashboard, 439
    database creation, 444
    database name, 445
    data import status, 457

INDEX

pgAdmin (*cont.*)
    data load status, 451, 452
    import/export data, 451, 456, 457
    pga_db database dashboard, 446
    pg_client2, 442
    pgdb1 database DDL, 440, 441
    pgdb1 database delete activity, 444
    pgdb1 database insert activity, 443
    pgdb1 database properties, 440
    pgdb1 database statistics, 441, 442
    row count validation, 452, 453
    schema creation, 446
    schema name, 447
    table columns definition, 449
    table creation, 447, 448, 454
    table data import, 450, 455, 456
    table name, 448, 449, 454
    table row count, 454
  register screen, 437
  servers section, 437
  versions, 429
pg_archivecleanup, 400
pgBackRest, 233
  backup types, 233
  installation and configuration
    check command, 243
    database and schema, 234–237
    database cluster configuration
      file, 242
    data directory, 241
    directories, 241
    .bash_profile, 241
    pgBackRest bin file, 241
    pgbackrest.conf, 240
    postgres database cluster, 242
    PostgreSQL database cluster, 233
    stanza, 242
    verification, 239

    version, 240
    yum command, 238
  stanza, 233
pg_createsubscriber tool, 716
pgdb1 database, 95, 116, 118, 176, 361, 390, 441
pg_filedump, 114–121
pg_hba.conf configuration file, 583
pg_hba.conf file, 173
  ALTER DEFAULT PRIVILEGE, 181, 184
  appuser1, 174
    create table, 182
    pg_client1, 175, 177–179
    pg_client2, 177
    pgdb1, 176
    pgdb1sch1.db1s1t2, 180
    testing, 182
  appuser2
    database connectivity, 185, 186
    pgdb2, 184
    pgdb2sch2, 184
    testing, 186, 187
  appuser3
    connectivity, 188, 189
    pgdb4, 187, 189
    privileges, 188
    updation, 187
  client authentication, 186
  client server, 174
  connected session, 175
  format, 174
  host-based, 173
  location, 173
  parameters, 174
  password-based authentication, 178
  pgdb1, 176
  pgdb1sch1.db1s1t2, 179, 180, 183
  privileges, 176

INDEX

    reload configuration, 174, 175
    updation, 184
    user connection, 173
pg_indexes_size(), 398
pg_relation_filepath() system, 94
pg_stat_user_indexes, 400
pg_stat_user_tables, 360, 388, 400
pg_table_size(), 359, 398
pg_total_relation_size(), 359, 398
Physical files, 13
    archived log files, 12
    data files, 8
    log files, 11
    WAL log files, 10
Point-in-time recovery (PITR), 4, 220, 221, 305
    archive log settings, 307
    current database server, 305
    current data directory, clean up, 309, 311
    database list, 305
    database restoration, 311–313
    db1 database/db1_schema1.db1tb1, 309
    pg_basebackup, 308
    postgres database cluster, 314
    postgresql.conf file, 313, 314
    restore and recovery, 314, 316
    schemas & tables, 306
    steps, 308
    table data, 307, 308
    WAL, 316
PostgreSQL, 19, 24, 39, 46, 47, 50, 55, 63, 64
    binaries, 31, 32
    binaries and data directory, 26
    binaries and extension modules, 35
    binary packages, 22
    cluster, 131, 133, 134
    configuration files, 40
    configure.log, 62
    connection parameters, 512
    database cluster, 35, 47
    database management system, 39
    download and install binaries, 22
    hardware configuration, 20
    install commands, 58
    libraries, 59
    module, 30
    pg_controldata, 41
    platforms, 20
    postgres, 26
    repository packages, 26
    RPM method, 27
    server, 38, 40, 49, 50, 72
    server process tree, 14, 15
    server shutdown, 48
    server version installation, 29
    service, 38
    setup script, 24
    software, 73
    software stage directory, 56
    source code, 68
    step-by-step process, 22
    systemctl status commands, 37
    system details, 21
    uninstallation, 74
    v16, 717
    v17, 316, 673, 717
    versions, 20, 24, 55
Postgresql16-contrib package, 34
Postgresql.auto.conf configuration file, 85
PostgreSQL 17, 673, 717
    combine I/Os, 717
    incremental backups
        "db1" database, 706

729

PostgreSQL 17 (*cont.*)
    full vs. incremental backups, 698
    get walsummarizer state, 712
    "/home/postgres/backups/ fullbackups" directory, 702
    "/home/postgres/backups/ incrementalbackup/" directory, 709
    pg_basebackup and pg_ combinebackup commands, 697, 699, 701
    pg_combinebackup tool, 713
    pg_walsummary, 710, 711
    pg_wal_summary_contents function, 712
    "summarize_wal", 699, 707
    "WAL Summarizer", 698
  installation method, 674
    .bash_profile file, 695
    binaries related to PostgreSQL 17, 693
    createdb command-line utility, 697
    data directories, 692
    disable built-in PostgreSQL module, 677
    initialize database and enable automatic start, 686
    install postgresql 17-contrib package, 683, 685
    install PostgreSQL v17 server binaries, 681
    Linux distribution selection, 675
    log in as "postgres" user, 690
    operating system family selection, 674
    OS platform, and architecture selection, 675
    pg_ctl, 696
    PostgreSQL Yum Repository section, 675
    postgres, template1, and template0, 691
    start/stop/status, PostgreSQL server, 687
  introduce split and merge partitions, 719
  logical replication from standby servers, 716
  query planner improvements, 718
postgres server, 35, 174, 184, 187, 301
Postmaster process, 2, 15, 16, 112, 173, 191
Postmaster process ID (PID), 80, 87
Predefined roles, 192
  appuser4, 194–196
  DML operation, 196
  pgdb4, 192, 193
  pg_hba.conf file, 194
  pg_write_all_data, 196

Q

Query Execution Stage, 113

R

Real-time system behavior, 413
  cpu consumption, 419, 420
  current session count, 414
  dead tuples, tables, 421, 423
  parallel session count, 415, 416
  queries, 413, 417, 418
  session active, 416, 417
  sessions, 413
  tables stats, 421
Recovery Point Objective (RPO), 217
Recovery Time Objective (RTO), 217

INDEX

Reindex in PostgreSQL, 392, 395–398
Routine maintenance, PostgreSQL, 359
    Analyze command, 360, 362, 363
    best practices, 401
    find and remove unused tables and indexes, 400
    find largest tables in database, 399
    log file maintenance, 402
    maintenance options, 359
    pg_indexes_size(), 398
    pg_table_size(), 398
    pg_total_relation_size(), 398
    reindexing, 392, 395–398
    Vacuum (*see* Vacuum in PostgreSQL)

S

Schema objects
    access, 148
    create user, 151
    grpaccount
        creation, 151
        privileges, 152
    pgdbhrm database, 154
    privileges
        levels, 148, 149
        operations, 149–151
        process, 149
        tables, 153, 154
Schema ownership, 162–164
Schemas
    CREATE TABLE command, 145, 146
    database name, 144
    database objects, 143, 148
    definition, 140
    dropping, 206, 207, 209
    hrmschema, 142
    hrmstaff table, 144
    meta command, 142
    non-public, 143
    pgdbhrm database, 145
    public, 141, 142
        tables, 143
    search path, 145–148
    syntax, 142
    tables list, 144
Server process
    background worker, 3
    postgres background process, 2
    postmaster processes, 2
Shared memory, 3, 5, 6, 15, 87
SH Schema database migration
    cost for CO schema, 543
    execute export_schema script, 546
    execute import_all.sh script, 548
    INSERT method, 543
    manual validation, 552
    migration project, 544
    migration report, 544
    objects, 543
    ora2pg -t INSERT command, 548
SQL Dump method, 218
Storage area network (SAN), 215
System Activity Report (SAR), 405–406
systemctl, 36–38, 43, 608
System memory
    local, 5
    maintenance operations, 6
    shared buffers, 6
    sub-areas, 5
    temp buffers, 7
    WAL buffers, 7
    work, 6
System resources and OS-level metrics
    iostat, 409
    iostat -d 5 5, 410

INDEX

System resources and OS-level metrics (*cont.*)
    iostat-help, 409
    iostat-x, 411
    netstat command, 412
    sar, 406
    SAR, 405
    sar-d, 407
    sar-help, 406
    sar-n Dev, 408
    sar-r, 407
    sar-u 10 8, 406
    sysstat rpm, 406
    top, 409
    TOP, 408
    top-help, 408
    vmstat, 412
    vmstat 5 5, 412
    vmstat-help, 412
System views, 423, 424
    cache hit ratios, 426
    deadlock and temp file monitoring, 427
    pg_class, 427
    pg_locks, 424
    pg_stat_activity, 424
    pg_stat_bgwriter, 425
    pg_stat_database, 426
    pg_stat_statements, 425
    pg_stat_user_tables, 425
    statistics, 426, 427

T

Tablespace, 99, 121–124, 128
    concept, 131
    database, 103, 106, 107
    database cluster, 102
    datafile, 112
    default, 100
    directory, 102
    layout, 109
    objects storage directory, 110
    pgdb1 and pgdb2, 110
    physical directory, 106
    physical filesystem, 100
    tspace1, 103
Temporary operations, 124, 126
Temporary tables, 7, 124–127, 386
Temp_tablespaces, 124
Tuples, 4, 111, 114, 121, 365, 382, 389

U

User attributes, 157
    connections test, 160
    grpaccount user, 158, 159
    max connections, 159, 160
    password expiry, 157
    version 16.3, 161
User, dropping, 205, 206
User renaming, 162
Utility process
    archiver, 4
    autovacuum, 4
    background writer, 3
    checkpoints, 4
    logical replication, 4
    logs, 4
    statistics collector, 4
    WAL Writer, 4

V

vacuumdb, 359, 389–391
Vacuum in PostgreSQL, 4

analyze command, 378, 379
Autovacuum, 366
bloating information for tables, 377
bloat SQL query, 378
flow of vaccum command, 382
objects under hrm schema, 369
purposes, 365
size, tables and indexes, 369, 370
standard vacuum, 366
vacuumdb, 389–391

Vacuum Full, 366
VACUUM FULL, 383, 385–388
Virtual Memory Statistics (VMSTAT), 411–412

W, X, Y, Z

WAL files, 10, 400
Write-Ahead Log (WAL), 4, 121, 305, 400–401, 707

GPSR Compliance

The European Union's (EU) General Product Safety Regulation (GPSR) is a set of rules that requires consumer products to be safe and our obligations to ensure this.

If you have any concerns about our products, you can contact us on

ProductSafety@springernature.com

In case Publisher is established outside the EU, the EU authorized representative is:

Springer Nature Customer Service Center GmbH
Europaplatz 3
69115 Heidelberg, Germany

www.ingramcontent.com/pod-product-compliance
Lightning Source LLC
LaVergne TN
LVHW080309260326
834688LV00038B/1014